The Behavioral Science of Firearms

American Psychology-Law Society Series

The Behavioral Science of Firearms

A Mental Health Perspective
on Guns, Suicide, and Violence

Gianni Pirelli

Hayley Wechsler

and

Robert J. Cramer

OXFORD
UNIVERSITY PRESS

OXFORD
UNIVERSITY PRESS

Oxford University Press is a department of the University of Oxford. It furthers
the University's objective of excellence in research, scholarship, and education
by publishing worldwide. Oxford is a registered trade mark of Oxford University
Press in the UK and certain other countries.

Published in the United States of America by Oxford University Press
198 Madison Avenue, New York, NY 10016, United States of America.

© Oxford University Press 2019

CIP data is on file at the Library of Congress
ISBN 978-0-19-063043-0

9 8 7 6 5 4 3 2 1

Printed by WebCom, Inc., Canada

This book is dedicated to the victims of firearm-involved suicide, violence, and domestic violence; to responsible gun owners and operators; and to all who promote mental health- and firearm-related education and training. Our humble aspiration in writing this book has been to move the discussion regarding firearms, mental health, and violence two steps forward and the gun "debate" a step back.

Contents

Series Foreword

This book series is sponsored by the American Psychology-Law Society (APLS). The APLS is an interdisciplinary organization devoted to scholarship, practice, and public service in psychology and law. Its goals include advancing the contributions of psychology to the understanding of law and legal institutions through basic and applied research; promoting the education of psychologists in matters of law and the education of legal personnel in matters of psychology; and informing the psychological and legal communities and the general public of current research, educational, and service activities in the field of psychology and law. APLS membership includes psychologists from the academic, research, and clinical practice communities as well as members of the legal community. Research and practice are represented in both the civil and criminal legal arenas. The APLS has chosen Oxford University Press as a strategic partner because of its commitment to scholarship, quality, and the international dissemination of ideas. These strengths will help the APLS reach its goal of educating the psychology and legal professions and the general public about important developments in psychology and law. The focus of the book series reflects the diversity of the field of psychology and law as we will publish books on a broad range of topics.

In the latest book in the series, *The Behavioral Science of Firearms: A Mental Health Perspective on Guns, Suicide, and Violence*, Gianni Pirelli, Hayley Wechsler, and Robert Cramer provide the foundation for understanding the behavioral science associated with firearms-related matters. Pirelli, Wechsler, and Cramer begin with a primer on firearms, firearm safety, and firearm-related subgroups and then move into a review of the professional literature and case law/legal statutes relevant to firearm development, use, laws, regulations, violence, suicide, and safety. In providing this review, the authors draw from psychology, sociology, criminal justice, and law as well as provide a multitude of media-rich examples. An overview of emerging roles for medical and mental health professionals related to firearms is presented, and a formal framework for conducting various assessments in this regard is provided. Throughout this book the authors focus on how the principles and empirical knowledge in behavioral science can inform and improve firearm-related policy, practice, and research.

The Behavioral Science of Firearms: A Mental Health Perspective on Guns, Suicide, and Violence presents a well-integrated review of various behavioral science literatures associated with firearms and related issues and guides the mental health professional through a number of evaluation- and treatment-related considerations and the corresponding implications for practice, research, and policy. Scholars, researchers, policymakers, and practitioners will undoubtedly find that this book has the potential to help to shape the future of our thinking, policy, research, and practice on firearms-related issues in behavioral science.

Patricia A. Zapf
Series Editor

Preface

It was the summer of 2013 and I was just 8 months into my newly launched private practice when I received a call to conduct an assessment in a gun forfeiture matter associated with a domestic violence incident. The man informed me that the prosecutor's office would consider reinstating his firearms purchaser identification (FPID) card and returning his guns if he could produce documentation from a psychiatrist or psychologist "clearing" him. I had never heard of such an evaluation, which was somewhat surprising given that I had graduated from one of the leading clinical-forensic psychology programs in the country and forensic evaluation was my area of specialization. Nevertheless, I did what any good scientist-practitioner would do, and I consulted the professional literature, and contacted past mentors and leaders in the field as well. The result was underwhelming. While there was an extensive professional literature pertaining to firearm-involved violence and suicide, there was really nothing I could find that provided guidance on conducting forensic mental health evaluations with civilians seeking reinstatement of their gun rights. Moreover, the experts with whom I consulted were generally unsure how to proceed other than to emphasize the need to adhere to the practice standards associated with violence and suicide risk assessment. So, that's what I did.

I reviewed all available records, conducted a clinical-forensic interview with and administered psychological testing to the man, and conducted collateral interviews with his wife and mother. Once I determined I could support his reinstatement, I wrote a report to that effect. It was pretty standard for a psychological evaluation: a review of the referral question, sources of data, referral incident, legal and violence history, and general background

information. I also included the collateral interview data and the findings
from psychological testing, followed by a detailed listing of all of the man's
risk and protective factors related to violence and suicide. In my conclusion
section, I summarized the data and opined that he was at low risk for engaging
in acts of violence toward himself or others in the foreseeable future, especially with a firearm. I spoke briefly about gun-specific issues, such as the need
for him to adhere to firearm safety principles, but not much because I did not
know anything about guns (personally or professionally). In hindsight, it was
a good risk assessment and report but a not-so-good firearm evaluation. At
the time, I knew I did well given what I had to work with from my training
and the professional literature, but I also felt rather strongly that there were
important pieces missing from my evaluation and report—I just did not know
what, exactly.

I began thinking more about the issues relevant to the case, and I continued to read firearm-related literature when I had a chance. The fact that
I could not find more specific information on conducting civilian firearm
ownership evaluations bothered me to an extent; but I started to tell myself
that it had probably been an anomalous request, and I put it all in the back of
my mind. Then, 7 months later, I received another call for a firearm evaluation.
However, this time it was a man who applied for an FID card and was denied
because of a 2-day voluntary hospitalization 20 years earlier stemming from
substance use, anger management, and depression-related problems he had
experienced over a brief period as a late teenager. I understood the concept
of guns being taken from people at times, such as in my prior evaluation, but
I never knew that someone could be blocked from owning firearms because
of a very brief hospitalization many years before. Incidentally, I have come to
find out that applicants are flagged for much less, including for engaging in
routine psychotherapy to treat relatively benign issues while living normally
in the community. Nevertheless, I expanded the breadth of my evaluation report in this case, such that I added and applied my analysis to the state firearm
ownership legal statute, consistent with forensic practice standards.

It was now early 2014, and I had a sense that these types of cases might not
actually be so anomalous after all. I proceeded to do something I had never
done in my life: I went to a gun range. Other than playing with toy guns as a
child, I had never been exposed to firearms before. In fact, I was fairly appre-
hensive about them. I was not even sure how to go about entering the facility,
and I had no idea what to expect. So, I did what any courageous man would
do: I brought my wife, selling it as a date night. As an aside, my wife is also a
psychologist (one of the best therapists I have ever met) who was historically
very liberal and, essentially, "antigun." Still, I somehow convinced her to try it
with me. When we entered the facility, Gun for Hire at Woodland Park Range,
I was immediately taken aback. It was clean, welcoming, and very nicely organized. The staff was inviting and helpful; they clearly dealt with newcomers
all the time. One of the range officers provided us with individual instruction
on firearm safety and use, and he stayed near to help us throughout the hour.

Needless to say, we had fun, and my wife shot better than I, which I was as-
sured was typical.

A lot of ideas were flashing through my mind that night, so I decided
to contact the owner, Anthony Colandro, the next day to introduce myself
and see if he would be willing to meet. He graciously accepted, and I headed
back to the range. I came to realize very quickly into my meeting with Mr.
Colandro that the types of situations I had been called upon to address in the
two evaluations I had conducted were not uncommon at all and represented
a much bigger issue for gun owners and applicants—and, therefore, for police departments, lawyers, and the courts. Mr. Colandro spoke of the importance of mental health in the firearm arena and invited me to teach a course
at his range on the topic. I have come to develop expertise in this area and
have since taught a number of courses at the Woodland Park Range, and Mr.
Colandro has also been instrumental in connecting me with other ranges and
the Second Amendment community in New Jersey, more generally, over the
past few years. I have had the opportunity to present at a number of their
conferences as well. What continues to stick out for me is that neither he nor
any of his counterparts have ever screened my presentations or even asked
me in advance what I would say. I have never once felt any pressure one way
or another. To the contrary, I have only found them and their members to be
inquisitive and completely respectful of my independent and objective role as
a forensic practitioner and educator. In that vein, I have also been invited to
speak to a wide range of groups, including schools, gun violence prevention
groups, and domestic violence/battered women groups; and I provide ongoing
continuing education trainings to mental health and legal professionals. All of
these groups have been equally inquisitive and respectful.

It is very rewarding to be able to interface with so many different groups in
the community, including those with completely divergent views on firearms
and firearm-related issues. This has also been a critical component of my developing professional and cultural competence in this arena. Learning about
the relevant subcultures, their views, concerns, and aspirations—regardless of
mine or how polarizing theirs may be—has been important and meaningful.
Too often we hear complaints about the gaps that exist between research,
practice, and policy. However, there frequently seems to be an unreasonable expectation assumed by many that bridges will be formed by some other
(unknown) third party based on a compelling recommendation or two—a
stance consistent with *belling the cat* à la Aesop.[1] Instead, professionals across
disciplines and community leaders must serve as the bridges and seek to not
only integrate research, practice, and policy-related concepts into their daily
work but also to come to the table and identify the common ground. Such was
the driving force and aspiration of this book: to serve as a singular resource
for everyone, regardless of their views, on the myriad of issues relevant to
firearms in America today. We are not the first to write a book in the firearms
arena. In fact, the literature is relatively vast, but we believe we have put together a resource that can be found on the bookshelf of a Second Amendment

advocate just as readily as that of someone on the other end of the spectrum. Indeed, this was our intention and goal.

Most of the existing professional literature will never reach or be read by those who own and interact with firearms, and most of the information related to guns, gun safety, and gun laws does not reach professional groups. Perhaps neither body of information reaches most policymakers or the public, more generally. These disconnects are concerning, but they are fixable. What is necessary, however, is a shared commitment to finding common ground guided by scientific principles and findings when possible. It is also essential that those writing about guns and gun owners actually gain some exposure to guns and gun owners. It is hard to imagine reading a book on motor vehicle accident analysis written by someone who has never seen a car or spoken with a driver, for example. This is true in most other areas as well, including those related to medicine, mental health, and the law. When it comes to firearm-related issues, though, there seems to be a collective complacency that has developed, whereby people fall into their respective places: the researchers say X, the practitioners say Y, the policymakers and advocacy groups say A or Z, depending on their affiliations. The media puts their spin on the information, and the general public is left to sort it all out. It is no wonder the divides are great in this arena. Perhaps, we can take something from the liberal, Obama-appointed Supreme Court justice Elena Kagan's experience, however. Namely, she has spoken of her hunting trips with her former colleague, the late conservative, Reagan-appointed Antonin Scalia:

> I shoot birds with him . . . I shot myself a deer. . . . The way this started, I'll tell the story. You know the NRA has become quite a presence in judicial confirmations, and that means when you go around from office to office, from chamber to chamber, I met with about 80 senators individually and quite a lot of them, both Republicans and Democrats, ask you about your views on the Second Amendment. But because you don't say anything about your views on anything, when they ask you, well, they'll try to figure out what your views on the Second Amendment are likely to be and they'll say, "Well, have you ever held a gun? Have you ever gone hunting? Do you know anybody who's gone hunting?" And you know me, Jeff, I grew up on the Upper West Side of Manhattan and this was not something we really did, you know. And so I kept on having these conversations where I would say no and no and no and I was—and finally somebody said to me, one of these sets of these questions, and so I said, "You know senator," I said, "if you were to invite me hunting, I would really love to go." And this look of total horror passed over his face. You know, "Has this woman just invited herself hunting with me?" And I thought, I've gone too far, and then I sort of pulled back and I said, "I didn't really mean to invite myself, but I'll tell you what, if I am lucky enough to be confirmed, I will ask Justice

Scalia to take me hunting." And I went to Justice Scalia when I got onto the court, and I said, "This is the only promise I made during my entire confirmation proceedings, so you have to help me fulfill it." And he thought it was hilarious. He thought it was a total crackup. And so, there you go. (Franke-Ruta, 2013)[2]

As for writing this book over the past 2 years, it has been somewhat of a rollercoaster. On the one hand, it is exciting to be addressing such timely topics and feeling that we can possibly make a meaningful contribution to a range of professional disciplines and, more importantly, to society as a whole. However, it is exceedingly difficult to write a book like this given the constant developments in this area—from ongoing shootings to law and policy changes, and everything in between. We have done our best to keep up and revise as needed, and the most upsetting part has been having to update the deadliest mass shooting in modern U.S. history twice while writing this book (i.e., 2016 Orlando, and 2017 Las Vegas). We have humbly tried to channel our sadness from these events into motivation to complete this book, in the hopes it will be educative, help effectuate change, and ultimately play a role in preventing firearm-involved violence and suicide. Still, it is likely that this book's greatest strength is also its greatest limitation: its timeliness. Like most books, portions will be outdated soon after hitting the shelves, but we have made concerted efforts to balance contemporary issues with foundational concepts and principles that will maintain relevance moving forward.

This book is somewhat lengthy. It is also complicated at times. These were not our goals, but they reflect the reality of the many firearm-related issues we address: they are often involved and complex. In light of the significant time, effort, and thought we have put in consistently over the past 2 years to more fully understand firearms and firearm-related matters, it is hard to watch as some professionals, politicians, journalists, and celebrities so easily identify and provide answers to the problems in an instant, equipped with a thought and a Facebook or Twitter account. The average broadcast news soundbite is 9 seconds, and the optimal length for most social media posts is 40 characters.[3] In this context, however, the best we can do is:

GUN ISSUES TOO COMPLEX, MUST READ ENTIRE BOOK

Thank you for taking the time to read this book. We appreciate it, and we are grateful for the opportunity to share it with you.

Gianni Pirelli, Ph.D.

Acknowledgments

We would like to thank Oxford University Press, particularly Sarah Harrington and Andrea Zekus, for their guidance and support in bringing this project through its various phases. We would also like to thank Dr. Patricia Zapf and the proposal reviewers for their feedback and support in having this book be a part of the book series of the American Psychology-Law Society, Division 41 of the American Psychological Association. Thanks also goes to Rachael Scheiter, B.A., for her assistance in developing the glossary of terms. Last, but certainly not least, we want to thank Kathryn Schrantz, M.A., for her tireless work in conducting extensive literature reviews, compiling reference lists, and providing a tremendous amount of overall foundational support for this project. Kathryn's efforts cannot be overstated, and we are very appreciative. Without Kathryn, this book would have taken twice as long to write, and it would have been half as informative.

Gianni

Thank you to my coauthors, Hayley Wechsler and Robert Cramer, for their collaboration on this book and for many years of friendship. Thank you to Lina, my wife, for providing me with the love, space, and time needed to complete this work and for taking care of our most precious treasures. Thanks also to Gemma, Marco, Ryan, Sandie, and my mother, Susan, for their ongoing love and encouragement. And to all of our beautiful children—Miguel,

Tiago, Milena, Luca, Arielle, and Louis—for reminding us how to love, play, and forgive.

Hayley

I would like to thank Gianni and Rob for all of their hard work on this book, as well as their invaluable mentorship while I completed my doctorate. I will continue to cherish their guidance as I progress through the early stages of my career as a psychologist. I would also like to thank Kathryn Schrantz for the many hours she spent helping put the book together. Finally, I want to thank my soon-to-be husband, Johnny, and the rest of my family for their unyielding support and patience.

Robert

Thank you, Gianni Pirelli, my friend and colleague, for your vision and leadership in this collective effort. Thank you, Hayley Wechsler, my mentee and friend, for your tireless efforts and energetic spirit. Gianni and I are both very fortunate to have you as a collaborator. I would like to dedicate this book to my friend and mentor, Dr. Stan Brodsky (Look Stan, I finally wrote part of a book!). Thank you also to my wife, Chelsea, for your unending patience and for your support and partnership moving across the country over the course of the completion of this book. Finally, thanks to my parents, Linda and Alan, for instilling in me the pursuit of science, health, knowledge, and empirical truth—personal values for which I am endlessly grateful.

Disclaimer

This book is designed to provide readers with education and information on mental health, suicide, and violence-related issues associated with firearms, including, but not limited to, their proper and improper use and relevant laws and procedures. Our primary goal is to promote awareness and education in this arena, especially as such relates to mental health. Please note that information presented in this book does not represent professional advice applicable to specific cases as such should be sought from attorneys and/or mental health professionals retained for that purpose.

Introduction

Approximately 30 firearm-involved homicides and 53 suicides are committed in the United States each day—a rate that is appreciably greater than that of 25 other industrialized countries; namely, 1.66 per 100,000 versus 0.14 per 100,000, annually (Centers for Disease Control and Prevention; CDC, 2013).[4] Correlates of firearm-related homicide and suicide risk continue to be identified by researchers, such as the presence of a firearm in the home (Dahlberg, Ikeda, & Kresnow, 2004)[5]; but causal relationships between variables largely remain unknown in this arena. For instance, the relationship between mental illness and violence and suicide is nuanced and complicated (American Psychological Association, 2013).[6] Nevertheless, these issues have become integral to our national discussions and are particularly salient following highly publicized, tragic events such as mass shootings (e.g., Sandy Hook Elementary School, Virginia Tech, the Colorado movie theater, the Tucson, Arizona, constituents meeting). These incidents all consisted of a mentally ill shooter using firearms with large-capacity magazines (Barry, McGinty, Vernick, & Webster, 2013).[7] In some cases, the shooters had diagnosable mental health problems (Jenson, 2007).[8] However, very few people diagnosed with severe mental illness engage in violence at all (3%–5%); and while mass and school shootings are the most sensationalized, they are by far the least common. In fact, firearm-involved violence and suicide is typically more closely associated with gangs and other organized crime organizations, domestic and intimate partner violence, and suicide, especially in law enforcement, correctional, and military populations. In this book, we certainly address mass and school shootings, but we also spend considerable time (i.e., whole chapters) addressing typically overlooked areas related to firearm-involved violence and self-injury, as well as to the pro-social uses of firearms.

The overarching topic, behavioral science and firearms, is a cutting-edge, emerging area of study. In this context, we address areas often bypassed or only briefly touched upon in the extant "gun violence" literature. In fact, you will find that we avoid the overarching term "gun violence" as much as possible and seek to address issues in the more nuanced manner we believe is necessary. Furthermore, many publications have focused on highlighting the correlates of firearm-involved violence and suicide and advocate for the prevention of such, but few include the range of perspectives needed to fully understand the issues at hand. The existing publications that address mental health, violence, and suicide do not speak to issues related to the historical uses of firearms, the various types of firearms available and how they work, pro-social uses and safety-related considerations, and the range of firearm-related subgroups within a cultural competence perspective. Our goal in writing this book was to have it serve as a singular resource on the myriad of issues relevant to firearms today—from their historical uses to firearm-involved violence and suicide to safety and self-care and the many emerging roles of mental health, medical, and legal professionals in this arena. We have sought to create an objective, data-driven, educative resource for a broad readership, regardless of perspectives on guns and related issues, such as gun control.

Scope and Format of This Book

Scope

In this book, we present the most relevant factors and considerations involved in the intersection between behavioral science and firearms. The intent of this book is to provide readers with a comprehensive review of these issues in the context of the professional literatures in these and related areas. It was designed to be an informational and educational source for a wide range of readers, including the general public and lawmakers. We also developed it to serve as a reference text for mental health and medical practitioners, institutional threat assessment team members and law enforcement personnel, and academicians and students in fields such as psychology, criminal justice, and public health. As an empirically focused educational resource, this book includes no politically based position statements but rather provides readers with the range and depth of information available, as well as the limitations of such data, in each respective area covered. Concepts are presented using a best-practices model that encourages and promotes engaging in empirically supported practice, research, policy, and decision-making, more generally. We believe this book is distinct from others published in this area, given its inclusion and integration of the following:

1. A focus on the behavioral science of firearm-related matters.
2. A primer on firearms, firearm safety, and firearm-related subgroups.

3. A review of the professional literatures and case law/legal statutes relevant to firearm development and use, laws, regulations, violence, suicide, and safety.

4. Considerations of and information from various relevant areas, including psychology, sociology, criminal justice, law, and others more specific to the general public (e.g., the media).

5. An overview of the emerging roles related to firearms for medical and mental health professionals who provide treatment and evaluation services, including firearm-specific evaluations. In this regard, we provide a formal framework for conducting assessments in gun application and forfeiture matters as well as mental health expungements. We also address potential applications for such groups as military, law enforcement and corrections personnel, and security and armed guards.

6. A particular focus on how the principles and empirical knowledge in the behavioral science arena can inform and improve firearm-related policy, practice, and research.

Format

This book consists of four parts comprised of 9 chapters, each of which corresponds with a major area of consideration in the intersection between behavioral science and firearms. Part I, "An Introduction to Firearms," includes two chapters. In Chapter 1, we provide a primer on guns, including information related to their history and general use, as well as national and state ownership statistics and various firearm-related subgroups and cultures. In Chapter 2, we review relevant national and state laws and policies related to firearms, including those specific to mental health–related issues. We also address matters pertaining to the legal liability of gun manufacturers and sellers as well as medical and mental health professionals. In addition, we discuss the media's impact on firearm policy and provide a comparative international analysis of firearm-related laws and policies.

In Part II, "Mental Health, Violence, and Suicide," there are four chapters. In Chapter 3, we provide the reader with an overview of psychopathology, the contemporary mental health diagnostic system per the *Diagnostic and Statistical Manual of Mental Disorders*, and some of the more prominent clinical and personality disorders. In Chapter 4, we provide an overview of violence by reviewing various definitions, types, and psychological components and theories related to such. We also highlight psychiatric diagnoses commonly associated with interpersonal violence and aggression. In addition, we delve more specifically into firearm-related violence and crime and present relevant statistics, theories, and research related to such. Lastly, we provide an overview of high-profile mass shootings in the United States, followed by a focused discussion on the association between mental illness and firearm-related violence. In Chapter 5, we solely focus on domestic violence (DV) and intimate partner violence (IPV), inclusive of definitions, types, and relevant statistics. We also highlight firearm use in these situations and present a number of high-profile cases that have occurred involving celebrities, athletes, citizens, and law enforcement personnel. In this chapter, we also review psychological theories of DV and IPV and discuss issues related to laws and regulations in this arena. In Chapter 6, we provide a comprehensive overview of concepts and statistics associated with suicide, in addition to the more specific association between firearms and suicide. We also review principles of suicide risk assessment, management, and prevention and various high-profile case studies that involved firearms.

Part III, "The Emerging Roles of Medical and Mental Health Professionals in Firearm-Related Matters," includes two chapters. Chapter 7 pertains to evaluation-related issues, including mental health screening in the community and outpatient and inpatient settings, and specific considerations for those who wish to conduct firearm evaluations as well as those who conduct psychological and forensic evaluations more broadly. We also address the need for professional development of cultural competence in these contexts. In Chapter 8, we focus on treatment and review some of the best-known therapeutic modalities and the ways in which such interventions are modified for use with violent offenders, victims of violence and DV, those who are suicidal, and youth, generally. In addition, we speak to considerations for health and wellness as well as firearm safety. Moreover, we discuss the barriers to treatment that exist for many people, including those who interact with firearms, and issues related to the restoration of gun rights. Lastly, we present a number of considerations associated with the emerging roles for treating professionals in firearm-related matters.

Part IV, "Future Directions for Practice, Research, and Policy," is comprised of the last and final chapter. In Chapter 9, we present the 30 main findings we have extracted from our comprehensive investigation into all of the aforementioned areas. We briefly summarize each and present the most salient corresponding implications for practice, research, and policy.

A Final Note

We hope you will find this book informative and useful. We also hope you find yourself disagreeing with us at times, identifying our blind spots and potential biases, and challenging our interpretations. Science works best that way. When all is said and done, though, we mostly hope that we have achieved our goal of promoting awareness, education, and productive dialogue in this area. This book was written for you, regardless of your views on guns or your political affiliation. We humbly sought to do our part in facilitating the balance between respecting individual rights and pressing for much more progress in the firearm-involved violence and suicide prevention arena. Know this: even if you only agree with some aspects of this book, there is a very good chance that your counterpart on the other side of the aisle does, too. We firmly believe there is common ground that continues to go unnoticed by many and, worse, intentionally ignored by some. We also believe that the *Even if we save one life, it's worth it* argument lacks utility and focus and encourages subpar initiatives dependent more on emotion than science. Saving that one life is necessary but insufficient. We can and should do more. And we must demand results and not simply be satisfied by movement.

> ALICE: Would you tell me, please, which way I ought to go from here?
> THE CHESHIRE CAT: That depends a good deal on where you want to get to.

ALICE: I don't much care where.

THE CHESHIRE CAT: Then it doesn't much matter which way you go.

ALICE: . . . So long as I get somewhere.

THE CHESHIRE CAT: Oh, you're sure to do that, if only you walk long enough.

—Lewis Carroll, *Alice in Wonderland* (1865)

About the Authors

The authors of this book have doctoral degrees in clinical and clinical-forensic psychology, and they have trained and worked in a wide range of inpatient and outpatient settings. They are also well published in the areas of psychology and law, forensic psychology, and public health, including in the mental health and firearms arenas. They have created a formal model of conducting psychological evaluations in firearm ownership–related legal and administrative matters, and they engage in ongoing efforts to educate the public and help clinicians develop professional and cultural competence in this area (see Pirelli, Wechsler, & Cramer, 2015; Pirelli & Witt, 2015, 2017; Wechsler, Pirelli, Struble, & Cramer, 2015; Wechsler, Pirelli, & Cramer, 2014).[9]

Gianni Pirelli, Ph.D.
Dr. Pirelli received his doctorate in clinical-forensic psychology from The Graduate Center at John Jay College of Criminal Justice. He is a licensed psychologist in New Jersey and New York. He maintains an independent group practice in clinical and forensic psychology, Pirelli Clinical and Forensic Psychology, LLC (www.gpirelli.com). Dr. Pirelli conducts a wide range of clinical and clinical-forensic evaluations in criminal and civil legal and administrative matters, including those involving firearms. He has conducted evaluations in 18 of 21 New Jersey counties and five states. Dr. Pirelli is the editor of the New Jersey Psychological Association's journal, the *New Jersey Psychologist*, and he is an editorial board member for a number of professional journals, including *Law and Human Behavior*. Dr. Pirelli also regularly gives presentations and teaches courses on firearm-related issues, including

continuing education workshops for mental health and legal professionals. He maintains an active research program and publication record, particularly in the areas of mental health and firearms, forensic mental health assessment, and ethics and standards of practice in forensic psychology. Dr. Pirelli is also in the process of co-authoring a book with Dr. Liza Gold of Georgetown University, titled: *Guns and Clinical Practice: A Handbook for Medical and Mental Health Professionals* (Oxford University Press). He has numerous other publications as well, including the 2017 edited book, *The Ethical Practice of Forensic Psychology: A Casebook* (Oxford University Press), and chapters in books such as *Handbook of Forensic Psychology* (4th ed.), *Violent Offenders: Understanding and Assessment*, and *Psychology in the Courtroom*. His articles have been published in journals such as the *Journal of Forensic Psychiatry and Psychology*, the *Journal of Forensic Psychology Practice*, *Professional Psychology: Research and Practice*, and *Psychology, Public Policy and Law*. Dr. Pirelli's research has been cited in amicus briefs to the US Supreme Court and to the New York Court of Appeals.

Hayley Wechsler, Ph.D.
Dr. Wechsler received her M.A. in forensic psychology from John Jay College of Criminal Justice and her Ph.D. in clinical psychology from Sam Houston State University. Her areas of professional interest include forensic evaluation, firearm ownership, wrongful convictions, scientific evidence in the courtroom, and judicial decision-making. Dr. Wechsler has experience in a range of clinical, forensic, and correctional settings, including county psychiatric centers, state and federal prisons, jails, juvenile detention centers, state hospitals, school clinics, and community supervision programs. She has a notable publication and professional presentation record. She completed her doctoral internship at the Department of State Hospitals–Atascadero, where she is now an admissions psychologist working toward licensure.

Robert J. Cramer, Ph.D.
Dr. Cramer received his Ph.D. from the University of Alabama in the psychology and law concentration of the clinical psychology doctoral program. After serving as a faculty member at Sam Houston State University and the University of Alabama, he is currently an associate professor of community and environmental health at Old Dominion University. Dr. Cramer's work has garnered international attention as he has served as a visiting member of the teaching or research faculty at the Prague Centre for Public Policy (Prague, Czech Republic) in 2014, Griffith University Institute of Criminology (Brisbane, Australia) in 2015, and the University of Central Lancashire School of Psychology (Preston, England) in 2016. He is currently editor of the *Journal of Aggression, Conflict and Peace Research*, an international multidisciplinary journal focusing on issues of interpersonal violence. Dr. Cramer's research spans issues of suicide prevention, hate crimes and interpersonal violence, LGBTQ health, and the intersection of social science, law, and public policy.

Having published more than 100 peer-reviewed articles and book chapters to date, his work has appeared in top-tier behavioral health, public health, psychology, and other interdisciplinary outlets such as *Law and Human Behavior*, *Journal of Interpersonal Violence*, and *Suicide & Life-Threatening Behavior*. His work has been funded by the Veterans Affairs Administration, the National Science Foundation, the American Psychological Foundation, and the US Surgeon General's Office. Adopting a community-engaged approach to scholarship, Dr. Cramer has experience partnering with courts, military, community health, judicial, and advocacy organizations, and many others. Dr. Cramer has extensive experience consulting and provides training on best practices in suicide risk assessment and prevention, publishing a framework for such training in *Training and Education in Professional Psychology*, *Teaching of Psychology*, and *Journal of Clinical Psychology*.

The Behavioral Science of Firearms

Part I

AN INTRODUCTION TO FIREARMS

1

Firearms

A Primer

In most cases, you can read an entire article or book on firearms and not be presented with the full range of information available because of the authors' narrow scope. This may be a result of the authors' particular views on firearms, the Second Amendment, or related issues, such as gun control. Unfortunately, presenting information with such a constricted focus leaves people walking away with only part of the story. In addition, people are more likely to adopt *confirmation bias*, which refers to the tendency to seek out or interpret information in a manner that confirms one's preconceived ideas, leading to statistical errors (Confirmation bias, n.d.). Put differently, we tend to listen to and read things that support our preexisting beliefs. As a result, many people are not inclined to search for, listen to, or read information from an opposing viewpoint—and if they do, they are more likely to do so critically and highlight flaws while dismissing potentially convincing points. With the concept of confirmation bias in mind, we need to determine if we are effectively reaching our target audiences with the full spectrum of available information. Again, in many instances, speakers, authors, and organizations have very narrow audiences, which is understandable. However, this may also be the reason that members of Second Amendment groups are unlikely to read academic peer-reviewed journal articles or scientific books on gun-involved violence and why gun violence prevention advocacy group members are unlikely to read about the history of firearms or about the roots of the long-standing subculture of firearm owners. Additionally, it is important to take into consideration that this issue is particularly emotionally charged; therefore, it is difficult for individuals to remain objective and dispassionate about this topic. Although reasonable minds can disagree, we must first establish that, no matter what our preconceived viewpoints might be, we are looking at the same set of information. Our primary goal in writing this book is to facilitate just that, by presenting the full range of available information related to firearms, objectively and independently.

In this chapter, we provide an overview in eight different areas intended to provide the reader with a primer on firearms, setting the stage for the remainder of the book. First, we review the history of firearms across numerous contexts, including military, law enforcement, corrections, civilian, and pop culture. We then outline the available statistics from various sources related to firearm ownership and use in the United States, as well as the breakdown across each of the 50 states. Next, we set forth important foundational information about firearms, including basic gun models, components, and functionality; firearm safety; ammunition and bullet calibers; and gun manufacturers. We then address issues related to the public sentiment and attitudes toward firearms, gun control, and related concepts. This provides the framework for our remaining sections wherein we review a wide range of Second Amendment groups; shooting sport groups; rod & gun clubs, hunting clubs, and shooting ranges; and gun control, gun violence prevention, and antigun groups.

The History of Firearms

Arms represent some of the earliest tools as they have been used for protection and to secure food since the formation of the earliest social groups. As Supica, Wicklund, & Schreier (2011) have indicated, undoubtedly, firearms have become the most effective type of arms and ensure that the most basic goals of a people are met, including obtaining food, enforcing the law, providing personal protection, defending territory, and liberating people. Of course, firearms can also be used improperly, such as to defy the law, steal, and harm and enslave others. This is the blessing and the curse of many, if not most, advancements in a society, including, but not limited to, those related to technology and medicine. If we are to benefit from the *use* of something, we must accept the potential *misuse* by some that may follow.

It is thought that gunpowder likely originated in China, but its exact origins are unknown. It is clear that gunpowder-based firearms were present in the 13th-century Middle East as well as in Europe around the turn of that century. Perhaps unsurprisingly, the earliest firearm-related records are in the context of warfare and battle. The basic firing mechanism remains in place today—ignited gunpowder to cause rapidly expanding gases to launch a projectile. The earliest firearms were essentially hand cannons and were even referred to as such. The role that arms played in warfare over many centuries cannot be understated, and such remains true today. Firearms have literally changed the world in many ways (McNab, 2009).

Key turning points in the evolution of firearms pertain to the ignition system and developments in gunpowder and designs that allowed repeat and more accurate shots. With respect to the ignition system, the first firearms used a matchlock system—literally requiring the operator to light a rope or cord (i.e., a fuse) with a match. One might visualize how a cannon, bomb, or firework is lit, for example. Obviously, this system posed problems in many respects, not the least of which were related to safety and effectiveness issues. Thus, the wheel lock system came into play in the 1500s, which relied upon striking a flint or similar substance against the steel to produce a spark. This system circumvented the problems with the matchlock, such as using it in inclement weather and remaining undetected by others (as a result of the smell). However, wheel lock firearms were pricier and more complicated to use; therefore, they did not gain much traction. Improvements were made, though, and a flintlock system was created by the second half of the 16th century. Flintlock firing maintained the same approach as the wheel lock, although it avoided the clock-like winding components of it and the like. In or around the time that the flintlock system was being solidified, improvements were made to the barrel to increase accuracy. Specifically, firearm designers adopted designs from archery arrows to create grooves inside the barrel, called *rifling*, which would facilitate the spin of the projectile. Additional improvements, such as gun sights (i.e., an apparatus attached to the firearm to help focus on the target), were made around that time as well (the interested reader is referred to Supica, n.d.; see also, American Firearms Institute, n.d.).

Firearms were brought to the United States in the 17th and 18th centuries by European settlers. Marksmanship was a valued and much needed skill, facilitating protection but also the gathering of food. Undoubtedly, firearms played an essential role in securing independence, and the new government readily moved to mass-produce arms for its military at the turn of the 18th century. Nevertheless, firearms continued to evolve, and a new firing system known as the percussion system gave rise to the creation of the modern revolver. The percussion system relies upon certain chemicals to ignite a spark rather than lighting a match or striking flint. This development ultimately led the way to firearms capable of repeat shots via a cylindrical revolving component. Samuel Colt is known for being the first to develop the most effective revolver in this context from his Paterson, New Jersey, manufacturing facility. Of course, many manufacturers have been instrumental in creating and innovating firearm designs, both before and after Colt. We present a number of them in the *Gun Manufacturers* section of this chapter. First, let us outline the involvement of firearms in military, law enforcement and corrections, civilian, and pop culture contexts.

Military

As noted, the role that firearms have played in military efforts cannot be understated. In fact, it would be hard to imagine modern military personnel or actions without thinking of firearms. In colonial America, the firearm of choice for settlers was the American or Kentucky long rifle—a derivative of European arms. Muskets subsequently became a mainstay in Europe and ultimately found their way to the newly developed United States. The government began mass-producing arms at facilities such as the Springfield Armory.

In addition, as is reflected in the *Gun Manufacturers* section in this chapter, a number of firearm manufacturing companies emerged and became primary suppliers for the military in essentially every military action and war to date. Of course, firearm designs evolved rather quickly over time, thereby increasing their capabilities and effectiveness—and, in turn, the nature of combat was completely changed. One can easily conceptualize the difference between firing a single-shot, match-lit firearm that took a fair amount of time to load and had limited accuracy at modest distances versus a modern-day sniper rifle that maintains pinpoint accuracy from over a mile away or even an automatic machine gun that can fire thousands of rounds per minute. Certainly, much advancement took place to get from the one end of the continuum to the other, but this progression occurred relatively quickly once modern-day firing mechanisms were discovered and refined. Undoubtedly, each type of firearm has served a particular purpose in the military. A crude distinction would be that of handguns, long guns, and automatic firearms—all of which remain a part of the military's artillery today. While choices were much more limited in early America, military personnel receive training on a variety of firearms and weaponry during their basic training. Infantry personnel and specialists, including snipers and Special Operations members, receive much more extensive firearms training.

Automatic firearms were developed in Germany at the turn of the 20th century but readily made their way into the United States. By the start of World War I, the submachine gun made its debut; one particularly notable type was the Thompson submachine gun, or *Tommy Gun*, which is perhaps best known for its association with mobsters of the 1920s. Nevertheless, these automatic firearms, or *assault weapons*, were continuously improved and refined, making them much more efficient, accurate, and reliable. Some contemporary semiautomatic firearms look similar to their automatic counterparts and predecessors, but such is an aesthetic similarity and not a functional one as semiautomatic firearms do not possess the capability of automatic assault weapons (McNab, 2009).

Handguns and long guns have certainly played an important role in military efforts throughout the country's history as well for different reasons and in different contexts. Although such level of depth and detail is outside of the scope of this book, it seems quite safe to say that, but for the presence of firearms in our country, countless critically important and formative events would have never occurred. For example, it is likely that the United States would have never been formed in the first place, neither slavery nor the Holocaust would have ended, and people such as Osama Bin Laden would remain at large.

Law Enforcement and Corrections

Law enforcement in the United States has its roots in England, particularly in the context of the Magna Carta and the authority contained therein. Shortly after the United States came to be, domestic protection was provided by local and state militias along with sheriffs, which was a political appointment. By the mid-19th century, many cities had established police forces in place. Notably, the eventual president Theodore Roosevelt served as police commissioner of New York City from 1895 to 1897 (Theodore Roosevelt biography in brief, n.d.), but the establishment of the modern police department has been credited to August Vollmer, the police chief of Berkeley, California, in 1910 (Supica et al., 2011). Although law enforcement officers appear to have always used firearms, the way in which they were used was by no means a standardized operation, and officers used what they personally owned (The history of firearms in law enforcement, 2016). As a result, officers' firearms ran the gamut from handguns to long guns, including muskets. As police commissioner, however, Theodore Roosevelt enacted the standardization and issue of firearms to officers. Today, there is a relatively wide range of firearms used by officers across departments throughout the country; however, most larger departments have policies that identify which firearm constitutes standard issue. Perhaps the most common handguns used are those manufactured by Glock, Smith & Wesson, Beretta, Sig Sauer, Heckler & Koch, Ruger, and Colt, whereas a Remington shotgun is often a favored long gun. Of course, there are numerous other firearms used, particularly by those in specialized units, such as emergency services units and Special Weapons and Tactics (SWAT) teams.

It is noteworthy that there are at least five countries wherein some police officers have traditionally not carried firearms as a matter of course—Britain, Ireland, Norway, Iceland, and New Zealand—in addition to about a dozen nations of the Pacific Islands (Noack, 2016). It is actually a misconception, however, that there are no armed police in places such as the United Kingdom, where there are specialist officers who carry firearms; and in Norway, for example, officers keep firearms in their cars rather than on their person (Kelly, 2014). Although traditionally these realities have remained relatively unnoticed and unspoken, officers in places such as England have begun making openly armed patrols with submachine guns and handguns in higher-crime areas (For some British bobbies, a gun comes with job, 2009).

Executions and the Death Penalty: The Firing Squad

The execution of a person via multiple firearms, or *fusillading*, has historically been a military and wartime endeavor. Its roots appear to predate firearms, such that bows and crossbows were used in Roman times as early as the 3rd century. While it is less common in the modern era, there are some countries throughout the world that continue to use it as a legal punishment for criminal soldiers and even political figures (Firing squad, n.d.). Nevertheless, the firing squad has rarely been used as a capital punishment method in the United States. There are sporadic accounts of its use in Nevada and Utah in the first half of the 20th century, but the death penalty was effectively abolished in the United States in 1972 per the Supreme Court ruling in *Furman v. Georgia*

(1972). However, it was essentially reinstated by the court just a few years later in *Gregg v. Georgia* (1976), and in 1977 Gary Gilmore was the first inmate to be executed since the moratorium—by firing squad in Utah on January 17, 1977. Only two other inmates have been executed in this manner since, also in Utah: John Taylor in 1996 and Ronnie Gardner in 2010 (Firing squad, n.d.).

Death by firing squad was an option for inmates in Utah along with lethal injection, and Idaho and Oklahoma considered it an option but have never implemented it in modern-day executions. Today, Oklahoma offers firing squad only if lethal injection and electrocution are found unconstitutional; and on March 23, 2015, firing squad was reauthorized in Utah as a method of execution but only in cases where the state is unable to obtain the drugs necessary to carry out a lethal injection execution. Although some have accused the firing squad method of being antiquated or seemingly out of the Wild West or movies, others, including Fordham Law School professor Deborah W. Denno, have highlighted the fact that the firing squad is the only capital punishment method "that involves experts specifically trained to kill human beings as well as a record of relative speed and certainty" (Denno, 2015). This sentiment is particularly salient given the relatively recent and ongoing challenges to lethal injection because of the number of botched and otherwise problematic execution attempts that have occurred in that context. As a result, some have contended that the firing squad could resurface as a viable means of execution, which is not a far-fetched thought given that recent bills have been proposed in Wyoming and Missouri in this regard (Morris, 2014). The Wyoming bill passed through the state's Senate but ultimately failed in the House (Jones, 2015).

As noted, it has been contended that the firing squad is, in fact, the only method implemented by those with specific training. In this procedure, the inmate is bound to a chair with leather straps across his or her waist and head, in front of a wall. The chair is surrounded by sandbags to take in the inmate's blood. A black hood is placed over the head. A physician locates the inmate's heart with a stethoscope and secures a circular white cloth target over it. Five shooters 20 feet away are armed with .30 caliber rifles loaded with single rounds, with the exception of one shooter, who has a blank round, with no one knowing who holds the blank. The shooters fire, and the inmate ultimately dies from blood loss due to a rupture to the heart or a large blood vessel or tearing of the lungs. The inmate loses consciousness when shock causes a fall in the supply of blood to the brain, although he or she may bleed to death slowly if the shooters miss the heart (Descriptions of execution methods, n.d.).

Civilian

Much of this book relates to civilians' involvement with firearms, and therefore, we only provide a brief overview of this topic here. Despite our delineation of subsections, it is not actually possible to make a clear distinction between civilian and noncivilian firearm use per se because such use predates many laws and regulations. American Revolutionary soldiers were essentially militiamen who, essentially by definition, were civilians who illegally used firearms. Confederate Civil War soldiers used nonregulated arms as well. Moreover, civilians used firearms in the context of exploring the new land and for hunting and self-defense. Thus, it lacks utility to try and separate the civilian use of firearms from other uses given the significant overlap in this regard in the early stages of this country's history. Certainly, the Second Amendment of the US Constitution (1791) reads, "A well regulated Militia, being necessary to the security of a free State, the right of the people to keep and bear Arms, shall not be infringed." Of course, the interpretation of the Second Amendment continues to be argued. In essence, the two main opposing interpretations are referred to as the *individual rights theory* and the *collective rights theory*, which reflect the primary question of whether or not firearm ownership is an absolute individual constitutional right (Second Amendment, n.d.). We provide a comprehensive overview of firearm policies and laws in Chapter 2 of this book and, therefore, direct the interested reader there. It is worth noting here, however, that Georgia passed the first law banning handguns in 1837—although it was ultimately ruled unconstitutional and dismissed (Longley, 2016).

Aside from military service, many, if not most, US presidents have interacted with firearms, including those such as President Obama, who reportedly engaged in skeet shooting "all the time" (Sonmez, 2013). Undoubtedly, early presidents and founding framers owned and used firearms, including George Washington, Thomas Jefferson, James Madison, Martin Van Buren, Grover Cleveland, and Theodore Roosevelt; but there have been numerous others in the modern day who have either owned or at least used firearms in some capacity—again, outside of military service. They include, but are not necessary limited to, Calvin Coolidge, Franklin Delano Roosevelt, Harry Truman, Dwight D. Eisenhower, John F. Kennedy, Gerald Ford, Jimmy Carter, Ronald Reagan, George H. W. Bush, Bill Clinton, George W. Bush, and Barack Obama, as noted (Pickhartz, 2016; Shea, 2017). Moreover, it has been reported that Ronald Reagan actually carried a firearm on his person during his presidency, although the timing of such remains unclear (Hawkins, 2016).

Perhaps unsurprisingly, the late Supreme Court justice Antonin Scalia was a hunter; however, it was unexpected when President Obama's newly appointed justice Elena Kagan began engaging in a number of hunting excursions with him in 2013 for deer, antelope, quail, and duck. Justice Kagan has indicated that, while she never used a gun prior, she had promised to keep an open mind on firearm-related issues given their relevance in our society (Mears, 2013). There are also a number of current celebrities who use firearms, including Johnny Depp, Robert DeNiro, Eric Clapton, Clint Eastwood, James Earl Jones, Marc Anthony, Howard Stern, Angelina Jolie, Brad Pitt, Demi Moore, and Whoopi Goldberg—who is also a member of the NRA (Burke, 2015; Celebrities with gun licenses, n.d.).

As we will outline throughout the remainder of the chapter, civilians own and operate firearms for a range of purposes, including hunting, target shooting, plinking, and various other types of shooting sports, in addition to self-defense. Moreover, it is worth recognizing the uses of toy guns among children and the other types of recreational activities wherein certain types of guns are used, including BB and airsoft guns and those used in laser tag and paintball, to name a few.

Pop Culture

We need not look far to find the presence of or, at least, reference to firearms in movies, television shows, music, books, theater, and video games. A review of these mediums is outside of the scope of this book and, in fact, would be a book in and of itself. Nonetheless, we can readily bring to mind the old John Wayne westerns, the numerous movies about gangs and mobsters, and Andy Warhol's famous gun art in 1981 and 1982. Moreover, guns are present in so many aspects of our pop culture that we may not readily recall their presence in subtler forms. For instance, guns are present in many Looney Tunes and Disney cartoons, where Yosemite Sam and Bugs Bunny wielded firearms, as did Davy Crockett, Gaston (*Beauty and the Beast*), and John Smith (*Pocahontas*)—and, of course, we recall the infamous moment when Bambi's mother was shot and killed. In addition, some firearms have become iconic in and of themselves, such as the Model 29 .44 Magnum Smith & Wesson revolver Clint Eastwood used in *Dirty Harry* and the numerous firearms used in the James Bond films over the years. With certainty, firearms remain as present in Hollywood today as they always have been, as they do across essentially all of our pop culture mediums (Hollywood and guns, 2013).

US and State Firearm Ownership Statistics

Because federal law prohibits the creation of a national gun registry, it is exceedingly difficult to measure firearm ownership in the United States. As such, research studies examining gun levels and their correlation to various variables, such as crime rates, often utilize proxies of gun ownership. Unfortunately, often either these proxies are invalid or their validity has yet to be established (Kleck, 2015). In an article discussing the research flaws in this particular body of literature, Kleck (2015) reviewed a few arguably more valid gun ownership measures that are existent in the research base: the percentage of suicides committed by guns (PSG), two survey measures of percentage of households with either a gun or a handgun, and one survey pertaining to the percentage of individuals with guns. Nevertheless, he asserts that only PSG shows strong validity in terms of measuring firearm ownership by area, while none of the proxies that have been used in prior studies were determined to be valid for purposes of examining trends of ownership over time (Kleck, 2004). Further, surveys, while having the benefit of being fairly direct modes of measurement, come with their share of measurement problems, namely in the form of underreporting firearm ownership and small sample sizes (Kleck, 2015).

Given the problems associated with these measures or proxies of gun ownership, contested gun ownership survey data will not be presented in this chapter. However, Tables 1.1–1.6, regarding firearm-related statistics from 2012, are included for the reader's edification. According to Kovandzic, Schaffer, & Kleck (2013), PSG is currently thought to be the best available proxy of firearm ownership by several researchers in the field. As such, along with other deaths related to firearms, firearm-related suicide deaths are included within these tables. Table 1.6 includes National Instant Criminal Background Check System (NICS) data, which include the number of checks conducted by state in 2012 to determine a person's eligibility to possess a firearm or explosive in accordance with federal law. The obvious problem with using the rate of background checks as a proxy to measure gun ownership is that these background checks are only conducted by licensed gun dealers who are selling guns legally (Giffords Law Center to Prevent Gun Violence, n.d.). Unlicensed, private sellers do not conduct these checks; and there are many additional flaws associated with the system, such as states failing to report the necessary records to the appropriate databases (Giffords Law Center to Prevent Gun Violence, n.d.). Even if the system was not so flawed, these numbers would only account for ownership by individuals who obtained their firearms legally, completing ignoring the subset of the population who obtain their firearms illegally.

Although the aforementioned concerns about validity of self-report surveys should be considered, some information is available regarding the use of firearms in America. According to a Gallup poll conducted in 2005, most gun owners reported using their firearms for the following three reasons: for protection against crime (67%), for target shooting (66%), and for hunting (58%). Because there was very little change from Gallup surveys conducted in 2000 and 2005, Gallup combined the data to provide the following more nuanced information. Gallup data indicated that male gun owners are more likely to use their guns for hunting or target shooting, while female gun owners are more likely to use their guns for personal protection. Also, younger gun owners are more likely to report using their guns for hunting and target shooting than older gun owners. Republicans are more likely to report using a gun for target shooting and hunting in comparison to Democrats; however, they are almost equally likely to say they use a gun for protection against crimes (Carroll, 2005).

Firearm Foundations

Imagine reading an entire book on airplanes and not knowing what the terms *cockpit* or *taxiing* meant before or after reading—or reading a book

Table 1.1 Death Statistics by State, 2012

State	Number of total deaths	Number of fatal injury deaths	Fatal injury deaths, percentage of total deaths	Rate of fatal injury deaths per 100,000	Number of firearm-related deaths	Firearm-related deaths, percentage of total deaths	Rate of firearm-related deaths per 100,000
Alabama	49,212	3,470	7.05%	72.03	831	1.69%	17.25
Alaska	3,912	596	15.24%	81.61	132	3.37%	18.07
Arizona	49,549	4,802	9.69%	73.30	946	1.91%	14.44
Arkansas	30,117	2,338	7.76%	79.26	490	1.63%	16.61
California	242,554	17,237	7.11%	45.36	3,068	1.26%	8.07
Colorado	33,133	3,761	11.35%	72.47	672	2.03%	12.95
Connecticut	29,316	1,938	6.61%	53.96	227	0.77%	6.32
Delaware	7,875	586	7.44%	63.90	96	1.22%	10.47
Florida	177,291	13,156	7.42%	68.09	2,473	1.39%	12.80
Georgia	72,847	5,638	7.74%	56.89	1,286	1.77%	12.97
Hawaii	10,274	724	7.05%	52.08	51	0.50%	3.67
Idaho	11,998	1,079	8.99%	67.62	207	1.73%	12.97
Illinois	102,433	6,769	6.61%	52.60	1,178	1.15%	9.15
Indiana	59,332	4,218	7.11%	64.52	800	1.35%	12.24
Iowa	28,389	1,851	6.52%	60.09	217	0.76%	7.06
Kansas	25,145	1,970	7.83%	68.27	377	1.50%	13.07
Kentucky	43,664	3,808	8.72%	86.95	655	1.50%	14.96

Louisiana	42,320	8.42%	77.44	845	2.00%	18.36
Maine	12,870	6.65%	64.43	130	1.01%	9.79
Maryland	44,477	7.43%	56.18	589	1.32%	10.01
Massachusetts	53,177	5.64%	45.13	233	0.44%	3.51
Michigan	89,901	6.74%	61.31	1,222	1.36%	12.37
Minnesota	40,016	7.81%	58.07	382	0.95%	7.10
Mississippi	29,544	8.06%	79.76	535	1.81%	17.91
Missouri	56,094	7.91%	73.68	882	1.57%	14.64
Montana	8,976	9.54%	85.13	171	1.91%	17.01
Nebraska	15,659	7.04%	59.40	167	1.07%	9.00
Nevada	20,785	8.94%	67.49	360	1.73%	13.007
New Hampshire	10,730	7.53%	61.14	117	1.09%	8.85
New Jersey	70,534	5.91%	47.01	444	0.63%	5.01
New Mexico	16,710	11.83%	94.84	323	1.93%	15.50
New York	148,991	5.72%	43.52	977	0.66%	4.99
North Carolina	81,925	7.58%	63.73	1,175	1.43%	12.05
North Dakota	6,038	7.42%	63.88	73	1.21%	10.41
Ohio	112,498	6.89%	67.08	1,263	1.12%	10.93
Oklahoma	36,870	9.32%	90.10	619	1.68%	16.22
Oregon	32,759	8.05%	67.62	443	1.35%	11.36
Pennsylvania	126,981	6.96%	69.24	1,453	1.14%	11.38

(continued)

Table 1.1 Continued

State	Number of total deaths	Number of fatal injury deaths	Fatal injury deaths, percentage of total deaths	Rate of fatal injury deaths per 100,000	Number of firearm-related deaths	Firearm-related deaths, percentage of total deaths	Rate of firearm-related deaths per 100,000
Rhode Island	9,354	669	7.15%	63.70	42	0.45%	4.00
South Carolina	43,198	3,427	7.93%	72.55	743	1.72%	15.73
South Dakota	7,333	600	8.18%	71.94	84	1.15%	10.07
Tennessee	61,956	5090	8.22%	78.85	995	1.61%	15.41
Texas	174,187	13,956	8.01%	53.55	2,743	1.57%	10.53
Utah	15,676	1,884	12.02%	65.99	324	2.07%	11.35
Vermont	5,491	441	8.03%	70.45	56	1.02%	8.95
Virginia	61,564	4,356	7.08%	53.21	840	1.36%	10.26
Washington	50,105	4,139	8.26%	60.03	681	1.36%	9.88
West Virginia	21,915	1,893	8.64%	101.96	278	1.27%	14.97
Wisconsin	48,384	3,802	7.86%	66.42	481	1.00%	8.44
Wyoming	4,481	509	11.36%	88.27	117	2.61%	20.29

Data collected from the Centers for Disease Control and Prevention, Web-based Injury Statistics Query and Reporting System (WISQARS) (2003). National Center for Injury Prevention and Control, Centers for Disease Control and Prevention (producer). Available from: www.cdc.gov/injury/wisqars/index.html. (Accessed March 20, 2015).

Table 1.2 Homicide Statistics by State, 2012

State	Number of total homicides	Homicide deaths, percentage of total deaths	Rate of homicides per 100,000	Number of firearm-related homicides	Firearm-related homicides, percentage of total deaths	Rate of firearm-related homicides per 100,000
Alabama	405	0.82%	8.41	306	0.62%	6.35
Alaska	38	0.97%	5.20	17*	0.43%*	2.33*
Arizona	394	0.80%	6.01	254	0.51%	3.88
Arkansas	238	0.79%	8.07	166	0.55%	5.63
California	2,010	0.83%	5.29	1,362	0.56%	3.58
Colorado	205	0.62%	3.95	115	0.35%	2.22
Connecticut	152	0.52%	4.23	114	0.39%	3.17
Delaware	62	0.79%	6.67	46	0.58%	5.02
Florida	1,200	0.68%	6.21	862	0.49%	4.46
Georgia	657	0.90%	6.63	481	0.66%	4.85
Hawaii	22	0.21%	1.58	<10	—	<10
Idaho	34	0.28%	2.13	18*	0.15%*	1.13*
Illinois	832	0.81%	6.47	645	0.63%	5.01
Indiana	345	0.58%	5.28	251	0.42%	3.84
Iowa	63	0.22%	2.05	33	0.12%	1.07
Kansas	103	0.41%	3.57	67	0.27%	2.32
Kentucky	236	0.54%	5.39	159	0.36%	3.63
Louisiana	550	1.30%	11.95	428	1.01%	9.30

(continued)

Table 1.2 Continued

State	Number of total homicides	Homicide deaths, percentage of total deaths	Rate of homicides per 100,000	Number of firearm-related homicides	Firearm-related homicides, percentage of total deaths	Rate of firearm-related homicides per 100,000
Maine	30	0.23%	2.26	15*	—	1.13*
Maryland	408	0.92%	6.93	294	0.66%	5.00
Massachusetts	133	0.25%	2.00	73	0.14%	1.10
Michigan	734	0.82%	7.43	579	0.64%	5.86
Minnesota	105	0.26%	1.95	61	0.15%	1.13
Mississippi	293	0.99%	9.81	216	0.73%	7.23
Missouri	424	0.76%	7.04	311	0.55%	5.16
Montana	24	0.27%	2.39	10*	0.11%*	0.99*
Nebraska	64	0.41%	3.45	46	0.29%	2.48
Nevada	123	0.59%	4.47	77	0.37%	2.8
New Hampshire	16*	0.15%*	1.21*	13*	.12%*	0.98*
New Jersey	405	0.57%	4.57	276	0.39%	3.11
New Mexico	133	0.80%	6.38	80	0.48%	3.84
New York	730	0.49%	3.73	436	0.29%	2.23
North Carolina	567	0.69%	5.82	422	0.52%	4.33
North Dakota	16*	0.26%*	2.28*	<10	—	—
Ohio	632	0.56%	5.47	437	0.39%	3.78
Oklahoma	270	0.73%	7.08	188	0.51%	4.93

Oregon	110	0.34%	2.82	53	0.16%	1.36
Pennsylvania	698	0.55%	5.47	547	0.43%	4.29
Rhode Island	30	0.32%	2.86	15*	0.16%*	1.43*
South Carolina	373	0.86%	7.9	273	0.63%	5.78
South Dakota	20*	0.27%*	2.4*	<10	—	—
Tennessee	471	0.76%	7.3	327	0.53%	5.07
Texas	1,324	0.76%	5	894	0.51%	3.43
Utah	46	0.29%	1.61	28	0.18%	0.98
Vermont	<10	—	—	<10	—	—
Virginia	335	0.54%	4.09	224	0.36%	2.74
Washington	227	0.45%	3.29	127	0.25%	1.84
West Virginia	103	0.47%	5.55	66	0.30%	3.55
Wisconsin	187	0.39%	3.27	126	0.26%	2.2
Wyoming	20*	0.45%*	3.47*	<10	—	—

* According to the CDC, rates based on 20 or fewer deaths may be "unstable" (i.e., unreliable).

— indicates a calculation that is not applicable.

Data collected from Centers for Disease Control and Prevention, Web-based Injury Statistics Query and Reporting System (WISQARS) (2003). National Center for Injury Prevention and Control, Centers for Disease Control and Prevention (producer). Available from: www.cdc.gov/ncipc/wisqars. (Accessed March 20, 2015).

Table 1.3 Suicide Statistics by State, 2012

State	Number of total suicides	Suicide deaths, percentage of total deaths	Rate of suicides per 100,000	Number of firearm-related suicides	Firearm-related suicides, percentage of total deaths	Rate of firearm-related suicides per 100,000
Alabama	724	1.47%	15.03	500	1.02%	10.38
Alaska	168	4.29%	23.00	98	2.51%	13.42
Arizona	1,156	2.33%	17.65	663	1.34%	10.12
Arkansas	485	1.61%	16.44	307	1.02%	10.41
California	3,893	1.61%	10.24	1,549	0.64%	4.08
Colorado	1,052	3.18%	20.27	533	1.61%	10.27
Connecticut	368	1.26%	10.25	111	0.38%	3.09
Delaware	125	1.59%	13.63	46	0.58%	5.02
Florida	3,002	1.69%	15.54	1,550	0.87%	8.02
Georgia	1,168	1.60%	11.78	750	1.03%	7.56
Hawaii	190	1.85%	13.63	43	0.42%	3.09
Idaho	297	2.48%	18.61	176	1.47%	11.03
Illinois	1,292	1.26%	10.04	490	0.48%	3.81
Indiana	940	1.58%	14.38	513	0.86%	7.85
Iowa	383	1.35%	12.46	175	0.62%	5.69
Kansas	502	2.00%	17.40	297	1.18%	10.29
Kentucky	724	1.66%	16.53	469	1.07%	10.71
Louisiana	567	1.34%	12.32	375	0.89%	8.15

Maine	209	1.62%	15.73	112	0.87%	8.43
Maryland	583	1.31%	9.91	272	0.61%	4.62
Massachusetts	604	1.14%	9.09	151	0.28%	2.27
Michigan	1,261	1.40%	12.76	623	0.69%	6.30
Minnesota	656	1.64%	12.19	310	0.77%	5.76
Mississippi	410	1.39%	13.73	296	1.00%	9.91
Missouri	914	1.63%	15.17	546	0.97%	9.06
Montana	233	2.60%	23.17	153	1.70%	15.22
Nebraska	232	1.48%	12.5	115	0.73%	6.2
Nevada	524	2.52%	19.02	274	1.32%	9.95
New Hampshire	202	1.88%	15.28	98	0.91%	7.42
New Jersey	683	0.97%	7.7	160	0.23%	1.8
New Mexico	442	2.65%	21.21	230	1.38%	11.04
New York	1,708	1.15%	8.72	516	0.35%	2.64
North Carolina	1,286	1.57%	13.19	709	0.87%	7.27
North Dakota	105	1.74%	14.97	63	1.04%	8.98
Ohio	1,542	1.37%	13.35	784	0.70%	6.79
Oklahoma	670	1.82%	17.56	411	1.11%	10.77
Oregon	724	2.21%	18.57	367	1.12%	9.41
Pennsylvania	1,647	1.30%	12.9	819	0.64%	6.42
Rhode Island	105	1.12%	10	26	0.28%	2.48

(continued)

Table 1.3 Continued

State	Number of total suicides	Suicide deaths, percentage of total deaths	Rate of suicides per 100,000	Number of firearm-related suicides	Firearm-related suicides, percentage of total deaths	Rate of firearm-related suicides per 100,000
South Carolina	673	1.56%	14.25	433	1.00%	9.17
South Dakota	141	1.92%	16.91	76	1.04%	9.11
Tennessee	978	1.58%	15.15	626	1.01%	9.7
Texas	3,037	1.74%	11.65	1,744	1.00%	6.69
Utah	550	3.51%	19.27	283	1.81%	9.91
Vermont	87	1.58%	13.9	50	0.91%	7.99
Virginia	1,063	1.73%	12.98	587	0.95%	7.17
Washington	1,038	2.07%	15.05	529	1.06%	7.67
West Virginia	326	1.49%	17.56	198	0.90%	10.66
Wisconsin	723	1.49%	12.63	348	0.72%	6.08
Wyoming	171	3.82%	29.66	102	2.28%	17.69

Data collected from Centers for Disease Control and Prevention, Web-based Injury Statistics Query and Reporting System (WISQARS) (2003). National Center for Injury Prevention and Control, Centers for Disease Control and Prevention (producer). Available from: www.cdc.gov/ncipc/wisqars. (Accessed March 20, 2015).

Table 1.4 Additional Firearm-Related Death Statistics by State, 2012*

State	Number of firearm-related deaths: Unintentional, percentage of total deaths	Rate of firearm-related deaths: Unintentional per 100,000	Number of firearm-related deaths: Undetermined, percentage of total deaths	Rate of firearm-related deaths: Undetermined per 100,000	Number of firearm-related deaths: Legal intervention, percentage of total deaths	Rate of firearm-related deaths: Legal intervention per 100,000
Alabama	14 (0.03%)	0.29	<10	—	<10	—
Alaska	<10	—	<10	—	<10	—
Arizona	<10	—	11 (0.02%)	0.17	13 (0.03%)	0.20
Arkansas	10 (0.03%)	0.34	<10	—	<10	—
California	30 (0.01%)	0.08	15 (0.01%)	0.04	112 (0.05%)	0.29
Colorado	11 (0.03%)	0.21	<10	—	<10	—
Connecticut	<10	—	<10	—	<10	—
Delaware	<10	—	<10	—	<10	—
Florida	22 (0.01%)	0.11	15 (0.01%)	0.08	24 (0.01%)	0.12
Georgia	36 (0.05%)	0.36	<10	—	13 (0.02%)	0.13
Hawaii	<10	—	<10	—	<10	—
Idaho	<10	—	<10	—	<10	—
Illinois	17 (0.02%)	0.13	12 (0.01%)	0.09	14 (0.01%)	0.11
Indiana	14 (0.02%)	0.21	<10	—	13 (0.02%)	0.20
Iowa	<10	—	<10	—	<10	—
Kansas	<10	—	<10	—	<10	—
Kentucky	17 (0.04%)	0.39	<10	—	<10	—

(continued)

Table 1.4 Continued

State	Number of firearm-related deaths: Unintentional, percentage of total deaths	Rate of firearm-related deaths: Unintentional per 100,000	Number of firearm-related deaths: Undetermined, percentage of total deaths	Rate of firearm-related deaths: Undetermined per 100,000	Number of firearm-related deaths: Legal intervention, percentage of total deaths	Rate of firearm-related deaths: Legal intervention per 100,000
Louisiana	33 (0.08%)	0.72	<10	—	<10	—
Maine	<10	—	<10	—	<10	—
Maryland	<10	—	<10	—	18 (0.04%)	0.31
Massachusetts	<10	—	<10	—	<10	—
Michigan	<10	—	<10	—	<10	—
Minnesota	<10	—	<10	—	<10	—
Mississippi	12 (0.04%)	0.40	<10	—	<10	—
Missouri	17 (0.03%)	0.28	<10	—	<10	—
Montana	<10	—	<10	—	<10	—
Nebraska	<10	—	<10	—	<10	—
Nevada	<10	—	<10	—	<10	—
New Hampshire	<10	—	<10	—	<10	—
New Jersey	<10	—	<10	—	<10	—
New Mexico	<10	—	<10	—	<10	—
New York	<10	—	<10	—	19 (0.01%)	0.10
North Carolina	29 (0.04%)	0.30	<10	—	<10	—
North Dakota	<10	—	<10	—	<10	—

State					
Ohio	<10	—	18 (0.02%)	0.16	16 (0.01%)	0.14
Oklahoma	12 (0.03%)	0.31	<10	—	<10	—
Oregon	<10	—	<10	—	12 (0.04%)	0.31
Pennsylvania	65 (0.05%)	0.51	<10	—	18 (0.01%)	0.14
Rhode Island	<10	—	<10	—	<10	—
South Carolina	26 (0.06%)	0.55	<10	—	<10	—
South Dakota	<10	—	<10	—	<10	—
Tennessee	25 (0.04%)	0.39	14 (0.02%)	0.22	<10	—
Texas	45 (0.03%)	0.17	32 (0.02%)	0.12	28 (0.02%)	0.11
Utah	<10	—	<10	—	<10	—
Vermont	<10	—	<10	—	<10	—
Virginia	11 (0.02%)	0.13	<10	—	12 (0.02%)	0.15
Washington	<10	—	<10	—	16 (0.03%)	0.23
West Virginia	<10	—	<10	—	<10	—
Wisconsin	<10	—	<10	—	<10	—
Wyoming	<10	—	<10	—	<10	—

* According to the CDC, rates based on 20 or fewer deaths may be "unstable" (i.e., unreliable).

— indicates a calculation that is not applicable.

Data collected from Centers for Disease Control and Prevention, Web-based Injury Statistics Query and Reporting System (WISQARS) (2003). National Center for Injury Prevention and Control, Centers for Disease Control and Prevention (producer). Available from: www.cdc.gov/ncipc/wisqars. (Accessed March 20, 2015).

Table 1.5 Handgun Data by State (2012)

State	Number of firearm-related handgun deaths, percentage of total deaths	Rate of firearm-related handgun deaths per 100,000	Number of firearm-related homicides with a handgun, percentage of total deaths	Rate of firearm-related homicides with a handgun per 100,000	Number of firearm-related suicides with a handgun, percentage of total deaths	Rate of firearm-related suicides with a handgun per 100,000
Alabama	—	—	—	—	—	—
Alaska	90 (2.30%)	12.30	<10*	—	67 (1.71%)	9.19
Arizona	—	—	—	—	—	—
Arkansas	—	—	—	—	—	—
California	—	—	—	—	—	—
Colorado	315 (0.95%)	6.07	13 (0.04%)*	0.25*	291 (0.88%)	5.61
Connecticut	—	—	—	—	—	—
Delaware	—	—	—	—	—	—
Florida	—	—	—	—	—	—
Georgia	871 (1.20%)	8.78	283 (0.39%)	2.85	562 (0.77%)	5.67
Hawaii	—	—	—	—	—	—
Idaho	—	—	—	—	—	—
Illinois	—	—	—	—	—	—
Indiana	—	—	—	—	—	—
Iowa	—	—	—	—	—	—
Kansas	—	—	—	—	—	—
Kentucky	263 (0.60%)	6.00	62 (0.14%)	1.42	193 (0.44%)	4.41

State						
Louisiana	—	—	—	—	—	—
Maine	—	—	—	—	—	—
Maryland	445 (1.00%)	7.56	234 (0.53%)	3.99	189 (0.42%)	3.21
Massachusetts	148 (0.28%)	2.23	34 (0.07%)	0.53	106 (0.20%)	1.59
Michigan	—	—	—	—	—	—
Minnesota	—	—	—	—	—	—
Mississippi	—	—	—	—	—	—
Missouri	—	—	—	—	—	—
Montana	—	—	—	—	—	—
Nebraska	—	—	—	—	—	—
Nevada	—	—	—	—	—	—
New Hampshire	—	—	—	—	—	—
New Jersey	73 (0.10%)	0.82	<10*	—	69 (0.10%)	0.78
New Mexico	224 (1.34%)	10.74	55 (0.33%)	2.64	161 (0.96%)	7.72
New York	—	—	—	—	—	—
North Carolina	822 (1.00%)	8.43	286 (0.35%)	2.93	508 (0.62%)	5.21
North Dakota	—	—	—	—	—	—
Ohio	719 (0.64%)	6.23	167 (0.15%)	1.45	524 (0.47%)	4.54
Oklahoma	410 (1.11%)	10.75	89 (0.24%)	2.33	302 (0.82%)	7.92
Oregon	309 (0.94%)	7.92	34 (0.10%)	0.87	264 (0.81%)	6.77
Pennsylvania	—	—	—	—	—	—

(continued)

Table 1.5 Continued

State	Number of firearm-related handgun deaths, percentage of total deaths	Rate of firearm-related handgun deaths per 100,000	Number of firearm-related homicides with a handgun, percentage of total deaths	Rate of firearm-related homicides with a handgun per 100,000	Number of firearm-related suicides with a handgun, percentage of total deaths	Rate of firearm-related suicides with a handgun per 100,000
Rhode Island	29 (0.31%)	2.76	<10*	–	19 (0.20%)*	1.81*
South Carolina	319 (0.74%)	6.75	67 (0.16%)	1.42	239 (0.55%)	5.06
South Dakota	–	–	–	–	–	–
Tennessee	–	–	–	–	–	–
Texas	–	–	–	–	–	–
Utah	225 (1.44%)	7.88	18 (0.11%)*	0.63*	201 (1.28%)	7.04
Vermont	–	–	–	–	–	–
Virginia	637 (1.03%)	7.78	176 (0.29%)	2.15	445 (0.72%)	5.44
Washington	–	–	–	–	–	–
West Virginia	–	–	–	–	–	–
Wisconsin	292 (0.60%)	5.10	96 (0.20%)	1.68	189 (0.39%)	3.30
Wyoming	–	–	–	–	–	–

Note. The source contained handgun data for the following states only: AK, CO, GA, KY, MD, MA, NJ, NM, NC, OH, OK, OR, RI, SC, UT, VA, WI.

* According to the CDC, rates based on 20 or fewer deaths may be "unstable" (i.e., unreliable).

— indicates a calculation that is not applicable.

Data collected from Centers for Disease Control and Prevention, Web-based Injury Statistics Query and Reporting System (WISQARS) (2003). National Center for Injury Prevention and Control, Centers for Disease Control and Prevention (producer). Available from: www.cdc-gov/ncipc/wisqars. (Accessed March 20, 2015).

Table 1.6 NICS Background Checks by State, 2012

State	Number of NICS background checks
Alabama	563,880
Alaska	93,405
Arizona	363,036
Arkansas	279,763
California	563,458
Colorado	514,658
Connecticut	294,338
Delaware	40,062
Florida	1,073,859
Georgia	527,885
Hawaii	17,416
Idaho	147,494
Illinois	1,280,613
Indiana	597,124
Iowa	160,062
Kansas	228,105
Kentucky	1,578,331
Louisiana	353,025
Maine	96,760
Maryland	231,182
Massachusetts	251,361
Michigan	503,979
Minnesota	525,774
Mississippi	231,711
Missouri	567,009
Montana	137,830
Nebraska	91,553
Nevada	146,892
New Hampshire	147,726
New Jersey	120,071
New Mexico	156,333
New York	353,064

(continued)

Table 1.6 Continued

State	Number of NICS background checks
North Carolina	574,622
North Dakota	85,812
Ohio	680,930
Oklahoma	380,634
Oregon	274,302
Pennsylvania	1,044,731
Rhode Island	26,666
South Carolina	335,695
South Dakota	92,055
Tennessee	600,869
Texas	1,633,278
Utah	324,604
Vermont	36,135
Virginia	498,426
Washington	561,122
West Virginia	248,952
Wisconsin	434,688
Wyoming	70,671

NICS, National Instant Criminal Background Check System.
NICS information collected from Everytown for Gun Safety Action Fund
website: http://act.everytown.org/sign/fatal-gaps.

on automobiles and not understanding how they run at the most basic level. Certainly, one would not necessarily require a sophisticated knowledge or understanding of the parts and functionality of a mechanism unless one were interested in operating it. However, in order to reflect intelligently upon concepts and issues relevant to it, it is critical to have, at the very least, a basic understanding of its various types, components, and functions. Such is absolutely the case with firearms. Namely, the fundamental pieces of information and language associated with firearms are absent in the gun literature, including in resources addressing issues germane to the Second Amendment, gun violence, and gun violence prevention. It is a rather glaring and peculiar omission. Again, one can readily contend that it is not important to know how a gun fires in order to adequately address gun violence among youth, for instance. While that may well be true in that specific example, we believe that it is necessary to possess at least a basic understanding of the types, components, and functionality of firearms to be an informed commentator and consumer of information related to them. Perhaps most importantly, however, is that scholars and readers must familiarize themselves with the vocabulary and terms associated with firearms in order to be able to speak and reflect intelligently upon issues in this regard. Failing to do so leads to miscommunication and misunderstanding, such as associating neutral or benign concepts with negative undertones. Terms such as *semiautomatic, assault rifle, large-capacity magazine*, and even *background checks* are used so freely and casually that they have become household words; but it is likely that many people are unsure of their actual meanings.

Simply put, terms and concepts must be properly defined and appropriately understood by everyone interested in firearm-related issues, to ensure that proper interpretations are made and the use of jargon is avoided. Therefore, in this section, we provide an overview of firearm-related foundational concepts and key terms. Specifically, we present information relevant to four areas: (i) basic gun models, components, and functionality; (ii) firearm safety; (iii) ammunition and bullet calibers; and (iv) gun manufacturers. It is important to note that these sections are not exhaustive, but rather, they are intended to provide the reader with a fundamental level of education and knowledge from which to draw. Please note that we define a number of firearm-related terms and summarize various notable legal cases because it is essential that readers be acclimated to such. These are included in the back of this book: *Glossary of Firearm-Related Terms* in Appendix A and *Glossary of Firearm-Related Law and Legal Cases* in Appendix B. All of those who interact with firearms should be familiar with these basic terms and cases, as should those engaged in firearm-related initiatives and discussions, including organizations, groups, researchers, authors, and professionals involved in all aspects of firearm issues and debates.

Basic Gun Components, Functionality, and Models

Perhaps the most basic distinction between firearms is that of *handguns* versus *long guns*. Certainly, there are more classifications, such as machine guns and other automatic weapons, antitank weapons and grenade and missile launchers, taser guns, air guns, BB guns, and even improvised or otherwise modified guns. We focus on handguns and long guns in this section. We also review some of the most common models of firearms within these categories as well as their fundamental components and functions. First, it is important to familiarize ourselves with the basic components and functions of firearms before discussing various types and models.

Essentially, all firearms have the following four components, which establish how they operate and are classified: muzzle, breach, hammer, and trigger. The *muzzle* is the opening on the front of a firearm whereby the bullet is projected. The *breech* is the back of a firearm. The *hammer* is the component that initiates contact with the bullet primer to ignite the gun powder and project the bullet out of the muzzle. This is the piece that one would see a firearm operator pull or click back with his or her thumb; however, hammers on most rifles and shotguns, and some handguns, are internal. With some firearms, a *firing pin* is used to contact the bullet primer rather than the hammer directly. Lastly, the *trigger* is the component that is pulled by one's finger to release the hammer, which fires the bullet (Guns 101, n.d.). In addition, some of the more common components include sights, action, frame, barrel, bore, chamber, cylinder release, firing pin, and receiver. There are certainly many other parts of certain firearms, some specific to handguns and some to long guns.

So, how do guns work? It depends. Different guns have different firing mechanisms, although bullets are essentially comparable across type and size. Early firearms, such as matchlock and flintlock guns, functioned in the manner in which the names imply: via lighting a match or producing a spark that would ignite the gunpowder. Modern firearms operate with the same premise but include additional steps: the ammunition, in the form of a bullet, sits in the barrel of the firearm; the operator pulls the trigger; the hammer snaps forward; the firing pin strikes the primer, which creates a spark, igniting the gunpowder, thereby creating an explosion that projects the bullet out of the firearm. While there are various types of firing mechanisms, these are the basic steps involved in shooting a gun.

Handguns

Although some handguns have been designed for hunting, they are most typically developed for the purpose of engaging in target shooting and other marksmanship-related activities and for self-defense. This is rather obvious given their compact nature, which facilitates easier handling and carrying, in addition to making them easy to conceal. There are essentially three types of handguns:

- single-shot pistols
- revolvers
- semiautomatic pistols

As the name signifies, *single-shot pistols* are firearms that contain a maximum of one bullet at any given time. Single-shot mechanisms are also available for rifles and shotguns. Once the operator fires the gun, he or she must load another bullet into the firearm. As we will see in the paragraphs that follow, single-shot firearms are clearly much less efficient than revolvers and semiautomatic pistols. Therefore, today, they would likely only be collected and used by those interested in such from a historic or novelty standpoint rather than as a practical matter. That said, there are rare exceptions, such as the Palm Pistol˚ (n.d.), a single-shot firearm "intended for seniors, disabled or others with grip limitations due to hand strength, manual dexterity or phalangeal amputations," as it can be fired using the thumb or combinations of other fingers. Please note that single-shot firearms should not be confused with single-action revolvers, whose type of revolver mechanism we will describe.

Most people would recognize revolvers from older police or western movies, although they are generally no longer used by on-duty law enforcement officers due to the higher level of firepower readily available to citizens, particularly those engaging in criminal activity. That said, revolvers remain popular and continue to be used today by officers as an off-duty gun, by armed security guards, and, of course, by average citizens. Revolvers were first called *revolving guns*, reflecting the movement of the aforementioned cylinder and the fact that they are repeating firearms, such that they allow the operator to fire multiple rounds without reloading. Each bullet is loaded individually, and the cylinder rotates when fired, lining up the next round for fire. Revolvers can be classified as either single-action or double-action. *Single-action revolvers* require the operator to manually pull back on the hammer, whereas *double-action revolvers* automatically rotate upon pull of the trigger. Most revolvers hold six bullets, which is where the moniker *six-shooter* was derived.

Despite the negative connotation often associated with the term, semiautomatic pistols essentially describe every modern handgun that is not a single-shot pistol or revolver. As such, it the type of handgun people are most likely to see on the news or even in the community given their use by law enforcement personnel. The defining feature of the semiautomatic pistol is the magazine clip that holds the bullets and snaps into the handle of the firearm. Unlike the rotating nature of revolvers, the semiautomatic handgun uses the energy of one shot to reload the chamber for the next bullet. This process is repeated at each trigger pull, until the magazine is empty (i.e., all of the bullets are used). It is for these reasons that semiautomatic firearms can be rapidly fired and quickly reloaded with a backup magazine clip—and, therefore, they are often used by those committing violent crimes but also by law enforcement in crime prevention efforts. For these reasons, they are popular among civilians for self-defense purposes as well but also because of their ease of use in target shooting and other marksmanship-related activities. The number of bullets held in a magazine varies, ranging from 5 to 30 and including everything in between, such as 10, 11, or even 15. Of note, certain states have restrictions on the magazine capacity, such as New Jersey's maximum of 15 (see Ciyou, 2017; Kappas, 2017; Supica, n.d.).

Long Guns

The term *long guns* refers to just what the name implies—those with longer barrels than handguns. Given the fact that laws differ as a function of the type of firearm in question (i.e., long gun versus handgun), laws across jurisdictions also differ in their definition of what constitutes a long gun (e.g., a barrel length between 16 and 24 inches). Given the size of these firearms, they are often designed to be held against the operator's shoulder; and they are also often less restricted because it is much more difficult to conceal them compared to handguns. For instance, in New Jersey, one must apply for a handgun permit for each handgun purchase, whereas there is no specific permit required for long guns. The ultimate purpose of long guns runs the gamut from hunting to home defense to marksmanship-related activities. At the core level, long guns can be broken down into two categories: shotguns and rifles.

Shotguns are firearms that project shells that are packed with ammunition of three types: birdshot, buckshot, and slugs. *Birdshot* shells have the smallest pellets, *buckshot* shells have the largest pellets, and *slugs* do not have pellets but, rather, pieces of metal. As a result, the gun is intended to fire a (circular) pattern of these many small projectiles. This function makes a shotgun useful for such activities as trap and skeet shooting and hunting, particularly for birds and other moving targets, as well as for self-defense. There are many types of shotguns, but perhaps the most commonly known are pump-action and double-barreled.

Rifles are long guns that have a "rifled" bore, which means that the inside of the barrel is grooved. These grooves spin the bullet upon firing, thereby greatly improving the accuracy of the shot. Thus, it is no surprise that rifles are the primary weapon of snipers, hunters, and marksmen seeking high levels of accuracy, especially from extended distances. Theoretically, a rifle can shoot over 4 miles, although accuracy is significantly compromised at that distance. More realistically, record sniper shots have generally been recorded at distances between 0.5 and nearly 1.5 miles, or 800 to 2,600 yards. That said, most amateur shooters practice at 50-, 100-, and 200-yard ranges, which also represents typical hunting distances. With regard to the ammunition, there is great variability, ranging from .22 caliber rifles (which are essentially on par with BB pellets) to much higher-level calibers, with the largest being .950 (Largest caliber rifle ever, 2013).

Civilian rifles are typically either bolt action or semiautomatic. A *bolt action* rifle functions by a manually operated bolt, whereas a semiautomatic rifle functions much like its handgun counterpart—by way of rounds loaded into a magazine clip. Readers are likely to have heard the term *assault rifle*, which refers to a fully automatic rifle that uses a detachable magazine. As the name implies, these firearms are used by the military. A term that is often used and likely misunderstood is *AR-15*. The AR-15 stands for ArmaLite rifle, named after the company that developed it in the 1950s. The AR-15 is a semiautomatic modern rifle, and it is simply one type of design within this category of firearms. As such, it is not an assault rifle, unless one uses a definition other than that of an automatic firing mechanism. Nevertheless, despite the negative attention they have received, rifles are commonly owned and operated by many civilians in the hunting and shooting sports communities.

Ammunition and Bullet Calibers

The primary components of *ammunition*, or *ammo*, are the case, primer, powder, and projectile. The *case* is the container that holds the other components together and is typically made of brass, steel, or copper. The *primer* is an explosive chemical compound that ignites the gunpowder once struck by the firing pin. There are two types of primer, *rimfire* and *centerfire*, which correspond to where the primer is located in the case—either in its rim or in the center of its base. *Gunpowder* is a chemical mixture that serves as a propellant as it burns quickly and becomes an expanding gas once ignited. Lastly, the *projectile* is the object expelled from the barrel, such as a bullet.

In the context of firearms, the *caliber* refers to the approximate internal diameter of the gun's barrel or the diameter of the projectile it fires. As such, it is associated with the size of the bullet a gun fires as measured in inches—specifically, in hundredths and even thousandths of an inch. Of note, the word *gauge* is used to refer to the diameter of shotgun barrels. There are literally hundreds of ammunition and gun calibers available, although some of the most common are .380, .22LR, .40 S&W, 9mm, .45ACP, .38 Special, and .357 Mag (see McNab, 2009).

Gun Manufacturers

As with gun calibers, a full review of all gun manufacturers is well beyond the scope of this book; therefore, we provide a concise overview of the more common brands that are more likely to be heard among those in the general population via media, news, music, movies, and other pop culture forums. For readers interested in more information, we have included the gun manufacturers' websites at the bottom of each overview paragraph for more information.

Benelli

Benelli is an Italian company founded by Giovanni Benelli in 1967. Located in Urbino, Italy, Benelli is most known for its high-quality shotguns used by many, including SWAT teams and other law enforcement personnel (www.benelliusa.com).

Beretta

Beretta, more formally known as Fabbrica d'Armi Pietro Beretta S.p.A. (Pietro Beretta Arms Factory), is an Italian company that dates back to 1526 and is currently in its 15th generation of lineage. After nearly 500 years of business, Beretta is one of the best-known and recognizable names in the firearm arena. The company produces a wide range of types and styles of firearms, which are used by civilians, military, and law enforcement alike (www.beretta.com/en-us).

Bushmaster

Bushmaster Firearms International, LLC, is a North Carolina–based company founded in 1973 that produces semiautomatic pistols and rifles, including M4 and AR-15 designs (www.bushmaster.com).

Century Arms

Century Arms is a Florida-based company founded in 1961 in Vermont, which is one of the largest importers and manufacturers of firearms in the country. Century Arms also imports and distributes ammunition (http://centuryarms.biz).

Colt

A post–Civil War slogan has been recounted as "Abe Lincoln may have freed all men, but Sam Colt made them equal." Such reflects Samuel Colt's development of a firearm not requiring reloading after each shot. At age 22, in 1836, Colt opened his first plant in Paterson, New Jersey. By 1851, Colt became the first American manufacturer to open a plant in England, securing his reputation in the international market. He ultimately became one of the ten wealthiest people in the United States and was awarded the honorary title of "colonel" by the governor of Connecticut. Today, Colt's Manufacturing Company, LLC, is based in Hartford, Connecticut, and continues to produce firearms for military, law enforcement, commercial, and international markets (www.colt.com).

CZ Firearms

Ceska zbrojovka Uhersky Brod, or CZ, was established in 1936 in Strakonice, a town in the South Bohemian region of the Czech Republic. The company has undergone numerous transformations and restructuring efforts over the years, including development of various factories throughout the Czech Republic. In 1997, the company expanded to the US market by creating CZ-USA. CZ manufactures a range of firearms, including handguns, rifles, and shotguns, as well as firearms for military and law enforcement (http://cz-usa.com).

Glock

In 1963, Gaston Glock began developing extensive experience working with plastics and metals and, in 1981, Glock GES.M.B.H. was founded. This resulted in the first commercially successful line of handguns with a *polymer* (synthetic plastic) frame. Today, Glock is the leading manufacturer of handguns, specifically designed to meet military and law enforcement specification requirements throughout the world. As such, it is perhaps the most commonly used service pistol in police departments across the United States. Undoubtedly, it remains very popular with military persons and civilians as well (www.glock.com/GlockLanding/index.html).

Heckler & Koch

Heckler & Koch (H&K) is a German defense manufacturing company that produces a range of firearms for military and civilian use. The Engineering

Office Heckler & Co. was developed by Edmund Heckler, Theodor Koch, and Alex Seidel subsequent to Germany's demise in World War II and changed its name to H&K in 1949. The company focused on developing military firearms and weaponry throughout the 1950s and 1960s until diversifying and expanding to develop firearms for law enforcement, shooting sports, and hunting. Today, the company maintains its operations in Germany, the United Kingdom, France, and the United States and characterizes itself as "a leading designer and manufacturer of small arms and light weapons for law enforcement and military forces worldwide" and "the maker of premier brand firearms for the sporting and commercial markets" (http://hk-usa.com).

Israel Weapons Industries

Israel Weapons Industries (IWI) is an Israel-based firearm manufacturer best known for the production of the UZI line of automatic submachine guns. The UZI was first developed by Uziel Gal (1923–2002), a captain in the Israeli army who won an internal competition for the design of a new submachine gun. The first prototypes appeared in 1950, and its first manufacturer, Israeli Military Industries, developed numerous variations, including handguns and semiautomatic firearms. The UZI has remained iconic in pop culture. For instance, a well-known scene is that of the attempted assassination on US president Ronald Reagan in 1981, wherein one of his bodyguards wielded an UZI from his jacket. It has also been presented in numerous movies, music videos, and songs over the years. Today, IWI produces a full line of UZIs, including the SMG, Mini, Micro, and Pistol. In addition, IWI manufactures knives, watches, stun guns, flashlights, tactical pens, and other related gear, such as handcuffs and batons (www.uzi.com).

Kel-Tec

Kel-Tec CNC Industries, Inc., is a Florida-based firearm manufacturing company that was founded in 1991. It began as a machine shop producing firearm components but started to manufacture firearms in 1995. Kel-Tec specializes in rifles and handguns that were designed for concealed carry by law enforcement personnel and qualified citizens. Additionally, it has become one of the top five handgun makers in the United States and one of the largest in the world. Among its innovative designs, its 2006 production of a 9mm handgun that was said to be the thinnest and lightest of its kind to ever be mass-produced (www.keltecweapons.com).

Kimber

With offices in Montana and New York, Kimber Manufacturing, Inc., is a US firearms manufacturing company that designs and produces handguns, pistols, and rifles. It was founded in 1979 in Oregon and underwent numerous transitions over the years, ultimately surviving as a well-known brand used by civilians as well as organizations, such as the USA Shooting Team, the Los Angeles Police Department SWAT Team, and the US Marines. Kimber has become known for the accuracy and customizability of its M1911-style handguns in particular, although its full line of firearms remains quite popular (www.kimberamerica.com).

Remington

Remington Arms Company, LLC, is a North Carolina–based firearm and ammunition manufacturing company that dates back to 1816, at which point Eliphalet Remington developed his first hand-built rifle. As E. Remington & Sons, the company was responsible for supplying countless pistols, carbines, rifles, and muskets to the Federal Army and Navy in 1861 in connection with the Civil War. The company was also a substantial supplier of firearms and ammunition to the United States and its allies during World War I and World War II. In addition, Remington's M24 Sniper Rifle served as the US Army's standard sniper rifle from 1988 to 2010. Of note, Remington also developed the world's first effective typewriter in 1873. As the oldest gunmaker in the United States, Remington maintains production facilities and offices throughout the country; and it also continues to produce firearms from its original product line (www.remington.com).

Ruger

Sturm, Ruger & Co., Inc., is a US firearms manufacturing company most commonly referred to as "Ruger." It was founded in 1949 by Alexander McCormick Sturm and William B. Ruger, and its motto is "Arms Makers for Responsible Citizens." Ruger produces a wide range of rifles, shotguns, and handguns; namely, 400 variations of more than 30 product lines. Moreover, Ruger has been ranked the number one US firearm manufacturer numerous times as a leading producer of firearms for hunting, target shooting, collecting, self-defense, law enforcement, and government agencies (www.ruger.com).

SIG Sauer

SIG Sauer is a New Hampshire–based firearm manufacturer originally developed in 1853 by Friedrich Peyer im Hof, Heinrich Moser, and Conrad Neher in Switzerland. The company started out as the Swiss Wagon Factory, producing wagons and railway cars, but ultimately became a world-renowned firearm manufacturer when it entered the competition to develop a state-of-the-art rifle with the goal of the Swiss Army adopting it. Sure enough, the Swiss Wagon Factory won the award 4 years later for its Prelaz-Burnand rifle, receiving an order for 30,000 firearms. In turn, the company changed its name to the Swiss Industrial Company—Schweizerische Industrie-Gesellschaft, known worldwide as SIG. The company proceeded to develop arms for military and law enforcement and, by the 1980s, sought an expansion to the United States. In 1985, SIGARMS', Inc., came to be in Virginia. In 2007, SIGARMS changed its name to SIG Sauer'. According to the company, approximately one in three law enforcement officers in the United States use its firearms, in addition to many civilians. Moreover, SIG Sauer maintains its worldwide presence and popularity across military, law enforcement, and civilian groups (www.sigsauer.com)

Smith & Wesson

Smith & Wesson is a Massachusetts-based firearm manufacturer developed by Horace Smith and Daniel B. Wesson in the mid-19th century. They formed their partnership in 1852 in Connecticut with the goal of producing a lever action repeating handgun that could use a completely self-contained cartridge. However, this was an unsuccessful venture, forcing them to sell their company to Oliver Winchester, who was a shirt manufacturer but later became the world-renowned developer of the Winchester Repeating Arms Co. In 1856, Smith and Wesson formed their second partnership, resulting in the creation of the first successful fully self-contained cartridge revolver available in the world. By 1870, Smith & Wesson had emerged as a worldwide leader in handgun manufacturing, highlighted by such clients as the US Cavalry and the Russian imperial government. Ultimately, Horace Smith retired at age 65 and sold his share of the company to Daniel B. Wesson. Nevertheless, Smith & Wesson remained successful and produced firearms that became iconic and are still produced today, including hammerless revolvers and the .38 Military & Police, which is currently known as the Model 10. According to Smith & Wesson, the Model 10 has been in continual production since its development and "has been used by virtually every police agency and military force around the world." In the 20th century, the company developed the first Magnum revolver, the .357 Magnum (1935), and the first American-made double action auto-loading pistol, the Model 39 (1955). The Model 29, famously known as the firearm used by Clint Eastwood in *Dirty Harry*, was produced in 1956. In addition, in 1965, Smith & Wesson launched the world's first stainless steel revolver. Although recognized for its innovations in the handgun arena, Smith & Wesson has continued to develop an extensive line of long guns, military weapons, and a range of related items and accessories, such as handcuffs, safes, apparel, watches, collectibles, knives, and air guns. In 2007, the company purchased Thompson/Center Arms (see *Thompson/Center Arms*). Furthermore, the company sponsors sport shooters under the moniker "Team Smith & Wesson."

Needless to say, Smith & Wesson remains a worldwide leader in firearm manufacturing and has maintained a strong presence in pop culture, including in movies and music (www.smith-wesson.com).

Springfield Armory

In 1777, during the American Revolutionary War, George Washington ordered the creation of the Springfield Armory based out of Springfield, Massachusetts, for the purpose of storing revolutionary ammunition and gun carriages. By 1794, the armory started producing muskets for the young country and served as a supplier for every major US conflict for the following 150 years. In 1968, the US government closed the armory, citing budgetary concerns. The site was preserved as the Springfield Armory National Historic Site and as part of the national park system. However, in 1974, the Springfield Armory name was licensed to Robert Reese and became Springfield Armory, Inc. Although the company is not directly related to the original armory and it is based out of Illinois, it cites "reverence for the legacy of The Armory" and notes that the Reese family "resurrected the most historically significant designs produced by The Armory." Today, Springfield Armory, Inc., is a leader in the production of contemporary sporting rifles and polymer handguns with its M-, XD-, and 1911 series (www.springfield-armory.com).

Thompson/Center Arms

Out of the collaboration between Warren Center and the K.W. Thompson Tool Company, Thompson/Center (T/C) Arms is a Springfield, Massachusetts–based firearm manufacturer that was established in 1967. The company is known for its interchangeable barrel single-shot pistols and rifles and its resurrection of muzzle-loading rifles. In 2007, T/C Arms was purchased by Smith & Wesson (www.tcarms.com).

Walther Arms

Walther Arms, Inc., is a German firearm manufacturer founded by Carl Walther in 1886, serving as a producer of hunting and target rifles. By the turn of the 20th century, the company began engineering handguns. The early years of the company included only variable success, but in 1929, Walther began to manufacture its *Polizeipistole* (police pistols) or "PP" models, followed by its "PPKs" (*Polizeipistole Kriminalmodell*), or Police Pistol Detective models. The company then encountered significant trouble when its factory was destroyed during World War II as it had reportedly used labor from a German concentration camp (*Neuengamme*). Nevertheless, the company was reestablished in the mid-1950s and has continued to develop into a worldwide leader in firearm manufacturing. Today, Walther remains in Germany but also maintains a US base in Arizona, producing a range of handguns from its P, PP, and PPK series, as well as Colt and H&K tactical rimfire replicas (www.waltherarms.com).

Winchester

Winchester Repeating Arms Company was created by Oliver Fisher Winchester in 1866 and in 2016 celebrated its 150-year anniversary. As noted,

Winchester purchased controlling interest in the firearms company initially developed by Smith and Wesson. Winchester quickly established its name by producing rifles and ammunition. It gained further notoriety as President Theodore Roosevelt's favorite hunting rifle. The brand also maintained connections with other US presidents. Frankly, Winchester's history and connection with American culture and war efforts is so extensive that even an attempt to summarize it comprehensively here would be impossible. Although the company experienced economic hardship and related troubles from the 1960s to the 1990s, it reemerged as a leader and remains so today. The company continues to produce its world-renowned rifles, shotguns, and ammunition (www.winchesterguns.com).

Firearm Safety

Although it is rarely presented in the professional mental health literature, firearm safety is one of the most, if not the most, paramount issues to address in the firearm arena. While law and policy issues are relevant to firearm-related violence and suicide prevention efforts, highlighting firearm safety at the individual level is critical given the many millions of people who own and operate firearms in this country. There are many firearm safety resources available to people in many different forms, including in-person education and instruction, as well as online and in print (e.g., Luciano, 2015). Two particular authorities have set forth basic safety rules: the National Shooting Sports Foundation (NSSF) and the National Rifle Association (NRA).

The NSSF has set forth 10 rules for safe firearm handling (National Shooting Sports Foundation, n.d.). We present them below along with our paraphrased summary of each rule:

1. *Always keep the muzzle pointed in a safe direction.* Essentially, this rule is paramount and underlies all others: namely, do not aim at something you do not intend to shoot. This rule applies even when loading and unloading a firearm as well as when cleaning one; this rule applies *at all times.* Following this rule would likely eliminate most, if not all, accidental injuries and deaths.
2. *Firearms should be unloaded when not actually in use.* A firearm should only be loaded when it is being prepared for use. Moreover, firearms and ammunition should be secured in a safe place, separately, and in an area inaccessible to children and unauthorized adults. When a firearm is being handled or transferred to another person, it should immediately be checked to determine if it is loaded (including checking the chamber, receiver, and magazine). Assume all firearms are loaded until they are determined to be otherwise.
3. *Don't rely on your gun's "safety."* Again, assume that all firearms are loaded until otherwise determined. Many firearms have what is referred to as a *safety*—a component that is intended to prevent unintended firing. However, some firearms do not have safeties,

some have fairly ineffective ones, and, in other cases, a handler can be mistaken as to whether the safety is engaged or not. Nevertheless, a safety should be in the "on" or "engaged" position until the operator is ready to fire. Of note is that a gun can fire in certain instances even when the trigger is not pulled, such as when it is dropped or otherwise struck hard enough to engage the firing mechanism.

4. *Be sure of your target and what's beyond it.* Do not fire a gun unless you are certain as to what the bullet will strike, including beyond the intended target. Once a gun is fired, the operator has no control over where the projectile will go or what it will strike. Therefore, it is critical that the operator take into account the target and beyond and where the projectile may travel if the shot is missed or otherwise ricochets.

5. *Use correct ammunition.* Some firearms allow for the use of various sizes of ammunition. It is critical that the operator only use the proper ammunition for the firearm, which will be outlined in its instruction manual. Relevant information in this regard will also be on ammunition boxes. Using improper ammunition can destroy a firearm and lead to injury. Firearms are designed, produced, and safety-tested based on the proper ammunition. Those who hand load or reload ammunition need to ensure that they adhere to the proper specifications as well. Ammunition should never be submerged in water, lubricated, or otherwise modified.

6. *If your gun fails to fire when the trigger is pulled, handle with care!* There are times when a firearm jams or simply does not fire when the trigger is pulled. During such instances, the firearm should be properly unloaded and the cartridge should be disposed. The firearm is loaded until the cartridge and all other ammunition is removed.

7. *Always wear eye and ear protection when shooting.* Eye and ear protection is necessary for obvious reasons. There are numerous types of materials that could lead to eye injury when using and even cleaning firearms, and noise exposure can lead to hearing damage.

8. *Be sure the barrel is clear of obstructions before shooting.* Any obstruction in the barrel, however small, can impact the firearm's pressures and lead to injury.

9. *Don't alter or modify your gun, and have guns serviced regularly.* Although there are approved accessories for firearms, such as sights, no one other than the experts who design them should modify firearms. Moreover, firearms require periodic inspection, adjustment, and service, like most other mechanical devices

10. *Learn the mechanical and handling characteristics of the firearm you are using.* The range of available firearms is seemingly endless, varying by brand, type, style, size, and functionality, as well as many other classifications and specifications. As such, people should only handle and operate firearms with which they have familiarity, including, but

not limited to, issues related to its loading and unloading, carrying, safety, and firing mechanisms.

These are consistent with the NRA's fundamental rules as well. The NRA adds two rules to the aforementioned list: never use alcohol or over-the-counter, prescription, or other drugs before or while shooting and be aware that certain types of guns and many shooting activities require additional safety precautions (NRA gun safety rules, n.d.).

Both the NSSF and the NRA have also developed firearm safety programs: *Project ChildSafe* and *Eddie Eagle GunSafe*, respectively.

The NSSF developed Project ChildSafe in or around 2003 as part of *Project Safe Neighborhoods*, a federal gun violence prevention initiative (Project ChildSafe, n.d.). Project ChildSafe has partnered with more than 15,000 law enforcement agencies (primarily police departments) who have distributed more than 36 million safety kits to firearm owners throughout all 50 states and the five US territories. According to the group, it received $90 million of federal funding from 2003 through 2008, but such funding was cut for a period of time thereafter. However, according to its 2015 annual report, the NSSF (see www.nssf.org/annual-review) was awarded a 2-year, $2.4 million cooperative agreement by the US Department of Justice, and the money was to go toward supporting firearm safety education. Specifically, gun locks and safety materials were to be provided to communities throughout the country in an effort to help reduce firearms misuse. The group has numerous additional supporters, including firearm manufacturers, hunting groups, and various other firearm-related organizations and companies. Project ChildSafe is a nonprofit charitable organization that focuses on promoting firearms safety via educational means, providing free firearm safety kits. The kits include a cable-style gun-locking device and a brochure (also available in Spanish) that discusses safe handling and secure storage guidelines to help deter access by unauthorized individuals. Furthermore, a primary initiative of the group is "Own it? Respect it. Secure it." According to the group, this initiative is "an industry-wide commitment to raise the public's consciousness on the issue of firearm safety and responsibility and encourage firearms owners to embrace the importance of proper storage" and to set forth the following message to gun owners: "Store your firearms responsibly when not in use." The group also has an "Own it? Respect it. Secure it." initiative toolkit available for people to promote and encourage responsible firearms ownership. They also ask firearm owners to sign and adhere to the following pledge:

> I choose to own a firearm and therefore accept responsibility for using and storing it safely. I commit to securing my firearm when not in use, being aware of who can access it at all times and educating others to do the same.

The NRA developed the Eddie Eagle GunSafe° program in 1988, which the group characterizes as a "gun accident prevention program that seeks to help parents, law enforcement, community groups and educators navigate a topic paramount to our children's safety." The primary mission is to teach pre-kindergarten through fourth-graders what to do if they ever come across a firearm (Eddie Eagle GunSafe Program, n.d.). The basic instructional steps are stop, don't touch, run away, and tell a grown-up. The program's website includes videos, activities, and a number of program resources. The program instructor guides were developed by Dr. Lisa Monroe, an assistant professor in the Department of Instructional Leadership and Academic Curriculum, University of Oklahoma, and a specialist in early childhood education. According to the program, it provides grant funding for schools, law enforcement agencies, hospitals, day-care centers, and libraries interested in bringing Eddie Eagle to children in the area.

Public Sentiment

Public sentiment regarding firearms continues to be divided in the United States. For some, firearms are a significant part of their family heritage and subculture, whereas others remain deeply opposed to anything related to guns. Mass shootings such as those at Columbine; Virginia Tech; Sandy Hook Elementary; Newtown; the Emanuel African Methodist Episcopal Church in Charleston, South Carolina; and most recently Orlando and Las Vegas gain media attention, thereby reinvigorating debates and discussions related to firearms and gun control. In fact, the *New York Times* set forth a page-one editorial for the first time since 1920, entitled "End the Gun Epidemic in America" (2015).

Researchers have investigated the effects that mass shootings and the media's subsequent response have had on public opinion related to various topics, such as firearms, mental illness, and gun violence prevention policies. Prior to the Newtown shooting, public opinion research pertaining to firearm-related topics was 15 years old. Two weeks following the Newtown shooting, in 2013, McGinty, Webster, & Barry (2013) fielded a national opinion survey to gauge support for public policy pertaining to firearm violence prevention. The authors found that large majorities of Americans (gun owners and non–gun owners alike) supported a range of gun violence prevention policies. Specifically, these policies included attitudes regarding the enhancement of background check systems for gun sales, prohibiting certain individuals deemed dangerous from possessing guns, and preventing people with mental illness from owning guns. Results suggest that stories about mass shootings heighten negative attitudes toward individuals with serious mental illness. Media coverage also raised support for gun restrictions for this specific group and for a ban on large-capacity magazines (McGinty et al., 2013). However, concerns later arose regarding the responses to the original survey being directly related to the tragedy (Barry, McGinty, Vernick, & Webster, 2015). At the end of 2014, a Pew Research Center poll asked the question "What do you think is more important—to protect the right of Americans to own guns or to control gun ownership?" The latter study reported a 7-point increase of respondents who affirmed the rights of gun owners in comparison, which may be related to the hypothesis that the recent tragedy somehow influenced the first survey. As such, the authors decided to examine how attitudes might have changed since Sandy Hook with a 2-year follow-up public opinion survey regarding 24 specific gun policies. Again, large majorities of Americans continued to support a range of gun violence prevention policies, often with little difference between gun owners' and non-owners' opinions. Specifically, little difference was noted for issues such as universal background check requirements for gun sales, barring individuals with temporary restraining orders pertaining to domestic violence from having guns, and certain regulations for licensed gun dealers (Barry et al., 2015).

Considering that the media seems to have considerable influence on public opinion, Perrin (2016) highlighted the need for psychologists to translate psychological science (related to these issues) for the media and public. She contended that the field needs to bring attention to the media's contribution to contagion regarding mass shootings. Similarly, McLeigh (2015) outlined the issues that arise when policies are implemented out of fear and without necessary knowledge and understanding. She also discussed the appointment of Vivek Murthy as the US surgeon general and guessed that he might move the government toward a "well-reasoned and scientifically grounded approach to gun violence" (p. 202). She proceeded to address the policies that are implemented out of fear and without necessary knowledge and understanding and how these policies may lead to deleterious effects. She reiterated the suggestion that "we need to invest in approaches that are preventive and that seek to build community, instead of policies and practices that further exclude and isolate individuals from communities" (McLeigh, 2015, p. 202). While such attention following noteworthy and tragic events such as mass shootings is warranted and understandable, the prosocial and appropriate use of firearms rarely, if ever, gains attention in our media. Given that one-third of our country are firearm owners—approximately 100 million people—it is fortunately the case that the vast majority own and operate firearms safely. However, such activities as hunting and sports shooting are rarely highlighted as they are likely not very well understood by many. This reality does not negate or minimize the significance of mass shootings or other types of firearm-related violence, but it is essential to understand firearms from a much broader perspective—one of our primary goals in this book. As such, we now provide an overview of Second Amendment groups; rod & gun clubs, hunting clubs, and shooting ranges; as well as gun control and gun violence prevention groups.

Second Amendment Groups

In this section, we provide an overview of a number of Second Amendment (2A) groups. The Second Amendment of the US Constitution reads: "A well regulated Militia, being necessary to the security of a free State, the right of the people to keep and bear Arms, shall not be infringed." As such, 2A groups believe that the Constitution provides for an individual right to own firearms for US citizens versus opposing views that highlight the "well regulated Militia" aspect of the amendment. What is clear is that there is great variability in the perspectives even among 2A groups; as we will see, some groups uphold a "no compromise" stance such that they will not entertain any negotiation related to gun control, whereas others present with much more flexibility on the issue—and, of course, there are groups that fall somewhere along the continuum. The set of groups presented below is by no means an exhaustive list of 2A groups, but it is a representative one that reflects a range of perspectives and organizational structures within the 2A community. Please note that we present the NRA first, given that it is likely the most recognizable to the broad readership, but then proceed by presenting groups alphabetically. Please also note that a full review of all 2A groups, including state and regional organizations, would essentially be a text in and of itself. Therefore, we have focused our review on national groups rather than those that are locally or regionally focused. Nevertheless, the interested reader would not have to look very far to find such groups as they are located in each state throughout the country (see www.allgungroups.org for more information), including in states with the strictest gun laws, for example, the California Rifle & Pistol Association (www.crpa.org) and the New York State Rifle and Pistol Association (www.nysrpa.org).

The National Rifle Association

In 1871, the NRA was formed by two Union veterans, Colonel William C. Church and General George Wingate, who were displeased by the problematic marksmanship of their troops and, therefore, sought to promote rifle shooting. Ultimately, the NRA received a charter by the state of New York in November of that year, and the Civil War general, former governor of Rhode Island, and US senator Ambrose Burnside became the NRA's first president. In subsequent years, rifle ranges and shooting practice grounds were developed in New York State, wherein matches were held annually. However, political opposition led the NRA to ultimately relocate its primary range to Sea Girt, New Jersey, in 1892. The NRA has been met with political opposition since its inception. Therefore, the NRA formed the Legislative Affairs Division in 1934 and, in 1975, the Institute for Legislative Action. The NRA has also developed and maintains three publications: *The American Rifleman, The American Hunter,* and the more recent *The American Guardian,* which has been renamed, *America's 1st Freedom.*

Despite the near constant political opposition, interest in the NRA has continued to grow. At the turn of the 20th century, the NRA began to encourage the development of rifle clubs across colleges and military academies in an effort to advance the involvement in shooting sports among young people. According to the NRA, programming for young people and youth remains a foundational aspect of the group. As such, more than 1 million youth participate in shooting sporting events and related programs in connection with various groups, including, but not limited to, 4-H, the Boy Scouts of America, the American Legion, the Royal Rangers, the National High School Rodeo Association, and others. Today, Camp Perry in Ohio serves as the home of the NRA's national matches—the primary platform for excellence in marksmanship—with approximately 6,000 annual participants.

The NRA was also involved in war efforts. According to the group, its call to assist in arming Britain in 1940 led to the collection of more than 7,000 firearms for Britain's defense against Germany, and it offered its ranges to the government, helped develop training materials, and reloaded ammunition for those guarding war plants during World War II.

The NRA also continued its educational and training efforts to the civilian population after the war. Namely, in 1949, the NRA joined the state of New York in developing the first hunter education program. Such courses are now offered by state fishing and game departments throughout the United States and Canada (details regarding hunter education training can be found at http://hservices.nra.org/state-fish-game-information.aspx). In addition, the NRA provides the Youth Hunter Education Challenge (YHEC), which is a program for young people to develop their hunter education skills. These YHECs are currently held in 43 states and three Canadian provinces and include an estimated 40,000 youth.

The NRA became the only national trainer of law enforcement officers with the introduction of its NRA police firearms instructor certification program in 1960. The group reports that there are more than 13,000 NRA-certified police and security firearms instructors today. Moreover, eight different pistol and shotgun matches are held each year at the National Police Shooting Championships in Albuquerque, New Mexico.

According to the NRA, it also has 125,000 certified instructors who train over 1 million firearm owners annually. It provides courses in such areas as basic rifle, pistol, shotgun, muzzle-loading firearms, personal protection, and ammunition reloading. In addition, approximately 7,000 certified coaches are trained to work specifically with young competitive shooters. Furthermore, the NRA established the Eddie Eagle GunSafe˙ program in 1988, which is a safety program (described in more detail under *Firearm Safety*) for pre-kindergarten to fourth-grade children to provide instruction for situations in which they might come across a firearm while unsupervised. The group notes that it has been provided to more than 28 million children and was developed by a task force comprised of educators, school administrators, curriculum specialists, urban housing safety officials, clinical psychologists, law enforcement officials, and NRA firearm safety experts. Furthermore, the NRA has provided Refuse To Be a Victim' seminars over the years for more than 100,000 men and women to develop their own personal safety plans and strategies. In addition, Trigger the Vote is the NRA's national non-partisan voter registration campaign sponsored by the NRA Freedom Action Foundation (NRA trigger the vote, n.d.). Chuck Norris is presented as its honorary chair. It represents the NRA's effort to ensure that gun owners across the country are registered to vote.

Armed Citizens United

According to the group, Armed Citizens United (ACU) is "an action based organization committed to lobbying, organizing, informing, empowering and educating at every level (Federal, State and Local) to ensure that the liberties originally and expressly stated in the 2nd Amendment are not infringed" (Armed Citizens United, n.d.). Its board consists of three members, including a 21-year veteran of the Tulsa Police Department and a US Marine Corps veteran, in addition to the support of a media and management group. ACU's mission statement is:

> Armed Citizens United is a membership based organization that stands to preserve and defend the inherent rights declared by the 2nd Amendment. We lobby, organize, inform, empower and educate to ensure that the liberties provided to us are not infringed.

The following represents the ACU's positions on various issues related to firearms:

- Nonviolent felons should have their rights fully restored "once their debt to society is paid."
- Students and faculty should be able to legally carry firearms on campus, including in class.
- Gun-free zones should be abolished.
- The government should not have the ability to tax or license a constitutional right.
- The passage of "constitutional carry" laws nationwide, such that all 50 states should be required to honor the concealed weapons permits of other states (e.g., Alaska, Arizona, Arkansas, Vermont, and Wyoming).
- The current NICS background check system should be eliminated.
- The National Firearms Act should be repealed.
- The Hughes Amendment to the Firearm Owners Protection Act should be repealed.
- Firearms safety instruction courses should be made available to all students.

- The right of all Americans is to carry their firearm either openly or concealed, and states should not determine such. Moreover, the ACU does not agree with carrying a concealed weapon license fees.
- All 50 states should have "stand your ground" and castle doctrine laws to provide citizens with the legal backing to the "inherent right" to self-defense.
- All gun owners and regular gun users should proactively be standing up for and supporting the Second Amendment.

Bullets & Bagels

Bullets & Bagels is a group founded in Orange County, California, in 2013 to provide Jewish people with a forum to express their interest in firearms and shooting. As such, the group provides "a comfortable and supervised venue for socializing, networking, eating quality food, learning about firearms, firearm safety, marksmanship, and recreational shooting for primarily Jewish members." However, the group indicates that it is non-exclusive, such that approximately 25% of its participants and members are not Jewish. The group holds recreational shooting events at various ranges in Southern California every other month, and, in addition to target shooting, their meetings include guest speakers, vendors from various industries, and food—to facilitate socialization and networking. The group notes that its guest speakers are typically law enforcement officers, legal experts, educators, or military figures who address a range of topics, such as California firearm laws, home firearm maintenance and storage, and an analysis of the Old Testament view of self-defense. Bullets & Bagels presents five primary volunteer NRA-certified range safety officers and instructors, including an advanced martial artist who holds a master's degree in modern Middle Eastern history and public history, a Marine Corps veteran, and a federal special agent. The mission of Bullets & Bagels is as follows:

> To provide the Jewish community and others a comfortable, supervised, no-pressure environment to experience the satisfaction and pleasure of learning to shoot a gun and to hone shooting skills.

Citizens Committee for the Right to Keep and Bear Arms

The Citizens Committee for the Right to Keep and Bear Arms (CCRKBA) is an advocacy group based out of Washington State, sharing an office with the Second Amendment Foundation, Jews for the Preservation of Firearm Ownership, and Keep and Bear Arms. Of note is that Alan M. Gottlieb is a foreperson of all of these groups. The CCRKBA consists of seven people on the board of directors, including a chair, vice chair, secretary, and treasurer. It has been reported to have over 650,000 members and is part of a network of 2A rights organizations overseen by its chair. The CCRKBA employs one full-time lobbyist in Washington, DC, and, unlike many 2A advocacy groups, has a political action committee that extends itself beyond firearm-related issues. Its mission is as follows:

> The *Citizens Committee for the Right to Keep and Bear Arms* is dedicated to protecting your firearms rights. Our role is to educate grass root activists, the public, legislators and the media. Our programs are designed to help all Americans understand the importance of the Second Amendment and its role in keeping Americans free.

Firearms Policy Coalition

The Firearms Policy Coalition (FPC) is a group based out of Roseville, California, that characterizes itself as a 501(c)4 grass-roots, non-partisan, public benefit organization (see www.firearmspolicy.org). The FPC sets forth the following purposes and objectives:

- To protect and defend the Constitution of the United States and the People's rights, privileges and immunities deeply rooted in this Nation's history and tradition, especially the inalienable, fundamental, and individual right to keep and bear arms;
- To protect, defend, and advance the means and methods by which the People of the United States may exercise those rights, including, but not limited to, the acquisition, collection, transportation, exhibition, carry, care, use, and disposition of arms for all lawful purposes, including, but not limited to, self-defense, hunting, and service in the appropriate militia for the common defense of the Republic and the individual liberty of its citizens;
- To foster and promote the shooting sports and all lawful uses of arms; and
- To foster and promote awareness of, and public engagement in, all of the above.

As such, the FPC seeks members and collects donations to support 2A advocacy. According to the group, it communicates its constituents' positions to elected officials, regulators, courts and others; funds pro-gun efforts and activities, including direct lobbying, grass-roots outreach, legal action, and education and coalitions; and keeps members apprised of the latest gun rights issues and news. According to the FPC, it has over 600,000 members and supports 12 partner organizations.

Gun Owners of America

The Gun Owners of America (GOA) is a nonprofit lobbying organization based out of Springfield, Virginia, formed in 1975 by retired senator H. L. (Bill) Richardson. The GOA indicates that its purpose is to preserve and defend Second Amendment rights of gun owners as it "sees firearms ownership as a freedom issue." The group reports that it represents the views of gun owners "whenever their rights are threatened," "from state legislatures and city councils to the United States Congress and the White House." The GOA notes that it has built a national network of attorneys to help fight such legal battles in almost every state, citing the fact that it fought for and won the right of gun owners to recover damages from the Federal Bureau of Alcohol, Tobacco and Firearms for harassment and unlawful seizure of firearms. It indicates that the Gun Owners of America Political Victory Fund serves as its political action branch, and the Gun Owners Foundation is the research branch of the group. The GOA indicates that it represents over 500,000 members (See a shrink, 2014) and, as such, provides a number of online articles and media resources. The group presents a quote from former Republican (Texas) US congressman Ron Paul on its website header: "The only no-compromise gun lobby in Washington."

Jews for the Preservation of Firearm Ownership

Jews for the Preservation of Firearm Ownership (JPFO) is a Washington State–based group founded in 1989. It characterizes itself as an "educational civil-rights organization, not a lobby," and sets forth three primary goals, which are presented verbatim here:

> Destroy so-called "gun control" (code words for disarming innocent people).
> Expose the misguided notions that lead people to seek out so-called "gun control."
> Encourage Americans to understand and defend all of the Bill of Rights for all citizens. The Second Amendment is the "Guardian" of the Bill of Rights. (http://jpfo.org/filegen-a-m/about.htm)

According to the group, it was initially created to educate the Jewish community about the historical tragedies Jews have suffered when they have been disarmed, although it welcomes those of all religious persuasions. It cites the Holocaust, for example, but also presents eight other instances where the occurrence of genocide is put in the context of gun control:

- Ottoman Turkey (1915–1917), 1–1.5 million civilians killed
- Soviet Union (1929–1945), 20 million
- China, Nationalist (1927–1949), 10 million

- China, Red (1949–1952, 1957–1960, 1966–1976), 20–35 million
- Guatemala (1960–1981), 100,000–200,000
- Uganda (1971–1979), 300,000
- Cambodia, Khmer Rouge (1975–1979), 2 million
- Rwanda (1994), 800,000

The interested reader can reference The Genocide Chart on JPFO's website for more detailed information, including the targets of such atrocities and the associated gun control laws enacted and enforced by the aforementioned governments (The genocide chart, 2002).

The JPFO also publishes numerous articles, open letters, documentaries, booklets, and books, including *Death by "Gun Control": The Human Cost of Victim Disarmament*, which was written by its founder Aaron Zelman along with Richard W. Stevens. The group's organizational team consists of a director, rabbinic director, operations manager, editor, and webmaster.

Keep and Bear Arms

Keep and Bear Arms describes itself as "a grassroots movement of the people, by the people, and for the people." Moreover, "It is a call to action, a call for self-education, and a 21-gun salute to the many good men and women who fought and died to bring America into being." The group consists of a president, vice president, secretary/treasurer, bookkeeper, web director, marketing director, two doctors, three advisors, a cartoonist, and numerous featured writers. According to the group's website (www.keepandbeararms.com/about/mission.asp), its mission is to advocate for the upholding of the Second Amendment by engaging in the following:

- Educate people via free email news and editorials, and by linking to and from the many organizations standing for our Second Amendment freedoms;
- Be an outlet for quality writers who offer ideas and information to share with the national community which uphold and strengthen our guiding principles;
- Stimulate new ideas and strategies;
- Generate simple, regular action by people with similar aims;
- Build an electronically-linked community of Liberty-motivated activists;
- Work effectively daily to move forward in the cause of Freedom.

National Association for Gun Rights

The National Association for Gun Rights (NAGR) is based out of Windsor, Colorado. The group characterizes itself as a "nonprofit, nonpartisan, single-purpose citizens' organization dedicated to preserving and protecting the Constitutionally-protected right-to-keep-and-bear-arms through an aggressive program designed to mobilize public opposition to anti-gun legislation."

Its leadership consists of a president, vice president of political affairs, vice president of marketing and development, and chair. The NAGR indicates that it has become the fastest-growing gun rights organization in the country with over 4.5 million members, that it maintains a "no compromise" perspective on the issue of gun control, and that its legal team is "constantly at work in the courts." The group also offers firearm training and publishes a quarterly newsletter, *The Gun Activist*. According to the NAGR, it is only similar to the NRA insofar as they are both gun rights organizations, indicating that "the similarities end there." Namely, the NAGR reports that it is not seeking "access to politicians" to pass a gun bill "just to get something done." The NAGR asserts that the NRA has supported and endorsed antigun politicians and reiterates its own position of "no compromise" in firearm legislation in contrast to its conceptualization of the NRA.

Second Amendment Foundation

The Second Amendment Foundation (SAF) was founded in 1974 as a Washington State–based nonprofit corporation. It describes itself as a group that has been "a pioneer in innovative defense of the right to keep and bear arms, through its publications, public education programs and legal action." The SAF is governed by a seven-member board of trustees. The SAF publishes TheGunMag.com as well as a women's firearms magazine, the quarterly *Women & Guns*; a monthly newsletter, *The Gottlieb-Tartaro Report*; and a quarterly member/supporter newsletter, the *SAF Reporter*. In addition, the SAF publishes the annual reference book the *Journal on Firearms and Public Policy*. The group is affiliated with the CCRKBA and Keep and Bear Arms. Their mission statement is as follows:

> The Second Amendment Foundation (SAF) is dedicated to promoting a better understanding about our Constitutional heritage to privately own and possess firearms. To that end, we carry on many educational and legal action programs designed to better inform the public about the gun control debate. (www.saf.org/mission/)

According to the group, it has "a noteworthy track record in bringing and supporting legal actions and amicus briefs, in cases affecting the right to keep and bear arms." It states that successful court actions have been brought in the US Supreme Court, such as in *District of Columbia v. Heller, 2008* and *McDonald v. Chicago, 2010*. The SAF further indicates that it is involved in as many as two dozen active court cases at a given time, including in successful cases that have been brought against the carry ban in Illinois (*Moore v. Madigan, 2012*), emergency powers acts (*Bateman v. Perdue, 2012*), self-defense outside of the home (*Ezell v. City of Chicago, 2011*), handgun prohibitions in public housing, denial of permits or sales to resident aliens, and other firearm-related issues. The SAF also contends that it was involved in numerous cases over many decades, such as overturning the San Francisco handgun ban and blocking a ban on the sale of handguns in New Haven, Connecticut.

The SAF also launched a project spearheaded by a California surgeon in 1994 which remains a functional subgroup today: Doctors for Responsible Gun Ownership (DRGO; see https://drgo.us for more information). DRGO is a nationwide network of physicians, scientists, medical students, and others who support the safe and lawful use of firearms. According to the group, its mission is as follows:

> Doctors for Responsible Gun Ownership (DRGO) values the foundational tradition of firearm ownership in the lives of Americans. Firearm policy must always accord with the enumerated individual civil right to keep and bear arms enshrined in the Second Amendment.
>
> DRGO educates health professionals and the public in the best available science and expertise about firearms, including gun safety and preventing injury and death through wise use and lawful self defense. We teach what science shows—that guns in responsible hands save lives, reduce injuries, and protect property by preventing violent crime.
>
> DRGO serves as a guard against biased, policy-directed pseudoscience that would hinder gun ownership under the guise of legitimate science. (https://drgo.us/mission/)

Students for Concealed Carry on Campus

Students for Concealed Carry on Campus (SCCC) was formed by Chris Brown, a political science student from the University of North Texas, immediately after the Virginia Tech shootings. Its board of directors consists of an assistant director of development, director of public relations, director of development, director of technology, and a board member whom spearheads product development. The SCCC also has regional directors in the Southeast, Rocky Mountain, Southwest, and Midwest regions. The group characterizes itself as "a national, non-partisan, grassroots organization composed of more than 43,000 college students, professors, college employees, parents of college students, and concerned citizens." SCCC has members in all 50 states and the District of Columbia, and it has over 350 established chapters on college campuses and universities. According to the group, it consists of members from a wide range of political persuasions, including "conservatives, moderates, liberals, Republicans, Democrats, Libertarians, Independents."

The SCCC indicates that it has two main functions: first, "to dispel the common myths and misconceptions about concealed carry on college campuses, by making the public aware of the facts" and, second, "to push state legislators and school administrators to grant concealed handgun license holders the same rights on college campuses that those licensees currently enjoy in most other unsecured locations" (http://concealedcampus.org/about/) As such, the SCCC does not advocate that every student and teacher carry handguns on campus but that those who are age 21 and older and who possess valid concealed handgun licenses/concealed carry weapons permits be afforded the same right to carry on college campuses that they are currently afforded in other settings. The group reports that its policy is "to push for change at the state level, rather than at the federal level" and notes that it is not affiliated with any other organization or political party. While the SCCC supports concealed carry on the campuses of both public and private colleges, it indicates that the issue of concealed carry at private colleges should be handled through negotiations with those respective school administrators as opposed to through legislation. The group maintains "no official positions on open carry, unlicensed concealed carry, or concealed carry" at primary or secondary schools.

Students for the Second Amendment

Students for the Second Amendment (SF2A) was founded in 2000, and it is based in San Antonio, Texas. It describes itself as a non-partisan, campus-based, student organization that is "dedicated to educating young people about their rights guaranteed in the Constitution of the United States, especially that right that is the guarantor of all the others—the Second Amendment" (www.sf2a.org/about.html). SF2A consists of 12 board members across various campuses, including a chair, executive vice chair, director of administration, vice chair of finance, director of legislative affairs, director of publicity, vice chair of membership, director of media relations, vice chair of coalitions, director of events, director of information systems, and national executive director. In addition, SF2A maintains chapters and state coordinators in 22 states. Of note is that the group has an advisory board comprised of 11 notable national figures, including retired congressman Ron Paul and Ted Nugent, as well as other members of Congress and retired law enforcement and military personnel.

The group hosts biannual skeet and trap shoots for college and university students. The group notes that it will work with any student who would like to start a chapter on his or her campus by providing "advice, start-up kits, affiliation agreements, assistance in battling hostile administrations, web space, graphic design work, and in rare cases, seed money." In 2002, SF2A initiated its Collegiate Firearms Instructor Program, in an effort to train college and university students to become NRA-certified firearms instructors. It notes that its instructors have subsequently volunteered their training services to programs outside of the academic community, including groups such as Boy Scouts, Girl Scouts, the 4-H Shooting Program, Youth Hunter Education Programs, Big Brothers & Sisters, Camp Fire USA, and Junior Reserve Officer Training Corps (JROTC) organizations. According to SF2A, the Collegiate Firearms Instructor Program has served over 4,100 youth and adults in south Texas by introducing them to the shooting sports.

US Concealed Carry Association

The US Concealed Carry Association (USCCA) is a self-defense-focused 2A group based out of West Bend, Wisconsin. The group was developed from the periodical first published in 2003, the *Concealed Carry Magazine*. The group indicates that it has members in every state and owns a nationally syndicated radio program called *American Radio*, which is broadcast in 36 cities throughout the United States. The group provides numerous resources, including a weekly newsletter, blogs and articles on an extensive set of topics, as well as equipment reviews.

Shooting Sport Groups

In this section, we present a number of shooting sport groups. These are groups that provide education, training, and often competitive forums for those interested in marksmanship-based activities and events that may include archery, crossbow, rifle, shotgun, and pistol. Activities such as archery appear to date back at least 12,000 years, and formally recorded shooting sports date back to approximately 3,000 years ago. According to the International Olympic Committee, the pentathlon was first held in the ancient Olympic Games in 708 BC and consisted of running, long jump, spear throwing, discus, and wrestling. The event was based on skills needed to be a soldier. The more contemporary event, known as the modern pentathlon, consists of fencing, swimming, and horse riding, followed by a combined running and shooting event. This event also reflects skills needed to be a soldier, albeit a cavalry soldier. The modern pentathlon was held over a 4- or 5-day period up until Atlanta 1996, when it was combined into a single day. The modern pentathlon continues to be a popular and internationally recognized sport, and, as such, was a part of the 2016 Summer Olympics in Rio de Janeiro, Brazil, for instance. In addition, 15 other shooting sport events will take place that include the use of rifle, pistol, and shotgun from various distances, positions, and contexts (e.g., trap, skeet). The Paralympic Games also holds various shooting sport events with the use of air pistol, free pistol, and long rifle. These events are for both men and women. For more information, the interested reader can visit the Olympic website (https://www.olympic.org/).

The International Shooting Sport Federation was developed at the turn of the 20th century and brought standardization and structure to shooting sports. Moreover, shooting sports remain popular across colleges and universities throughout the country. According to the Association of College Unions International, there are at least 165 shooting collegiate teams and clubs, including those at Harvard, Yale, and Fordham universities (see www.acui.org/claytargets/directory). Furthermore, the National Collegiate Athletic Association (NCAA) has held its rifle championship at the Division I, II, and III levels for both men and women since 1980 (Rifle, n.d.).

The following is an overview of representative, but not exhaustive, national and international shooting sport advocacy groups, presented alphabetically.

Civilian Marksmanship Program

The Civilian Marksmanship Program (CMP) is a national organization dedicated to training and educating US citizens in the responsible use of firearms and air guns through gun safety training, marksmanship training, and competitions. The CMP is governed by an 11-member board of directors, including a chair/chief executive officer and a chief operating officer. Its southern headquarters is located in Anniston, Alabama; and its northern headquarters is located at Camp Perry, Ohio. According to its 2015 Annual Report, the CMP opened a 500-acre marksmanship facility, Talladega Marksmanship Park, in Alabama. The organization reports that it is one of the most advanced outdoor facilities in the world as it includes a 600-yard rifle range, a 100-yard multipurpose range, and a 50-yard pistol range, in addition to trap and clay fields. In 2015, over 5,000 competitors participated in events with approximately 2,000 spectators. The CMP notes that its origins date back to 1903, when Congress and the president established the National Matches and National Board for the Promotion of Rifle Practice. However, in 1996, Congress privatized the program by creating a federally chartered, not-for-profit corporation known as the Corporation for the Promotion of Rifle Practice and Firearm Safety, Inc.—more commonly known as the CMP. The federal law enacted in 1996 (Corporation for the Promotion of Rifle Practice and Firearms Safety, 1996) that created the group specifically indicates that "the corporation shall give priority to activities that benefit firearms safety, training, and competition for youth and that reach as many youth participants as possible" and identifies its primary functions as:

- To instruct citizens of the United States in marksmanship;
- To promote practice and safety in the use of firearms;
- To conduct competitions in the use of firearms and to award trophies, prizes, badges, and other insignia to competitors.

The CMP notes that its priority is firearm safety:

> The CMP believes that gun safety training is the foremost means of ensuring the safe and responsible use of firearms and air guns. Every CMP program has a teaching component that includes safety doctrine, safety training and safety controls. Every CMP training course includes a gun safety presentation. The use of gun safety flags is mandatory in all CMP events. Rifle purchasers must show proof of marksmanship activity where safety training was given. Gun safety locks are available for all rifles sold by the CMP.
> (2015 Annual Report, p. 5; http://thecmp.org/wp-content/uploads/AnnualReport15.pdf)

Consistent with its mission, the CMP offers extensive training, education, and competitions, particularly geared toward youth, including JROTC cadets across Army, Navy, Marine, and Air Force Cadet Commands. During the 2014–2015 school year, such cadets participated in CMP competitions. In addition, the CMP awarded 173 $1,000 higher education scholarships to qualified students who would also participate in marksmanship activities for the upcoming academic year. It also awarded $200 4-H Shooting Sports State Grants in 2015.

According to the group, it is affiliated with nearly 5,000 clubs, schools, teams, and other shooting sports organizations. The CMP also publishes its quarterly magazine, *On The Mark*, for youth shooting sports leaders and JROTC instructors, with over 8,500 mail recipients. CMP also publishes an online magazine, *The First Shot*, which it distributes electronically to over 47,000 e-mail subscribers.

International Defensive Pistol Association

The International Defensive Pistol Association (IDPA) is based out of Berryville, Arkansas, and serves as the governing body of a shooting sport that uses practical equipment, including full-charge service ammunition, to simulate "real-world" self-defense scenarios using practical handguns and holsters suitable for self-defense. As such, it represents itself as an organization and a sport, where the main goal is to test the skill and ability of an individual, not equipment or gamesmanship. The IDPA matches or courses are either in self-defense or standard exercise formats. The IDPA was founded in 1996 and has a membership of more than 20,000 people across the United States and 50 foreign countries. The IDPA notes: "If you're interested in using truly practical pistols to solve challenging and exciting defensive shooting problems, then IDPA is the sport for you."

International Practical Shooting Confederation

According to the International Practical Shooting Confederation (IPSC), it is a non-political group based out of Oakville, Ontario (Canada), that was established to promote, maintain, and advance practical marksmanship. Competitive IPSC-style shooting originated in Southern California in the late 1950s but continued into various regions of the world, including Australia, Central and South America, Europe, and southern Africa. Given the interest in competing in a structured setting, the IPSC was formally established in 1976. The IPSC is now active in more than 90 countries, and 16 world championships and a number of additional continental championships have been held since its inception. The IPSC does not accept individual members but rather members of IPSC-affiliated bodies. It also has an executive council consisting of a president, general secretary, secretary, treasurer, regional directors, and president and vice president of the International Range Officers Association. The IPSC maintains a 20-page constitution, which includes, but is certainly not limited to, an outline of its guiding principles as well as its governing bylaws. The IPSC also has a comprehensive website, which includes information related to its competitions, rules, and other related information.

National Shooting Sports Foundation

The NSSF is based in Newtown, Connecticut, and describes itself as the "trade association for the firearms industry." Its mission is "To promote, protect and preserve hunting and the shooting sports." The NSSF was formed in 1961 and maintains a membership of more than 13,000 manufacturers, distributors, firearms retailers, shooting ranges, sportsmen's organizations, and publishers. The group indicates that it is active in defending gun rights on Capitol Hill and in state capitols nationwide, which has resulted in many key legislative wins for over a decade. The NSSF supports numerous programs for shooters and hunters, including grant opportunities for college students. It also maintains an extensive library of resources for its members, including printed guides, webinars and videos created for ranges and related businesses, as well as access to NSSF's team of range compliance consultants. In addition, the group publishes a monthly newsletter for shooting facilities, *The Range Report*, as well as a weekly e-newsletter, *Bullet Points*, and weekly updates on topics related to political and legislative issues relevant to the firearm community.

Shoot Like a Girl

Shoot Like a Girl (SLG²) is a women's shooting sports group founded in 2008 by its president, Karen Butler, and its chief operations officer, Cristy Crawford. It was launched at the 2009 World Archery Festival. The group has 43 female pro staff members located in various states. Its mission is "To grow the number of women who participate in shooting sports by empowering them with confidence." Namely, SLG² provides the opportunity for women to try equipment in safe and controlled environments. Moreover, the group notes the benefits of engaging in shooting sports in the context of increasing family time and socialization as well as improving physical fitness and decreasing stress. Furthermore, SLG² indicates that it promotes the conservation efforts of the North American HUNTING MODEL and regional organizations and notes that hunting is a choice women can make to provide organic food for their families. According to SLG², their efforts help protect the environment, manage wildlife, and preserve hunting heritage. The group hosts archery and firearms tournaments to raise money for such organizations as the National Breast Cancer Foundation (NBCF). Specifically, SLG² indicates that it has raised over $40,000 for the NBCF since 2010 from its archery tournaments.

Youth Shooting Sports Alliance

The Youth Shooting Sports Alliance (YSSA) is based in North Augusta, South Carolina, but was originally incorporated in Virginia in 2007. It is classified as a private foundation that provides grants and raises money to promote the recruitment and retention of youth in the shooting sports. According to the group,

> The YSSA was organized to address two important challenges regarding the recruitment and retention of new shooters:
>
> • Identify and support the needs of successful and safe youth programs
> • Provide leadership in the development and promotion of family-friendly shooting range facilities to encourage continued participation in the shooting sports (www.youthshootingsa.com/)

The YSSA provides a directory of youth shooting sports programs throughout the country in the areas of shotgun, rifle, handgun, air rifles/BB guns, muzzleloaders, and archery. The group also conducts a National Youth Shooting Sports Program Needs Assessment to aid in identifying limitations to program growth attributed to the need for shooting sports equipment and supplies. Invitations to participate in the national assessments are sent to Boy Scout Councils, JROTC brigades, district and area managers, National 4-H Shooting Sports state contacts, Royal Rangers region and district leaders, and state association leaders.

Rod & Gun Clubs, Hunting Clubs, and Shooting Ranges

It would require a full book to list and describe the extensive number of rod & gun clubs, hunting clubs, and shooting ranges throughout the United States. Therefore, we will only discuss them briefly here and encourage interested readers to conduct their own searches for those in their respective area. First, we provide an overview of one particularly active and long-standing group in this context: the Sportsmen's Alliance.

The Sportsmen's Alliance began in 1977, known as the Wildlife Legislative Fund of America and Wildlife Conservation Fund of America, after Ohio Ballot Issue 2 threatened Ohio's trapping community. It was then called the US Sportsmen's Alliance, but it changed its name to the Sportsmen's Alliance in 2015 for the purpose of brevity and ease of name recognition. It is comprised of a relatively sizeable board and staff, which includes a chief financial officer, interim president & chief executive officer, vice president of government affairs, vice president of operations, vice president of development & membership, vice president of communications and marketing, government affairs coordinator–western US operations, senior director of western US operations, California State director, director of federal affairs, vice chair, secretary/

treasurer, 13 additional board members, and a graphic designer, digital media specialist, director of education, membership administrator, receptionist, executive assistant, fundraising coordinator, and account manager.

According to the Sportsmen's Alliance, it has continued to fight for, protect, and advance the heritage of hunting, fishing, and shooting across the country, politically and otherwise. In 2001, the group created the Trailblazer Adventure Program to develop a new generation of hunters and anglers by introducing youth and their families to an outdoor lifestyle. It has also created the Families Afield program, which it characterizes as a collaborative effort by Sportsmen's Alliance, the NSSF, and the National Wild Turkey Federation with support from the NRA and the Congressional Sportsmen Foundation, to establish an apprentice (or "mentored") hunting license. It notes that such legislation has been passed in 35 states and that 1.2 million apprentice licenses have been sold.

The Sportsmen's Alliance also created the Sportsmen's Legal Defense Fund as a branch solely aimed at defending sportsmen's rights in the courts. It notes that this branch continues to win precedent-setting cases for sportsmen today. For example, it notes a victory in 2010, whereby it prevailed over the Humane Society of the United States to ensure hunting access on 100 million acres of the National Wildlife Refuge system; and in 2010, the US Fish and Wildlife Service granted its request to delist the Western Great Lakes Region wolves from the endangered species list to ensure the reestablishment of wolf hunting seasons. In addition, the Sportsmen's Alliance has continued to work against restrictions upon the sporting dog community by the animal rights lobby, noting that it has monitored and worked on more than 350 bills in this context. It notes that, as a result of its efforts, no bills have passed in any state that restrict sportsmen in raising and utilizing hunting dogs to date.

Rod & Gun Clubs

Rod & gun clubs are located throughout the country, from Holmes Harbor Rod & Gun in Washington State (www.hhrodandgun.com) to Stuyvesant Rod & Gun Club in Flushing, Queens, New York, and even in Hawaii (e.g., Schofield Rod & Gun) and Puerto Rico (e.g., AAA Gun Shop). Rod & gun clubs are typically social clubs that offer a venue for shooters to congregate and engage in a variety of activities, such as target shooting, trap and skeet shooting, archery, and even camping, fishing, hiking, and wildlife conservation efforts.

Hunting Clubs

Hunting clubs are very diverse in nature and format but essentially share the common goal of providing a venue for hunters and even fishers to not only gather but have access to a safe and formally managed recreational property. The types of hunting available are wide-ranging and may include big game or small game, which varies greatly across clubs and regions. Big game includes such wildlife as moose, elk, bear, mountain lion, caribou, bison, and deer. Small game includes upland and migratory game birds, squirrel, rabbit, fox, coyote, and even reptiles and amphibians. Wildlife will be classified as either protected or unprotected in certain jurisdictions, which is associated with regulations relevant to hunting such animals. Moreover, hunting licenses are needed, and local regulations designate not only the season in which people can hunt but also the permissible methods when doing so (e.g., rifle, shotgun, handgun, air gun, muzzle-loader, crossbow, bow and arrow). These parameters can be quite specific, such that a particular season for a specific classification of wildlife may extend a few months but will be delineated by method and even location. For instance, the following are just some examples of rules set forth by the New York State Department of Environmental Conservation (Hunting, n.d.):

Big Game: Deer and Bear

- A legally antlered deer must have at least one antler that is three inches or longer measured by the base of the burr.
- The number of deer taken is dependent upon the licenses and privileges purchased.
- Only one bear may be taken by gun or bow each license year.
- It is unlawful to take the deer or bear while it is in water, to use a firearm or bow with any artificial light or laser that projects toward the target, or to use dogs.
- There are very specific tagging, reporting, transportation, and sales-related rules to adhere to upon killing a deer or bear.

Small Game: Upland and Migratory Game Birds, Small Game Mammals (e.g., squirrel, rabbit), Furbearers (e.g., fox, coyote), and Reptiles and Amphibians

- You may not use a rifle or handgun to hunt pheasant or migratory game birds.
- You may not take a turkey with a rifle, or with a handgun firing a bullet. You may hunt turkey with a shotgun or handgun only when using shot no larger than #2 and no smaller than #8.
- Air guns may be used to hunt squirrels, rabbits, hares, ruffed grouse, and furbearers that may be hunted (e.g., raccoons and coyotes) and unprotected species. Air guns may not be used to hunt waterfowl, pheasant, wild turkey, or big game.
- A fishing or hunting license is required to take frogs with a spear, club, hook, or by hand. A hunting license is required to take frogs with a gun, bow, or crossbow.
- Dogs may be used to hunt small game, except, you may not use dogs to hunt wild turkey in the spring; you may not possess a rifle larger

than .22 caliber rim-fire or possess a shotgun loaded with slug, ball or buckshot unless you are coyote hunting with a dog; and crossbows may not be used while hunting with a dog for any small game (except for coyotes) in the Northern Zone.

Hunting is a very popular sport. According to the US Fish and Wildlife Service, there are approximately 14 million hunters in the United States over age 16. Such popularity is true even in states known for strict gun control laws. For example, according to the New York State Department of Environmental Conservation, hunting is one of the most popular types of wildlife recreation in the state, with approximately 700,000 New Yorkers and over 50,000 nonresidents engaging in such activities there annually. Therefore, there is a plethora of organizations and hunting clubs throughout the country. There are also extensive education and training resources available in this regard. The interested reader can consult the NRA's Hunter Services division (http://hservices.nra.org) for more information about hunting, hunting clubs, and destinations. There are also resources specifically designed for such. For instance, HuntClubListing.com, launched in 2007, is a website comprised of free listings of private and commercial hunting clubs in the United States. It also provides news pages and message boards for visitors. For each club, the site presents its name, state, county, city, acreage, dues, and if it has a Quality Deer Management program, as well as if the club is seeking members. The site lists over 350 clubs, 15,000 members, and over half a million site hits.

Shooting Ranges

Shooting ranges are facilities specifically designed for firearms practice. They may be indoors, outdoors, or a combination of the two. The setting is typically dependent on the area as indoor ranges are more commonly located in cities and suburban areas, whereas outdoor ranges are typically located in more rural or, at least, more isolated areas. They are supervised by range masters or range safety officers. Shooters may engage in stationary target practice, such as what the movies and television often depict when law enforcement officers are training and shooting at paper silhouettes. They may also engage in *plinking*, which is the informal target shooting of nonstandard targets, such as aluminum cans and rimfire steel or clay circular targets. As such, plinking is often viewed as a particularly fun activity among shooters, given the nature of the targets and their reaction to being struck (e.g., breaking, spinning). Shooting ranges have continued to grow in popularity, particularly when one considers that gun owners outnumber hunters by a 5 to 1 margin (Burke, 2013). As such, there are numerous ranges throughout the country, and the interested reader can reference such resources as those provided by the NRA (http://findnra.nra.org) for more information, as well as websites specifically designed to search for ranges, such as RangeListings.com.

Gun Control and Gun Violence Prevention Groups

In this section, we provide an overview of a number gun control, gun violence prevention, and antigun groups. As with the 2A groups, there is great variability in the perspectives among the groups in this section. Namely, on one end of the spectrum, there are gun control and gun violence prevention groups that support the Second Amendment right to bear arms but advocate for stricter laws and policies to prevent violence and related problems. On the other end, there are groups that are essentially against all firearm ownership and use at the civilian level. And, as would be expected, there is much variability in perspectives along the continuum. Again, the set of groups presented below is by no means an exhaustive list of gun control, gun violence prevention, or antigun groups; but it is a representative one that reflects a range of perspectives and organizational structures within such circles. Please note that the groups are presented alphabetically. Please also note that a full review of all gun control, gun violence prevention, and antigun groups, including state and regional organizations, is beyond the scope of this book and, therefore, our review is particularly focused on national groups. Nevertheless, just as with the 2A groups, interested readers can easily locate local and regional groups in this regard, such as North Carolinians Against Gun Violence (www.ncgv.org) and New Yorkers Against Gun Violence (www.nyagv.org). There are many such groups throughout the country (for a representative list, see www.gunfreekids.org/resources). It is also important to note in this context that many of the national groups presented below are actually comprised of mergers between and among various groups, and, as such, many are campaigns and coalitions rather than stand-alone groups per se. Furthermore, many gun control, gun violence prevention, and antigun groups are relatively newer as they are often developed in response to particular mass shootings and tragic events, such as the Sandy Hook Elementary and Newtown tragedies.

There are also various groups that include gun violence prevention as one of their primary initiatives but are not solely focused on such, and therefore, we do not review them here. Such groups include the Joyce Foundation (www.joycefdn.org) and the Center for American Progress (www.americanprogress.org). Another such group is Moms Rising; whereas gun violence prevention is one of approximately 10 issues they actively address, others include maternity and paternity leave, healthcare for all, fair wages, paid sick days, nutritious food for kids, and immigration fairness. The Washington State–based group indicates that it has more than a million members, and, in the context of its Gun Safety Campaign, it argues for criminal background checks for all gun purchases, a ban on military-style assault weapons and high-capacity magazines, and a federal antigun trafficking statute "with real penalties to crack down on *straw purchases*" (Rowe-Finkbeiner, 2015; see www.momsrising.org for more information).

Similarly, the National Physicians Alliance (NPA) is a Washington, DC–based nonprofit organization led by medical doctors in place to develop research and education programs that "promote health and foster active engagement of physicians with their communities to achieve high quality, affordable health care for all." The NPA was created in 2005 by former leaders of the American Medical Student Association. According to the NPA, the organization provides a forum "for physicians across medical specialties who share a commitment to professional integrity and health justice." Gun violence prevention is one of six projects in which the group engages, including, but not limited to, secure healthcare for all and promoting good stewardship in the medical profession. As part of this initiative, the NPA partnered with the Law Center to Prevent Gun Violence to create a white paper addressing gun safety and setting forth policy recommendations in this regard. These include extending background checks, repealing prohibitions against requiring the disclosure or collection of information about gun ownership from patients, removing impediments (e.g., funding) to conducting firearm-related research, restricting "unusually dangerous" firearms and assault weapons, design safety standards for firearms, laws that require written and performance-based tests to ensure that firearm applicants possess knowledge on safety and storage, and increasing accountability among firearm sellers and manufacturers (see National Physicians Alliance, n.d.).

Americans for Responsible Solutions

Americans for Responsible Solutions is a Washington, DC–based nonprofit advocacy group and political action committee that was founded by Congresswoman Gabby Giffords and her husband, Mark Kelly, a retired Navy captain and astronaut. The organization was created in response to the January 8, 2011, Tucson, Arizona, shooting where Congresswoman Giffords was shot in the head and six of her constituents were killed and 12 others wounded. Americans for Responsible Solutions was launched on the second anniversary of that tragic event. The group indicates that Congresswoman Giffords and her husband are gun owners and strong supporters of the Second Amendment, and they want to protect gun rights for collection, recreation, and protecting while seeking gun violence prevention. Americans for Responsible Solutions acknowledges the complexity of the issues related to gun violence but believes that one reason for the rate of firearm-related deaths and injuries is bad legislation. As such, the group's commitment is to facilitate changes in that regard. Americans for Responsible Solutions presents ongoing firearm-related news stories on its website along with relevant statistics and forums to contact Congress and sign a petition to expand background checks, inform friends and family via e-mail about these issues, sign a petition, and join one of their three groups: Doctors, Gun Owners, or Veterans for Responsible Solutions.

Brady Campaign to Prevent Gun Violence

The Brady Campaign to Prevent Gun Violence is a gun control group based out of Washington, DC, named after James Brady, who was permanently disabled as a result of the attempted assassination of President Ronald Reagan in 1981. The group formerly operated under the National Council to Control Handguns from 1974 to 1980 before serving under the name Handgun Control, Inc., between 1980 and 2000. It was renamed the Brady Campaign to Prevent Gun Violence in 2001. Its sister organization, the Center to Prevent Handgun Violence (CPHV), was founded in 1983 as "an educational outreach organization dedicated to reducing gun violence"; and the CPHV subsequently set forth the Legal Action Project in 1989 to "take the fight against gun violence into the courts." The Brady Handgun Violence Prevention Act is typically referred to as the Brady Act and the Brady Bill. The legislation was originally introduced in Congress in 1991 but was not enacted until 1993, signed by President Bill Clinton, thereby amending the Gun Control Act of 1968. The law mandated federal background checks on firearm purchasers in the United States and imposed a 5-day wait period on purchases, until the NICS was created in 1998, which extended checks to long guns in addition to handguns. According to the group, the Brady law has prevented over 2.1 million gun sales to "dangerous" people. In 2014, the Brady Campaign launched its Stop Bad Apple Gun Dealers Campaign, which includes lawsuits against irresponsible dealers, noting that 5% of gun dealers account for 90% of crime guns in the United States.

The Brady Campaign consists of a president, chief operating officer, director of the legal action project, senior national policy director, national field director, director of marketing and communications, and director of finance. The Brady Campaign is comprised of a 21-member board, which includes a chair, vice chair, treasurer, and secretary as well as the group's president and a Million Mom March representative. The Brady Center has an 18-member board, comprised of most of the same members as the campaign. The Brady Campaign is an affiliate of the Million Mom March, and it indicates that it has 94 chapters throughout the United States. The group publishes a quarterly newsletter titled *The Brady Report*. Its mission is "to create a safer America for all of us that will lead to a dramatic reduction in gun deaths and injuries," and its primary goal is to cut the number of US gun deaths in half by 2025.

According to the group's most recently posted annual report, it generated $9.5 million in revenue in 2012 and had $6 million in expenses, $2 million for public education and $1.2 million for fundraising efforts. In 2013, its revenue approached $12 million, as did its expenses. Of particular note is that the group reports spending $520,082 for legal action efforts in 2012, which substantially increased to $2.6 million in 2013. Such appears connected with the group's report that 2013 was "a record year for the passage of strong state gun laws," which included 21 states passing gun reform measures, and 25 Brady chapters in California worked to pass "a record" 16 gun reform bills, nine of which were signed into law as part of the Life Act.

In addition to its collaboration with the Million Mom March, the Brady Campaign is very active in organizing rallies, providing education and awareness, and engaging in legislative efforts throughout the country. For instance, the group notes its assistance in organizing rallies subsequent to the tragedy at Virginia Tech in 2007 and developing the We Are Better Than This campaign in 2012 subsequent to the Aurora, Colorado, theater shooting and the Voices Against Violence campaign that same year in response to the tragedy at Sandy Hook Elementary School. The group also started the ASK campaign years ago, which reminds parents and guardians of the importance of asking if there is an unlocked gun in the homes where their children play. It is also responsible for launching Gun Industry Watch, the Campaign Against Illegal Guns and has played a role in passing the NICS Improvement Amendments Act. The campaign has also been involved with legal cases against gun dealers, such as Smith & Wesson and Bushmaster.

Campaign to Unload

According to the group, Campaign to Unload (C2U) is a Washington, DC–based group of more than 50 organizations across the country that have united to hurt the funding of who they believe to be are irresponsible gunmakers. Its goals are to prompt the gun industry to adopt common-sense, publicly backed reforms, such as universal background checks and smart gun technology, by securing the support of major institutional investors and pension fund managers. C2U characterizes itself as a divestment campaign in that it seeks to defund aspects of the gun industry by having investors sell their stocks in companies; namely, firearm manufacturers. They note that investors may not even realize that they own shares in such companies through their mutual funds, retirement accounts, exchange-traded funds, or other products. The group cites past successful divestment campaigns, such as those that effectuated changes in US tobacco policy and the end of apartheid in South Africa. C2U indicates that it has the support of dozens of established national civic organizations, local grass-roots groups, educators and youth groups, and elected leaders, including, but not limited to, Bill de Blasio, MoveOn.org, MillionHoodies Movement for Justice, Catholics United, National Association for the Advancement of Colored People New York State Conference, and the American Federation of Teachers.

According to the C2U, its "current target" is Cerberus Capital Management, L.P. According to C2U, Cerberus is a private equity firm that owns the vast majority (94%) of the world's largest firearms and ammunition manufacturer in the world: Freedom Group. C2U indicates that Cerberus pledged to sell its $700 million interest in Freedom Group but had not done so and continued to profit from gun violence. C2U's other primary campaigns are to "pressure" the University of California and other schools to divest from gun violence,

UnloadYour401k.com—Divest Your Retirement, and Tell Your 401k Manager to Divest Gun Stocks, whereby it lists eight mutual funds that reportedly invest in guns. For instance, in a previous press release, C2U indicated that, in the context of a partnership between Unload Your 401k and the antigun violence campaign No Guns Allowed, entertainment icon Snoop Dogg and tech leader Ron Conway were joining forces to call for divestment from the gun industry (see also Richinick, 2015). On its website, C2U posts additional press releases, news, a blog, and resources, such as a Divestment Toolkit, as well as opportunities to sign up and make donations.

Coalition to Stop Gun Violence

The Coalition to Stop Gun Violence (CSGV) is a Washington, DC–based nonprofit organization formed in 1974. The organization is comprised of 47 national organizations working to reduce gun violence, including religious and social justice organizations, child welfare advocates, and public health professionals. The CSGV indicates that its guiding principle is that all Americans have a right to reside in communities without gun violence. The association has set forth a three-step strategy to effectuate gun control reforms, including aggressive political advocacy, seeking legislative change, and exposing the NRA's hypocrisy:

The CSGV indicates that it's the first gun violence prevention group to address these issues in terms of democratic values and to use the term "insurrectionism" to describe the NRA's "treasonous interpretation of the Second Amendment." The group consists of a seven-member staff, which includes a president emeritus, executive director, director of communications, director of development, Virginia State director, legislative director, and general counsel. It is also comprised of a 14-member board of directors, which includes a venture capital investor, a number of attorneys, a university professor, and a Presbyterian Church pastor. The group indicates that the "victims and survivors of gun violence on our staff are the leaders in [this] lobbying effort." On its website, the group maintains news stories, campaign-related information, a blog, an action center, and information related to job opportunities, internships, and a forum to contribute.

Everytown for Gun Safety

Everytown is a New York–based nonprofit group founded in 2014 subsequent to the merger of Mayors Against Illegal Guns and Moms Demand Action for Gun Sense in America, with the support of Everyday Americans of All Stripes. It notes that Mayors Against Illegal Guns was formed in 2006 by former New York City mayor Michael Bloomberg and former Boston mayor Thomas Menino as a coalition of 15 mayors; it now consists of more than 1,000 current and former mayors nationwide to fight for common-sense gun legislation. Moms Demand Action was created in response to the Newtown, Connecticut, tragedy; and they indicate that they are the largest grassroots organization of mothers collaborating to reduce gun violence. Everytown also has a Survivor Network for gun violence survivors to connect with one another in-person and online forums. Everytown is comprised of a 26-member advisory board, which includes such people as Bloomberg, former Philadelphia mayor Michael Nutter, and Warren Buffet as well as a number of victims and parents of victims of gun violence. The group presents its primary issues as background checks, domestic violence, preventable deaths (e.g., safe storage), and gun trafficking.

The group provides a number of resources on its website as well as press-related information. Despite its relatively new development, Everytown indicates that it has already influenced Facebook to take steps to limit illegal gun sales on its platforms and, most recently, indicates that Facebook has moved to ban private gun sales on its website and Instagram.

Faiths United to Prevent Gun Violence

Faiths United to Prevent Gun Violence is a Washington, DC–based organization comprised of 51 groups that reportedly represent "tens of millions of Americans in faith communities across the nation." The organization was formed on Martin Luther King Day in 2011 by 24 national faith groups "to confront America's gun violence epidemic and to rally support for policies that reduce death and injury from gunfire." The organization is quite diverse and includes such groups as the African Methodist Episcopal Church, Catholics in Alliance for the Common Good, Islamic Society of North America, and Jewish Council for Public Affairs. Faiths United indicates that it supports legislative action in terms of increasing background checks and related measures. Faiths United highlighted the aforementioned points in its 2013 letter to Congress and includes additional areas of support in its National Resolution document. On its website, the organization includes numerous resources, news updates, and blogs, as well as opportunities to donate to and join its efforts.

Gun Free Kids

Gun Free Kids is a New York–based gun violence prevention group that encourages political activism at the grassroots level across states. One of its primary campaigns is Keep Guns Off Campus, an initiative to oppose legislative policies that would allow the concealed carry of guns on campuses (see The campaign to keep guns off campus, n.d.). According to the group, this initiative has prevented such legislation in 18 states, and it is the only national organization to address such issues at the higher education level. Furthermore, the group reports that, as of December 2015, the American Association of State Colleges and Universities, over 420 individual colleges and universities in 42 states, and 48 college presidents have signed a resolution that opposes legislation that would mandate that colleges and universities allow students to carry concealed handguns on campus. Its sister site is ArmedCampuses.org, which is presented as a resource for parents regarding where concealed guns are and are not permitted on campus. Gun Free Kids presents news, resources, voter registration, and opportunities to sign petitions to Congress and to donate on its site.

Law Center to Prevent Gun Violence

The Law Center to Prevent Gun Violence (LCPGV), formerly known as the Legal Community Against Violence, is a nonprofit national law center based in San Francisco, California, that is aimed at offering legal expertise in support of gun violence prevention and "smart" gun laws. The group was formed by lawyers and provides free public education on issues related to gun laws and gun violence prevention in the United States. It indicates that it has become the leading resource on firearms law and policy in the country. The LCPGV asserts that its work is dedicated to the victims of the shooting at 101 California Street, San Francisco, on July 1, 1993, and to their families, which was also the impetus of the group's development. As such, one of its first initiatives was to support the enactment of the 1994 federal assault weapon ban. The group maintained its efforts in California until its national expansion in 1999. In 2012, it changed its name to reflect the broad scope of its work. Namely, the LCPGV reports that it has monitored all Second Amendment legislation and litigation nationwide since the landmark Supreme Court decision in *District of Columbia v. Heller* (2008). On its website, the LCPGV provides numerous resources and information on issues related to laws and policies, the Second Amendment, studies, and statistics. It also includes its annual reports as well as opportunities to donate to and become involved with the group, such as by signing petitions, attending events, and engaging in pro bono assignments that may involve speaking at public meetings and hearings, drafting amicus curiae briefs, or authoring op-eds.

Moms Demand Action for Gun Sense in America

Moms Demand Action for Gun Sense in America describes itself as a "non-partisan grassroots movement to mobilize moms and families to advocate for stronger gun laws." It was founded in 2012 in response to the Sandy Hook Elementary School tragedy by Shannon Watts, a stay-at-home mother, who modeled it after Mothers Against Drunk Driving to demand action from state and federal legislators, companies, and educational institutions to establish gun reforms. In 2013, the group united with Mayors Against Illegal Guns, which ultimately resulted in the formation of Everytown for Gun Safety. According to Moms Demand Action, they support the Second Amendment but believe solutions are available to reduce gun violence The group indicates that it now has a chapter in every state across the country and that its focus is to educate, motivate, and mobilize mothers and families to take action that would lead to stronger gun control laws and policies. Initiatives of Moms Demand Action include, but are not limited to, #GroceriesNotGuns, whereby the group is asking Kroger, the country's largest grocery retailer, to prohibit open carry in its supermarkets; the Mother's Dream Quilt Project (see Mother's Dream Quilt Project, n.d.) to symbolize the repercussions of gun violence and to honor victims of such; and the Corporate Responsibility campaign, whereby Moms Demand Action provides information on company policies so that certain companies with gun sense can be praised and those that do not can be pressured. The group provides resources, relevant news and information on its website. It also seeks pledges to be a "gun sense voter" and notes endorsements from numerous members of Congress nationwide and various attorney generals and state senators throughout the country.

Newtown Action Alliance

Newtown Action Alliance is a nonprofit issue advocacy organization based out of Newtown, Connecticut. It was founded by Newtown residents subsequent to the Sandy Hook Elementary School shooting tragedy there in December 2012. The group indicates that it maintains an open membership policy and that it is "dedicated to reversing the escalating gun violence epidemic in this nation through the introduction of smarter, safer gun laws and broader cultural change." Newtown Action Alliance indicates that one of its strategies to effectuate change is to connect rural and urban victims and communities impacted by gun violence. Its immediate goals are to support gun control legislation and policies, and to collaborate to create safer schools and residential areas. Newtown Action Alliance distributes a newsletter and provides numerous resources on its website, including blogs, op-eds, and various professional and media highlights. The group has also created a teen organization called the Junior Newtown Action Alliance, which it describes as the "next generation of American leaders and voters." An affiliated group is the Newtown Foundation, which is also a nonprofit group but one that is not involved in legislative or electoral activities: "Instead it is focused on educational, healing and cultural programs including a focus on first responders and teachers to help them move forward." The foundation also works to help teens and provide them with opportunities to network and engage in prosocial activities and focuses on developing community educational and enrichment programs.

Sandy Hook Promise

Sandy Hook Promise (SHP) is a nonprofit organization that was founded and led by a number of people whose loved ones were killed at Sandy Hook Elementary School in December 2012. The group lists 13 primary team members, including three managing directors, an operations director, national field director, program manager, finance director, senior development manager, social media manager, two Ohio organizers, an office manager, and a bookkeeper. SHP's mission is to prevent gun deaths of all types. SHP's legislative platform is based on the fact that the group supports gun rights and it does not support bans. It does not believe guns are the primary cause of gun violence. SHP has an Action Fund that advocates for the development and enforcement of existing gun violence prevention laws, policy, and regulations in the areas of mental health & wellness, gun safety, gun lethality, and research.

SHP's focus is to develop a national movement of parents, schools, and community organizations that will set forth gun violence prevention programs and effectuate legislative change. SHP indicates that 146,000 educators, parents, community leaders, and students have been trained on their programs and practices. According to the group, 660,341 people from all 50 states have made the following promise:

> I promise to do all I can to protect children from gun violence by encouraging and supporting solutions that create safer, healthier homes, schools and communities.

States United to Prevent Gun Violence

States United to Prevent Gun Violence is a New York–based nonprofit group representing an affiliation of 30 state gun violence prevention groups and 150,000 grass-roots supporters who advocate for gun control laws and antiviolence education. States United's mission is to support gun violence prevention organizations, and they set forth a number of goals related to such prevention as well. In addition, States United supports state-based gun violence prevention organizations in many ways, including, but not limited to, helping to develop effective policy and best practices; organizing local action to highlight gun violence impacts and costs; providing fact-based input to local elected representatives and members of Congress about gun policy to help foster progress; providing technical support for website development and social media; providing a shared e-newsletter; and connecting members to groups of like-minded organizations for policy and program support and instruction. On its website, States United provides information about its state affiliates, relevant firearm-related issues and actions, news and blogs, and an opportunity to become involved with and donate to the organization.

Student Pledge Against Gun Violence

The Student Pledge Against Gun Violence is a national program based out of Northfield, Minnesota, that began in 1996, supported by a unanimous US Senate resolution and presidential proclamation by Bill Clinton, which both called for a Day of National Concern about Young People and Gun Violence as well as a national distribution of the Student Pledge. The resolution was introduced by Senators Bill Bradley (NJ), Arlen Specter (PA), and Paul

Wellstone (MN) and 81 of their Senate colleagues. The Student Pledge Against Gun Violence is focused on the role young people can play in reducing gun violence. On its website, the group provides numerous resources to educate and increase awareness on issues related to gun violence, including books, articles, curriculum suggestions, websites, press releases, newsletters, and music and videos. In addition, there is information related to the Day of National Concern, such as suggested activities and ideas for those interested in hosting an event at their respective school. According to the group, over 10 million students have signed the following pledge since 1996:

> I will never bring a gun to school;
> I will never use a gun to settle a personal problem or dispute;
> I will use my influence with friends to keep them from using guns to settle disputes.
> My individual choices and actions, when multiplied by those of young people throughout the country, *will* make a difference.
> Together, by honoring this pledge, we can reverse the violence and grow up in safety.
> (www.pledge.org/the-pledge/)

Violence Policy Center

The Violence Policy Center (VPC) is a Washington, DC–based organization aimed at reducing gun violence via research, education, advocacy, and collaboration. Namely, the group describes itself as a national tax-exempt educational organization based on research, investigation, analysis, and advocacy. The VPC provides information to policymakers, journalists, organizations, advocates, and the general public. The group was founded in 1988 by Josh Sugarmann, its executive director and former press officer at Amnesty International, Inc., and communications director for the National Coalition to Ban Handguns. The VPC continues to engage in its work at the federal, state, and local levels and reports that it has an extensive record of achievements that have effectuated legislative change and reduced the power of the gun lobby. For instance, the group indicates that one of its studies resulted in federal policy changes that reduced the number of gun dealers from 250,000 to 56,000. The VPC indicates that it led the coalition that passed the federal Domestic Violence Offender Gun Ban as well as the ban against .50 caliber sniper rifles in California. The group lists a number of other accomplishments over the years and notes that it publishes annual reports and ongoing research in this area. The VPC provides numerous resources on its website, including blogs, publications, and press releases.

2

Firearm Law and Policy

Highly emotional events, such as mass shootings, are typically followed by calls to revisit existing laws and policies. The emotionality is often reflected in the name of the bills proposed as they are often named after incidents or victims—so-called apostrophe laws. As with many laws and policies, those proposed and enacted in the firearms context are often set forth with the best intentions but suffer from problems with implementation and unintended consequences. That said, there are certainly some laws and policies that have been beneficial in many ways; yet, measuring their effectiveness is no simple feat. Doing so is in line with what social scientists refer to as *policy* or *program evaluation* research, which is fairly complicated business given that it involves acquiring baseline data and accounting for variables to even be able to consider the potential of causality. Moreover, the nature and quality of the research conducted are quite relevant, particularly when our overarching goal is to employ evidence-based interventions (e.g., see Kazdin, 2006 and 2008, for a review of these issues in the mental health treatment context). Nevertheless, one might find it uncomfortable to oppose laws and policies that are ostensibly positive and intended to reduce societal problems. In the context of firearms, such includes, but is certainly not limited to, more extensive background checks, domestic violence restrictions, and banning high-capacity magazines and firearms that resemble "assault" rifles. This problem is not unique to the firearm arena, however; think Drug Abuse Resistance Education (D.A.R.E.) and Scared Straight—two programs that received significant attention, praise, funding, and support for many years, despite being found to be ineffective in accomplishing their primary goals. Entire careers in law enforcement were built around the D.A.R.E. program, even though the program itself acknowledges that it was ineffective for at least its first 26 years.[1] Scared Straight programs were established in the 1970s and used throughout the country to deter juvenile crime, and entire television series have been devoted to them as well. However, in 2011, the US Department of Justice indicated that Scared Straight programs not only were ineffective but could also be harmful to youth; in fact, the Office of Juvenile Justice and Delinquency Prevention has noted that it does not fund such programs and indicates that they may be in violation of federal law.[2]

As we will see in this chapter and throughout this book, research support for the effectiveness of firearm laws and policies has been quite mixed despite the significant amount of resources and support driving them. For instance, President Obama addressed firearm issues directly numerous times and with notable conviction but without effectuating much change at all due, in part, to limits in presidential power (Keneally, 2016). One reason may be that he had to work against opposition in the form of a Republican Congress throughout his presidency, but another may be that he simply focused on the wrong issues in the firearm arena. For instance, while most Americans support more extensive background checks, it is also the case that there is a very weak link between mental illness and firearm-related violence. Despite that empirical reality, in his January 4, 2016, executive order regarding gun control, President Obama used the terms "mental health" and "mental illness" almost 30 times without ever defining them, and he committed $500 million "to increase access to mental health care" (Fact sheet, 2016). In his corresponding town hall at George Mason University 3 days later, the president emphasized mental health again, although he conflated the concepts of violence and suicide when doing so: "And—the problem, when we talk about that guns don't kill people, people kill people, it's primarily a mental health problem, or it's a criminal and evil problem, and that's what we have to get at." However, the president later clarified, "Out of the 30,000 deaths due to gun violence, about two-thirds of them are actually suicides. Now, that's part of the reason why we are investing more heavily also in mental health under my proposal" (Guns in America, 2016). Although some (e.g., Jenson, 2007) have agreed with President Obama's views, such that more attention (i.e., education, research, policy) should be devoted to connecting violence and mental illness, many contemporary leading scholars in the firearms arena opine that the link between mental illness and firearm-related violence is relatively weak, whereas mental illness and firearm-involved suicides are certainly much more closely associated. That said, the constructs of violence and suicide should not be combined in reference to "gun violence." Although there is overlap and these concepts can be thought of as interpersonal and self-directed violence, respectively, there is too much risk of confusion when considered a unitary construct in this context. As we address in greater detail in Chapter 4, most mass shooters are not mentally ill, and mental illness is not a leading or even primary predictor of firearm-involved violence, more generally. A very small percentage of such violence is attributable to mental illness per se. As Knoll and Annass (2016) articulated it:

Laws intended to reduce gun violence that focus on a population representing less than 3% of all gun violence will be extremely low yield, ineffective, and wasteful of scarce resource. Perpetrators of mass shootings are unlikely to have a history of involuntary psychiatric hospitalization. Thus, databases intended to restrict access to guns and established by gun laws that broadly target people with mental illness will not capture this group of individuals. . . . Gun restriction laws focusing on people with mental illness perpetuate the myth that mental illness leads to violence, as well as the misperception that gun violence and mental illness are strongly linked. Stigma represents a major barrier to access and treatment of mental illness, which in turn increases the public health burden. (Gold & Simon, 2016, p. 82)

Trestman, Volkmar, & Gold (2016) added:

Mass shootings by individuals with serious mental illness are very rare events and therefore cannot be predicted. People who are at high risk for violence, with or without firearms, often cannot be identified and treated against their wishes before they become violent . . . available evidence does not support the belief that voluntary or involuntary mental health treatment can reduce or prevent mass shootings by individuals with or without mental illness. (Gold & Simon, 2016, pp. 185–186)

Price, Recupero, & Norris (2016) echoed these sentiments and noted the link with suicide:

Laws that seek to restrict firearm acquisition through background checks and increased reporting of persons with mental illness may help to reduce rates of suicides by firearms but are unlikely to achieve the desired aim of preventing future acts of mass violence. (Gold & Simon, 2016, p. 128)

These empirically based findings have gained attention in the mainstream media as well (e.g., Rosenwald, 2016) but have yet to change the politically driven push to enact certain laws and policies that are inconsistent with the behavioral science literature in this area. It seems as though the sensationalized image of the "mentally ill mass shooter" continues to prevail in some circles. Fox and DeLateur (2014) may have shed some light on the reason for this as they expressed concerns with the assumptions that are often made about mass murder and set forth numerous *myths* and *misconceptions* related to mass shootings and multiple homicides:

- mass murderers snap and kill indiscriminately
- mass shootings are on the rise
- recent mass murders involve record-setting body counts
- violent entertainment, especially video games, are causally linked to mass murder

- greater attention and response to the telltale warning signs will allow us to identify would-be mass killers before they act
- widening the availability of mental health services will allow unstable individuals to get the treatment they need and avert mass murders
- enhanced background checks will keep dangerous weapons out of the hands of these madmen
- restoring the federal ban on assault weapons will prevent these horrible crimes
- expanding "right to carry" provisions will deter mass killers or at least stop them in their tracks and reduce body counts
- increasing physical security in schools and other places will prevent mass murder
- having armed guards at every school will serve to protect students from an active shooter and provide a deterrent as well

In addition to addressing the general effectiveness of laws and policies, we must remember that significant heterogeneity exists within our country's legislative makeup. There are 50 states, but the issues go well beyond that. Namely, there are 19,492 municipalities (an area which has its own local government) in the United States according to the National League of Cities (Number of municipal governments, n.d.). Keep in mind that New Jersey, for example, is the fourth smallest state (followed by Connecticut, Delaware, and Rhode Island), but it still has 565 municipalities within 21 counties (Municipalities, n.d.). Thus, while there is one federal law and 50 state laws, there are nearly 20,000 potentially different policies that guide firearm-related procedures across the country. Anecdotally, we have seen great variation within the jurisdictions in which we work. For example, one of us (G.P.) regularly conducts firearm evaluations and has had cases wherein applicants have been cleared by one municipality subsequent to a mental health evaluation but denied once they moved to another (nearby) municipality in the same state. In addition, municipalities are willing to accept a diverse range of clearances; we have seen everything from one-page letters from physicians, including primary care doctors, psychiatrists, and even gynecologists, to "approvals" from medical doctors written on a prescription pad. In other cases, a comprehensive, 10-page forensic psychological evaluation including a clinical interview, psychological testing, and collateral documents and interview is conducted. Indeed, there is great variability in the firearm arena. Nevertheless, whether or not we can affect legislation, it is incumbent on us to continue to work toward developing practice standards for mental health professionals interfacing with firearm-related issues. In other words, we must think globally and act locally.

In this chapter, we first provide an overview of federal- and state-level firearm laws, including landmark cases, the impact of various types of firearm laws, and the limitations of the research in this regard. We then address the mental health components of firearm legislation at the federal and state levels, with particular attention to suicide, violence, and domestic violence–related considerations. Next, we review issues pertaining to liability for gun manufacturers, dealers, and mental health professionals. We then discuss how the media affects firearm policy in this country, before finally turning to a comparative analysis of international laws and perspectives on firearms.

Federal and State Firearm Laws

Firearm regulations have been present since our country's inception and have routinely been revisited and revised since. As US government expert Robert Longley noted, many believe the gun control debate began after the assassination of President John F. Kennedy because of the relative lack of control the United States previously had over the sale and possession of firearms (Longley, 2016). Namely, prior to 1968, firearms and ammunition were readily available to adults throughout much of the nation, including via over-the-counter purchases and even mail-order magazines and catalogues. Nevertheless, the regulation of firearms certainly began in 1791, embedded in the Bill of Rights. In his review, Longley provided an outline of landmark legislation and related events in the firearms arena:

- **1791**—Bill of Rights, Second Amendment gains final ratification.
- **1837**—Georgia passes a law banning handguns, which is ruled unconstitutional by the Supreme Court and subsequently thrown out.
- **1865**—After Emancipation, several southern states adopt laws that forbade black people from owning firearms.
- **1871**—The National Rifle Association (NRA) was formed, intended to improve civilians' marksmanship in preparation for war.
- **1927**—Congress passes a law which banned the mailing of concealable weapons.
- **1934**—National Firearms Act of 1934: Congress approves the regulation, manufacturing, sale, and possession of fully automatic firearms (e.g., submachine guns).
- **1938**—Federal Firearms Act of 1938: places the first limitations on selling ordinary firearms. Firearms sellers are required to obtain a federal firearms license and to keep a record of names and addresses of persons to whom firearms are sold. The act prohibited the sale of firearms to violent felons.
- **1968**—Gun Control Act of 1968: enacted for the purpose of "keeping firearms out of the hands of those not legally entitled to possess them because of age, criminal background, or incompetence." The act regulates imported guns, increases the gun dealer licensing and record keeping requirements, and places additional limitations on handgun sales. The list of individuals who are prohibited from purchasing guns is extended to those who have been convicted of non-business-related

felonies, users of illegal drugs, and those who have been found mentally incompetent.

- **1972**—The Bureau of Alcohol, Tobacco and Firearms (ATF) is created with the mission to control the illegal use and sale of firearms and enforce federal firearm laws. The ATF conducts licensee qualification and compliance inspections while also issuing firearms licenses.
- **1977**—Washington, DC enacts an anti-handgun law, which also requires the registration of all rifles and shotguns within the jurisdiction.
- **1986**—Several laws are enacted:
  o Armed Career Criminal Act: increases penalties for individuals found in possession of firearms who are not qualified to own them (under the Gun Control Act of 1968).
  o Firearms Owners Protection Act (Public Law 99-308): relaxes some of the restrictions on gun and ammunitions sales while also establishing mandatory penalties for individuals who are in possession of a firearm during the commission of a crime.
  o Law Enforcement Officers Protection Act (Public Law 99-408): bans the possession of bullets that can penetrate bulletproof clothing, also known as "cop killer" bullets.
- **1989**—The Roberti-Roos Assault Weapons Control Act of 1989: California bans the possession of certain semiautomatic weapons after five children were shot to death on a school playground.
- **1990**—The Crime Control Act of 1990 (Public Law 101-647): enacted to ban semiautomatic weapon production and importation into the United States. Also, "gun-free school zones" are established with penalties for violators.
- **1994**—The Brady Law and Assault Weapon Ban
  o The Brady Handgun Violence Prevention Act: mandates a 5-day wait period before the purchase of a handgun and requires local law enforcement to conduct background checks on individuals attempting to purchase a handgun.
  o The Violent Crime Control and Law Enforcement Act of 1994: Over a 10-year period, the manufacture, possession, sale, and import of specific types of "assault weapons" were banned. Of note, however, is that Congress did not reauthorize this ban in 2004.
- **1997**—Several initiatives are set forth:
  o *Printz v. United States*: The Supreme Court rules that the background check requirement as established by the Brady Handgun Violence Prevention Act is unconstitutional.
  o The Florida Supreme Court upholds a jury's decision that Kmart owes $11.5 million after selling a gun to an intoxicated man who then shot his estranged girlfriend.
  o Major gun manufacturers in the United States agree to include child safety trigger devices on all new handguns.

- **1998**—Many notable developments:
  - o June: A report by the Justice Department indicates that 69,000 people were barred from purchasing handguns in 1997 due to the Brady presale background check requirement.
  - o July: An amendment requiring the inclusion of a trigger lock mechanism on all handguns sold in the United States is defeated in the Senate. However, the Senate approves an amendment requiring gun dealers to have trigger locks available for sale and creating federal grants for firearms safety and education programming.
  - o October: New Orleans becomes the first city to file a lawsuit against gun makers, firearms trade associations, and gun dealers in an effort to seek recovery of costs associated with firearm-related violence.
  - o November 12: Chicago, Illinois, files a suit against gun dealers and makers for $433 million alleging that the oversupply of firearms to the local market provided guns to criminals.
  - o November 17: A negligence suit filed by a California family against the Beretta company after their 14-year-old son was killed by another boy with a Beretta handgun is dismissed by a California jury.
  - o November 30: Permanent provisions of the Brady Act go into effect, enforcing the requirement that gun dealers initiate a presale criminal background check of all gun buyers through the newly created National Instant Criminal Background Check (NICS) computer database.
  - o December 1: The NRA files a federal lawsuit against the FBI attempting to prevent it from collecting information about firearm buyers.
  - o December 5: President Bill Clinton announced that the NICS had prevented 400,000 illegal firearm purchases, to which the NRA responded by stating the claim was "misleading."
- **1999**—Several developments:
  - o January: Bridgeport, Connecticut, and Miami-Dade County, Florida, both file civil suits against gun makers for firearm-related violence costs in their respective areas.
  - o April 20: The Columbine shooting renewed the national debate regarding the need for more restrictive gun control laws.
  - o May 20: The US Senate passes a bill which requires trigger locks on all newly manufactured guns in the United States and extends the waiting period and background check requirements to gun show firearm sales.
  - o August 24: The Los Angeles County Board of Supervisors bans the Great Western Gun Show from the Pomona, California, fairgrounds, where it had been held for the past 30 years. It was billed as the "world's largest gun show."

- **2004**—A number of developments:
  - o September 13: After lengthy and divisive debate, the Violent Crime Control and Law Enforcement Act of 1994 (which banned the sale of 19 different types of military-style assault weapons) was allowed to expire.
  - o December: Project Safe Neighborhoods, President George W. Bush's 2001 gun control program, is no longer funded by Congress. In addition, Massachusetts becomes the first state to implement an electronic firearms sales background check system that utilizes fingerprint scanning for gun licenses and purchases.
- **2005**—Two notable developments:
  - o January: the .50 caliber Browning machine gun rifle's manufacture, sale, distribution, and import are banned by the state of California.
  - o October: President Bush signs the Protection of Lawful Commerce in Arms Act, which protected firearms manufacturers and dealers. Specifically, the act limits the ability of victims of crimes committed by firearms to sue manufacturers and dealers. Additionally, the law enforced the requirement for all new guns to come with trigger locks.
- **2008**—A landmark year:
  - o January: President Bush signed the National Instant Criminal Background Check Improvement Act, requiring gun buyer background checks to screen for legally declared mentally ill individuals as they would be ineligible to purchase firearms. Both gun control advocates and opponents were largely in favor of this law.
  - o June 26: *District of Columbia v. Heller*—The US Supreme Court ruled that the Second Amendment affirmed the rights of individuals to own firearms, which also overturned the 32-year ban on the sale and possession of firearms in Washington, DC.
- **2012**—President Obama enacted a federal law that allowed licensed gun owners to bring firearms into national parks and wildlife refuges, as long as firearms are allowed by state law.
- **2016**—President Obama called on Congress to either enact or renew a law that would prohibit the possession and sale of "assault-style" weapons and high-capacity ammunition magazines after Omar Mateen killed 49 people in an Orlando, Florida, nightclub.

Federal Law and Landmark Cases

Before we can even entertain federal laws and landmark legal cases, we must start at the beginning, as it were, with the Second Amendment of the Constitution of the United States of America (1791):

A well regulated Militia, being necessary to the security of a free State, the right of the people to keep and bear Arms, shall not be infringed.

In providing a historical overview of our country's firearm laws, James Lindgren (2015), a law professor from Northwestern with a J.D. (Yale) and a Ph.D. (University of Chicago), noted that the two prevailing theories of the Second Amendment had traditionally been the *individual rights* and the *states'* (or *collective*) *rights* perspectives. However, there is little evidence from the time period around the enactment of the Second Amendment supporting the individual rights view and essentially no evidence to support the states' rights view. Lindgren contended that, as a result, a *civic rights* view was developed by the "states' rights academics," whereby "the right to keep and bear arms was an individual right, but it could be exercised only with the permission of the state in a militia" (p. 707). However, as Lindgren reiterated, there was no available evidence from the founding framers' era to support this position, either. In fact, there is contradictory evidence from the 1790s, such as St. George Tucker's edition of the *Blackstone Commentaries*, wherein the Second Amendment was viewed as guaranteeing an individual right *not* limited to members of a militia, consistent with the views of those such as Samuel Nasson, Samuel Latham Mitchell, and Samuel Adams. As Lindgren pointed out, the US Supreme Court substantiated the individual right set forth by the framers in *District of Columbia v. Heller* (2008), while the minority opinion of the court embraced the civic rights view—"a view that had not even been invented a decade earlier" (p. 709). He continued:

> The biggest surprise was that it was a five-to-four split decision, with the majority garnering only five votes for a position giving nontrivial content to a constitutional right explicitly guaranteed in the Bill of Rights. (p. 709)

A second landmark case in this context was that of *McDonald v. City of Chicago* (2010), wherein the US Supreme Court ruled that the Fourteenth Amendment included the Second Amendment and applied it to the states, thereby finding Chicago's firearm ban to be unconstitutional. Thus, the individual rights perspective is the prevailing view at this time, at least in the higher courts. Please note that a brief review of these cases follows, as does a summary of landmark cases at the end of this book in the *Glossary of Firearm-Related Law and Legal Cases*, Appendix B.

Lindgren (2015) contended that the discussion can, therefore, move to policy:

> On historical issues, I agree with the gun rights crowd that in the Second Amendment the Framers recognized an individual right to own guns. On policy issues, however, I tend to believe that some forms of gun control probably save more lives than they cost, but unfortunately the net effects are probably not that large one way or the other. (p. 705)

Lindgren supported his position, in part, by citing the National Research Council reports on the state of the extant firearm research and noted the irony was that the one type of gun control initiative that the council believes may be effective is targeted law enforcement interventions but that such policing in high-crime areas is precisely the type of gun control that those advocating for more firearm restrictions tend to oppose.

District of Columbia v. Heller (2008)

The District of Columbia had banned handgun possession by both criminalizing the ownership of unregistered firearms and prohibiting the registration of handguns. Although one was not allowed to carry an unlicensed handgun, the DC law had authorized the chief of police to issue 1-year licenses. Further, it stated that those who legally owned firearms must keep said firearms disassembled or bound by a device, such as a trigger lock. Heller, a DC special police officer, applied to register a handgun he could keep at his residence. The district refused his application. As a result, he filed a suit on Second Amendment grounds, seeking "to enjoin the city from enforcing the bar on handgun registration, the licensing requirement insofar as it prohibits carrying an unlicensed firearm in the home, and the trigger-lock requirement insofar as it prohibits the use of functional firearms in the home" (p. 1). Although the district court initially dismissed the case, the DC Circuit Court reversed, stating that the Second Amendment protects an individual's right to possess firearms. As such, the court held that DC's handgun ban and its requirement that firearms be kept in the home in a nonfunctional state, even when necessary for self-defense, violates the Second Amendment.

McDonald v. City of Chicago (2010)

Similar to *District of Columbia v. Heller* (2008), this case centered on an individual's right to firearm ownership. While the *Heller* case reasoned that the Second Amendment was applicable since the original ban was enacted under the authority of the federal government, the *McDonald* case argued that the Second Amendment should also apply to state and local governments. The case arose in 2008, when Otis McDonald, a retired custodian, along with others, filed a suit to the US district court regarding a 1982 Chicago law, which both banned the new registration of handguns and made it illegal to possess firearms without registration. The Supreme Court eventually granted a decision, after the case had been heard by the district and appellate courts, stating that the Second Amendment is applicable to the states through the due process clause. The court opined that the individual right to possess and use firearms for lawful purposes is a fundamental American right, specifically regarding the "scheme of ordered liberty and system of justice" (p. 1).

In the context of the *McDonald* ruling, Nieto (2011) posited that the court's analysis would have been stronger if it incorporated the privileges or immunities clause of the Fourteenth Amendment rather than the due process clause. Specifically, the privileges or immunities clause provides that federal rights are paramount: "[n]o State . . . shall abridge the privileges or immunities of citizens of the United States." As Nieto noted:

> Thus, when looking to the fundamental rights that would be encompassed by the Privileges or Immunities Clause, it is appropriate to encompass those that are heavily steeped in the nation's history and tradition, such as gun ownership for self-defense. . . . The Court in *McDonald* logically expanded upon *Heller* by holding that the Second Amendment right to bear arms is a fundamental right of U.S. citizens. (pp. 1125–1126)

Based on his legal analysis, Nieto concluded that reliance on the Fourteenth Amendment's due process clause has become a catch-all mechanism that lends itself to judicial activism—"a tool for judges to legislate from the bench" (p. 1128). Nieto further pointed out that federal and state rights should be cumulative and not competitive. In his dissent in *McDonald*, Justice Breyer contended that there was no public consensus on firearm ownership; however, there were amicus briefs submitted by 58 senators and 251 representatives and from 38 states, urging the court to maintain the right to keep and bear arms. As Nieto articulated in his concluding remarks:

> There are many people who are still uncomfortable with the thought of incorporating Bill of Rights protections against the States, citing concerns of federalism and worrying that it will lead to widespread restrictions of state rights. However, the Privileges or Immunities Clause exists to protect historic, fundamental rights that Congress intended with the passage of the Fourteenth Amendment to immunize from government interference, whether state or federal. Instead of allowing for the rampant judicial activism that is possible through the Due Process Clause, a decision via privileges or immunities would properly cabin the right in the manner intended by Congress. Moreover, the Second Amendment is just the kind of traditional right that should be incorporated through the Privileges or Immunities Clause. Though the Court has punted on the issue a handful of times in a 150-year span, courts are more comfortable incorporating rights than they were when the Court decided the *Slaughter-House Cases*.[3] It is time for the Court to stop punting the issue further and further into the future, and consider the intention with which Congress wished it to apply. (p. 1130; footnote added)

National Legislation

Professor William Vizzard of California State University Sacramento had a 27-year career as a special agent, supervisor, and manager in the ATF. In a recent article, he provided a historical account of US firearm laws and considerations for policy in this regard (Vizzard, 2015). He cites the Gun Control Act of 1968 as a turning point in American focus on these issues but notes that national gun control policy has generally remained unchanged since the early 1990s, following the Brady Handgun Prevention Act and the subsequent Republican congressional victories in 1994. As Vizzard indicated, no gun control legislation has passed either house of Congress since the sunset of the assault weapons ban; however, state legislatures have been much more active on both sides of the issue. He further contended that firearm regulation in the United States has followed a consistent pattern. Specifically, attempts were made by states to restrict handguns in the early 1900s, which were followed by their repeal and a lengthy period of inactivity. Then, landmark legislation came about in the 1930s, such as the National Firearms Act and the Federal Firearms Act. A period of general activity followed once again, until the assassination of President John F. Kennedy in 1963, which was followed by elevated crime rates and the ultimate murders of Martin Luther King, Jr., and Bobby Kennedy in 1968. These events paved the way for the Gun Control Act of 1968. However, nearly 20 years passed once again before any notable new federal legislation passed. Namely, the Firearms Owners Protection Act (FOPA) of 1986 revised much of the 1968 Gun Control Act. For instance, it redefined what a "gun dealer" was and exempted certain activities in that regard, it permitted the interstate sale of long guns in certain situations, it repealed some record-keeping requirements, and it permitted the interstate transportation of unloaded firearms by those who were not prohibited by federal law (i.e., the so-called safe passages clause). Thus, in many respects, the FOPA was much less restrictive than the Gun Control Act, although certain restrictions were certainly added, such as a ban on machine guns, record-keeping requirements for collectors, and harsher mandatory sanctions for those using firearms during the commission of certain crimes. As Vizzard noted, the FOPA is the primary federal law regulating firearm commerce and possession with one notable addition: the Brady Law of 1994, which expanded waiting periods and background checks to those seeking to purchase firearms. In sum, Vizzard (2015) suggested:

> Thus, federal policy relating to firearms possession and commerce has experienced only three notable changes in the past seventy-five years. Since the 1968 enactment of the GCA, one of these policy changes, FOPA, has significantly weakened gun policy. Although the issue has recurrently intruded on the public policy agenda, received significant media attention, and stirred passions, particularly among opponents of control, Congress has not acted on any significant legislation for two decades. (p. 884)

That said, Vizzard reminded us of the "monumental action" taken by the US Supreme Court during this time period à la *Heller* and *McDonald*. As such, he concluded that "any attempt at prohibition or quasi-prohibition of firearms not currently prohibited would appear to fail the constitutional standard. Thus, future fights will likely focus on concealed and open carry laws, licensing, and registration" (p. 892). Therefore, Vizzard recommended that advocates focus on specific, pragmatic goals that include reducing gun possession and carrying by high-risk individuals and by prohibited persons and utilizing firearms laws to incapacitate violent, career offenders. As he reiterated, the real movement has been at the state level in recent years—an area of consideration to which we now turn.

State-Level Legislation

As we indicated earlier, there are nearly 20,000 municipalities in the United States of America. It is a nation of laws—very many laws, and even more policies. Those of us whose work interfaces with the law regularly encounter the challenges of keeping up with even the most rudimentary, broad-based laws across states. We can compare and contrast dark blue and red states to illustrate the differences in laws related to contemporary social issues (e.g., the death penalty, abortion), but that type of academic exercise merely scratches the surface as to the extensive variability in laws throughout the country. In fact, let us take two of the most liberal states in the country and consider a fairly benign issue: it is legal to hunt bobcat in New York but illegal in New Jersey (see General hunting regulations, n.d., and Bobcat hunting seasons, n.d.). There is also *intrastate* variability—not with respect to laws but regarding procedures, such as the time taken to process new applications and the general acceptance of them (e.g., see Hill, 2015). Of course, there is also a rather significant amount of discretion afforded to prosecutors' offices regarding their pursuits in gun forfeiture matters. Thus, firearm-related policies occur at the municipality level, and most matters are typically settled at the county level; but it still behooves us to address the state-level laws and policies that drive these practical issues.

One salient issue is safety. Discussions regarding gun safety, gun-involved violence, and suicide prevention often arise in the wake of firearm-related tragedies, particularly school shootings. Some have questioned if armed guards should be stationed in schools, and initiatives have been taken in that context as well. For example, New Jersey legislatures have been pursuing a bill that would put armed, retired police officers who are under age 65 and in good standing in the schools (Senate Bill 86, 2016). Some jurisdictions have already implemented these types of initiatives. For example, a school district in central Colorado recently purchased 10 semiautomatic rifles with which to arm the district's security patrol (Tan, 2016). Even more recently and of particular note is that one Colorado school district has voted to allow teachers and other school staff the opportunity to carry firearms on campus to protect students (Colorado school district, 2016). One of the reasons the district voted on this matter is because it takes law enforcement 20 minutes to arrive at the schools in an event of a mass shooter. Also, board members expressed concern that there was a marijuana-growing operation in the vicinity that is believed by some to be connected to foreign cartels.[4]

Still, firearm regulations also arise in response to increasing crime rates and not only singular tragic incidents. For instance, acts of civil disturbance related to labor struggles, a rapidly growing population and immigrant influx, and Prohibition around the turn of the 20th century in Chicago led to the development of certain firearm laws in Illinois as firearm-related homicide rates increased (Weaver, 2002). Nevertheless, as Bridge (2012) noted, despite their landmark significance, *Heller* and *McDonald* left questions unanswered in the context of constitutionality of state and local firearm regulations. Bridge presented various cases of out-of-state tourists who had been arrested in New York for naively bringing their firearms into the state. For example, he described the case of Meredith Graves, a 39-year-old medical student from Tennessee who was arrested in Manhattan 3 days before Christmas in 2011 when she asked a security guard at the 9/11 Memorial where she could check in her handgun. She was in the city to attend a job interview at a hospital on Long Island. Graves spent a number of days in jail before making bail; she was facing between 3.5 and 15 years in prison for the felony offense. However, she pled guilty to a misdemeanor weapons possession charge and was fined instead.[5] Bridge (2012) indicated that "Graves' arrest was just the latest in a string of unwitting out-of-state tourists who have recently run afoul of New York's strict gun laws," and he cited various other people who were similarly charged for bringing handguns into New York City that they were legally permitted to carry in other states. Bridge also provided an overview of New York's firearm laws, which are some of the strictest in the state and date back quite some time, such as the Sullivan Dangerous Weapons Act of 1911. He noted its origins:

> At least part of the motivation behind the Sullivan Act was a desire to keep firearms out of the hands of recent immigrants from Italy and Southern Europe—perceived to be prone to violence—by giving the New York Police Department (NYPD) the power to grant or deny permits. (p. 151)

As Bridge pointed out, it remains illegal to possess a handgun anywhere in New York State without a license, and doing so represents (at least) an automatic class A misdemeanor. Moreover, New York does not make an exception for firearms kept in the home or use at a shooting range.[6] In his review of the state's gun laws, Bridge concluded that New York interprets the law to mean that the possession of firearms is a privilege, not a right—which he asserted, "clearly contradict[s] the explicit holdings of *Heller* and *McDonald*" (p. 165). As he fully articulated it:

> Thus, despite the clear language in both *Heller* and *McDonald* that the Second Amendment protects an individual's *right* to possess a handgun in the home for self-defense, in New York possessing the license that is required to possess a handgun is not a right, but a privilege. Similarly, despite *Heller*'s rejection of rational-basis review, New York state courts

will apparently only overturn the NYPD License Division's decision to deny a handgun license application if it is arbitrary and capricious. However, if an applicant were to challenge the denial of a license in federal court on Second Amendment grounds, then New York's "privilege not a right" doctrine and arbitrary-and-capricious standard of review would likely be declared unconstitutional, since they clearly contradict the explicit holdings of *Heller* and *McDonald*. (p. 165)

Furthermore, Bridge questioned the constitutionality of the "good moral character" component of New York's firearm application, noting that such is "highly discretionary and is not defined anywhere in the Penal Law" (p. 165). Bridge also challenged the fees for handgun licenses in New York. Namely, he indicated that the statute allows for $3–$10 fees, but the Penal Law provides the New York City Council and Nassau County Board of Supervisors authority to determine the fee schedule. Thus, those in New York City are required to pay $340 every 3 years, for example, leading Bridge to conclude: "Since the enactment of the Sullivan Law, New York City has deliberately imposed high fees for handgun licenses and registration in order to discourage poorer residents from obtaining weapons" (p. 170).

Bridge's (2012) review of New York firearm laws illustrates just some of the controversial nuances within a single state alone. Certainly, there are lists of contentions to existing and proposed laws in every state and on each side of the issue. As such, the complexity of firearm laws and policies among and within states cannot be understated. Although we present additional examples below, the interested reader is directed toward Kappas (2017) and Ciyou (2017) for informative outlines of existing firearm laws throughout the country; and one can read the proposed firearm-related bills online by conducting a keyword search (e.g., "firearm") within each state's legislative agenda on the respective legislature website (for example, New Jersey, www.njleg.state.nj.us).

Other states with comparatively more stringent gun laws continue to tighten as well. For example, California governor Jerry Brown has recently signed six stringent gun control measures restricting high-capacity magazines; mandating background checks for ammunition sales, including checks and licensing of sellers; and outlawing new firearms with a "bullet button," which was seen as a loophole to California's weapons assault ban. Those who previously owned firearms with bullet buttons would have to register them. In addition, transactions will be recorded, and those who are loaned firearms by non–family members will have to undergo background checks. McGreevy (2016) outlined the gun control measures approved by the California Senate:

- *Ammunition regulation*: requires background checks to buy ammunition, and creates a license to sell ammunition and a new system for collecting information about those sales.
- *Ban on large ammunition magazines*: bans the ownership of any ammunition clip that holds more than 10 rounds.

- *Bullet buttons*: expands the legal definition of an "assault weapon" to include a group of rifles with ammunition clips that can be quickly swapped out by using a bullet to push a small release button.
- *Theft*: requires reporting most lost or stolen guns within five days.
- *"Ghost guns" (a plastic pistol made by 3D printer)*: requires a person to get a serial number from state officials before making or assembling a gun.
- *Gun violence research*: creates a new University of California center for researching firearm-related violence.

States like California have also sought to pass much narrower laws aimed at curtailing gun violence and mass shootings by regulating dangerous people based on clear and convincing evidence of risk (see Paglini, 2015). The state of Hawaii has been considering adding gun owners to a federal database that would automatically notify the police if an island resident is arrested anywhere else in the country. Gun rights advocates are against this bill as they feel as if they should not be entered into a database just to enjoy a constitutional right. Supporters of the bill, such as a staff attorney at the Law Center to Prevent Gun Violence, regard the bill as "groundbreaking," however. At the present time, gun owners only undergo a background check when registering a new weapon (Riker, 2016).

Massachusetts is another example of a state with strict gun laws, but one that has recently had pivotal legal rulings. As the National Constitution Center's constitutional literacy advisor, Denniston (2016) addressed the recent case, *Caetano v. Massachusetts* (2016), whereby the US Supreme Court sought to expound upon the meaning of the right "to keep and bear arms." Denniston noted the unanimous opinion of the court to vacate Massachusetts' highest state court upholding of the flat ban on possessing stun guns for personal self-defense. An excerpt of the opinion set forth by Justice Alito, joined by Justice Thomas, is as follows:

> If the fundamental right of self-defense does not protect [the threatened woman in this case], then the safety of all Americans is left to the mercy of state authorities who may be more concerned about disarming the people than about keeping them safe. . . . [The woman in this case] didn't need physical strength to protect herself. She stood her ground, displayed the stun gun, and announced: "I'm not gonna take this anymore." . . . The gambit worked. The ex-boyfriend got scared and he left her alone. (*Caetano v. Massachusetts*, 2016)

Massachusetts had flatly banned stun guns from use by anyone other than law enforcement and military personnel. In this case, a woman threatened to use a stun gun against her ex-boyfriend, who had repeatedly assaulted her. The police found her in possession of the stun gun, however, and she was prosecuted. The Supreme Court came to the aforementioned brief, unsigned opinion that vacated the decision to ban stun guns in the state. Denniston (2016) set forth some possible implications of the ruling:

- The Supreme Court is paying attention to what the states and lower courts are doing with regard to Second Amendment issues, which is noteworthy given that the Court has denied review of various related cases in recent years. Thus, the Court may be waiting to intervene when it finds a lower court ruling that has gone too far.
- This ruling does not signal any desire by the Supreme Court to reconsider or reverse the *Heller* (2008) ruling, especially considering no dissents to the opinion were issued.
- This is the first time the Supreme Court has recognized the right to bear arms in a public setting for self-defense, outside of the home. Whether the Court will expand upon the right to bear arms in favor of public carry or public use of guns remains to be seen.
- There are at least five votes for the Court to rule in favor of a somewhat enlarged scope for the right to keep and bear arms. However, it is possible that this specific case did not receive as thorough of a review because it was not a major gun rights case per se.

The Massachusetts Supreme Judicial Court also recently analyzed the validity of the Massachusetts Safe Storage Statute in *Commonwealth v. McGowan* (2013), which required firearms to be secured in a locked container or equipped with a safety device that would make the firearm inoperable by anyone other than the owner or an authorized user, when not carried or under the control of said owner or user (see Stidham, 2015). The Supreme Judicial Court found that the statute falls outside of the scope of the right to bear arms and, therefore, outside of the protection of the Second Amendment. As such, they opined that it passed constitutional muster easily, under rational basis scrutiny. However, some such as Stidham (2015) argue that the statute does fall within the scope of the Second Amendment and, therefore, should be held unconstitutional.[7]

Gun laws can differ significantly due, in large part, to the state's political climate. In comparison to states like New York, California, and Massachusetts, with relatively stringent gun laws, gun laws in states like Texas are comparatively more lax. For example, although Texas requires the reporting of mentally ill individuals to the federal database of firearm purchaser background checks, firearm dealers are not required to obtain a state license, there is no limit on the number of firearms that can be purchased at one time, and there are no regulations on the transfer or possession of assault weapons or large-capacity ammunition magazines (Texas State law background, n.d.).

Similarly, Florida does not license firearm owners, require the registration of firearms, or regulate unsafe firearms, such as "Saturday night specials" (Florida State law background, n.d.). Legislators have proposed several law changes for 2017. For example, SB140 would allow for the open carry of handguns by concealed weapon permit holders in elementary schools, public college and university campuses, airport passenger terminals, and legislative meetings, among other settings (Clark, 2017).

While a discussion of the existing and proposed firearm-related laws and initiatives throughout the United States is important, it represents an initial step in understanding the issues at hand. Namely, what is particularly essential is to assess the impact of such laws and policies. As an example, a recent report issued by the Violence Policy Center in January 2017 stated that, according to data from 2015, states with weak gun violence prevention laws and higher rates of gun ownership (e.g., Alaska, Louisiana) have the highest rates of overall gun death in the nation (States with weak gun laws, 2017). Conversely, the report indicated that states with the strongest gun violence prevention laws and lower rates of gun ownership (e.g., Hawaii, Massachusetts) have the lowest overall gun deaths, although even in these areas the human toll of gun violence is far above the death rates that exist in other industrialized countries (States with weak gun laws, 2017). Data like these are important to take into consideration, especially since the impact of firearm-related policies and laws is of the utmost importance. However, as will be discussed elsewhere in this book, the issues at hand and the research behind them are complicated and sometimes should not be accepted at face value. We address laws and policies throughout the book along with the research associated with them, but first we provide an introduction to some of these issues.

Impact of Firearm Laws and Policies

Much of the research on firearm-involved suicide, violence, and other re-lated areas relies upon *proxy* variables and data. In other words, various types of data are impossible or difficult to attain, leading some researchers to col-lect related data from which they will make inferences. For example, some researchers use firearm-related homicide and suicide data to estimate rates of firearm ownership. Furthermore, most researchers use retrospective data that are made publicly available from government agencies rather than engaging in independent, prospective data collection. As such, there are virtually no available data that have been gathered directly from law-abiding citizens who interact with and own firearms, for example. This reality is quite peculiar for an issue that has remained almost squarely in the forefront of our national discussion for some time and given that the firearm-owning population has been estimated to be over 100 million people. Social scientists manage to con-duct research on some of the most vulnerable and least accessible populations, which makes the dearth of research on this extremely large and highly ac-cessible population of firearm owners and operators very striking. These are some of the reasons why we have relatively few empirical studies on the impact and efficacy of firearm laws and policies, or what is known as "policy anal-ysis"—a type of research that is akin to treatment outcome or program eval-uation studies that are conducted in the medical and mental health research arenas. As we will highlight in Chapter 5 of this book, some of this type of research has been conducted in specific areas, such as in the context of domestic and intimate partner violence prevention programs, policies, and laws. Otherwise, many researchers simply rely upon the aforementioned proxy-variable studies to make (often) far-reaching inferences about the efficacy of firearm laws, policies, and related programs. One common example is when researchers simply calculate the statistical correlation between the number of firearm owners in a region and the crime rate. These types of analyses are typically uninformative at best and can even be quite misleading, particularly because the sound bites pulled from them do not and cannot appropriately reflect the extensive limitations and caveats associated with this type of research. Nevertheless, we must work with what we have for the time being and point out limitations, where applicable. In the following subsections, we provide an overview of the contemporary research on some of the more pressing issues in the firearm arena: background checks, the castle doctrine or "stand-your-ground" laws, right to carry laws, and considerations related to child access prevention and storage.

Background Checks

The push to implement more extensive background checks is, perhaps, the most oft-cited concern by gun violence prevention advocates. Indeed, in President Obama's January 4, 2016, executive order, two out of four of his stated goals pertained to background checks. He noted that the NICS received more than 22.2 million background check requests in 2015 alone, corresponding to more than 63,000 per day, on average. The president's first stated goal in the order was to "Keep guns out of the wrong hands through background checks." Specifically, he indicated that everyone selling firearms must get a license and conduct background checks, regardless of the sales venue. Moreover, he wrote that the FBI was overhauling its system so that it could conduct checks 24 hours a day, 7 days per week, while improving communication with local authorities when a prohibited person attempts to purchase a firearm. In addition, the FBI was to hire more than 230 additional examiners and other staff to assist in the background check process. The third stated goal was to "Increase mental health treatment and reporting to the background check system," such that the Social Security Administration would begin to include information in the background check system regarding those who receive benefits and who may be prohibited from possessing a firearm for mental health reasons. Additionally, the order noted that the Department of Health and Human Services was "finalizing a rule to remove unnecessary legal barriers preventing States from reporting relevant information about people prohibited from possessing a gun for specific mental health reasons" (Fact sheet, 2016). Many other politicians and advocates also cite the need for improved background checks, and even public opinion generally supports such; but how effective are they?

As we illustrate in Chapter 4 of this book, the paradox is that many of the high-profile shootings that have prompted firearm-related legislation would not have been prevented by many of the laws and policies set forth, including background checks. Swanson and Felthous (2015) pointed out that there has been a notable increase in the reporting of mental health records to the NICS index, which is likely attributable to the media's sensationalizing mass shootings by those with mental health problems. However, they suggested that it is unclear if even an improved background check system would have deterred such psychologically disturbed mass shooters. Still, they noted that the combination of suicide and violence risk may be a particularly important consideration in these contexts:

> Mental conditions that are not uncommonly reported in mass killers are depression, sociopathy, psychosis, alcohol abuse and intoxication, jealousy, and paranoia, and they often experience some disturbance in their closest relationships. Thus, clinically it is important not to compartmentalize suicide and homicide risk potential, but to consider the possibility of combined homicide and suicide risk in certain individuals for whom hospitalization and perhaps firearm restriction, depending on jurisdictional law, might be more appropriate than restriction of other large categories of persons with mental disorders. (p. 170)

Nevertheless, there appears to be some association between background checks and lower firearm-related homicide and suicide rates, although the typical caveats related to correlation and causality are applicable. Ruddell and Mays (2005) examined the relationship between state firearm background checks and firearm-related homicides and found that states with less stringent background check policies were significantly associated with more firearm homicides. They acknowledged that, because there are so many guns circulating in our country, a motivated individual will likely be able to gain access to a gun through a secondary market. However, effective state background checks may "temporarily frustrate an unauthorized person from obtaining a firearm," which might contribute to lower firearm-related homicide rates (p. 127).

Sen and Panjamapirom (2012) investigated the relationship between the types of background check information required by states prior to firearm purchases and firearm homicide and suicide deaths, using data from the Surveys of State Procedures Related to Firearm Sales and the Web-based Injury Statistics Query and Reporting System (WISQARS) of the Centers for Disease Control and Prevention (CDC). The results indicated that more background checks were associated with fewer firearm-related homicides and suicides. Additionally, firearm-related homicides were fewer in states where background checks included restraining orders and fugitive status. For firearm-related suicides, the rates were lower in states where background checks look for mental illness, fugitive status, and misdemeanors. Sumner,

Layde, & Guse (2008) compared firearm deaths among states that utilize different background check systems. Specifically, firearm deaths were analyzed among states that use a federal background check system, states that use a state background check system, and states that use a local background check system. Results suggested that lower firearm deaths, related to both suicide and homicide, were associated with local-level background check systems. The authors note that lower rates of firearm-related deaths among states that utilize local-level background checks could be, at least in part, due to more thorough background checks conducted by local agencies. This could be because states that utilize local agencies to conduct background checks are likely states that place additional value on gun control, and as such, more resources (i.e., financial, law enforcement, legal) are devoted to the issue.

Castle Doctrine—"Stand Your Ground"

Between the years 2000 and 2010, over 20 states passed new or revised legislation related to the castle doctrine, or what is known as a "stand your ground" law, which civilly and criminally protects those who use physical force to protect themselves or their home. Wallace (2014) investigated the potential influence that this legislation has had on firearm acquisition and ownership, as measured by two proxy variables: the number of background checks and the proportion of suicides attributed to firearms. She found that the castle doctrine was associated with a long-term increase in the number of federal background checks, but the opposite relationship was found for firearm-related suicides, such that the legislation was associated with a decrease in suicides by firearm. However, results related to the proportion of suicides by firearm were limited. See Table 2.1, created by Wallace (2014), which displays information pertaining to castle doctrine legislation by state.

Although there has not been much research conducted regarding the castle doctrine, Wallace (2014) indicated that evidence has been found of racial disparities regarding whether a shooter would be ruled justifiable, whereas others have found no evidence that castle doctrine served as a deterrent for burglary, robbery, or aggravated assault. In fact, in states with castle doctrine legislation, murder and non-negligent manslaughter rates increased by 8%. In addition, it had been found that castle doctrine legislation passed in Arizona was associated with a lasting increase in robberies. Of course, these correlations must be considered in context given that violent offenders do not typically stay abreast of their state's legislation to guide their criminal activities and planning.

Right to Carry

Some contend that the Second Amendment does not simply afford people the right to own firearms but also the right to carry (i.e., to keep *and bear* arms). However, there is a lack of consensus in the professional literature in

Table 2.1. Castle Doctrine Legislation 2000–2010 by Store

State	Region	Effective date	No duty to retreat extended beyond the home	No duty to retreat anywhere one has a legal right to be	Presumes reasonable fear of bodily harm	No civil liability
Alabama	South	4/4/06	Yes	Yes	No	Yes
Alaska	West	6/22/06	Yes	No	Yes	Yes
Arizona	West	4/24/06	Yes	Yes	Yes	Yes
Florida	South	3/23/05	Yes	Yes	Yes	Yes
Georgia	South	3/24/06	Yes	Yes	No	Yes
Idaho	West	4/14/06	No	No	No	Yes
Illinois	Midwest	7/28/04	No	No	No	Yes
Indiana	Midwest	3/28/06	Yes	Yes	No	Yes
Kansas	Midwest	3/30/06	Yes	Yes	No	Yes
Kentucky	South	4/14/06	Yes	Yes	Yes	Yes
Louisiana	South	3/28106	Yes	Yes	Yes	Yes
Maine	Northeast	9/21/07	No	No	No	Yes
Maryland	South	5/21/10	No	No	No	Yes
Michigan	Midwest	7/20/06	Yes	Yes	No	Yes
Mississippi	South	3/28/06	Yes	Yes	Yes	Yes
Missouri	Midwest	7/3/07	Yes	No	Yes	Yes
Montana	West	4/27/09	Yes	Yes	Yes	No
North Dakota	Midwest	4/27/07	Yes	No	Yes	Yes
Ohio	Midwest	6/10/08	Yes	No	Yes	Yes
Oklahoma	South	5/12/06	Yes	Yes	Yes	Yes
South Carolina	South	6/9/06	Yes	Yes	Yes	Yes
South Dakota	Midwest	2/28/06	Yes	Yes	No	No
Tennessee	South	5/23/07	Yes	Yes	Yes	Yes
Texas	South	3/20/07	Yes	Yes	Yes	Yes
West Virginia	South	3/28/08	Yes	Yes	No	No

From Wallace (2014).

this regard, particularly as such pertains to *Heller's* impact on the law (see e.g., Neil & Neil, 2009). The existing laws are nuanced, though. Namely, there are laws related to the *concealed carry* versus the *open carry* of firearms. However, the states are very specific in their requirements. For instance, concealed carry is legal in even the strictest states, such as New Jersey, but only for very select persons who are approved for such (e.g., those engaged in security work and former law enforcement officers). In actuality, most states allow some form of carrying firearms by some types of approved persons. The empirical literature is mixed. Some have found right to carry laws in "shall issue" states associated with increased homicide rates, whereas "may issue" states have been associated with decreased homicide rates by roughly 20%–30% (Valle & Glover, 2012). The associated increase in firearm-related homicides is consistent with past research (e.g., McDowall, Loftin, & Wiersema, 1995). However, others have not found support for the notion that right to carry laws either increase or decrease the number of mass public shootings (Duwe, Kovandzic, & Moody, 2002) or crime rates (Phillips et al., 2015).

While the aforementioned detailed debates, research studies, and legal challenges continue, a more contemporary issue has emerged: the right to carry on college campuses—a setting that is inextricably linked to the national gun debate, more generally. Arrigo and Acheson (2016) contended that the competing demands that comprise the concealed carry on campus debate (i.e., Second Amendment liberties versus personal safety versus learning environment interests) have yet to be appropriately balanced in current policy. In their review, they addressed three key dimensions in this context: individual, institutional, and societal conditions. According to Arrigo and Acheson, the individual conditions are those that pertain to the social–psychological dynamics of gun control policy, including, but not limited to, the relationship between individuals' perspectives on carrying on campus, their demographic variables (e.g., state of residency, sex, political affiliation), and their personal experiences with firearms and crime. The institutional conditions are those related to the governmental and educational dynamics of gun control policy, namely, the power dynamics, partisan politics, and differing interests between state legislatures and public colleges and universities. Lastly, the societal conditions surrounding the campus carry discussion include the political, economic, and media dynamics associated with gun control policy. In this context, Arrigo and Acheson highlighted the significant role that special interest groups and lobbyists play in shaping gun control policy but also the less obvious role that the media plays by sensationalizing certain events. As they articulated it:

> The media's ability to make the rare event of mass shootings appear relevant to individuals is due to its ability to play on human psychology. . . . In other words, infotainment news and commentary cultures take what is otherwise a non-issue, and create a moral panic in which society believes that the non-issue requires immediate, critical, and ongoing attention. (p. 8)

This sentiment appears consistent with that of the country as a whole, given that Americans' trust in the media is currently at its lowest point in 20 years, such that only 32% of people report having at least a fair amount of trust in the media (Swift, 2016). But what does the social science research indicate?

Perhaps unsurprisingly, the professional research reflects notable regional differences in students' perspectives on campus carry policies. For example, students in Washington State have been found to be exponentially more uncomfortable with guns on campus compared to their counterparts from Texas (see Cavanaugh, Bouffard, Wells, & Nobles, 2012). Bouffard, Nobles, Wells, & Cavanaugh (2012) also surveyed approximately 1,400 undergraduate students from a Texas university regarding concealed carry on campus and found that 16% already had a concealed handgun license. In addition, 50%–100% of those students indicated that they would carry on campus if the university allowed it, which would potentially lead to 20%–100% of classrooms on that campus containing a concealed handgun. Of note is that student perceptions have been found to be more related to political and weapon socialization factors than fear or victimization factors (Jang, Dierenfeldt, & Lee, 2014).

Moreover, Arrigo and Acheson (2016) cited research indicating that a significant majority of police chiefs disagreed or strongly disagreed that concealed carry would prevent some or all of the murders on college campuses. Nevertheless, the case law has been rather variable in this regard. For example, in *University of Utah v. Shurtleff* (2006), the state Supreme Court held that the university did not have the authority to ban guns on campus, and it was not up to the court to decide whether the university's policy was necessary to achieve an educational and safety mission; therefore, firearms were allowed on Utah campuses. Similarly, in *Regents of the University of Colorado v. Students for Concealed Carry on Campus, LLC* (2012), the university had a policy prohibiting weapon possession on campus, but the appellate and Supreme Court found that this policy violated the state's legislation and that the university does not have authority to restrict possession of firearms on campus. However, in *DiGiacinto v. The Rector and Visitors of George Mason University* (2011), the state Supreme Court ruled that the university did not violate the state or federal constitution by adopting a concealed carry ban on campus and, as such, endorsed the university's autonomy to protect the population on campus as it saw fit. Based on their review and analysis, Arrigo and Acheson (2016) concluded: "if consensus-building is to be achievable on matters of firearms legislation (including the concealed carry ban controversy), then attention to additional scientific research is required and a renewed focus on ethical accountability among political stakeholders is essential" (p. 14). Specifically, they emphasized the need for research on the structural (i.e., media-driven political economic factors), institutional (i.e., government and educational influences), and individual-level (i.e., social-psychological forces) dynamics that serve as barriers to consensus-building legislation.

Child Access Prevention and Storage

Safety and security are paramount concerns in the firearm arena, particularly as they relate to our youth. As we discussed in Chapter 1, programs have been developed to teach children about firearms and how to remain safe should they be around or otherwise encounter them (e.g., Project ChildSafe and Eddie Eagle GunSafe'). Thus, particular attention has been paid to child access prevention (CAP). We address related issues, such as the presence of firearms in the home, at various points throughout this book; but some research has specifically investigated CAP and storage practices. For example, Prickett, Martin-Storey, & Crosnoe (2014) examined the relationship between state firearm legislation, CAP firearm legislation, parental firearm ownership, and storage safety practices. They found that fewer families owned firearms in states with more restrictive firearm laws and CAP laws compared to families in less restrictive states without CAP laws. Of note was that unsafe storage practices were least likely among families in states with strong firearm legislation and CAP laws.

According to Price and Norris (2010), safe storage laws seem to have been successful in lowering suicide risk among adolescents. However, these findings are nuanced. For instance, Gius (2015) investigated the relationship between CAP, minimum age laws, youth firearm-related suicide at the state level, and unintentional death rates. The results suggested that state-level minimum age laws had no effect on youth suicides or unintentional deaths. Additionally, state-level CAP laws had no effect on unintentional deaths. However, states with CAP laws had lower rates of youth suicide, and after the enactment of a federal minimum age limit, both types of death decreased. Gius concluded that, given the mixed results regarding minimum age levels at the state level, perhaps nationwide handgun restrictions for youth would be primarily effective in lowering both youth suicide and unintentional deaths. Another study pertaining to CAP laws conducted by Webster, Vernick, Zeoli, & Manganello (2004) found similar results. Specifically, the results suggested that state CAP laws were associated with a modest reduction in suicide among adolescents aged 14–17. Also, consistent with the aforementioned study, the authors concluded that minimum age restrictions (as implemented during the time of the study) did not appear to reduce overall rates of suicide among youth.

Regarding firearm storage practices, more generally, a study of unintentional firearm deaths (Miller, Azrael, Hemenway, & Vriniotis, 2005) discovered that a disproportionate number of unintentional firearm-related fatalities occurred in states where gun owners are more likely to store their firearms loaded. Further, states where loaded firearms were more likely to be stored unlocked were at greatest risk for unintentional firearm deaths. In another study of the association between gun storage practices and the risk of unintentional and self-inflicted firearm injuries, Grossman et al. (2005) concluded, "The 4 practices of keeping a gun locked, unloaded, storing ammunition locked, and in a separate location are each associated with a protective effect and suggest a feasible strategy to reduce these types of injuries in homes with children and teenagers where guns are stored" (p. 707).

Mental Health and Firearm Laws

Mental health issues have become inextricably linked to firearm legislation and policies for a whole host of reasons, including, but not limited to, sensational media portrayals of the stereotyped "mentally ill shooter." We address the connection between firearms and violence in Chapter 4, but as we will outline, the relationship between suicide and firearms is actually much stronger, which we highlight in Chapter 6. Nevertheless, many of the prohibitors in the context of firearm ownership are related to mental health (e.g., violence and domestic violence, suicide, substance abuse, psychiatric history, current mental health problems). Indeed, Part III of this book pertains to the emerging roles of mental health professionals in firearm-related matters, particularly in the context of treatment and evaluation (Chapters 7 and 8) but also in research, which we address throughout the final chapter. However, before we can reflect upon those more advanced concepts, we provide an overview of existing and proposed federal and state legislation associated with mental health concepts, followed by a general discussion related to the ways in which firearm laws reflect concerns with suicide, violence, and domestic violence—issues we delve into in much more detail in their respective chapters.

Federal

The Gun Control Act of 1968, in part, prohibits possession of a firearm by any person who has been adjudicated "mental defective" or committed to a mental institution or who is addicted to any controlled substance. Specifically, the federal firearms prohibition under 18 U.S.C. § 922(g)(4)[8] indicates that any such person is banned from shipping, transporting, receiving, or possessing any firearm or ammunition per the following:

> A person is "adjudicated as a mental defective" if a court, board, commission, or other lawful authority has made a determination that a person, as a result of marked subnormal intelligence, mental illness, incompetency, condition, or disease:
>
> - Is a danger to himself or to others;
> - Lacks the mental capacity to contract or manage his own affairs;
> - Is found insane by a court in a criminal case; or
> - Is found incompetent to stand trial, or not guilty by reason of lack of mental responsibility, pursuant to articles 50a and 72b of the Uniform Code of Military Justice, 10 U.S.C. §§ 850a, 876b.

A person is "committed to a mental institution" if that person has been formally committed to a mental institution by a court, board, commission, or other lawful authority. The term includes a commitment:

- To a mental institution involuntarily;
- For mental defectiveness or mental illness; or
- For other reasons, such as for drug use.

The term *does not include* a person in a mental institution for observation or by voluntary admission.

Moreover:

The term "mental institution" includes mental health facilities, mental hospitals, sanitariums, psychiatric facilities, and other facilities that provide diagnoses by licensed professionals of mental retardation or mental illness, including
a psychiatric ward in a general hospital.

A person is *not* prohibited if:

The person received relief from Federal firearms disabilities under 18 U.S.C. § 922(g)(4) by:

- The Bureau of Alcohol, Tobacco, Firearms and Explosives under 18 U.S.C. § 925(c);
- or
- A proper Federal or State authority under a relief from disabilities program that meets the requirements of the NICS Improvement Amendments Act of 2007, Public Law 110-180.

The mental health adjudication or commitment was imposed by a Federal department or agency, and the:

- Adjudication or commitment was set aside or expunged;
- Person was fully released from mandatory treatment, supervision, or monitoring;
- Person was found to no longer suffer from the disabling mental health condition;
- Person has otherwise been found to be rehabilitated; or
- Adjudication or commitment was based solely on a medical finding without opportunity for hearing by the Federal department or agency with proper jurisdiction.

As Price and Norris (2010) noted, the Brady Handgun Violence Prevention Act of 1993, also known as the "Brady Act" or "Brady Bill," spurred the creation of the NICS, which is administered by the FBI. An NICS background check includes access to three databases maintained by the FBI: the Interstate Identification Index (includes criminal history plus adjudications of legal insanity or incompetency), the National Crime Information Center (information on civil protection orders and arrest warrants), and the NICS Index (information from federal and state agencies about individuals prohibited for other reasons, such as disqualifying mental health history and undocumented persons).

Thus, federal law prohibits those who have had certain mental health problems. But what do the leading scholars have to say about complete prohibitions based on a mental health history or diagnosis alone? A multidisciplinary group of gun violence prevention and mental health experts formed the Consortium for Risk-Based Firearm Policy (McGinty et al., 2014) in an effort to advance an evidence-based policy agenda on the issue of mental illness and firearms. They agreed on a guiding principle for future policy recommendations:

> Restricting firearm access on the basis of certain dangerous behaviors is supported by the evidence; restricting access on the basis of mental illness diagnoses is not. (p. e22)

At the end of a 2-day meeting, the experts also agreed on the following points, which they contended are supported by the best available evidence (p. e22):

- The vast majority of people diagnosed with mental illnesses do not engage in violence against others, and most violence is caused by factors (e.g., substance abuse) other than mental illness per se.
- At certain times, such as the period surrounding a psychiatric hospitalization or first episode of psychosis, small subgroups of individuals with serious mental illness are at elevated risk of violence.
- Mental illnesses such as depression significantly increase the risk of suicide, which accounts for more than half of gun deaths in the United States each year.

The consortium's perspectives are consistent with those of many other leaders in the field (e.g., see Gold & Simon, 2016). A position statement on firearm-related issues from the American Psychiatric Association was also recently set forth by Pinals and colleagues (2015b) and, in part, includes the following policy recommendations:

- The vast majority of gun violence is unrelated to mental illness; therefore, the broader problem of firearm-related injury needs to be the focus, with interventions that reduce the risk of harm
- Guns should be banned for people whose conduct indicates they present a risk for harming themselves or others, whether or not they have a diagnosable mental health disorder
- Disqualification criteria should be carefully defined and there should be a fair and reasonable restoration process

- Improved identification and access to care for people with mental disorders is important, but will have a limited impact on overall rates of violence due to the small percentage of violence attributable to mental disorder in the first place.

Swanson and Felthous (2015) echoed the American Psychiatric Association's sentiment that involuntary commitment exclusions would not prohibit many people with concerning mental health conditions. As they articulated it:

A number of common mental health conditions—including personality disorders, post-traumatic stress disorder, and alcohol use disorder—tend to be associated with this risky mix of pathological anger with gun access. However, only a small proportion of angry people with guns has ever been hospitalized for a mental health problem—voluntarily or involuntarily—and thus most would not be prohibited from firearms under the involuntary commitment exclusion. (p. 169)

Moreover, as Mattaini (2012) noted:

Apparently simple solutions often are not. At the moment, there appears to be near universal political agreement on the potential value of enhanced background checks for firearms purchases, for example. How to word a law in such a way as to identify those with mental health issues who should not have access to guns without stigmatizing mental illness has proved difficult however, records are incomplete, and a majority of states do not regularly report such data. (p. 2)

Vernick, McGinty, & Rutkow (2015) examined the laws and professional literature to determine if temporary, emergency mental health holds (as opposed to a full involuntary commitment) would disqualify a person from gun ownership. They noted the factors that increase the risk for violence among those diagnosed with mental illnesses (i.e., substance abuse, childhood trauma and victimization, unemployment) and how the prevalence of these factors—especially substance abuse—are increased for these individuals. Moreover, although most violence in this country is not committed by individuals with diagnosable mental health problems, there is a small minority of those with serious psychiatric conditions who are at increased risk for violence during particular periods. Vernick and colleagues further noted that neither the Gun Control Act nor the ATF's subsequent regulations specify whether temporary emergency detentions fall under the restricted category. Thus, in *United States v. Rehlander* (2012), Rehlander argued that a temporary hospitalization under an ex parte proceeding should not disqualify him from purchasing or possessing firearms under *Heller*. The court ultimately concluded that *Heller* did not apply to a temporary hospitalization, although this might be a different case if the Gun Control Act provided for a *temporary* prohibition from possessing firearms.

Simpson (2007) presented a number of additional notable cases related to firearms and mental health. For instance, in *Redford v. U.S. Dept. of Treasury,*

Bureau of Alcohol, Tobacco and Firearms (1982), a man challenged the seizure of his gun due to a previous not guilty by reason of insanity determination, but the court upheld the seizure, stating: "We believe people of common intelligence would understand that language [in the statute] to include persons found not guilty of a criminal charge by reason of insanity" (ref. 12, p. 473). In *United States v. Hansel* (1973), Hansel was involuntarily committed but not by judicial or administrative proceedings; in fact, the examining physician later testified he did not have a serious mental illness, nor was he mentally ill or in need of hospitalization. Therefore, the appeals court found that Hansel was not committed for the purposes of the Gun Control Act. In *United States v. Giardina* (1988), the Fifth Circuit Court of Appeals held that admission by emergency certificate did not constitute a commitment for the purposes of the Gun Control Act, stating that "[t]emporary, emergency detentions for treatment of mental disorders or difficulties, which do not lead to formal commitments under state law, do not constitute the commitment envisioned" (ref. 17, p. 1337). Simpson pointed out other similar cases related to commitments to psychiatric hospitals and firearms as well (e.g., *United States v. Waters*, 1994; *United States v. Chamberlain*, 1998; *United States v. Dorsch*, 2004). Most recently, the Sixth Circuit Court of Appeals reversed and remanded a previous decision made by the district court for the Western District of Michigan in *Tyler v. Hillsdale County Sheriff's Department* (2014), which we discuss in the subsection pertaining to state laws that follows.

Nevertheless, as Price and Norris (2010) have pointed out, while the link between mental illness and suicide is well established, researchers continue to debate the relationship between mental illness and violence. They suggest that it is unclear whether legislation aimed at persons with mental illnesses will be an effective tool to combat firearm-related violence, although they note that the "gun show loophole" (whereby unlicensed sellers are not required to perform background checks) permitted a bypass of NICS. Still, they stated, "the legislation was also unlikely to have any significant impact on the illegal firearm market" (p. 328), particularly given that our background check system is dependent on the states' transmission of information related to prohibited persons to the NICS for entry into the databases; and in *Printz v. United States* (1997), the US Supreme Court held that the federal government cannot mandate state officials to administer or enforce a federal regulatory program, under Tenth Amendment protections. As a result, by 2006, reports were available for only 235,000 of the 2.7 million prohibited people who had been involuntarily committed since the NICS came into effect (i.e., 9%), and only 22 states had voluntarily contributed mental health records to the NICS by 2007, much of which was considered incomplete even by the FBI.

A series of high-profile shootings over the years, perpetrated by those with mental illness, prompted additional legislation. For instance, the Our Lady of Peace Bill was introduced by US Representative Carolyn McCarthy, whose husband was killed and whose son was wounded by Colin Ferguson in the 1993 Long Island Railroad shooting. The bill would have provided financial incentives to states to automate records and create databases, along with disincentives for failing to do so. However, it did not have enough support to pass in the Senate. A similar bill was subsequently set forth in response to the Virginia Tech massacre. Namely, 2016 vice presidential candidate and Virginia governor Tim Kaine filed Executive Order 50, which required law enforcement to enter involuntary orders for psychiatric care into the state mental health database as well as send that information to federal law enforcement. Thus, involuntary outpatient treatment was deemed equivalent to involuntary admission to a mental health facility.

Price and Norris (2010) also noted that part of the national response to the Virginia Tech shooting was the enactment of the NICS Improvement Amendments Act of 2007, a bipartisan amendment to the Brady Act that was supported by organizations on both sides of the gun debate. The act included, but was not necessarily limited to, improving the transmission of information from the states to the system and providing protection and recourse for prohibited persons (e.g., a diagnosis alone is insufficient). As Price and Norris indicated:

> Prior to the enactment of the NICS Improvement Act, the federal barrier for persons with a disqualifying mental health history was, in effect, lifelong. The new act requires that all federal agencies that issue mental health adjudications or commitments provide a process for "relief from disabilities." Moreover, mental adjudications or commitments by federal agencies or state agencies are considered "not to have occurred" for the purpose of the NICS check when those adjudications or commitments have been "set aside or expunged." (p. 329)

The act provided funding for states to develop and maintain *relief from disabilities programs*, which 29 states already had in place; and it also required federal agencies (e.g., the Department of Veterans Affairs) to employ such programs as well. However, Price and Norris pointed out the concerns set forth by those such as the American Psychiatric Association, who have noted the issues surrounding fundamental fairness and the potential associated with these types of laws and policies in facilitating discrimination against those diagnosed with a mental illness. One unintended consequence may be that people avoid seeking treatment for mental health and substance use problems. As Price and Norris (2010) articulated it:

> Persons who have jobs that require a firearm license or who are hunters might be especially reluctant to risk identification as a prohibited person. This reluctance might be especially great in states that define the disqualifying mental health history much more broadly than required by the federal statutes. (pp. 329–330)

Indeed, we have observed this reluctance to seek help from law enforcement and correctional officers for some time now (Steinkopf, Hakala, & Van Hasselt, 2015; Karaffa & Tochkov, 2013; Miller, 2004).

State

There are a number of resources authored by attorneys that provide an overview of firearm-related laws across the country (e.g., Ciyou, 2017; Kappas, 2017), as well as those more detailed and specific to certain states, such as Evan Nappen's books on New Hampshire (2015) and New Jersey (2017) gun laws. As noted earlier, there is significant variability with regard to state laws across the country (see Norris, Price, Gutheil, & Reid, 2006; Price & Norris, 2010; Simpson, 2007; US Department of Justice, 2006). One such area pertains to the searches and seizures conducted by law enforcement officers when it is believed that a person poses a risk because of mental health problems. In 2005, Indiana passed a law (HEA 1776, PL 187-2005) in response to the shooting death of a police officer by a paranoid man that allowed law enforcement to seize firearms without a warrant if they believed someone was dangerous due to mental illness and not compliant with psychiatric medication or had the propensity for violence or unstable conduct. The empirical literature is scant in this specific area, although Parker (2010) investigated 133 gun seizure cases in Indianapolis in 2006 and 2007 and found that most firearm confiscations were from white men (over 80%) and most (64%) were related to suicide risk. Only 16.5% of revocations were due to violence risk concerns, followed by concerns related to domestic disturbance (14%) and active psychosis (10%). Just over one-quarter of cases were related to substance use concerns. In his follow-up review of the effects of this legislation from 2006 to 2013, Parker (2015) reiterated that firearms were most often removed due to risk of suicide, consistent with the firearm and mental health literature more generally, and he concluded:

> Overall, the Indiana law removed weapons from a small number of people, most of whom did not seek return of their weapons. The firearm seizure law thus functioned as a months-long cooling-off period for those who did seek the return of their guns. (p. 308)

Olivero and Pinals (2015) highlighted the right of people diagnosed with mental illnesses to keep and bear arms in their review of *Tyler v. Hillsdale County Sheriff's Department* (2014). In Tyler, the Sixth Circuit of Appeals reversed and remanded a previous decision made by the district court for the Western District of Michigan. The district court had dismissed a claim by Mr. Tyler, who had argued that the federal statute that prohibits individuals committed to mental institutions from possessing guns was unconstitutional as applied to him, especially as there was no relief program with an opportunity to challenge the prohibition in place. The appeals court stated that he had cited a valid violation of the Second Amendment. From *Tyler*, one quote is particularly noteworthy: "not all previously institutionalized persons are mentally ill at a later time, so the law is, at least somewhat, overbroad" (p. 332). And, of course, the question: "Are previously institutionalized persons sufficiently dangerous, as a class, that it is permissible to deprive permanently all such persons of the Second Amendment right to bear arms?" (p. 333). The court held that Mr. Tyler should be able to exercise the right to bear arms in any state he chooses to live, regardless of whether the state has chosen to accept federal grant money to fund a relief program. The court further stated that Congress designed the law that enforces prohibitions on this group of people only during periods in which the person is deemed dangerous, which does not necessarily equal a lifelong prohibition. Ultimately, the court did not order that Mr. Tyler's rights be restored immediately but provided him with the opportunity to prove that he had regained mental stability and that his mental illness did not pose a risk to himself or others.

In their survey of Massachusetts police chiefs tasked with certifying firearm ownership qualification, Silver, Fisher, & Silver (2015) found that some have broadened the scope of their background checks to include information and experiences gleaned from officers who have had personal experiences with applicants. This survey preceded significant legislative reforms in the state that centralized database commitments to include all mental health and substance abuse facilities, which facilitated the identification of all commitments occurring in the state. This new database could streamline the background check process, but Silver and colleagues indicated that they were interested in how this new system may change police chiefs' practices. In that regard, they expressed concerns related to potential unintended consequences, such as the treatment-avoidance concerns we mentioned above. As they articulated it:

> As noted here, the evolution and decentralization of the inpatient mental health system long ago rendered obsolete and ineffective the practice of contacting the DMH [the Department of Mental Health] as a means of conducting mental health background checks, as had been required by the pre-reform statute in Massachusetts. As the survey data indicate, many police departments had continued to make that query in the pre-reform era, but some had expanded their investigations to include in their assessments the impressions of their officers regarding suitability. By mandating the creation of a centralized commitment database, the Massachusetts legislature in 2014 brought the query function in line with 21st century systemic realities. While the new database will increase the efficiency of the background check process, questions arise, as has been noted, about who is and is not included, and what the effects might be on the willingness of some persons to seek treatment. (p. 288)

Barnhorst (2015) compared California's firearm ownership disqualification system with the federal system, as well as those used by other states. The federal guidelines (i.e., adjudication as mentally defective or commitment to a mental institution) are followed by most states, but California has a stricter disqualification requirement—a lower threshold for gun prohibition based on mental illness. According to California law, firearm ownership prohibition is tied to admission to a psychiatric facility for dangerousness. Under the federal

guidelines, "commitment" refers to a formal judicial commitment that typically occurs subsequent to admission to a facility. Additionally, the *Tarasoff*
statute (CA Civil Code 43.92, n.d.) and court-ordered outpatient commitment
provide additional ways in which individuals can be barred from owning guns,
particularly during times of perceived heightened dangerousness. The legal
criteria related to mental illness in many other states are often unhelpfully
vague, while other states (i.e., Colorado, Tennessee, Texas, Nebraska, Kansas)
do not mention mental illness whatsoever.

California's prohibition differs in duration from the federal one as well—
California's lasts 5 years, while the federal is indefinite or lasts until steps are
taken to restore rights. In California, individuals can request a hearing at any
time during their prohibited time period, at which point they have to prove
by a preponderance of the evidence that they can safely and lawfully use a
firearm. However, no mental health evaluations are necessary at this juncture,
despite the fact that an admission to a psychiatric facility triggered the entire
process in the first place. Barnhorst also noted California's and federal laws
regarding alcohol and drug prohibitions, as well as gun violence restraining
orders (GVROs), which will be discussed in more detail in Chapter 5. GVROs
were modeled after domestic violence restraining orders; however, potential
petitioners were expanded to include law enforcement officers and family
members, in addition to domestic partners. Barnhorst concluded:

> Currently, California is a national leader in enacting firearm legislation
> targeted at groups who have been identified by researchers as having an
> elevated risk for violence. This represents an important shift away from
> targeting people with mental illness who may not, as a whole, be at
> increased risk, and who can be difficult to identify and report on at an
> individual level. (p. 254)

The American Psychiatric Association, in a 2015 resource document
pertaining to access to firearms by people with mental disorders, reiterates the
necessity of providing individuals with a fair opportunity for restoration of the
right to purchase a firearm after what would be determined a "suitable waiting
period" (Pinals et al., 2015a; p. 191). The document notes that these waiting
periods should ultimately be reflective of the individual's need for, as well as
participation in, mental health care. Further, because psychiatrists can describe and interpret one's mental health history, current mental status, effects
of treatment, and exacerbating or mitigating factors related to one's condition,
psychiatrists' evaluation and testimony should be a required component of
the restoration process. Nevertheless, it asserts that review panels established
by state agencies or other judicial bodies should be responsible for making the
ultimate decision regarding restoration, considering they will be more able
to weigh the constitutional right to bear arms against the safety of the public.

Fisher, Cohen, Hoge, & Appelbaum (2015) reviewed issues related to
mental health prohibition and restoration of gun rights in New York. They
noted that the NICS Improvement Act of 2007 encouraged states to create

processes that would allow individuals who had been prohibited from firearm possession for mental health reasons to acquire relief from these restrictions. Under federal law, judicially ordered involuntary hospitalizations, formal determinations of incapacity, and findings of psychiatric impairment related to criminal proceedings lead to indefinite restrictions on firearm possession. Some states have expanded the mental health–related reasons that lead to such restrictions. The authors noted that 20 states have enacted policies that would help individuals restore their firearm rights; however, the heterogeneity among these policies is considerable. For instance, psychiatrists participate in the process of deciding whether firearm rights should be restored in New York, while psychologists manage the process in other states.

Britton and Bloom (2015) described two programs in Oregon designed to comply with federal gun laws pertaining to reporting requirements of individuals who have received mental health adjudications in criminal and civil courts. One of the programs requires that records are submitted to the NICS once an individual is adjudicated. The second program requires the state to provide a qualifying gun restoration program for individuals who want to be requalified for gun ownership. In 2009, Oregon's legislature developed an administrative approach to gun restoration, requiring the Oregon Psychiatric Security Review Board—primarily responsible for the supervision and treatment of insanity acquittees—to conduct hearings on the restoration of firearm rights. While the gun restoration program was initiated in 2010, only three completed petitions requesting restoration of gun rights have been received.

Luther (2014) presented issues related to the restoration of gun rights in Virginia. He contended that individuals who voluntarily admit themselves to a psychiatric hospital should not have the same "firearms disability" as someone who was involuntarily committed by the court. He noted that losing one's firearms rights might deter some from seeking treatment, and, as such, he argued for an amendment of this policy. Luther highlighted a Virginia Supreme Court case, *Paugh v. Henrico Area Mental Health and Developmental Servs.* (2013), wherein it was decided that a de novo appeal from the order of involuntary commitment was moot after an individual was released from the facility. The Virginia Supreme Court opined that Paugh was no longer involuntarily committed on the day his circuit court hearing was docketed; therefore, he no longer met the criteria that caused him to be involuntarily committed months before. Thus, the involuntary commitment was moot, and he could maintain his firearm rights.

Proposed Laws

New legislation is proposed regularly in the firearm arena and a portion of such legislation is directly related to mental health issues. For example, a new California law that took effect at the beginning of 2016 allowed for law enforcement to seize firearms for 21 days from individuals determined by a judge to be a potential threat to others (Lucas, 2015). The law allows for

GVROs, again discussed in detail elsewhere in this book, which would restrict firearm access for individuals, even without an involuntary hospitalization. In Seattle, a heavy tax on guns and ammunition was put into effect, which would create between $300,000 and $500,000 per year in revenue but was actually implemented to prevent gun violence. In Texas, where firearm-related measures are often significantly more lenient, a new law allowed individuals with concealed carry permits to carry a holstered weapon in plain view (Lucas, 2015). In 2016, three states adopted permitless carry, and more are considering adopting these laws, which would allow individuals to carry concealed weapons without receiving any training or permits from a state government (Friedman, 2017). Thus far, Idaho, Mississippi, Missouri, and West Virginia have either established or strengthened these permitless carry laws, in addition to Alaska, Arizona, Kansas, Maine, Vermont, and Wyoming, which are states that already do not require individuals to possess a license to carry a concealed weapon (Friedman, 2017).

Under President Trump's administration, a standing rule established by the Obama administration was repealed, wherein "the SSA must identify and report to the National Instant Criminal Background Check System (NICS) individuals who are unable to work because of severe mental impairment and can't manage their own Social Security financial benefits, and thus make them ineligible to buy guns" (Gorman, 2017, n.p.). Individuals who oppose the repeal assert that the rule would make it more difficult for the federal government to put individuals with severe mental illness or who pose a risk to public safety on the list of those who are prohibited from purchasing guns. On the other hand, individuals in favor of the repeal state that the previous law resulted in reporting people to the gun ban list who should not be on the list and that it deprived Americans of their constitutional rights (Gorman, 2017).

Suicide and Violence

Mental health–related firearm laws are typically driven by general concerns associated with risk of suicide, violence, and domestic violence, although some specifically target each of these areas. However, as Price and Norris (2010) articulated: "The impact of specific firearm laws on the rates of homicide and suicide remains controversial" (p. 331), and empirical evidence to support the benefit of such laws in this context has been insufficient. For example, Hahn and colleagues (2005) noted that evidence available from identified studies was inadequate to determine the effectiveness of firearm laws that had been reviewed. This does not mean that there is evidence the laws are ineffective, but it means the evidence is unclear. Therefore, the Task Force on Community Preventative Services reviewed the available evidence to evaluate the effectiveness of firearm laws in reducing gun violence. To demonstrate the complicated impact of said laws, a logic model was utilized (Figure 2.1) to depict the flow of influences from the laws on firearms, through their manufacture, distribution, acquisition, storage, carrying, and use, including possible violent

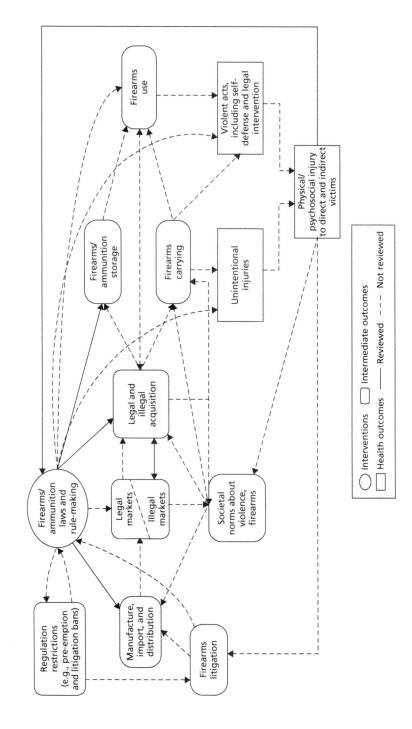

Figure 2.1. A Model of the Impact of Firearm Laws

Legend:
- ○ Interventions
- ▢ Intermediate outcomes
- ▭ Health outcomes
- —— Reviewed
- - - - Not reviewed

Firearms/ammunition laws and rule-making

Regulation restrictions (e.g., pre-emption and litigation bans)

Manufacture, import, and distribution

Firearms litigation

Legal markets

Illegal markets

Societal norms about violence, firearms

Legal and illegal acquisition

Firearms/ammunition storage

Firearms carrying

Unintentional injuries

Firearms use

Violent acts, including self-defense and legal intervention

Physical/psychosocial injury to direct and indirect victims

acts and injury to others. Not surprisingly, the model suggested that the enforcement of these firearm laws plays a role at various stages in this process. Adequate enforcement could limit access to illegal guns, thereby reducing violence, while inadequate enforcement could diminish the effect of a law, making it difficult to assess its true potential. Additionally, the model indicates that violent outcomes may result in consequences that affect the legislative process through feedback loops. For example, one might consider the effects of mass shootings on efforts to pass firearm-related laws.

More recently, Webster and Wintemute (2015) reviewed the professional literature between 1999 and 2014 with respect to policies aimed at keeping high-risk individuals from accessing guns. Based on their research, they concluded that "Roughly half or more of those who commit gun crimes do not meet any of the prohibiting conditions under federal law" (p. 34). Although they found that some prohibitions for high-risk individuals are associated with lower rates of violence, such as domestic violence restraining orders and comprehensive background checks, they indicated that other restrictions have not affected violent crime rates (e.g., minimum age requirements and domestic violence misdemeanors). On the other hand, accountability-focused initiatives seem to have at least some effectiveness; for instance, stricter regulation and oversight of gun dealers and requirements that gun owners report lost and stolen firearms in a timely fashion.

As we indicate throughout this book, the association between suicide and firearms is appreciably stronger than that related to violence, such that firearm availability has been associated with an increased risk of suicide and restricting access to at-risk persons has also been correlated with lower suicide rates (Crifasi, Meyers, Vernick, & Webster, 2015). Despite the notably higher association between suicide and firearms, laws and policies are largely focused on gun *violence* prevention measures. Much of this focus has been driven by highly emotional and tragic events, such as school shootings. That said, there has also been a fair amount of community policing and deterrence-based legislation and policies geared toward reducing gang- and youth-related firearm violence. We briefly review each below, followed by a discussion of domestic violence laws. Please recall that we cover all of these issues in significant depth in Chapters 4 and 5 of this book as well.

School Shootings

Miller and Kraus (2008) characterized school violence as a public health initiative and advocated for a four-step process to reduce it: (1) data collection of violence-related problems, assets, and resources; (2) assessment of the possible causes of violence through risk factor identification; (3) the establishment and evaluation of violence prevention strategies; and (4) the dissemination and implementation of effective strategies. They set forth recommendations for primary, secondary, and tertiary levels of prevention, including violence prevention programs that integrate social skills training, teacher–student bonding, counseling and supportive services for youth exposed to violence, and psychoeducational strategies. They contended that the key goals of prevention-oriented programs should include having a network of involved students who understand their own peer culture and serve as a resource themselves, providing alternatives for antisocial, violent, and delinquent behavior. In that vein, Chapin and Coleman (2006) investigated the impact of optimism bias on a school violence prevention program and asserted that, because students believe violence is less likely to happen to them and at their school, educational campaigns aimed at addressing the optimism bias could be a means of reducing violence. Chapin and Coleman described the first program to incorporate optimism bias into a campaign aimed at promoting violence awareness among youth. However, the empirical support for this notion is lacking—but what about the effectiveness of laws in this context?

Schildkraut and Hernandez (2014) investigated the efficacy of laws enacted in response to school shootings by reviewing those associated with some of the more high-profile school tragedies. For example, the Extended Juvenile Jurisdiction Act proceeded from the 1998 Westside Middle School shooting near Jonesboro, Arkansas, whereby 11-year old Andrew Golden and 13-year old Mitchell Johnson killed a teacher and four students and injured 10 others. In response, the act permitted the state to charge a person of any age with capital or first-degree murder provided that a juvenile understood the charges and the trial process. Prior to this change, it was presumed that individuals aged 7–13 were incompetent to stand trial. Additional changes were related to record-keeping and jurisdictional issues, such that juvenile records would be transferred to adult court if the individual is convicted of and receives an adult sentence. This is relevant because it keeps a juvenile with convictions from legally purchasing a firearm. The second incident addressed is that of the 1999 Columbine High School shooting, which prompted a debate of what is referred to as the *gun show loophole*. Namely, an extensive number of bills sought increased regulation at gun shows, such as those in the context of background checks; however, most were never passed. In fact, in the year following Columbine, 800 firearm-related bills were introduced, and only 10% were passed. In contrast, the 2007 Virginia Tech shooting resulted in legislation that did pass in many states regarding increased reporting to the NICS system. However, notable limitations remained. As Schildkraut and Hernandez noted:

> Nearly $500 million in additional grants were made available to state courts to help establish or update systems for criminal history reporting (H.R. 2640, 2007). Five years after the Virginia Tech shooting, around $50 million of these funds had been appropriated by states; although a million records were added to the NICS, as many as 24 states submitted less than 100 mental health records to the system. . . . However, the Brady Campaign . . . noted there should be nearly twice as many records disqualifying individuals from firearms purchases in the system. (p. 367)

Ultimately, Schildkraut and Hernandez concluded that most laws and policies, including the NICS Improvement Act, have not been shown to be particularly successful and may simply function as "feel better" laws. As they articulated it:

> In his research on mass shootings in schools, Gary Kleck noted, "the specific gun control measures proposed in their aftermath were largely irrelevant and almost certainly could not have prevented the incidents or reduced their death tolls" (2009, p. 1447). Further examination into the cases discussed in this paper support Kleck's statement as each shooter was, in some way, in violation of existing laws. Andrew Golden, Mitchell Johnson, Eric Harris, and Dylan Klebold each had weapons in their possessions as juveniles, which was illegal under the AWB [Federal Assault Weapons Ban]. The sawed-off shotguns used in the Columbine massacre were in deliberate violation of the National Firearms Act of 1934. The TEC-9 semi-automatic handgun used by Klebold was expressly banned under the AWB, which was in effect at the time of the shooting. Although he cleared the background check as a result of failed reporting by the mental health system, Seung- Hui Cho violated the Gun Control Act of 1968 and the Brady Law by purchasing guns after multiple members of the medical community had declared him mentally ill. The question still remains, then, whether existing bills and laws, as well as bills and laws that are introduced in response to such tragedies, can prevent the next shooting. Though none of the measures to close the gun show loophole have yet to be successfully enacted into legislation, other bills, such as the NICS Improvement Act, have been implemented. But are they successful? One could argue that in fact they are not. (p. 370)

Community Policing and Deterrence and Prevention Programs

Focused deterrence strategies are part of the developing evidence-based gun injury prevention programs available to policymakers. According to Braga and Weisburd (2015), the focused deterrence approach seeks to target underlying risk factors and other causes of recurrent, violent gun injury problems. The approach also develops specific responses to these underlying conditions while also measuring the impact of these programs once implemented in the community. In the context of existing theoretical principles, such as *general deterrence* (i.e., the general population is deterred from committing crimes after it sees punishment following the commission of a crime) and *specific deterrence* (i.e., punish a criminal to deter him or her from committing crimes again in the future), a focused deterrence strategy for firearm-related violence would likely target very specific behaviors typically enacted by a small number of chronic offenders who are highly vulnerable to criminal justice sanctions.

For instance, gang-involved youth would be targeted with information about how continued gun-related offending will not be tolerated and exactly how the justice system will respond to violations. Focused deterrence strategies are a recent addition to the existing literature on gun violence prevention, and the available scientific evidence suggests that focused deterrence strategies generate gun violence reductions.

Boston's Operation Ceasefire initiative was an interagency prevention program that focused on providing resources and targeted law enforcement to a small number of young gang-involved offenders who were at the heart of the violence problem in the city (Kennedy, Piehl, & Braga, 1996). In the late 1990s, the focused deterrence strategy was associated with a near two-thirds drop in youth homicide (Piehl, Cooper, Braga, & Kennedy, 2003), and as such, the Department of Justice embraced the program as an effective approach to crime prevention. However, evaluation of the prevention program was relatively weak and left some uncertainty regarding the size of the effect on gang violence in Boston (Braga, Hureau, & Papachristos, 2014). Braga et al. (2014) subsequently conducted a more rigorous evaluation of the program, which resulted in findings that the Ceasefire intervention was associated with significant reductions in gun violence trends among gangs involved in the treatment. Further, results indicated that sharp reductions in gun violence among treatment-involved gangs followed immediately after the intervention. Total shootings decreased by 31% for Boston gangs subjected to the treatment, suggesting that focused deterrence strategies should be adopted by additional jurisdictions.

Project Exile is another example of a focused deterrence gun program. The program, which was developed in Virginia, is based on the theory that stiffer penalties for gun offenders will ultimately reduce gun violence (Payne & Gainey, 2008). The program, which was developed in the mid-1990s, uses existing firearms laws to send firearm offenders to federal court, even if they were apprehended by local authorities. Payne and Gainey (2008) explain, "In principle, Project Exile meets these ideals in that federal law provides stiffer sentences for offenders (meeting the element of severity), in an efficient manner (meeting the element of swiftness), and with a degree of certainty in that all offenders prosecuted through this manner would receive a stiffer sentence" (p. 184).

As time has progressed, more and more firearm reduction strategies have been studied. One study by Petrosino et al. (2015) conducted a rapid evaluation assessment of 129 studies to identify effective, cross-sector, multiagency urban youth firearms violence reduction strategies. Ten studies indicated sizeable reductions in violence, and based on their findings, they described several broad implications of future firearm violence reduction efforts. First, they suggested that the focus of such efforts needs to be on the most violent gang offenders as a small number of high-risk youth are responsible for a vast majority of shootings. Second, programs need to prepare for and limit potential backfire effects. Specifically, some programs found that outreach workers' attention to gang members led to increased cohesion among the gangs. Also, a credible message needs to be effectively communicated to gang members. Law enforcement messages and services messages need to be consistently communicated through a variety of outlets. Finally, a leadership team that coordinates the initiative and ensures that different departments are collaborating is an important component.

As a detective and Ph.D. candidate at Old Dominion University, William Patterson (2010) wrote an article about the Virginia Beach Police Department's Gun Trace Unit. In 2008, the department disbanded its joint task force with the ATF and created its own internal unit tasked with investigating firearm-related crimes. Patterson wrote:

> Anthony Braga and his colleagues argue, in an article published in the journal Crime and Justice, that "local police departments can quite possibly be effective at disrupting local gun markets, but only if they concern themselves with gathering the necessary intelligence and acting on it".... It is precisely with those purposes in mind that the Virginia Beach Police Department's Gun Trace Unit was developed. (p. 270)

According to Patterson, the primary function of the Gun Trace Unit was to investigate the illegal transfer and possession of firearms. Their e-Trace system provides the identity of the individual who originally purchased the gun, and the investigation goes from there, usually with a major focus on the *straw* purchase and illegal transactions. Another successful initiative of the Gun Trace Unit was its monthly check of pawnshop records. The department's Pawn Unit runs a computerized criminal history on all individuals who pawned or sold firearms to the shops; then information about those who are otherwise prohibited from selling or possessing firearms is forwarded to the Gun Trace Unit for further investigation, often leading to arrests for illegal possession. Per Patterson, qualitative evidence suggests that the unit's endeavors were at least as effective as the former task force strategy. Because secondhand gun transactions by private party gun sellers are not regulated by the federal government, Braga and Hureau (2015) examined whether state-level private firearm transfer data could be used to inform deterrence strategies to reduce the supply of handguns to violent criminals. Traced crime handguns originally sold by licensed dealers in Boston were matched to state secondhand gun transfer data. According to their results, important transaction data regarding in-state sources were not readily available to law enforcement for 63% of recovered crime handguns on the secondary market. As such, Braga and Hureau concluded that strong, private transfer gun laws, in addition to the enforcement of reporting requirements, are needed in order to develop necessary interventions.

Other researchers have explored the effectiveness of various programs aimed at reducing firearm-related violence. For instance, Phillips, Dae-Young, & Sobol (2013) examined gun buy-back programs and found limited support for them, only insofar as decreasing gun robbery levels. They indicate that such programs may take years to affect crime numbers. However, Rosenfeld, Deckard, & Blackburn (2014) investigated targeted policing intervention directed at reducing firearm assaults and robberies in St. Louis, and although they found that incidences of nondomestic firearm assaults decreased, firearm robberies did not. Wyant, Taylor, Ratcliffe, & Wood (2012) examined whether police firearm arrests reduce future shootings in the area in the days immediately following the arrests. They found that shootings declined significantly up to a few blocks away following a firearm arrest but that these effects last only a few days. This may be related to the research indicating that people from nearby communities were more likely to carry firearms than those who lived in the community in which they were arrested (Payne & Gainey, 2008).

In their meta-analysis of 29 studies on the effectiveness of policies and programs that attempt to reduce firearm violence, Makarios and Pratt (2012) found that comprehensive community-based law enforcement initiatives have performed the best compared to other programs in terms of firearm violence reduction. Such is consistent with the extant professional literature. However, Makarios and Pratt also found that a number of politically popular strategies show little or no promise of success, such as gun buy-back programs, waiting periods, background checks, and enhanced prison sentences. In fact, the only laws that seemed marginally successful at reducing gun violence were those related to bans on the sale of firearms. Moreover, certain types of policies and programs showed more promise in reducing gun violence. Again, they found law enforcement programs to be clearly more effective than gun laws. They noted that prosecutorial strategies evidenced marginal success in reducing violence, while directed patrol policing strategies have had a moderate impact on firearm violence. Probation-based strategies have been quite successful but lack research support.

Organized Crime and Gang Violence

Gagliardi (2012) posited that transnational organized crime and firearm violence are interrelated and, therefore, that firearm forensic intelligence should be shared internationally through Interpol's Interpol Ballistic Information Network program. He contended this would be an integral component of intelligence-led law enforcement strategies aimed at combating cross-board gun-related crimes:

> With such a network in place, frequently mobile criminals who use firearms to further their illicit activities can no longer escape detection merely by crossing into another jurisdiction or by leaving evidence of their crimes scattered across boundary lines. (p. 94)

McGarrell and colleagues (2013) investigated the Comprehensive Anti-Gang Initiative (CAGI) implemented in 12 jurisdictions throughout the United States. CAGI cities saw significantly reduced firearm homicides postintervention. The authors concluded that their findings suggested that funding for comprehensive gang programming should be prioritized in jurisdictions with high risk of gang activity. They further stated: "Efforts like CAGI would benefit from a planning period that would allow for the establishment of intensive and timely prevention and re-entry programs to run in conjunction with suppression activities" (p. 33). And finally, they asserted that the field needs to build reliable and valid measures of gang crime.

Domestic Violence

Please note that, given its substantial importance, we have devoted an entire chapter to domestic and intimate partner violence in this book (Chapter 5), but it is important to first set the foundation here. According to Everytown (https://everytownresearch.org), women in the United States are 11 times more likely to be murdered with a firearm in comparison to women in other high-income countries, making it the most dangerous place for a woman in the developed world with regard to gun violence. It also reports that intimate partner homicides have been committed with guns more than all other weapons combined over the 25 years prior to 2014, and those with a history of domestic violence are five times more likely to murder an intimate partner when a firearm is in the house. It noted that 19 states and DC prohibit nonfelony domestic violence offenders from having guns, and 22 states and DC prohibit those under domestic violence restraining orders from buying or owning firearms. The interested reader should refer to Everytown for Gun Safety's website (i.e., https://everytownresearch.org/wp-content/uploads/2014/10/Guns-and-Violence-Against-Women-Appendix.pdf),   which contains a table that provides a summary of each state's domestic violence–related firearm laws. The table indicates whether each state requires domestic violence misdemeanants from buying or owning firearms, requires domestic violence misdemeanants to dispose of firearms already in their possession, prohibits subjects of restraining orders pertaining to domestic violence from buying or owning firearms, and requires subjects of domestic violence restraining orders from disposing of firearms already in their possession. Of note, California, Colorado, Connecticut, Hawaii, Illinois, Iowa, Minnesota, New York, and Tennessee are the only states with all four prohibitions/requirements.

It is also important to note that, while states may not have restrictions or sanctions explicitly stated in their laws, law enforcement personnel and judges certainly maintain the ability to order such actions as firearm revocation in many cases. In their review of gun removal laws throughout the country, Frattaroli and Vernick (2006) noted that states' laws fall into one of two categories: (i) police gun removal laws, whereby police officers are authorized to remove guns from batterers' possession while responding to a domestic complaint, and (ii) court-ordered removal laws. Examples of states that have these mechanisms but do not necessarily have explicit domestic violence– and firearm-related laws across the board include, but are not limited to, Arkansas, Arizona, Indiana, New Jersey, Oklahoma, and Utah. Nevertheless, Everytown (2014) expressed concerns with gaps in four areas of law pertaining to domestic and intimate partner violence, which it believes are particularly harmful. In their words:

- First, federal law does nothing to keep guns out of the hands of abusive dating partners or convicted stalkers.
- Second, in 35 states, state law does not prohibit all people convicted of misdemeanor domestic violence crimes and all people subject to restraining orders from buying or using guns.
  o Only 15 states prohibit all domestic violence misdemeanants and subjects of restraining orders from buying or owning guns: California, Colorado, Connecticut, Delaware, Hawaii, Illinois, Iowa, Louisiana, Minnesota, New York, New Jersey, Tennessee, Texas, Washington, and West Virginia.
- Third, federal law (and the law in most states) allows domestic abusers and stalkers to easily evade gun prohibitions by purchasing guns from unlicensed, private sellers.
- Finally, forty-one states do not require all prohibited domestic abusers to relinquish guns they already own. (p. 3)

With respect to the existing laws in this area, Price and Norris (2010) noted:

The Violent Crime Control Act of 1994 made it a federal offense to possess or receive a firearm while subject to a restraining order that protected an intimate partner or a child of an intimate partner. Protective orders qualifying for the federal firearm exclusion are limited to those issued following a hearing in which the alleged abuser has an opportunity to participate. The Lautenberg Amendment of the Gun Control Act of 1996 prohibited possession or receipt of a firearm by anyone who had ever been convicted of a qualifying misdemeanor crime of domestic violence. Some states have laws that require confiscation of firearms in domestic violence situations and that may have further broader restrictions on transfer or possession, such as applying the prohibition in the presence of a temporary restraining order only. Some state laws also expand the definition of an intimate partner. (p. 331)

Recently, in *Voisine v. United States* (2016), the US Supreme Court upheld the ban for convicted domestic abusers to possess firearms. Namely, the court ruled that a "reckless domestic assault" qualifies as a "misdemeanor crime of domestic violence" that prohibits convicted felons from possessing firearms. Regarding the case background, two men who pled guilty to domestic abuse argued that their convictions should not restrict them from owning guns as their conduct did not fall under intentional and knowing acts of abuse. Rather, they asserted that their abusive behavior was committed recklessly and that reckless abuse means the abuser is aware that his or her conduct holds a risk of causing injury but is not certain that it will. Justice Kagan, writing the majority opinion, stated that, if the law were to exclude misdemeanors in which a person acted recklessly, it would "substantially undermine the provision's design." Meanwhile, Justice Thomas, who wrote the dissent, stated, "Under the majority's reading, a single conviction under a state assault statute for recklessly causing an injury to a family member—such as by texting while driving—can now trigger a lifetime ban on gun ownership." He added: "We treat no other constitutional right so cavalierly." Justice Sotomayor agreed that if Congress wanted to cover all reckless conduct, it could have written the law differently (see also, Supreme Court upholds, 2016).

But what is the efficacy of these laws? Vigdor and Mercy (2006) investigated the impact of three types of laws on intimate partner homicide: laws that limit access to firearms for people who are the subject of a restraining order, laws that limit access to firearms for those who have been convicted of a domestic violence misdemeanor, and laws that allow law enforcement to confiscate guns at a domestic violence scene. They obtained data related to intimate partner homicide across states from the FBI Supplementary Homicide Report files for the years 1982 through 2002, and they generated estimates by comparing homicide rates before and after the passage of relevant laws. They noted, "Although we cannot be certain that we are isolating the impact of the laws, the time variation in the effective dates of the laws reduces the likelihood that we are capturing the effect of an omitted shock affecting all IPH rates" (p. 323). Based on their analyses, their results suggest that female intimate partner homicide decreased by 8% as a result of domestic violence restraining order laws; however, they found no effect related to domestic violence misdemeanor laws or laws that allow law enforcement to confiscate firearms at a domestic violence–related scene. Again, we address these issues in much greater depth in Chapter 5 of this book.

Firearm Laws and Liability

Questions related to responsibility and accountability invariably arise in the wake of shooting deaths. In some cases, the actual firearms are readily overlooked and the focus is on the perpetrators (think gang-involved and inner city violence); in other cases, the attention paid to the firearms is much greater (think mass shootings or youth suicide). Indeed, liability lawsuits are much more likely to be filed against gun and ammo manufacturers and sellers subsequent to the latter situations as opposed to the former. We present these examples in the next subsection, followed by a review of liability-based legislation associated with mental health professionals.

Gun Manufacturers and Sellers

When someone who is permitted to own a firearm does so with the unlawful intention of giving it to a prohibited person, it is referred to as a *straw sale*. Licensed firearm dealers have been characterized as a key source for criminals and gun traffickers, accounting for a majority of guns diverted to the illegal market (Bureau of Alcohol, Tobacco and Firearms, 2000a). However, it is a small proportion of dealers that are associated with the majority of gun trafficking problems. In fact, the Bureau of Alcohol, Tobacco and Firearms (2000b) found that only 1% of dealers initially sold more than 50% of all guns traced to crime. However, progress has been made over the years in reducing gun trafficking as a result of a series of undercover law enforcement stings and the formation of local government coalitions. Nevertheless, Vernick, Webster, Bulzacchelli, & Mair (2006) reviewed state oversight statutes and concluded that many states impose little to no regulation of dealers. Namely, they found:

- 26 have explicit gun sales record-keeping laws
- 23 address the retention of records
- 23 either permit or mandate the inspection of dealers
- 17 mandate a dealer license
- 13 have storage security requirements to prevent theft
- 11 require some conditions to obtain a license
- 6 mandate the reporting of stolen guns

Vernick and colleagues also pointed out that even in states where these laws exist, enforcement is often lenient. For instance, while 23 states permit police inspection of dealers, only two states (Massachusetts and Rhode Island) require that such occurs regularly. The authors further contended that the federal licensing system is flawed, with various limitations, limited resources, and weakened penalties for those dealers who do actually get prosecuted. Based on their research, Vernick and colleagues recommended the following:

- States should license gun dealers
- Conditions are needed to ensure that only qualified persons obtain a license
- State laws should mandate dealer record-keeping and retention
- States should require periodic inspection of dealers
- States should impose mandatory theft reporting by dealers
- Store security requirements should include rules requiring that inventory be locked up when not being shown to a customer
- States must enforce each of these laws

In a follow-up to their review, Webster, Vernick, & Bulzacchelli (2009) examined 54 cities in the United States with respect to their utilization of laws related to gun sales, a survey of law enforcement's efforts to promote compliance with these laws, and crime gun trace data to examine the association between these policies and practices with gun trafficking indicators. They found that lower levels of intrastate gun trafficking were associated with comprehensive regulation and oversight of gun dealers, as well as the state regulation of private gun sales. According to Webster and colleagues, "Intrastate gun trafficking was two to four times higher in cities located in states without the gun sales regulations, with the greatest differences associated with strong gun dealer regulations and discretionary handgun purchase permit licensing" (p. 531). Moreover, cities with laws restricting handgun purchases to one person per month were associated with the lowest gun trafficking. However, they found no relationship between law enforcements' reports of undercover stings of gun stores and gun trafficking. Webster and colleagues concluded:

> Our findings indicated that comprehensive regulation and regular compliance inspections of retail gun dealers as well as the regulation of private handgun sales were each associated with significantly lower levels of gun trafficking. As would be expected, these relationships were strongest for guns originally sold within the same state in which they were recovered from criminals. Although cities in states with the most comprehensive gun sale regulations attract some guns from states with weaker gun laws, the combination of strong gun dealer regulations and regulation of private handgun sales were [sic] still associated with fewer trafficked guns even after controlling for local levels of gun ownership. (p. 533)

In one of the most recent and high-profile cases in this context, the Brady Center to Prevent Gun Violence organized a lawsuit against Lucky Gunner, an online ammunition retailer, following the mass shooting that took place in the Aurora, Colorado, movie theater. According to the family of one of the victims of the shooting (Phillips & Phillips, 2015), they wanted to bring the case against the company as they were outraged that a company selling ammunition would not be required to gather information about the individuals to whom they sell their products. The judge ultimately dismissed the case, stating:

> It is apparent that this case was filed to pursue the political purposes of the Brady Center and, given the failure to present any cognizable legal claim, bringing these defendants [Lucky Gunner] into the Colorado court . . . appears to be more of an opportunity to propagandize the public and stigmatize the defendants than to obtain a court order. (Brady vs. Lucky Gunner, n.d., paragraph 4)

According to the blog post about the lawsuit (Phillips & Phillips, 2015), the case was dismissed because the online company had "special immunity from the general duty to use reasonable care under the federal Protection of Lawful Commerce in Arms Act and a Colorado immunity law" (paragraph 5). They note that the Colorado immunity law (HB000-208) states that if you bring a civil case against a gun or ammunitions seller and then lose in court, you have to pay your opponent's legal fees. As such, the judge then ordered them (and/or The Brady Center who represented them pro bono in court) to pay $203,000 in legal fees. The Phillips family continued to fight the issue as they do not believe it is right that guns and ammunitions dealers get what they consider to be special privileges. Further, they believe laws like those that exist in Colorado bar individuals from attempting to effect change.

Lucky Gunner was not the first liability lawsuit in this context, however. In 1997, the Florida Supreme Court upheld a decision that Kmart must pay a woman who was shot by her boyfriend over $11 million after a salesperson sold the rifle to him while he was drunk (Kmart held liable, 1993). In October 1998, New Orleans became the first city to file a lawsuit against gun companies and trade groups saying that they should be held responsible for the financial burden (e.g., medical bills, police expenditures) of handgun violence (Duggan & Torry, 1998). In November 1998, Chicago filed a $433 million lawsuit against gun companies alleging that they oversupply firearms to the local market, which in turn provides more guns to criminals (Butterfield, 1998). Also in November 1998, firearm manufacturer Beretta won a negligence lawsuit brought by the family of a California boy who was shot by a handgun purportedly without safety features. In 1999, cities in Connecticut and Florida filed civil suits against gun makers for firearm-related violence costs in their respective areas (Longley, 2016). Following these various suits throughout the country, in 2005, President Bush signed the Protection of Lawful Commerce in Arms Act, which protected firearms manufacturers and dealers by limiting the ability of victims of crimes committed by firearms to sue (Longley, 2016).

Legislation Related to Medical and Mental Health Professionals

We outline the emerging roles of medical and mental health professionals in firearm-related matters in Chapters 7 and 8 of this book, but we must first ask: What are the laws pertaining to their liability in the context or firearms? The *Tarasoff* rule, which spread to many states following a California Supreme Court ruling in 1976, states that psychotherapists have a duty to protect or warn a third party if the therapist predicts or believes that a client or patient poses a serious risk of inflicting bodily injury upon a reasonably identified victim (Ewing, 2005). In the original case, *Tarasoff v. Regents of the University of California* (1976), a patient told his psychotherapist that he planned to kill an unnamed but easily identified person, which he subsequently did. The victim's parents sued the therapist for failing to warn their daughter about the imminent danger. The California Supreme Court ultimately opined that the therapist bears a duty to exercise reasonable care to protect a foreseeable victim from future danger.

Although mental health professionals are likely to have increased involvement in this arena as time progresses (e.g., see Appelbaum, 2017a; Gold & Simon, 2016; Pirelli, Wechsler, & Cramer, 2015; Pirelli & Witt, 2017), as Falls (2011) has pointed out, several states have considered legislation in recent years that would prohibit physicians from asking their patients questions about firearm ownership, and some states have already passed such legislation. For example, Florida's 2011 Privacy of Firearm Owners Act prevents medical personnel from asking questions about gun ownership, documenting information concerning firearms in a patient's medical record, and denying care for patients who refuse to answer questions about firearm ownership. Shortly after the law was passed, the Florida chapters of the American Academy of Pediatrics, the American Academy of Family Physicians, the American College of Physicians, and the American Medical Association filed a lawsuit challenging the new law's constitutionality. Namely, in *Wollschlaeger v. Farmer* (2011), the petitioners argued that various provisions of the act violate the First and Fourteenth Amendments of the US Constitution. In this matter, the plaintiffs stated that the act violated the First Amendment by preventing communication with their patients about ways to maintain safety related to firearms. The court, in this case, issued an injunction against the provisions of the act, stating that they violated the First Amendment right of free speech. In a subsequent lawsuit, *Wollschlaeger v. Governor of Florida* (2015), Wollschlaeger, other medical professionals, and various Florida chapters of medical organizations sued the governor of Florida and the state (officials) for setting forth the Firearm Owners Privacy Act. Again, the plaintiffs argued that the act violated the First Amendment by preventing "open and free exchanges of information and advice with their patients about ways to reduce the safety risks posed by firearms" (*Wollschlaeger v. Governor of Florida*, 2015,,p. 2). According to Tomazic (2015):

> Other national professional organizations have filed amicus curiae
> briefs and have expressed their opposition to restrictions of physician
> speech regarding gun ownership and safety. Restriction of physician
> speech is likely to remain an issue of national attention and heated
> debate since at least two states have passed laws similar to Florida's
> Firearm Owners' Privacy Act and several more have bills with similar
> intent and language presented to their state legislatures. (p. 683)

In *Wollschlaeger v. Governor of Florida* (2015), the Eleventh Circuit ultimately upheld the Firearm Owners Privacy Act, which banned medical doctors from asking their patients questions about firearm ownership. According to the court, because the law only restricts speech uttered in doctors' examination rooms, it is exempt from First Amendment scrutiny, which otherwise allows freedom of speech.

On February 16, 2017, a federal appeals court ruled on what came to be known as Florida's "Docs v. Glocks" lawsuit (Federal appeals court, 2017). The court issued two majority opinions, ultimately asserting that portions of the law threaten loss of license to doctors based on their conversations with patients, which violates First Amendment rights. Regarding the matter, Moms Demand Action for Gun Sense in America issued an amicus brief in support of doctors' speech regarding gun safety with their patients (Amicus brief: *Wollschlaeger v. Governor, State of Florida*, 2015). Since Florida attempted to pass the "Docs v. Glocks" law, 10 other states have tried and failed to pass similar bills (Allow doctors, 2017). However, some managed to pass laws that were related to the doctor–patient relationship. As an example, in 2014, Missouri managed to pass a law that makes it difficult for doctors to ask patients about firearm safety. Among other things, the law states that doctors cannot be compelled by law to ask patients about firearms, record data pertaining to firearms in medical records, or notify government agencies about who owns guns (Doctor gag order laws, 2015). For more information on laws pertaining to firearms and the doctor–patient relationship, the interested reader is directed to Doctor gag order laws (2015) and Appelbaum (2017b).

The Media and Firearm Policy

Americans' trust in the media is currently at its lowest point in over two decades, such that only 32% of people report having at least a fair amount of trust in the media (Swift, 2016). However, as we will address in greater detail in Chapter 4, media attention plays a role in the public's perception of firearms, particularly given the high levels of coverage for such tragedies as mass shootings, including school shootings. But what is the effect of this type of attention on firearm laws and policies?

One salient example is that of the infamous Columbine shooting, one of the most notorious events in modern American history. Although it received significant media attention, Birkland and Lawrence (2009) posited that its effect on the nature and substance of public policy was limited, as was its effect on public opinion. Rather, the attention surrounding Columbine appears to have spurred the more rapid implementation of existing policies and tools that were already available to schools. As Birkland and Lawrence articulated it:

> Columbine formed the peak of public attention to the problem of school shootings, but media framing of school violence subsequently shifted, the national school shootings "problem" faded from view, and enduring public attitudes thwarted attempts to change, in particular, gun policy in response to the tragedy. (p. 2)

Immediately post-Columbine, there was a slight increase in support for stricter gun laws; however, the main trajectory of this particular public opinion topic quickly settled back to where it was pre-Columbine. Birkland and Lawrence opined that this change in public opinion was likely due to many factors, such as the passage of time, changes in media attention, and how the topic is "framed" (i.e., blaming violence in the media vs. blaming guns). One of the explanations for the limited policy changes is that post-Columbine members of Congress made claims in the media that were inconsistent with both existing laws and realistic policy options for addressing the issues associated with school shootings. The most obvious examples of this are the emotionally laden calls for action made by politicians following mass shootings, despite continued congressional restrictions on funding for firearm-related research by the CDC (which studies almost every other type of violence).

In an earlier analysis, Lawrence and Birkland (2004) examined how different aspects of an event-driven problem compete for attention in the media and governmental agendas and noted: "Agenda divergences are amplified when prominent politicians cue the media to follow particular storylines that depart from actual legislative activity" (p. 1193). Indeed, Elson & Ferguson (2013) set forth the possibility that the Obama administration's efforts to call for specific research "in the midst of moral panic" (i.e., public response to the Sandy Hook shooting) might actually introduce biases and further distract from issues of greater importance. They further indicated that ideological rigidity has repeatedly shaped past research on media violence and that a responsible dialogue pertaining to the media effects and firearm-related violence is needed. Moreover, Elson and Ferguson contended that the gaps in empirical research and academic debate need to be closed in order to inform public policy, while remaining vigilant to the potential influences of society and politics.

The media also covers firearm violence in starkly different ways, depending on where the violence takes place and what populations are affected. Parham-Payne (2014) focused on the ways in which structural and policy resolutions intended to address gun violence involving low-income as well racial/ethnic minority individuals are overlooked from national and political discourse, stating, "The convergence of local news broadcasts and national news media has set forth an indelible depiction of Blacks as criminally inclined and the collective antithesis of vulnerability or innocence" (p. 762). As a result, large numbers of black children lose their lives, even on school grounds, and the media and political arena hardly address it at all. This sentiment is consistent with that of Schildkraut and Muschert (2014), who contended that the media covered the "worthy victim" more than the shooter vis-à-vis the Sandy Hook shooting. In their analysis, Schildkraut and Muschert employed a two-dimensional analytic framework to examine the frame-changing differences between Columbine and Sandy Hook. They noted that, although the Columbine shooting set the precedent for the way in which the media covered school shootings, the Sandy Hook coverage was different and might have changed the way these events are covered in the future. Specifically, the media seemed to have emphasized different aspects of the story over time, keeping it new and fresh. Additionally, the media was able to frame the shooting in a way that coincided with various political agendas, thereby influencing public opinion. Whereas other shootings were perceived as isolated incidents, it seems as though Sandy Hook was conceptualized as a reflection of broader social problems in the United States. To explore that perspective more formally, we now turn to a review of firearm-related issues throughout the world.

Comparative International Analysis

Like many topics we address in this book, an entire volume could be devoted to firearm-related issues throughout the world. Although the scope of this book pertains to such considerations in the United States, an overview of international issues and perspectives is warranted as our primary goal is to provide the reader with a comprehensive resource on firearms. Therefore, in the sections that follow, we present various international considerations and statistics related to firearms as well as a review of legislation and policies throughout the world, including in North America (Canada and Mexico), South America, Europe, Asia, the Middle East, Africa, and Australia.

International Considerations and Statistics

In the mental health professions, we place significant emphasis on the need to be culturally competent practitioners. *Cultural competence* has been generally defined as "the ability to understand, appreciate and interact with people from cultures or belief systems different from one's own" (DeAngelis, 2015, p. 64). Indeed, the way in which we define, conceptualize, and treat mental health conditions is heavily grounded in our societal norms and the Western medical model. Namely, the primary source for clinicians who diagnose, research, and treat mental health conditions in the United States is the *Diagnostic and Statistical Manual of Mental Disorders*, 5th edition (DSM-5; American Psychiatric Association, 2013). The DSM was first published in 1844 to classify institutionalized psychiatric patients and has evolved considerably since that time. The latest revision, DSM-5, includes both categorical and dimensional approaches to making certain diagnoses; and it also highlights the need to account for developmental and cultural considerations in this context.[9] As the manual indicates:

> The boundaries between normality and pathology vary across cultures for specific types of behaviors. Thresholds of tolerance for specific symptoms or behaviors differ across cultures, social settings, and families. Hence, the level at which an experience becomes problematic or pathological will differ. The judgment that a given behavior is abnormal and requires clinical attention depends on cultural norms that are internalized by the individual and applied by others around them, including family members and clinicians. Awareness of the significance of culture may correct mistaken interpretations of psychopathology, but culture may also contribute to vulnerability and suffering (e.g., by amplifying fears that maintain panic disorder or health anxiety). . . . Culture also affects the conduct of the clinical encounter; as a result, cultural differences between the clinician and the patient have implications for the accuracy and acceptance of diagnosis

as well as for treatment decisions, prognostic considerations, and clinical outcomes. (p. 14)

One particular goal of the DSM publisher, the American Psychiatric Association, has been to harmonize it as closely as possible with the *International Statistical Classification of Diseases and Related Health Problems*, which is a medical classification list published by the World Health Organization (WHO) and used throughout much of the world. The mental health and medical professions account for the fact that statistics and data, more generally, are dependent on the way in which emotional and behavioral problems are recognized and defined across cultures. Of course, the same is true for laws.

There are three main issues to consider in this context. The first is based on the letter of the law (i.e., what is legal/illegal); the second is the enforcement and application of the law; and the third is the classification of lawbreaking (i.e., recording crimes and corresponding statistics). For instance, a data analysis would reflect no traffic violations in a society without traffic laws, but one can certainly "speed" legally or illegally. Namely, one may drive above the speed limit in a particular area, whereas a NASCAR driver going 200 mph at Talladega will not only be speeding legally but may just get some prize money and the win. Though the underlying principles remain, perhaps these examples do not parallel firearm laws closely enough. Let us consider crimes then. Similarly, some acts are legal in certain places and illegal elsewhere. For instance, loose-fitting swim trunks are not allowed in public pools in France, it is illegal to chew gum in Singapore, and stepping on currency is a crime in Thailand (23 unusual laws around the world you probably didn't know about, 2016).

Of course, these are some of the more peculiar examples, and many states in the United States have very quirky laws as well. For example, in Alabama, it is illegal to wear a fake mustache that might induce laughter in church. In Connecticut, a pickle cannot legally be considered a pickle unless it bounces; and in Iowa, one-armed piano players might perform for free. In Utah, it is illegal not to drink milk; and in Minnesota, a person may not cross state lines with a duck atop his or her head (Bratskeir, 2016). Some are more serious, however. For example, there is no minimum age for marriage in Saudi Arabia; in fact, in 2008, a Saudi court denied an 8-year-old a divorce from her 58-year-old husband (Saudi court, 2008). Extramarital sex, including being the victim of rape, is illegal in Dubai; and recently, a woman who was allegedly gang raped was arrested and incarcerated for engaging in sex outside of wedlock when she reported the attack to the police (Boyle, 2016). According to a news article, in Greece, anyone can be forced by the police to be tested for human immunodeficiency virus with little evidence to indicate suspicion (Artavia, 2013). Specifically, the article states, "If tested positive, the consequences can mean the loss of your job and release of personal information to the media. Additionally, according to the measure's language, a positive person

'should be evicted from their homes, without any alternative being offered'"
(Artavia, 2013).

The second and third issues in this context pertain to law enforcement
and data collection and analysis. In this context it is critical to remember
that statistics are dependent on both the presence and enforcement of laws.
As we illustrate throughout this book, there are significant challenges with
respect to operationally defining firearm-related constructs and, therefore,
with collecting and analyzing data appropriately in this area of study in the
United States alone. These challenges are notably amplified when we attempt
to conduct cross-cultural data collection and analyses. Kopel, Gallant, & Eisen
(2003) expressed this sentiment with regard to the difficulties in obtaining an
accurate assessment of the number of deaths that result from armed conflicts
throughout the world—which should theoretically be easier data to ascertain
than the narrower firearm data we aspire to collect. As Kopel and colleagues
noted, the numbers used to come to estimates of fatalities from armed
conflicts (e.g., 500,000 deaths annually is a widely cited one) are sometimes
derived using the median or mean of widely disparate estimates and are provided solely as a reference point. Ultimately, they recommended against the
use of existing estimates and believe the statistics listed by the WHO are an
overestimate. Incidentally, in the context of firearms, they further contended
that not all wartime deaths are a result of firearms, which is unlike what the
United Nations "implicitly claims," and asserted that "wartime deaths from
small arms usually account for less than half of all wartime deaths" (p. 121).[10]

In this vein, it is relevant to note that violence and weapons, especially
firearms, are often conflated, particularly when international comparisons are
being made. It is not uncommon for there to be a hyperfocus on US firearm-
related data, including those associated with homicide and suicide. While the
statistics may be accurate, we always run the risk of being misleading when
making cross-cultural comparisons, particularly given how different the
United States is from most countries, including those considered to be part
of the "Western world." By focusing solely on firearm-related homicide and
suicide from an international perspective, we also run the risk of overlooking
such acts committed via different methods or even violence against animals
(e.g., honor killings in the Middle East and Africa, self-immolation and sep-
puku in Asia, celebratory killing of animals in countries such as Spain, and the
more general acts of violence and terrorism committed with knives and even
vehicles in Europe).

Still, while we acknowledge the limitations of all research, we must
work with what we have and seek to remain transparent and improve our
methods as many researchers have attempted to tackle internationally relevant firearm questions. For instance, Lankford (2016) examined data on
people who killed four people or more between 1966 and 2012 to compare
and contrast offenders in the United States to those elsewhere. Data were from
the New York City Police Department's 2012 *Active Shooter* report. Results
suggested that public mass shooters in the United States were significantly

more likely to arm themselves with multiple weapons and to attack at school or a workplace compared to offenders from other countries, who were more likely to attack military sites. The authors hypothesized that these differences may be attributed to both American gun culture and American "strains" (e.g., is there something that makes students and workers more likely to commit these atrocities? a gap between individuals' boundless aspirations and reality, inclusive of their struggles?).

Killingley (2014) wrote of the US relationship with guns and how it differs from that of other nations. For instance, the Small Arms Survey, a Swiss Organization, estimated the gun ownership rate in the United States to be 89 firearms for every 100 people, while for the United Kingdom, the rate is 6.2 firearms per 100 people. Killingley also noted that, according to the CDC, there were over 11,000 firearm homicides in the United States in 2010, whereas there were only 58 in England and Wales in 2011. Killingley further noted that, in fact, in Leesburg, Virginia, one restaurateur (owner of The Cajun Experience) offered a 10% discount to customers who bring their licensed handguns to his establishment on Open Carry Wednesday (although that restaurant is now closed). These differences led Killingley to ask, "Why do guns captivate so many Americans and energise them into vocal opposition at the first hint of regulation?" (p. 543), to which he highlighted the fact that America was founded upon a common concept of liberty, as opposed to ethnicity.[11]

Ajdacic-Gross et al. (2006) compared changes in the proportion of firearm suicides to changes in the proportion of firearm ownership since the 1980s in Western countries. They indicated that, for the countries in which firearm suicide rates are declining, the firearm legislation and licensing of firearm ownership have become more restrictive. Some of the policies that these countries enacted include:

- Requiring mandatory registration for all weapons
- Extending the "prohibited weapons" category
- In order to obtain license approval, the licensee must substantiate the specific reason for which the weapon is needed
- Setting a new minimum age for licensing (e.g., 18 instead of 16)
- Requiring a 28-day waiting period before individuals can purchase a firearm
- Periodic examination and renewal of licenses
- Interviewing new firearm owners and applicants and visiting them at home before approving a license and/or renewing one

Legislation and Policy

As Cukier (2005) aptly noted, firearm policy is the subject of debate throughout the world, although there are notable distinctions among the ways in which the issues are framed and the policy goals are formulated. While many industrialized countries began to require firearm licenses and registration in the wake of their respective shooting tragedies, there has been significant variability in the levels of support for and resources devoted to legislation in these places and, therefore, in the time required to pass it. Cukier posited that "the scale and sophistication of resources brought to bear on gun policy in the US are not seen anywhere else in the world," noting that gun control movements in places like Canada, Australia, Great Britain, and South Africa "have been led primarily by tiny organizations relying mainly on volunteers with limited budgets and little political influence" (p. 228). Regardless, Cukier highlighted the fact that "laws must not only be passed, they must be effectively implemented and they must be vigilantly defended . . . [and] we must differentiate achieving political goals from achieving effective outcomes" (p. 229).

North America (Canada and Mexico)

Many characterize Canada's gun laws as stricter than those in the United States. Federal regulations in Canada require that all gun owners, who must be 18 years of age, obtain a license which requires a background check and a safety course (Masters, 2016). Canada also categorizes firearms by type: nonrestricted, restricted, and prohibited. Nonrestricted firearms are ordinary rifles and shotguns, while restricted firearms are handguns, semiautomatic rifles and shotguns, and sawed-offs. This latter category of firearms requires a federal registration certificate (Masters, 2016). A registration certificate, according to the Royal Canadian Mounted Police, differs from a license in that it identifies a firearm and links it to its owner so that it can be tracked, if necessary (Canadian firearms program, 2013). Prohibited firearms are automatic weapons (Masters, 2016). Many of the state's firearm laws are credited to prior incidences of gun violence, such as an incident in 1989 where a disgruntled student killed 14 of his classmates and injured several more when he entered an engineering school with a semiautomatic weapon (Masters, 2016). While prior violence often energizes laws such as these, continued research is needed on the effects to which these laws contribute.

Langmann (2012) investigated whether three separate firearm laws passed by the Canadian Parliament had an effect on homicide or spousal homicide rates but found no significant associations between them. Specifically, no effects were found related to the implementation of licensing in 2001 or the registration of rifles and shotguns in 2003. McPhedran and Mauser (2013) examined the effect of the 1995 Firearms Act in Canada on female firearm homicide victimization. Based on their research, they concluded:

> There was little evidence to suggest that increased firearms legislation in Canada had a significant impact on preexisting trends in lethal firearm violence against women. These results do not support the view that increasing firearms legislation is associated with a reduced incidence of firearm-related female domestic homicide victimization. (p. 875)

McPhedran, Baker, and Singh (2011) compared Canada, Australia, and New Zealand due to their similar social histories but different legislative regimes' long-term firearm homicide trends. They found that the most pronounced decline occurred in New Zealand. Because Canada and Australia have stricter firearm laws, they concluded that other issues must be at play (e.g., socioeconomic factors, such as New Zealand's lower unemployment rate, as well as illicit activities and socioeconomic disadvantage) regarding the decline in firearm homicides.

Mexicans, like Americans, have a constitutional right to own firearms (Podnar, 2015). However, considering there is only one gun store in all of Mexico, this creates some logistical problems for Mexicans who want to own guns legally. The store is known as the Directorate of Arms and Munitions Sales, and it is run by the nation's military. Nevertheless, there are legal requirements for individuals to own guns and obtain a firearm permit there. To be a gun owner, one must be at least 18 years of age, a member of a shooting club, physically and mentally able to safely operate a gun, and free of criminal convictions. Further, individuals must fulfill military service. In order to carry a firearm outside of the home, individuals must have an additional permit, and they must need to carry their weapon for occupational purposes, such as law enforcement or security (Podnar, 2015).

South America

In the wide range of firearm restrictions that we see from country to country— from relatively permissive to substantially more restrictive—South America typically falls somewhere in the middle (Podnar, 2015). In Argentina, citizens can own firearms, including semiautomatic weapons, with a permit. The permit is provided to individuals who are at least 21 years old, have no criminal record, pass both a physical and a mental examination, participate in firearm training, provide proof of income, and are fingerprinted. Further, the government implemented a program that encourages individuals to turn in their firearms. Brazilians who are 25 years or older can apply for a firearm permit to own handguns or semiautomatic weapons. Automatic weapons are outlawed, as are toys that resemble real firearms. Although firearm ownership is relatively easy to achieve in Brazil, permits to carry a firearm are much more difficult to obtain. Firearm carry permit applicants must provide a written statement pertaining to why they need to carry a gun, and they must pass a psychological evaluation completed by a state-approved psychologist. Further, a background check and proof of training are required.

Chile, like Brazil, allows for firearm ownership, although it is not a constitutionally protected right. To become a gun owner, one must endure a lengthy permit application process, including passing a psychiatric examination, completing firearm training, providing a home address, and (if applicable) applying for another application to carry the firearm outside of the home. In Venezuela, a firearm owner must obtain a license, which requires an identified genuine reason to own a gun, a background check, and third-party references. The permit length depends on the specific stated rationale to own the gun. Also, Venezuelans can only carry ammunition that is appropriate given the firearm they are licensed to own (Podnar, 2015).

Europe

In the United Kingdom, modern gun control efforts have largely been reactionary, precipitated by acts of violence that brought about public outrage, eventually leading to political change (Masters, 2016). In August 1987, the Hungerford massacre occurred, which involved a lone gunman who went on a 6-hour shooting spree west of London, killing 16 people and eventually himself. He used two legally owned semiautomatic weapons and a handgun. As a result of the tragedy, the Firearms (Amendment) Act was introduced, which expanded the list of weapons that were banned (e.g., certain semiautomatic weapons) and increased the firearm registration requirements. After another horrific tragedy in 1996, in which a gunman in Scotland killed 16 school children and one adult before ending his own life, even stricter gun laws went into effect. The incident prompted a public campaign referred to as the Snowdrop Petition, which drove legislation pertaining to banning handguns and instituting a temporary gun buy-back program. The buy-back program was credited with successfully removing tens of thousands of illegal and unwanted guns from the public. Of note, analysts reported that firearm-related crimes increased significantly in the late 1990s through the early 2000s, despite the strict gun laws in Britain (Masters, 2016).

More recently, Hallsworth and Silverstone (2009) examined the increase in gun violence in the United Kingdom. Specifically, the authors noted that others have attributed this increase to a burgeoning "gun culture" or to the arrival of American-style gangs on UK streets—"gang culture." However, the authors rejected these explanations as too vague or too general. They instead examined the "life world" of two different types of gun users: successful violent career criminals and the street-based world inhabited by violent young men (termed "on road" there). They stated that the problem with using terms such as "gang culture" and "gun culture" is that different populations use guns for various reasons, including the fact that there are many kinds of street organizations that are not necessarily gangs (e.g., drug traffickers, armed robbers, and mid- to upper-level drug dealers with long-standing businesses). The authors noted that previous research has indicated that "criminal contacts are preeminent in determining the ease with which quality illegal firearms can be obtained; the better connected someone is, both in terms of numbers and seniority of contacts, the easier it is to get hold of a gun" (p. 363). When guns are used, the use is invariably justified on business grounds as the criminal elite knows that indiscriminate weapon use can bring down an enforcement response. The life world of those who are "on road" is considered to be enmeshed in a more violent and volatile street culture. Being "on road" means for many that they could find a form of authentic sovereignty, where they are free from the constraints of what is perceived to be a hostile society. Surviving "on road" requires a certain mastery of violence—you either survive or are a victim. Firearms possession for this group of individuals often holds a sense of power. Additionally, gun use for individuals who are "on road" is much less instrumental and planned and far more erratic and situation-dependent. In this world, gun use is often territorial. The authors draw comparisons to the gang culture in the United States, stating, "While the 'on road' culture described here constitutes the destination for young poor people drawn from a range of different ethnicities, its stylistic features are, however, profoundly shaped by media images of a black urban ghetto culture as this has evolved in the United States" (p. 370). In conclusion, according to Hallsworth and Silverstone's (2009) research, it seems that the life worlds of both groups involve the possession of weapons but that these weapons are utilized for different reasons and under different circumstances. For professional criminals, violence is regulated. Regarding the "on-road" life world, the authors state, "This is a world that is volatile because the violence rules that exist within it license escalation while precluding the breaking mechanisms that would delimit the possibility of violence from erupting and spreading. Because of this, conflict situations abound, vendettas proliferate and young men tragically shoot at each other with fatal consequences" (Hallsworth & Silverstone, 2009, p. 372).

In other parts of Europe, different firearm-related problems require scientific attention. For instance, Junuzovic and Eriksson (2012) examined unintentional firearm-related hunting deaths in Sweden. This was deemed an important topic of research considering that during 1983–2008 48 out of 90 (53%) unintentional firearm deaths were hunting-related. The authors ultimately found that over the past few decades these numbers have dropped, which seemed to be at least partly due to more restrictive firearm legislation in Sweden (e.g., all firearms must be stored in authorized safety lockers) and a mandatory hunter's exam (enacted in 1985). Human error was deemed the main cause of the hunting fatalities.

In Norway, gun control had never been considered a prominent political issue, with a high gun ownership rate yet relatively restrictive gun laws (Masters, 2016). Perhaps this is because, although Norway ranks tenth in the world regarding gun ownership, it ranks very low on firearm-homicide rates. As a reference point, the United States ranks almost 64 times higher in terms of firearm-homicide rates. Nevertheless, gun ownership became significantly more politicized after Anders Behring Breivik killed 77 people in July 2011. After the tragic event, critics stated that the country's gun control laws were ineffective and expressed beliefs such as those who are willing break the law to murder are not going to be dissuaded by the regulation of firearms and will get hold of firearms regardless of whether it is legal to do so. In fact, many argued that, perhaps, so many people would not have died if more people had been armed. Others on the opposite side of the argument recommended tightening

Norway's gun restrictions by prohibiting pistols and semiautomatic weapons outright (Masters, 2016).

According to Donohue's (2015) summary of firearm laws and policies throughout the rest of Europe, laws differ significantly from country to country. In Germany, one must be at least 25 years of age and able to pass a psychiatric evaluation to buy a gun. In Finland, handgun license applicants can only purchase a gun if they can prove they are active members of regulated shooting clubs, pass an aptitude test and police interview, and prove they have a proper gun storage process. In Italy, prospective gun owners must establish a genuine reason to own a firearm and pass a background check that includes a consideration of both criminal and mental health records. In France, firearm applicants must pass a comprehensive background check of criminal, mental, and health records, while also considering the reason for the gun purchase.

Asia

Japan holds the record as having the lowest gun-homicide rate in the world, which many lend credit to the fact that most firearms are illegal to own and, as a result, gun ownership rates are very low (Masters, 2016). The only guns that are legal to own are air guns, shotguns, guns used in competitions, and guns that are utilized for research or have industrial purposes. Even then, in order to obtain the privilege of owning a gun, the prospective gun owner must undergo formal instruction and pass a variety of different tests, including mental, written, and drug tests. Further, a rigorous background check must be passed, owners must provide information to the authorities about how the firearm is used and stored, and the firearm must be presented on an annual basis for inspection (Masters, 2016).

On the other end of the spectrum, Thailand's reported rate of gun-related deaths is twice as high as that of the United States and one of the highest in Asia, in part due to a gun culture on par with that of the United States but also partly due to a thriving black market (Domínguez, 2016). Firearm law indicates that one can only obtain a license to own a gun for one of a few reasons: self-defense, protection of property, or hunting and sport. Further, the applicant must be at least 20 years old and pass a background check. The background check considers the applicant's personal conduct, criminal records, and living conditions. According to Domínguez (2016), it is quite easy to obtain an illegal firearm that has been smuggled in from across the border. Further, the Thai government has exacerbated firearm problems in certain parts of the country as it supplies civilians with firearms in areas where there are problems related to insurgent attacks.

The Middle East

In the Middle East, governments are known to set strict laws pertaining to firearm possession and ownership (Ziabari, 2012). In fact, the ownership of handguns and rifles is mostly prohibited in the regional countries. In this section, we will briefly discuss unique gun policy in two Middle Eastern countries: Israel and Turkey.

In Israel, military service is required, and firearms are entrenched in everyday life. According to the law, most 18-year-olds are drafted, psychologically screened, and provided with weapons training after high school (Masters, 2016). However, after serving 2–3 years in the military, young Israelis are discharged and must abide by civilian gun laws. Civilian gun laws are relatively strict in Israel, such that assault weapons are banned and individuals who want to own or possess a firearm are required to register ownership with the government. In order to obtain a firearm license, individuals must have various qualifications; for example, they must be an Israeli citizen or permanent resident, be at least 21 years old, and speak some Hebrew. Similar to Australia's gun laws, they must show genuine cause to carry a firearm. However, genuine cause appears to be slightly more liberal in that self-defense and hunting are considered legitimate. Critics argue that these measures may not be restrictive enough as almost the entire population has indirect access to an assault weapon by being either a soldier or reservist or by being related to one of the former (Masters, 2016).

In Turkey, psychiatrists conduct a medical evaluation with anyone who applies for a firearm license; according to Özalp & Karakiliç (2007):

> The psychiatrist is designated as an expert in the process of licensing and is not required to provide medical treatment but instead is required to provide an expert medical opinion and to make a medical examination to address a question posed by Law no. 6136: namely, does the applicant have any psychopathology that should prevent him or her from receiving a gun license? (pp. 99–100)

In this situation, the definition of *psychopathology* is narrowed to include only cases in which capacities of judgment and reality testing are impaired. These psychiatrists are tasked with a daunting challenge, which is to predict a potential gun owner's mental capacity to be a gun owner, based on one evaluation. Complicating matters further, these evaluations are not standardized, and there is no agreed-upon format for said diagnostic evaluations. In fact, there is a wide variation among psychiatrists' examinations, especially between urban and rural settings. Although the specifics pertaining to these evaluations are not defined by the law, the conditions that would prevent individuals from gun ownership are. The conditions that would prevent an individual from owning a gun are the following: established psychiatric disorders, personality disorders, alcohol and substance abuse disorders, and impulse control disorders. Critics argue that these practices are flawed in many ways, and the fact that firearm ownership and firearm homicides have reached major proportions leads many to reach the conclusion that there is a need for the development of improved policy (Özalp & Karakiliç, 2007).

Africa

Firearm laws differ significantly throughout the continent of Africa, but we present information about Egypt and South Africa here.

In Egypt, the right to bear arms is not protected by the constitution, and as such, it is not a guaranteed right for citizens. According to Polk (2014): "gun control laws are extremely restrictive forcing citizens to either have connections within the government's security forces that issue licenses, bribe officials, or attempt to acquire illegal weapons and risk prosecution in order to arm themselves." Rifles, long-range guns, and assault weapons are prohibited. To obtain a license to possess a legal firearm, the applicant must be determined to be both physically and mentally fit and provide a valid reason for owning the weapon. The applicant must provide a description of the weapon to be purchased, as well as information about his or her profession. Former government officials are entitled to own a firearm without a license, which allows them to circumvent an otherwise seemingly impossible system. Specifically, Polk (2014) asserted, "Without having connections within the government, the application of an average citizen without the ability to bribe numerous officials is denied."

In South Africa there is a comprehensive firearm regulation regime in place, which makes it difficult to obtain permission to own guns, especially certain firearms which are prohibited except for in very limited circumstances (Firearms-control legislation, n.d.). To obtain a license for firearm ownership, one must state a basis for needing one. As an example, when applying for a firearm license based on self-defense, one must demonstrate a need for a weapon, as well as an inability to provide protection through alternative methods. In order to obtain a license, the application must include a competency certificate, which is provided after it has been established that the applicant does not have a proclivity toward violence or a substance abuse problem. Further, the individual must successfully complete a training on safe and efficient handling of a firearm (Firearms-control legislation, n.d.).

Australia

In 1996, Australia firearm legislation was "tightened significantly" due to the National Firearms Agreement (NFA), which resulted in a series of studies investigating the impact of the legislative changes (Baker & McPhedran, 2015). The NFA was put into effect after a series of mass shootings in Australia that resulted in public outrage (Chappell, 2014). The NFA stated that in order to own or possess a firearm, an individual must have a legitimate reason to own it; and personal protection was not recognized as such a reason. A national firearm registration was put in place, along with a procedure for license refusal or cancellation and seizure of previously owned firearms. Removal of guns from individuals who were not fit to own guns due to a mental or physical condition was a part of this program. While firearm laws vary throughout the world, most nations seek a way to limit access to guns by individuals with mental illness, as does Australia (Chappell, 2014). However, Chappell (2014) notes that policy should prioritize the implementation of sensible and enforceable policies regarding general access to firearms, rather than worrying about identifying and screening out individuals with a pathological condition that would deem them a danger to themselves or others.

Research indicates that, while observed and predicted homicide trends did not differ significantly post–legislative changes, firearm-involved suicide, non-firearm suicide, and non-firearm homicide were all significantly lower than predicted (Baker & McPhedran, 2015). Brief descriptions of some of the studies investigating the impact of legislative changes are provided here. McPhedran and Baker (2008) attempted to make sense of the differing opinions (despite remarkably consistent results) in the literature regarding the NFA, which not only prohibited certain types of firearms but also enacted a firearm buy-back scheme. They note the importance of taking into consideration that firearm deaths are often largely represented by suicides, not only homicides. As such, some studies that found declining firearm deaths saw declines of firearm suicides. However, they warn it would be unwise to draw conclusions about the relationship between NFA and firearm suicides as there was also a decline in non-firearm suicides. They conclude, "The extant literature is extremely consistent in its findings—namely, that there was no significant change in the rate of decline in firearm homicides following the legislative intervention, and that there was a significant acceleration in the rate of decline in firearm suicides" (p. 15). Disagreements, therefore, seem to come from the various conclusions at which authors arrive, not their statistical analyses.

In another article regarding firearm legislation and its effects in Australia, McPhedran (2013) reported preliminary findings pertaining to levels of legal firearm ownership and violent firearm-related crime in New South Wales, Australia. No evidence was found to suggest that increasing levels of firearm ownership are associated with increasing levels of crime. Modest negative associations were found between gun ownership and violent firearm-related crime. The author states in conclusion that firearm crime reductions can exist in the context of increasing levels of legal ownership. In a more recent article, McPhedran (2016) made the argument that in order to inform international policy development aimed at addressing firearm misuse, other countries' experiences with gun law amendments need to be studied. Her study identified five evaluation-focused studies that examined the impact of legislative reform pertaining to firearm homicide in Australia (after the previously mentioned significant changes made to gun laws in the mid-1990s). These studies did not find statistical evidence of any significant changes in firearm homicide rates due to legislative impact. McPhedran asserted:

It may be reasonable to suggest that policy changes may have been "effectively achieved", in the sense of implementing changes in processes

around regulating firearm ownership, but seems prudent to avoid
equating the process of legislative and policy change with outcomes
resulting from that process of change. (p. 70)

An obvious question arises: Why would such a major legislative change seem
to make no significant impact? It could be a misspecification of "high-risk"
populations or an inappropriately designed policy. Policymakers are left with
another important question to ponder: What interventions might be more
successful? McPhedran noted that, perhaps, interventions to improve social
equality and address social and economic disadvantage are an important
next step.

Part II

MENTAL HEALTH, VIOLENCE, AND SUICIDE

3

Mental Health

With each revision of the *Diagnostic and Statistical Manual of Mental Disorders* (DSM) it seems that an almost endless list of new or modified psychiatric disorder categories appears. As very few mental health providers and researchers have all disorders memorized, it would be unreasonable to expect the reader to meaningfully consume information about each disorder. Thus, it is our intention in this chapter to provide a broad overview of various major psychiatric disorders, their symptoms, and some current theoretical and empirical thought underlying these disorders. In providing a primer concerning mental health, we first review the latest iteration of the DSM, the fifth edition (DSM-5; American Psychiatric Association, 2013), with respect to how psychopathology is defined and the nature of the diagnostic system. We then shift to definitions, key examples, and various theories for: (i) *clinical disorders*, (ii) *substance use disorders*, and (iii) personality disorders. Before moving to the overview, a few caveats are warranted. First and foremost, reading this chapter does not qualify you to diagnose yourself, your friends, or your family. Second, the DSM-5 is intended for clinical use by trained and licensed mental health professionals. This chapter draws heavily from the DSM-5 for educational and illustrative purposes within the broader context of discussing key issues in the behavioral science of firearms and related concerns.

What Is Psychopathology?

A basic definition of *psychopathology* would note that thoughts, feelings, and/or behaviors outside of social norms may be deemed "abnormal" or "disordered." However, psychopathology is much more intricate than that. As we elaborate on more in Chapter 8, historical views of pathology were often rooted in religious perspectives. For instance, demonic possessions and religious exorcisms often defined what was considered "pathological." Among the first modern and meaningful conceptualizations of psychopathology was that offered by Emil Kraepelin in his 1883 text *Compendium der Psychiatrie*. While the full scope of Kraepelin's diagnostic categories and disorder types is beyond the scope of this chapter, his basic definition of a *syndrome* is paramount. In short, he was the first to offer the notion that a "syndrome" (later defined by the DSM as a "disorder") reflected a combination or constellation of identifiable symptoms grouped together. This basic idea laid the groundwork for the diagnostic scheme and array of grouped mental health symptoms we see today in the DSM-5. Later notions of psychopathology or psychiatric disorders also rely on socially defined norms for what constitutes normal versus abnormal symptoms of mental illness.

The DSM-5 contains important considerations when trying to understand the basic nature of psychopathology. For example, some symptoms may be indicative of or related to more than one disorder. Therefore, clinical expertise and careful assessment are required in diagnosing psychopathology. To illustrate, severe changes in sleep habits may fit within the diagnostic criteria of many disorders, such as major depression, generalized anxiety, or various stress-related disorders, to name a few. Thus, it is necessary for a qualified professional to conduct a thorough evaluation to conceptualize how such a symptom best fits an individual client. Most central to the point at hand, the DSM-5 specifies the following criteria for a mental disorder to be present (adapted from American Psychiatric Association, 2013, p. 20):

- Clinically significant disturbance in thinking, emotional regulation, and behavior
- Reflection of a dysfunction in the psychological, biological, or developmental processes underlying mental functioning
- Associated with distress or disability in social, occupational, or other activities

The DSM-5 provides further distinctions in that neither culturally normative responses to stress nor socially deviant behaviors in and of themselves qualify as a mental disorder or psychopathology. In all, psychopathology is best understood as a set of clusters of symptoms out of the ordinary for a given person, involving significant impacts on thoughts, feelings, and/or behavior. Observations of associated impaired functioning and distress are critical considerations in distinguishing normative conditions from mental disorders.

The DSM-5 Diagnostic System

The broad diagnostic structure of the DSM-5 is rather straightforward. Simply, the attending mental health professional documents diagnoses, important psychosocial or contextual factors, and level of impairment or disability (i.e., level of functioning). As noted, the set of disorders we identify in our society is vast. The DSM-5 consists of approximately 300 disorders described in over

900 pages of text. We provide the overarching categories identified in the DSM-5 here along with examples of conditions that are likely to be recognizable to most readers:

- Neurodevelopmental Disorders
  - o Autism Spectrum Disorder
- Schizophrenia Spectrum and Other Psychotic Disorders
  - o Schizophrenia
- Bipolar and Related Disorders
  - o Bipolar I Disorder
- Depressive Disorder
  - o Major Depressive Disorder
- Anxiety Disorders
  - o Panic Disorder
- Obsessive–Compulsive and Related Disorders
  - o Body Dysmorphic Disorder
- Trauma- and Stressor-Related Disorders
  - o Posttraumatic Stress Disorder
- Dissociative Disorders
  - o Dissociative Amnesia
- Somatic Symptom and Related Disorders
  - o Conversion Disorder
- Feeding and Eating Disorders
  - o Anorexia Nervosa
- Elimination Disorders
  - o Enuresis
- Sleep–Wake Disorders
  - o Narcolepsy
- Sexual Dysfunctions
  - o Erectile Disorder
- Gender Dysphoria
- Disruptive, Impulse-Control, and Conduct Disorders
  - o Intermittent Explosive Disorder
- Substance-Related and Addictive Disorders
  - o Alcohol-Related Disorders
- Neurocognitive disorders
  - o Major neurocognitive disorder (formerly Dementia)
- Personality Disorders
  - o Borderline Personality Disorder
- Paraphilic Disorders
  - o Pedophilic Disorder
- Other Mental Disorders
  - o Unspecified Medical Disorder Due to Another Medical Condition
- Medication-Induced Movement Disorders and Other Adverse Effects of Medication
  - o Tardive Dyskinesia

The DSM-5 structure also provides a fairly comprehensive list of "other conditions" that may be a focus of clinical attention, addressing issues such as abuse and partner violence. Each major category listed here also contains further subclassification. To illustrate, neurodevelopmental disorders include intellectual disabilities, communication disorders, autism spectrum disorders, attention-deficit/hyperactivity disorder, specific learning disorder, motor disorders, and other neurodevelopmental disorders.

Anyone familiar with psychiatric disorders knows that not all versions of the same disorder look alike (i.e., there is often heterogeneity even within the same diagnostic classification). For instance, one patient's depression may present primarily as mood and social withdrawal, whereas another's presents with fatigue and other symptoms. Critical issues like the onset, severity, and duration of a particular disorder are significant in planning treatment. The DSM-5 classification system accounts for varied presentation, onset, and severity (among other details) through the use of diagnostic criteria and descriptors, as well as subtypes and specifiers. Reflecting back on Kraepelin's notion of sets of symptoms clustering together, each DSM-5 diagnosis is defined by a set of potential affective, cognitive, and behavioral symptoms, along with a minimal time criterion for which symptoms must have been present. Importantly, the DSM-5 maintains that each set of diagnostic criteria is a "guideline" (p. 21), suggesting that a diagnosis may be made in the absence of essential criteria or vice versa.

Subtypes and *specifiers* offer further nuance to account for variation in mental disorders. Subtypes denote mutually exclusive subcategories of a particular disorder. Specifiers, on the other hand, offer clinical detail that may be optionally added if such criteria are satisfied. Let us take the instance of major depressive disorder. This diagnosis has no subtypes; that is, there is only one category of major depressive disorder. However, a range of specifiers may highlight severity (e.g., mild versus moderate), prominent features (e.g., with psychotic features), and other notable content (e.g., in partial remission). With the ability to add more than one specifier, diagnoses can account for a great deal of nuance from patient to patient.

To fully grasp the scope and nuances of the DSM-5 system, a few other important notes are worth highlighting. As time has gone on and mental health research has advanced, there has been an upward trend in attending to developmental aspects of psychopathology. That is, fields of psychology and psychiatry (among others), have attended to age-related differences and aging processes as they influence psychopathology. The DSM-5 takes obvious note of this idea. For example, the groupings of disorders above are listed by typical age at onset (e.g., neurodevelopmental in childhood or bipolar in adolescence). Further, summaries within each diagnostic category often note related research findings or considerations addressing developmental processes. Equally vital to the DSM-5 system is the need to recognize cultural considerations. Quite overtly, the DSM-5 accounts for familial and social norms, as well as other cultural aspects. Moreover, sample tools are provided for cultural assessment, and there exists a "Glossary of Cultural Concepts of Distress" to assist the clinician. Furthering the highlighting of culture, the DSM-5 provides clinically useful guidance concerning cultural syndromes, cultural idioms of distress, and cultural explanations or perceived cause (of a disorder). Such specifiers should prompt an assessing or treating clinician to carefully weigh the role of the patient's unique cultural beliefs and experiences in formulating psychopathology diagnoses. While nowhere near perfect, the DSM-5 has made strides compared to prior iterations in terms of intentional attention to cultural variation in normative behaviors and psychopathology. Finally, the DSM-5 allows for multiple diagnoses provided that criteria for more than one disorder are satisfied and rule-outs do not preclude such instances. Mental health providers are to note the principal diagnosis, however; the methods for determining such varies by treatment setting. For inpatients, the principal diagnosis is typically the one chiefly responsible for the hospital admission. Similarly, for outpatients, the primary diagnosis would be that which led to the seeking of treatment.

Clinical Disorders

Overview

We present common psychological disorders apart from personality and substance use disorders for sake of ease in understanding. It merits noting, however, that: (i) the DSM-5 did away with prior coding schemes that differentiate personality disorders from clinical syndromes (i.e., Axis I versus Axis II) and (ii) many clinical, personality, and substance disorders are often comorbid, or co-occurring. The clinical disorders presented here were selected either due to their relevance in public and lay discourse or for their documented association, or lack thereof, with firearms and associated issues covered in the rest of this book (e.g., suicide risk, violence risk).

Overall, clinical disorders share in common the fact that each is defined or diagnosed along a set of symptoms or criteria. Oftentimes those symptoms overlap across diagnostic categories, further reflecting the need for careful clinical assessment and differential diagnosis. However, as illustrated by the selected examples below, clinical disorders vary greatly with regard to issues like theoretical causes, course (i.e., onset, duration, severity, response to treatment), and other key aspects. Where possible, we present sets of diagnostic criteria, associated features, and risk and protective factors paraphrased or shortened from the DSM-5. However, to avoid redundancy, we limit this review to more commonly occurring disorders and symptoms. Many disorders also require specific additional items; for instance, diagnosis of many disorders requires impairment of social or occupational functioning as well as subjective feelings of distress. Recalling our review of the DSM-5 definition of a mental disorder, let us focus here on the key domains of symptom presentations and lists. Finally, DSM-5 diagnostic criteria often specify rule-outs, or other conditions that cannot be the cause of symptoms. For instance, symptoms in a diagnosis of schizophrenia cannot be due to psychotic features of another diagnosis (e.g., depression) or a substance use problem. We do not report such criteria in our review; the interested reader is referred to the DSM-5 itself for details we do not cover here.

Prominent Clinical Disorders: A Primer

Schizophrenia

Schizophrenia is classified as a disorder under the broader category of "schizophrenia spectrum and other psychotic disorders."[1] The five defining symptom types for this category of disorders, including schizophrenia, are: delusions (concerning, for instance, fear of persecution, grandeur, or nihilism), hallucinations (sensory experiences not consistent with external sources), disordered thinking (speech), abnormal motor behavior (often consisting of catatonia or lack of verbal/motor responding), and negative symptoms (such as lack of emotional expression, speech, or social interaction). A formal diagnosis of schizophrenia must satisfy a certain number and combination of criteria, for a certain period of time depending on onset. A complete list of diagnostic criteria for schizophrenia can be found in the DSM-5. Further, schizophrenia can be elaborated on with the following specifiers: first episode, currently in acute episode; first episode, currently in partial remission; first episode, currently in full remission; multiple episodes, currently in acute episode; multiple episodes, currently in partial remission; multiple episodes, currently in full remission; continuous; unspecified; or with catatonia.

Many perspectives exist concerning causes of schizophrenia. Moreover, thought varies somewhat concerning the underlying roots of so-called active or positive symptoms such as hallucinations and delusions compared to negative symptoms (e.g., catatonia). Regarding the latter symptom category, many theorized explanations are rooted in the neurobiology of brain development and neurotransmitter function. This is not to say that environment and social interaction (i.e., "nurture") cannot play a role in the onset or maintenance of schizophrenia. However, neurobiological thought concerning schizophrenia commonly offers support for the primacy of "nature" in this particular disorder. Howes & Kapur (2009) provide a review and scientific update regarding perhaps the most common theory of schizophrenia: the dopamine hypothesis. Dopamine is a key neurotransmitter indicated in the functioning of many human abilities, as well as the pathology of a range of medical and mental disorders. In brief, these authors summarize that older versions of the dopamine hypothesis were grounded in ideas of over- and/or underactive dopamine pathways in the brain, especially in the prefrontal cortex. In their review, Howes & Kapur bring together considerable genetic, neurochemical imaging, environmental risk, and animal studies to update the dopamine hypothesis.

Labeled the "final common pathway," these authors explain dysregulated dopamine functioning as a result of genetic predisposition in combination with dysfunction in the temporal and frontal lobes of the brain, as well as the impact of environmental influences of high stress and psychoactive drugs/substances. Active or positive symptoms are said to be caused or exacerbated by these underlying interactions, whereas they can be ameliorated by appropriate application of antipsychotic drugs. It should be noted that the dopamine hypothesis is not the only common theory of schizophrenia. For instance, Fatemi & Folsom (2009) provide an overview of the neurodevelopmental hypothesis. This neurobiological perspective presupposes that brain injury as early as the first trimester influences the onset of pathological neural pathways during adolescence and young adulthood. This perspective too sees evidence from multiple domains of the research literature, such as brain pathology, genetics, and environmental factors, as well as their interactions.

Bipolar I and Bipolar II

While other diagnoses exist under the category of "bipolar and other disorders," we focus mainly on bipolar I versus II. This group of disorders features both depression and mania, the latter representing a cluster of symptoms of hyper- or overactivity in mood, thoughts, and behaviors. In short, this group of disorders represents the contemporary view of "manic depression" (i.e., bipolar I), as well as less severe forms of the disorder. Bipolar II is primarily differentiated from bipolar I disorder in that it requires only one hypomanic episode.

For a DSM-5 diagnosis of bipolar I disorder, it is necessary to meet the criteria for a manic episode. The manic episode may have been preceded by and may be followed by hypomanic or major depressive episodes. A manic episode consists of a specific period of significantly elevated, expansive, or irritable mood and notably increased goal-directed activity or energy, lasting at least 1 week. Furthermore, during this period, the person must also present with such symptoms as grandiosity, decreased need for sleep, pressured speech, racing thoughts, distractibility, psychomotor agitation, or excessive engagement in risky behaviors (e.g., spending sprees or sexual indiscretions).

On the other hand, bipolar II disorder requires satisfying the criteria for a past or current hypomanic episode and at least one depressive episode without a manic episode. A hypomanic episode consists of similar symptoms but to a lesser degree. Whereas manic episodes often lead to notable impairments and even psychiatric hospitalizations, hypomanic episodes may actually be rather functional for those who experience them. In contrast, a major depressive episode consists of such symptoms as depressed mood, loss of interest in activities once enjoyed, weight loss or gain—or effects on appetite, sleep disturbance, psychomotor agitation or retardation, fatigue or loss of energy, feelings of worthlessness or guilt, concentration problems, and/or recurrent thoughts of death or suicidal thoughts.

Thought concerning the mechanisms or causes of the range of bipolar disorders includes the role of both biology and the environment. One prominent view grounded in both social learning and predisposition perspective is the behavioral approach system (BAS) activation/dysregulation theory. A fairly dense literature summarizes the tenets and empirical support for this perspective (e.g., Boland et al., 2016; Nusslock et al., 2009). This collective literature maintains that humans possess two physiologically based systems aimed at regulating behavior. The BAS, one of these two systems, is theorized to regulate behavior toward the goal of seeking simple rewards and avoiding punishment (hence, a social learning basis). Importantly, the types of rewards/punishments can emanate from the person (e.g., cognition/thinking) or the environment. Two pathways may occur which influence one's relative behavioral (dys)regulation. First, BAS-activating stimuli, for example, personal goals or social challenges, can yield regulatory thoughts and actions. Moreover, BAS-deactivating experiences like loss can yield negative regulation. According to Boland and colleagues (2016), individuals with bipolar disorders are thought to possess hypersensitive or overreactive BAS systems. In other words, ineffective regulation systems account for the highs and lows associated with bipolar symptoms and episodes.

Major Depressive Disorder and Persistent Depressive Disorder (Dysthymia)

The overall category of depressive disorders is quite expansive, covering additional disorders like premenstrual dysphoric disorder and disruptive mood dysregulation disorder. We focus here primarily on major depressive disorder and persistent depressive disorder (formerly known as dysthymia). Importantly, we covered key diagnostic criteria for major depression within the bipolar section in light of the critical diagnostic role depressive episodes play in such disorders. Major depressive disorder represents a contemporary manifestation of what we used to call "clinical depression" and, in short, requires clearly observable changes in thoughts (e.g., suicidal ideation), feelings (e.g., hopelessness), and behaviors (e.g., social interaction) for at least 2 weeks. Persistent depressive disorder, on the other hand, is defined by lower-grade severity of many of these same symptoms for at least 2 years.

For a formal major depressive disorder diagnosis to be rendered, the criteria related to a major depressive episode that we outlined in the bipolar section must be met. The DSM-5 further qualifies major depression with the following potential specifiers: (i) mild, moderate, or severe (severity); (ii) single or recurrent episode; (iii) in partial or full remission; (iv) with psychotic features; (v) unspecified; or (vi) with anxious distress, mixed features, melancholic features, atypical features, mood-congruent psychotic features, mood-incongruent psychotic features, catatonia, peripartum onset, and/or seasonal pattern.

Per the DSM-5, diagnostic criteria for persistent depressive disorder reflect a combination of symptoms from DSM-IV-defined chronic major depressive disorder and dysthymic disorder. Such includes a depressed mood for most of the day, more often than not, for at least 2 years, in addition to such symptoms as appetite problems, sleep disturbance, low energy or fatigue, concentration difficulties, and/or hopelessness. Of particular note is that to reach this diagnosis there must have never been a manic or hypomanic episode. Many of the identical specifiers apply to persistent depressive disorder as for major depressive disorder. Persistent depressive disorder can further be qualified as: (i) early or late onset and (ii) with pure dysthymic syndrome, persistent major depressive episode, intermittent major depressive episodes with current episode, or intermittent major depressive episodes without current episode.

Depressive spectrum disorders have been the subject of perhaps the greatest number of psychological and other disciplinary theories compared to other disorders. Of the array of theoretical explanations, cognitive perspectives have seen a great deal of exposure and theoretical support. Cognitive theories are also discussed later in this book, in Chapters 6 (Suicide) and 8 (Treatment). McGinn (2000) reviewed some of the early work of noted psychiatrist Aaron Beck. Specifically, the outline of Beck's early theory of depression suggests that depression is primarily a function of negative thinking and errors in thinking styles. In other words, persons who experience depression tend to:

- Possess a negative self-concept, in forms such as low self-esteem and high self-criticism
- Hold negative views of the "cognitive triad": themselves, their social world, and the future
- Engage in misperceptions or irrational thinking (e.g., dichotomous thinking, or seeing the world as all good or bad/black and white)

Clark & Beck (2010) elaborate on key aspects of the cognitive theory of depression, extending it to include anxiety, and account for the role of early life events and stress. Namely, negative self-schema are hypothesized to be rigid, influenced by negative core beliefs (e.g., "nobody loves me"), yielding biased ways in which the person interprets information. Early negative life events like childhood stress are thought to influence the formation of negative schema, playing out later in life. Overall, persons exhibiting these cognitive characteristics are understood to possess cognitive "vulnerability" or risk for depression and other disorders.

An extension of cognitive theory, hopelessness theory, also merits attention. Although this stance is reviewed in greater detail in Chapter 6, the nature of hopelessness warrants mention to fully understand the nature of depression. Haeffel and colleagues (2017) summarized hopelessness theory well. Specifically, cognitive vulnerabilities such as those emanating from the

Beck perspective may interact with life stress and other factors, yielding three necessary thinking patterns placing one at risk for hopelessness:

1. Negative events are global (i.e., all-encompassing in one's life) and stable (i.e., will never improve).
2. Further negative consequences will come from a negative event.
3. Negative events are internal (i.e., caused by and a reflection of the fact that the person is unworthy and blameworthy).

Both general cognitive theory and hopelessness theory have witnessed considerable empirical support and are often the treatment targets of leading psychotherapies. Although we focus our depression review on cognitive and affective perspectives, biologically heavy frameworks also exist. For instance, the social signal transduction theory of depression posits that depression results from a biological–environmental interaction response to stress (Slavich & Irwin, 2014). In particular, in the face of social distress or threat, immune responses influencing inflammation processes are increasingly activated. Neuroinflammatory sensitization in the brain is thought to increase subsequent risk for depressive symptoms such as sadness, sleep disturbance, and social withdrawal. A take-home point regarding theories of depression, as well as many other disorders, is the notion that many mental health conditions are best understood as biopsychosocial phenomena. That is, we must view mental health as a result of the intersection of neurobiology (e.g., genes, neurotransmitter functioning), psychological makeup (e.g., thinking styles, emotions), and social conditions (e.g., early life events, social support).

Social Anxiety Disorder (Social Phobia) and Generalized Anxiety Disorder

The anxiety disorder category contains one of the most varied and voluminous sets of pathologies in the entire DSM-5. We address two key subtypes, social anxiety disorder (social phobia) and generalized anxiety disorder (GAD), largely because of their prevalence in the general population as well as their associations with critical issues in this book (e.g., suicide risk). Overall, anxiety disorders share in common the concepts of fear and anxiety/worry. Very simply, fear is one's reaction to actual or perceived threat (think "fight or flight"), whereas anxiety concerns worry or anticipation of a *future* threat. Fear and anxiety are, in and of themselves, common emotions and, in many instances, can be healthy or adaptive. For instance, the fear an individual may experience in a dangerous setting or situation (e.g., military conflict, criminal victimization) may actually prompt responses allowing one to survive. Moreover, a tried-and-true principle of professional performance holds that a healthy level of fear, anxiety, or arousal can actually enhance performance (known as the *Yerkes-Dodson curve* or *law*; Cherry, 2016).

Normal fear or anxiety crosses into psychopathology when its level grossly exceeds or is out of proportion with what would be expected by the perceived threatening cue. Let us jump to an example most, if not all, can appreciate—spiders (the non-poisonous kind). For most, spiders are benign and, perhaps to the practicing arachnologist, very interesting. If you are like some people, however, you are fearful of spiders to the point of running from the room. This is likely a phobia. This is fear-in-action out of proportion with the actual threatening stimulus. And, overall, learning theory has taught us that anxiety often results from associative learning/pairing and is maintained through negative reinforcement. A basic example we often utilize in our undergraduate courses to illustrate the point includes a car accident on a bridge. For most of us, driving over a bridge is a rather uneventful, harmless experience. However, if one was to get into a car accident, one may then associate that bridge (and all bridges for that matter, through a process called generalization) with fear, worry, or anxiety. Driving over bridges moving forward becomes an almost impossible task. In fact, the process of negative reinforcement, or removal of a negative stimulus, may maintain that bridge-related anxiety. Think about it this way—the next time that person drives toward a bridge, he or she may turn around, alleviating or removing the sense of worry in favor of calm (i.e., removing the anxiety-inducing cue of the bridge), which in turn perpetuates the disproportionate fear.

A key concept differentiating anxiety disorders then is the stimulus causing the anxiety. As illustrated in the case of social anxiety disorder (social phobia), in many cases the object or stimulus can be very specific. The DSM-5 criteria for this disorder include a notable fear or worry about social situations whereby the person may be scrutinized by others (e.g., a work meeting or class presentation), and the fear is that he or she will exhibit anxiety symptoms that will be negatively viewed by others (e.g., embarrassment leading to social rejection). Moreover, such situations nearly always provoke such anxiety, which is out of proportion; therefore, the person avoids these situations. As noted, the source of the anxiety is social situations, and the (irrational) anticipation concerns social judgment or scrutiny of others. A specific subtype of this disorder can be seen in scenarios in which the person fears performance situations only (e.g., athletic or arts/music performance). Finally, we should note that social anxiety disorder is different from panic disorder and other specific phobias.

Much of the current clinical zeitgeist surrounding anxiety argues that anxiety and depressive symptoms can be classified under a broader umbrella of "internalizing" disorders; evidence for this perspective includes the overlapping symptoms between depressive disorders and many anxiety disorders. GAD is perhaps the strongest illustration of this pattern; when reviewing these symptom criteria, we encourage the reader to consider the conceptual similarities to and differences from the key features of major depression and persistent depression. The symptoms of GAD are excessive anxiety and worry about numerous issues, such as academics or work performance; and the person has difficulty controlling these symptoms. Furthermore, the condition includes the presence of additional symptoms, such as restlessness, fatigue, concentration difficulties, irritability, and sleep disturbance.

Not surprisingly, some of the theoretical underpinnings associated with anxiety are the same as those for depression. Indeed, Beck's cognitive theory has been extended to anxiety (Clark & Beck, 2010). However, additional perspectives exist, largely grounded in cognitive-behavioral and related concepts. Here, we again center our focus on GAD, though many theoretical concepts extend to the formation of other anxiety disorders. Behar et al. (2009) provide a helpful review of major theories of anxiety, categorizing them along three domains: cognitive models, experiential/emotional models, and an integrated model. Here, we provide one sample from each of these categories. A prominent cognitive perspective, the avoidance model of worry and GAD, posits that worry may function as a maladaptive approach to problem-solving, yielding unsuccessful management of a perceived threat; moreover, worry may yield avoidance of important emotional experiences and, therefore, becomes reinforced. An example experiential theory can be seen in the metacognitive model of GAD. To fully grasp this perspective, it is necessary to first understand the construct of metacognition. From a psychoeducational purview, a simple way to define *metacognition* is "thinking about thinking" or "thinking about our thoughts." Applied to GAD, there are two types of thinking about worry. Type 1 is healthy, positive, and adaptive (e.g., worry can function as coping). Type 2 is characteristic of those with GAD, reflecting failed attempts at cognitive coping with worry such as avoiding anxiety, provoking triggers, or suppressing thoughts. Finally, an integrated model can be seen in the acceptance-based model of GAD. This view posits that, in response to a threatening cue, a chain reaction occurs involving negative internal experiences, an unhealthy relationship with those experiences, experiential avoidance (i.e., worry, fear), and ultimately unhealthy behaviors. A feedback loop exists in which heightened distress re-energizes the initial negative internal states. The reader is referred to Behar and colleagues (2009) for a detailed review regarding the empirical support and treatment implications of these and other theories of GAD.

Posttraumatic Stress Disorder

Posttraumatic stress disorder (PTSD) is likely the best-known and most investigated disorder within the broader domain of trauma- and stress-related disorders. All mental health disorders in this cluster share in common exposure to a traumatic or stressful event. However, it is critical for the reader to understand that what qualifies as a traumatic/stressful event is both subjective and varied. In other words: (i) the traumatic nature of an event is somewhat in the eye of the beholder and (ii) traumatic events may be personal injuries/events or those that have been witnessed (e.g., witnessing a car accident.) Some witnesses to such an event would likely be able to move on with their day with little disruption. Others, on the other hand, may experience seeing such an event as stressful to the point of suffering symptoms causing subjective distress and functional impairment. Finally, a recent development in thinking regarding PTSD is that the diagnostic features vary by age, especially with respect to younger children. These dissimilarities can be observed in the DSM-5 criteria. For a diagnosis of PTSD to be rendered for a person 6 years of age or older, there must have been exposure to actual or threatened death, serious injury, or sexual violence, as well as the presence of intrusion symptoms (e.g., bad memories, nightmares), avoidance symptoms, negative changes in thoughts and mood, and notable changes in arousal and reactivity related to the trauma. In addition, these symptoms must be present for more than 1 month. PTSD in those 6 years of age or older can be qualified by the following specifiers: (i) with dissociative symptoms, derealization, or depersonalization or (ii) with delayed expression. The diagnostic criteria for a person 6 years of age or younger are comparable in type but differ in terms of their severity and ultimate manifestations. Nevertheless, the same specifiers apply to PTSD across age groups.

The theoretical understanding of PTSD varies widely and could be the subject of its own chapter or book. For the sake of our discussion, a review by Brewin & Holmes (2003) provides a useful summary. The authors highlight three valuable conceptual frameworks worth attending to: (i) emotional processing theory, (ii) dual representation theory, and (iii) cognitive theory. Up front, we should note that these are only three of a bevy of perspectives, and the reader is referred to Brewin & Holmes' (2003) historical overview. Emotional processing theory is an updated framework of earlier network theory. Key tenets of this perspective include: (i) pretrauma self-concepts that one is highly competent and that the world is safe are severely compromised by a traumatic event, yielding PTSD and negative cognitions; (ii) negative appraisals of events can contribute to severe, chronic PTSD; and (iii) an array of mechanisms within exposure therapies can help counter negative appraisals of the self and world. Grounded in information processing, dual representation theory holds that traumatic memories are truly distinct from regular memories. Reconciling traumatic memories, therefore, involves retraining one to frame traumatic memories as normal experiential narratives. A fundamental assumption of this perspective, then, is that multiple parallel information processing systems exist, one of which is centrally involved in the associative processing of traumatic events. PTSD is thought to operate on both systems, yet differing symptoms are pertinent to each information processing stream. Finally, an updated cognitive theory of PTSD posits that the disorder is rooted in appraisal of severe threat to the self, future, or safety. A range of negative appraisals or thinking styles (e.g., overgeneralization) exacerbate symptom presentation; these negative appraisals may concern safety/danger, one's own actions, or life details. Moreover, mental states such as defeat or helplessness are thought to contribute to the course of PTSD.

Intermittent Explosive Disorder

Intermittent explosive disorder falls under a broader category of disruptive, impulse-control, and conduct disorders. This class of disorders shares in common externally driven aggression involving violation of the rights of others (e.g., interpersonal harm, property damage). Intermittent explosive disorder is specifically defined by poor regulation of emotion, leading to externalizing aggression. This disorder only applies to individuals age 6 or older. A diagnosis of intermittent explosive disorder requires the presence of recurrent behavioral outbursts reflecting a lack of control of aggressive impulses as evidenced by either verbal or physical aggression, including damage to property or injury to animals. The aggressiveness must be out of proportion to the provocation or related stressors, and such is not premeditated or committed to achieve some tangible objective.

Contemporary views of this psychological disorder are not atheoretical per se; however, compared to the dense theoretical literatures for disorders like depression and PTSD, the scope for intermittent explosive disorder is rather narrow. Two recent bodies of clinical psychological science literature may provide the best conceptual grounding for the primary constructs involved in intermittent explosive disorder: social–emotional cognition (e.g., Coccaro, Solis, Fanning, & Lee, 2015; Coccaro, Fanning, Keedy, & Lee, 2016) and negative urgency/emotional control (e.g., Ahmed, Green, McCloskey, & Berman, 2010; Puhalla et al., 2016). Regarding thinking styles, empirical evidence suggests that intermittent explosive–type aggression is associated with hostile cognitive styles (e.g., aggressive automatic thinking; Coccaro et al., 2015) as well as negative emotional response styles and hostile attributions of others' acts (Coccaro et al., 2016). Paralleling the role of emotion-based cognitive styles are recent data demonstrating that a characteristic called "negative urgency" (i.e., negative emotional drive) is a driving force of intermittent explosive–style aggression (Puhalla et al., 2015). The prominent role of negatively charged emotional impulsivity in intermittent explosive disorder is further supported by epidemiological evidence confirming the unique nature of impulsive aggression among those with this disorder (Ahmed et al., 2010). Collectively, pathways to intermittent explosive disorder may be best conceptualized as a combination of poor emotional control and angry views of one's social world leading to aggression toward other persons and their property.

Conduct Disorder

Conduct disorder also falls under the disruptive, impulse-control, and conduct disorders umbrella. However, it is very clearly defined by aggressive behaviors that "violate the rights of others or that violate major societal norms" (American Psychiatric Association, 2013, p. 460). As such, conduct disorder is often linked in the long term to criminality and/or development of antisocial personality disorder. A formal diagnosis of conduct disorder requires a chronic pattern of problematic behavior, whereby the rights of others or societal norms and rules are violated, including such behaviors as bullying, intimidating, physically fighting or harming other people or animals, stealing from or robbing others, forced sex, destruction of property, lying, violating curfews, running away, and/or truancy from school. Age at onset is a critical specifier for this disorder. As such, conduct disorder can be subtyped as childhood-onset type (prior to age 10), adolescent-onset type (after age 10), or unspecified onset (insufficient information to determine onset). Severity can be labeled as mild, moderate, or severe. Reflecting the variety of presentations of this disorder, additional specifiers include limited prosocial emotions, falling under four possible sublabels: lack of remorse or guilt, callousness or lack of empathy, unconcerned about performance, or shallow or deficient affect.

Krol, Morton, & De Bruyn (2004) reviewed several psychological and criminological theories of conduct disorder. Prior to summarizing their major tenets, it is worth noting that the authors of the review maintain, with empirical support, that no single theory can fully explicate the variety of conduct disorder presentations; therefore, multilevel causal thinking is necessary to fully capture the causal essence of this disorder. Pertinent major frameworks of conduct disorder include, but are not limited to, the violence inhibition mechanism (VIM) model, the social information processing model of aggression, the coercive parenting model, and the theory of life-course antisocial behavior. Although acknowledging biologically based predispositions for aggression, the key notion with the VIM model is that individuals may possess a cognitive mechanism by which they cease aggression when they recognize withdrawal or submission cues by the target. The VIM model holds that this cognitive ability is likely stunted in those with conduct disorder and related conditions. A social information processing perspective suggests that conduct-disordered behavior may be a function of hostile cognitive styles (e.g., attributions) differentially predisposing such persons to both reactive and instrumental aggression. A coercive parenting approach to understanding this disorder presupposes that a child learns to exert control over parents through repeated instrumental aggression. Such mechanisms become automatic, yielding long-standing patterns of aggressive and antisocial behavior. Finally, a criminological perspective called life-course persistent antisocial behavior suggests the conduct and associated disorders emanate from two paths: the interaction between pathways of neurodevelopmental deficits (e.g., brain abnormality) and unhealthy interactions with parents. Readers should remember that these are simplified summaries of each theory and are therefore referred to Krol and colleagues (2004) for further elaboration.

Substance Use Disorders

Substance use disorders comprise a sole class of disorders covering a range of drug types, along specific manifestations of disorder. Overall, this type of disorder is signified by behavioral and other symptoms originating from excess substance use and occurring in the face of psychosocial and other problems (caused by the substance use). There is also a heavy biological component to substance use disorders. For instance, all subtypes are thought to (over)activate the brain reward system, and physiological symptoms for many disorders persist after cessation of use. Likewise, low self-control or high impulsivity, as a biologically grounded trait, is a key risk factor for this group of disorders. The 10 substances covered with the DSM-5 definition of substance use disorders are: alcohol, caffeine, cannabis, hallucinogens (i.e., phencyclidine, other hallucinogens), inhalants, opioids, sedatives/hypnotics/anxiolytics, stimulants, tobacco, and other. Two broad classes of substance disorders can be diagnosed: use and induced disorders. Substance-induced pathologies include intoxication, withdrawal, and other substance/medication-induced mental disorders. Diagnostic criteria for substance use disorders generally cover four domains: impaired control (e.g., taking the substance in larger amounts for the same effect), social impairment (e.g., failure to fulfill home, work, or school obligations), risky use (e.g., recurrent use in spite of knowing it worsens physical and mental health problems), and pharmacological impairment (e.g., increased tolerance). Severity can be qualified as mild, moderate, or severe; moreover, specifiers include in partial remission, in sustained remission, on maintenance therapy, and in a controlled environment.

Here, we provide further detail concerning alcohol use disorders as an exemplar. The reader is referred to the DSM-5 for insight on how diagnostic criteria and other details vary by substance. The following criteria must apply for the diagnosis of alcohol use disorder: problematic use of alcohol that leads to clinically significant impairments or distress, as evidenced by such symptoms as increased tolerance; inability to decrease or control use; spending notable amounts of time trying to obtain, use, or recover from alcohol; cravings; use that negatively impacts major responsibilities at work, school, or home; continued use despite continued problems; and withdrawal symptoms. This diagnosis is distinguishable from alcohol intoxication, which consists of recent alcohol use that has caused clinically noteworthy and problematic behavioral or psychological changes and symptoms such as slurred speech, unsteady gait or coordination, nystagmus, attention or memory impairments, and/or coma. Highlighting the earlier noted role of physiology and issues surrounding cessation of a substance, alcohol withdrawal is characterized by the stopping of notable and prolonged alcohol use, whereby certain symptoms develop within hours to days, for example, sweating, increased pulse, tremors, insomnia, vomiting, hallucinations, anxiety, and seizures. There is also a final generic subcategory of other alcohol-induced disorders, which are specifically listed under the respective clinical disorder types (e.g., alcohol-induced depressive disorder).

The theoretical exposition on substance use literally warrants an encyclopedic length of coverage. We focus in this book on a few of the prevailing perspectives, highlighting many of the concepts noted in the general overview of defining features of substance use disorders. Otten, Mun, & Dishion (2017) provided a recent review of perhaps the best-known lay understanding of substance use progression: gateway theory. A basic premise of the gateway perspective is that early use, for instance, during adolescence, of more benign substances (e.g. alcohol) activates brain mechanisms creating desire and eventual use of more severe substances (e.g., cocaine). The authors note that evidence for the gateway viewpoint is considerable, especially for younger persons and for substances such as alcohol and tobacco. Otten and colleagues' own work demonstrated prospective evidence of gateway paths from cannabis and tobacco to illicit drugs over an adolescent to young adult transition. Another psychosocial framework for understanding substance use disorders concerns coping skills theories. Carver (1997) provides a representative summary of this idea. Based on prior theories of coping grounded in self-regulation, Carver highlights that coping skills or strategies typically fall into one of two broad categories: (i) active/healthy coping (e.g., problem-solving, seeking social support) or (ii) passive/unhealthy coping (e.g., denial, self-blame). Substance use falls in the latter grouping. Importantly, framing of substance use as a maladaptive coping strategy has witnessed a wealth of empirical support as well, suggesting that this mode of understanding substance is valid and clinically useful.

Theoretical views concerning substance use disorders also commonly address biologically based explanations. For instance, a personality-based explication of substance use relies on the trait of self-control or impulsivity. Citing young adult alcohol use/binge drinking rates among other data, Arnett (2000, 2016) frames emerging adulthood (i.e., ages 18–25) as a time of low "volitional control" (i.e., low self-control). One of the most common manifestations of this high trait impulsivity, due in large part to lack of full prefrontal cortex and other brain development, is substance use in often large quantities. Recall too that the DSM-5 perspective of substance use disorders is founded on the idea of activation of brain reward systems. Reflecting that key idea is the theoretical premise of reward sensitivity or incentive sensitization. Arulkadacham et al. (2017) provide an example of incentive sensitization in the context of alcohol and caffeine usage. This model holds that two critical drivers of substance use are liking and wanting and that each of the two functions from a different neurological underpinning. Over time, it is thought that biological systems involved in wanting become rewired, yielding enhanced sensitization. The authors report data in support of this theory for alcohol, but not caffeine, use.

Personality Disorders

Personality disorders comprise a rather unique type of mental disorders, often rather distinct from clinical syndromes. The DSM-5 provides the following definition of a personality disorder: "an enduring pattern of inner experience and behavior that deviates markedly from the expectations of the individual's culture, is pervasive and inflexible, has an onset in adolescence or early adulthood, is stable over time, and leads to distress or impairment" (American Psychiatric Association, 2013, p. 645). This definition is indeed complicated. Let us break it down a little further. First, personality implies traits, or biologically based characteristics that yield stable reaction patterns across situations. An easy, "common," or "normal" (read everyday trait) characteristic we all have some conception of is extraversion. A person high on this trait may be talkative, seek social situations, enjoy social engagement, be assertive, and so forth. Another way to think about personality disorders is that they represent extremes of personality traits (as reflected by expressed thoughts, feelings, and behavior) that are largely unchanging and tend to cause problems, be they social, academic, romantic, or otherwise. Whereas most disorders we have covered thus far are based in emotions or behaviors that are largely malleable, personality disorders tend to be resistant to change and therefore resistant to psychotherapy. In other words, treatments for personality disorders often concern *managing* symptoms, not resolving them. And with few exceptions, personality disorders are not typically diagnosed in persons under the age of 18 because personality is still in flexible development in youth and adolescence.

Personality disorders are currently classified under three "clusters," with each represented by a unifying personality style theme. The current cluster classification is:

- Cluster A: "Odd and eccentric"—paranoid, schizoid, and schizotypal personality disorders
- Cluster B: "Dramatic, emotional, and erratic"–antisocial, borderline, histrionic, and narcissistic personality disorders
- Cluster C: "Anxious and fearful"–avoidant, dependent, and obsessive–compulsive personality disorders

This clustering system has come under quite a bit of criticism, including inconsistent empirical validation. Moreover, a dimensional trait-based description exists within the DSM-5 (i.e., alternative DSM-5 model of personality disorders) that we address at the end of this section. Here, we focus on a review of antisocial and borderline personality disorders because they arguably (i) are the subject of the most research in the professional literature and (ii) contain symptoms and correlates most closely associated with critical issues in this book (e.g., impulsivity, anger, violence, and suicide proneness). We will review diagnostic criteria for both disorders first, followed by discussion of some recent conceptual thought explicating both disorders.

Per the DSM-5, antisocial personality disorder is characterized by a pattern of disregard and violation of the rights of others since age 15, including such behaviors as failure to conform to societal norms and rules, lying, impulsivity, irritability and aggressiveness, irresponsibility, and lack of remorse. The person must be at least 18 years old, and there must have been evidence of the onset of conduct disorder before age 15. A diagnosis of borderline personality disorder is characterized by a pattern of unstable relationships, self-image, and affect. These symptoms are evidenced across contexts and include such manifestations as significant efforts to avoid abandonment, alternating idealization and devaluation in relationships, poor self-image, potentially self-damaging impulsivity, suicidal or self-mutilating behavior, chronic feelings of emptiness, anger problems, and dissociation.

Meloy & Yakeley (2014) provided a useful summary of some of the contributing factors to antisocial personality disorder in their larger summary of assessment and treatment considerations. One perspective they provide from the literature is that development of an antisocial personality may be influenced by childhood events and personality traits. Specifically, one subtype tends to possess high levels of anxiety, perhaps due to early childhood trauma. On the other hand, a second subtype displays traits indicative of psychopathic characteristics displayed as early as childhood (e.g., callousness, low remorse, low anxiety). Another purview these authors summarize is based on narcissism; angry, narcissistic behavior may function as a defense against emotional injury, covering up for early life trauma or feelings of inadequacy. Some instances of narcissistic aggression, however, are also thought to be authentic, unrelenting, and apart from serving as a defense. The reader is referred to this text for further psychoanalytically based explanation of antisocial personality disorder as well. One may be unsurprised to learn that cognitive theory also exists contextualizing antisocial personality disorder. Beck, Freeman, & Davis (2004) describe the cognitive underpinnings of one with antisocial personality disorder. For instance, such individuals tend to view the world through a self-focused, or perhaps better labeled "selfish," lens. As such, antisocial behaviors are easily justified, manifesting as self-serving appraisals or attributions of events and persons. Such cognitive styles fit Beck's general notion of thinking errors or distortions, in this case assuming forms such as justification (i.e., rationalizing behavior via self-serving explanations), personal infallibility (i.e., assuming one is always correct), or the impotence of others (i.e., other people's perspective is irrelevant), among others.

The most prominent theory of borderline personality disorder coincides with a leading type of psychotherapy: dialectical behavior therapy (DBT; discussed in more depth in Chapter 7 of this book). The collective works of the prominent scholar and clinician Marsha Linehan (e.g., Koerner & Linehan, 2007; Lieb et al., 2004) summarize many of the main conceptual tenets of DBT and, by proxy, borderline personality disorder (note: DBT was originally developed as a borderline-specific treatment toward the goal of regulating the erratic and often binary cognitive, emotional, and behavioral symptoms of the disorder). Causal factors include considerable evidence of genetic contributions; moreover, unresolved childhood trauma such as abuse or neglect is thought to influence the development of borderline characteristics such as distrust and erratic affect. A core theme in the developing person with borderline personality concerns instability; for instance, over time persons with borderline personality manifest unpredictable mood shifts, unstable relationships, and other patterns of instability. Such instability is thought to be rooted in deficits or underdeveloped abilities to regulate emotions, cope with stress or crises, assert and communicate needs, and manage ruminative or obsessive thinking. In their review of cognitive perspectives on borderline personality disorder, Beck et al. (2004) highlight a common characteristic of the disorder: splitting. Based on a research review, they also identify the following contributing factors to the development of borderline personality disorder: disorganized attachment styles; childhood sexual, physical, and emotional abuse; and meaning ascribed to childhood trauma experiences (e.g., abandonment, self-blaming). Further cognitive patterns or styles hypothesized to contribute to the onset or maintenance of borderline personality include, but are not limited to:

- Common thinking patterns regarding topics like rejection, abandonment, and unlovability
- Core beliefs surrounding a dangerous world, personal powerlessness, and low self-worth
- Self- and other schemas characterized by failed protection by adults, abused child, and angry child
- Frequent presence of dichotomous thinking (e.g., seeing people or the world as all good or bad)

In addition to acknowledging the legitimacy of Linehan's view of this disorder, Beck and colleagues proffer their cognitive take. In addition to the schemas and dichotomous thinking, a number of cognitive errors or biases are said to perpetuate borderline symptoms. In particular, the manner in which a child makes meaning of trauma (e.g., abuse, neglect) influences the development of negative core thinking styles, yielding lifelong patterns such as themes of powerlessness and low self-worth.

As summarized in the DSM-5 alternative model for personality disorders, another prevailing view of this type of disorder concerns pathological or extreme levels of personality traits and functioning. This view is a stark departure from the checklist-style diagnostic criteria of thoughts, feelings, and behaviors and is grounded in a considerable empirical literature investigating dimensional personality trait theories (e.g., the five-factor model; McCrae & Costa, 2003). A dense personality trait literature has reported extreme high and low levels of traits associated with varying personality disorder diagnoses. Importantly, not all personality disorders fit within this alternative model. However, borderline and antisocial subtypes do. Nevertheless, the relative strengths and weaknesses of the ways of diagnosing personality disorders have been and remain the subject of contentious debate. Suffice it to say that, moving forward, personality-based understandings of antisocial and border-line personality disorders will become increasingly salient, especially for the clinical and legal matters covered in this book.

Conclusions

In reviewing definitions of diagnosable mental health disorders, as well as prominent conditions and theories, we can extract the following overarching themes.

Variation from the norm: Even dating back to Kraepelin's work, mental disorders have been understood, in part, through the lens of variation from social or cultural norms. Moreover, defining features of the DSM-5 perspective include this feature, as well as necessary subjective distress or functional impairment.

Appreciation for nuance: Details such as DSM-5 specifiers and the range of potential symptoms point to the need for viewing mental disorders through a flexible lens. For instance, one person's GAD may look different from another's. Even within broad classes of disorders, the sheer array of subtypes is astounding. Schizophrenia provides an apt exemplar as the range of observable defining features can run from positive psychotic symptoms (e.g., hallucinations, delusions) to more rigid negative symptoms (e.g., catatonia or absence of speech). To fully appreciate mental disorders, it is necessary to move beyond stigmatized stereotypes of specific disorders and take a more malleable view.

Common symptom clusters: While we need to appreciate nuance, we can also identify common themes in symptoms. At the simplest level, disordered thoughts, feelings, and/or behaviors are easily identified. Moreover, the same symptomatic concern may be potentially indicative of a multitude of concerns. A fitting example of this idea can be seen in sleep disturbance, which not only is characteristic of many disorders covered in this chapter (i.e., bipolar disorder, GAD, PTSD) but is also the subject of its own class of disorders (i.e., sleep–wake disorders). Common symptom clusters can be helpful in practice (e.g., linking internalizing pathologies, differential diagnosis) and in research. Moving forward, we can expect more emphasis to be placed on trans-diagnostic indicators of pathology.

The value of biopsychosocial perspectives: We covered just a small snippet of the endless number of theories underlying psychopathology. Such theories often address one or more aspects of a biopsychosocial framework. Linehan's purview of borderline personality, for instance, acknowledges genetic and trait influences, identifies social learning processes, and addresses cognitive concerns such as dichotomous thinking. In today's clinical-research view of mental disorders (and mental health for that matter), it is becoming increasingly critical to operate from this comprehensive perspective to fully appreciate each individual presentation of a mental health case. As such, when learning about the conceptual explanations of a disorder, we strongly encourage anybody to seek more than one perspective.

4

Violence

In this chapter, we address four areas particularly relevant to understanding violence[1] in the context of firearms. First, we provide a general overview of violence, setting forth commonly recognized definitions and types of violence, psychological components and theories of violence, and psychiatric disorders most closely associated with violence. Second, we address firearm-related violence and crime with respect to national- and state-based statistics as well as the theories and empirical research in this domain. Third, we discuss high-profile shootings; namely, we present an overview of some of the more infamous mass shootings in the modern-day United States, followed by the theories and research relevant to mass shootings, including school shootings. Lastly, we address the relationship between mental illness and firearm-related violence.

Overview of Violence

Defining Violence

As with all constructs, we must define the term *violence* before we begin to address it; namely, we must *operationally* define it. In other words, we must turn the abstract concept of violence into a concrete variable that we can measure. This is necessary in order to conduct research on violence but also to facilitate communication among professionals and members of the community. Put differently, we need to make sure we are all referring to the same thing when we are discussing "violence." However, constructs in social science, such as violence, are complicated to operationally define and measure. This is one of the reasons that the field of medicine has the appearance of a hard science, whereas social science—including the mental health field—may seem like a pseudoscience to some. After all, medical terms such as *blood pressure* are also constructs that once needed to be identified, named, and operationally defined.[2]

The second important step when working with constructs such as violence is to identify consensus among professionals with respect to how they are operationally defined and measured. As is clear in the example above, the concept of blood pressure and its measurement did not gain acceptance among medical professionals for nearly two centuries. However, we would expect nothing other than to have a cuff placed around our arm to measure our blood pressure during a medical evaluation. Such is true regardless of the situation we are in—be it in a doctor's office in New York City or in an ambulance in Milwaukee. Frankly, many medical procedures appear to be more scientific than those in psychology because they have received consensus and not necessarily as a result of being more accurate or reliable. In fact, psychological test validity has been found to be strong and compelling, overall, and comparable to that of medical tests (Meyer et al., 2001). This is not the public perception, though—again, largely because of the lack of consensus among mental health professionals. Whereas medical doctors essentially measure blood pressure, weight, and other vital signs in only one way at this point, an evaluating psychologist in New York City may administer the Rorschach inkblot test to assess an examinee's personality functioning, whereas one in Milwaukee may use a version of the Minnesota Multiphasic Personality Inventory. This is not a regional issue, however, as it is not uncommon to find psychologists within the same office, agency, or institution using different tests to measure the same construct. Research on psychological test usage has shown that practitioners use a range of measures when conducting various types of clinical, neuropsychological, and forensic evaluations (Archer, Buffington-Vollum, Stredny, & Handel, 2006; Camara, Nathan, & Puente, 2000). Moreover, test publishing companies, such as Pearson, Psychological Assessment Resources, and Multi-Health Systems, offer an extensive array of tests for psychological evaluators across a number of domains (Pearson Education, 2017; Psychological Assessment Resources, 2017; Multi-Health Systems, n.d.). There are literally hundreds, perhaps thousands, of psychological tests available—particularly if we include measures published in the professional literature but not commercially available. For instance, there are literally dozens of tests available to measure such constructs as depression, anxiety, anger, intelligence, attention, legal competencies, and even the feigning of psychological symptoms.

To return to the original point, the reader will note that we present statistics and terms throughout this book from a wide range of sources. However, it is important to highlight the fact that we cannot assume that they actually refer to the same concepts even when a seemingly common term such as *violence* is used. Perhaps the most notable example is the annual oft-cited statistical figures related to firearm violence. For instance, reports indicate that, in 2012, there were 32,288 deaths from "firearm violence" in the United States. However, what is typically omitted from that statistic is that 20,666 of those deaths were suicides, which is particularly troubling given that there are very distinct differences and noteworthy considerations associated with firearm-involved suicide compared to homicide. For example, as Wintemute (2015b) indicated, suicide is the most common type of fatal firearm violence and is increasing, whereas homicide rates are decreasing. Moreover, homicide risk is strongly concentrated among black males across age groups, and these rates have remained stable, whereas suicide risk is highest among white males in early adolescence, and these rates have increased. These are just a few examples of the important nuances and differences that exist between firearm-involved suicide and violence. The oft-cited, misrepresented "total gun deaths" statistic further highlights the root of problems in miscommunication and misunderstanding that arise when terms are conflated or defined in otherwise unconventional ways. An additional example is the commonly used term *mass shooting*, which also lacks a consensus definition (Ingraham, 2015). In fact, when the FBI released its study on *active shooters* from 2000 to 2013 (Blair & Schweit, 2014), it was criticized by a number of prominent criminology scholars because of the definitions it employed (Sanburn, 2014). Namely, the FBI's report on active shooters does not necessarily mean that anyone was killed or even injured in such incidents, and the majority of incidents would not meet the federal definition of *mass killing* (i.e., three or more deaths). According to the report, 40% would have met the definition, which, incidentally, was previously defined as at least *four* deaths prior to President Obama's 2013 mandated change in the federal definition (Investigative Assistance for Violent Crimes Act of 2012, 2013).[3] Moreover, the FBI reported 1,043 *casualties* as a result of the 160 shootings during that time period. However, it combined injuries *and* deaths to constitute casualties, which is very misleading, particularly given that the majority of the 1,043 were injuries and not deaths. An even more concerning example is the way in which the term *school shooting* is used by some groups (e.g., see Everytown's use described in Chapter 9, main finding 6).

While every shooting is problematic, we must come to a consensus on how these terms are operationally defined to ensure accurate communication and that the appropriate responses are set forth. Until then, we will continue to conflate terms, such as *active shooter, mass killing, mass shooting*, and the like. Moreover, changing the definitions of certain terms can artificially (and arbitrarily) reflect changes and patterns that may not in actuality exist. Another example is when the Obama administration was subject to significant scrutiny in the wake of the 2009 Fort Hood shooting, when US Army Major Nidal Hasan killed over a dozen people and injured 30 more. The administration characterized the event as an act of *workplace violence* rather than an act of terrorism despite Hasan's ties to and ongoing communication with Anwar al-Awlaki, a senior recruiter for al-Qaeda, in addition to other factors associated with terrorism (Dem Blames, 2013; Berkowitz, 2013; Basu, 2013). President Obama and his administration continue to be criticized for an unwillingness to recognize certain acts of terrorism or to use the term in conjunction with Islam. The White House was reported to have censored a video of French president François Hollande speaking at an event on terrorism with Obama, such that Hollande's words "Islamist terrorism" were muted, which the White House attributed to a "technical" error in the audio recording (Howell, 2016). President Obama is certainly not the only public official who has received such scrutiny. During a press conference in early January 2016 in response to the shooting of one of his city's police officers, Philadelphia mayor Jim Kenney stated, "In no way shape or form does anyone in this room believe that Islam or the teaching of Islam has anything to do with what you've seen on the screen," despite the fact that the shooter himself confessed that he shot the officer "in the name of Islam" (Mayor Kenney, 2016; Gunman shoots Philadelphia police officer, 2016). This type of misclassification of events is concerning given that there has been an increase in lethal violence directed at law enforcement officers in recent years (Craun, Detar, & Bierie, 2013). Nevertheless, these examples illustrate the issues that arise when trying to define or categorize acts of violence, which in turn affects statistics and, therefore, interventions and prevention efforts that follow. Undoubtedly, the implications greatly differ, from acts of workplace violence or a random shooting of an officer to those of terrorism.

In addition, broad-based definitions do not reflect details of incidents, which are very relevant to ascertain when drawing implications for practice and policy. Examples include, but are certainly not limited to: How and why did the incident unfold? Which situational and personal characteristics were present? What was the likely motivation of the shooting? Were there opportunities for prevention? How did the incident resolve or otherwise end? Which type of firearm was used? How was it acquired, and was it done legally? How could the incident have been prevented?

In response to this need, various psychological test developers, scholars, and organizations have set forth their operational definitions of violence. For example, two commonly used measures designed to assess violence risk are the Historical-Clinical-Risk Management-20, Version 3 (HCR-20[v3]; Douglas, Hart, Webster, & Belfrage, 2013), and the Violence Risk Appraisal Guide (VRAG; Quinsey, Harris, Rice, & Cormier, 2006). The HCR-20[v3] definition of violence is: "Any actual, attempted or threatened harm to a person or persons (Douglas et al., 2013, p. 159).

The VRAG, which predicts violent recidivism, separates criminal conduct into violent and non-violent offenses, whereby examples of violent offenses are: homicide, attempted murder, aggravated assault, assault with a weapon, sexual assault, armed robbery, and gross indecency. Alternatively, non-violent offenses include robbery, arson, threatening with a weapon, fraud, impaired driving, and indecent exposure. Krause (2009) noted that the most common ways in which violence is categorized are based on the meaning and purpose of the act, the scope of the perpetrators, and the nature of the act itself. With respect to the meaning and purpose of the violent act, Krause outlines four distinctions: politically motivated, economically motivated, socially conditioned, and interpersonal.

Krug, Mercy, Dahlberg, & Zwi (2002) set forth the World Health Organization's (WHO's) definition: "The intentional use of physical force or power, threatened or actual, against oneself, another person, or against a group or community, that either results in or has a high likelihood of resulting in injury, death, psychological harm, maldevelopment or deprivation." Such includes all types of violence via commission or omission and regardless of the outcome (i.e., death, injury, or otherwise). In this context, violence is delineated into three main areas: self-inflicted, interpersonal, and collective. As Krug and colleagues noted, "Violence cannot be attributed to a single factor. Its causes are complex and occur at different levels" (p. 1085). Using the WHO model, they outlined four such levels: biological and personal factors, close relationships, community context, and broad societal factors.

Lee (2015) contended that there is little consensus regarding how to properly define and measure the concept of violence across professional disciplines, and she suggested a new definition: "The intentional reduction of life or thriving of life in human being(s) by human being(s), through physical, structural, or other means of force, that either results in or has a high likelihood of resulting in deprivation, maldevelopment, psychological harm, injury, death, or extinction of the species" (p. 202). In her proposed definition, the term *power* is avoided and accidents are not included, such that the term *threatened* is removed. Moreover, Lee's definition seeks to characterize violence as a public health concern, thereby shifting the emphasis from criminology, law, and politics to public health, preventive medicine, and mental health. She stresses the importance of conceptualizing violence as a public health issue in this regard. She further contends that a definition of violence should be flexible and reflective of the emerging research, and she illustrates such by highlighting, for example, that we have come to realize the deleterious effects of rejection and neglect. Lee concludes:

> Violence is a human phenomenon that seems so abnormal, so bizarre, and so outside the realm of most behavior, to bring about the death of the self and others of one's kind, that we cannot satisfy ourselves with superficial explanations. It seems not only one of the most important subjects of study, on which hinges our very survival as a species, but one of the greatest intellectual challenges of our time. (p. 203)

In partial contrast to Lee's contention that violence should be broadly defined and flexible, Waddington, Badger, & Bull (2005) have suggested that including the "enormously broad spectrum" of what constitutes violence, threats, and intimidation in the definition could potentially cause more problems. As they articulated, "both analytically and normatively/politically, there are considerable drawbacks associated with such an inclusive definition that becomes so broad that almost any situation that any person finds disagreeable can be described as a form of 'violence'" (p. 158). Waddington and colleagues noted that doing so would lend itself to analysts referring to quite different events within the same umbrella term of *violence*. Therefore, they propose a set of specifiers to define violence more accurately, which include, but are not limited to, the relationship between parties, conflictual entry (e.g., police entering an already violent scenario), the duration and intensity of the act as well as the target, and the victim's vulnerability.

It is likely that most people associate the term *violence* with acts of physical harm. However, at its most foundational level, violence includes physical, sexual, and verbal acts. We address each in the following section (*Types of Violence*), in addition to highlighting particular considerations in the context of youth violence.[4]

Types of Violence

Physical

Because violence is a complex phenomenon, it is difficult to provide a precise and inclusive definition of physical violence. According to the authors of the *World Report on Violence and Health* (Krug et al., 2002), the definition of *violence* is more a judgment than an exact science. This is particularly true of physical violence as a result of the constant evolution of social and cultural norms and values, in addition to the changing consensus of what constitutes acceptable behaviors or harm. As an example, although it may have been previously acceptable for teachers to strike a child with a foreign object in school as part of the institution's regular punishment protocol, many parts of the country, even the world, would now consider this sort of physical contact to be unlawful (Krug et al., 2002). Despite the lack of consensus regarding what might characterize physical violence, it should be noted that worldwide we experience 1.6 million deaths per year from human violence (First ever global report, 2002). Additionally, this number does not include many million more instances in which people suffer from nonfatal injuries, non-injury-related health consequences, and less visible forms of related trauma, such as psychological and social trauma (Lee, 2015). What is more is that the reverberating effects of physical violence extend through generations of families, communities, economies, and society at large (Lee, 2015). According to the WHO's 2014 *Global Status Report on Violence Prevention*, fatal physical violence is disproportionately experienced by young males. For women who die by violence, their male partners are typically responsible for the act. Finally, although the mechanism of fatal injury differs significantly by region, one in two homicides throughout the world is committed by use of a firearm (World Health Organization, 2014).

While the definition is not precise or widely agreed upon, a multitude of actions and behaviors are considered physical violence, such as slapping, stabbing, ambushing, assailing, battering, choking, gagging, hitting, grabbing, kicking, punching, pushing, and assaulting. Not surprisingly, there are many different types of physical violence, and they can occur simultaneously, rendering them not mutually exclusive (Rutherford, Zwi, Grove, & Butchart,

2007). Another way of conceptualizing violence is through the different forms it takes. Forms of violence are sometimes grouped together by perpetrator and/or intended victim. Specifically, physical violence can be categorized as follows: self-directed violence, interpersonal violence, and collective violence. Self-directed violence broadly includes suicidal actions (both ending in successful completion of suicide and nonfatal suicide attempts) and self-harm (Rutherford et al., 2007). Interpersonal violence occurs between family members, intimate partners, acquaintances, or strangers and is not specifically intended to further the aims of any group or cause (Waters, Hyder, & Rajkotia, 2005). Collective violence is defined by Zwi, Garfield, & Loretti (2002) as "instrumental use of violence by people who identify themselves as members of a group . . . against another group or set of individuals, in order to achieve political, economic or social objectives." Acts included in the definition of collective violence include war, terrorism, organized violent crime, and violence perpetrated by states (e.g., genocide, torture; Rutherford et al., 2007). Of note, other categories of violence, including sexual and verbal violence, can also be considered acts of collective violence.

Sexual

According to the Centers for Disease Control and Prevention (CDC), sexual violence is defined as "sexual activity when consent is not obtained or not given freely" (Centers for Disease Control and Prevention, 2017, para. 1). Results of a nationally representative survey conducted by the CDC indicate that 1 in 5 women and 1 in 71 men report experiencing rape at some point in their lives. Additionally, in the year leading up to the survey, 1 in 20 women and men reported experiencing sexual violence in some other way (e.g., being made to penetrate someone else, sexual coercion, unwanted sexual contact, or non-contact unwanted sexual experiences; Centers for Disease Control and Prevention, 2012).

Because of the scale of sexual violence perpetrated in this country, as well as the effects this type of violence has on victims, individuals who sexually offend are taken very seriously by the criminal justice and mental health systems in the United States. Sex offenders, both youth and adults, are psychologically assessed for various reasons, pre- and post-adjudication. Yet, despite a widely perpetuated belief that sex offenders are likely to reoffend (i.e., recidivate) at some point in the future (Hanson, 2003) and are incapable of change (Wevodau, Cramer, Gemberling, & Clark, 2016), the best empirical evidence to date suggests that only a small minority of sex offenders recidivate (Mercado et al., 2011). Nevertheless, after being convicted of a sexual offense but prior to the sentencing process, many jurisdictions require a psychological evaluation of sexual offenders to determine their risk of reoffending. Depending on the determined risk of recidivism, the judge then has several options to consider while deciding on the appropriate sentence for the offender. As an example, in New Jersey, the judge will likely sentence the offender to a comprehensive treatment program (often in a highly secure environment), to a state prison, or to community probation. Further, within the United States, 20 states have enacted sexually violent predator (SVP) civil commitment legislation. Individuals who are thought to pose an elevated risk for recidivism are potentially eligible in these jurisdictions for post-sentence indefinite civil commitment (Mercado et al., 2011). In order to be eligible for SVP commitment, offenders typically must meet the following criteria: they must have a mental abnormality, have a history of sexual offending, and exhibit evidence of a volitional impairment and there must be a connection between the abnormality and the individual's risk so that he or she is likely to reoffend (Miller, Amenta, & Conroy, 2005). According to Gookin (2007), only an estimated 10% of individuals who have been committed as SVPs have been released or discharged. The literature is relatively vast on these topics; therefore, for more information on the complex issues associated with sexual violence, as well as sex offender risk, treatment, and related laws, the interested reader can see Breiner & Witt (2017); DeMatteo, Murphy, Galloway, & Krauss (2015); Mercado et al. (2011); Pirelli (2016); and Prentky, Barbaree, & Janus (2015).

Verbal

Although verbal acts of violence may not initially come to mind, one can readily think of threats that constitute criminal offenses, such as terroristic threats. Terroristic threats, which became unlawful acts after the terroristic activity the United States experienced on September 11, 2001, are a relatively new type of criminal offense that exists on both the state and federal levels. Although the exact definition varies depending on the jurisdiction, a terroristic threat involves the threat to commit a violent crime in an effort to terrorize another or cause public panic (Shoener, 2016). Verbal acts of violence, including threats and verbal abuse, also often lay the foundation for such court-imposed restrictions as restraining and no-contact orders, which are typically seen in cases involving domestic violence and intimate partner violence (covered in Chapter 5). Nevertheless, there are additional forms of verbal violence, for example, acts of bullying, which often have a verbal or emotional component, such as taunting, harassing, humiliating, shaming, or ridiculing (Phillips, 2007). Verbal violence of this nature has been shown to lead to a variety of mental health problems, including diminished self-esteem, depression, anxiety, posttraumatic stress disorder, and even suicidal ideation and attempts (Arseneault, Bowes, & Shakoor, 2010). Another form of verbal aggression that has received significant attention in recent years is cyberbullying, which is considered to be serious, intentional, and harmful repetitive and aggressive behavior (Huang & Chou, 2010). In fact, researchers have found that children and adolescents behave more aggressively online than they do in real life (Huang & Chou, 2010). Further, high levels of verbal aggression exist in inpatient hospital wards, where verbal abuse, shouting, threats, angry behavior, and racist comments have been shown to have notable negative consequences for staff members and other patients (Stewart & Bowers, 2013). These are just a few examples in a long list of forms of verbal violence experienced by people throughout the world.

Youth

It had been a long-standing assumption that adolescents functioned similarly to adults across a wide range of areas. As a result, juveniles were treated in the same manner as adults in the legal and criminal justice systems up until the first juvenile court was enacted in 1899. However, landmark reforms in the juvenile justice system pertaining to juveniles' rights did not occur until the mid- to late 1960s (*Kent v. United States*, 1966; *In re Gault*, 1967), which was ultimately followed by a shift from a more rehabilitative to a responsibility- and accountability-based model in the 1980s and 1990s. Namely, it was at that time that juveniles began getting "waived up" to adult courts and receiving harsher sentences than they had before. The system has since undergone another reformation, however, such that juveniles began to be considered in a different light from adults around the turn of the 21st century—a trend that has remained intact for over two decades. This most recent reform has been primarily in response to the now fairly extensive scientific research literature that has demonstrated the stark differences between juvenile and adult groups across a range of functional areas due to their incomparable neurological makeup. In other words, juveniles and adults simply do not have the same brains, neither anatomically nor functionally, overall. Anatomically speaking, we have come to realize that the human brain does not fully develop until one is in one's 20s and that the frontal lobe is the last part of the brain to develop, which is a particular issue in this context because it is the area of the brain responsible for emotional control and decision-making, as well as other important functions (e.g., emotional expression, planning); and it is, essentially, the basis of our personalities.

Thus, once researchers began applying the neuroscience to legal concepts, it became clear to our judicial system that a unique set of considerations was required when adjudicating juveniles; and as a result, significant changes have been implemented over the years (Steinberg, 2013). Three particularly noteworthy US Supreme Court cases in this context are: *Roper v. Simmons* (2005), *Graham v. Florida* (2010), and *Miller v. Alabama* (2012). In *Roper*, the court held that the death penalty could not be imposed on juveniles under 18 years old—extending the 1988 ruling in *Thompson v. Oklahoma*, which barred capital punishment for those under age 16. In *Graham*, the court found that life without parole sentences for non-homicide juvenile offenders was unconstitutional, which was extended to all offenses, including homicide, shortly thereafter in *Miller*. In all three landmark cases, the primary issue at hand was whether an adolescent's developmental immaturity reduced his or her criminal culpability, such that certain types of punishment would be disproportionate and, therefore, unconstitutional. Undoubtedly, the neuroscience and neuropsychology research literature played a role in the court's decision, particularly such work as the seminal article by Steinberg and Scott (2003). However, in his dissenting opinion, Justice Scalia highlighted the fact that, just 14 years earlier, the court itself sanctioned the death penalty for those at least 16 years old in *Stanford v. Kentucky* (1989). As such, Scalia chastised the court for contradicting its earlier position, for considering constitutional rights to be those that evolve, and for making "legislative judgments." Moreover, Scalia noted that, while the majority court relied upon "scientific and sociological studies," it did not consider if such research was methodologically sound or the potential error contained therein. Therefore, Scalia contended that the court was "picking and choosing" studies that supported its position. For instance, Scalia noted that the majority court integrated the position of the American Psychological Association (APA), "which claims in this case that scientific evidence shows persons under 18 lack the ability to take moral responsibility for their decisions." However, the APA had "previously taken precisely the opposite position" before the court. Scalia pointed out: "In its brief in *Hodgson v. Minnesota*, 497 U.S. 417 (1990), the APA found a 'rich body of research' showing that juveniles are mature enough to decide whether to obtain an abortion without parental involvement." Scalia further noted that, in *Stanford*, the court had previously struck down the counterargument that states prohibit those under age 18 from voting, serving on juries, or even marrying without parental consent because of the different levels of maturity and abilities involved; as Scalia put it: "Whether to obtain an abortion is surely a much more complex decision for a young person than whether to kill an innocent person in cold blood."

In response to Justice Scalia's dissent in *Roper*, Professor Steinberg and his colleagues authored a paper in which they contended that adolescents exhibit adult levels of cognitive ability earlier than emotional and social maturity (Steinberg et al., 2009).

Therefore, they argued that adolescents would possess the required cognitive abilities to make an informed choice about having an abortion but are less mature than adults in the context of mitigating criminal responsibility. Essentially, their position was that the developmental science research has demonstrated that age boundaries related to decision-making must be considered on an independent basis, such that they are contingent upon the particular demands placed on an individual in a given circumstance. Put differently, adolescents—particularly those 16 and older—have been found to possess comparable levels of (cognitively based) competence to their adult counterparts (Grisso et al., 2003); however, they function at a much lower level in areas related to psychosocial or developmental maturity, such as in impulsivity, sensation-seeking, future orientation, and susceptibility to peer pressure (Cuffe & Desai, 2016; Scott, Reppucci, & Woolard, 1995; Steinberg & Cauffman, 1996). Continued research in this area has illustrated that juveniles' developmental immaturity has been associated with problems in a number of legal areas that rely upon their decision-making, including, but certainly not limited to, sex offender registration (Najdowski, Cleary, & Stevenson, 2016), waiver of *Miranda* rights (Roesch, McLachlan, & Viljoen, 2008), and plea bargaining (Daftary-Kapur & Zottoli, 2014).

These foundational concepts related to the adjudication and management of youth offenders are critically important to understand, but it is also imperative to understand why these offenses happen in the first place, particularly those involving firearms. First and foremost, negative childhood experiences, such as abuse and household dysfunction, are risk factors for violence in adolescence (Duke, Pettingell, McMorris, & Borowsky, 2010), as are psychiatric conditions—particularly substance use disorders (Elkington et al., 2015). In order to adequately assess youth for their risk of future violence, a number of violence risk assessment measures have been designed, such as the Early Assessment Risk List (EARL-20B and EARL-21G; Augimeri, Webster, Koegl, & Levene, 2001; Levene et al., 2001), the Structured Assessment of Violence Risk in Youth (Borum, Bartel, & Forth, 2006), the Short-Term Assessment of Risk and Treatability: Adolescent Version (Nicholls et al., 2010), the Youth Level of Service/Case Management Inventory (Hoge & Andrews, 2006), and the Youth Assessment and Screening Instrument (Orbis Partners, 2007). There is considerable overlap in the types of risk factors included in these measures as they tend to include items in three primary areas: environmental (e.g., household, school, community), individual (e.g., attitudes, behavior, psychiatric symptoms), and response to interventions. When evaluating young people, it is particularly important to assess their home life, including their family relationships and dynamics, and any problems their caregivers may be having that would affect them (e.g., legal, substance use, domestic violence). In addition, it is essential to recognize that mental health symptoms are usually manifested quite differently in youth compared to adults. For example, children often experience physical rather than cognitive symptoms in response to stress and anxiety, such as gastroenterological symptoms, rather than rumination or worry about the future. Moreover, depressive symptoms may come across as irritability and agitation rather than the low mood and melancholy often seen in adults. These unique features and considerations related to youth must be recognized, assessed, and taken into account when developing appropriate interventions and violence prevention plans.

Certain high-risk youth, such as those with drug problems and assault histories, are also at higher risk to engage in future firearm-related violence compared to their peers (Carter et al., 2015). Although firearm deaths among youth in the United States have declined since the early 1990s, they remain high in comparison to other developed countries and relative to the historical rates in the United States (Fingerhut & Christoffel, 2002). It is also well established that the highest rate of firearm-related violence is that which is perpetrated by and experienced by minority youth, particularly African American youth, residing in urban environments (Fingerhut & Christoffel, 2002; University study, 2016). Spano and colleagues have demonstrated that gang membership, exposure to violence, violent behavior, and poverty are primary risk factors that are associated with gun carrying (Spano, 2012; Spano & Bolland, 2011; Spano, Pridemore, & Bolland, 2012). They view gun carrying via a cumulative risk model, such that youth ultimately come to it through a progression of steps and experiences. Namely, they found that violent behavior among African American youth living in extreme poverty increased the likelihood of initiation of carrying a gun by 76% after controlling for exposure to violence. This is consistent with the *stepping stone* model as youth who were both exposed to violence and engaged in violent behavior were more than 2.5 times more likely to initiate gun carrying in the future in comparison to youth who did not experience such exposure or behavior. We will address additional considerations with respect to youth and firearm violence in the sections that follow, particularly in the *High-Profile Mass Shootings in the Modern-Day United States* section later in this chapter.

Psychological Components and Theories of Violence

The fact that human beings engage in acts of violence is not a new phenomenon. In fact, recent reports suggest that the earliest known form of human violence dates back 150,000–200,000 years in southern China, where a skull was discovered from a person who suffered "blunt force trauma" likely due to "interhuman aggression" (Wu, Schepartz, Liu, & Trinkaus, 2011). Clearly, human violence and aggression have remained constant throughout our history, both prehistoric and modern. The rise and fall of civilizations and empires reflect such, and, depending on how one defines it, people have been engaged in war more than 90% of the time over the past 3,400 years of recorded history (Hedges, 2003). Although this number may seem striking, it appears as though human violence has actually *decreased* significantly. According to Harvard psychology professor and cognitive scientist Steven Pinker, we may be living in the most peaceful time in our species' existence. In his recent book, *The Better Angels of Our Nature: Why Violence Has Declined* (2011), Pinker illustrates that our modern times are relatively calm and nonviolent compared to our history. For instance, the murder rate of Medieval Europe was 30 times greater, tribal warfare was nine times as deadly as war and genocide in the 20th century, and crimes such as rape, hate crimes, child abuse, and cruelty to animals have notably declined along with acts of slavery, sadistic punishments, and executions. Sadly, these types of crimes and cruel acts remain present in our world today but, again, at an appreciably lower level than before. Still, the question remains: Why do people engage in acts of violence in the first place?

Perhaps, in its most general conceptualization, theories of violence consider it to be a condition of human nature or a consequence of a damaged mind (King, 2012). Essentially, violence can be considered at the societal or individual level. Many years ago, there was a nature versus nurture debate about the basis of human behavior, but we have come to a general consensus in the mental health fields in recognizing that human behavior is a function of nature and nurture. Thus, the *biopsychosocial model* assumes that interactions between one's genetic makeup (i.e., biology) and psychological and social factors ultimately lead to a particular illness or behavior. With respect to a person's biology, we know that some people are genetically predisposed to develop certain conditions or engage in certain behaviors based on their biological precursors. Psychological factors may include a person's mood or personality, and social factors are those related to one's family, culture, situation, or even physical environment. It is the combination of factors from all three of these domains that is relevant—it is nature *and* nurture. Although this is an oversimplified explanation of illness and behavior, it provides us with a good working framework from which we can begin to understand violence, as well as suicide and other related concepts we address in this book.

Violence can be further delineated for classification purposes. For instance, McEllistrem (2004) and Meloy (2006) have contended that there was an empirical basis and viable forensic application of a *bimodal* theory of violence, which consists of *predatory* and *affective* types. Predatory violence has been described as "planned," "instrumental," and "cold-blooded" and is generally defined as "violent behaviors that are more purposeful and controlled and that lack an emotional display" (Declercq & Audenaert, 2011, p. 580). Affective violence typically includes behaviors described as "hot-blooded" or "impulsive" and has been described as "acts of aggression in response to a perceived threat, acts that are typically emotionally charged and relatively uncontrolled" (Declercq & Audenaert, 2011, p. 580). However, it should be noted that these modes of violence should be considered on a continuum rather than as discrete categories due to the complex nature of human behavior, as well as the reality that the same violent action can contain both predatory and affective attributes (Declercq & Audenaert, 2011). In the creation of The Aggression Questionnaire, Buss & Perry (1992) found aggression to be constructed by four distinct factors, physical aggression, verbal aggression, anger, and hostility. Further, a statistical analysis determined that anger served as "the bridge" between physical and verbal aggression, as well as hostility (p. 452). Ching, Daffern, & Thomas (2013) noted that aggression has historically been classified dichotomously—as either *reactive* or *instrumental*, depending on the motivation behind the behavior. Reactive aggression includes hostile and impulsive types of aggression, which derives from anger and impulsivity and reflects a motivation to hurt something. Such aggression is thought to be the most common type among youthful offenders. On the other hand, instrumental aggression is usually premeditated and motivated by another tangible goal. However, Ching and colleagues (2013) note that strict adherence to such a dichotomous classification scheme is limiting and does not account for a range of violent acts that may be committed. Therefore, they addressed another type of violence, *appetitive violence*, which is considered to be separate from and incompatible with the aforementioned typologies. Appetitive violence is that which is perpetrated for the purpose of pleasure or entertainment and, as such, is not motivated by emotional or social factors. Moreover, we can look to McMurran, Jinks, Howells, & Howard (2010, 2011), who set forth a tripartite typology—another type of classification model based on categorizing violent acts based on their ultimate goal: (i) violence in pursuit of non-social, profit-based goals; (ii) violence in pursuit of social dominance goals; and (iii) violence as defense in response to threat.

Haas & Cusson (2015) conducted a comparative analysis of six major categories of theories of violence: (i) social conflict and reaction, (ii) differential association and learning, (iii) rational choice and lifestyle, (iv) control, (v) childhood trauma, and (vi) psychopathology. According to social conflict and reaction theories, people are not born deviant, but social disadvantage (e.g., resorting to illegal means to achieve social success due to lack of alternative methods) and social reaction to deviant behavior (e.g., authorities scapegoating the powerless) contribute to delinquency and criminal behavior. Nevertheless, Haas & Cusson (2015) found that these theories poorly predicted violence, whereas they were much better at predicting non-violent acts. Per differential association and learning theories, criminal behavior, including violent behavior, can be learned through interpersonal interactions via reinforcement and rewards. These theories were more predictive than social conflict and reaction theories. The third category, rational choice and lifestyle, is based on people's opportunities and the perceived necessity to commit crimes. Under this theoretical umbrella, violence can be thought of as a rational means to gain immediate reward in the context of emotional or material profit (e.g., power, revenge) (Cornish & Clark, 1987). Still, although situational inducements offered the best prediction for violent behavior, there was no empirical support for the notion that anybody can turn to violence as a consequence of pure exposure to many social situations. The next concept is control theory, which essentially addresses the reality that most people do not commit crime, but some do not react accordingly to social control mechanisms. Per control theory, social attachments and bonds are developed in early childhood within the context of socialization in the family structure and are later reinforced in school. This theory seems to predict positive or successful outcomes but is much less useful in predicting poor or negative outcomes.

Childhood trauma theories are based on the fairly extensive research that has found a significant relationship between childhood maltreatment and subsequent delinquency, although such has been found to be dependent on other factors, including gender, race and ethnicity, socioeconomic status, type of maltreatment, and type of delinquency. Nevertheless, this relationship is just that—correlational—and not causal. In other words, while not having a trauma history is a protective factor, such a history alone is not causally related to later violence per se. Of course, as Haas & Cusson (2015) noted, trauma histories may be predictive of other concerning outcomes (e.g., covert aggression, mental health problems), but notable proportions of people with trauma histories do not go on to perpetrate violence, just as many who do commit acts of violence do not have such histories. Finally, Haas & Cusson (2015) noted the psychopathology-based theory of violence, which is grounded in psychiatric diagnostic classification systems—the *International Statistical Classification of Diseases and Related Health Problems,* tenth revision (ICD-10) (World Health Organization, 1992), and the *Diagnostic and Statistical Manual,* fifth edition (DSM-5) (American Psychiatric Association, 2013)—that are predicated on the assumptions that lack of parental care, biological predispositions, and trauma can all lead to mental health and behavioral problems. Namely, the theory suggests that violence is not directly caused by childhood risk factors but that such negatively impacts such areas as one's ability to cope with stressors, which ultimately leads to violence. Haas & Cusson (2015) found this model to come the closest to a complete interdisciplinary model of violence. Nevertheless, they concluded that many theories in social and medical science are complementary and not contradictory.

That said, Hass & Cusson (2015) noted that each theory they analyzed was very effective at predicting non-violence (95.0%–99%) but that none of them could recognize more than 30% of the violent cases in their research. On its face, this finding is discouraging; however, Haas & Cusson (2015) pointed out that some of the theories address factors that are indirectly related to violence and, therefore, are important to recognize. For instance, factors such as early trauma are important to account for when assessing violence, and many theories address the importance of developing good relationships and coping skills and avoiding negative social networks—all of which can allay the effects of such trauma histories. These findings support the need to consider risk, protective, static, and dynamic factors when assessing violence risk and to focus on *prevention* rather than *prediction,* which is critically important (Skeem & Monahan, 2011). Although it is important to account for factors that are empirically associated with violence, we will certainly miss opportunities to reduce acts of future violence if our goal is to predict rather than to prevent such. And, as Haas & Cusson (2015) remind us: "Human behavior is certainly influenced by circumstantial, social, medical and biographical factors. . . . We suspect that unexplained part of the variance, appearing in all prediction scales, has a systematic significance: it might stem from the individual free will" (p. 82).

Common Psychiatric Disorders

We provided an overview of mental health conditions/psychiatric disorders in Chapter 3 of this book. In consideration of these conditions and disorders, the question becomes: Which are most commonly associated with violence? Note that the operative term is *associated with* rather than *cause.* As we outlined in the context of the biopsychosocial model, there are many factors that come together to ultimately lead to particular behaviors, including acts of violence. Therefore, while we cannot say that a particular mental health disorder causes a person to act violently, there is an extensive empirical scientific literature that demonstrates strong relationships between violence and certain conditions as opposed to others. As we will see, in some instances, violent or otherwise problematic behavior is actually what leads to a particular mental health diagnosis—presenting a chicken–egg problem of sorts. Therefore, it is critically important that the reader keep in mind the fact that *correlation does not equal causation*: just because a person has been diagnosed with a certain mental health condition does not mean he or she will commit an act of violence. First, we are much better at post-diction than we are at prediction, as a general rule. Second, diagnostic labels will only serve to be pejorative if they do not have functional value in leading to treatment or other relevant interventions. Nevertheless, diagnostic considerations provide one starting point in understanding violence, and it is particularly important to focus such considerations at the symptom level.

Our diagnostic system is based on symptom combinations or clusters; therefore, there can be significant heterogeneity within diagnostic categories. For example, Galatzer-Levy & Bryant (2013) found that there are over 630,000 possible symptom combinations that can lead to a diagnosis of posttraumatic stress disorder (PTSD) per the DSM-5. Although diagnosing PTSD tends to be more intricate and involved due to the numerous criteria that must be met, many diagnostic categories function similarly with respect to their potential for numerous symptom combinations. As a result, we must focus on the functional aspects of the diagnosis—again, at the symptom level—to understand what someone may be experiencing and how that person may subsequently behave. Further, there is often a significant amount of overlap pertaining to victim versus perpetrator status in regard to violence. As an example, one study investigating the overlap of community violence perpetration and victimization among mentally ill adults found that while these adults with mental illness were unlikely to report violent outcomes, when they did they tended to report both perpetration and victimization (Johnson, Desmarais, Van Dorn, & Grimm, 2015). These so-called victim-perpetrators were more likely to be young, to be black, and to have a variety of psychiatric diagnoses, such as bipolar disorder, major depressive disorder, substance use disorder, or "other" (p. 522).

Some of the most common psychiatric disorders present in the context of interpersonal violence include anxiety, depressive, and substance use disorders (Cerdá, DiGangi, Galea, & Koenen, 2012). In fact, those diagnosed with anxiety and depressive disorders have been found to be four times more likely to report engaging in violence in comparison to those without psychiatric disorders and those diagnosed with bipolar or substance use disorders were eight times more likely (Corrigan & Watson, 2005). However, an important distinction must be taken into account as it has been found that violence directed toward others (i.e., externalizing behavior) is most closely associated with substance use and personality disorders, whereas self-directed violence (i.e., internalizing behavior) is more closely associated with mood and anxiety disorders (Harford, Yi, & Grant, 2013). As such, it can be useful to conceptualize the behavioral manifestations of psychiatric disorders as either externalizing or internalizing (the latter concept we address in detail in Chapter 6 in the context of suicide and self-injury). Nevertheless, while certain disorders are associated with an elevated risk of engaging in violent behavior compared to others, the majority of people diagnosed with psychiatric disorders do not engage in violent behaviors; and, therefore, the public perception and stereotypes of mentally ill individuals appear to be unwarranted (Pulay et al., 2008). This has also been found to be the case within criminal populations, such that the presence of severe mental health disorders, including substance use, has not convincingly predicted violent crime post-incarceration within these groups above and beyond their inmate counterparts without such problems (Teplin, Abram, & McClelland, 1994).

Still, the presence of a mental illness, including substance use, is important to consider as a risk factor on an individual basis to facilitate treatment planning and other efforts aimed at reducing and managing one's violence risk. However, the presence of a mental illness is a relatively weak predictor of violence, and adjusting violence rates by population base rates suggests that demographic variables, such as ethnicity and gender, are better predictors (Corrigan & Watson, 2005). That said, there are certain psychiatric disorders that are very behaviorally based and do not fall under the umbrella term *major mental illness* per se, although they often lead to significant problems for the person and others. Within the context of the DSM-5, our primary diagnostic classification system, these conditions are what are referred to as the disruptive, impulse-control, and conduct disorders; and they include: oppositional defiant disorder, intermittent explosive disorder, pyromania, kleptomania, and conduct disorder. These conditions are those that involve problems in the self-control of emotions and behaviors and are distinguishable from other mental health problems because they specifically include the violation of rights of others, rules, or societal norms. The DSM-5 diagnostic approach is *atheoretical* and, as such, reflects the notion that the causes of such problems and associated behaviors can vary considerably. Nevertheless, these conditions are very behaviorally driven, such that the diagnostic emphasis is on the lack of self-control of emotions and behaviors.

Oppositional defiant disorder is defined by the presentation of a pattern of angry or irritable mood, argumentative or defiant behavior, or vindictiveness lasting at least 6 months and observed in the interaction with at least one person who is not a sibling. *Intermittent explosive disorder* is defined by recurrent behavioral outbursts reflecting a failure to control aggressive impulses in the context of either verbal or physical aggression that occurs twice weekly, on average, over a 3-month period or three such incidents within a 12-month period. The operative components of this diagnosis are that the "magnitude of aggressiveness expressed during the recurrent outbursts is grossly out of proportion to the provocation or to any precipitating psychosocial stressors" and that the outbursts are not premeditated or committed to achieve a tangible objective (American Psychiatric Association, 2013, p. 466). *Pyromania* is characterized by: (i) deliberate and purposeful fire-setting on more than one occasion; (ii) tension or affective arousal before the act; (iii) fascination with, interest in, curiosity about, or attraction to fire and its "situational contexts," such as paraphernalia and the effects of the fire; and (iv) pleasure, gratification, or relief when setting fires or when witnessing or engaging in their aftermath. Moreover, pyromania can be diagnosed when the fire-setting is not done for a secondary reason, such as for monetary gain or to conceal a crime, or as a result of another mental health condition (e.g., in response to psychotic symptoms, such as delusions). *Kleptomania* is defined by the recurrent failure to resist impulses to steal objects not needed for personal use or for their monetary value. In addition, the person must experience an elevated sense of tension immediately prior to stealing and a sense of pleasure, gratification, or relief at the time of the act. Moreover, the theft must not be done as an expression of anger or retaliation or as a result of another mental health problem.

A final condition in this group is *conduct disorder*, which is defined by a repetitive and persistent pattern of behavior in which the basic rights of others or societal norms or rules are violated. There must be at least three such behaviors present in the last 12 months, with at least one present in the last 6 months. In the DSM-5, there are 15 behaviors noted across four domains: (i) aggression to people and animals, (ii) destruction of property, (iii) deceitfulness or theft, and (iv) serious violations of rules. In addition, conduct disorder may have a childhood or adolescent onset, with age 10 being the diagnostic marker in that regard. In addition, the diagnosis can be further specified if there are limited prosocial emotions present, such as: a lack of remorse or guilt; callousness and lack of empathy; lack of concern about performance in school, work, or other important activities; or a shallow or deficient affect. Conduct disorder is related to a diagnosis known as *antisocial personality disorder*. Although not all youth diagnosed with conduct disorder will go on to develop antisocial personality disorder, one must have exhibited evidence of conduct disorder with onset before 15 years old in order to be diagnosed with antisocial personality disorder. In addition to that precursor, one must be at least 18 years old for this personality disorder diagnosis and must have demonstrated a pervasive pattern of disregard for and violation of the rights of other since age 15 in at least three of the following areas:

1. Failure to conform to social norms with respect to lawful behaviors as indicated by repeatedly performing acts that are grounds for arrest
2. Deceitfulness, as indicated by repeated lying, use of aliases, or conning others for personal profit or pleasure
3. Impulsivity or failure to plan ahead
4. Irritability and aggressiveness, as indicated by repeated physical fights or assaults
5. Reckless disregard for safety of self or others

6. Consistent irresponsibility, as indicated by repeated failure to sustain consistent work behavior or honor financial obligations
7. Lack of remorse, as indicated by being indifferent to or rationalizing having hurt, mistreated, or stolen from another

As with most mental health conditions, the manifestation of the disruptive, impulse-control, and conduct disorders and antisocial personality disorder should be conceptualized on a continuum. Just as most of us have felt down or blue at some point but did not meet the clinical criteria for major depressive disorder, one may present with a particular behavior or trait listed in the criteria of one of the aforementioned conditions and yet still not have the diagnosis. As we previously discussed, diagnoses are made when certain symptom combinations or clusters are present and when these symptoms reach a particular clinical level—often involving the individual's level of clinical distress or functional impairment related to said symptoms. Thus, many teenagers engage in episodes whereby they test limits and boundaries by being defiant toward their parents but would not necessarily be diagnosed with oppositional defiant disorder; many of us have lost our temper disproportionally to the situation at hand but would not be classified as having intermittent explosive disorder; some youth experiment with fire but not necessarily to a level of meeting the diagnostic criteria for pyromania, and the same is true for stealing and kleptomania. Again, these conditions are very behavior-based, and professionals tasked with making diagnoses must ensure that such behaviors and traits rise to a clinical level worthy of a diagnosis. Otherwise, these diagnostic labels will simply stigmatize and negatively impact people (see Schomerus et al., 2012, for more on social stigma and mental illness), which is in direct contrast to the point of diagnosis—to facilitate treatment, interventions, and additional community support and services. Nevertheless, the behaviors and traits related to the aforementioned conditions are often associated with violence; and, certainly, the diagnoses of conduct disorder and the related antisocial personality disorder are associated with criminal behavior, including acts of violence. In fact, according to the DSM-5, "The highest prevalence of Antisocial Personality Disorder (greater than 70%) is among most severe samples of males with alcohol use disorder and from substance abuse clinics, prisons, and other forensic settings" (p. 661). Moreover, gang members have been found to show high levels of mental health problems and needs (Coid et al., 2013). Relatedly, the prevalence of antisocial personality disorder is higher in classes of individuals affected by adverse socioeconomic and sociocultural factors, such as poverty and migration. The research is clear that people diagnosed with antisocial personality disorder possess aggression-related attitudes, maladaptive thoughts, and anger—all of which are associated with violence (Gilbert & Daffern, 2011).

Another particularly noteworthy condition in this context is *psychopathy*. The term *psychopath* or *sociopath* is the likely reference point here for most of us. Please note that the term *psychopathy* should not be confused with *psychopathology*, which simply refers to the scientific study and classification of mental illnesses. Psychopathy is a personality disorder characterized by a range of traits and behaviors that extend well beyond those associated with antisocial personality disorder. Although psychopathy is not included as a formal diagnosis in the DSM-5, it has been recognized among mental health professionals as a bona fide mental health problem for quite some time. The concept was ultimately delineated and refined by Hervey Cleckley, a psychiatrist at the University of Georgia School of Medicine, when he published his 1941 book *The Mask of Sanity: An Attempt to Clarify Some Issues About the So-Called Psychopathic Personality* (Cleckley, 1955). Cleckley reduced his original 21-characteristic conceptualization (Hare & Neumann, 2008) of the characteristics of psychopaths to a clinical profile of 16:

1. Superficial charm and good intelligence
2. Absence of delusions and other signs of irrational thinking
3. Absence of nervousness or psychoneurotic manifestations
4. Unreliability
5. Untruthfulness and insincerity
6. Lack of remorse and shame
7. Inadequately motivated antisocial behavior
8. Poor judgment and failure to learn by experience
9. Pathologic egocentricity and incapacity for love
10. General poverty in major affective reactions
11. Specific loss of insight
12. Unresponsiveness in general interpersonal relations
13. Fantastic and uninviting behavior with drink and sometimes without
14. Suicide rarely carried out
15. Sex life impersonal, trivial, and poorly integrated
16. Failure to follow any life plan

As the mental health field developed, so did efforts to formally measure such constructs as psychopathy. A measure known as the Hare Psychopathy Checklist (PCL; Hare, 1980) and its revision, the PCL-R (Hare 1991, 2003), have become the best known in this regard. In the 1970s, Professor Robert Hare became concerned about the lack of formalized tools to assess psychopathy and, therefore, applied much of Cleckley's clinical conceptualization of the condition to develop items within a semistructured interview format, which are subsequently scored on a 3-point rating scale (see Hare & Neumann, 2008). The 20 items are:

1. Glib and superficial charm
2. Grandiose (exaggeratedly high) estimation of self
3. Need for stimulation
4. Pathological lying
5. Cunning and manipulativeness
6. Lack of remorse or guilt

7. Shallow affect (superficial emotional responsiveness)
8. Callousness and lack of empathy
9. Parasitic lifestyle
10. Poor behavioral controls
11. Sexual promiscuity
12. Early behavior problems
13. Lack of realistic long-term goals
14. Impulsivity
15. Irresponsibility
16. Failure to accept responsibility for own actions
17. Many short-term marital relationships
18. Juvenile delinquency
19. Revocation of conditional release
20. Criminal versatility

The presence of these behaviors or personality traits is clearly related to violence, and, as such, the PCL-R has become a staple in many violence and sexual risk assessment protocols. In fact, the assessment of psychopathy is mandated in certain risk evaluations (e.g., sexually violent predator) in certain states, and the PCL-R's use specifically is mandated by statute in several states (Spiegel, 2011). As an example, California now requires the use of the PCL-R for certain parole fitness evaluations and for prisoners sentenced to indeterminate terms, including life in prison (Guy, Kusaj, Packer, & Douglas, 2015). Further, use of the PCL-R in court has become more popular through time. For instance, from 1991 through 2004, the PCL-R was used in 15 states and was also used in federal district and appellate courts. During this time, the PCL-R was used in court in California, Florida, Hawaii, Illinois, Iowa, Minnesota, New Jersey, New York, North Dakota, Ohio, Oklahoma, Texas, Virginia, Washington, and Wisconsin (DeMatteo & Edens, 2006). From 2005 to 2011, the PCL-R was used in 214 cases in 19 states, with California, Texas, and Minnesota accounting for more than half of the usage (DeMatteo et al., 2014). Although measuring psychopathy is not the same as measuring violence risk, the research has consistently shown how strong of a predictor it is in that context (e.g., Reidy et al., 2015, Dolan & Doyle, 2000). In fact, in terms of dispositional factors, psychopathy has been shown to be one of the strongest predictors of aggression and violence (Aharoni & Kiehl, 2013; Neumann & Hare, 2008). Nevertheless, only 16% of adult males in prison or jails or on parole or probation meet such criteria (Kiehl & Hoffman, 2011; Rice & Harris, 1997). Thus, characterological deficits of this magnitude are fortunately somewhat uncommon even among our most serious offender groups. That said, Professor Hare has shown us that psychopathy may be more prevalent than we may have thought, particularly in non-violent populations. In his books *Without Conscience: The Disturbing World of the Psychopaths Among Us* (Hare, 1999) and *Snakes in Suits: When Psychopaths Go to Work* (Babiak

& Hare, 2006), he addresses the presence of psychopathy among some of those we interact with in our communities and places of employment.

A final, yet very important diagnostic category to consider in the context of violence and crime is that of the substance-related and addictive disorders. The DSM-5 recognizes a number of classes of drugs: alcohol; caffeine; cannabis; hallucinogens; inhalants; opioids; sedatives, hypnotics, and anxiolytics; stimulants; and tobacco. The substance-related disorders are bifurcated into substance use disorders and substance-induced disorders. Substance-induced conditions may be classified as intoxication or withdrawal or may fall under various other mental health disorders that were induced by substances or medication. Per the DSM-5, the "essential feature of a substance disorder is a cluster of cognitive, behavioral, and physiological symptoms indicating that the individual continues using the substance despite significant substance-related problems" (p. 483). Undoubtedly, substance-related problems may be interpersonal or legal problems that include acts of violence. We address acts of domestic and intimate partner violence in detail in Chapter 5, but it is relevant here to highlight the role that substances often play in other acts of violence and criminal activity, more generally.

The empirical research has clearly shown that alcohol and drug use increases the likelihood that one will engage in and become a victim of violence, particularly among female groups (Chavira et al., 2011). In fact, 80% of criminal offenses that lead to incarceration in the United States involve situations in which alcohol or drugs are implicated, and approximately 60% of individuals arrested for most types of crimes test positive for drugs upon their arrest (National Council on Alcoholism and Drug Dependence, 2015). Of note, alcohol is a factor in 40% of all violent crimes today (National Council on Alcoholism and Drug Dependence, 2015). Moreover, certain environments, such as bars and restaurants or other "alcohol outlets," are associated with more simple assaults as opposed to aggravated assaults (Pridemore & Grubesic, 2013). This is not particularly surprising given the social context of such settings in conjunction with the presence of alcohol—a commonly used disinhibitor. As such, alcohol-related violence has been classified by three particular goals: (i) violence in pursuit of non-social, profit-based goals; (ii) violence in pursuit of social dominance goals; and (iii) violence as defense in response to threat (McMurran et al., 2010). However, the relationship between illicit drugs and violent crime (even crime more generally) is a little more complex, in part because it is unclear whether drug use leads to additional criminal activity or whether individuals who use drugs are predisposed to criminal behavior. What is known is that those with drug dependencies are more likely to be arrested for crimes committed in an effort to feed the habit. For example, in 2004, 17% of state prisoners and 18% of federal prisoners reported that they committed their instant offense in an effort to obtain money for drugs (National Council on Alcoholism and Drug Dependence, 2015). Striving to disentangle the relationship between violence and drug use, researchers have started conducting brain-imaging studies. Brain researchers (e.g., Schiffer et al., 2011) have found interesting differences in the brains of violent criminals and drug abusers, which could explain, at least in part, the disproportionate number of violent criminals who are also drug users. Specifically, those individuals with a history of drug use were more likely to have reduced brain volume in areas that are involved with self-control. Essentially, this means the addicted brain is typified by the equivalent of faulty breaks. Meanwhile, individuals with a history of violence, aggression, and higher scores on the PCL-R were more likely to have greater brain volume in areas involved with desire, craving, pleasure, and motivation. In other words, a more powerful engine, which drives impulsive behaviors, may characterize individuals prone to violence. In combination, the drug-addicted violent offender has a more powerful engine with weaker breaks, which results in a greater desire to engage in pleasure-seeking behavior (e.g., drug use, violence, other criminal activities) and a reduced ability to manage said desires effectively (Schiffer et al., 2011).

Firearm-Related Violence and Crime

Now that we have set a foundation for our understanding of violence and mental illness, generally speaking, we can turn to the more specific scope of our book: firearm-related violence and crime. In this section, we present national and state-based firearm-related statistics and relevant theories and research findings, and we also address issues related to gun availability and ownership, police-involved shootings, limitations of the research, and international perspectives.

US and State Firearm-Related Violence Statistics

According to statistics presented by the Giffords Law Center to Prevent Gun Violence (http://lawcenter.giffords.org), which collects data from sources such as the CDC and the US Department of Defense:

- Guns were used in 11,078 homicides in the United States in 2010, comprising almost 35% of all gun deaths and over 68% of all homicides.
- On average, 33 gun homicides were committed each day for the years 2005–2010.
- Regions and states with higher rates of gun ownership have significantly higher rates of homicide than states with lower rates of gun ownership.

For more detailed information regarding firearm injuries in this country (i.e., firearm-related deaths, suicides, homicides), please see Tables 1.1–1.6. Nevertheless, while gathering data and presenting statistics are important first steps, they are insufficient. These data must be analyzed and investigated at a deeper level to facilitate appropriate and meaningful interpretation—an effort in which we engage in the sections that follow.

Theory and Research

General Findings and Trends

In his recent epidemiological study, Wintemute (2015b) outlined the statistics and related trends in firearm violence in the 21st century in the United States. A primary finding is that the mortality rate from firearm violence has not appreciably changed since the late 1990s, whereas there were low rates in the 1950s and 1960s before a notable and rapid increase in the mid-1970s. A second increase in such rates occurred in the early 1990s, followed by a rapid decline from 1994 to 1999. He noted that firearm violence trends have been different from those related to non-firearm violence. He indicated that such injury rates dropped by 50% and firearm deaths dropped 30% from 1993 to 1999, and then both rates stabilized from 1999 to 2012. While firearm-related homicide, unintentional death, and assault-related nonfatal injury rates declined during those time periods, suicide rates increased nearly 20% from 2006 to 2012. He also highlighted the fact that "Mass killings in public places account for a very small percentage of deaths from firearm violence" (p. 8.4), which we address further in the *High-Profile Mass Shootings in the Modern-Day United States* section later in this chapter. Nevertheless, Wintemute highlighted the fact that most deaths from firearm violence are, in fact, suicides and not homicides. Namely, suicides by firearm averaged a rate of 60.5% from 2002 to 2012, and "Over the past 30 years, suicide has exceeded homicide even when firearm homicide rates were at their highest, and it was also the case for most of the twentieth century" (2015b, pp. 8.2–8.3). Moreover, Wintemute indicated: "There has been a notable divergence in firearm suicide and homicide rates since 2006; homicides have decreased, but suicides have increased by a like amount" (2015b, p. 8.3). Thus, he demonstrated that there is essentially no correlation between firearm-related suicide and homicide. Wintemute's (2015b) findings are consistent with those of Fowler, Dahlberg, Haileyesus, & Annest (2015), who also noted that annual rates of firearm-related suicide are approximately double those of homicide. For instance, more than 32,000 people, on average, died each year in the United States from 2010 to 2012; over 20,000 (62%) of these were suicides, over 11,000 (35%) were homicides, and approximately 600 (2%) were unintentional.

With regard to nonfatal firearm injuries and crime, Wintemute (2015b) noted that the data in this regard are limited. Nevertheless, the CDC's National Electronic Injury Surveillance System–All Injury Program, which includes reports from 66 hospital emergency departments, estimated that there were 63,163 persons treated for injuries from firearm violence, including 59,077 for injuries related to assaults and 4,086 for injuries related to self-harm in 2012. In addition, he noted that, in the same year, the National

Crime Victimization Survey estimated that firearms were used in 460,718 serious violent victimizations, including approximately one-third of robberies and aggravated assaults. Others have substantiated these findings as well (e.g., see Fowler et al., 2015). Although these are estimates, they clearly illustrate that firearm-related injuries are predominantly the result of violent crime. Wintemute's findings are consistent with the extant research in that way and in that such crime primarily occurs in inner cities. Grommon & Rydberg (2015) also recently found that critical injuries from gunshots are more likely among older victims, victims who know their assailants, and victims who are not cooperative with the police. In addition, firearm-related injuries place a heavy financial toll on the country. For instance, Coben & Steiner (2003) found that the cost in 1997 was $802 million and that 29% of patients admitted for injuries were uninsured. As such, firearm-related injuries ranked highest of all conditions among the number of uninsured hospital stays.

Which specific factors are related to firearm-related violence? While ecological factors, such as day of the week, temperature, and even weather conditions (e.g., rain), have been associated with the incidence of firearm-related injuries and crime (Kieltyka, Kucybala, & Crandall, 2016), these are certainly not causal factors. Causality is much more difficult to ascertain compared to correlation. Nevertheless, additional correlated factors include: sex, age, race and ethnicity, and geography.

Sex

Nearly all (90%) firearm-related deaths reviewed by Fowler et al. (2015) were males, with disproportional rates of 7:1 males to females for suicide and 5:1 males to females for homicide. This number is not particularly surprising given that males are much more inclined to attempt suicide with a firearm and that 85% of such attempts end in completed suicides compared to less lethal methods (e.g., overdosing on medication). In addition, Fowler and colleagues noted that nearly all nonfatal firearm injuries occur among males (90%) and are treated in emergency departments in the United States each year.

Age

Fowler and colleagues (2015) found that young adults between ages 25 and 34 have the highest rates of fatal firearm injuries (15.1 per 100,000) among all age groups, followed by those between 15 and 24, whereas those under age 15 have the lowest rates. Furthermore, people under age 35 account for almost three-quarters of all nonfatal firearm injuries each year. However, firearm-related suicide is highest among those 65 and older (10.9 per 100,000), followed by the two successive younger age groups: 55–64 and 45–54, respectively. In contrast, firearm-related homicide rates are highest among adolescents and young adults, but this decreases with age. Nevertheless, rates among those aged 15–24 and 25–34 range from approximately 2 to 10 times higher than those over age 34. These groups also had the highest rates of unintentional firearm-related deaths, albeit at very low rates; and of note is that children under age 15 had the lowest rates of unintentional firearm deaths.

Race

Fowler and colleagues (2015) found that non-Hispanic blacks had firearm-related homicide rates that were 10 times higher than those of non-Hispanic whites and 4–15 times higher than those of other racial groups. Moreover, non-Hispanic black youth between ages 15 and 24 have firearm-related homicide rates 5 times higher than those of Hispanics and 19 times higher than those of whites. That said, whites have approximately 3–6 times higher suicide rates than their counterparts in other racial groups. In fact, non-Hispanic white males commit 75% of all firearm-related suicides, with the highest rates in the 70 and older age group (35.3 per 100,000).

Ethnicity and Geography

Wintemute (2015b) substantiates the oft-cited finding that homicide risk is significantly higher among black males. Namely, at ages 20–29, the firearm homicide rate for black males was at least 5 times higher than that for Hispanic males and at least 20 times higher than that for white males; this was true for females within these groups as well. In fact, the homicide rate for black females even exceeded that of white males. On the other hand, risk for firearm-related suicide is generally concentrated among white males, which we will address in greater detail in Chapter 6.

Of course, subcultural and geographical considerations are particularly relevant in the firearm violence arena. Although the distribution of homicide types varies across cities throughout the United States, there are notable regional differences. Fowler and colleagues (2015) noted that nearly half of all firearm deaths occur in the South, at an annual rate of 12.6 per 100,000, whereas the Northeast has the lowest percentage and rate of firearms deaths in the country. These findings are consistent with those of Ousey & Lee (2010), who studied what they referred to as the "southern culture of violence" (SCOV). In their research, they investigated firearm violence rates across 141 cities in the United States at three different time points: 1980, 1990, and 2000. In sum, they found that cities with a higher percentage of people born in the South are more differentiated toward "argument homicides," which are those that are felony-, gang-, or drug-related, compared to cities with lower percentages born in the South. They concluded that "the evidence suggests that for the most part the primary measure of the SCOV perspective discriminatively predicts argument homicide relative to other homicide types" (p. 272).

As noted, Wintemute (2015b) has illustrated that there is essentially no correlation between firearm-related suicide and homicide. In fact, states with both the highest and lowest rates of firearm suicide are among those with low rates of firearm homicide. Namely, states in the New England region represented low-suicide, low-homicide areas; the rural Northwest represented the high-suicide, low-homicide states; and high-suicide, high-homicide states were primarily in the Southeast. There have also been clear developmental trends, or what has been referred to as "highly volatile micro-level trends," at a select number of specific locations in urban environments, such as inner-city areas of Boston in the late 1980s and early 1990s (Braga, Papachristos, & Hureau, 2010). However, firearm violence is not even equally dispersed within such communities but rather occurs in very specific areas where criminality is quite high. In fact, Braga and colleagues found that approximately 75% of firearm violence in Boston over a 29-year period occurred in only 5% of the city blocks and intersections.

As Burgason, Thomas, & Berthelot (2014) found, gun incidents are more prevalent in cities with a high level of socioeconomic disadvantage and violence, and black individuals are more likely to be victims of gun crimes. However, "In those areas where the code of the streets is strongly ingrained into the culture, those assaulted or robbed by gun wielding offenders are likely to facilitate a smooth transaction and thus decrease the likelihood that they will sustain injuries" (p. 388). Moreover, the quality of social ties is relevant in the context of gun victimization. Social capital, or the ability of an individual or network of individuals within a social group to utilize resources—particularly in the context of trust—has been found to reduce the likelihood of firearm-related victimization (Medina, 2015). Based on their study of homicides in Chicago between 1980 and 1995, Griffiths & Chavez (2004) concluded: "We confirm findings from past cross-sectional research that indeed a small number of communities experience extremely elevated levels of lethal violence, that this violence can be largely attributed to gun violence, and that these communities are clustered in space" (p. 966). They found disproportionate amounts of street gun violence in these communities, which they noted were not adjacent to non-violent communities. Perhaps the more interesting finding, however, was that homicide rates increased as a result of street gun violence, whereas lethal violence by other means actually declined. Griffiths & Chavez referred to this as the "weapon substitution effect," such that the levels of violence essentially remained constant but homicides notably increased because the method changed and became more lethal (i.e., firearms). Nevertheless, they noted that the regions with significant increases in street gun homicide rates were likely also those plagued by activities associated with gun violence, including drug markets and gang activity. They opined that this could lead to a process whereby residents may arm themselves for protection against those from notoriously violent communities nearby.

As noted, however, media attention plays a role in the public's perception of firearms. Mass shootings, including school shootings, receive high levels of media coverage. In fact, most people learn of mass shootings through mass media (Wallace, 2015), and media violence may be part of an interrelated set of social, cultural, and political factors that impact the risk of school shootings

(De Venanzi, 2012). Nevertheless, high levels of media attention help perpetuate the perceived association between gun violence and mass shooters with "assault weapons"—a very rare event—rather than the actually compelling statistics related to crime in specific areas of inner cities. The following is quite illustrative: as this book is being written, there were 69 people shot in Chicago just on Memorial Day weekend (2016) alone.[5] During the same weekend, a gorilla in the Cincinnati Zoo was shot and killed when a 3-year-old boy fell into the exhibit and the animal began dragging the boy (Nickeas, Wong, Chachkevitch, & Mahr, 2016; Thorbecke, 2016). The news coverage of these incidents was quite disparate, however, as the gorilla story received 54 times the amount of press coverage than the 69 shooting victims in Chicago on that same weekend (Richardson, 2016).

Papachristos, Grossman, Braga, & Piza (2015) investigated the relationship between the social proximity to a gang member in one's co-offending network and the likelihood of being shot. They found that being either directly or indirectly linked to a gang member within one's co-offending network significantly predicts the likely of being a gunshot victim. Furthermore, they found an "extreme concentration" of gunshot injuries within a small social network. For instance, nearly one-third of all shootings in Newark, New Jersey, occur in a network that contains less than 4% of the city's total population. Such is consistent with the aforementioned findings of Braga and colleagues (2010) in Boston and that of Griffiths & Chavez (2004) in Chicago. Given the saliency and consistency of these findings, it is important to take a closer look at the criminological factors related to firearm possession, violence, and crime.

Criminological Considerations

According to the FBI's *Uniform Crime Reports* on murders committed in 2014, 67.9% of all homicides in the United States were conducted by firearm. Of all the homicides in the Northeast, 65.3% involved a firearm, 70.8% of homicides in the Midwest were via firearm, 69.6% of homicides in the South were firearm-related, and 64.2% of the homicides in the West were committed using a firearm. The vast majority of murder weapons used to perpetrate homicides in the United States were handguns. Specifically, there were 5,562 homicides committed using a handgun versus 1,567 homicides committed using a knife or other cutting instrument. Regarding robberies during this time period, 40.3% were committed using a firearm, with the South in the lead for most robberies committed using a firearm (49.9%), followed by the Midwest (45.3%), then the Northeast (31.1.%), and finally the West (29.3%). Firearms were used 22.5% of the time during the commission of aggravated assaults in the United States, with the South again leading with 26.7% of aggravated assaults being firearm-related. Following the South, firearms were used in 25.1% of all aggravated assaults in the Midwest, 18.1% of aggravated assaults in the West involved a firearm, and 14.6% of aggravated assaults in the Northeast involved a firearm.

Barragan, Sherman, Reiter, & Tita (2016) conducted in-depth interviews with 140 inmates who were incarcerated in the Los Angeles County jails on gun charges to delineate the reasons why these offenders chose to illegally own and carry firearms. Two main themes emerged from the study: the offenders' experiences with violence in their communities made them feel unsafe and in need of protection with a firearm, and they did not trust law enforcement, generally, and doubted their authority and ability to ensure their safety. The overarching finding that the offenders possessed firearms for the purpose of protection is consistent with non-offending groups as it is the most common rationale set forth by those who own firearms (Carlson, 2015; Cook & Goss, 2014). Barragan and colleagues also found that the vast majority of the offenders were victims of gun violence and that half were gang-involved. Specifically, almost 75% of their sample reported being direct victims of firearm-related crimes, and more than half had family or friends who had been victims of such. Moreover, regardless of the offenders' gang involvement or lack thereof, concerns regarding gang violence were a primary motivator to possess a firearm. Paradoxically, many offenders in the sample agreed that some level of gun control is necessary; however, their mistrust of the police and personal safety concerns outweighed such considerations. An additional finding was that many of the offenders disliked being grouped into the category of firearm-related offenders along with those such as mass shooters.

Cook, Parker, & Pollack (2015) also investigated inmates' firearm use and attitudes. Specifically, they surveyed 99 inmates at Cook County Jail in Chicago, Illinois, and found that the majority of respondents obtained their guns from their social network as opposed to gun shows or gun theft. They often share guns or hold guns for others. Furthermore, Cook and colleagues found that gang members in the Chicago area also played a pivotal role in organizing gun purchases and distribution. They noted that police in the area did play a significant role in deterrence, however, as the inmates had been concerned about being arrested for either selling a gun to an undercover police officer or informant or being caught with a gun that had been fired in a crime (i.e., a "dirty" gun). Brandl & Stroshine (2011) investigated the dynamics of illegal firearm markets in Milwaukee, Wisconsin, by analyzing over 1,500 federal and state law enforcement records associated with firearms that were purchased legally but later confiscated. They found that the overwhelming majority of firearms in that area were acquired based on *straw* purchases, whereby they were legally obtained by someone without a criminal record but sold to another person who is not legally permitted to purchase or own a firearm. The fastest time-to-crime purchases (i.e., less than 1 year) were by minority females who lived in high-crime areas of the city. They were also more likely to be purchased by one particular store and were larger-caliber, semiautomatic firearms. That said, when the data are considered overall and regardless of time, most of the buyers (82%) were males and minorities (59%) and most of the firearms were medium-caliber (56%) semiautomatic handguns. Furthermore, the guns were only reported stolen 19% of the time, and most crimes (53%) were committed 5 years or longer after the purchase. Sevigny & Allen (2015) investigated gun carrying in the context of illegal drug markets across the United States. They found that the drug offenders who were most likely to possess a firearm were those who: (i) used illicit drugs at the time of their offense, (ii) had been previously threatened or victimized with a gun, (iii) had a prior weapon conviction, (iv) were involved with methamphetamine and controlled larger and more valuable amounts of drugs, (v) operated from a residential rather than a public location, and (vi) were younger males.

Most of us will not find the aforementioned connection between illegal drug markets, gangs, and guns to be particularly surprising; but what about the mere presence of a firearm? In the next section, we investigate the relationship between firearm availability and ownership and firearm violence.

Firearm Availability and Ownership

Research findings on violence and crime in the context of firearm availability and ownership have been mixed. The United States has higher rates of firearm ownership than other developed countries, such that almost 40% of households have a firearm and more than 200 million firearms are in circulation in this country (Hepburn, Miller, Azrael, & Hemenway, 2007). It is important to note, however, that there is quite a range of prevalence across states. The average rate of firearm ownership of all states has been found to be 58%, and Hawaii has been found to have the lowest rates at 26%, whereas Mississippi has the highest at 77% (Siegel, Ross, & King, 2013). Siegel and colleagues found that the average percentage of firearm ownership dropped from 61% to 52% from 1981 to 2010. Nevertheless, given that the United States also has relatively higher homicide rates than other developed countries, the link between gun ownership and violent crime has continued to be a topic that is given much attention.

Miller, Hemenway, & Azrael (2007) conducted one of the first studies to examine the relationship between household firearm ownership and homicide victimization across all 50 states, and they found that houses with higher rates of firearm ownership had significantly higher homicide rates for men, women, and children. However, they noted the numerous limitations inherent in this line of research. In particular, the use of aggregate data rather than individual-level information precludes us from knowing the actual circumstances of the violent crimes, including the fact that it is not possible to know where the firearm used in a given homicide even came from. As Miller and colleagues accurately pointed out, their study "does not establish a causal relationship between guns and homicide," and it may be the case that "individuals in states with historically high homicide rates acquired more guns . . . as a defensive response to actual homicide rates in their communities" (p. 663). However, the authors ruled out that possibility because gun ownership was not significantly associated with rates of non-firearm homicide or other crimes in their study. Nevertheless, this concept is referred to as *reverse causation*, and it is an inherent limitation to all correlation research. We will address this issue later in the chapter (see *Limitations of the Firearm-Related Violence Research*).

More recently, Monuteaux et al. (2015) examined the relationship between state-level ownership of guns and violent crime. They also found that higher levels of ownership were associated with higher firearm violence rates (i.e., assault, robbery, and homicide). Siegel and colleagues (2013) investigated archival federal data from all 50 states from 1981 to 2010 to examine the relationship between household firearm ownership and suicides and homicides completed with a firearm. They also found that gun ownership significantly predicted firearm homicide rates, such that states with higher rates of firearm ownership also had disproportionately large numbers of firearm-related deaths. However, the availability of firearms does not influence levels of violence in a uniform manner (Altheimer & Boswell, 2012). Most studies have focused on homicide, bypassing other types of violent crimes. However, Hoskin (2011) also included robbery and aggravated assault in his study. He analyzed retrospective survey data from the CDC's Behavioral Risk Factor Surveillance System across 120 of the most populated counties in the country, and, as such, the study was correlational in nature. Hoskin found that counties with higher rates of household firearm ownership also had higher rates of homicide and aggravated assault but not robbery. Therefore, Hoskin concluded, "The view that the availability of firearms plays no role in violence [*sic*] crime receives little support" in his study and that there was "no support" for the notion that firearm ownership deterred violent crimes (p. 133).

Wallace (2015) investigated the effects of six mass shootings that occurred between 2000 and 2010 by analyzing gun acquisition data from the National Instant Criminal Background Check System (NICS). The results suggest that there is a positive but delayed association between mass shootings and the number of NICS background checks. She further concluded that the effects are temporary, and it is largely unclear how firearm ownership is actually affected by these events. Such is consistent with Pirelli & Witt's (2015) notation that NICS background checks doubled in New Jersey from 2011 to 2013, going from 60,256 to 120,071 checks, although such appears more likely in response to gun control efforts (i.e., the threat of prohibition) rather than a mass shooting or otherwise high-profile event. Nevertheless, another relevant question that has been asked is: Do people who have concealed carry licenses engage in more criminal behavior? To address this, Phillips et al. (2013) investigated the differences in criminal convictions between holders and non-holders of concealed handgun licenses (CHL) in Texas. They found that CHL holders were much less likely to be convicted of crimes and that there were differences in the types of crimes committed. Namely, non-holders were more likely to be convicted of higher-prevalence crimes (e.g., burglary, robbery, simple assault), while holders were more likely to be convicted of lower-prevalence crimes (e.g., sex offenses, gun offenses, or offenses involving a death). Phillips and colleagues concluded that concealed carry may increase the risk of certain types of crimes, including those that are quite serious and involve weapons. Nevertheless, they indicated that CHL holders "were almost universally a law-abiding population" who committed crimes in "rare instances" (p. 90).

Police-Involved Shootings

Tension between certain communities and law enforcement represents one of the most pressing issues in the United States at this time. As we are writing this book, the second Baltimore police officer to be tried, Edward Nero, has just been found not guilty in the death of Freddie Gray, Jr. A mistrial was declared in the trial of Officer William Porter, and it is unclear if he will be retried; four additional officers face serious charges in the death. The Gray death did not involve a shooting, and the sentiment is perhaps even more emotional when such is the case. The 2014 case of Michael Brown in Ferguson, Missouri, did involve the police shooting of an unarmed suspect, as did the case of Tamir Rice in Cleveland, Ohio that same year. Of course, such incidents have also been associated with retaliatory acts of violence and aggression toward police, including riots and protests. We merely scratch the surface of this topic here but recognize the importance of this emerging area of study, which will undoubtedly have numerous publications solely dedicated to it in the foreseeable future.

For nearly four decades, it has been recommended that law enforcement agencies be required to collect data on police-involved shootings that would be publicly available—from the US Commission on Civil Rights in 1981 to the President's Task Force on 21st Century Policing in 2015 (White, 2016). It is unclear as to why this has not been implemented by this point, and even former FBI director James Comey has said, "It's ridiculous that I can't tell you how many people are shot by police in this country right now" (McCarthy, 2015). Although some may contend that such data are available, Comey has also indicated that FBI and Bureau of Justice statistics in this context should not be taken "at face value." That said, police use of force is a rare event as it has been consistently shown to occur in less than 2% of all encounters with civilians and typically to a minor extent (Hickman, Piquero, & Garner, 2008). The use of deadly force by officers is an even much smaller percentage of what is already a rare event (White, 2016). Nevertheless, without having a national, publicly available database, we cannot fully examine questions such as the frequency of firearm use against citizens and the factors related to such, for instance. Still, it has been suggested that integrating concepts from *social learning* and *terror management theories* can provide some explanations for police shootings of unarmed suspects. Maskaly & Donner (2015) proffer that social learning theory reflects the process officers experience through their training and immersion in the police subculture. They learn about appropriate and inappropriate conduct through a series of reinforcements and expectations instilled in them. An almost inherent "us versus them" mentality ensues, whereby citizens are thought to be potentially dangerous, which strengthens the associations between officers and weakens those with community members. This essentially comes down to a matter of self-protection and survival. According to Maskaly & Donner, though, this alone does not explain the shooting of unarmed suspects. The missing link is what is referred to as *mortality salience priming*, which is the constant reminding of officers that their own death is a potential part of the job. After all, as they point out, officers go to work each day wearing bulletproof Kevlar vests and are equipped with firearms. Moreover, they are required to qualify with their weapons each year, if not twice per year. Taken together, the nature of the subculture reinforces the learned principles of the job and mortality salience that correspond to particular worldviews. Some (if not many or most) officers enter police work because they incorrectly believe it revolves around adventure, action, and the use of force; moreover, the subculture idealizes aggressive and authoritative actions within the paramilitary structure; and, lastly, the subculture often focuses on tactical interventions, conflict, and weapons. Maskaly & Donner contend that the resulting and overarching worldview in this context is that of the need to remain safe and secure and, therefore, annihilate any threats. Another is derogation, whereby officers may draw a distinction between themselves and civilians. Nevertheless, the sequence of events that leads to the shooting of unarmed suspects may certainly be best explained by the aforementioned interaction between the underpinnings of social learning and terror management theories.

In contrast to police actions toward civilians, there are data readily available on violence against police. There are numerous reasons for this, not the least of which is that personnel records require it, as they correspond to such facets as employment disability and workers' compensation claims. Hopefully, departments would also collect and analyze these data to assist in the training and equipping of officers. In their study of the Orlando Police Department, which includes over 700 officers who serve a population of 250,000 full-time residents and over 55 million tourists annually, Covington, Huff-Corzine, & Corzine (2014) examined violent acts against officers from 2006 to 2008. There were 391 such cases during that time period, in which 457 officers were battered. Covington and colleagues found that these events were more likely to occur on weekend nights and against officers who were white (72%) and male (91%). With respect to the offenders, most were also male; however, fewer than half were white, whereas 43% were black and 11% were Hispanic. Such reflects a notable racial discrepancy between victims and perpetrators. Moreover, the odds of an officer battery were significantly greater in multiple-officer rather than single-officer situations. This finding may seem counterintuitive at first glance, but it corresponds to research showing that when multiple officers respond to calls, they tend to be more volatile. Furthermore, offenders may feel more threatened in multiple-officer situations, thereby leading to a potentially more dangerous dynamic. Perhaps the least surprising finding was that those who consumed alcohol were more likely to batter officers. Lastly, the authors found no significant relationship between call type or the use of intermediate weapons (e.g., Tasers) and battery of officers.

Gibbs, Ruiz, & Klapper-Lehman (2014) investigated data regarding line of duty death in the Baltimore Police Department from 1808 to 2006. The main finding was that officers with *social investment* were less likely to be killed while on duty than their lesser invested counterparts. Specifically, the researchers were interested in whether officers were married and had children and their level of experience. Gibbs and colleagues found that 123 Baltimore Police Department officers died in the line of duty between 1808 and 2006, of whom 59% were feloniously killed and 41% died accidentally. The majority were married, but most had no children; and experience ranged from a few months to more than 44 years. In predicting felonious deaths, they found that marriage was an important predictor but not children; they also found that less experienced officers were more likely to be killed in the line of duty than those with more experience. To the extent that social investment is defined by marriage and level of experience, this research supports the notion that such decreases the likelihood of felonious death in the line of duty. This is consistent with research that has found marital problems to increase one's likelihood in that regard. Researchers have also found that fatal assaults on officers vary by region, such that the South has consistently had the most officers feloniously killed (Boylen & Little, 1990), which is consistent with the more general southern culture of violence literature we outlined earlier in this chapter. Furthermore, robberies in progress and domestic violence scenarios are linked to more fatalities, as are deaths via handguns; however, Boylen & Little (1990) found that such were mostly with the officers' own firearms, whereas Johnson (2008) found few of those instances.

Of course, a separate topic altogether is that of *suicide by cop* incidents, whereby citizens intentionally create a scenario in which the police will be compelled to shoot them—a subject we touch upon in Chapter 6.

Limitations of the Firearm-Related Violence Research

There are limitations associated with all research studies. However, there are inherent limitations to studies that employ *correlational* rather than experimental designs. This is essentially unavoidable in the firearm arena, though, given the nature of the research questions involved. We simply cannot conduct experiments to address most relevant questions. We can come close, such that we can create laboratory-based shooting scenarios and the like; but such simulation studies come with their own set of limitations and caveats. Therefore, in most cases, we are retrospectively reviewing data or information to investigate the relationship among variables. As such, we can only speak to *correlation* and not *causation*, and questions such as "Do more people own firearms because of high crime rates in a given area, or is the crime higher because more guns are present?" remain unanswered. This concept in particular has been described as *reverse causation, post-diction* (as opposed to prediction), and, more colloquially, the chicken and egg problem, or, as Kleck (2015) more formally articulated it:

> Beginning students in research methods are taught that in order to establish that one variable, X, has a causal effect on another variable, Y, one must establish that (1) there is a statistical association between X and Y, (2) this association is not spurious, that is, it is not completely the product of confounder variables (antecedent variables that affect both X and Y), and (3) X is causally antecedent to Y, rather than (or in addition to) the reverse. (p. 41)

In his recent article, Mattaini's (2012) opening sentence is, perhaps, the most telling when he notes that the data tell us "not so much." He points out the way in which distortions in data, methodologically weak studies, and publication biases (among other things) have impacted the quality of the literature on guns and violence. Mattaini notes, however, that one of the most significant concerns is that research on firearm-related violence by the CDC was halted for over a decade due to a block on funding (see The missing data on gun violence, 2016). Nevertheless, Kleck (2015) found notable methodological problems in research that has investigated the impact of gun ownership rates on crime rates. He examined 41 studies that tested the theory that higher gun prevalence rates cause higher crime rates, particularly higher homicide rates. A primary finding of his was that the research quality in this area of research is poor, noting that only about one-third of the studies' findings were based on valid measures of gun prevalence and only 7% were based on sufficient methods to demonstrate causation. Kleck found three primary types of shortcomings in the firearm prevalence research literature: (i) most studies do not use a valid measure of gun ownership levels; (ii) most researchers do not control for confounding variables; and (iii) virtually no studies properly modeled the potential two-way relationship between gun levels and violence rates, such that they may have confused the effect of crime rates on gun levels. Additionally, Kleck (2004) indicated that most studies investigating the impact of gun levels on crime and violence rates use proxies of macro-level gun ownership, oftentimes yielding uninterpretable findings due to poor or unknown validity. As noted in more detail in Chapter 1 of this book, he asserts that, "the best measure for cross-sectional research is the percentage of suicides committed with guns" (Kleck, 2004, p. 3). With respect to confounding variables, Kleck (2015) noted that they are considered such when they are significantly correlated (statistically) with both predictor and outcome variables. However, he found that few studies accounted for such and that even those that did accounted for few. Moreover, fewer than one-third of findings in the research literature reflected positive associations between firearm ownership levels and crime rates, although there was a stronger connection for homicide rates, specifically. However, Kleck found that the "findings of lower quality studies are diametrically opposed to those of higher quality studies" (2015, p. 46). Namely, he noted that when researchers employed an invalid measure of gun prevalence, 62% of the homicide findings were positive as opposed to the 36% of findings when a valid measure was used. As such, Kleck concluded: "Technically weak research mostly supports this hypothesis, while strong research does not" (2015, p. 40).

Others, such as Wallace (2015), have pointed out that certain data, such as NICS background checks, are only an approximation of ownership statistics and that macro studies cannot address why people may choose to obtain a firearm post-shooting. Stroebe (2013) contended that firearms merely provide a means to achieving the goal of killing oneself or someone else and, therefore, that the possession of a firearm cannot be a primary cause of homicide or suicide. Nevertheless, he points out that firearms are a very effective way of committing such acts, which is the reason for the correlation between firearm possession and homicide and suicide rates. He further indicates that macro-level studies of cultural, demographic, and economic variables related to homicide and suicide do not account for the motivating factors behind such acts. Still, Stroebe opined that firearm ownership increases suicide and homicide rates as easy access to firearms increases the likelihood of dying from violent causes. It may be the case that the presence of firearms increases aggressive behavior and that individuals who own them may have characteristics that put them at increased risk of being shot. Of course, the lethality of a firearm goes without saying, but there may be an issue of reverse causality in this context. Namely, research shows that the likelihood of handgun ownership is greater in cities with high crime rates. Still, this does not fully explain the aforementioned connection between gun ownership and homicide rates. Moreover, it does not appear that guns simply serve as a substitute for other means of homicide, nor does the research support self-defense or deterrence hypotheses. However, the aforementioned reverse causality issue is unavoidable. Firearms are lethal and, therefore, a very effective means of committing suicide and homicide. Thus, people use them for those purposes. Also, a cyclical relationship exists in the context of homicide and crime: "Easy access to guns increases homicide rates and increased homicide rates motivate people to buy guns for self-protection" (p. 719).

Eckberg (2015) also raised concerns subsequent to analyzing data from the National Crime Victimization Survey (NCVS) and the FBI's *Uniform Crime Report* (UCR). Namely, notable trend differences related to estimates of serious injury and mortality were found when using the NCVS versus the UCR data. The fact that different patterns emerged from two comparable data series is concerning and, as Eckberg stated, "The trend differences raise serious problems of data choice for the researcher" (p. 59). Barber & Hemenway (2011) conducted an extensive and in-depth analysis of the accuracy of mortality data regarding unintentional firearm fatalities in the United States. Specifically, they examined data from the National Violent Death Reporting System (NVDRS) and investigated every firearm death reported as an accident by any NVDRS data source—the NVDRS abstracter, the State Vital Statistics Registry (i.e., the ICD-10 underlying cause of death code and manner of death from the death certificate), the medical examiner's or coroner's report, and the police supplementary homicide report. They found that, although the NVDRS data were accurately classified, the State Vital Statistics Registry had great inaccuracies. Over half of unintentional shootings by another person were misclassified as homicides, not accidents. Barber & Hemenway also found that many unambiguous homicides and suicides were reported as accidents. Somewhat unbelievably, a primary reason for the errors is a software processing issue of the CDC's National Center for Health Statistics. For instance, if manner of death is pending or missing from a death certificate, the software uses "accident" as the default. Additional reasons for errors in the data include, but are not necessarily limited to: (i) the way in which firearm-related deaths are classified by coroners and medical examiners in the first place; (ii) inaccuracies in the state of residence data when state lines are crossed; (iii) unintentional shooting deaths, or "other-inflicted accidents," classified as homicides; and (iv) deaths that occur after notable time passes following an accidental injury. Taken together, there has been a great overreporting of unintentional deaths, and this is clearly a major problem considering the implications that have been drawn based on these data. Many true accidents seem to be missed, while many suicides and homicides are mistakenly classified as accidents. Barber & Hemenway concluded:

> In over half of the cases in which one person unintentionally shoots another, the case is coded as a homicide, not accident, for underlying cause of death. However, at the same time, many firearm homicides and suicides are mistakenly captured as accidents, apparently largely as a result of a coding algorithm in the software that was designed to improve and standardize cause-of-death coding. Official mortality data are therefore an unreliable source of data on unintentional firearm deaths because they miss many true positives and report many false positives. The problem is particularly acute in certain states. The National Violent Death Reporting System, on the other hand, applies a case definition for unintentional firearm deaths with consistency and accuracy. (p. 731)

International Perspectives

Research has indicated that there are more guns in US households than in those of any other comparable country (Killias, van Keseteren, & Rindlisbacher, 2001). Furthermore, Wintemute (2015b) found that the US firearm-related violence and suicide mortality rates notably exceeded those in other industrialized nations. However, this finding does not appear to reflect a predisposition to violence in this country as it ranks among the lowest in its prevalence of assaults. Such is consistent with the research conducted by Altheimer (2008), whose sample was comprised of 45,913 individuals across 39 cities in developing nations. Namely, those results suggested that individuals who reside in cities where firearms are more widely available had higher odds of being the victim of firearm assault or firearm robbery compared to individuals who live in cities with fewer guns available but that gun availability does not influence one's likelihood of overall crime victimization. In a follow-up study, Altheimer & Boswell (2012) noted that the relationship between gun availability and violence is shaped by sociohistorical and cultural processes occurring across nations. They found the most significant relationship between gun availability and firearm-related homicide in Latin American nations, which is the opposite of what is found in eastern European countries. van Kesteren (2014) analyzed data from 26 developed countries and came to the same conclusion: particularly, that handgun ownership was positively related to serious violence but not for less serious violent crimes. As such, international homicide rates and gun violence are distinct issues from other types of violence (Felson, Berg, & Rogers, 2014). In sum, violence is not an "American problem" but rather a global one.

For instance, bank robberies in Australia doubled from the 1990s to 2001 before stabilizing; however, the rates of firearm use in such robberies remained extremely low and unchanged (Willis, 2006). In fact, unarmed bank robberies were the most prevalent from 1995 to 2005, followed by other weapons. But why the stabilization? Certainly, a focus on firearms would not have affected the crime and violence rates. Rather, Willis suggested that such is attributable to increased security measures in banks, or *target hardening*, and a reduced heroin market. Furthermore, approximately 4,400 people die each day from acts of violence, and the World Health Assembly declared violence a major public health issue in 1996 (Krug et al., 2002).

According to the WHO's most recent *Global Status Report on Violence Prevention* (World Health Organization, 2014), there were 475,000 deaths in 2012 as a result of homicide. Males between the ages of 15 and 44 comprised 60% of these deaths, making homicide the third leading cause of death for males in this age group. Additionally, within low- and middle-income countries, the region of the Americas had the highest estimated rates of homicide, followed by the African region. Nevertheless, between 2000 and 2012, homicide rates are estimated to have declined by just over 16% on a global scale and by 39% among high-income countries. Low- and middle-income countries have shown fewer declines. Importantly, deaths are only a portion of the burdens arising from violence. The report indicates that women, children, and the elderly bear the brunt of nonfatal physical, sexual, and psychological abuse. However, most instances of said abuse do not come to the attention of law enforcement, authorities, or service providers, making it difficult to collect data to inform prevention strategies. Additionally, while countries throughout the world are beginning to invest in violence prevention, it is not yet at a scale that is commensurate to the burden. The WHO report outlined seven "best-buy" strategies to prevent or respond to violence, in an effort to both reduce violence and help decrease the likelihood of the perpetration of violence by individuals or becoming a victim. These strategies are:

- Developing safe, stable, and nurturing relationships between children and their parents and caregivers
- Developing life skills in children and adolescents
- Reducing the availability and harmful use of alcohol
- Reducing access to guns and knives
- Promoting gender equality to prevent violence against women
- Changing cultural and social norms that support violence
- Victim identification, care and support programs

The WHO report goes on to discuss important risk factors that can be targeted through policy and other means. Two crosscutting risk factors discussed in the report are ease of access to firearms and other weapons and alcohol use, which are strongly associated with multiple types of violence. One of the main recommendations set forth in the report is to strengthen data collection as while more than half of countries collect data pertaining to intimate partner violence and sexual violence, fewer than half conduct population-based data collection regarding other types of violence, such as elder abuse, youth violence, and child maltreatment (World Health Organization, 2014).

Perhaps the greater issue, then, reverts back to how we define and measure violence, particularly when our intention is to make cross-national and cross-cultural comparisons. Krause (2009) addressed just that in his analysis of these issues. From an international perspective, the only comparable event recorded aside from war- or conflict-related death is violent death, or *criminal homicide*. Perhaps unsurprisingly, the vast majority (75%) of the 208,400 conflict-related deaths between 2004 and 2007 occurred in just 10 countries: Iraq, Sudan, Afghanistan, Colombia, Democratic Republic of Congo, Sri Lanka, India, Somalia, Nepal, and Pakistan. Moreover, those in Afghanistan, Iraq, Somalia, Sri Lanka, and Sudan in 2007 accounted for more than two-thirds of the deaths. There was more than double the number of deaths due to homicidal violence in 2004 alone, however. Namely, 490,000 people died from such in that year, but it was also highly concentrated in southern Africa, Central America, and South America—with substantially higher rates in South Africa, Brazil, Colombia, Guatemala, and El Salvador. In summarizing the data, Krause highlighted three notable problems: (i) undercounting and narrow definitions, (ii) indirect victims of conflict violence, and (iii) the relationship between lethal and non-lethal forms of violence.

First, the accurate reporting of data is an inherent problem to this type of research. For instance, consider the likely colossal underreporting by Yemen, which only records approximately 850 intentional homicides annually and no conflict-related deaths. In other countries, such as Somalia, Pakistan, and Peru, official statistics are simply not maintained in certain contexts or are greatly distorted. The other significant problem in this regard is determining what constitutes conflict-related versus homicidal violence. This distinction is not as clear as one may think, especially in higher-conflict regions. Furthermore, such figures may not include the nuanced forms of intentional death, such as *manslaughter* or those related to self-defense. As Krause aptly noted, "The problem is that one cannot simply add homicide and manslaughter figures without knowing much more about the nature of the event and the legal system in question" (2009, p. 350). For instance, relying on raw data alone cannot tell us if it was a vehicular homicide or if the recorded crime is based on a plea bargain and, therefore, does not reflect the actual event in question. An additional problem is related to the reporting of the crimes in the first place. Krause points out that, "if one does not have faith in one's government, one will not report a crime" (p. 350). He notes that reporting is much more likely in wealthier countries, such that a theft in Egypt or India is much less likely to be reported than one in Austria or Finland, for example. In addition, there is the issue of including suicide in the violence statistics. The FBI has done so; but such is unlikely in many other places—particularly because of the stigma associated with it. Krause (2009) also highlighted the problem with disregarding statistics related to the indirect victims of violence. He points out that the data do not include what is referred to as *excess mortality*, or the indirect deaths caused by war-induced displacement and deprivation of basic needs like clean water, food, shelter, and healthcare. He notes, "Excess mortality in almost all contemporary conflicts vastly exceeds the number of violent deaths" (p. 351) and provides the striking example of the war in the Democratic Republic of Congo from 1998 to 2002. Specifically, estimates indicate that 5.4 million people died as a result of that war, but fewer than 10% died violently. Almost all of the deaths (4.8 million) were the result of preventable diseases and malnutrition. Krause also considered the relationship between lethal and non-lethal forms of violence, consistent with the studies we outlined initially in this subsection. Comparing and contrasting non-lethal forms of violence across countries presents one of the greatest dilemmas in many respects because of the aforementioned issues with reporting and defining such. Namely, certain acts that are classified as violent in the United States either are not considered so in other places or are simply tolerated (e.g., domestic, sexual, and gender-based violence). At the most extreme end of the continuum lay such acts as honor killings and the use of certain lethal weapons other than firearms, such as machetes and fire.

Gerard, Whitfield, Porter, & Browne (2016) examined 28 school shooting cases in the United States, Canada, Finland, Germany, Scotland, and Australia. The researchers established common characteristics of the offender and offense, the differences between adult and youth offenders, and underlying themes of offender characteristics. The results suggest that the majority of offenders were Caucasian, were US citizens, and had suffered from depression. Most commonly, the offenses were well planned, resulted in more than three deaths, and ended in the shooter committing suicide. About half of offenders had been victimized via bullying, abuse, or neglect; and 60% had a history of violence. There were significant differences between adult and youth offenders, such that youth were more likely to have experienced depression, be citizens of the United States, and be somehow associated with the school. Additionally, they were more likely to have made threats prior to the incident and to have stolen their firearms. Agnich (2015) compared attempted and completed mass murder and rampage-style attacks that have taken place on campuses, in addition to a comparison of incidents that involved firearms to others that involved different deadly weapons. Of particular note is that Agnich defined a school-based mass murder as a homicide that involved two or more victims in a school or on school grounds, and she gathered data only for cases that have been reported in newspapers. The database included 282 cases across 38 nations. Based on her analysis, Agnich found that high schools in rural areas were particularly vulnerable compared to other settings, that very few instances involved hostages, and that bullying was reported as a motive in approximately 20% of the cases. In addition, about one-third of mass shooters commit suicide. The average age of perpetrators of mass killings is 28, and although the majority of mass shooters in the United States are white, the perpetrators of mass killings not involving firearms are significantly less likely to be white. For example, incidents of mass stabbings in schools in rural China have increased. Agnich also notes that mass killings involving explosives result in more deaths and injury than those involving firearms. Undoubtedly, mass shootings have received the most attention in the United States; and, therefore, we address such in great detail in the following section.

High-Profile Mass Shootings in the Modern-Day United States

As in most cases, statistics can be interpreted to fit particular views on gun control issues, but high-profile shootings invigorate the debate and seem to make the numbers disappear. Rather, we remember names: Sandy Hook, Virginia Tech, Columbine, the Colorado movie theater—Jared Loughner, Colin Ferguson, Major Nidal Hasan, and, most recently, Omar Mateen. Undoubtedly, these tragedies prompt proposals for sweeping gun reform and evoke strong feelings throughout the country. It is not coincidental that certain laws carry the names of the unfortunate victims, referred to as *apostrophe laws*. Although these laws seem to be on the decline for various reasons (Hampson, 2013), consider apostrophe laws enacted in various contexts, such as Megan's Law, Kendra's Law, and the Adam Walsh Child Protection and Safety Act. In this section, we review some of the details involved in the United States' more recent high-profile shootings, followed by the theory and research behind shootings that involve multiple victims.

Overview of Cases

Colin Ferguson (Long Island, New York, 1993)

On December 7, 1993, Colin Ferguson, a 35-year-old Jamaican native, went through an evening rush-hour Long Island Railroad train, shooting passengers as the train entered Merillion Avenue station. Ferguson's onslaught resulted in him killing six people and injuring 19. He was ultimately sentenced to six consecutive life sentences. However, the Colin Ferguson case was particularly noteworthy because of the mental health questions that were raised. Namely, his attorneys' defense strategy was to demonstrate that Ferguson's actions were not willful but rather born of years of harbored anger living in an oppressive, race-based society. However, Ferguson disagreed with this approach and fired them, thereby choosing to defend himself. Although his competency to do so was questioned, he was found competent by the court and allowed to proceed with one of his initial attorneys serving as an assistant counsel. Ferguson's self-directed defense strategy was to convince the jury that he was framed for the shooting and someone else committed the murders. During his cross-examination of witnesses, including some of his victims, Ferguson engaged in lengthy, nonsensical diatribes and even accused law enforcement of conspiring against him. On February 17, 1993, the jury found him guilty of the murders. Ferguson's attorney subsequently withdrew from the case and brought his competency back into question. Nevertheless, Ferguson proceeded, and during his sentencing hearing he set forth a 3-hour summation and reiterated his entire defense theory. He also compared himself to John the Baptist of the Christian Bible's New Testament and contended that history would vindicate him. Despite questions about his competency and sanity, Ferguson was sentenced accordingly (see Colin Ferguson—The Long Island Railroad gunman, n.d.). Current correctional records indicate that Ferguson is to serve 315 years and 8 months in prison in New York, with a parole eligibility date of 2309. According to the Violence Policy Center, Ferguson legally purchased his handgun, a Ruger P-89 9mm, at a sporting goods store in California, passing the background check and waiting the mandatory 15 days before picking up the firearm (Violence Policy Center, n.d.a).

Eric Harris and Dylan Klebold (Littleton, Colorado, 1999)

On April 20, 1999, Eric Harris (age 18) and Dylan Klebold (age 17) engaged in a shooting spree at Columbine High School in Littleton, Colorado, which resulted in them killing 13 people and injuring more than 20 before they committed suicide. Reports indicate that Harris and Klebold prepared their weapons, which included guns and bombs, at their respective homes before proceeding to the school around lunchtime. A now infamous video of the event depicts the tragedy, whereby students were shot in and around various parts of the school, including the cafeteria where students hid under tables. Teachers attempted to contain the situation by directing students and communicating with 911. Although police arrived within 5 minutes of shots being fired, they did not enter the school—a decision for which the Jefferson County Sheriff's Office was harshly criticized by parents and loved ones, particularly because Harris and Klebold shot additional students subsequent to the officers' arrival. Sheriff John Stone ultimately stated that the shooting represented a "unique set of circumstances, the magnitude of which no one had dealt with before" and indicated that the officers acted in a manner consistent with their training given the obstacles that prevented them from entering the building (e.g., bombs, booby traps, uncertainty about the number of gunmen). However, reports indicate that, by 12:06 p.m., 47 minutes had passed by the time the first SWAT team was assembled and prepared to enter the building and 75 police officers had surrounded Columbine High School. Just 2 minutes later, at 12:08 p.m., Harris and Klebold committed suicide; however, approximately 3 hours passed before this was known. Law enforcement was further criticized, given that reports indicate about 1,000 officers and rescue personnel from 47 agencies came to the scene; but many were left without assigned tasks despite the fact that some victims were severely injured. It took approximately 2 hours after shots were fired for a SWAT team to enter the west side of the school building, wherein victims were awaiting help. One student waited with an injured teacher, Dave Sanders, for over 3 hours after he was shot before police came to his aid at 2:42 p.m.; however, a paramedic did not arrive for an additional 42 minutes, at which point Sanders was dead (see Kohn, 2001). By no means was this the first school shooting in the United States, but it certainly struck a particular chord with the public due to its unique circumstances and number of casualties. According to the Violence Policy Center, four firearms were used in the shooting, two handguns and two shotguns: an Intratec TEC-DC9 assault pistol, a Hi-Point 9mm carbine, a Savage 67H pump-action shotgun, and a Savage 311-D 12-gauge shotgun. These firearms were illegally obtained, however. Namely, they purchased the shotguns and the 9mm carbine from a friend who bought them at a gun show in 1998 from unlicensed sellers—an illegal *straw purchase*. They bought the TEC-DC9 from a pizza shop employee who knew they were too young to purchase it (Violence Policy Center, n.d.b).

Seung-Hui Cho (Blacksburg, Virginia, 2007)

On April 16, 2007, Seung-Hui Cho killed 32 people, injured 17, and committed suicide at Virginia Polytechnic Institute and State University in what has been referred to as the "Virginia Tech" shooting.[6] The shooting is the deadliest committed by a single gunman at a school in US history. Cho was a 23-year-old senior at Virginia Tech, majoring in English. He was a South Korean national who became a permanent US resident in 1992. In December 2005, Cho was accused of stalking female classmates at least twice, and he was ultimately court-ordered to be psychiatrically evaluated because he made suicidal statements to his roommates. He was taken to a hospital for such but released with orders to receive outpatient treatment. Reports subsequent to the 2007 shooting indicate that, although he had not specifically targeted any of his victims, he was a loner with the aforementioned mental health history, he was bullied at a young age, and his class assignments submitted well before the shooting raised concerns among faculty and classmates because they reflected anger and violence. Prior to the incident, in February and March 2007, Cho purchased two firearms: a .22 Walther P-22 and a Glock 19 9mm. He obtained both legally, passing federally mandated background checks, although some groups have contended that his mental health history should have precluded him (Alfano, 2007). Nevertheless, on April 16, he perpetrated his first round of shootings around 7:15 a.m., resulting in two victims. At 9:01 a.m., Cho mailed a package containing video, photos, and writings to NBC News in New York City, although they did not receive it until the April 18 because it was addressed incorrectly. At 9:45 a.m., a second round of shootings was reported, whereby 30 students and faculty were killed (and Cho ultimately killed himself as well). The university communicated with students throughout the morning via e-mails and text messages, providing them with direction and information. At 10:35 a.m., students received an e-mail that the police had one gunman in custody; Cho was formally named the following day. Private donations were subsequently made to the families of each of the 32 victims, such that they were to receive $180,000 each, and those injured were to receive between $40,000 to $90,000 plus tuition waivers. In April 2008, Governor Kaine announced that a "substantial majority" of the victims' families agreed to an $11 million settlement from the state, with the contingency that they could not sue the university, state, or local government in the future. In June 2008, it was reported that a judge approved the settlement and that 24 of the 32 victims families accepted it, along with the 18 who were injured. In December 2010, the US Department of Education released a report that the university had, in fact, failed to notify students in a "timely manner" per the Clery Act. In March 2012, a jury agreed with that sentiment and awarded $4 million each to both of the families who sued the state for wrongful death. However, in October 2013, the Supreme Court of Virginia overturned the jury verdict, indicating that "there was no duty of the Commonwealth to warn students about the potential for criminal acts" by Cho. In April 2014, the university paid $32,500 to the Department of Education for violating the Clery Act by not providing students with timely notification of campus safety information (see Virginia Tech shootings fast facts, 2017; Virginia Tech shooting leaves 32 dead n.d.; Seung-Hui Cho, 2014).

Major Nidal Malik Hasan (Fort Hood, Texas, 2009)

On November 5, 2009, US Army officer and psychiatrist Major Nidal Malik Hasan killed 13 people and injured more than 30 others when he opened fire at a processing center in Fort Hood, Texas. He was 39 years old at the time. It was the worst mass murder at a US military installation, resulting in the death of 12 service members and one Department of Defense employee.

Hasan reportedly shouted "Allahu akbar!" meaning "God is great," prior to targeting soldiers in the center and firing an excess of 200 shots from an FN Herstal Five-seven handgun, which he purchased legally (Hancock, 2011). The shooting lasted approximately 10 minutes before Hasan was shot by a civilian police officer and apprehended; he was left paralyzed from the waist down as a result. With respect to his background, Hasan was born in Virginia, the son of Palestinian immigrants. He graduated from Virginia Tech University and completed his psychiatry training in 2003 at the Uniformed Services University of Health Sciences in Bethesda, Maryland. He was subsequently employed at Walter Reed Medical Center in Washington, DC, treating soldiers returning from war. In May 2009, Hasan was promoted to the rank of major in the Army, and he was transferred to Fort Hood in July. Pentagon and US Senate investigations found that Hasan's supervisors continued to promote him despite concerns that had been raised pertaining to him becoming radicalized by Islamic extremists and, as noted earlier in this chapter (see *Overview of Violence*), the Obama administration was harshly criticized for classifying the shooting as workplace violence rather than an act of terrorism despite Hasan's ties to and ongoing communication with Anwar al-Awlaki, a senior recruiter for al-Qaeda. The FBI and Defense Department also received criticism for missing numerous warning signs. Namely, it was reported that Hasan carefully planned the attack, including training at a local shooting range and researching jihad on his computer. In 2013, Hasan was tried in military court and served as his own attorney. Reports indicate that he informed the judge that he shot at soldiers at Fort Hood who were being deployed to Afghanistan in an effort to protect Muslim and Taliban leaders there. He was reportedly scheduled to be deployed there a few weeks after the shooting as well. Hasan attempted to plead guilty prior to the trial, but military rules governing capital punishment cases do not allow for such. During the trial, Hasan did not call any witnesses, set forth limited evidence, and made no closing argument. He was subsequently found guilty of 45 counts of premeditated murder and attempted premeditated murder by a jury and, ultimately, sentenced to death (see Army major kills 13 people in Fort Hood shooting spree, n.d.; Kenbar, 2013). He was transferred to the military's death row at the US Disciplinary Barracks in Fort Leavenworth, Kansas, where he remains with five others, although the military has not executed anyone since 1961 (Death Penalty Information Center, n.d.). Of note is that, in 2014, Hasan wrote to the head of Islamic State, requesting to become a "citizen" of the group (Chumley, 2014).

Jared Lee Loughner (Tucson, Arizona, 2011)

On January 8, 2011, 23-year-old Jared Lee Loughner killed six people and injured 13 when he fired shots at an event in Tucson, Arizona, where Democratic Representative Gabrielle Giffords was meeting constituents. Giffords was one of those injured; she was shot in the head but survived. In

November 2012, Loughner was sentenced to seven life terms and 140 years in prison without parole. Loughner was born in 1988 and raised by his parents in northern Tucson. Reports indicate that he had a troubled life, exhibiting psychotic symptoms as early as high school. Namely, he wrote and said illogical statements, his thought process was disorganized, and he developed a pathological obsession with the US Constitution. He demonstrated similarly concerning behavior during his time at Pima Community College, where he reportedly made disturbing statements about terrorism and engaged in otherwise inappropriate behavior. Loughner was ultimately suspended from the college in the fall of 2010 subsequent to repeated disruptions there and for posting concerning videos online, wherein he would make such claims as the college was "illegal." Loughner chose to withdraw from school rather than engage in the mental health risk evaluation the school required for him to return. His parents became increasingly concerned about him and attempted to keep him home when possible; but Loughner continued to post anti-government videos online, and there is no indication that he was ever psychiatrically evaluated or treated during that time. On January 8, Loughner went to a Tucson grocery store where Congresswoman Giffords was holding a meet-and-greet event. He brought a Glock 19 9mm handgun, which he purchased legally 2 months prior after passing a background check and which he was legally allowed to conceal (Grimaldi & Kunkle, 2011). Loughner proceeded to fire 31 shots in a span of 30 seconds, hitting 19 people—six of whom died, including a 9-year-old girl, a congressional aide, and a district judge. As noted, Giffords was shot in the head and badly injured, leaving her right arm and leg paralyzed as well as impairing her speech and vision. During the subsequent investigation, an envelope was found in Loughner's home on which he had written that he "planned ahead" the "assassination" of "Giffords." FBI reports have also indicated that Loughner began focusing on Giffords prior to the shooting, such as watching her speeches online at the city library. Reports further indicate that Loughner may have met Giffords in 2007 when she spoke at his high school, when he asked her an odd question and found her answer unacceptable ("Loner" Jared Loughner, 2011). Loughner initially pled not guilty to the murder and attempted murder charges against him. However, he was found incompetent to stand trial in May 2011 due to impairments related to his schizophrenia diagnosis. He was cleared to proceed the following year, in August 2012, at which point he entered into a plea agreement and pled guilty to 19 charges in exchange for the removal of the death penalty for consideration (see Jared Lee Loughner, 2015). Loughner was initially held at the Federal Correctional Institution in Phoenix before being transferred to the US Penitentiary in Tucson; however, records indicate that he was most recently housed at the US Medical Center for Federal Prisoners in Springfield, Missouri, before being transferred to his current placement at the Federal Medical Center in Rochester, Minnesota (Loughner moved to MN facility, 2016).

Adam Lanza (Newton, Connecticut, 2012)

On December 14, 2012, Adam Lanza (age 20) shot and killed 20 first-graders and six adults at Sandy Hook Elementary School in Newtown, Connecticut, before committing suicide. The shooting is the second deadliest committed by a single gunman at a school in US history (the first is that of Virginia Tech in 2007). According to the Connecticut Office of the State Attorney's report (2013), Lanza was born in New Hampshire in 1992 and raised by his parents along with his older brother. At age 16, Lanza's parents divorced; and he moved to Stamford, Connecticut, with his mother. In 2010, his older brother moved out of state after college; he attempted to contact Lanza a few times after moving, but Lanza never responded. They had had no contact since 2010. Lanza had not had contact with his father since that time as well. Reports indicate that Lanza was diagnosed with Asperger's disorder in 2005—one of the previously separated subtypes of autism that now fall within the autism spectrum disorder classification. Others described him as someone who had "significant social impairments and extreme anxiety." Reports also indicate that he lacked emotion and was extremely particular, such that he did not allow anyone in his room, he disliked birthdays and holidays, and he prevented his mother from putting up a Christmas tree or having a pet cat. He did not like to be touched, so when he had his hair cut, he would sit with his hands in his lap and look down; he did not like the sound of the shears. Those who worked on the property had to speak to Ms. Lanza outside and had to make prior plans to use power equipment because he had problems with loud noises. He was evaluated numerous times over the years, which revealed speech and language deficits, seizures, and concerning behaviors early on, including repetitive behaviors, tantrums, smelling things that were not there, excessive handwashing, and eating idiosyncrasies. It was reported that in school he had "extreme anxiety" with "changes, noise, and physical contact with others" (Moreno, 2013). Despite his severe problems, Lanza refused to take medications and engage in recommended behavioral therapies. Of note, however, is that he never engaged in acts of violence or gave indications of such to professionals with whom he had interacted. That said, Lanza made various anonymous postings on websites and online video games indicating that he was going to perpetrate a school shooting and commit suicide just days before the incident. On the morning of December 14, Lanza shot his mother in the head, killing her, and then took her car to drive the 5 miles to Sandy Hook Elementary School. As noted, he shot and killed 20 first-grade students as well as six staff members, including the principal and school psychologist. Two additional teachers were shot but survived. Lanza then killed himself. It remains unclear as to why he targeted the elementary school, however, or what triggered him to engage in the shooting in the first place. However, the subsequent investigation revealed that Lanza had a strong interest in firearms, which his mother also shared; they had numerous weapons in the home as well as ammunition. In fact, Ms. Lanza wanted to purchase, and had already made out a check for, a CZ 83 handgun for him for Christmas. They went target shooting and took NRA safety courses together. According to the state attorney's report, the following weapons were recovered in the course of this investigation: (i) a Bushmaster Model XM15-E2S semiautomatic rifle, found in the same classroom as Lanza's body (all of the 5.56mm shell casings from the school that were tested were found to have been fired from this rifle); (ii) a Glock 20, 10mm semiautomatic pistol found near Lanza's body, which was determined to have been the firearm he used to commit suicide; (iii) a Sig Sauer P226, 9mm semiautomatic pistol found on Lanza's person, although there was no evidence it was fired; (iv) an Izhmash Saiga-12, 12-gauge semiautomatic shotgun found in the trunk of Lanza's car in the parking lot outside the school, although there was no evidence it was fired either; and (v) a Savage Mark II rifle found at Lanza's home, which he used to kill his mother. Lanza used his mother's legally obtained and registered firearms to commit the homicides and suicide. The state attorney's report also indicates that Lanza was preoccupied with mass killings, particularly Columbine, and that he had a spreadsheet with mass murders over the years along with information about each shooting. Digital evidence seized from the home included Internet bookmarks for such topics as firearms, mass murder, and ammunition, as well as videos depicting suicide by gunshot, commercial movies with mass shootings, a computer game entitled "School Shooting," images of Lanza holding a handgun and rifle to his head, and various other disturbing (and benign) items (see Adam Lanza, 2016).

James Eagan Holmes (Aurora, Colorado, 2012)

James Eagan Holmes, then age 24, killed 12 people and injured 70 when he perpetrated a mass shooting at a Colorado movie theater on July 20, 2012. Holmes was born in San Diego, California, and graduated from high school in Rancho Penasquitos, California, in 2006. He subsequently completed a bachelor's degree in neuroscience from the University of California, Riverside, in 2010. In 2011, he enrolled in the University of Colorado's doctoral program in neuroscience at the Denver campus. In early 2012, he began seeing a psychiatrist at the campus clinic but stopped when he withdrew from school that summer. On July 7, 2012, Holmes bought a ticket online for the July 19 showing of *The Dark Knight Rises* at the Century Aurora 16 Multiplex Theater in Aurora. On July 19, he entered the theater for the midnight showing of the movie but left an exit door leading to the parking lot propped open. Eighteen minutes into the movie, just after midnight, Holmes threw tear gas canisters into the theater and fired into the audience. He was apprehended by police within 7 minutes of the first 911 calls near the theater, wearing a gas mask and body armor; his hair had been dyed red, which was purportedly to resemble "the Joker," a notorious Batman villain. Reports indicate that Holmes planned the shooting approximately 4 months prior and that he received a high volume of deliveries to his apartment and to the university during that time period. He also purchased various firearms during that time and had four guns on him during the shooting: an AR-15 assault rifle, a Remington 12-gauge 870 shotgun, and two 40-caliber Glock handguns. He obtained all of these firearms legally; he passed all required background checks (Carbone, 2012), and he purchased more than 6,000 rounds of ammunition online. Holmes also reportedly told authorities that he had booby-trapped his home; but all makeshift bombs were disarmed, and no personnel were injured. It was also reported that Holmes had mailed a notebook about his mental health problems and homicidal thoughts to his prior psychiatrist hours before the shooting, although it was not discovered until days later. Subsequent to his arrest, Holmes was held in Arapahoe Detention Center, where he reportedly experienced psychotic episodes and attempted suicide, leading to a hospitalization. In late July 2012, Holmes made his first set of court appearances and was charged with 24 counts of first-degree murder and 116 counts of attempted murder, in addition to weapons charges. In March 2013, Holmes attempted to plead guilty to avoid the death penalty, but prosecutors rejected the offer and sought to move forward with trial. In May 2013, Holmes pled not guilty by reason of insanity. His trial ultimately began on April 27, 2015, and ended 11 weeks later. On July 16, 2015, after 12 hours of deliberation, a jury found him guilty on all 24 counts of first-degree murder and 140 counts of attempted murder as some counts had been added. He was also found guilty of possession or control of an explosive or incendiary device (see James Holmes, 2015; Aurora theater shooting, n.d.; New photos, 2015). He ultimately received 12 life sentences, one for each person he killed, plus 3,318 years in prison for the additional 70 he attempted to kill and the plan to detonate his apartment (Hernandez & Ingold, 2016). Holmes had been housed in the Colorado State Penitentiary in Canon City as of March 2016; however, he was assaulted by another inmate (despite being in a no-contact setting) and was moved out of state to an (initially) undisclosed facility. Of note is that, while a transfer is not atypical in such cases, the fact that his whereabouts were unknown to the public for some time is quite uncommon (Margolin & McKinley, 2016). Nevertheless, a search as of September 2017 indicates he is housed in US Penitentiary in Allenwood, Pennsylvania.

Omar Mateen (Orlando, Florida, 2016)

As this book was being written, what had been the deadliest mass shooting in US history (until Las Vegas 2017, see following section) was perpetrated by Omar Mateen. Mateen, age 29, killed 49 people and injured 53 more in a gay nightclub in Orlando, Florida, on June 12, 2016. He was armed with legally purchased weapons, an AR-15-type rifle and a Glock 17 handgun. After a 3-hour standoff with the police, he was killed in the nightclub, after a hostage situation had developed. According to the ongoing investigation, Mateen was a US citizen born in New York to parents who had emigrated from Afghanistan. Several sources have since come forward revealing that

Mateen talked about killing people frequently and that he hated women, blacks, lesbians, and Jews. In fact, a former police officer who had frequent contact with the perpetrator, told the press that he complained several times that Mateen was dangerous, especially after Mateen started texting him 20–30 times per day, as well as leaving him more than a dozen phone messages. Sources indicated that Mateen's actions were not surprising given his previous behavior. His ex-wife also commented on his past behavior and mental health, reporting that he physical abused her regularly and that he was "mentally unstable and mentally ill [and] obviously disturbed, deeply, and traumatized." Additionally, the perpetrator had a history with the FBI as he had allegedly made inflammatory remarks to co-workers regarding affiliations with a terror group. Nevertheless, the FBI was never able to substantiate any connections with actual terror groups prior to the shooting. According to news reports, Mateen called 911 prior to his attack and declared his allegiance to Islamic State. His motivations were likely complex and not readily apparent, and many have speculated about what factors may have contributed to this deadly attack. As an example, his ex-wife commented that he showed "no sign" of radicalism, although he was religious. His father stated, "This has nothing to do with religion" and added that Mateen had recently been infuriated after he witnessed a public display of affection between two gay men, which he guessed may have been related to his son's later actions. Days after the shooting, the massacre was determined to be both an act of terrorism and a hate crime. However, it has not been substantiated whether Islamic State was connected to the attack, although it has reportedly claimed responsibility (Teague, Ackerman, & Safi, 2016; Perez, Brown, & Almasy, 2016).

Stephen Paddock (Las Vegas, Nevada, 2017)

On the evening of October 1, 2017, Stephen Paddock, age 64, perpetrated what is now the deadliest mass shooting in US history, killing 58 people and injuring over 500 at a country music festival near the Mandalay Bay Resort and Casino in Las Vegas, Nevada. Despite an immediate response and call for action, including for policy changes (e.g., bans on "bump fire" stocks and gun control initiatives, more generally), by various politicians, media personnel, and celebrities, the underlying motives and explanations of what drove Paddock to commit this heinous act remain largely unknown—as this book is being written, even 1 month later (see Ellis & Chavez, 2017). It is believed that he shot from his window on the hotel's 32nd floor and that he had approximately two dozen firearms with high-capacity magazines, but we will not speculate further given the general uncertainty that remains regarding this incident. It is noteworthy, however, that his father, Benjamin Paddock, was a career criminal and spent years on the FBI's most wanted list (see Philipps & Haag, 2017).

Theory and Research

In this section, we take a closer look at the statistics and motives behind mass shootings in the United States. The reader will note that nearly all of the shooters highlighted in the previous section obtained their firearms legally, passing background checks. In fact, the vast majority of guns used in mass shootings have been obtained legally (Buchanan, Keller, Oppel, & Victor, 2016; Chuck, 2015). It is somewhat difficult to find incidences where *illegally* obtained firearms were used. The Columbine tragedy fits that exception in the previous section, although there are instances such as Sandy Hook where a legally owned and registered firearm was stolen and used by the shooter. Another example is the more recent 2014 Marysville-Pilchuck High School shooting in Washington State, where Jaylen Fryberg used his father's handgun to kill four other students, injure one, and commit suicide (Marysville shooter texted before killings, 2016). Others include the 2007 Westroads Mall shooting in Omaha, Nebraska (Friedberg & Davey, 2007), and the 2005 Red Lake High School shooting in Red Lake, Minnesota (Enger, 2015); but these occurrences are few and far between. Such is true in high-profile shootings, more generally, as well (Violence Policy Center, n.d.c). On the other hand, illegally obtained and operated firearms are likely more commonly used than not by those committing various other crimes, including, but not limited to, selling drugs, robbery, burglary, carjacking, rape, and, of course, murder (see *Criminological Considerations* above). Regarding illegally obtained guns, a survey of inmates in a state prison, conducted in 1991, indicated that among those who had possessed a firearm 9% had illegally acquired their firearm through theft, while 28% acquired their firearm through an illegal market (Zawitz, 1995). Further, in March 1995, the FBI's stolen gun file contained 2 million reports of stolen firearms, the majority of which were handguns (Zawitz, 1995).

The Statistics

The group Everytown published its 2015 report on mass shootings, in which it investigated such incidents from January 2009 to July 2015 across 39 states (Everytown, 2015). Specifically, the group investigated the 133 mass shootings that occurred during that time identifiable through FBI data and media reports. The report described the events in detail, including their locations, the number of casualties, and information about the shooters as well as the firearms, ammunition, and gun purchase. The group utilized the FBI definition of *mass shooting*: any incident whereby at least four people are murdered with a gun. Everytown noted that "Less than one percent of gun murder victims recorded by the FBI in 2012 were killed by incidents with four or more victims" (p. 2). However, during the 7-year period, no more than 3 months had passed without a mass shooting. Although 85% of gun homicide victims are male, there is no such divide between victims of mass shootings (i.e., 50% male and 50% female). Perpetrators of mass shootings are older, on average, than others who commit murders with a firearm, with the median ages being 34 and 26, respectively. High-capacity magazines or "assault weapons" were only used in 11% of the incidents, although they led to three times as many injuries and twice the number of deaths when used. With regard to mental health considerations, only one shooter of the 133 was prohibited by federal law from possessing guns due to severe mental illness. Moreover, only in 11% of the incidents were concerns about the mental health of the shooter previously brought to someone's attention. Moreover, in most cases (62%), the shooter was not prohibited from possessing the firearm for any reason. In nearly half (44%) of the shootings, the shooter committed suicide during the incident; but in only 11% of the shootings were law enforcement or military officers injured or killed. Only 4% of the shootings occurred at the shooter's current or prior workplace, and only 4% were perpetrated in schools, including primary and secondary schools as well as colleges. In contrast, most incidents (71%) occurred in private residences, and only 13% of the shootings occurred in "entirely" public places that were characterized as *gun-free zones*.

In 2014, the FBI published an unclassified report of active shooter incidents between 2000 and 2013 (Blair & Schweit, 2014). The report indicated that the agreed-upon definition of an active shooter by US government agencies, including the White House, the US Department of Justice/FBI, the US Department of Education, and the US Department of Homeland Security/Federal Emergency Management Agency, is: "an individual actively engaged in killing or attempting to kill people in a confined and populated area" with the use of a firearm (p. 5). As such, the FBI's study is not one of mass shootings and, furthermore, it excluded "shootings that resulted from gang or drug violence—pervasive, long-tracked, criminal acts that could also affect the public" (p. 5). From 2000 to 2013, the FBI identified 160 active shooter incidents in the United States resulting in 1,043 casualties. However, the majority of that number (53%) were people injured and not killed. Furthermore, it classified mass killings as those that resulted in three or more deaths; as such, it reported that 40% of the incidents constituted a mass killing, with the highest casualty counts in the Aurora, Virginia Tech, Fort Hood, and Sandy Hook incidents outlined in the previous section.

That said, of the 160 active shooting incidents identified by the FBI between 2000 and 2013, 48 would be considered a mass killing according to the definition that required four or more deaths, while 65 would be considered a mass killing according to the FBI's classification of mass killings. Nevertheless, all but two of the 160 active shooting incidents identified by the FBI from 2000 to 2013 included a single shooter, and only six involved female shooters. Of note is that five shooters remained at large. With respect to the duration of the incidents, in the 63 shootings where the time could be ascertained, 70% ended in 5 minutes or less, approximately one-third ended in 2 minutes or less, and 67% ended before police arrived. In approximately one-quarter of the 160 shootings the shooter committed suicide at the scene before police arrived. In 13% of the shootings, the situation ended because citizens restrained the shooter, half of whom were school staff. In only five of the incidents did individuals who were non–law enforcement personnel exchange gunfire with the shooters to end the incident, and only two incidents ended when off-duty officers engaged the shooters. On-duty officers were injured or killed in half of the 45 shootings where they engaged shooters, resulting in nine deaths. With respect to location, approximately half occurred in commerce-related environments (e.g., businesses both open and closed to pedestrian traffic) and one-quarter occurred in educational environments, including two school board meetings. Other shootings occurred in open spaces (9.4%), government properties (10.0%), other (non-military) government properties (6.9%), residences (4.4%), houses of worship (3.8%), military properties (3.1%), and healthcare facilities (2.5%). Of particular note is that the study did not focus on the motivation of the shooters, which is essential to understanding why these shootings occur and how we can best prevent them in the future.

Etter & Swymeler (2010) investigated 114 courthouse shootings from 1907 to 2007 by contacting 500 of the 3,084 sheriff's departments in the United States. They found that the majority (61%) occurred between 1987 and 2007 and that California (14) and Texas (13) have had notably more than other states, although this is not particularly surprising given their respective sizes. In three-quarters of the shootings, firearms were brought into the courthouse by the shooter, whereas approximately 20% were taken from a deputy. Domestic violence and related problems were the motivation in one-third of the shootings, assassination was attributable for another third, and escape was the motive in one-quarter of the cases. In most cases (59%), litigants or other court officials were the victims, followed by law enforcement officers (33%) and judges (8%). Approximately 60% of the shooters were apprehended; the remaining either were shot by security or committed suicide. In the majority of cases (58%), a gang member or a member of an extremist group was on trial. Unfortunately, 91% of the courthouses actually had metal detectors in place, although their usage was clearly poor.

Nekvasil, Cornell, & Huang (2015) examined the prevalence and offense characteristics of homicides involving multiple victims across locations using data from the FBI's National Incident Based Reporting System, which included nearly 19,000 incidents involving more than 25,000 victims between 2005 and 2010. In the vast majority of cases (78%), homicide incidents included a single victim, and 22% involved two or more victims. Specifically, 15.4% had two victims, 3.9% had three victims, 1.5% had four victims, and only 1% had five or more victims. Moreover, most homicides occurred in residences (52%), followed by highways/roads/alleys (24%), and parking lots/garage/terminals (6%), whereas just 0.3% occurred in schools. With respect to weapon use, most (68%) involved a firearm, and the most common offender–victim relationship was acquaintance (46%), followed by close relations (38%); just 16% involved strangers. Regarding the offenders, 90% were male and most (69%) were age 18–39, followed by 40–65 (23%). Based on the data, Nekvasil and colleagues concluded that schools are not a high-risk location for homicides, whereas other areas (which do not receive comparable media attention) are more likely to experience multiple-casualty shootings. The authors highlight the fact that hundreds of professional organizations and other entities set forth position statements recommending school security and related interventions; however, this is based on the misperception that schools are "risky places that need more protection from violent attacks than other locations," which led them to question the "massive allocation of public funding and human resources to school security" (p. 241). As a result, such resources are pulled away from the areas and contexts that are of much greater risk in this respect. But, as the authors quipped, "'restaurant violence' has not been identified as a public safety concern" (p. 242). Furthermore, the data clearly illustrate that multiple-casualty homicides, particularly mass shootings, are very rare events that comprise a very low percentage of all homicides in this country. Undoubtedly, firearms are a risk factor for multiple-casualty homicides given the ability to harm more people quicker than other means. However, these incidents are rare, as noted, and fatal shootings in environments such as schools are no more likely to be perpetrated than homicides with other weapons.

The Reasons

Public misconceptions regarding firearm-related injuries and deaths have been largely attributed to media coverage and attention (Nekvasil et al., 2015; Perrin, 2016). These also contribute to myths and misunderstandings about firearms and the associated statistics. In this context, Fox and DeLateur (2014) expressed concerns with the assumptions that are often made about mass murder and set forth a number myths and misconceptions related to mass shootings and multiple homicides. We addressed these in Chapter 2 of this book, but it is useful to highlight those applicable to the issues we are considering in this chapter. Recall that the myths they set forth were:

1. Mass murderers snap and kill indiscriminately
2. Mass shootings are on the rise
3. Recent mass murders involve record-setting body counts
4. Violent forms of entertainment, especially video games, are causally linked to mass murder
5. Greater attention and response to the telltale warning signs will allow us to identify would-be mass killers before they act
6. Widening the availability of mental health services will allow unstable individuals to get the treatment they need and avert mass murders
7. Enhanced background checks will keep dangerous weapons out of the hands of these madmen
8. Restoring the federal ban on assault weapons will prevent these horrible crimes and expanding "right to carry" provisions will deter mass killers or at least stop them in their tracks and reduce body counts

9. Increasing physical security in schools and other places will prevent mass murder
10. Having armed guards at every school will serve to protect students from an active shooter and provide a deterrent

It is relevant to point out that myths 9 and 10 reflect the findings of Nekvasil and colleagues (2015) delineated in the previous section. We will address number 6 in the mental health section that follows in this chapter, but let us focus on myths 1, 4, and 5 here. Namely, that mass murderers snap and kill indiscriminately; violent forms of entertainment, especially video games, are causally linked to mass murder; and greater attention and response to the tell-tale warning signs will allow us to identify would-be mass killers before they act. However, the research investigating these topics, for example, the connection between violent media and violent behavior, is mixed at best (Ferguson & Konijn, 2015). So, if these are myths, what are the actual motivations behind such heinous acts? According to Fox & DeLateur (2014), the motives for mass murder revolve around five primary themes that can occur independently or in combination:

1. Revenge (e.g., a deeply disgruntled individual seeks payback for a host of failures in career, school, or personal life);
2. Power (e.g., a "pseudo-commando" style massacre perpetrated by some marginalized individual attempting to wage a personal war against society);
3. Loyalty (e.g., a devoted husband/father kills his entire family and then himself to spare them all from a miserable existence on earth and to reunite them in the hereafter);
4. Terror (e.g., a political dissident destroys government property, with several victims killed as "collateral damage," to send a strong message to those in power); and
5. Profit (e.g., a gunman executes the customers and employees at a retail store to eliminate all witnesses to a robbery). (p. 3)

As we will see in the following section, there is a clear distinction between mass shootings perpetrated in the community and school shootings. Let us take a closer look at school shootings, which have gained the most media attention and public outcry and have prompted the most policy change as a result.

School Shootings

Although the names *Columbine* and *Virginia Tech* readily come to mind in the context of modern-day school shootings, they in no way represent the beginning of school massacres in this country. In actuality, the first was the Enoch Brown school massacre in Greencastle, Pennsylvania, in 1764. It occurred following a particularly gruesome series of murders by both Native Americans and English settlers in the mid-1700s during the Pontiac War. Indian resistance, followed by retaliatory attacks by English settlers, led to many deaths during this time. As time progressed, white settlers slaughtered an entire tribe of Native Americans, which subsequently led to the aforementioned massacre. On July 26, 1764, a group of Native Americans entered a schoolhouse and clubbed and scalped the schoolmaster and 11 young students, leaving them for dead. The schoolmaster and all but one student died, while one child survived to tell the story of what happened (Strait, 2010). This is a little-known fact and one that is rarely set forth because the concepts of school massacres, school shootings, and mass shootings are typically conflated. That is, most commentators choose to classify an incident as a school shooting based on the number of resultant deaths rather than simply as *a shooting perpetrated at a school*. All other firearm-related incidents, such as someone bringing a gun or an attempted shooting, are excluded as well. Therefore, most accounts lead us to believe that the first school shooting in the United States was the University of Texas shooting in 1966, when Charles Whitman killed 14 people and injured 31 (An ex-Marine goes on a killing spree, n.d.), which disregards the preceding 120 plus school shootings throughout the 19th century and the first half of the 20th century. Moreover, other tragedies are overlooked by exclusively considering *shootings*, such as the Bath Consolidated School massacre in Michigan in 1927, when Andrew Kehoe killed 37 children, a teacher, his wife, and himself. Kehoe was a school board member and town clerk who killed his wife and set fire to their home and other farm buildings to divert community members toward the fires. He then drove to the school and planted hundreds of pounds of dynamite, which he set off that morning, killing 37 children (mostly between the ages of 6 and 8) and one teacher and injuring many more (Andrew Kehoe, 2014).

The 1999 Columbine High School shooting became a defining event in this country's modern history. As Muschert (2007) put it, *Columbine* has become associated with a complex set of emotions pertaining to youth, risk, fear, and delinquency in the early 21st Century United States. Before the Columbine shootings, many school shootings were based on revenge; however, Columbine redefined such acts as a manner of protest against bullying, intimidation, social isolation, and public rituals of humiliation; and many subsequent shooters referenced it as an inspiration (Larkin, 2009). *Columbine* has certainly become a keyword for school shootings, more specifically, although *Virginia Tech* and *Sandy Hook* may resonate more with the younger generation at this point. Nevertheless, much of the public's understanding of school shootings comes from media sources rather than social science, which is in part due to the lengthy process involved in conducting conceptually meaningful and methodologically sound research (Muschert & Spencer, 2009). Namely, it takes literally seconds for a live feed or online posting to "go viral" and reach millions, whereas properly conducted research studies can easily take 1–2 years before being published, if they are ever published at all (i.e., the *file-drawer problem*; see Rosenthal, 1979). Simply put: social science cannot compete with social media. Therefore, it is critical, perhaps now more than ever, for social scientists and mental health professionals to use various media and community platforms to educate the public on the state of the field. As such, social science need not compete with social media but rather embrace it and utilize it as the information *vehicle* it was intended to be and not *the source* of information in and of itself. So, what does the contemporary research tell us about school shootings?

The term *school violence* is one that developed from the early 1990s into the 21st century. Programs, such as bullying, and student-of-concern committees that are now commonplace and even legally required, were never even a consideration before. Furlong & Morrison (2000) noted that research on school violence was rare in the 1970s and remained fairly stagnant until the 1990s, and it had been thought of as a law enforcement issue, such that educators often had no particular role in the process. They further impress upon us the need to distinguish between *school violence* and *violence in the schools*, which is dependent on our use of the term *school*—as a physical location or a system. Consider the Enoch Brown and Bath school massacres compared to Columbine. This is a distinction that makes a difference, although not one that we can ascertain from looking at statistics alone. Thus, let us take a closer look at the concept of school shootings in the systematic, rather than the physical location, sense.

Furlong & Morrison (2000) summarized the research in two particular areas. First, they set forth five statements supported by the empirical literature regarding violent and aggressive behavior at school: (i) males are most involved in school violence, (ii) violence varies by student age, (iii) student experiences vary by their racial/ethnic identification, (iv) student experiences differ slightly by location of the school, and (v) individual student attitudes are associated with school patterns. The first is not particularly surprising as violence and aggression have always been found to be much more prevalent among males compared to females. The second issue is also one commonly highlighted, with certain behaviors (e.g., bullying) being more common in younger groups, such as upper elementary school level, compared to others that more commonly occur in high school, such as those associated with weapon and drug possession. The third corresponding to race reflects the finding that African American students have reported higher rates of violent victimization than other groups, which is also consistent with the broader community violence research. This is also associated with the fourth statement, which indicates that crime victimization is more likely to occur in urban locales compared to suburban or rural environments. Lastly, students' attitudes are associated with their involvement in violence, both as perpetrators and as victims. For example, students who derive satisfaction from hitting others are more likely be perpetrators, and those who are mistrusting and disconnected from teachers are more likely to be victims; moreover, students who engage in frequent substance use are more likely to both commit and be victims of violence. Furlong & Morrison (2000) also delineated eight factors associated with firearm and other weapon possession at school:

1. Self-reported gun possession rates are higher in anonymous self-report surveys
2. Schools are a barrier to weapon and gun possession
3. Males are predominantly involved in gun possession
4. Self-reported gang affiliation is associated with gun possession
5. Youth who own guns are disproportionately involved in aggressive behavior at school
6. Students who admit to frequent alcohol or drug use at school have higher gun possession rates
7. Students bring weapons, including guns, to school for protection and other reasons
8. Youth involved with violence at school may have multiple risk factors

The National Center for Education Statistics publishes an annual report, *Indicators of School Crime and Safety*, wherein they address such topics as victimization, teacher injury, bullying and cyberbullying, school conditions, fights, weapons availability, student use of drugs and alcohol, student perceptions of personal safety at school, and criminal incidents at post-secondary institutions. They note that indicators of crime and safety are compared across different population subgroups and over time, and data on crimes that occur away from school are offered as a point of comparison when possible. The 2015 report (Zhang, Musu-Gillette, & Oudekerk, 2016) indicates the following firearm-related statistics:

- During the 2013–2014 school year, there were 1,501 firearm possession incidents at a rate of 3 per 100,000 students, and three states had rates above 10 per 100,000 students: Louisiana, Arkansas, and Vermont. However, between 1993 and 2013, the percentage of students in grades 9–12 who reported carrying a weapon on school property at least 1 day declined from 12% to 5%.
- The percentage of 12- to 18-year-old students who had access to a loaded gun without adult permission decreased from 7% in 2007 to 4% in 2013.
- There was only one unintentional firearm-related death in schools between 1992 and 2013, which occurred during the 1994–1995 school year.
- In the 2013–2014 school year, approximately 88% of public schools had a written plan of procedures in the event of a shooting and 70% of those schools had drilled students on said plan. Of note is that 94% had a natural disasters plan and 83% of those schools ran drills in that regard.

Mongan, Hatcher, & Maschi (2009) delineated the factors that are most prevalent among individuals who follow through with school shootings, as well as the clusters of variables seen in school shooting cases. They note that school shootings are very rare and that the only variable that connects every shooter is that they are male; however, one particularly salient cluster of risk factors includes marginalization, access to guns, and masculinity. Such factors have also seemed to impact every shooter leading up to the violence. Perhaps the best example of marginalization is bullying, which has a strong connection to school shootings, although ignoring and not including students is also a relevant factor in this context. Of course, access to guns is a critical factor. That said, some shooters had easy access to firearms and some attained them illegally and via violent means; still, it is clearly problematic for already volatile people to have access to weapons. The concept of masculinity has begun to gain attention in the context of school shootings. Namely, some shooters have been subject to "gay baiting" and attacks on their manhood. This is more than bullying as it serves to emasculate them. Dr. Peter Langman, an expert on school shooters, has described the issue as one of "damaged masculinity" (Rosenwald, 2016). Dr. Langman has pointed out that Eric Harris, one of the Columbine shooters, had a birth defect in his leg and a noticeable sunken chest, which likely precluded him from following in his father's footsteps into the Marines. However, he found power and control in guns. In his journal, Harris wrote, "I am (expletive) armed . . . I feel more confident, stronger, more Godlike" and, without guns, he referenced himself as "The weird looking Eric kid." Dr. Langman has pointed such issues out in numerous other school shooters as well. For instance, he cited Elliot Rodger, who killed six people near the University of California–Santa Barbara in 2014. Rodger wrote that he felt "left out" and "never had the experience of going to a party with other teenagers, I never had my first kiss, I never held hands with a girl, I never lost my virginity." However, after he purchased a Glock handgun, he noted: "After I picked up the handgun, I brought it back to my room and felt a sense of power. I was now armed. Who's the alpha male now, bitches?"

Langman (2009) has also set forth a tripartite typology of school shooters: (i) psychopathic shooters who feel no connection to others or guilt or remorse; (ii) psychotic shooters who are not grounded in reality and who may even be severely mentally ill; and (iii) traumatized shooters who may have experienced emotional, physical, or sexual abuse. Nevertheless, Mongan and colleagues (2009) emphasize that there is no actual profile of a school shooter and that attempts to construct one would likely be problematic as they would marginalize students who already feel alienated. However, they contend that it is useful to apply a stages-of-change model to understand the etiology of school shootings. Namely, there are six stages a student would move through before perpetrating a shooting:

Stage 1: Precontemplation: has thoughts about planning or engaging in a school shooting
Stage 2: Contemplation: feels unfairly treated; has "grandiose" ideas of getting back at the school or others

Stage 3: Preparation: weighs the pros and cons of attempting a school
   shooting; has morbid fantasies of death; develops a plan of attack
Stage 4: Action: commits to follow through on plan; withdraws from
   others; obtains weapons for attack
Stage 5: Maintenance: establishes a plan and sets a date for the attack;
   spends time rehearsing plan (i.e., thinking about it or practicing)
Stage 6: Termination: feels attack is justified; completes the attack
   (murder and/or suicide)

Rocque (2012) notes that school rampage (or mass) shootings are distinct
from other types of violence due to the fact that they more commonly occur in
low-crime suburban and rural settings, they lack planned individual targets,
and there are higher death tolls. Moreover, the shooters are nearly all middle-
to lower-class white males. Rocque also notes the issue of masculine identity,
such that the shooters have often struggled with theirs and the shootings have
predominantly taken place in conservative states that emphasize masculinity
and gun culture. Despite the distinctions between school shootings and other
forms of violence, Rocque (2012) concluded, "it is unclear whether this form
of violence is sufficiently unique to warrant separate theories or responses"
(p. 310). He suggested that our perceptions in this regard are likely attributable to the disproportionate level of media attention these events receive.
Harter, Low, & Whitesell (2003) examined variables identified in media accounts of the histories of 10 high-profile school shooting cases since 1996.
They studied the predictors and mediators of suicidal and violent ideation
among their sample of youth. Perceptions of competence or adequacy and social support among peers and parents, an adjustment/depression composite,
and anger-induced physical aggression predicted both types of ideation. The
authors were particularly interested in the emotional reaction of humiliation
in the context of these variables. Perceptions of social support and adequacy,
depressed affect, lower self-esteem, hopelessness, and anger-induced aggression were related to violent ideation. Violent ideators reported higher levels
of homicidal and suicidal ideation. Leary, Kowalski, Smith, & Phillips (2003)
examined 15 school shooting case studies between 1995 and 2001 to determine if social rejection plays a role in precipitating school violence. Acute or
chronic rejection (e.g., ostracism, bullying, romantic rejection) was present
in all but two of the cases. Additionally, shooters tended to be characterized
by one or more of three additional risk factors: interest in firearms or bombs,
fascination with death or satanism, or psychological problems such as depression, impulse control, or sadistic tendencies.

In outlining their National Science Foundation report for Congress and
all of America's governors, Bushman and colleagues (2016) highlighted the
distinction between rampage and street shootings. Consistent with others,
they stated that school shootings usually occur in close-knit, small rural towns
and that the shooter is typically a white teenage male without a history of disciplinary problems. Moreover, school shooters usually have no documented

mental health history despite the fact that some have shown signs of such difficulties. Bushman and colleagues noted that symptoms of mental illness may be either overlooked or attributed to the result of bullying and social rejection. School shooters typically have above average intelligence and academic achievement but lack social skills and certain physical attributes often valued within their peer group. Bushman and colleagues further noted that shooters have not actually been "loners" but rather youth who have attempted to join peer groups, albeit unsuccessfully because of their social awkwardness. As a result, school shooters end up on the periphery. Ultimately, the quest for fame may be a motivating factor to perpetrate a shooting as the youth could come to realize that such is the only way to gain notoriety in life. Moreover, many shooters have an obsession with firearms, and they often commit suicide after killing many people. Of course, as Bushman and colleagues point out, street shootings most commonly occur in densely populated, urban, high-crime areas. In contrast to school shooters, urban street shooters do typically have a history of behavioral difficulties. They also tend to be non-white and come from high-poverty neighborhoods, wherein drug and gun markets are commonplace, as are rates of incarceration, with few opportunities for meaningful employment or educational advancement. Another notable distinction is that street shooters typically have loyalty to their neighborhood and close ties, albeit nefarious, and are seldom involved in random acts of violence. The issue of masculinity is present but functions differently and has a much different connotation for urban street shooters compared to rural or suburban school shooters. In addition, street shooters are more likely to obtain guns from people they know, and they rarely commit suicide after shooting others. Nevertheless, Bushman and colleagues concluded that rampage school shootings are rare and that schools remain the safest environment for children. Moreover, they noted that "Street shootings take the lives of far more people in one year than all the school rampage shootings put together" and that street violence in the country's poorest neighborhoods is "far more costly in terms of human life, family disruption, and the destabilization of communi- ties engendered by chronic fear and trauma" (p. 34).

Moreover, Dr. Dewey Cornell, a preeminent expert in this area, reminds us that school homicides are very rare. As he articulated it:

Objectively, student-perpetrated homicides are rare events in the nation's 119,000
   schools. There were 103 such cases during the 12 school years from 1992–93 to 2003–04,
   which means an average of 8.58 per year. Although even one school homicide is too
   many, an event that affects an average of 8.58 schools out of 119,000 means that the
   average school can expect a student-perpetrated homicide about once every 13,870 years

(119,000 divided by 8.58 ...). Clearly the fear of school homicides as imminent or pervasive events is inaccurate. In contrast, every school must deal with student fights, threats, and bullying on a regular basis. School authorities should not lose perspective on the need for fair and proportionate discipline policies and practices for these frequent problems (p. 1, Cornell, 2007; see also, Cornell & Allen, 2011; Cornell, Sheras, Gregory, & Fan, 2009)

Limitations of the Mass Shooting Research

As Nekvasil et al. (2015) noted, mass shooting research contains several well-known limitations, such as the fact that many related studies rely upon correlational connections between variables, making it difficult to establish a causal relationship or to determine the direction of the effects (i.e., we cannot assert that firearms cause multiple-fatality homicides, although the correlation between use of firearms and number of victims suggests that firearms lead to an increased number of fatalities in comparison to other weapons). Additionally, many databases used in this type of research are flawed in that only cases known to law enforcement are typically utilized, and even then, a surprising amount of data are missing from said databases. Moreover, Furlong & Morrison (2000) reported that while there has been a plethora of research on school violence, the research has been addressed through various disciplines, from disparate professional perspectives, and potentially from different points of interest. As such, school violence has been defined in many different ways, through the lens of various public policy foci. While it is not contested that school violence is a multifaceted construct, comprised of many dimensions, the literature lacks a definitive statement regarding the specifics about these dimensions. Because of this, as has been discussed in prior sections of this chapter, these data should be considered with caution, especially regarding the conclusions and implications that can be made about school violence as a whole.

Harris & Harris (2012) have contended that the current approaches to conducting violence research are ill-fitting with efforts to reduce rampage shooting violence. Consistent with what we noted earlier, they point out that one area of poor fit relates to "the structured pace of scholarly research versus the need for quick, decisive responses to such public tragedies" (p. 1055). They further noted that the policy response to the 2007 Virginia Tech shooting has been considered to be the most comprehensive response to such an event, and it was completed within 1 year. Harris & Harris (2012) believe a second limitation in the research is the lack of interdisciplinary collaboration and focus; for example, law enforcement and mental health professionals are likely to have different approaches and perspectives, which can be useful to integrate but can be quite confusing otherwise. A third and particularly salient limitation is the lack of policy outcome research. Simply put: how do we know if our policies, efforts and interventions are even working at all? The lack of re-search in this regard is deeply troubling. Harris & Harris (2012) highlighted a very concerning conclusion from a 2004 National Research Council study on efforts aimed at children to reduce firearm violence:

> There is almost no empirical evidence that the more than 80 prevention programs focused on gun-related violence have had any effect on children's behavior, knowledge, attitudes, or beliefs about firearms. (p. 1055; see also Wellford, Pepper, & Petrie, 2004)

Harris & Harris (2012) concluded that transdisciplinary research is needed in this area, as is a systems-based research focus on school shootings and policy outcome research. They also noted the need for quantitative analyses and case–control studies, and not simply the qualitative analyses that are typically employed in this area of study.

Finally, Elsass, Schildkraut, & Stafford (2015) asserted that the random nature of school shootings presents various complications for those studying these events. The authors addressed the related concerns and suggested ways in which these issues can be overcome so that research can move forward. For example, they noted that utilizing a deductive approach to studying school violence can be problematic as finding a testable theory can be challenging, and the data are limited regarding the perpetrators of such violence since the majority of them commit suicide. The authors suggested that studying individuals' responses to school shootings may be more advantageous as it provides the opportunity to test the effects of such incidents on a larger sample, one that has considerably more influence on related policy decisions. Additionally, Elsass et al. (2015) contended that, while studying these effects, assessing fear of crime and perceptions of risk following these events is an important area of study but one difficult to measure and that these sepa-rate constructs are sometimes confounded. Because the two constructs are essentially measuring different outcomes, the authors recommended that both should be included and measured separately in an effort to facilitate a more complete understanding of the individual effects of school violence. Furthermore, the authors referenced a point made by Warr (2000), which is that studying possible changes in attitudes as a result of violent crime can be difficult to capture in their full complexity without a pretest measure, which is often lacking due to the relative scarcity of such events.

Given the constraints and limitations inherent to research on school shootings, many of which are touched upon in this chapter, Elsass et al. (2015) provided the following recommendations as "best practices" for studying school shootings:

- Employ a universally accepted definition of the phenomenon.
- Ensure that the data being used is accurate and that it is collected in accordance with the agreed upon definition.
- Utilize theoretical perspectives to support the findings.

- Ground the findings in the context of homicide in the U.S. and relevant statistical risk of victimization.
- Expand the resource focus to explore new avenues and unanswered research questions.
- Combine quantitative and qualitative methodologies to increase the robustness of the body of literature and individual studies. (p 458)

Mental Illness and Firearm-Related Violence

In his January 4, 2016, executive order to reduce gun violence, President Obama used the terms *mental illness* and *mental health* nearly 30 times without defining them once (Fact sheet: New executive actions, 2016). Despite acknowledging, "Individuals with mental illness are more likely to be victims of violence than perpetrators," the president noted "incidents of violence continue to highlight a crisis in America's mental health system." Therefore, the administration proposed a $500 million investment to increase access to mental health care and vowed to "help those suffering from mental illness get the help that they need," which was a very emotional endeavor for Obama (Cillizza, 2016). But what is the actual connection between mental illness and firearm-related violence? After all, there are over 300 diagnosable psychiatric conditions covered in our 900-plus page diagnostic manual, the DSM-5 (American Psychiatric Association, 2013).

As with many topics covered in this book, an entire book could be devoted to the topic; and, in fact, one recently has been published. In their edited book *Gun Violence and Mental Illness* (2016), Drs. Liza Gold and Robert Simon have made an important and timely contribution to the field by outlining the most relevant aspects of the relationship between firearm-related violence and mental illness. The chapter authors cover a wide range of salient topics in this area of study, including gun violence and serious mental illness, firearms and suicide, urban youth, mass shootings, school shootings, the NICS, involuntary commitment, accessing mental health care, violence risk assessment, and violence and suicide prevention considerations. We revisit a number of these topics in Chapters 6–8 of this book but focus on the specific association between mental illness and violence here. In the introduction to the book, Gold noted:

> Although of little comfort to grieving families, survivors, and shattered communities, mass shootings are not the primary link between mental illness and firearm deaths and injuries. As horrific as mass shootings are, their sensational nature unfortunately obscures our view of the real associations between gun violence and mental illness. Until we understand the nature of the relationship between these two major

problems, we are not likely to be able to decrease the devastating toll that each takes on our society. (p. xx)

Gold indicated that, "Anyone who dies from firearm violence has died from a preventable injury" but that two-thirds of firearm deaths are a result of suicide and that the remaining one-third are related to interpersonal violence. Moreover, the chapter authors present the following conclusions, which they refer to as "evidence-based facts":

- Most people with serious mental illness are never violent, although small subgroups are at increased risk during specific high-risk periods; only 3%–5% of all violence, including, but not limited to, gun violence, is due to serious mental illness; and people with serious mental illness are, in fact, more likely to be victims of violence (McGinty & Webster, 2016).
- From 1994 to 2010, homicide rates among youth aged 10–24 years decreased by 50%; urban youth gun violence is a complex problem that involves various biological, psychological, and sociological considerations; but programs geared toward decreasing such have been shown to be effective over the past century (Bell, 2016).
- Mass shootings by people with serious mental illness represent less than 1% of all annual firearm-related homicides, the overall contribution of people with such illnesses to violent crimes is only approximately 3%, and an even lower percentage involve firearms (Knoll & Annas, 2016).
- Only a very small percentage of gun-related homicides and injuries to young people take place in schools or at colleges or universities, there is no known profile that facilitates the early identification of a mass killer, only a small proportion of school shooters have a psychotic mental health condition, and mass school shootings are planned and not impulsive acts (Ash, 2016).
- Mass shootings by individuals with serious mental illness are very rare events and therefore cannot be predicted (Trestman, Volkmar, & Gold, 2016).
- The most statistically significant association between guns and mental illness is suicide by firearm (Simon & Gold, 2016).

The aforementioned conclusions are consistent with the findings of many other contemporary researchers and scholars. As Dr. Jeffrey Swanson, professor of psychiatry at Duke University, recently said, "I say as loudly and as strongly and as frequently as I can, that mental illness is not a very big part of the problem of gun violence in the United States" (Beck, 2016). Media attention has once again played a major role in the misconception. McGinty, Kennedy-Hendricks, Choksy, & Barry (2016) investigated a random sample of 400 news stories about mental illness from 1995 to 2014 and found that news stories in the second decade of study were more likely to include mass shootings by people with mental illnesses despite the fact that the actual rates of such remained stable over the years. Nevertheless, while mental health problems may not be predictive of firearm-related violence, they are certainly present in various shooting cases. However, once again, we must be more specific when defining and discussing the very broad term *mental illness*. We certainly must also be clear as to the types of shootings to which we are referring, as we have seen in the context of the rampage school shooting versus urban street shooting distinction.

It is likely that most people are thinking of serious mental illnesses (e.g., psychotic disorders, bipolar disorder) when using the term *mental illness* and not many other psychiatric conditions (e.g., learning disorders, eating disorders, sexual disorders). It is also likely that substance use disorders are not being considered in this context despite the connection between them and crime, more generally. Wintemute (2015a) investigated the relationship between alcohol misuse, ownership, access to and use of firearms, and the perpetration of firearm-related violence. He noted, "In an average month, an estimated 8.9 to 11.7 million firearm owners binge drink" (p. 15) and ultimately concluded that acute and chronic alcohol misuse has a positive association with firearm ownership, risk behaviors involving firearms, and risk for perpetrating violence. As such, he recommended restricting access to firearms for individuals who misuse alcohol as a violence prevention measure. In his other published article that same year, Wintemute (2015b) noted that mental illness is not, in and of itself, a primary contributor to interpersonal violence but rather does contribute to firearm-related suicide. In fact, he indicated that abuse of alcohol or other controlled substances is a predictor of future firearm-violence risk, regardless of whether other mental health problems are present.

Metzl & MacLeish (2015) addressed four assumptions that commonly arise following a mass shooting in the United States: (i) mental illness causes gun violence, (ii) psychiatric diagnosis can predict firearm-related crimes, (iii) shootings represent the deranged acts of mentally ill loners, and (iv) gun control will not prevent another mass school shooting. They opined that these assumptions are true in certain circumstances but believe that the connection between mental illness and firearm violence is less causal and more nuanced and complex than public opinion reflects. Specifically, they posited:

> The findings cited earlier in this article suggest that neither guns nor people exist in isolation from social or historical influences. A growing body of data reveals that US gun crime happens when guns and people come together in particular, destructive ways. That is to say, gun violence in all its forms has a social context, and that context is not something that "mental illness" can describe nor that mental health practitioners can be expected to address in isolation. (p. 246)

5

Domestic and Intimate Partner Violence

In the United States, the concept of domestic violence (DV) as a national concern was only introduced within the last half-century as laws and social science research developed in this area. Although media attention and resources for victims have increased substantially over the years as a result, the public is rarely presented with the nuances involved in DV and intimate partner violence (IPV) situations. In this chapter, we cover a broad spectrum of issues related to DV and IPV. We first provide an overview of these concepts, including definitions and particular types, prevalence and general statistics, homicide and suicide, firearm use in these situations, and law enforcement–related considerations. Next, we present psychological components and theories of DV and IPV, including, but not limited, to battered woman syndrome, and the applications of such theories to legal cases. We then review high-profile DV and IPV incidents that involved firearms among a range of subgroups, including celebrities, athletes, citizens, and law enforcement personnel. Lastly, we provide an overview of laws, regulations, and protective orders related to DV and IPV situations.

Overview of DV and IPV

In this section, we provide an overview of DV and IPV. Namely, we present some of the ways in which these terms have been defined by various agencies, nationally and internationally, followed by different types of DV and IPV and relevant national statistics in this context. We then turn to a discussion of homicide and suicide and firearm use in these situations, followed by law enforcement–related considerations

Definitions and Particular Types

The National Coalition Against Domestic Violence (NCADV) defines DV as the "willful intimidation, physical assault, battery, sexual assault, and/or other abusive behavior as part of a systemic pattern of power and control perpetrated by one intimate partner against another." NCADV's definition includes physical, sexual, and psychological violence as well as emotional abuse (National Coalition Against Domestic Violence, 2015). The NCADV emphasizes the fact that, although the frequency, severity, and type of abuse can vary considerably, the themes of *power* and *control* are present across DV situations. Similarly, the US Department of Justice (DOJ) defines DV as "a pattern of abusive behavior in any relationship that is used by one partner to gain or maintain power and control over another intimate partner" (US Department of Justice, n.d.). The DOJ also notes that such abuse may be physical, sexual, emotional, psychological, and even financial; but the key component is the influential component of the behavior. As articulated, DV includes behaviors that "intimidate, manipulate, humiliate, isolate, frighten, terrorize, coerce, threaten, blame, hurt, injure, or wound someone." These definitions are also generally consistent with those set forth by other major agencies. For instance, the Centers for Disease Control and Prevention (CDC) definition includes physical, sexual, and psychological harm as well and further indicates that DV and IPV occur in both heterosexual and same-gender couples and do not require an association with sexual intimacy (Centers for Disease Control and Prevention, n.d.). According to the World Health Organization (WHO), IPV "refers to behaviour by an intimate partner or ex-partner that causes physical, sexual or psychological harm, including physical aggression, sexual coercion, psychological abuse and controlling behaviours" (Violence against women, 2017).[1]

Other classification terms have been used in the DV context as well. For example, Frye et al. (2006) examined factors related to two distinct forms of IPV: *intimate terrorism* and *situational couple violence*—a delineation set forth by Johnson (1995). Intimate terrorism is defined as the efforts of one partner (usually the male) to systemically control the other partner (usually the female) and the relationship. Moreover, this type of IPV is thought to occur more frequently in the relationship, resulting in injuries and escalating over time. In contrast, situational couple violence is considered to be typically less serious and severe, whereby both members of the couple often engage in the acts of violence. As Frye and colleagues noted: "Intimate terrorism is thought to be more characteristic of clinical, emergency department, criminal justice (at least in the past), and domestic violence shelter populations, whereas situational couple violence is thought to be more common at the population level" (p. 1287). As such, the original conceptualization as set forth by Johnson (1995) was based on the premise that classifying IPV was determined by the level of control perpetrators seek (i.e., high to low).

Despite the clarity and consistency with which these definitions are presented, there remains room for interpretation. In Chapter 4, we addressed the need, but also the limitations, related to operationally defining seemingly obvious terms, such as *violence*. Thus, the violence component of DV and IPV is subject to interpretation. However, this is also true for the *domestic* and *intimate partner* components of the term. Must the victim live with the perpetrator for the relationship to be considered *domestic*? And what exactly constitutes an *intimate* partnership? There is no unequivocal answer. If we return to the aforementioned definitions provided by the NCADV and DOJ, DV is, by definition, between intimate partners. However, the terms *domestic violence* and *intimate partner violence* are used interchangeably by some yet delineated by others. For instance, some classify an intimate partner as a current or former spouse, boyfriend, or girlfriend but categorize DV more broadly to include others, such as parents, children, siblings, or other relatives (e.g., Truman & Morgan, 2014). Moreover, it is not uncommon for the nature of the relationship to be defined by the victim, although involved others, such as courts and researchers, may ultimately make their own subjective classifications.

In addition to the need for consensus when operationally defining terms, it is important to recognize that factors related to DV and IPV may vary across different subgroups. In the mental health field, our education, training, and continuing education are largely devoted to the development and maintenance of cultural and professional competence. In other words, we must not make assumptions about clients or paint a clinical picture with broad strokes; we must dig deeper and take individual, cultural, and other related factors into consideration. Conducting (and consuming) research is no different: we must explore the possibility that a particular psychological phenomenon or theory will manifest itself differently from group to group.

For example, much of the earlier research conducted in this area of study focused on urban environments, but Shuman and colleagues (2008) investigated IPV against women in rural areas in the southern United States (i.e., "the South"). In their sample of women from Georgia, they found that IPV female victims were older, were less educated, and had more children than their peers who were never victimized. Furthermore, victims were approximately three times more likely to have been divorced, to have been pregnant prior to age 20, and to have moved within the past year. In addition, victims were more likely than their peers to have financial hardship, such that they were five times more likely to be unemployed or only intermittently employed. IPV victims also reported notably more psychosocial problems compared to their non-victim peers; namely, they were five to seven times more likely to report having low self-esteem, emotional problems, and substance use. They were also approximately 10 times more likely to have been abused as a child. They also reported having less social support than their counterparts. With respect to the perpetrator characteristics, IPV victims were 10 times more likely than their non-victim peers to report that their partner used drugs. They were also 40 times more likely to report that they had fought about money with their partners and nine times more likely to have had a suspicion of infidelity as a component of their current or most recent relationships. Although some of these findings are comparable to those related to urban samples, one of the strongest predictors of abuse in this southern, rural sample was *older* age of the victim, which is starkly different from what we find in urban samples, whereby victims are more commonly between 18 and 30 years old. Shuman and colleagues suggest that either southern, rural life in the United States may be a unique environment for older women in terms of IPV risk or, perhaps, they are simply more inclined to report such in the South (see *southern culture of violence*, as noted in Chapter 4). Regardless, what is clear is that IPV victims and perpetrators tend to have notably troubled histories and significantly more problematic ongoing issues in many areas of their lives.

According to the WHO's 2002 *World Report on Violence and Health*, a large collection of studies from both industrialized and developing countries have outlined a notably consistent list of possible triggering events that tend to lead to partner violence (p. 95):

- Not obeying the man;
- Arguing back;
- Not having food ready on time;
- Not caring adequately for the children or home;
- Questioning the man about money or girlfriends;
- Going somewhere without the man's permission;
- Refusing the man sex;
- The man suspecting the woman of infidelity.

The report also lists factors associated with a man's risk for abusing his partner (p. 98):

- Young age
- Heavy drinking
- Depression
- Personality disorders
- Low academic achievement
- Low income
- Witnessing or experiencing violence as a child.

Relationship-specific factors include:

- Marital conflict
- Marital instability
- Male dominance in the family
- Economic stress
- Poor family functioning

Community factors include:

- Weak community sanctions against domestic violence

- Poverty
- Low social capital

And, finally, societal factors include:

- Traditional gender norms
- Social norms supportive of violence

Another recent example relates to Wincentak, Connolly, & Card's (2016) meta-analysis of 101 studies investigating teen dating violence (TDV)—both physical and sexual—for youth aged 13–18. They found that 20% of youth reported experiencing physical TDV and 9% reported sexual TDV. However, there were notable gender differences; specifically, higher levels of physical perpetration were reported for boys, but no gender differences were found for victimization. Regarding sexual TDV, girls reported lower rates of perpetration than boys (3% versus 10%) but higher rates of victimization (14% versus 8%). Higher rates of sexual TDV were found among older teens, whereas cultural minority girls and those in disadvantaged neighborhoods had higher rates of physical TDV.

These examples truly highlight how nuanced and specific research findings are often found to be. It takes time and thought to get a real handle on not only what researchers have found but also their methods and the conceptual underpinnings of their studies. In reality, these important details are quickly lost in the sound bites and headlines of our modern society. We can easily imagine the headlines based on the results of the two aforementioned studies:

"SOUTHERN DOMESTIC ABUSE VICTIMS 10 TIMES MORE LIKELY TO HAVE BEEN ABUSED AS A CHILD"

"20% OF TEENS HAVE BEEN PHYSICALLY ABUSED BY THEIR DATING PARTNERS"

While accurate, these statements do not come close to capturing the studies' findings, particularly their *main* findings. Therefore, mental health and medical practitioners and researchers now have the heightened responsibility of appropriately conveying (often dense) scientifically based information to a public that has become more and more conditioned to building its knowledge base 140 characters at a time.

Prevalence and General Statistics

Alhabib, Nur, & Jones (2010) meta-analyzed studies conducted between 1995 and 2006 on the prevalence of DV against women aged 18–65. Specifically, they reviewed 134 studies conducted in North America, Europe, Asia, Africa, and the Middle East and found that levels of physical and sexual violence were comparable across groups. However, proportionally higher levels of physical violence were observed in Japanese immigrants to North America (47%), who also had the highest levels of emotional violence (78%). Levels of emotional violence were also relatively higher than levels of physical and sexual violence within South American, European, and Asian groups, ranging 37%–50%. Based on their research, Alhabib and colleagues concluded, "Violence against women has reached epidemic proportions in many societies and suggests that no racial, ethnic, or socio-economic group is immune" (p. 373). They further noted three salient factors to consider in the epidemiological study of DV against women:

- Surveys measure the number of women who are willing to disclose abuse, which may not equal the actual number of victims.
- The definition of violence against women and views related to such vary across and even within cultures.
- There are notable problems with the measurement of domestic violence and the methodology employed by researchers, which affects the data gathered and the way in which it is interpreted.

With respect to research efforts solely focused in the United States, the National Intimate Partner and Sexual Violence Survey was an initiative launched by the CDC's National Center for Injury Prevention and Control. It is an ongoing, nationally representative telephone survey inquiring about experiences of sexual violence, stalking, and IPV among non-institutionalized English- and Spanish-speaking women and men in the United States, aged 18 and older. Data were collected for the first time in 2010 from 16,507 people (55% female), and the main findings were as follows:

- 18% of women and 1.4% of men have been raped at some point in their lives.
- 51% of those women were reportedly raped by an intimate partner and 41% by an acquaintance, whereas 52% of the men were raped by an acquaintance and 15% by a stranger.
- 80% of female victims experienced their first rape before age 25 and 42% before age 18, whereas 28% of male victims experienced such at age 10 or younger.
- 16% of women and 5% of men have been victims of stalking, mostly perpetrated by an intimate partner or acquaintance.
- 36% of women and 29% of men have been the victims of violence from an intimate partner at some point in their lives, and such has been predominantly from one perpetrator.

The US Department of Justice's Bureau of Justice Statistics analyzed data from the National Crime Victimization Survey and recently issued a report on acts of nonfatal DV from 2003 to 2012 (Truman & Morgan, 2014). It found that DV accounted for 21% of all violent victimizations during that time period, with the majority being committed against females (76%). Of note, however, is that the rate of DV declined 63% from 1994 to 2012, which was comparable to the 67% decline in the overall crime rate in the United States during that time period. The data further indicate that stranger perpetrators accounted for the highest number of violent acts at 38%, followed by well-known or casual acquaintances (32%), intimate partners (15%), immediate family members (4%), and other relatives (2%). In addition, most acts of DV (77%) occurred near the victim's residence. The majority of DV during this time period (64%) was classified as simple assault, and most acts (77%) did not involve a weapon. Of further note is that acts of violence by immediate family members were highest in rural areas, whereas urban areas had the highest rates of stranger violence.

Vest, Catlin, Chen, & Brownson (2002) investigated acts of IPV in a sample of approximately 19,000 women from eight states who were 18 or older via the Behavioral Risk Factor Surveillance System, a telephone-based interview developed by the CDC. They defined IPV as acts of physical violence or sexual abuse within the last 12 months perpetrated by a date or current or former boyfriend, girlfriend, or spouse. Emotional abuse and threats were excluded. They found that there was a 2.3% annual prevalence of IPV in the year preceding the interview and that the factors most associated with IPV were young age, divorced/separated or single marital status, and low household income, all of which were consistent with other national surveys and databases. Other variables found to be associated with IPV were lack of health insurance, receipt of Medicaid, cigarette smoking, children in the home, self-reported fair/poor health, and frequent mental distress. These findings are consistent with those of Weinbaum and colleagues (2001), who investigated the prevalence of IPV in California and found the following factors to be related to IPV victims: poor physical and mental health; pregnancies at early age; smoking status; nutritional needs; low income; participation in the Special Supplemental Nutrition Program for Women, Infants, and Children program; children younger than 18 in the household; and limited access to healthcare.

Frye and colleagues (2006) collected data from a sample of women from 11 cities in the United States who survived attempted homicides and their counterparts without such experiences but included those with and without abuse histories. They found that women who reported having been physically abused by their partners were also more likely to report that their partner exhibited controlling behavior. However, the presence of intimate terrorism was relatively uncommon, even in the subsample of women with abuse histories. As Frye and colleagues articulated it:

> It may be, then, that the smaller population of women who experienced assault, control, and either violence or injury (or both) are the women who domestic violence advocates, service providers, and researchers, relying on clinical samples, know as battered or abused women, which is anywhere from 10% to 35% of women who are physically assaulted by their partner. (p. 1303)

When present, intimate terrorism was associated with the victim's young age, escalating violence in the relationship, partner's access to guns, arrest history related to DV, poor mental health, and previous suicide attempts and threats.

With regard to race, Ramos, Carlson, & McNutt (2004) examined the similarities and differences between black ($n = 126$) and white ($n = 365$) women in relation to their abuse histories. Specifically, they measured seven abuse-related variables in addition to demographic variables:

- Recent partner physical abuse
- Recent partner emotional abuse
- Recent partner sexual abuse
- Adult past physical abuse
- Adult past sexual abuse
- Child physical abuse
- Child sexual abuse

The groups differed in some respects regarding their demographic information, such that white women had more post–high school education than black women, whereas black women were much more likely to report having household incomes below $20,000 and more than three children aged 5–12. However, the groups were comparable with respect to the hours they worked each week and in having a current romantic partner, although black women were notably less likely to have a male partner living in the home compared to their white counterparts. Of particular relevance is that the groups did not differ significantly across most of the aforementioned abuse-related variables measured. Black women (32%) were more likely to report recent emotional abuse than white women (20%). However, there were no notable differences between the groups in terms of their experience of recent, past, or even childhood abuse. Black and white women were comparable with respect to having been victims of recent physical (8%, 9%) and sexual (2%, 3%) abuse, past physical (21%, 23%) and sexual (16%, 21%) abuse, and childhood physical (5%, 7%) and sexual (13%, 11%) abuse, respectively. In general, women who experienced physical and sexual abuse as children were more likely to have experienced all types of recent and past abuse as adults. Moreover, lifetime abuse is associated with higher levels of depression and anxiety for both groups of women, although the rates were notably higher among black women. Furthermore, black women (46%) reported much higher rates of excessive jealousy by their partners than white women (28%). Nevertheless, Ramos and colleagues demonstrated that there are many more similarities than differences between these groups.

Firearm Use and DV and IPV

The Giffords Law Center to Prevent Gun Violence (http://lawcenter.giffords. org/domestic-violence-and-firearms-statistics/) provides the following information:

- Firearms increase the likelihood of fatalities in incidents of DV
- Between 1990 and 2005, guns were used to murder more than two-thirds of the victims of spousal (current or former) homicide
- Firearm-involved DV assaults are 12 times more likely to result in fatality than those involving other weapons or bodily force
- The probability that abused women will be killed by their abusers is five times higher if the abuser owns a gun
- According to a survey of female residents of DV shelters in California, more than one-third of the residents reported having been threatened or harmed with a firearm
- Laws that prohibit the purchase of a firearm by a person subject to a DV restraining order are associated with a decreased number of intimate partner homicides
- Between 1990 and 2005, victims of homicide who were killed by their current intimate partners made up almost half of all spouse and current intimate partner homicides
- A study of applicants for DV restraining orders in Los Angeles indicated that applications were more likely to mention firearms when the parties had not cohabitated and were not married

The US Department of Justice's recently reported on acts of nonfatal DV from 2003 to 2012 (Truman & Morgan, 2014). Based on their research, most acts (77%) did not involve a weapon. However, a weapon was involved in a larger percentage of violence committed by "other" relatives (26%) compared to intimate partners (19%) and immediate family members (19%). Nevertheless, when weapons were involved, firearms were present in a smaller percentage of situations (3.7%) than were knives (7.8%) and other weapons (8.3%). This pattern is the case for intimate partners and immediate family members, although "other" relatives have used firearms and knives at comparable rates (10%). Further, only stranger-perpetrators used firearms more than knives (i.e., 10.4% firearm vs. 6.6% knife), but their use of "other" weapons was found to be comparable to that of firearms.

The findings of Kernsmith & Craun (2008) were consistent with those of the DOJ. Namely, they investigated the correlates of weapon use during DV incidents reported to the police within a sample 369 randomly selected cases handled by the San Diego County sheriff's department. They found that 25% of the cases involved a weapon and that a telephone was actually the most commonly used type of weapon, followed by other types of property. The use of a knife (3.1%) or firearm (0.8%) was very rare in this sample.[2] The suspect used alcohol or drugs in about one-third of cases, and there were protective orders in place in 17% of cases, overall, but in 48% of cases wherein a weapon was used. Although most suspects were male (81%), women were more likely to use a weapon when perpetrating DV in their sample (37% vs. 22%). DV was present most often in relationships of 1–5 years (39%), followed by those lasting 6–10 years (20%). However, there were no appreciable differences, overall, with respect to weapon use as a function of relationship length, other than the fact that weapon use was least common in relationships of less than 1 year. In contrast, Farr (2002) analyzed police reports and interviews with women who survived *near-lethal* attacks by a domestic abuser. In most cases, the female left or had informed the perpetrator that she was leaving the relationship. In *all* cases, the victims reported being physically assaulted within 1 year of the attempted homicide and that the offenders had problems with alcohol. Farr found that a firearm was used in 23% of cases, whereas beating and choking were perpetrated in two-thirds of the cases. We further highlight the distinctions between the more common versus severe DV and IPV cases in the *Homicide and Suicide* section that follows.

Consistent with the broader violence literature we outlined in Chapter 4, some researchers have also investigated the potential correlation between firearm ownership and DV or IPV. However, there are no compelling data to support a relationship between firearms in the home and acts of IPV (e.g., Vest et al. 2002). Shuman and colleagues (2008) also found no difference in reported gun possession between abused and non-abused women, although victims of IPV were six times more likely to report that their partner carried a weapon (i.e., a gun or knife) on him. In her review of national data, Sorenson (2006) examined the relationship between general firearm ownership and firearm use in the commission of intimate partner homicide (IPH). A particularly noteworthy finding was that, while the number of stranger homicides of women has decreased, homicides by intimate partners with handguns have increased. She aptly noted that firearms can be used in ways that do not result in injuries, such as for coercion for sex and to threaten. Based on her review of the data, Sorenson concluded that, when there was a firearm in an abusive home, it was often used against the woman—primarily to threaten her. Certainly, that does not suggest that having a firearm in the home leads to abuse but rather that it becomes a particular risk factor in homes where DV is already present. As Folkes, Hilton, & Harris (2013) articulated, weapon use is a known risk factor for DV severity, particularly lethality; but it is unclear whether access to the weapon is a risk factor in and of itself or if firearm use is a characteristic of a certain type of offender who is more likely to commit severe and repeated acts of domestic abuse. This point will be abundantly clear in the next subsection pertaining to homicide and suicide.

Despite the lack of empirical support for the broad-based correlation between firearm ownership and DV or IPV, study limitations and overzealous interpretations by researchers can perpetuate a false impression of the actual state of the behavioral science in this arena. For example, Sprinkle (2007) conducted research with a sample of fourth-, fifth-, and sixth-graders across three counties in South Carolina to investigate the relationship between and effects of DV, rates of gun ownership, and parental educational attainment on aggressive beliefs and behaviors. Although she reported finding a connection between these factors, Sprinkle acknowledged that she was unable to account for other types of violence exposure (e.g., TV, movies, video games, community) that may affect these factors, nor was she able to determine if there was even direct exposure to DV in the home. Despite these and other limitations of the research and the fact that she indicated that the relationship between rates of DV and the aggressive beliefs and behaviors of school-aged children in the state is "tentatively supported" (p. 146), Sprinkle still concluded, in part:

> With regard to social construction, the laissez-faire attitude of the state toward gun ownership and gun control does little to deter criminals from buying guns in bulk and employing these weapons in illegal activities such as robbery, rape, murder, and gun sales to minors or convicted felons. The ability of South Carolina's citizens to amass an unlimited amount of firearms and never have to register them legitimizes and encourages even illegal gun possession. (p. 146)

> limitations must be placed on the number of firearms an individual can purchase in a twelve month time span, safety key locks should be required, and the legislature should make it a felony offense to buy guns as gifts for children and adolescents or to allow minors access to firearms. (p. 149)

The aforementioned conclusions by Sprinkle are simply not at all connected to the data she gathered and analyzed. In fact, she did not even account for most of the factors in her research that she ultimately spoke to in her conclusions and recommendations. Of course, every study has limitations, and researchers should not be criticized for that inherent reality; but it is incumbent on researchers to adhere to the scientific method and its associated principles, as well as research ethics and standards. Failure to do so reflects a departure from social science to social activism, which is particularly problematic for mental health professionals purporting to engage in objective research and practice. Lay persons, including the media, will gravitate to the ultimate findings of a research study and extract sound bites or headlines, without examining important factors such as those related to the study sample and the specific variables studied and the way in which they are operationally defined.

Domestic and intimate partner murders seem to have always been considered particularly shocking and intriguing. As Barnard, Vera, Vera, & Newman (1982) put it: "Killers of members of their own families have long fueled the archetypical imagination. Our myths, literature, and popular arts are full of such characters as Cain, Oedipus, Medea, Othello, Hamlet, and Bluebeard" (p. 271). Undoubtedly, intrafamilial murder has continued to have a strong presence in our contemporary literature and cinema (e.g., *Sleeping with the Enemy, Gone Girl, The Godfather, The Lion King*) as well as capturing the attention of the media in true crime cases (e.g., Andrea Yates, Scott Peterson, Lyle and Erik Menendez). Family-involved murders are often specified by their own specific monikers, such as *familicide* (killing one's spouse, child(ren), and/or other relatives, which may include a suicide), *filicide* (a parent killing a child), *fratricide* (killing one's brother), *infanticide* (killing one's infant child), *matricide* (killing one's mother), and *patricide* (killing one's father). A distinct area entirely is that of *honor killings*, which refers to the killing of a family member who was believed to bring shame upon the family. Although this does not seem to have much of a presence in the United States outside, perhaps, of mafia and gang contexts, the United Nations Commission on Human Rights has indicated that honor killings have occurred in Great Britain, Brazil, India, Ecuador, Israel, Italy, Sweden, and Uganda, as well as in numerous Muslim nations, including, but not limited to, Turkey, Jordan, Pakistan, and Morocco (see e.g., Chesler, 2010).

In the United States, IPH and homicide–suicide scenarios are a qualitatively different phenomenon in many respects from the range of other, albeit very concerning and problematic, behaviors in which DV perpetrators engage. Campbell et al. (2007) delineated the most notable risk factors associated with IPH that have been identified in the empirical literature. They found past DV to be a primary risk factor but also firearms, estrangement, having a stepchild in the home, forced sex, threats to kill, and nonfatal strangulation. Shooting via firearm represents the method used in the majority of IPHs. Moreover, Campbell and colleagues noted that women are nine times more likely to be killed by an intimate partner than by a stranger. However, they noted that IPH has decreased significantly since the 1970s, which they attributed to DV resources and changes in DV and firearm-related policies. They further indicated that unemployment is a major factor for IPH rather than race per se and that a risk factor for intimate partner homicide–suicide is a history of mental health problems for the perpetrator. These findings are comparable to those of Garcia, Soria, & Hurwitz (2007), who also analyzed the empirical literature in this domain. Garcia and colleagues further noted that family and intimate assaults are 12 times more likely to end in death if firearms are involved.

In the context of a research study of 230 domestic homicides in the state of Florida, Johnson, Lutz, & Websdale (1999) have noted that men kill women more than women kill men; and biological fathers and mother's boyfriends made up two large blocks of perpetrators of killing children—as a general rule, when men kill children, they do so violently, while women kill children mainly out of neglect or a milder view of child abuse. They outlined 10 high-risk factors in lethal DV situations:

- Prior history of DV
- Marital estrangement
- Obsessive–possessiveness, including extreme jealousy, stalking, and suicide attempts or threats
- Prior police involvement
- Prior criminal history of the perpetrator
- Threats to kill
- Substance use problems
- Protection orders

- Acute perceptions of betrayal
- Child custody disputes

Although this publication is rather dated, the risk factors remain highly relevant and have received much empirical support over the years.

Smith, Moracco, & Butts (1998) analyzed data from the North Carolina Office of the Chief Medical Examiner and from interviews with law enforcement officers to investigate 108 partner homicides in North Carolina in 1989. They defined the term *partner* broadly as they included intimate and non-intimate relationships (e.g., cohabitants). They also excluded same-gender relationships, one-night stands, and relationships involving prostitutes. Smith and colleagues found that most of the homicide victims were females (62%) and that a slight majority was African American (53%). More specifically, 30% of the victims were white women, 30% were African American women, 23% were African American men, and 12% were white men. Only 17% of all victims had post–high school education. They ranged in age from 19 to 97, with the average age of female victims being 35 and that of male victims, 44. The perpetrators also ranged in age considerably, from 19 to 88. Only half of the couples were married at some point, but most (78%) were still in a relationship at the time of the homicide. The vast majority (71%) of the homicides occurred in the home or nearby, mostly in the bedroom. The majority of victims (64%) died at the scene of the crime, and the offenses were witnessed by others, including family members and police, approximately one-third of the time. Smith and colleagues delineated various themes based on their analyses: both leaving an abusive partner and staying are dangerous; protective measures for battered women were inadequate; DV was not necessarily private, such that there are often witnesses; and alcohol and firearms often accompany homicide. Namely, most of the male victims (70%) had alcohol in their systems, whereas only one-third of females did; furthermore, firearms, primarily handguns, were used in 67% of the homicides, followed by knives. In addition, Smith and colleagues found that there was a DV history in 96% of cases wherein such information was available. As such, they concluded that "The overriding theme to emerge from these cases was that partner homicide is most often the final outcome of chronic women battering" (p. 411), which had been previously known to others, including law enforcement, and primarily resulted from "habitual male aggression" (p. 415).

A study of risk factors for IPV among lesbian women found that minority stress (e.g., discrimination and internalized homophobia) and subsequent anger were related to the perpetration of psychological aggression as well as physical violence in these relationships. Further, anger was associated with alcohol use and alcohol-related problems, which were also related to the perpetration of violence (Lewis, Mason, Winstead, & Kelley, 2016).

DeJong, Pizarro, & McGarrell (2011) examined data from over 700 homicides in two metropolitan cities (Newark, New Jersey, and Indianapolis, Indiana) to determine what factors differentiate intimate and non-intimate partner homicides. Their findings indicate that females were more likely to be involved as both victims and offenders in IPH when compared to non-IPH. DeJong et al. found that Newark had higher rates of (street) homicide, although fewer cases involved intimate partners, which the authors attributed to greater levels of disadvantage and poverty. Moreover, IPHs in Newark were more likely to be committed by using a knife (47% vs. 20%), whereas such homicides in Indianapolis were much more likely to be committed with a firearm (66% vs. 21%). There were similarities between the two sites, however. For instance, IPH victims and perpetrators in both cities were older and more likely to be female, although race was not a particularly noteworthy differentiating factor. In addition, rates of firearm in non-intimate homicides did not differ as they were involved in 71% of such cases in both cities.

Hanlon, Brook, Demery, & Cunningham (2016) analyzed neuropsychological test data from forensic examinations of 153 murders in Illinois, Missouri, Indiana, Colorado, and Arizona to examine differences between spontaneous domestic homicide (33%) and non-domestic homicide offenders (61%). The domestic offenders were more likely to manifest psychotic disorders but less likely to be diagnosed with antisocial personality disorder or to have prior felony convictions than their counterparts. In addition, domestic offenders exhibited significantly worse neuropsychological impairments, including reduced performance in intellectual functioning (i.e., IQ scores), attention, executive functioning, memory, and language-related abilities. Of note, however, is that only 14% of domestic offenders used a firearm compared to 59% of non-domestic offenders. The authors conclude, "These findings corroborate the notion that spontaneous domestic homicide may represent a discernible criminological phenotype" (p. S168).

Glass et al. (2008a) conducted a study to identify risk factors associated with young adult intimate partner femicide. Specifically, across 11 cities, they analyzed 23 cases of 16- to 20-year-old females murdered by an intimate partner between 1994 and 2000. Data were gathered from police and medical examiner reports as well as from family members. Glass and colleagues then compared the murder victims to a group of young women who had been physically abused by an intimate partner within the past 2 years, and they found significant differences between the two groups. Specifically, the murder victims were more likely to be African American and to have a larger age gap with the perpetrator (5 years versus 1 year). Moreover, the perpetrators who killed their victims were significantly more likely to be unemployed, have a gun in the house, and have a history of threatening, choking, and controlling their partners as well as abusing them during pregnancy.

Considering that a substantial portion of cases involving DV include evidence of stalking behavior, it is important to briefly discuss a few findings from the research regarding the dangers of violence from stalking versus non-stalking abusive intimate partners. One study of police records of DV found that cases with elements of stalking were overall more threatening and violent than cases with no elements of stalking (Klein et al., 2009). Further, several studies indicate that women who were stalked after seeking a protective order were more likely to experience almost every other kind of abuse and violence in comparison to women who were not stalked after obtaining a protective order (Logan & Walker, 2009, 2010).

DV-related suicide is another important issue. A suicide that is considered DV-related is defined by the Utah Department of Health (2006) as a suicide in which one of the circumstances surrounding the event involved violence or the threat of violence between intimate partners, family members, or roommates. The research on DV-related suicide alone is rare. Nevertheless, Davis (2010) contended that the majority of those deaths are actually those of males, not females, and that researchers have historically viewed the issue of DV through a feminist lens, leading to improper conclusions.

According to the CDC's National Violent Death Reporting System (n.d.), there are substantial differences between IPH, intimate partner suicide, and IPH followed by suicide (i.e., homicide–suicide). Among the 16 funded states (Alaska, Colorado, Georgia, Kentucky, Maine, Maryland, North Carolina, New Jersey, New Mexico, Oklahoma, Oregon, Rhode Island, South Carolina, Utah, Virginia, and Wisconsin), the amount of intimate partner suicides far exceeded both homicides and homicide–suicides. Specifically, 42,743 reported intimate partner suicides, while there were only 1,721 homicides and 779 homicide–suicides in comparison. Of the homicides, 941 involved firearms, while 21,902 of the suicides involved firearms, as did 670 of the homicide–suicides.

The above data demonstrate that there are obvious differences between IPHs and homicide–suicides. However, it is important to ascertain specifically how they differ in order to move toward violence prevention in this crucial domain. Banks, Crandall, Sklar, & Bauer (2008) investigated 124 cases of female IPH and female intimate partner homicide–suicide cases in New Mexico between 1993 and 2002 and compared them in an effort to elucidate relevant risk factors and prevention strategies. They found that 63% of the cases were classified as solely homicides, whereas 37% were homicide–suicides. Furthermore, marital relationship, age, blood alcohol, and the use of firearms differed between the two types of cases. Namely, most homicide–suicides (70%) occurred within spouse/ex-spouse situations, whereas homicide-only cases occurred equally within spouse/ex-spouse and nonmarried intimate partner relationships. Furthermore, homicide–suicides tended to occur in older couples, such that they were in their 40s as compared to their 30s in homicide-only cases. In addition, victim blood alcohol levels above 0.02 mg/dl were present in a much higher proportion of homicide-only cases than they were in homicide–suicide situations (43% vs. 22%). With respect to the method of injury, the vast majority of homicide–suicide deaths (89%) included a firearm, whereas firearms were only used in 45% of homicide-only cases. In sum, Banks and colleagues noted that "Female intimate partner homicide–suicide was most often perpetrated by middle-aged to older, married, or formerly married men who used a firearm" (p. 1073), which was in contrast to homicide-only deaths. They concluded that treating professionals should focus on behavioral indicators and not just the patient's presentation:

> The interaction of firearms, substance abuse, depression, and intimate partner violence puts both members of a couple at substantial risk. . . . Homicide prevention in these cases may be better thought of as suicide prevention, suggesting that interventions aimed at the prevention of suicide, including screening and treatment for depression and chemical dependence in the battering partner and targeted removal of firearms, should be considered in the prevention efforts of domestic violence. (p. 1075)

As noted above, DV-related murder occurs outside of intimate partner relationships as well, although this is significantly understudied. Much of what is published in this context is in a case study–based format and the like. However, some have empirically investigated these phenomena in large samples. For instance, Kunz & Bahr (1996) studied the characteristics of people who have killed their minor children by reviewing over 3,000 cases included in the FBI's *Uniform Crime Reports* between 1976 and 1985. They found that 39% of the homicides were of children under age 1 and 67% were of children less than 2 years old. The rates generally stabilized among older children. The majority of victims were male (55%) and white (53%), whereas 39% were African American. A trend can be observed with respect to weapons and means of killing. Namely, "personal" weapons (e.g., hands, feet, asphyxiation) were used in more than half of the murders of children under age 1, which decreased significantly among older victims (e.g., <2% in victims 16–18 years old). The opposite was true for firearms: they were only used in less than 10% of murders of children less than 1 year old but 83% of the time when victims were between 6 and 18. Knives were used in 4%–13% of cases across all age ranges.

Sibling violence is thought to be relatively common yet is also often overlooked in the professional literature. Walsh & Krienert (2014) investigated over 1,000 sibling murders utilizing the FBI's *Supplemental Homicide Report* data from 2000 to 2007. The victims' characteristics were evenly distributed across age and race, although most were male (73%). The offenders were also mostly male (83%) but tended to be between 13 and 17 years old (53%) and were older than the victims in two-thirds of the cases. A gun was used in relatively more situations (43%), followed by a knife (31%) and other weapons and means (26%). The precipitating motivation was mostly in response to an argument (54%) and rarely characterized as a felonious homicide (12%).

In the context of yet another distinct area of study, Heide (2013) compared victim, offender, and case correlates in incidents where mothers and stepmothers were killed (i.e., matricide and step-matricide). Specifically, she analyzed the FBI's *Supplementary Homicide Report* data gathered from 1976 and 2007 to investigate comparisons between these two victim types. Heide found a number of similarities between groups;

for example, the perpetrators were primarily adult sons. However, several significant differences were reported with respect to specific age, involvement in multiple offender incidents, and weapon use. Namely, 64% of the stepchildren were under age 25 at the time of arrest compared to 35% of the biological children. In addition, a greater percentage of juvenile offenders were involved in multiple incidents involving mothers in comparison to their adult counterparts. Offenders who killed their stepmothers were significantly more likely to use guns than those who killed their biological mothers (49% vs. 37%), whereas use of knives was comparable (29% vs. 25%) in addition to other weapons and means of killing. Age differences were also detected with respect to firearms, however. Notably more juvenile matricide offenders used firearms compared to their adult counterparts (60% vs. 33%) as adult offenders were more likely to use knives and other weapons and means. No such age differences were found among step-matricide offenders. Gender differences were detected only in the context of knives, such that stepdaughters used knives at a notably higher rate than stepsons (45% vs. 21%).

Another area of consideration pertains to mass and active shooter situations. Although they are not typically thought of in terms of DV- or IPV-related scenarios, some data indicate at least some connection. For example, in their report on mass shootings, Everytown indicated that there was a relevant connection between mass shootings and DV or family violence. Namely, they found that perpetrators shot a current or former spouse or intimate partner or other family member in 57% of the cases they reviewed, and the shooters had prior DV charges in approximately one-quarter of those cases (Everytown for Gun Safety, 2015). In the FBI's 2014 active shooter analysis, however, much lower numbers were found. Specifically, shooters only targeted family members or current, estranged, or former wives and girlfriends in fewer than 10% of the cases; and they moved on to another location to continue shooting in just over half of those incidents. This specific area warrants further study and attention in the professional literature, particularly because anecdotal evidence suggests a potential (problematic) connection between some of these shooters and their family members.

A Note on Law Enforcement

Historically, police have been the ones to respond to violence in the home because of their on-call availability. However, the tide changed from reactive to proactive from the 1970s to the 1990s amid social pressures and public opinion about the need for more resources (Morgan, Nackerud, & Yegidis, 1998). Moreover, law enforcement personnel have been generally reluctant to intervene in DV matters for a variety of reasons, not the least of which is that they can be rather dangerous situations for officers. Nevertheless, DV- and IPV-related issues within law enforcement families are a significant concern as well.

The law enforcement community has certainly had its share of DV-related concerns related to officers themselves. In fact, some have suggested that DV may actually be more common among law enforcement families, with prevalence estimates as high as 20%–40% (see, e.g., Neidig, Russell, & Seng, 1992). The research literature in this area is scant, however, which is not surprising given the difficulty of acquiring these types of data. As Oehme and colleagues (2011) put it: "The lack of information may result in part from the distinctive culture of law enforcement. A conspicuous feature of that culture is the tendency of officers to think of themselves as separate and apart from the citizens whom they serve" (p. 85).

Although data specific to law enforcement DV are hard to come by, some researchers have found ways to explore the issues surrounding officer-involved DV matters through other means. For instance, Saunders, Prost, & Oehme (2016) recently investigated police officers' perspectives in the context of hypothetical examples. The study included a national sample of officers across all 50 states and found that officers expressed very supportive attitudes for victims, overall. However, officers were somewhat less likely to recommend that a perpetrator-officer seek counseling or contact an employee assistance program. Officers were even less likely to recommend couples' counseling, and the reported likelihood of arresting a perpetrator-officer was generally mixed but rather low in comparison to other options. However, officers were more inclined to suggest firmer responses, including arrest, when details about the presence of severe violence were presented. Nevertheless, officers' responses were largely dependent on their length of experience and supervisory status, such that those with more time on the job and working within higher titles were more likely to recommend interventions such as counseling and even sanctions.

With respect to officers' perspectives on themselves, Anderson & Lo (2011) analyzed data from the Baltimore police stress and DV study (Gershon, 2000) conducted between 1997 and 1999. The authors focused on self-reported physical aggression toward a domestic partner and its correlates. Over 1,000 officers participated in the study, and 9% of them reported losing control and becoming physically aggressive with an intimate partner. Of those, 41% were white males, 28% were African American males, 27% were African American females, and 4% were white females. Such behavior was most attributable to stressful life events, "authoritarian spillover" (which involves the unquestioning obedience that often coincides with the law enforcement mentality), and negative emotions associated with police work. As such, Anderson & Lo noted that their findings were consistent with *general strain theory*'s premise that stress leads to negative emotions that may trigger deviant behavior and with *angry aggression theory* as authoritarianism and angry emotional states may serve as maladaptive coping strategies to deal with stress.

Although many types of problems that occur within officers' families, including DV and IPV, may be kept secret even among their own departments and colleagues, police-involved homicide–suicides obviously cannot be hidden. Therefore, this type of information is arguably much more available than information on what might be considered more benign officer-related issues. Research findings in this context have been consistent in at least one respect: officer-involved homicide–suicides are almost always perpetrated by males who kill their current or former female spouses or girlfriends with their service weapons. Klinoff, Van Hasselt, & Black (2015) recently investigated 43 police-perpetrated homicide–suicides committed between 2007 and 2014 throughout the United States. The victims ranged in age from 7 to 56 and were predominantly female (82%). The majority of victims (81%) were current or former spouses or girlfriends. Nearly all of the perpetrators (98%) were males who used a service firearm to commit the offenses, the majority of whom (65%) were patrol officers. Klinoff and colleagues' primary finding was that officer-involved homicide–suicides occurred in the context of DV, despite the fact that the majority of perpetrators were employed and in good standing with their respective departments. Based on their findings, the researchers noted the importance of DV prevention programs within departments, as well as increased access to mental health services, and the need to decrease the stigma often associated with seeking such services.

A study conducted by Violanti (2007) consisted of an investigation of newspaper accounts of 29 cases of police family homicide–suicides from 2003 to 2007 in the United States. Victims' ages also ranged from 7 to 56 and were primarily females (83%) who were either current or former wives (55%) or girlfriends (28%). The perpetrators ranged in age from 24 to 57 and were almost exclusively males (93%) and local officers (76%) as opposed to state or federal officers. However, the perpetrators were evenly split between patrol (52%) and higher-ranking (48%) officers. Of note is that the service firearm was the weapon used in 90% of cases. Consistent with the broader DV literature, domestic abuse was present at the time of the offense in most cases (62%) and in the vast majority of the couples' histories (70%); the motivating factors were primarily DV (42%) and divorce or estrangement (35%). In light of the findings, Violanti contended that the primary trigger for homicide–suicide among officers is the presence of DV coupled with officers' exposure to violence and aggression. Thus, he concluded: "The key to prevention of homicide–suicide may thus lie with reduction of domestic violence" (p. 102). Indeed, law enforcement agencies have developed protocols to address these types of concerns over the years. One example is that of Florida's response to DV-related issues among officers, whereby the state adopted Responding to Domestic Violence, Model Policy Number Two for Florida Law Enforcement, in 1999 (see Oehme et al., 2011, for a review).

Psychological Components and Theories of DV and IPV

Particular attention has been paid over the years to investigating the effects of DV and IPV on victims. Ehrensaft, Knous-Westfall, & Cohen (2016) investigated the association between IPV and offspring trauma-related symptoms. They employed a 25-year longitudinal study of parents and their children born between 1965 and 1974 across 100 neighborhoods in upstate New York. Ehrensaft and colleagues found that IPV was, in fact, associated with trauma symptoms in children. However, differences were found based on who perpetrated the abuse (i.e., fathers or mothers). Namely, fathers' behavior had a more direct impact on children's risk for trauma symptoms, whereas mothers' subsequent stressful life events and mental health problems contributed to children's symptoms in addition to the presence of IPV. Nevertheless, positive parenting was found to moderate the relationship between IPV and trauma-related symptoms. In their study, Jouriles et al. (1998) examined three groups of young children:

- Those who observed the use or threat of violence with a knife or gun
- Those who did not observe such violence but it recently occurred in the home
- Those who did not have such occur in their home recently

Children in the "observed" group displayed more behavioral problems than children in the "neither" group. However, children in the "observed" group did not differ significantly from the children in the "occurred" group (i.e., those who did not witness the violence but violence had occurred nonetheless).

Slovak, Carlson, & Helm (2007) examined the impact of exposure to violence on youth attitudes regarding violence and guns. Approximately 500 youth in rural middle and high schools were surveyed in the context of various types of their reported recent and past violence exposure: (i) threats, (ii) slapping/hitting/punching, (iii) beatings, (iv) knife attacks, (v) gun violence, and (vi) sexual abuse. Consistent with the preexisting research, Slovak and colleagues found that males reported higher levels of violence exposure compared to their female counterparts, as did younger students compared to older students. Nevertheless, the research illustrated that youth in the sample were exposed to relatively high levels of violence across various settings, although school settings represented the greatest likelihood of such, followed by the neighborhood. However, the most severe forms of violence exposure (i.e., being physically abused) were most likely to occur in the child's own home. Despite the fact that home-based violence occurred at the relatively lowest levels of frequency, it had the most significant impact on the youth. Moreover, attitudes toward violence and guns were significantly influenced by both violence exposure in the home and being male. These findings are not particularly surprising as they are consistent with a fairly extensive literature base pertaining to the negative effects of violence in the home and child abuse.

With regard to the effects on adult victims, Morgan & Wells (2016) investigated male victims' experiences of being perpetrated against by their female intimate partners. Seven victims were interviewed, and four essential themes were revealed:

- They identified themselves as victims of multiple forms of abuse, including, but not limited to, physical abuse.
- They identified themselves as victims of "controlling" abuse, such as through the use of children and isolation.
- They experienced manipulation through gendered stereotypes of abuse.
- They felt their experiences were different because they were men, such as getting the help they needed. In some instances, the men felt that society does not even fully accept the fact that men could be victims of IPV, which in turn can enable abuse in these contexts.

Coker and colleagues (2002) analyzed data from the National Violence Against Women Survey of nearly 14,000 women and men aged 18–65 to assess the physical and mental health consequences of psychological and physical IPV among victims. Perhaps unsurprisingly, they found that both psychological and physical IPV were associated with significant physical and mental health consequences. Specifically, although women were more likely to report being victimized sexually (4% versus 0.2%) or physically (13% versus 6%) by an intimate partner in their lives, physical IPV victimization was associated with higher risk for both men and women in the following areas: current poor health, depressive symptoms, substance use, development of a chronic disease, chronic mental illness, and injury. Of particular note is that this was the first study to provide population-based estimates of psychological IPV among men and women, and Coker and colleagues found that men were more likely to only experience psychological IPV (17%) compared to women (12%). Nevertheless, the primary finding and associated implications remain: IPV is associated with negative outcomes and may lead to long-term adverse physical and mental health effects, which, for women, some believe may lead to the development of a specific condition referred to as "battered woman syndrome."

Battered Woman Syndrome

Over 30 years ago, Dr. Lenore Walker coined the term *battered woman syndrome* (BWS) to describe the psychological effects a woman may experience after being repeatedly physically, sexually, or seriously psychologically abused (Walker, 1979, 1984). Walker contended that the traditional diagnostic system (i.e., the *Diagnostic and Statistical Manual of Mental Disorders*) did not adequately capture the symptom picture of this condition, although she noted that the diagnosis of posttraumatic stress disorder came the closest. Namely, victims would often experience "recurrent thoughts of the abuse incidents, avoidance, numbing, or depression to avoid dealing with the situation which frequently changes interpersonal relationships, feelings, and lifestyle, and increased arousal symptoms such as pervasive anxiety, panic attacks, phobias, and hypervigilance to cues of further harm" (p. 23, Walker, 1991). Moreover, women in such situations will often put their partner's needs before their own and remain in a dependent and passive role in the abusive relationship as a coping mechanism or matter of survival. They often try to find ways to control the environment and keep everything calm to avoid abusive reactions by the partner. They may also learn ways to dissociate to avoid physical or psychological pain, and many battered women build up high levels of anger, resentment, and rage after years of abuse. Furthermore, they may confuse emotional and sexual intimacy. Such women are likely to be vulnerable to suggestions, even by treating professionals, who must approach assessment and treatment cautiously and thoughtfully. Walker highlighted the need for mental health professionals to assess for potential lethality in the situation, including the presence of weapons and particularly physically assaultive behavior in the relationship. Additionally, Walker emphasized the need for mental health professionals to design an escape plan with the person. She further noted the importance of reminding the woman that she is being assisted to heal from an abusive experience rather than being treated for a mental illness, which should help to decrease resistance to therapeutic interventions and allay her fear of being labeled "crazy." As Walker (1991) put it, "The primary goal of treatment is the woman's *re-empowerment*" (p. 25).

The concept of BWS is based on the theoretical foundations of the *cycle of violence* and *learned helplessness* theories (Biggers, 2003). Per Walker's conceptualization, a woman must go through at least two cycles of violence to be considered a battered woman, and there are three different phases that constitute a cycle:

1. The tension-building stage
2. The acute battering stage
3. The loving contrition stage, whereby the batterer demonstrates very loving and remorseful behavior

In addition, a battered woman is prone to experiencing *learned helplessness*, or a feeling of powerlessness that can lead to thoughts that she cannot be helped. As a result, she may not seek assistance or attempt to leave the situation. Some scholars have questioned the empirical support for the syndrome, however, noting that the research has not shown that all battered women experience the entire cycle of violence or experience learned helplessness as Walker defined it. In fact, some have pointed out that many battered women do, in fact, retaliate "or engage in other active efforts to resist, avoid, escape, and stop the violence against them (Gordon, 1996, p. 65). Indeed, some have researched this very topic.

The empirical literature has shown that the majority of women who killed their partners and subsequently received prison sentences had received specific threats from the batterers indicating that they would kill the women at some point (van Wormer, 2008). Based on their analysis of partner homicides,

Smith et al. (1998) concluded that, while partner homicide is "a complex phenomenon not given to easy generalizations," there are certain themes that tend to emerge, such as the presence of woman battering and the dangerousness associated with both staying and leaving an abusive partner, as well as the fact that DV is not necessarily private violence and alcohol and firearms are often involved in fatal acts of violence. Smith and colleagues also highlight that these concepts are not new ones, noting that research in this area dates back to the 1940s. For instance, they note the term *victim-precipitation*, which Wolfgang (1958) coined in the context of his homicide research:

> *Victim*-precipitation is applied to those criminal homicides in which the victim is a direct, positive precipitator in the crime. The victim-precipitated cases are those in which the victim was the first to show and use a deadly weapon, to strike a blow in an altercation—in short, the first to commence the interplay of resort to physical violence. (p. 252)

In the Courtroom

The concept of self-defense has been long-standing in our legal system, but its practical applications have not necessarily fit well in the context of women who kill their abusers. Traditional self-defense doctrines do not account for a history of repeated acts of violence or the fact that some women kill their abusers during a calm period—one wherein they are not confronted with imminent danger. Therefore, legal defense approaches based on theories, such as BWS, served to account for the nuances of the situational factors that differentiate it from typical self-defense situations, with the first being *Ibn-Tamas v. United States* (1979). Despite its admission in legal cases, BWS evidence has been subjected to criticism by psycholegal scholars, and it has led to relatively mixed results in actual legal cases and mock jury studies (e.g., Kimmel & Friedman, 2011; Terrance, Plumm, & Kehn, 2014). Undoubtedly, there are challenges to demonstrating such concepts to jurors as a woman's perception of imminent fear even during a calm, apparently safe time period and addressing the *reasonableness* components of the law related to the natural questions of: Why didn't she just leave? Why didn't she call for help? Why did she resort to a deadly weapon when she could have left instead? (Schuller & Vidmar, 1992, p. 277).

Overall, studies appear to indicate that BWS is not a successful legal defense. In a study that analyzed 100 cases of women who killed their abusers, approximately 75% of these women were convicted (Costanzo & Krauss, 2010). Further, according to a trend analysis performed by the National Clearinghouse for the Defense of Battered Women, in cases involving a woman killing her abuser, BWS testimony was not significantly decreasing convictions, nor was it helping to reduce crimes from murder to manslaughter

(Parrish, 1996). Further, the trend analysis suggested that in appellate court cases of women who were convicted at trial after attempting a BWS defense, there was a 20% increase in affirmation of their convictions (Parrish, 1996).

Messing & Heeren (2009) investigated issues related to the sentencing of perpetrators in DV matters. They analyzed newspaper databases, Lexis-Nexis and Proquest, and ascertained a sample of individuals who killed multiple people in a single DV incident between 1993 and 2002. Of course, this is a relatively small sample, but it is informative, nonetheless. Approximately one-half of all murderers used a gun to kill their victims, and one-third used a knife; 22% of women and 63% of men used a firearm in the commission of their killings. They found that women who killed their children with a knife or firearm were disproportionately sentenced to death, however, such that the death penalty was sought for the majority of men who used a firearm but was sought in *all* of the women's cases. Women were also much more likely than their male counterparts to face a death penalty trial when a knife was used in the murder (75% vs. 20%). Although having a history of violence is an aggravating factor and should, therefore, be associated with harsher sentences, men who killed in the context of a separation (e.g., a partner leaving or being unfaithful) were granted leniency in regard to the death penalty. On the surface, the findings may seem counterintuitive; however, Messing & Heeren point out that the research has shown that women who commit "masculine-type" crimes are more likely to be punished more harshly, which explains the death penalty being sought against women who used weapons to commit murder, particularly of their children. They further contend that the criminal justice system is gender-biased due to the fact that it allows a separation-based scenario to be a mitigating factor for men who murder their partners, even when a DV history is present. As Messing & Heeren articulated it:

> Rather than forcing men to take responsibility for their homicidal tendencies, the criminal justice system removes their responsibility and excuses (to varying degrees) their homicidal actions. That the criminal justice system is predicated on a male model allows mitigation in this context. Women have acted in a manner not culturally scripted, whereas men have fulfilled cultural expectations. Further research must be done to understand the impact of gender on sentencing. (p. 185)

Despite a trend toward stronger prosecution in DV offenses, the issues related to sentencing disparity between DV-related cases and non-DV-related cases are underresearched (Bond & Jeffries, 2014). A study conducted in Australia found that individuals convicted of crimes related to DV are less likely than those convicted of crimes outside of DV to be sentenced to prison terms. Additionally, of those who receive prison sentences, DV offenders receive shorter terms (Bond & Jeffries, 2014).

Another study pertaining to mock jurors' sentencing of DV offenders found that jurors delivered less severe sentencing when the female victim was perceived as provoking as opposed to not provoking (Kern, Libkuman, &

Temple, 2007). Additionally, during predeliberation sentencing, female jurors delivered more severe sentences. However, the effect of gender disappeared during postdeliberation sentencing, which suggests that deliberation produced some sort of compromise between male and female jurors (Kern et al., 2007).

High-Profile DV and IPV Incidents Involving Firearms

DV and IPV have received increased media attention over the years, particularly in light of the advent of social media venues and the associated decrease in personal privacy. Although the personal lives of celebrities and athletes have traditionally been much more exposed than those of civilians and even those in other professions, such as law enforcement, expectations of privacy are generally a thing of the past. While some may elect not to actively pursue an online presence, such is often unavoidable given that friends, family, and employers are likely to have either a website or some type of social media outlet with which they engage. Moreover, situations requiring police involvement are often readily accessible on the Internet via police blotters, local and national news sites, and real-time filming by civilians. After all, a number of significant incidents have been and continue to be videotaped by citizens with cell phones; in fact, such videos are the only available evidence in many court cases. In this section, we present a number of high-profile DV and IPV matters that involved firearms within celebrity, athlete, civilian, and law enforcement populations. The cases we present are not necessarily representative of other DV and IPV cases among these groups, either in content or in process; but they certainly illustrate the types of situations that make the local and national news.

Summary of Cases

Celebrities

Relationship issues, including domestic disputes, have been a part of the Hollywood news and gossip culture for some time. Notable cases include, but are certainly not limited to, those related to Ike and Tina Turner, Mike Tyson, O. J. Simpson, Tommy Lee and Pamela Anderson, Bobby Brown and Whitney Houston, and Chris Brown and Rihanna (Domestic abuse accusations, 2015). However, these matters are not known to have involved firearms. In fact, it is fairly difficult to find DV-related incidents that have, although a few well-known examples are described below.

One well-publicized event involved actor-comedian, Phil Hartman, known for his many roles on *Saturday Night Live*. Mr. Hartman's third wife, Brynn, had a history of cocaine and alcohol addiction and became increasingly jealous of his growing fame in the late 1990s. Brynn's behavior contributed to a tense home life, and eventually Mr. Hartman grew distant and spent more and more time with his friends. On May 27, 1998, Brynn, after consuming alcohol, shot her husband at close range with one of his guns, a Smith & Wesson .38. She later crawled into bed beside her husband's body and shot herself with a Charter Arms .38, killing herself. Brynn's brother later sued Zoloft's manufacturer, Pfizer, for wrongful death as it was suspected that a combination of alcohol and Zoloft may have caused the tragedy. The company later settled (Getlen, 2014).

In 2013, Curtis James Jackson III, or the rapper known as 50 Cent, was ordered to turn in his firearms as a result of DV charges. Namely, he was accused of kicking the mother of his second child and destroying property in her condominium in Los Angeles. In addition to the revocation of firearms, Jackson was issued a protective order, requiring him to keep a distance from the victim (Snider, 2013). He ultimately pled no contest to one count of misdemeanor vandalism (Williams, 2015).

Athletes

Increased media attention regarding professional and college athletes' criminal activity might make it seem like athletes are disproportionately involved with the criminal justice system. However, a research study by Leal, Gertz, & Piquero (2015) found that the overall arrest rate among the general population was nearly twice as high as the arrest rate among NFL players between 2000 and 2013. The researchers also found that NFL players had a higher rate of violent crime in comparison to the general population during 6 of the years studied. Unfortunately, the researchers could not calculate which violent crimes were DV-related as those data were not available to them (Leal et al., 2015).

When considering the issue of DV among athletes, it is important to consider the likelihood that some crimes, especially those connected to influential people, go unreported, unpublicized, or unprosecuted. A search of newspaper articles published between 2010 and 2014 found that there were 64 cases of DV or sexual assault perpetrated by athletes in the MLB, NBA, and NFL during this period of time (Withers, 2015). However, only one athlete was convicted of the alleged crime (although four players pled guilty to lesser charges and one pled no contest), seven players were punished by their respective league, and two were punished by their team. Withers (2015) noted that the likelihood of a professional athlete being punished for DV or sexual assault is probably even lower than what is evidenced by studies involving media reports of such incidents. This is for two reasons: (i) many victims of assault do not report to the police and (ii) even when victims have the courage to report to the police, allegations often go unreported by the media until formal charges are pressed (Withers, 2015).

Following various stories in the media regarding DV among professional athletes (several of which will be discussed below), the NFL revised its DV policy. Several actions were identified in an effort to improve its response as an organization to allegations of DV and sexual assault. These actions included new and enhanced educational programming for all NFL personnel, information dispersed to NFL families about available resources and services, and enhanced disciplinary procedures for offenders of DV and sexual assault.

Below are several examples of athletes who were involved in DV disputes involving firearms.

In February 2002, Jayson Williams, a former NBA star who played for the Philadelphia 76ers and New Jersey Nets, was giving a group of people, including his limo driver, a tour of his mansion. Included in the tour, Mr. Williams showed the group his gun collection in his bedroom. While showing the group his double-barreled, 12-guage shotgun, Mr. Williams admittedly failed to properly check the safety mechanism. He only checked one of the two barrels before snapping the gun shut, which then fired, striking his limo driver once in the chest, killing him. After a complicated 8-year legal battle, Mr. Williams ultimately pled guilty to aggravated assault and received a 5-year prison sentence.

In 2009, New York Giants wide receiver Plaxico Burress was sentenced to 2 years in prison after accepting a plea deal on a firearm charge following an incident in which he suffered a self-inflicted gunshot wound to his thigh when his gun went off in a Manhattan nightclub. He faced a minimum sentence of 3.5 years if convicted at trial.

In 2012, Kansas City Chiefs linebacker Jovan Belcher killed his girlfriend, who was the mother of his 3-month-old daughter, and then drove to the team's practice facility and killed himself in front of the team's coach and general manager. Belcher was 25 years old and a starting player for the Chiefs. Reports indicate that, after he shot his girlfriend, he stood in front of the doors of the practice facility, holding a gun to his head. He ultimately shot himself upon the police's arrival (Wilson, 2012).

In February 2014, New York Knicks player Raymond Felton was accused of threatening his wife with a firearm. He was charged with various felony and misdemeanor weapons offenses and turned in a Belgian-made FN Herstal pistol. Reports indicated that he had filed for divorce just prior to the allegations (Felton arrested, 2014). Felton ultimately pled guilty in exchange for no incarceration time but received a fine and community service (Knicks' Raymond Felton, 2014).

In May 2014, NFL player Greg Hardy was charged with misdemeanor assault for allegedly assaulting a woman by picking her up and throwing her into the tub area of the bathroom. He also reportedly dragged her into the bedroom and choked her before throwing her on a couch that was allegedly covered in loaded firearms. The allegation was that he threatened to shoot her if she reported the assault (Rose, 2014). Hardy was found guilty of the assault, but he appealed to have a new trial in front of a jury in a superior court. The case was ultimately dismissed as a result of a reported settlement (Butt, 2015).

In June 2016, Jerry "The King" Lawler, a professional wrestler, was arrested, alongside his young fiancée, due to DV allegations. While the two sides of the story differed significantly, both agreed that a firearm was involved. Lawler's fiancée stated that he hit her, pushed her, and then provided her with a gun telling her to kill herself, while Lawler stated that she pulled out the gun after attacking him. The WWE issued a statement saying that Lawler was suspended indefinitely per the organization's zero tolerance policy regarding matters pertaining to DV (Jerry "The King" Lawler, 2016).

Citizens

Of all the groups we discuss here, it is certainly the easiest to find seemingly endless examples of DV-related incidents among average citizens that involved firearms in some respect. Indeed, much of this chapter has been devoted to addressing that very context. Nevertheless, most DV- and IPV-related incidents do not actually *involve* firearms per se but, rather, involve the revocation of firearms as a consequence or condition of a court order. Incidents that actually involve the use of firearms are undoubtedly more severe and include homicide–suicides, as we have addressed in various sections in the chapter. Here, we present some of the more extreme and sensational case examples.

In 1990, Billie Wayne Coble shot and killed his wife's parents and brother, and he was subsequently sentenced to death in Texas. Karen Vicha was Coble's third wife, whom he married in 1988. However, they began experiencing significant marital problems within a year's time, and Vicha wanted a divorce. In response, Coble would attempt to dissuade her from such and would show up at her place of employment and call her. He also kidnapped her one night, when he hid in her car while she was at a bar with a friend. Coble threatened her with a knife at that point; but Vicha stated that she would reconsider the divorce, so he let her go. Vicha subsequently spoke to her brother, a police officer, who encouraged her to report the kidnapping. The arresting officer became very concerned and warned Vicha's brother about Coble. A few days later, Coble told Vicha that he saw she now had a "big mean" dog, and she ultimately found her dog dead in front of the house. Nine days after the kidnapping, Coble went to Vicha's home and found her three daughters and nephew there; he handcuffed them, tied up their feet, and taped their mouths closed. He also cut the phone lines to the house. Coble proceeded to ambush and shoot Vicha's father, mother, and brother as they came home. Coble returned to Vicha's home after the three murders and waited for her to come home. When she did, he informed her about the murders and told her to kiss her children "goodbye," which she did. He then handcuffed her; however, Vicha convinced Coble to leave the house with her. He agreed but said he was going to take her away for a few weeks and torture her. Vicha attempted to escape from the vehicle as Coble drove; the car went into a ditch, and she tried to shoot him with one of his guns; but it did not fire. Coble pistol-whipped

Vicha until she could not see from all the blood in her face. A witness began yelling at Coble, but he drove away. He reportedly threatened to kill Vicha if she got blood on his clothes and told her his reputation was ruined because she had him arrested, but he also rubbed her between her legs during the ride. Coble drove to a deserted field, where he threatened to rape Vicha. He eventually drove out of the field, but a sheriff's vehicle began to follow them, prompting Coble to stab Vicha's chin, forehead, and nose while he was driving. He stated that he did not want to die in prison, so he accelerated into a parked vehicle. Both were injured in the crash, and Coble was found with .37 and .38 caliber revolvers. Upon further investigation, it was found that Coble had an extensive mental health history and a history of engaging in violence. He was evaluated by a psychiatrist when he was 15, and he was noted to have a sociopathic personality disturbance with a poor prognosis. At age 17, Coble entered the US Marines and was sent to Vietnam. He was honorably discharged, but he was not recommended for re-enlistment because of numerous violations and convictions during his duty. Throughout his life, he abused and molested women as he physically abused both of his prior wives and sexually assaulted multiple young girls, including relatives. Moreover, he was raised by a mentally ill mother and an alcoholic stepfather. Coble remains on Texas' death row to this day (*Billie Wayne Coble v. The State of Texas*, 2010).

In 2009, after his wife had informed him that she was leaving him for another man, James Harrison returned to his mobile home and shot and killed his five children. He then drove to a parking lot and shot and killed himself in his car. According to the state Children's Administration, Mr. Harrison had physically abused at least one of his children in the past, and the state had been called to the home due to matters related to neglect (Yardley, 2009).

In 2011, estranged husband Tan Do shot and killed his wife and several of her family members before killing himself at his son's 11th birthday party at a roller skating rink in Texas. Six other individuals at the rink were injured; however, Tan Do asked his children to leave the snack area prior to the rampage. No children were injured. When she was contemplating a divorce in 2010, he allegedly dragged her into a closet, fired his gun through the ceiling, and threatened her. Due to a pattern of physical violence and threats, Ms. Do obtained a protective order. Prior to the rampage, she had requested that the court withdraw the order as her husband had promised to change and work on their marriage for their kids. According to the affidavit, she stated, "I hope I am making the right decision" (Tree, 2011).

Also in 2011, 73-year-old Carey Hal Dyess shot and killed his ex-wife and four other individuals during a 6-hour shooting rampage. Dyess was allegedly disgruntled as a result of his divorce, which involved allegations of DV by both parties and led to mutual protective orders. Years after the divorce, in addition to his ex-wife, Dyess shot and killed her friends who had supported her throughout the divorce, along with her divorce attorney. He ultimately pulled over and shot himself, without leaving a note or any kind of explanation (Fry, 2011).

In 2016 in Jefferson, Maine, Shane Prior waited in the woods with a handgun, only to shoot his estranged girlfriend in the arm once she exited her vehicle. After fleeing the scene, Prior led the police on a chase and ultimately shot himself in the head. According to data collected by the Maine Domestic Abuse Homicide Review Panel, about half of all homicides in the last several years have been caused by DV (Eichacker, 2016). Between 2014 and 2015, 24 of 46 homicide victims in Maine were murdered by family members or intimate partners (Byrne, 2016).

In 2016 in St. George, Utah, Michael Dean Hughes, a prominent attorney in the area, pled guilty to a felony aggravated assault charge after "shooting in the direction" of his wife during a middle-of-the-night domestic dispute. However, his wife was reluctant to inform the police about the shooting, which confounded the investigators. The story became even more complicated after several individuals in California and Idaho contacted news outlets wondering if perhaps Hughes was the victim in a longer-standing DV situation with his wife as his wife had previously been incarcerated and was still serving a probation term related to her career as an attorney in Idaho. Despite initial concerns about Hughes' report to the police, especially considering he had been on several medications for mental illness, the prosecution ultimately decided that Hughes being the shooter matched the evidence best (Jenkins, 2016).

In 2016, in Katy, Texas, Christy Sheets, 42, shot and killed her 22- and 17-year old daughters after she called a family meeting that involved her husband. After shooting her two daughters, they attempted to flee with their father; but Sheets ran after them, and both of her daughters ultimately died. Her husband ran to the end of the street at the point when police arrived and ordered Sheets to drop her gun; she ignored their orders, prompting an officer to shoot and kill her. The murder weapon was a five-shot .38 caliber handgun. Those who knew the family were reportedly shocked by the news. However, it was reported that the couple had been having marital problems. In fact, the Fort Bend Sheriff's Office had responded to 14 calls to the residence since January 2012. Per reports, three of the calls were for suicide attempts, but the call details were not published (Muddaraj & Chapin, 2016).

On August 6, 2016, Mark Short killed his wife, three children, and himself just 3 weeks after his wife called the police on him after a domestic dispute on July 18, 2016. Megan Short had informed law enforcement that she was afraid of her husband at that time, and investigators ultimately stated that she was in the process of moving out. However, the bodies of Mark, Megan, and their 8-, 5-, and 2-year-old children were found in their living room. The dog was also killed. Reports indicate that Short brought his children to an amusement park the day prior and that he was supposed to rent a moving van to help his wife move on the day of the murders. Investigators found a homicide–suicide note on the table, which was apparently written after he murdered his family; he reportedly indicated that he purchased the firearm to commit the murders. Further investigation revealed a prior domestic dispute at a hotel in early June 2016. Although Ms. Short was informed of how to seek a protective order, she never sought one. She did, however, post an allegation on Facebook that she had been abused. The district attorney noted that law enforcement did all that it legally allowed to do in the matter but acknowledged the danger involved in leaving an abusive relationship and urged those in similar situations to develop a safety plan and seek assistance from a local DV agency. Of note is that Short was demoted from his job as a loan officer just prior to the murders and that the family had been featured in news stories about their challenges in securing medication for their youngest child, who had undergone a heart transplant. Ms. Short had previously indicated that she had developed posttraumatic stress disorder as a result of their child's condition (DA: Pa. dad took kids, 2016).

Law Enforcement

As we noted earlier in the section titled, "A Note on Law Enforcement," officers are not immune to DV- and IPV-related problems, and some evidence suggests that the rates may even be higher in this population. While officers and departments have historically been overwhelmingly secretive in the context of personal matters, severe acts of DV and IPV cannot be hidden and certainly draw significant levels of attention. The following examples represent relatively well-known homicide–suicides perpetrated by police officers.

In April 2003, Tacoma, Washington, police chief David Brame committed a homicide–suicide. Reports indicated that the chief and his wife arrived at a shopping center parking lot in separate cars, and their 8- and 5-year-old children were in the mother's vehicle. The chief took the children into his car and proceeded to engage in a verbal altercation with his wife, prompting him to shoot her and then himself. During their divorce proceedings, Ms. Brame reportedly accused the chief of choking and threatening her; in turn, he contended that she physically and verbally abused him. These problems did not appear to be known to most city officials or colleagues (Tacoma police chief, 2003). However, the allegations that Brame was abusive toward his wife were made public the day prior to the shooting (Kids saw, 2003). It was also reported that Brame sought professional counseling to manage the stress from his impending divorce. However, Ms. Brame never sought a restraining order, nor did she ever file charges as she wanted to keep their problems quiet because of her husband's position. Concerns about officer-involved DV were raised in response to the shooting, and the state attorney general, Chris Gregoire, called the department under Brame "culturally corrupt," prompting policy reforms and the development of a DV center (Robinson, 2013). In addition, the Tacoma City Council approved a $12 million legal settlement to Ms. Brame's family (Brame family, 2005).

In 2014, Lindon, Utah, police officer Joshua Boren killed his wife, two children, mother-in-law, and himself. Per reports, Boren's wife text-messaged him hours prior, threatening to leave him and take their children and confronting him for raping her. The couple had been separated for some time already, but they had exchanged contentious text messages the night and morning before the shootings. Boren's therapist informed police that he had drugged his wife and videotaped himself sexually assaulting her more than once. His wife reportedly learned of the tapes in 2013 and told friends, but she did not report it because she did not want to end his career. Reports further indicate that Boren was sexually abused as a child and that he struggled with drug and pornography addiction throughout his life. Boren reportedly hated his mother as she began using drugs and seeing several men after his father committed suicide when he was 5 years old. Boren had been working for the Lindon Police Department for only 3 months at the time of the shooting, although he was a Utah County sheriff's deputy for 7 years prior. Reports indicate that he used his service weapon to commit the homicides and suicide, but the autopsy did not reveal any drugs or alcohol in his system. Friends and family subsequently reported that Boren was not living in the family home but that he went there every morning to help the children get ready for school and picked them up every afternoon. A lieutenant in the department noted that Boren had been considered an excellent father (Police: Officer who killed family, 2014).

On the morning of June 16, 2015, Philip Seidle, a former police sergeant, called his wife incessantly, asking if her new boyfriend was in the home. When she hung up on him, he called back and told her he was going to kill her. Then, with his 7-year-old daughter in the car, he chased his wife through the streets before wedging her car into a parked car. When she tried to exit her car, he pushed her back in and shot her 12 times. At his trial, his children testified regarding their disturbing childhood, stating they grew up amid DV, manipulation, and infidelity. The nine children often heard their mother screaming behind closed doors, sometimes calling for help, yet their father would threaten to kill them if they ever came to her aid (Hopkins, Gecan, & Park, 2016).

Because his wife never signed DV complaints against Seidle, the disputes never triggered a mandatory investigation or disarming. However, in 2012, he was suspended and disarmed from the police department for which he worked after a doctor declared he was unfit for duty after he tried to cancel a call for help that his wife made to the police. He returned to duty 11 months later, and his firearm was returned to him. In 2013 he was suspended again but not disarmed (Hopkins et al., 2016).

Psychological Aspects

There are two main ways in which research can be conducted: quantitatively and qualitatively. A *quantitative* analysis involves examining data that are numerical in form (or coded to be) to generate frequencies, averages, and correlation coefficients with the intention of making probabilistic statements about group differences or the relationship between variables. A *qualitative* analysis may be structured and mathematically based as well but is often focused on the descriptive nature of data, which leads to a particular narrative based on the review. That said, book chapters such as this are essentially qualitative research reviews rather than quantitative reviews, although they may include meta-analyses and the like. Therefore, although we have already reviewed several types of data in this chapter, it is important to highlight the fact that we cannot and should not simply "look" at case examples (like those described in the last section) from afar and make generalizations with any real confidence, at least none that is scientifically based. We may have become somewhat desensitized to this type of caveat, however. For instance, the 2016 election for the US presidency was well underway as we were writing this book, and the scientific and non-scientific polls continued to be used interchangeably as talking points. It is unclear if the general public makes a distinction.

Nevertheless, the take-home message in this context is that we cannot make *conclusions* by simply eyeballing the details in the aforementioned case examples, but we can note commonalities and generate *research questions* and *hypotheses* that can be investigated empirically in the future. So which considerations can be drawn from the types of cases we have presented? First and foremost, there seem to be distinct differences among the groups. In other words, it seems likely that pooling DV- and IPV-related information and data from celebrity, athlete, civilian, and law enforcement populations is inappropriate. This concept in quantitative research synthesis, or meta-analysis, is referred to as *garbage-in, garbage-out*. In other words, if you aggregate data from heterogeneous groups, the results will likely be incorrect, if not misleading. For instance, making conclusive statements about "sex offenders" is inherently problematic given the stark differences among the subgroups within the classification (e.g., child molesters, rapists, exhibitionists, voyeurs, statutory and incest offenders). The same holds true for "domestic abusers." Still, we know there are factors that often cut across DV and IPV situations, such as controlling behaviors, constant jealousy or possessiveness, threats, substance use, and stalking by the abuser (Glass et al., 2008b). Additional factors may include the victims' fear of reinforcing negative stereotypes, secrecy of the abuse, and the failure of others to take victims who seek help seriously. The presence of psychopathic personality traits has been found to be associated with perpetration of IPV in both clinical and non-clinical samples, regardless of gender or alcohol use (Okano, Langille, & Walsh, 2016), as has the presence of borderline personality disorder traits and anxiety disorders (Davoren et al., 2016). Some have also begun to explore the role certain neurotransmitters and neurochemicals play in these situations (e.g., Corvo & Dutton, 2015).

If we entertain an arms-length look at the case examples, however, we may suggest that celebrities have certainly had their share of DV- and IPV-related problems; but it is exceedingly rare to find incidents involving firearms. This may be attributable to the fact that celebrities identify as liberal at an exponentially higher rate than the general public and, therefore, are considerably less likely to own or even interact with firearms. There are some exceptions, of course, as a smaller subset of celebrities are gun owners, including Whoopi Goldberg, Johnny Depp, Robert Downey, Jr., Shannen Doherty, James Earl Jones, Angelina Jolie, Kelsey Grammar, and Clint Eastwood (Blosser, 2015; Von Glinow, 2012).

Regarding firearm ownership and DV, athletes represent a different group entirely. The term *athlete* is overly broad, of course; but certain sport associations seem to have disproportionately high rates of DV- and IPV-related problems. As discussed earlier in this chapter, in the section entitled, "High-Profile DV and IPV Incidents Involving Firearms," the media has showcased several stories regarding DV among athletes, prompting professional sports agencies and leagues to revise their DV policies and seek prevention strategies. That said, we also know that many of these athletes experience notably high rates of head injuries. In fact, research has shown that more than 40% of retired NFL players exhibit signs of traumatic brain injury (Andrews, 2016). This has been linked to chronic traumatic encephalopathy (CTE)—a condition that can only be diagnosed at autopsy but has continued to raise great concerns in recent years and has been associated with the suicides of players such as Junior Seau, Terry Long, Andre Waters, and Ray Easterling (Bahk, 2016). More research is needed to determine the nature of the link between CTE and DV, if there is one. However, research out of Boston University suggests there may indeed be a link between such brain injuries and increasingly violent outbursts (Traumatic brain injury, n.d.). Some scientists have compared the effects of CTE to being heavily intoxicated as CTE seems to reduce inhibition, making it more difficult for individuals to control intense emotions (Traumatic brain injury, n.d.). Of note, there is also the possibility that, at least to some extent, a hidden third variable (e.g., aggression) connects athletes and IPV- or DV-related problems (see also New York State Office for the Prevention of Domestic Violence, n.d.).

Of course, civilian groups are extremely heterogeneous and are considered throughout this chapter and book. Due to their heterogeneity, it may be more difficult to find a single common thread that puts civilians at risk for DV as it is likely a unique combination of risk factors in most situations. Nevertheless, general violence risk factors (including gun violence and DV) are discussed in various chapters of this book. As for law enforcement officers, issues related to potentially higher DV rates, a traditionally secretive subculture, and the ever-available service firearm prove to be a problematic combination for some. Again, these considerations are intended to represent fodder for future research with these subgroups and are not conclusive in any respect.

Laws, Regulations, and Protective Orders

In Chapter 2, we provided a comprehensive overview of firearm-related laws and policies, but here we focus on those related to DV and IPV, such as laws pertaining to protective or restraining orders and the surrender and revocation of firearms.

The Legal Backdrop

The US courts and laws have not provided much protection to domestic abuse victims, historically (Price, 2014). However, DV-related laws began to develop over 40 years ago and have continued to evolve in response to the "battered women's movement" in the 1970s, consistent with the civil rights and feminist movements. In addition, three class-action lawsuits in the mid-1970s in New York, Cleveland, and California prompted the development of policies directing the mandatory arrest, prosecution, and incarceration of spousal abusers (Morgan et al., 1998). These laws have become a mainstay in each state across the country by this point. Over time, DV laws began to include firearm-related restrictions.

Per federal law, a DV restraining order can be filed against a current or former spouse, a current or former cohabitant, or a person with whom the applicant shares a child (Violence Against Women Act, 1994). Moreover, this federal legislation made it illegal for a person with a protection order to own, ship, or receive a firearm or ammunition in interstate or foreign commerce via the Violence Against Women Act's amendment to the Gun Control Act of 1968. In 1996, the US Senate voted 97–2 in favor of Bill S. 1632, which prohibited those convicted of felony or misdemeanor DV from owning or possessing firearms (see Morgan et al., 1998, for a more in-depth discussion on the evolution of the law). The resulting law, P.L. 104-208, became an amendment to Title 18 of the US Code and of the Federal Gun Control Act of 1968. Per P.L. 104-208 (1996), p. Stat. 3009-371:

> The term "crime involving domestic violence" means a felony or misdemeanor crime of violence, regardless of length, term, or manner of punishment, committed by a current or former spouse, parent, guardian of the victim, by a person with whom the victim shares a child in common, by a person who is cohabiting with or has cohabited with the victim as a spouse, parent, or guardian, or by a person similarly situated to a spouse, parent, or guardian of the victim under the domestic or family violence laws of the jurisdiction in which such felony or misdemeanor was committed.

This congressional addition to the Gun Control Act of 1968, known as the Lautenberg Amendment, made it unlawful for a person convicted of a misdemeanor crime of DV to possess a firearm. Per the amendment, a misdemeanor crime of DV is comprised of two elements: the offense must be a misdemeanor under federal, state, or tribal law and the offense must have included the use or the threatened use of physical force against a person within a domestic relationship. The domestic relationship component of the law caused notable debate and legal interjection with respect to its statutory interpretation. Namely, many federal and state courts historically held that a domestic relationship was not a requirement as an element of the predicate offense until *United States v. Hayes* (2007), wherein the US Court of Appeals for the Fourth Circuit determined that such was, in fact, a requirement. The US Supreme Court ultimately overturned the decision, but the background is noteworthy. In 1994, Randy Hayes pled guilty in West Virginia to a misdemeanor battery offense for hitting his wife. Ten years later, in 2004, police were called to Hayes' home for a DV report. While searching the premises, they found a Winchester rifle and proceeded to arrest Hayes for possessing a firearm after being convicted of his 1994 misdemeanor DV offense because it is unlawful in West Virginia for someone with such a conviction to possess a firearm. Hayes contended that his prior conviction did not constitute a DV crime under the statute, but the US District Court for the Northern District of West Virginia rejected his argument. Hayes appealed, and, as noted, the Fourth Circuit Court reversed the district court's decision, holding that a misdemeanor battery offense does not qualify as a DV offense, even if the battery occurred against his wife. Again, the focus of the decision was on the "domestic" relationship aspect of the initial case, and there was question as to whether the domestic relationship was a specified element of the initial offense. The case was heard by the US Supreme Court in *United States v. Hayes* (2009), which reversed the decision with a 7–2 vote (i.e., Chief Justice Roberts and Justice Scalia dissented). The court determined that statutes did not require the existence of a "domestic relationship" as an element of the crime to qualify as a misdemeanor crime of DV, as defined by the Gun Control Act of 1968. Namely, the court held that the predicate offense statute must only include "the use of force" as an element of the crime and not the additional "domestic relationship" element. In fact, if the latter element was a requirement, it would have nullified the Lautenberg Amendment in most states, and it would also make federal law dependent on state law (see Islam, 2010, for a thorough law review of *Hayes*).

Some have contended there may be notable, albeit unintended, consequences to DV laws with firearm restrictions. For instance, Morgan and colleagues (1998) noted that law enforcement personnel were, perhaps, even more directly affected by the Lautenberg Amendment because of the relatively high rates of DV-related problems within their own families. As a result, they reported that law enforcement allied with Second Amendment advocates to oppose the law. Price (2014) suggested six additional potential repercussions:

- A lack of awareness of the laws by those affected
- The potential for fewer protection orders granted by judges
- Disempowerment of victims who want the abuse to stop but not the associated sanctions
- Interference by DV advocates
- The potential for mutual orders of protection
- Employment consequences for those who may need to interact with or be in the presence of firearms

Moreover, Price highlighted the ever-present problems with the enforcement of these types of laws and restrictions, which includes judges' modifications to orders as well as issues related to having law enforcement officers carry them out. Price also noted the potential for the misuse of protection orders by those making unsubstantiated or completely frivolous claims. Perhaps the most striking example is that of Colleen Nestler, a woman from New Mexico who reported that television host David Letterman harassed her via his broadcasts in 2005. In her application, she reported that Letterman used code words and gestures in an attempt to manipulate her, and she also noted the involvement of Regis Philbin, Kathie Lee Gifford, and Kelsey Grammer in her complaint. Despite the fact they had never met and Letterman already had a history of dealing with a mentally ill stalker, Judge Daniel Sanchez of the district court in Sante Fe actually granted Nestler a temporary restraining order against David Letterman (Pace, 2005).

Still, some believe the extant firearm-related DV laws are insufficient. In its 2014 report titled *Guns and Violence Against Women*, Everytown contended:

- Federal law does nothing to keep guns out of the hands of abusive dating partners or convicted stalkers;
- In 35 states, state law does not prohibit all people convicted of misdemeanor domestic violence crimes and all people subject to restraining orders from buying or using guns;
- Federal law (and the law in most states) allows domestic abusers and stalkers to easily evade gun prohibitions by purchasing guns from unlicensed, private sellers; and
- 41 states do not require all prohibited domestic abusers to relinquish guns they already own. (p. 3)

Given concerns with the "loopholes" it believes are associated with the existing laws, Everytown recommended the following:

- Congress should close the loopholes in the federal gun prohibitions to ensure that stalkers and dating partners are barred from gun ownership just like other dangerous abusers;
- States should adopt or strengthen their domestic violence prohibitions;
- Congress should require comprehensive background checks and ensure that prohibited domestic abusers cannot easily evade background checks by buying guns from unlicensed sellers.
- States should pass legislation requiring background checks on all gun sales.
- States should create effective and enforceable laws and policies for prohibited domestic abusers to relinquish their guns. (p. 10)

The group has also conducted a pointed analysis of states' laws. For example, in its subsequent analysis of domestic abuse protective orders between 2012 and 2014 in Rhode Island, Everytown (2015) noted that Rhode Island courts are not required to make prohibited abusers turn in their previously acquired firearms, although the courts can if they are so inclined. Nevertheless, only 5% of domestic abusers, overall, and 13% of those associated with a firearm threat were court-ordered to turn in their guns during the aforementioned time period. This is particularly striking given that it found that one in four final protective orders in the state resulted from evidence indicating that a firearm was present or that the abuser threatened to use one against the victim.

Everytown (2015) also investigated DV-related homicides with firearms in Arizona between 2009 and 2013. It found 105 homicides in the state, where the victims were murdered with a gun by a current or former partner. The victims were women in 89% of cases, and 13% of shooters had been previously prohibited from possessing firearms as a result of their criminal histories or an active protection order. However, Everytown indicated that only one in six perpetrators who were under an active order of protection had been required to turn in their firearms. It further noted that firearms were used primarily to kill an intimate partner rather than in self-defense against an abusive one, such that there was only one person whose self-defense claim was upheld in court. Victims in four additional cases had purchased a firearm for the purpose of self-defense but either were unable to use it or had it used against them. Everytown reported that firearms were the primary method of murder in the sample as 62% included firearms and 38% included various other methods (e.g., fire, asphyxiation, strangulation, blunt object, knife or cutting instrument). It is important to reiterate that the research did not include DV incidents, more generally, which is likely the explanation of the proportionally high rates of firearm usage. Everytown also reported that there were protective orders sought in only 13 cases (12%), only seven remained active at the time of the shooting, and only one person had been court-ordered to turn in his firearms. Everytown concluded: "While the cases are devastating, the deaths were not inevitable. Domestic violence gun homicides can be prevented by strengthening weak gun laws so abusers are denied access to firearms" (p. 16).

Frattaroli & Vernick (2006) noted that, as of 2004, only 18 states had police gun removal laws and 16 states had court-ordered removal laws. A more recent study of removal laws was conducted by Webster et al. (2010), who surveyed DV victims in Los Angeles and New York City, two areas where laws include firearm surrender provisions in DV cases. The authors found that despite these laws, judges issued firearm surrender orders in only 26% of cases involving protective orders against armed abusers. Further, in some cases, victims reported that judges did not issue a surrender order, despite their explicit requests to have their abusers' firearms removed.

Law and Policy Evaluation Research

In order to ascertain whether laws and policies pertaining to DV are effective, various research projects have been conducted. However, laws vary significantly from state to state and are enforced to varying degrees. As such, research findings are rarely generalizable to all communities within the United States. Nevertheless, research studies in this area are imperative as laws and policies that demonstrate effectiveness in reducing DV and firearm casualties can pave the way for other communities. Below are summaries of various studies evaluating DV policies and laws.

In their research, Bridges, Tatum, & Kunselman (2008) examined whether states that have adopted specific DV laws have significantly lower rates of domestic homicide and IPH. With only two exceptions, these data indicated that state laws pertaining to DV were *not* correlated with homicide rates across the country. Additionally, relevant state laws were not related to the homicide rates, overall. However, one important exception was the potential effectiveness of protective orders. Specifically, "the family homicide rate decreased across 47 states as the number of states restricting firearms during a restraining order increased, or vice versa" (p. 127).

Zeoli & Webster (2010) examined the relationship between IPH and relevant public policies, including police staffing levels, from 1979 to 2003 across 46 of the largest US cities. They used data from the FBI's *Supplementary Homicide Reports*. Their findings suggest that state statutes that limit access to firearms for individuals with DV restraining orders, as well as laws that allow the warrantless arrest of violators of such orders, are associated with reduced total and firearm IPHs. Specifically, there was a 19% decrease in IPHs and a 25% decrease in firearm IPHs associated with state laws restricting access to those under restraining orders, as well as a 16% decrease associated with DV restraining order violation warrantless arrests. In addition, police staffing levels were associated with decreased IPHs and firearm IPHs. However, there were no statistically significant effects found in this regard for state laws reducing a DV misdemeanant's access to firearms or those that allow police officers to confiscate firearms from the scene of DV.

Sorenson & Shen (2005) analyzed the data related to the 227,941 protective orders that were in place against adults in California as of June 2003. Of note is that not all orders were for DV, although they estimated that approximately 200,000 had been. Based on their analysis, Sorensen & Shen found that only 3% of the orders were non-expiring, whereas about half were to expire in 18 months and the remaining half would expire in an increment of 1 year or less. Most of the restraining orders (72%) involved a restrained male and a protective female, and 63% of those restrained were of an ethnic minority group. The average age of restrained persons was 35 years. With regard to the orders' content, approximately half included so-called stay-away information, but only 5% of the orders addressed child custody–related issues. Per California law, a restrained person is prohibited from purchasing firearms regardless of whether this is specifically included in the order. Nevertheless, no such restrictions were noted in nearly 10% of cases. In half of the cases, restrained persons were prohibited and required to relinquish their firearms, and the remaining 40% were prohibited but not required to relinquish. Based on their research, Sorenson & Shen noted that there are as many active protective orders in place on any given day in California as there are marriages during a 1-year period there. Approximately 8% of the 1 million orders issued nationally in the United States come from California. However, one in six of the state's orders had not even been served; therefore, the restrained person was unaware that the order was even in place. Moreover, even many of those who are aware of the order may be unaware of its specific firearm-related restrictions. Sorenson & Shen concluded:

> Most restraining orders are for intimate partner violence. What should happen and what does happen with restraining orders differs across time and across judges or commissioners. Some counties have created domestic violence courts without substantially increasing costs by consolidating existing resources. Such courts, in which domestic violence cases including restraining orders are heard by specially trained and assigned judges or commissioners, could reduce jurisdictional inconsistency in the issuance and follow-up on restraining orders, including decisions regarding violated restraining orders. Greater consistency in the application of the law may increase confidence in the court system as well as increase the safety of those who are to be protected. (p. 930)

In a subsequent study, Vittes & Sorenson (2006) examined data gathered from the Los Angeles County Bar Association's Barrister's Domestic Violence Project. Specifically, they analyzed over 1,300 DV restraining order applications filed against intimate partners from 2003 and 2004 in Los Angeles County. Most applicants were females (92%) between the ages of 14 and 76, with an average age of 32. Most defendants were males (93%) between 16 and 79 years old, with an average age of 35. Applicants and defendants came from diverse ethnic backgrounds, but the majority was Latino (i.e., approximately 70% for each group), followed by black (20%), white (5%), and Asian (3%). Of particular note is that police were involved in at least one abusive incident in 71% of the applications, and approximately half of those defendants had been arrested at least once. Nevertheless, emergency protective orders were far less common (16%) despite the fact that violence and threats of violence were quite common. Namely, nearly 60% of applicants reported being threatened by the respective defendants, which included threats to kill (36%), harm (31%), kidnap the applicant's child or children (13%), harm or kill others such as family and friends (13%), and commit suicide if the applicant did not do what the defendant wanted (6%). Just over 40% of applicants noted (external) weapons in the applicants, which included firearms (16%), knives (12%), motor vehicles (4%), and other weapons (18%). Furthermore, the vast majority of applicants (87%) reported having been physically or sexually assaulted by the defendant, with being hit, beat, kicked, and/or pushed the most common forms (85%), followed by being choked (18%) and sexually assaulted (13%). It was rare for applicants to have been previously cut, however (2%). Moreover, children witnessed the abuse in half of the applications, and they were harmed by the defendant in 14% of the cases. As noted, firearms were mentioned in 16% of the applications. A higher proportion of such cases involved black applicants and defendants, people who were not married and had not lived together, and defendants younger than 18 years. In addition, Vittes & Sorenson found that a mention of a firearm was associated with eight abuse-related characteristics: threats to harm or kill, threats against others and to commit suicide, a history of choking and stalking, and a history of police involvement and injury. Furthermore, restraining orders were granted in most cases (89%), and the presence of child witnesses to abuse notably increased the odds of issuance.

Webster et al. (2010) found that only 15% of protective orders from Los Angeles County and New York City involved a firearm. They found the firearm-involved cases to be similar, demographically, to those that did not involve a firearm. However, victims with abusers who had a firearm were more likely to report that there was no intimate or cohabitating relationship with the abuser, and they were less likely to be foreign-born. Moreover, about two-thirds of the victims whose abusers had guns experienced severe types of IPV, and they were more likely to be victimized multiple times and by a gun or knife. Nevertheless, prior threats or use of a weapon did not increase the likelihood of judges' removal orders. Furthermore, only 26% of abusers with firearms were required by judges to surrender their firearms or have them removed, but only 12% actually surrendered them or had them confiscated. Victims only explicitly asked for such in half of the cases that involved firearms. Webster and colleagues point out that California laws require judges to include a firearm surrender component in nonemergency DV restraining orders and that, although New York law requires a judge to order a firearm surrender if the incident related to the protective order involved a firearm-related assault, they are not required to do so based on risk alone.

Vittes et al. (2013) examined a pilot program for two sheriff's offices in California funded by the California Department of Justice aimed at better enforcing the firearm surrender requirement for individuals under certain DV restraining orders. The authors describe interviews with 17 restraining order recipients regarding their experiences and feelings about the removal of firearms from their abusers. Most of the participants (15 of 17) reported being the victims of non-firearm-related physical abuse in the 6 months prior to obtaining a temporary protective order, including being pushed, shoved, or grabbed. Consistent with the typical base rate cited in the professional literature, three (18%) reported being abused or threatened with a firearm during that time. Of note is that all of the restrained persons owned at least one firearm. More than half of the women requested that the firearms be surrendered or removed, and this actually occurred in most cases. Most women reported feeling safer as a result. While all of the women reported that the physical abuse ended subsequent to the protective order, approximately one-third had to call the police due to threats of violence.

Wintemute et al. (2014) reviewed the screening procedures in two Californian counties with respect to restraining orders and revocation of firearms. They investigated all such cases between 2007 and 2010, which consisted of approximately 8,000 orders. Only 18% of respondents were linked to a firearm, and a total of 665 firearms were ultimately recovered, including 305 handguns, 291 long guns, and 69 of an unknown type. Of the handguns, 36% were not in the Automated Firearms System, which is California's record system that has tracked both handgun purchases and denied firearm purchases (of all types) since 1996. Furthermore, most firearms were revoked without incident. These findings led the authors to conclude that "it is possible to enforce prohibitions on firearm possession among persons subject to domestic violence restraining orders," noting that hundreds of firearms were recovered without any associated problems.

As Vigdor & Mercy (2006) noted, firearms are not typically used in DV incidents; however, they contribute significantly to IPHs. Therefore, they highlighted the importance of examining the effectiveness of state laws in reducing fatal and nonfatal incidents in DV situations. As they indicated, however, data are not maintained on DV outcomes, with the exception of homicide data. Thus, they focused on IPHs across states by accessing the FBI's *Supplementary Homicide Report* files between 1982 and 2002. Vigdor & Mercy found that all types of IPH decreased during the 20-year period, including those that were firearm-related. The highest rates were in the mid-1980s—in contrast to the majority of other violent crimes that increased into the early 1990s before declining. With respect to their primary research questions, Vigdor & Mercy found that states with restraining order laws had significantly lower rates of IPHs committed both with and without firearms. Namely, they found an 8%–10% reduction in IPHs each year, resulting in approximately two fewer homicides each year in states that have these laws in effect. Of note is that the rate reductions remain comparable for IPHs regardless of whether or not a firearm was used. They found the same trend for states with restraining order laws that incorporate purchase restrictions. Moreover, they found no difference in IPH rates when DV misdemeanor or firearm confiscation laws were in effect at the state level. Based on their analyses, Vigdor & Mercy "cautiously conclude[d] that laws restricting access to firearms by abusers under restraining orders reduce IPHs" (p. 337). Specifically, they found that states passing such laws see a reduction in IPH rates by approximately 8%, averaging nearly three homicides annually. As noted, the effects are comparable for IPHs with or without firearm involvement. Nevertheless, they found no effect from DV misdemeanor or confiscation laws that allow police to revoke firearms at a DV scene. However, they note that it may be the case that it is simply easier to enforce firearm restrictions at the time of attempted purchase rather than when someone already owns a firearm, particularly because owners are not always identifiable because of inadequate record-keeping systems. Of course, an onus remains on those tasked with enforcing the laws and restrictions in the first place (e.g., law enforcement, courts, firearm dealers).

Based on their review of published studies between 1999 and 2014, Webster & Wintemute (2015) concluded that there are weaknesses in federal laws and policies designed to keep firearms from high-risk individuals in the United States. They cite growing empirical support for the effectiveness of certain laws that prevent prohibited persons from accessing firearms. For instance, criminals who are prohibited from purchasing firearms from licensed dealers are less likely to engage in violent crime, and DV restraining orders and convictions for misdemeanor violent crimes appear to reduce violence. However, restrictions such as those related to a minimum age for purchasing or possessing handguns and DV misdemeanors are not associated with a reduction in crime.

Thus, there is some indication that laws in this context may be effective in preventing DV and IPV homicides but not necessarily DV or IPV in general—particularly misdemeanor DV. Nevertheless, the aforementioned problems with implementation and enforcement of these laws and restrictions remain, which is not terribly surprising given that states (and even towns and cities within states) notably differ with respect to their issuance of firearm permits in the first place. For example, states wherein citizens are allowed to carry a concealed handgun are either considered *may-issue* states, whereby the local police chief has discretion, or *shall-issue* states, whereby the permit must be issued if the applicant passes the background check. Within this context, Hemenway & Hicks (2015) surveyed 121 police chiefs throughout Massachusetts regarding "may-issue" and "shall-issue" laws and found that the large majority of police chiefs favored retaining police discretion to refuse to issue a permit. Furthermore, results suggested that chiefs set forth a median of two discretionary denials per year, for such reasons as the applicant providing false information, having a history of assault (often DV) or substance abuse, or a mental health history. As such, the notable differences found in relation to court orders and their enforcement are not unexpected.

Frattaroli & Teret (2006) analyzed 30 cases in the context of the Maryland Gun Violence Act, which became law in 1996 and authorized courts to order batterers to turn over their guns through civil protective orders. The law provided law enforcement with the duty to remove firearms when responding to a DV complaint. Frattaroli & Teret noted that Maryland's court-ordered surrender policy involves a multistep process, which begins when victims file hearing requests for batterers to surrender their firearms. They conducted 11 days of observation in a civil DV court and identified 27 protective order hearings that fell under the firearms surrender provision. Victims reported that firearms were part of the abuse in five of these matters. Namely, in the first case, a woman was seeking to divorce her husband of 19 years and reported how he has threatened to shoot her recently and in the past; in the second case, a male petitioner reported that he was threatened with being shot by a female; the third case involved an incident whereby the petitioner alleged that the respondent pointed a gun at her; in the fourth case, the petitioner reported being assaulted with a gun; and in the fifth case, the petitioner sought a protective order after being told by a friend that the respondent was talking about shooting at her house. Although protective orders were issued in these cases, none of the orders required respondents to surrender their firearms despite the fact that three different judges presided over these five cases. Frattaroli

& Teret noted that a judge did revoke a respondent's firearms in a sixth case, although the petitioner did not allege any firearm-related abuse. Based on their analysis, the researchers concluded that the implementation of the DV and firearm laws and policies varied across a number of urban, suburban, and rural sites in the state. They attributed this to challenges related to both the policies themselves as well as the people involved in interpreting and carrying them out. As such, they recommended further clarity in the language of the laws, training and support for those tasked with their implementation, and monitoring and assessment of their effectiveness.

Reflections and Revisions

Although judges and law enforcement personnel tend to absorb the responsibility associated with the implementation and enforcement challenges observed in this area, some state attorneys have acknowledged their role in the process. As a former city attorney of San Diego in the San Diego District Attorney's Office, Casey Gwinn (2006) reflected on his experience and noted:

> Over the past 20 years as a domestic violence prosecutor, I have failed to deal appropriately with firearms in many domestic violence cases I have handled. And I am not alone. Too often in dealing with firearms issues in domestic violence cases, we in the criminal justice system, including police officers, prosecutors, and judges, have relied on laws that are never enforced, assumed levels of safety that never existed, and depended on voluntary compliance that never occurred. (p. 238)

Paul Seave was a special assistant attorney general and director of the California attorney general's Crime and Violence Prevention Center. He was also on the attorney general's Task Force on Local Criminal Justice Response to Domestic Violence. In 2003, the attorney general convened a 26-member task force to assess the DV-related policies and practices of numerous agencies operating across California's 58 counties. The task force focused on four primary inquiries: (i) how DV restraining orders were obtained and enforced; (ii) how prosecutors' offices handle DV cases, given that most were misdemeanors; (iii) how batterer intervention programs, together with courts and probation departments, held convicted batterers accountable; and (iv) how law enforcement responded to mandated reports of DV from health practitioners. It focused on 10 of the 58 counties, although it collected data on restraining orders throughout the state. The task force also collected data by conducting hundreds of interviews, privately and publicly, which included 69 practitioners. Seave (2006) summarized the findings and recommendations based on the task force's subsequent report. Perhaps unsurprisingly, the task force found significant variation across counties throughout the state. In some counties, nearly all family court protective orders issued included firearms prohibitions, whereas other counties had relatively high rates. For example, 19% of the orders issued in San Francisco did not include firearm prohibitions, which was notably higher than the state averages of 3%–5%. Of note, however, is that Seave reported that San Francisco's rate notably diminished to less than 1% in 2005, once a new police chief was appointed. Nevertheless, as the state average reflected, most DV restraining orders in California prohibited batterers from owning, purchasing, possessing, or receiving firearms. Seave concluded that those who were subject to permanent family court protective orders were, on average, "more dangerous than those prosecuted criminally" (p. 263); but there was a significant challenge in enforcing prohibition of firearms when there was no evidence the person possessed them.

While DV- and IPV-related research, laws, and policies have developed over the last half-century, more recent efforts have been aimed at increasing awareness and revising laws and policies, as needed, based on the empirical research in this area. For instance, President Obama made October 2012 National Domestic Violence Awareness Month (Presidential proclamation, 2012),[3] and the Affordable Care Act required most insurance plans to make DV screening and counseling available for women and adolescent girls without copays or deductibles since August 2012. Moreover, January has been marked as National Stalking Awareness Month since 2003 by Congress in response to the extensive stalking and ultimate murder of Peggy Klinke, a University of New Mexico student, by her estranged boyfriend (National Stalking Awareness Month, 2013). States' efforts are also notable. For example, recent laws in Maine have mandated the use of evidence-based risk assessment procedures by law enforcement officers following DV arrests to assist bail commissioners and district attorneys in their decision-making (Colpitts & Niemczyk, 2012). Another law mandated notification of victims when offenders are released on bail. Additional laws refocused bail decisions and even gave strangulation special consideration as a criminal act. Colpitts & Niemczyk also noted the development of a California law in 2012 that allows the prohibition of alimony awards to domestic abusers. Another new law developed that year requires the court to ensure that a search of records is conducted prior to a protective order hearing, which includes the presence of a legal history and registered firearms. It also provides authorities with more confiscation power. In addition, Alaska engaged in a series of major revisions to its DV-related laws and policies over the past two decades (see Trostle, Barnes, & Atwell, 2000). For instance, it began to train police and others in handling DV situations and increased resources for victims. The state has made DV an independent and punishable crime to include the mandatory arrest of perpetrators as well as those who violate protective orders and release conditions.

In conclusion, while several jurisdictions have implemented laws and policies that are aimed at reducing DV by removing firearms from the possession of potentially dangerous reoffenders, these efforts require continued improvement. First, additional research and clarification are needed regarding the disparate laws and policies that are currently in existence throughout the United States. At the present time, it seems some laws and policies contribute to no significant reduction in DV incidence in general, while others are related to decreased homicide-related deaths. Second, the lack of uniform interpretation and implementation of laws and policies needs to be addressed. As a result of the varied and discrepant interpretation, additional training and monitoring of individuals tasked with carrying out these policies and laws are necessary. Further, considering that certain laws and policies seem to be effective at preventing DV- or IPV-related deaths, it is essential to clarify who is responsible for enforcing them as it seems there has been some disparity in the past as to who holds this burden and under what circumstances.

6

Suicide

In this chapter we cover the critically important area of suicide, both generally and in association with firearms. First, we provide a detailed review of suicide-related terminology and definitions. We do so because an existing and pressing problem in mental health and related professions is the use of confusing, inconsistent language surrounding suicide. Common understanding about suicide becomes critically important especially when considering the professions that interact with suicidal persons with firearms, including law enforcement personnel, but also those in the mental health and medical fields. Second, grounded in the best available data concerning suicide rates, we provide an overview of primary theoretical perspectives as to why people commit suicide, as well as key risk and protective factors in this regard. This lays the groundwork for a review of firearms and suicide; specifically, we review firearm-related suicide statistics, risk and protective factors, and a sample of laws and set forth a critique on the limitations of available data. We then turn our attention to the crucial role of dealing with firearms (and other lethal means) in the context of suicide risk assessment, management, and prevention. Finally, we tie up this discussion with sample case studies of firearm-related suicides to try and draw lessons that can inform best practices concerning suicide and firearm management.

Overview of Suicide

What Is Suicide?

There is no simple answer to this question. In fact, there is an unfortunate level of inconsistency in suicide terminology (Silverman & De Leo, 2016), though in the lay public it seems to be one of those issues that you "know when you see it." A common understanding of suicide is critically important for several reasons. First, it provides common communication and understanding among medical and health professionals, ranging from physicians to psychologists, who regularly assess and treat suicidal persons (Bryan & Rudd, 2006). Related to this point, law enforcement, military, and many other lay community professionals interface with suicidal persons. They too need a common understanding in order to effectively communicate. As suicide often becomes an ethical or legal issue, precise definitions of key terms become necessary. For instance, many laws concerning suicide address circumstances under which someone can be psychiatrically hospitalized against his or her own will, including being a "threat to self." Legal clarity is of the utmost importance in these circumstances. Finally, clear phraseology and common communication are vital in order to advance the suicide assessment and prevention science and training (De Leo et al., 2006).

The operational definition of suicide can be informed by several expert sources, including the professional mental health and medical literatures, the Centers for Disease Control and Prevention (CDC), and the World Health Organization (WHO). As with defining violence (see Chapter 4), expert consensus provides one valuable approach to defining suicide. Expert-driven clinical literatures (e.g., Bryan & Rudd, 2006; De Leo et al., 2006; Silverman et al., 2007) provide the following general guidance on defining suicide. First, as summarized by De Leo and colleagues (2006) in their review of classic suicide definitions (e.g., Durkheim, 1897; Ivanoff, 1989), suicide is any self-directed injury with the *intent to die*. It follows that suicide and suicide attempts fall under a broader umbrella of *suicide-related behavior* (SRB). SRB covers a continuum of thinking and behavior. *Suicidal ideation* generally describes thinking, which covers the range from thoughts of death (in the context of a desire to die) to suicidal fantasies to developing intent and the preparation toward a suicide attempt. In a classic breakdown of SRB, O'Carroll et al. (1996; later reviewed and modified by Silverman et al., 2007) provided a framing for behavioral aspects. This framing breaks SRB into instrumental (i.e., suicidal behavior for another gain) versus suicidal acts. This is not to say that "instrumental" suicide implies that the behavior should not be taken seriously. All suicidal behavior should be taken seriously. Rather, the distinction between instrumental suicide and suicidal act helps contextualize the underlying thinking and motivation for anyone working with a particular patient. Clinical guidance on suicide definitions further recommend defining both types of suicide attempt or behaviors with qualifiers of "with injuries" or "without injuries" in order to denote whether bodily injury has occurred (Bryan & Rudd, 2006; Silverman et al., 2007).

Expert clinical guidance also highlights the importance of understanding intent specifically. Intent, a basic cognitive aspect of SRB, is also unfortunately ill-defined in the literature (Hasley et al., 2008). For instance, from a research standpoint, intent is often measured inconsistently and framed as both a predictor and an outcome variable in suicide studies. What we do know about suicidal intent is that its severity is linked to other SRB issues, such as eventual suicide attempt, suicide completion, and lethal means (Bryan & Rudd, 2006; Hasley et al., 2008). In fact, mental health professionals often infer the presence of suicidal intent from the presence of a firearm (Hasley et al., 2008). Also concerning intent is the oft-used phrase *parasuicide*. As outlined by De Leo and colleagues (2006), although often used mistakenly as an interchangeable term along with *suicide attempt* in the literature, *parasuicide* and *suicide attempt* are actually mutually exclusive. A view favored in the United States, parasuicide represents SRB with little intent to die. That is, a suicide attempt or other SRB can possess varying levels of intent and be driven by other factors. The term *suicide attempt* is favored where clear high intent to die is present.

The CDC and WHO often frame discussion of suicide as *self-directed violence* (SDV). For example, the CDC (n.d.a) definition reflects this shift: death caused by self-directed injurious behavior or violence with an intent to die as a result of the behavior. Such definitions shift the conversation about suicide from one of mental illness and clinical issues to one of public health and SDV prevention (and perhaps a better fit with the framing of this book). As evidence of a change in how we discuss suicide, recent important suicide and violence prevention documents put forth by the CDC (e.g., Crosby, Ortega, & Melanson, 2011) and the WHO (e.g., World Health Organization, 2015) frame suicide as SDV. Research using clinical and forensic (e.g., Swogger, Van Orden, & Conner, 2014), as well as general (e.g., Cramer et al., 2017), populations consistently reports a strong association between experiences of SDV and interpersonal violence victimization or perpetration. The SDV framing, therefore, holds potential value for issues such as firearm-involved violence and suicide.

A critical element of an SDV framing of suicide is the inclusion of self-injurious behavior. Distinguished from suicide, *self-injury* reflects intentional SDV without the goal of death (Gratz, 2001). That is, the individual engages in self-harming behaviors (e.g., cutting, pill overdose) for some end or goal other than death. Like suicide, many phrases for self-injury are mistakenly used interchangeably in the literature. In short, *self-injury, self-destructive behavior,* and *self-harm* are terms appropriately used in the general public. Deliberate self-harm (DSH) phrasing is consistent with mental health practice and research literature. For example, the Deliberate Self-Harm Inventory (DSHI) is a common self-report tool used in research and practice to quantify types and frequency of self-harm (Gratz, 2001; Lundh, Karim, & Quilisch, 2007). Among the most common types of self-harm captured by the DSHI are cutting, burning, carving in skin, scratching, biting, and dripping acid onto one's body (Lundh et al., 2007), although this is a far from exhaustive list of known methods of DSH (e.g., firearm-inflicted injury). Finally, the phrase *non-suicidal self-injury* (NSSI), although used in the research literature, is also consistent with the American Psychiatric Association's definition of self-injury in the *Diagnostic and Statistical Manual,* fifth edition (DSM-5; American Psychiatric Association, 2013). NSSI falls under the classification of V-codes, or issues warranting clinical attention in the DSM-5. The theoretical and empirical literature (e.g., Nock & Prinstein, 2004; Gratz, 2003) provides a bevy of potential functions of self-injurious behavior such as short-term emotional relief, self-punishment, attempt to communicate with others (e.g., head-banging for someone without emotional expressivity skills), avoidance of hurting others, and general emotional expression (e.g., release of psychic pain).

In understanding suicide risk assessment and prevention, it is also important to define the following related concepts: risk factor, protective factor, and thoughts of death. According to the Suicide Prevention Resource Center (n.d.), a *risk factor* is any variable that increases the likelihood of the occurrence of an event. Put in a day-to-day example, a risk factor for catching the common cold is having a child (for those of you who are parents, you are well acquainted with the lovely amounts of germs your children bring home from school!). A *protective factor* is just the opposite—any variable that decreases the probability of an event or act. Another simple example: regular exercise is a well-documented protective factor against the chance of having a heart attack. The sheer number of documented risk and protective factors for SRB is astounding, with individual studies in the literature yielding an almost too-high-to-count total number of factors. Turning again to the expert clinical literature (e.g., Bryan & Rudd, 2006; Van Orden et al., 2008), we can provide tangible examples of the best-known risk factors. As summarized by Bryan & Rudd (2006), among the necessary risk factors mental health professionals should attend to are a person's history of SRB, symptoms of depression and other mental illness, indicators of impulsivity or low self-control (e.g., fighting, substance use), and hopelessness (e.g., giving up on the future). To the contrary, well-supported protective factors for SRB include, but are not limited to, the presence and use of social support (e.g., friends, family), history of positive coping skills, and fear of suicide or death.

A final definitional nuance worthy of our attention is that of *thoughts of death*. This particular issue can be a tad of a conundrum in defining SRB and associated issues like risk. Have you ever thought about death? (most of us have). Did it mean you were suicidal? (likely not). Thus, the point is well illustrated: thoughts of death may or may not be indicative of suicide or related SRB/SDV. One end of the spectrum concerning thoughts of death frames them as normative, day-to-day issues, just as thrill-seeking and other behaviors can be considered (see Silverman et al., 2007). Topics related to death may fall into other categories such as religious or philosophical discourse. Where thoughts of death become potentially problematic is when they occur out of character and in the context of other distressing issues. For instance, the DSM-5 (American Psychiatric Association, 2013) specifically lists suicidality/thoughts of death as one diagnostic indicator of major depression. Thoughts of death under such circumstances often take the form of thinking about ending one's life, wondering what it would be like to be dead, or wishing one could no longer be alive. In essence, a nuanced understanding of the exact nature and backdrop of thoughts of death is necessary; thinking of death is not by straightforward definition indicative of suicide.

In summary, let us agree on the following basic points concerning a definition of suicide moving forward: (i) suicidality, such as attempts and completion, presupposes the intent to die; (ii) the degree of intent is important in understanding nuance in suicide (e.g., lethality, plan, and preparation); (iii) a mental health framing of suicide is best thought of from the perspective of SRB; (iv) a public health prevention perspective of suicide operates from an SDV understanding; (v) self-harm and its various conceptualizations are related to, yet distinct from, suicide (but do fall under the umbrella of SDV); and (vi) risk and protective factors, as well as thoughts of death, are important factors in defining suicide risk. And on a promising closing note, recent work by Silverman & De Leo (2016) aims at moving toward a global approach to common suicide vernacular. We encourage the reader to follow this work closely for developments in suicide-related definitions and nomenclature.

Suicide Statistics and Relevant Laws

One role of public health agencies pertains to the surveillance of major health concerns on the national, international, and local levels. Suicide and related conditions comprise one such area tracked by the CDC, among other agencies. In this section we provide a basic overview of major recent prevalence data for SRB in the United States—we address demographic and other characteristics associated with elevated rates below (see *Key Risk and Protective Factors and a Theoretical Overview*). CDC (Centers for Disease Control and Prevention, 2015, 2016) reports provide the following notable patterns of SRB:

- suicide is among the top 10 causes of death annually
- between approximately 33,000 and 43,000 documented suicides occur annually for instance, 41,149 suicides occurred in 2013 with 21,175 via firearm
- rates of nonfatal SRB remain high, with 3.9% of adults experiencing suicidal ideation and 0.6% of adults making a suicide attempt in a 12-month period

The American Association of Suicidology also provides valuable SRB-related surveillance information. In 2014, 42,773 documented suicides occurred (an average of about 117 per day), with an estimate of over 1 million suicide attempts occurring in the same year (Drapeau & McIntosh, 2015). Importantly, recent years have seen a budding upward trend in documented suicides in the United States after a decade of stabilization and even decline (Drapeau & McIntosh, 2015).

We must, of course, frame these best available base rates within their respective and obvious limitations. Namely, SRB rates are truly hard to confidently estimate, especially in terms of specific thinking and behavior. For instance, a commonly accepted truism in the mental health field is that we likely underestimate rates of suicidal thinking because it is an impossibility to know what patients are thinking unless they tell you. Further complicating the issue is trying to reach every citizen in need without knowing who they are. Regarding suicide attempts, expert sources note that completed suicides are likely underestimated (e.g., Katz, Bolton, & Sareen, 2016) for a variety of reasons such as inconsistent definitions and reporting, as well as lack of clarity in many deaths of undetermined cause. For example, many single-person, single–motor vehicle accidents resulting in death may have been suicide, but we will never know.

While many US state and federal laws are relevant to our discussion, two types are particularly relevant because they specifically address SRB: those that (i) address criteria for psychiatric hospitalization and (ii) define the (il) legality and details of physician-assisted suicide (PAS). We provide a short framing of these issues as they may be informative to the broader understanding of issues impacting firearms and mental health. The first category of laws generally concern civil psychiatric hospitalization. In everyday discourse, you may hear these laws referred to as *psychiatric holds, civil commitment*, and other related terms. What they share in common is that a medical or mental health professional, under certain circumstances, may evaluate the mental condition of a community member with the possibility of a determination of need for psychiatric hospitalization. Most laws within the United States include as one of the potential reasons for such hospitalization: "threat to self" or "imminent danger to self" (among others). Alternatively, any person may have himself or herself voluntarily psychiatrically hospitalized as well. The Treatment Advocacy Center (2014) in Arlington, Virginia, recently summarized state laws concerning psychiatric hospitalization. This valuable summary is publicly available, although the caveat exists that some laws may have been updated since 2014. To illustrate psychiatric hospitalization laws, let us turn to the state of Texas.

Two Texas laws directly address SRB in the medical determination for psychiatric hospitalization or forced medication administration. The first (Tex. Health & Safety Code, 2012b) defines a hospitalization criterion as a person having a mental illness that "is likely to cause serious harm to himself." SRB is perhaps the most commonly defined condition qualifying as threat to self in this instance, although others exist (e.g., loss of cognitive abilities or impulse control). The second Texas state law (Tex. Health & Safety Code, 2012a) example concerns circumstances under which medical professionals may forcibly administer emergency medications, commonly preceding the need for psychiatric hospitalization. In this case, "medication-related emergencies" under the law allow for forced medication whereby probable death or injury may otherwise occur because "the patient . . . overtly or continually is threatening or attempting to commit suicide or serious bodily harm." A related issue, and one pressing for mental health approaches to the gun control debate, is the potential role of psychological fitness evaluations for civilian gun ownership. This topic applies in the legal review because threat to self, influenced or defined by suicide risk, is a proposed requirement to address in such evaluations (Pirelli, Wechsler, & Cramer, 2015; Pirelli & Witt, 2015). The role of mental health evaluations in civilian firearm ownership is discussed in greater depth in Chapter 7.

Shara Johnson, a forensic psychologist, and her colleagues (2014, 2015) provided a useful review of the history of PAS legalization. Passed in 1994, the first state law legalizing PAS was the Oregon Death with Dignity Act (1995). Basic requirements for an Oregon resident to request PAS included: state residency, minimum of 18 years of age, a documented terminal illness (within 6 months), and being deemed competent to make the request. Much more nuance applies to the request process, however, such as the fact that the sick individual must be deemed terminally ill by two independent physicians. Further, the applicant must provide two written requests at least 48 hours apart. As you may imagine, the use of PAS is contentious in both the medical field and the public (Johnson et al., 2015), with many moral, legal, and political arguments on both sides of the issue. Three other states followed Oregon's model very closely, enacting the Washington Death with Dignity Act (2008), the Montana Death with Dignity Act (*Baxter v. Montana*, 2009), and the Vermont Patient Choice and Control at the End of Life Act (2013). Importantly, a recent development in US-defined PAS laws since Johnson's work has happened in California. Although modeled after the Oregon Death with Dignity Act, California's Assembly Bill No. 15 (2015) allows a terminally ill patient to request death-hastening medication under the following conditions: (i) diagnosed as terminally ill (i.e., death occurring within 6 months), (ii) deemed competent to make medical request, (iii) two oral requests are made to physicians within 15 days of each other, and (iv) a consulting physician must confirm points 1 and 2 (Cain, 2016). Colorado adopted a similar position with its End of Life Act in 2016 (see www.colorado. gov/pacific/cdphe/medical-aid-dying).

Key Risk and Protective Factors and a Theoretical Overview

Recalling our previous review, a risk factor is any variable associated with an increased chance of an event, and a protective risk factor is just the opposite. So, a word of caution is necessary here. As we review the key risk and protective factors for SRB or SDV, we need to bear in mind the difference between correlation and causation. Most risk and protective factor research tends to fall within a retrospective (think looking backward) or a cross-sectional research design. A notable problem with this source of evidence is that we cannot infer causality; that is, we cannot say that factors directly cause or prevent suicide (with a few exceptions). In fact, a recent meta-analysis examining the strongest available research came to a troubling conclusion: current risk factor knowledge is almost no better at predicting suicide over time than flipping a coin (Franklin et al., 2017). Why then take the time to review and use research-informed risk and protective factors? Simple: because this body of literature represents the best available scientific understanding of the likelihoods and contingencies under which SRB is most likely to occur. No, we cannot predict SRB looking forward with great precision. But, yes, we can understand contributing factors and conduct empirically informed risk assessments aimed at suicide risk management and prevention strategies to employ in mental and public health programming.

The Centers for Disease Control and Prevention (n.d.b) provides a user-friendly way of organizing risk and protective factors for health-related conditions. This tiered approach is called the social-ecological model (SEM). The SEM was designed with the intention of ultimately informing multi-level prevention efforts. Though there are slight variations of the framework, the SEM organized contributing factors to any health or disease risk in four top-down categories: societal, community, interpersonal/relational, and individual. Societal factors are those determined by the majority, such as social norms and laws. Societal factors may also be naturally occurring, for example, season or climate. Community-level factors center on resources or characteristics of a given region, ranging from service provision to support staff. They also encompass physical characteristics of an environment, such as those defining safety or hazard risk. Relational factors concern those influenced directly by interpersonal relationships, be they with family, romantic partners, work colleagues, health professionals, or others. Individual characteristics include an individual's demographics, attitudes, personality traits, health status, behaviors, and additional qualities.

As you can likely imagine, there exists a great deal of commentary and publicly available information concerning suicide risk and protective factors. We are actually remarkably well educated as a public in this regard. And we have government and private organizations such as the National Institute of Mental Health, the American Association of Suicidology, and the CDC to thank for this level of public health education. The scientific literature also includes a great deal of high-quality review articles to help guide public information efforts. In an effort to integrate the CDC's SEM approach and make the sheer number of risk and protective factors more palatable for the reader, we have constructed Table 6.1, a compilation of key suicide risk and protective factors organized by the SEM. Although not exhaustive, this list was generated from information gleaned during our review of both empirical studies and systematic reviews in the scientific literature (i.e., Bernard, Geoffroy, & Bellivier, 2015; Bryan & Rudd, 2006; Calear et al., 2016; Linehan, Goodstein, Nielsen, & Chiles, 1983; Van Orden et al., 2010), as well as from publicly available key organizational resources (i.e., American Association of Suicidology, n.d.; Centers for Disease Control and Prevention, n.d.c; Drapeau & McIntosh, 2015; National Institute of Mental Health, 2015; Suicide Prevention Resource Center, n.d.). There are undoubtedly other quality sources available in the public and scientific arenas—we merely endorse this set as representative of best current knowledge concerning suicide risk and protective factors. An important practical matter concerns the best use of summary information like this. We caution lay readers against using this table as a checklist-style count

Table 6.1. Compilation of Major Suicide Risk and Protective Factors from Expert Sources Organized by Levels of the CDC's Social-Ecological Model

Risk factors	Protective factors
Societal	*Societal*
1. Economic downturn/depression	1. Healthy economy
2. Living location with less restrictive firearm laws	2. Living location with more restrictive firearm laws
3. Seasonal variation	3. Mental health funding
4. Stigma about mental health and treatment	4. Northeast United States
5. Air pollutants	
6. Viruses/parasites	
7. Poverty	
8. Mountain region of the United States	
9. Western & southern United States	
Community	*Community*
1. Exposure to community violence	1. Crisis support lines/hotlines
2. Local suicide epidemic	2. Healthcare/mental healthcare access
3. Barriers to healthcare access	3. Effective mental healthcare
	4. Trained gatekeepers
	5. Community involvement
	6. School-based support and intervention programming
Interpersonal/relationship	*Interpersonal/relationship*
1. Living in household with firearm	1. Presence of social support
2. Exposure to suicide/contagion	2. Use of social support
3. Family violence	3. Perceived social support
4. Family conflict	4. Concerns suicide is harmful to child/family
5. Family history of mental illness	5. Sense of responsibility to family
6. Family history of suicide/attempt	6. Healthy long-term committed relationship/marriage
7. Relationship instability	7. Help-seeking behavior
8. Death of a loved one	8. Children presence in the home
9. Severing of romantic relationship	9. Pregnancy
10. Social isolation/withdrawal	10. Pulling together
11. Combat exposure	11. Caring letters
	12. Social connectedness
	13. Contact with caregivers
	14. Support for connection with healthcare providers
	15. Cognitive-behavioral therapy
	16. Dialectical-behavior therapy

(continued)

Table 6.1. Continued

Risk factors	Protective factors
Individual	*Individual*
1. Male sex (completions)/female sex (attempts)	1. Coping skills
2. Lesbian, gay, bisexual, or other sexual orientation minority identity	2. Problem-solving skills
3. Religiosity/spirituality (i.e., suicide as a resolution to problems)	3. Religiosity/spirituality (i.e., beliefs about suicide being wrong)
4. Native American ethnicity	4. Moral objections to suicide
5. Hispanic or Asian/Pacific Islander ethnicity	5. Survival beliefs/desire to live
6. Whites (compared to non-whites)	6. Fear of suicide/death
7. Older adult age	7. Fear of social disapproval
8. Middle adult age	8. Treatment motivation
9. Mental health diagnoses/symptoms such as depression, bipolar, posttraumatic stress disorder, anxiety, and active-phase schizophrenia	9. Optimism
10. Personality disorders such as borderline personality	10. Hopefulness/positive future orientation
11. Substance/alcohol use/abuse	11. Life satisfaction
12. Prior suicide attempt	12. Intact reality testing
13. Current suicidal thinking	13. Selective serotonin reuptake inhibitor usage
14. Presence of suicidal intent	14. Lithium/mood stabilizer treatment
15. Presence of suicide plan	15. High self-esteem/self-efficacy
16. Access to/presence of lethal means	16. Resiliency
17. Preparatory behaviors (e.g., giving away prized possessions)	17. Extraversion
18. Prior or current non-suicidal self-injury	18. Additional reasons for living
19. History of other suicide (e.g., ideation)	
20. Hopelessness	
21. Low self-control/high impulsivity	
22. Aggression	
23. Agitation	
24. Emotion dysregulation	
25. Severe mood change	
26. High-risk professions (e.g., military, law enforcement)	
27. Firearm ownership (and storing a gun unlocked and loaded)	
28. Incarceration	
29. Childhood abuse	
30. Feelings of burdensomeness	
31. Rejection/thwarted belonging	
32. Recent discharge from psychiatric hospital	
33. Chronic illness	
34. Acute health symptoms	
35. High perceived/subjective stress	
36. Job loss/unemployment	
37. Financial strain	

Table 6.1. Continued

Risk factors	Protective factors
38. Fatigue	
39. Sleep disturbance/disorders	
40. Neuroticism	
41. Introversion	
42. Limited openness to experience	
43. Perfectionism	
44. Serotonin dysfunction	
45. Homelessness	
46. Low self-esteem	
47. Shame	
48. Physical pain tolerance	
49. Fearlessness of suicide/death	
50. Thinking errors/negative thinking	
51. Psychache/psychic pain	

This list is intended to be reflective of major factors but not exhaustive; sources for this review include: American Association of Suicidology (n.d.); Bernard et al. (2015); Bryan and Rudd (2006); Calear et al. (2016); Centers for Disease Control and Prevention (n.d.c); Drapeau and McIntosh (2015); Linehan et al. (1983); National Institute of Mental Health (2015); Suicide Prevention Resource Center (n.d.); Van Orden et al. (2010).

for themselves or people they know. It is for educational purposes only. For mental health professionals, on the other hand, this table consists of factors that should be considered in evaluating and managing suicide risk.

The table is self-evident. We limit comments to a few key contextual points of interest. First, you may have noticed that most of our current knowledge is at the individual and interpersonal levels. This may explain our current inability to predict suicide attempts over time (see caveats above). Careful inspection of the organizational framework reveals inclusion of biological (e.g., serotonin dysfunction), climatological (e.g., seasonal variation), medical (e.g., chronic medical condition), social (e.g., social support), mental health (e.g., depression), cognitive (e.g., thinking styles), and other aspects. The variety of risk and protective factors documented to date suggests that the best understanding of SRB most decidedly requires a true multilevel biopsychosocial approach. Finally, and perhaps most relevant to firearm-related suicide, firearm-related factors are present at every level of the SEM, either directly or indirectly. For instance, individual firearm ownership itself is a direct risk factor. Situational and policy factors also indirectly involve or are associated with firearms and are linked to SRB. For example, at the interpersonal level, combat exposure and family violence often involve firearms. The same holds true for community-level violence exposure. Finally, laws and policies addressing firearm access have been linked to SRB rates.

Whereas risk and protective factors for suicide help us understand issues associated with likelihoods and probabilities, we are still left wondering why. What explanations exist, if any, to help us understand how someone could commit what for most of us is an unthinkable act? Here is where we address theories of suicide. The basic elements of a theory are thus: (i) it provides hypotheses or suppositions that are testable through the scientific method, which (ii) explains the occurrence of a given phenomenon (Glanz, Rimer, & Lewis, 2015; Whetton, 1989). So, a formal theory of suicide would define concepts that (i) make direct statements investigated via research that (ii) offer some understandable reason or explanation why people attempt or die by suicide. Truth in advertising being important, there are two buyer-beware messages for consuming theories. First, just because someone tells you it's a theory doesn't mean it's a theory. In other words, some theories fall short of providing an actual explanation, instead offering technical descriptions of nothing more than risk and protective factors. For the sake of our discussion, let us refer to these as "models" (yes, they are included in the discussion of theories). Second, and unfortunately, many theories of suicide suffer from lack of sufficient empirical testing or support. This limitation follows in line with the risk and protective factor limitation of our collective inability to confidently predict future SRB.

Many, many behavioral and other scientific theories of suicide exist. One of the leading current suicide scholars, David Lester, reviewed many of the historical (including some outdated) theories of suicide in a key 1994 article appearing in *Suicide & Life-Threatening Behavior*. Among them were the psychoanalytic and psychodynamic perspectives of Adler, Jung, and Freud. We will focus our theory review on either historical theories that have remained most relevant or recent developments in the last few decades. In so doing, we aim to keep the conversation simple by defining the basic theoretical ideas, subtypes, or explanations of suicide.

Sociological Theory

Sociologist Emil Durkheim (1897) proffered one of the first, and longest-lasting in impact, theories of suicide in a seminal work, *Le Suicide*. He explained suicide as a function of two social occurrences: integration and regulation (Lester, 1999). When examining the intersection of social *integration* (the clustering of people in social groups) and *regulation* (the extent of rituals and customs being influenced by societal norms), suicide can be categorized into four differing types: egoistic, altruistic, fatalistic, and anomic. All four stem from an individual's reaction to social or sociological change. *Egoistic* suicide serves the function of attention in response to feelings of social rejection or isolation. *Altruistic* suicide is intended to save face in response to group or social pressures. *Fatalistic* suicide results from excessive hopelessness due commonly to interpersonal loss. *Anomic* suicide is driven by the stress of urbanization and rapid social change.

Impulsive Suicide

Schneidman (1981) articulated a three-piece model to explain a specific type of suicide: one characterized as an impulsive act. Such an act is theorized to possess the following qualities: (i) the attempter believes the act will be fatal, (ii) the choice to commit the act is made suddenly, and (iii) indirect observable cues to the act happening may exist, but the attempter makes no overt indication. Extreme levels of three psychological characteristics must be present for this impulsive suicide to occur: stress, agitation, and psychache (i.e., emotional pain). Ultimately aimed at reducing the psychache, the impulsive suicide is further qualified by inimicality (self-perceived negative attributes), perturbation (excessive sense of upset), and constriction of thinking (narrowing of cognition or focus).

Cognitive Perspectives

Cognitive perspectives of suicide are grounded in psychiatrist Aaron Beck's early work developing a theory of depression (Beck, Rush, Shaw, & Emery, 1979). As a root of suicide, he and his colleagues articulated the idea of cognitive vulnerability for depression, comprised of several qualities in one's thinking. The first is a negative self-schema or negative self-perception (e.g., low self-esteem, sense of failure). The second is a tendency to engage in what Beck has called "thinking errors" or cognitive errors. These are an array of thinking styles not grounded in a rational perception of reality. Examples include dichotomous thinking, or the tendency to see the world in black and white, and overgeneralization, or drawing conclusions based on one small fact or sampling of evidence. These cognitive styles (i.e., schemas and error) contribute to a person's tendency to hold negative thoughts about himself or herself, the world around him or her, and the future (sometimes in the form of hopelessness). Importantly, Beck's theory of suicide has yielded some of the gold standard research and clinical practice tools in the form of the Beck Depression Inventory-II (Beck, Steer, & Brown, 1996) and the Beck Scale for Suicidal Ideation (Beck & Steer, 1991).

Building on Beck and colleagues' work, Abramson, Metalsky, & Alloy (1989) put forth a hopelessness theory of depression, which has subsequently been tested as a precursor to suicide (e.g., Abramson et al., 1998). As with the cubic model, Abramson and colleagues hypothesized that hopelessness-driven depression, and thereby suicide, represented one subtype. The basic mindset of this subtype is depressive in nature; that is, the individual views negative life events such as loss or failure as resistant to improvement (i.e., "stable"), all-encompassing (i.e., "general"), and self-caused (i.e., "internal") (Abramson et al., 1998). This pattern is associated with an increased chance of suicide ideation and attempt. Hopelessness is a key feature in that it is theorized to explain how a depressive thinking style leads to suicide. Hopelessness, in forms such as seeing no chance of getting better or having no sense of optimism about the future, leads one to consider suicide as an option to end negative feelings and self-blame.

Personality Approaches

Personality-based perspectives to understanding suicide have generally taken two forms: personality pathology and common personality trait models. Personality psychopathology has been part of the mental disorder diagnostic spectrum for decades, with the most recent iteration reflected in the DSM-5 (American Psychiatric Association, 2013). Borderline personality disorder (BPD) is generally considered a personality pathology category most associated with suicide (see Anestis, Dixon-Gordon, & Gratz, 2015). Common BPD characteristics empirically linked to suicide are the inabilities to appropriately express and regulate emotions (e.g., Ammerman et al., 2015). Based on the BPD perspective, Selby and colleagues (2008, 2009) developed an emotional cascade model to explain how emotional dysfunction associated with BPD can lead to a wide range of self-harming behaviors, including suicide. In short, a person with BPD may experience a great degree of obsessive thinking. Triggered by an emotionally charged event, emotional cascades are thought to develop as a function of a back and forth between obsessive thinking and unregulated negative emotionality (e.g., anger, despair; Selby, Anestis, Bender, & Joiner, 2009). Seeking alleviation from the "cascade," or cumulative negative domino effect of obsessive thinking and negative emotions, a person is thought to engage in self-harm as a distraction. Suicide, as one of these potential self-harming behaviors, in essence occurs as a result of seeking relief from the synergy of obsessive thinking and negative affective experience.

Understanding suicide can occur beyond persons with pathological personality structures; the literature has also examined common personality trait models associated with suicide. The five-factor model (Costa & McCrae, 1992; McCrae & Costa, 2003) is based on the premise that all persons can be characterized along five primary trait domains; that is, we all possess some level of each trait. Further, each broad trait domain can be described by six subcomponents. The five broad domains are neuroticism (i.e., emotional instability), extraversion, openness to experience, agreeableness, and conscientiousness. To illustrate subcomponent-level detail, neuroticism is comprised of an individual's degree of trait depression, anxiety, impulsiveness, self-consciousness, stress vulnerability, and hostility. Being a general model of personality, the five-factor model has been widely tested with domains of health (see Murray & Booth, 2015, for a review). Concerning risk for suicide, particular levels of two traits are most consistently linked to suicide: high neuroticism and low extraversion (i.e., high introversion) (see Cramer, Moore, & Bryson, 2016, for review). Described more generally, high neuroticism may feature trait patterns of high sadness, worry, anticipation, emotional reactivity, anger, or impulsivity (McCrae & Costa, 2003). Low extraversion may manifest in social isolation, quietness, passiveness, avoidance or fear of social contact, or a preference for stability and structure. Such patterns can heighten risk for suicide, although exploration of causal explanations for these associations is largely lacking.

Interpersonal-Psychological Theory

In an attempt to provide a universal framework explaining suicide, Thomas Joiner (2005), a psychology professor at Florida State University, penned a seminal work entitled *Why People Die by Suicide*. He proposed a three-component interpersonal-psychological theory of suicide (IPTS). These components are perceived burdensomeness, thwarted belongingness, and acquired capability (Joiner, 2005; Van Orden et al., 2008, 2010). Briefly, perceived burdensomeness reflects a thinking style concerned with self-hatred and being a liability to others (Van Orden et al., 2010). Thwarted belongingness is a thinking pattern concerned with a sense of loneliness and absence of reciprocal care and support of others. Where both of these depressive thinking styles are high, Joiner (2005) hypothesized that a desire to commit suicide formed. The third variable, acquired capability, is biological, emotional, and behavioral in nature. Based in biological mechanisms such as serotonin mechanism dysfunction, the acquired capability for suicide represents both a fearlessness of death and behavioral habituation to pain developed through processes including impulsivity, exposure to suicide, and self-harming/suicidal behavior itself (Joiner, 2005; Van Orden et al., 2010). Where all three components of the IPTS are very high, it is hypothesized that suicide attempt or completion occurs. Interestingly, a recent review reported generally strong support for the cognitive aspects of the IPTS, with mixed findings concerning acquired capability-related interactive influences (Ma, Batterham, Calear, & Han, 2016).

Information-Processing Approaches

Information-processing concepts are more recently being applied to assist in understanding suicide. Two examples are implicit processing associated with death and attitudes concerning how one takes in affective and cognitive information. The notion of implicit association is not new; the idea that we have unconscious preferences in thought (i.e., implicit processes/associations) is a cognitive psychology idea dating back to at least 1998 when Project Implicit (n.d.) scholars provided publicly available tests of our unconscious preferences or biases based on demographic and visual stimuli (e.g., race, age, skin tone). Generally speaking, implicit association tests operate by having a person rapidly respond to positively and negatively valenced words associated with visual stimuli of varying categories (e.g., a white versus black face). A series of recent studies (e.g., Barnes et al., 2017; Ellis, Rufino, & Green, 2016; Randall et al., 2013) show promise in understanding suicide and related issues (e.g., self-harm) from an implicit association perspective. Specifically, an unconscious preference for or orientation toward death appears to be associated with suicidal ideation and attempt. Being a novel approach, this approach is in need of further study to identify causal agents and contingent boundaries.

Augmenting implicit cognition, another recent cognitive approach to suicide is grounded in dual-process models of information processing. In short, dual-process models posit two parallel methods by which people assimilate new information: heuristic (i.e., mental shortcut) and systematic (i.e., effortful thinking) processes (Kahneman & Frederick, 2002). Although applied widely to other areas of decision-making, individual differences approximating these two information-processing streams have only recently been applied to suicide. Cramer, Bryson, Gardner, & Webber (2016) drew on individual difference characteristics of need for cognition (Cacioppo & Petty, 1982) and need for affect (Maio & Esses, 2001) to approximate overt attitudes or preferences in processing cognitive and emotional information, respectively. High need for cognition, characterized by appreciation of informational complexity and preference for difficult cognitive tasks, represents a tendency toward systematic information processing (Reinhard, 2010). Low need for cognition, characterized by avoidance of effortful thinking and preference for easy tasks, is akin to heuristic information processing. Need for affect further reflects information-processing streams to the extent to which one tends to engage emotions, a surface-level cue sometimes associated with heuristic decisions, or avoids emotion in favor of cognition, potentially basing decisions on systematic processing. In the only empirical test of a preference-in-information-processing perspective, Cramer, Bryson, Gardner, & Webber (2016) found suicide risk to be associated with three patterns: (i) a straightforward preference to avoid emotions (i.e., high need for affect avoidance), (ii) effect 1 being more pronounced among persons with simultaneous elevated depressive symptoms, and (iii) a combination of high need for cognition and high emotional approach (i.e., high need for affect approach). This perspective is also in need of further study in light of the preliminary findings.

An Attempt at Integrating Theories

You may be asking yourself at this point—why so many explanations? Why so many theories? We wonder this as well. Suicide theory literature is vastly underdeveloped with respect to integrating explanations. In a recent attempt to do so, Rory O'Connor (2011) of the University of Stirling summarized a series of studies laying the groundwork for the integrated motivational-volitional model of suicidal behavior. Suicide is framed as a three-phase process: pre-motivational, intention formation, and behavioral action. The pre-motivational phase is thought to encompass preexisting risk factors such as biological, environmental, and social/stress risk

factors. Those higher in these risk factors become susceptible to a motivational phase in which suicidal thinking develops and worsens (yielding
ultimate intent to die by suicide). The pathway to intent begins in feelings
of defeat and humiliation that progress to a sense of entrapment and end
in suicidal intent. O'Connor hypothesizes two substeps within this phase in
which moderating factors can influence the formation of suicidal thinking.
For example, coping skills and thinking styles (what he terms "threat to
self moderators") can positively or negatively impact the step from defeat/
humiliation to entrapment. Next, interpersonally themed issues (what he
terms "motivational moderators") such as perceived burdensomeness or
social support can mitigate the step from entrapment to suicidal desire. The
final transition into behavioral action phase, or the suicide attempt, is further influenced by what he terms "volitional moderators." This set of characteristics, thought to promote the ability to move from suicidal thinking to
action, includes factors such as impulsivity, suicide planning, and (relevant
to firearms) access to lethal means. While also promising, this theory of suicide is limited in research support.

Firearms and Suicide: Statistics, Risk and Protective Factors, and Prevention Potential Under the Law

A wealth of research evidence links firearm ownership with an elevated risk for
SRB (e.g., Brent & Bridge, 2003; Miller et al., 2009; Miller, Warren, Hemenway,
& Azrael, 2013). A great summary of much of this body of literature was provided by Anglemyer, Horvath, & Rutherford (2014). Their pooled analysis of
existing observational studies in the literature shows that firearm ownership
is associated with an approximate three times increase in the likelihood of
suicide. Additional reviews suggest that firearms do more than just serve as
more lethal means (compared to other methods such as cutting); they actually
worsen the likelihood of suicide death above other means (Stroebe, 2013).
Public health surveillance data generally follow this same trend; that is, state-
and national-level data routinely highlight firearms among the most common
methods of suicide attempt and completion. Key trends in this collective body
of evidence (e.g., American Foundation for Suicide Prevention, n.d.; Centers
for Disease Control and Prevention, 2015, 2016; Drapeau & McIntosh, 2015;
Mathews, Woodward, Musso, & Jones, 2016) show that (i) between 21,000
and 22,000 firearm-related suicides occur annually and (ii) firearms account
for between 46% and 50% of total suicides annually. Even more pressing are
time-based examinations showing a recent national upward trend in the
number of firearm-related suicides (Fowler, Dahlberg, Haileyesus, & Annest,
2015). While these data are concerning, they also may not represent the full
picture, for two reasons. First, as noted in general suicide surveillance data,
we may not fully grasp all known suicide attempts and completions involving

firearms. Second, following from this general data limitation, recent empirical data suggest that about half of mental health patients experiencing SRB have accurate firearm ownership information in their records (Betz et al., 2016). Generally speaking, we may have an incomplete or underestimated view of firearm ownership and likelihood of experiencing SRB.

We also want to convey that these data, while valuable and likely representative, lack nuance. In statistical language, there are factors that *moderate* the association of firearm ownership and SRB risk. But what is statistical moderation? Simply put, *moderation* means that the relationship between two variables depends on another one (think about every time a psychologist, scientist, or political pundit on TV answers a straightforward question leading with the phrase "it depends . . ."—this is probably moderation). We also refer to these as "contingent" or "conditional" associations because the influence of one variable on another is contingent upon the absence or presence of another (Hayes, 2013). Consider the following example. Your risk for heart disease is connected to your family history. What can you do to mitigate or moderate this risk? Exercise. Maintain a healthy diet and healthy living. In other words, the link between family history and your risk for a heart attack *depends* on, or is moderated by, healthy behaviors or the lack thereof. Turning back to firearms and SRB risk, risk and protective factors serve as the moderating factors. That is, many of the factors listed in the multilevel risk and protective factors table will moderate the association of firearm ownership and risk for SRB. We provide a few of these examples from the literature to emphasize the need for nuance in discussing the firearm–suicide polemic.

The following are illustrative examples that can buffer or exacerbate the influence of firearms on SRB risk (although they do not represent a complete set of factors from the professional literature). An intuitive place to start concerns suicide risk among military personnel. When compared to general rates (about 44%–49%), firearms account for more than two-thirds of suicides among military personnel (e.g., Anglemyer, Miller, Buttrey, & Whitaker, 2016; McCarten, Hoffmire, & Boassarte, 2015). Thus, military profession is a moderating risk factor of the link between firearms and suicide risk. The role of military profession is further mitigated by other firearm-related factors. For instance, improper storage and keeping firearms loaded directly exacerbate risk for firearm suicide (e.g., Shenassa, Rogers, Spalding, & Roberts, 2004), while also being linked with suicidal ideation and self-perceived likelihood of committing suicide in the future among military personnel (Khazem et al., 2016). Although beyond the full scope of this review, it is worth noting that law enforcement officers are at similarly high risk for suicide overall (O'Hara & Violanti, 2009); moreover, a recent study of suicide method among law enforcement personnel found that about 91% of suicides involved firearms (Violanti et al., 2012).

Other demographics also provide context. For instance, sex and race play an intricate role in moderating the firearm–suicide association. Sex demonstrates a straightforward pattern in which men are more likely to use firearms for suicide (Hempstead, Nguyen, David-Rus, & Jacquemen, 2012). Straightforward comparisons of rates demonstrate that white males possess the highest suicide rates (Drapeau & McIntosh, 2015). However, in the context of firearm suicides, Joe, Marcus, & Kaplan (2007) found that African American men are twice as likely as white men to die by firearm suicide (controlling for a number of other factors). To further complicate the matter, Kaplan, McFarland, & Huguet (2009) analyzed the firearm–suicide link varying by gender to identify psychosocial factors that differentially increase or decrease firearm suicide risk. Among their important findings is that military service, older age, living in locations with increased firearm access (per state laws), and relationship problems all exacerbate firearm suicide risk for men. For women, age, military status, and living location also increased risk; however, death of a loved one, being married, and being depressed also increased firearm suicide risk only for women. Kaplan and coauthors also found a number of protective factors against firearm suicide risk by gender. For men, alcohol use, mental health diagnosis, and a history of suicide attempts actually decreased the odds of using a gun for suicide. For women, physical health problems and prior treatment for a mental health disorder did the same. We hope this short overview of demographic and psychosocial moderators (i.e., individual and relational CDC-defined factors) highlights the importance of nuance and digging deep into firearm suicide information.

Several other important empirical findings are worth noting in the area of moderating factors. For example, one variable that does not explain the firearm ownership–SRB association: mental health symptoms (Sorenson & Vittes, 2008). That is, despite oft-portrayed media representations, public commentary or cherry-picked examples, on the whole mental health symptoms do not explain why people with access to or who own guns are more likely to die by firearm suicide. Also, while we do not spend a tremendous amount of time on international data, it is worth noting that US trends of firearm involvement in suicides (Grinshteyn & Hemenway, 2016) and suicide–homicides (Panczak et al., 2013) are among the highest in the world.

Along the societal level of the CDC's public health approach, a considerable amount of data exist concerning SRB risk levels by state firearm and related laws. Firearm-related laws largely vary by topic and state, so rather than provide an overview of firearm-related laws (see Chapter 2 for more details), we review key studies concerning states and laws with available associated suicide data. Perhaps the most common or, at least, well-known type of firearm law is a background check. Sen & Panjamapirom (2012) analyzed the influence of a variety of types of background check laws on state suicide rates over a 10-year period. Overall, implementation of any and all background check laws was associated with a slight decrease in suicide rates, although this may also be a function of a large study sample size as opposed to a sizeable impact. This caveat concerns estimation of the size, as opposed to statistical significance, of this finding. The effect size (or magnitude estimate) in this case is called an *odds ratio*, defined as an approximation of how much greater or lesser one's odds are to experience a certain event (in this instance, suicide). In the research literature we often employ a range around an estimate, called a *confidence internal*, to allow for error. You see this all the time in public opinion polls—something to the effect of ±2 percentage points in surveys such as presidential approval polls. Odds ratio confidence intervals including the value of 1.0 translate into an equal odds of experiencing the event or not; in other words, there is no more than a 50/50 odds of suicide rate reduction in this case. Therefore, this trend must be viewed with caution. Firearm suicide reduction was more meaningfully associated with state implementation of background checks for mental illness and fugitive status, whereas background checks for misdemeanor records showed the same equivocal association with suicide reductions as the general patterns of any background check. Crifiasi, Meyers, Vernick, & Webster (2015) examined whether changes in permit-to-purchase laws in two states were associated with suicide rates, presumably lowering suicide rates by making it more difficult to purchase firearms. In brief, permit-to-purchase laws set up several steps necessary for purchasing a firearm such as an in-person application, firearm safety training completion, and a considerable waiting period. Background checks under these laws are intended to capture concerns such as mental illness, domestic violence charges, and so forth. Examination of data from Connecticut and Missouri demonstrated equivocal effects of the laws on overall state suicide rates. However, firearm suicides declined by approximately 15% in Connecticut after law implementation and increased more than 16% after repeal in Missouri. Permit-to-purchase law data then show potential promise to positively impact firearm suicide rates.

Anestis & Anestis (2015), psychologists from the University of Southern Mississippi, provided one of the most critical firearm law–suicide analyses to date. Their work advances knowledge over other analyses because they (i) evaluated several types of laws in relation to both overall suicide and firearm suicide rates and (ii) sought to identify explanatory pathways or reasons why laws may be working in instances where they are associated with suicide rate reductions. The following four types of firearm laws were shown to have influence (controlling for demographic and other associated factors): waiting periods, universal background checks, gun locks, and open carry regulations. Where implemented, all four types of laws were associated with lower firearm-related suicide rates. Further, three of four (with the exception of waiting periods) were associated with lessened overall suicide rates. Anestis & Anestis provided critical information on why these reductions in overall suicide rates seem to occur by identifying patterns of decreases in overall suicide attempt numbers, lessened average number of firearms in a home, and a decrease in lethality of means (i.e., using methods of suicide attempt such as cutting that are less likely to result in death). Often, a combination of these factors accounted for declines in overall state suicide rates.

Firearm-related laws have been investigated for influence of suicide among specific subpopulations in the United States. For instance, Gius (2015), an economist at Quinnipiac University, evaluated firearm laws directly addressing youth access and suicide risk. Two types of state laws specifically examined were child access prevention and minimum age laws. The former type is intended to promote safer firearm practices among adults who have children by imposing criminal responsibility among adults who allow youth unsupervised firearm use. Minimum age laws typically impose a minimal age for independent purchase or ownership (usually 21 years), although where these laws exist the age and details (e.g., intent of use of firearms for activities such as hunting) vary. Gius concluded that states with child access prevention laws observed lower youth suicide rates, whereas no meaningful influence of minimum age laws was noted.

Hoyt & Duffy (2015) provided a conceptual analysis of firearm regulations for US Army service members, including policies contained in federal law (e.g., restricting access to firearms for those who are mentally ill) and military policy (e.g., restriction of firearm carrying for those convicted of domestic violence). All regulations were framed from the standpoint of restricting access to firearms as a means for suicide. Among the bevy of suggested firearm means restriction approaches for military service members put forth by authors are: (i) barracks restriction, (ii) voluntary disabling of firearm while in the field, (iii) involving social support such as family or fellow service members, (iv) training of commanders and unit heads as a prevention strategy, (v) voluntary turnover of privately owned firearms to a unit arms room, and (vi) firearm storage outside of the military installation. While many of these approaches are grounded on sound principles and data from general suicide prevention literature (e.g., involving social support), the influence of these military-specific laws or mandates is in need of further empirical testing.

Again, with an international account of firearm laws and suicide being beyond the scope of this discussion, we think it is still useful to provide a cross-cultural exemplar. To that end, Kapusta, Etzersdorfer, Krall, & Sonneck (2007) evaluated the influences of European Union country–informed firearm policy changes on suicide in Austria. Austria specifically adopted decreased access to larger-sized guns and imposed the requirement that a firearm purchase needed a specified reason. To acquire handguns or semiautomatic weapons, policy implementation included psychological testing and background checks for first-time buyers and a minimum age requirement (21 years). Finally, a waiting period and stricter gun safety storage regulations were specified for long firearms, rifles, and other guns. During the 10-year period following gun restriction laws, firearm suicide rates dropped by more than 4% annually. Moreover, other suicide methods did not increase as a result. This example lends further support to the potential positive impact of firearm laws on firearm-related suicides.

294 Mental Health, Violence, and Suicide

Several conclusions can be drawn from the overall scope of firearms, firearm-related laws, and SRB risk. First, firearms are associated with elevated general and firearm-specific suicide risk; this is offset by a current lack of data on the association of firearm ownership/access and suicide ideation, attempts, and other aspects of SRB. Further, the firearm–suicide risk link is moderated by many factors (e.g., sex, ethnicity, military status), a fact that reinforces the need for a nuanced approach to the firearm–suicide discussion. Overall, firearm regulation laws show promise in impacting suicide rates, although the effects may be more impactful for firearm-specific suicides. With the exception of one study (Anestis & Anestis, 2015), reliable analyses identifying explanatory pathways from firearm regulation laws to suicide rates could not be located. Finally, firearm laws targeting special populations such as youth or the military are in great need of further inquiry and implementation.

Suicide Risk Assessment, Management, and Prevention for Medical and Mental Health Professionals: The Role of Firearms

The role of firearms in suicide-related mental health practice is key. As noted, firearms are associated with an elevated risk for suicide, and they are regularly among the top chosen methods in suicide attempts and deaths. They also can increase suicide risk when stored improperly and kept loaded. How then should mental health professionals incorporate firearms into professional suicide assessment, prevention, and management practice? The answer to this question begins with understanding more specific SRB terminology, namely suicide *planning, preparation,* and *access to (lethal) means.* The first two phrases are valid on their face. That is, suicide planning is just what it sounds like—the extent or type of planning one has done toward making a suicide attempt. Likewise, preparation is an extension of that planning. To be more precise, however, we can think of suicide planning as primarily cognitive. A person contemplating suicide may begin to think and even read about ways to make an attempt. Where the line blurs between planning and preparation is in the cognitive rehearsal of a suicide attempt. Suicidal persons often mentally visualize themselves making the attempt, potentially as part of the process of readying themselves or habituating themselves to the idea of ultimately committing a suicide attempt. One can also think of preparation as behavioral. Recalling the overview of suicide risk factor above, preparatory behaviors are a risk factor for suicide attempt and, in fact, often an immediate warning sign or precursor. Preparatory behaviors range from talking about death and making wills (out of character or situation) to giving away prized possessions and obtaining the means or instrument for the suicide attempt. We hope by now you begin to understand both that picking apart these suicide-specific factors can be difficult and that it is necessary for effective assessment and prevention (e.g., Bryan & Rudd, 2006).

The role of firearms in suicide assessment, management, and prevention then becomes most critical when dealing with the issue of access to means. No, not every person who owns a gun is at elevated risk for suicide. However, as reflected in the statistics and risk factors, firearms represent a pressing issue for mental health professionals working with persons at elevated risk. Luckily, there is considerable helpful guidance on the topic of dealing with lethal means of suicide, including firearms. First and foremost, where any plan or preparation is indicated, and really where any suicide risk is elevated, access to lethal means should be completely restricted (Jobes, 2009). Noted clinical professor of psychiatry Robert Simon (2007) provided more specific advice for involving social support in the removal of lethal means such as firearms. The best-case approach assumes joint responsibility between the clinician, patient, and contacted support person(s). The approach overtly identifies one responsible social support person in the patient's life to remove all firearms and ammunition, relocating them to another location unknown to the patient. Specific phone confirmation between the clinician and support person is a must, and Simon advised not discharging psychiatrically admitted persons until such confirmation of lethal means restriction occurred. Importantly, means restrictions strategies such as this do show empirically based promise in helping reduce the likelihood of suicide attempt (Yip et al., 2012).

An emerging practice for mental health professionals in the context of suicide risk assessment and management concerns evaluating firearm risk. For example, Slovak & Brewer (2010) surveyed licensed social workers to evaluate the promise of firearm assessment and safety counseling with suicide patients. Social workers held generally positive attitudes about this approach. The notion of firearm safety counseling as a form of means restriction has gained further traction. For instance, recent experimental data support usage of the phrase "means safety" over "means restriction" to increase the likelihood of patient compliance with firearm management for persons at elevated suicide risk (Stanley et al., 2016). Training and guidance in counseling-based approaches to managing suicidal means, especially firearms, have become publicly available and are yet in need of further empirical evaluation to substantiate their effectiveness. An example of such publicly available resources is a Substance Abuse and Mental Health Services Administration–funded online training in means restriction counseling for mental and medical health professionals (Substance Abuse and Mental Health Services Administration, 2014). The content of the training addresses methods of asking a patient about lethal means such as firearms, as well as best-approach techniques to manage or remove those means.

A cutting-edge approach to firearms-based suicide prevention may also be of use or worthy of attention to mental health professionals. Vars, a member of the law faculty at the University of Alabama (2015), along with Vars, McCullumsmith, Shelton, & Cropsey (2017) set forth the notion of voluntary enlistment of mental health patients on a "no firearm" list. In short, the approach would offer patients the opportunity to place themselves on a 7-day period of inability to purchase a firearm, either with or without the need for further judicial hearing to reinstate the option of purchasing firearms. Preliminary attitudinal data obtained by Vars and colleagues suggested that almost half of those surveyed would be willing to be listed on a "do-not-sell" type of list. Although this strategy may best fit under a public health approach to suicide prevention, it is worth noting here that clinicians could work with their patients on similar voluntary surrendering of firearms or restriction in ability to purchase, potentially empowering the patient to take control of his or her own suicide risk management and well-being. This approach is in need of future research and implementation.

Case Studies and Information Concerning Firearms and Suicide in the Modern United States

A seemingly endless list of examples of suicides via firearms exists. Here, we provide a few illustrative cases across several categories of suicides involving firearms. In these cases, much of the chapter's content, such as examples of different fact-based patterns as well as instances of potential exceptions to empirical trends, can be seen. Specifically, we provide infamous examples of suicides by firearm, including murder–suicide and suicide-by-cop. We end the discussion with commentary and data concerning firearm involvement in terroristic suicide.

Suicide by Firearms

We have reviewed prevalence and other data concerning firearm-related suicides. The following famous examples illustrate some of the other key risk or influential factors that may contribute to a firearm suicide.

Kurt Cobain

Kurt Cobain was the founder and lead singer of the famous alt-rock band Nirvana (Kurt Cobain, n.d.). Born on February 20, 1967, Cobain tended to be socially withdrawn and introverted, especially after his parents divorced when he was 9 years old. His teen years were marred by anger toward his father, distance from his stepmother, and a severe path of illicit drug use. After 1982, Cobain lived a largely transient lifestyle, bouncing between relatives' and friends' homes. During this time period, his artistic and musical passions excelled but were tempered by a property destruction and public intoxication arrests. Between 1987 and 1988, Cobain began playing with bassist Krist Novoselic, dating his first serious girlfriend, and playing frequent gigs with new band Nirvana. After beginning a romantic relationship with Courtney Love in 1990, Cobain and Nirvana became an international success in 1991 with such top hits as, "Smells Like Teen Spirit." Between 1991 and 1994, Cobain's life included domestic violence occurrences toward Love, continued drug abuse, and apparent struggles with depression. A 1993 domestic violence incident revolved around Cobain keeping a gun in the residence where Love also resided. On March 4, 1994, Cobain attempted suicide via (pill) overdose, and he also left a suicide note. After the attempt, Cobain became a recluse, surrounding himself with drugs, pills, and guns. On April 5, 1994, Cobain died by suicide, specifically from one shotgun blast through his mouth and head.

Junior Seau

Born January 19, 1969, Tiaina Baul "Junior" Seau became a National Football League (NFL) Hall of Fame inductee because of his years as a linebacker for the San Diego Chargers, Miami Dolphins, and New England Patriots . Seau's early years were highly grounded in family and Samoan culture, yielding an intense need to please other people, among other characteristics. A highly decorated multisport high school athlete, Seau attended the University of Southern California as a member of the football team. Sitting out the first year of college due to low SAT scores, he experienced a notable level of social relationship difficulties as a result. Nicknamed the "Tasmanian Devil," he successfully made the NFL Pro Bowl more than 10 times and received numerous defensive player honors. In 2010, Seau was arrested on domestic violence charges, hours after he suffered injuries in an automobile accident. On May 2, 2012, Seau died of a self-inflicted gunshot to the chest, also scribbling song lyrics on a piece of paper suggesting that he had regretted the person he had become. Postmortem examination of Seau's brain showed evidence of chronic traumatic encephalopathy, arguably due to repeated head trauma over the course of his football career (Fainaru-Wada, Avila, & Fainaru, 2013).

Hunter S. Thompson

A noted activist and journalist, Thompson was born July 18, 1937. He grew up in poverty and lost his father during high school. Thompson became infamous for both breaking the rules and his writing talent. His early criminal mischief included robbery and property crimes. Faced with a judge's forced decision between jail and military service, Thompson entered the Air Force. After an early discharge from the military, Thompson began a prolific journalism career equaled by a wealth of substance abuse and firearm obsession.

His unique writing style, garnering the name "gonzo journalism," made Thompson a well-regarded anti-establishment figure. Printed in *Rolling Stone* in 1971 and as a hardcover book in 1972, perhaps his most famous work was *Fear and Loathing in Las Vegas*. In later life, he suffered from various physical health issues, which led him to experience chronic depression. Thompson died of a self-inflicted gunshot wound to the head on February 20, 2005 (Hunter S. Thompson, n.d.).

Murder–Suicide

Overall rates of murder–suicide, also known as homicide–suicide, fall somewhere between 200 and 300 instances annually in the United States (e.g., Regoeczi et al., 2016; Violence Policy Center, 2015). Concerning firearms and violence, more than 90% of these incidents involve a firearm and almost three-quarters are committed by intimate partners (Violence Policy Center, 2015), raising concerns about murder–suicide as an ultimate outcome of escalation of intimate partner violence. Unsurprisingly, the vast majority of perpetrators are male. Determining what qualifies as a murder–suicide in the data, however, is sometimes complicated by crime characteristics or lack of clarity in data reporting (e.g., Byard, Veldhoen, Kobus, & Heath, 2010; McNally, Patton, & Fremouw, 2016); therefore, these estimates likely contain a great deal of error.

Sahel Kazemi & Steve McNair

Steve McNair, a very successful NFL quarterback, was the victim in this infamous instance of murder–suicide. Born February 14, 1973, McNair grew up in a rural impoverished area of Mississippi (Steve McNair biography, n.d.). Surrounded by a close-knit family, McNair developed a sense of determination as a youth that facilitated athletic and other success. A multisport high school athlete, McNair attended Alcorn State as the football team's quarterback. Drafted by the Houston Oilers (later the Tennessee Titans) in 1995, McNair enjoyed a stellar career including a Super Bowl appearance and league co–most valuable player award. On July 4, 2009, he was shot twice in the head and twice in the chest while lying on a couch in his girlfriend's home (Sahel Kazemi, a 20-year-old waitress). Kazemi subsequently shot herself as well. By many accounts, Kazemi was highly distressed leading up to the event due to financial strain, a recent driving under the influence citation, and suspicion that McNair was cheating on her (Merrill, 2010).

Seung-Hui Cho

Although this incident fits many definitions of mass murder, it also fits established framings of a murder–suicide. We also addressed the case of

Seung-Hui Cho and the 2007 Virginia Tech shooting in Chapter 4. For the sake of illustrating pertinent murder–suicide details here, however, recall that Cho murdered 32 Virginia Polytechnic Institute and State University students and staff on April 16, 2007. Following this, Cho committed suicide by firearm. Pertinent biographical information about Cho relates to him being a South Korean national who became a permanent US resident in 1992. In 2005, Cho was accused of stalking a female classmate. Afterward, he was court-ordered to be psychiatrically evaluated because of suicidal thinking and expressions. After this evaluation, he was released with no required follow-up observation. Cho was born in South Korea in 1984 and emigrated to the United States at age 8. By history, Cho was a loner with a documented mental health history and was bullied as a youth. In the months leading up to the shooting, Cho legally purchased two pistols (Seung-Hui Cho, n.d.).

Suicide-by-Cop

Suicide-by-cop represents a relatively infrequent occurrence compared to other forms of violence reviewed in this and other chapters. DeGue, Fowler, & Calkins (2016) provided one of the most reliable overviews of rates and correlates of suicide-by-cop based on National Violent Death Reporting System data from 17 states. Over a 4-year period, from 2009 to 2012, they observed a total of 145 cases of suicide-by-cop. They also set forth an important definition of *suicide-by-cop*: incidents in which "evidence from witness/ LE [law enforcement] accounts suggests that victim was actively suicidal and engaged in criminal behavior directed at LE to elicit use of lethal force" (p. S176). Compared to other types of incidents, those who died by suicide-by-cop were more likely to be white, have a positive alcohol toxicology screen, and be armed with a firearm; moreover, the incident was more likely to occur in the home. From the viewpoint of IPTS, suicide-by-cop and other murder–suicide events are theorized to be driven primarily by an intent to die as opposed to a desire to kill others (Hagan, Podlogar, & Joiner, 2015).

Trepierre Hummons

Trepierre Hummons was 21 years old when he was involved in an incident with Cincinnati, Ohio, police on June 19, 2015 (Molski, 2015). Known to be gang-involved yet by many reports a warm and caring youth, Hummons called the police on himself. Noting that he had violated parole, media reports suggested he was facing an additional criminal charge (unconfirmed in public record review). Reports suggest that Hummons was acting odd in the streets while armed with a firearm. When approached by law enforcement, he shot and killed one officer, resulting in law enforcement's response of fatal gunshots.

De-Identified Officer Case

Arias and coauthors (2008) provided a valuable example of de-identified federal case data, including an active-duty police officer who committed suicide-by-cop. We include this case for two additional reasons: (i) it demonstrates that all community members are at risk of getting caught in the crossfire and (ii) it provides a case example from a high-risk profession (see Table 6.1 of risk and protective factors). The authors referred to the case of A. A. (de-identified initials), providing the following prominent information: the individual was a 36-year-old male who had served as a sheriff's deputy for 13 years. His position at the time of the incident, and for the 5 years prior, was as an evidence technician. In the weeks preceding the event, A. A. reported financial and marital strain, as well as depression. His professional record was exceptional. At the time of the event, the toxicology report came back positive for amphetamines and cocaine. On the day of the incident, A. A. filled his van with gas and left without paying. He subsequently led police on a high-speed chase in excess of 100 mph. When stopped, he exited his van armed with a semiautomatic firearm, shooting at and wounding several officers. A. A. was fatally shot shortly after he began firing at officers.

Terroristic Suicide

Rather than trying to evaluate famous case studies, we highlight the innovative scholarship by Adam Lankford (2012), a criminologist from the University of Alabama. Drawing on a variety of scholarly, federal, and other sources, he extracted details concerning 81 mass shootings inclusive of 12 suicide terrorist events. Acknowledging obvious limitations in obtaining these quantitative data, Lankford reported the following prominent characteristics among terroristic suicides: all men, many experiencing key historical suicide risk factors that were included in the data set (i.e., history of social marginalization, work/school problems, and a precipitating personal crisis). Also, although Lankford did not code for exact method of suicide, the majority of terroristic suicides were committed by forcing others to do the killing (e.g., suicide-by-cop or airplane collision), a notable departure from other types of mass shooter suicides (e.g., school shooters) where the majority died by self-inflicted means like gunshot. Lankford also provided a list of the specific names and locations of terroristic and other mass shooting suicides (for the interested reader).

Conclusion

Suicide is inextricably linked with firearms. Based on the chapter overview, we hope you can appreciate the complexity of this intersection and the need to consider the role of personal practices such as firearm storage, professions at elevated risk, and current best practices for policy and educational prevention and intervention efforts. While the limitations of current scientific firearm suicide data are important to note, suicide prevention efforts moving forward can draw on knowledge from this review. We set forth numerous practice, research, and policy recommendations related to firearm-involved suicide prevention in Chapter 9.

Part III

THE EMERGING ROLES OF MEDICAL AND
MENTAL HEALTH PROFESSIONALS
IN FIREARM-RELATED MATTERS

7

Evaluation

In this section of the book (Part III), we present considerations related to the emerging roles of mental health professionals in firearm-related matters. However, it is important to note that mental health and medical professionals have been addressing firearm-related issues, directly and indirectly, for quite some time in various settings and contexts. In this chapter, we first present some of those contexts, which essentially fall under the *mental health screening* umbrella. We then provide an overview of traditional psychological assessment, followed by the more specialized area of forensic mental health assessment (FMHA) and the even more specific emerging practice area: firearm evaluations. In our earlier developmental work in this area, we contended that, while they should be grounded in FMHA principles, firearm evaluations "represent a unique class of assessments with a particular set of considerations" (Pirelli, Wechsler, & Cramer, 2015, p. 250; see also Pirelli & Witt, 2015, 2017; Wechsler, Struble, Pirelli, & Cramer, 2015; Wechsler, Pirelli, & Cramer, 2014). As we continue to engage in research and practice in this area, we only feel more confident in our initial sentiment: firearm evaluations truly represent a subspecialty area, which requires specific professional and cultural competency. The saliency of firearm-related issues in this country cannot be understated; indeed, this represents one of our most pressing social issues. The level of public, media, and legislative attention that firearms receive must be met with equal—or even greater—careful attention by mental health and medical professionals. Therefore, as we will illustrate in the sections that follow, firearm-specific education and training are necessary for most mental health and medical practitioners—our society's primary gatekeepers in this regard.

Mental Health Screening

Screening for the presence of mental health problems is a fundamental component of all mental health and many medical intakes. If we think of the questions many of us have been asked (either verbally or in print) by physicians and other treating professionals, we would likely recall inquiries pertaining to such issues as anxiety, depression, and suicidality. This is especially true prior to undergoing certain medical procedures; in fact, more in-depth mental health assessments may be required in specific instances, such as in the context of elective, semi-elective, and even emergency surgeries (e.g., bariatric, organ donation, transplants, neurosurgery). In some cases, mental health professionals are called to see medical patients subsequent to a medical episode or procedure if they begin to experience new mental health symptoms, such as postpartum depression, or if they have a preexisting mental health history. Most hospitals and medical facilities have a consultation-liaison service, where professionals and trainees in the areas of psychiatry, psychology, and social work conduct assessments, provide brief treatment, set forth recommendations, and set up follow-up services for patients in need.

Some may continue to subscribe to the idea of mind–body *dualism*, which is often associated with René Descartes' 17th-century philosophy that considers the mind and body as distinct entities. However, many contemporary medical and mental health practitioners believe that consciousness is a function of the brain (materialistic monism) or that physical objects and events are, at least, reducible to mental objects (phenomenalistic monism or subjective idealism). Regardless of one's nuanced belief, the mind–body connection is quite clear and can be illustrated by the interplay of common emotional states and physical reactions, such as sadness and crying or embarrassment and blushing. At a more complex level, we can consider medically unexplained illnesses or symptoms, which are among the most common and frustrating challenges in primary care practices (see Edwards et al., 2010; Johnson, 2008). Some examples include chronic fatigue syndrome, fibromyalgia, multiple chemical sensitivity, Gulf War syndrome, and irritable bowel syndrome. Of course, there are also various more common symptoms many of us experience, such as general muscle, back, and joint pain; headaches; tiredness; chest pain; and stomach pain. Indeed, psychological stress has been cited as: a $1 trillion health epidemic—above the combined cost of cancer, smoking, diabetes, and heart disease; a factor in five of the six leading causes of death; and related to 75%–90% of all doctor visits (Robinson, 2013). Furthermore, more than 10% of Americans in the community take psychotropic medications—almost double the numbers from the late 1980s and early 1990s—and this number does not include those who are institutionalized or incarcerated or those who are prescribed general medications used for psychiatric purposes (Munsey, 2008). We must also consider the notable US substance abuse statistics in this context as well as a form of self-medicating, including the abuse of prescription medications.

To return to the original point, mental health screening is the primary scope of mental health intakes and many medical intakes because it provides practitioners with an overview of clients' histories and presenting problems and allows them to begin to form their case conceptualization and preliminary hypotheses. A strong case conceptualization and set of hypotheses are critical for effective treatment and, almost as importantly, to avoid certain interventions that may be contraindicated in a particular case. Assessment is the foundation for proper treatment and recommendations, but the mental health and medical professions have largely drifted away from formal and in-depth assessment procedures, such that it has become a specialty area rather than a core component of all practitioners' skill sets. For instance, psychiatrists and social workers are not trained in psychological testing; and in their quest to specialize, many psychologists have to specifically identify themselves as assessment psychologists. In fact, evaluators are often met with confusion from the public when they indicate that they do not provide therapy services, but such is not the case for those who provide treatment—most of whom do not conduct evaluations. This is an ironic shift in the field given that formal psychological evaluation is what sets psychologists apart from other mental health professionals, including psychiatrists, social workers, and counselors. Nevertheless, it is incumbent upon all treating professionals to be able to at least screen for particular areas of concern. Namely, treating professionals have an obligation to assess for violence, domestic violence, and suicide risk when applicable. Although they are not required to be specialists in the assessment or treatment of these issues, they must at least be able to screen for such and refer out when necessary. In fact, practitioners are often required to break confidentiality, report their concerns, and set up appropriate transitional services for those who are deemed at risk for harm to themselves or identifiable third parties or who report active child or elder abuse, consistent with their jurisdiction's *duty to warn and/or protect* statutes. However, there are gaps in training and education that we must acknowledge.

Let us consider mental health screening questions in the context of assessing suicide and violence risk levels. Mental health and medical professionals receive fairly extensive education and training on substance abuse, and questions regarding such use are a part of essentially all mental health assessments. A typical line of inquiry would consist of a review of all substances a client has tried, including the date of first use for each as well as the frequency, amount, and date of last use. There are also a whole host of formal substance use screening measures available to clinicians (e.g., see National Institute on Drug Abuse, 2015). In addition, a number of more in-depth substance use assessment measures have been published, and many general psychological assessment instruments include substance use–related scales (see the *Psychological Assessment* section below). But where are the firearm inquiries and specialized measures?

Imagine the following scenario. A man goes to the hospital, reports feeling extremely depressed, and asks for help. He is sent to the emergency room to be screened by mental health staff. The psychiatrist begins her screening and comes to the substance use portion of her assessment. She asks, "Do you have access to alcohol?" The man replies, "Yes," and the psychiatrist then begins to ask about the man's relationship status, never to return to follow up on the alcohol inquiry. This would likely represent a fairly negligent screening procedure, but it is also likely one that is commonplace in the context of firearm-related inquiries, regardless of the setting and scope of the evaluation. Given that mental health and medical professionals do not receive formal professional education and training on firearm-related issues, the vast majority likely do not know how to possibly follow up once they ask a person if he or she has access to a firearm. As a result, clinicians are likely to engage in dichotomous decision-making in this regard, whereby access to a firearm is only considered to be a factor associated with high risk. Although the presence of a firearm is certainly a potential risk factor, it is simply insufficient to begin and end there. In fact, all factors inquired about represent potential risk factors, which is why they are asked in the first place. But there is a reason that mental health and medical professionals engage in many years of education and training: clinical decision-making is context-specific and often complex. As with any formal assessment measure, a screener can help *facilitate* such decision-making, but it certainly cannot and should not substitute for it. It would be insufficient to fully evaluate a person by merely checking boxes "yes" or "no"—a screener is intended to *start* a line of additional inquiry rather than *end* it.

As we will see in the sections that follow, mental health and medical professionals work in many different settings, where they engage in a wide range of roles and are responsible to address various types of issues. Still, there is a common set of mental health–related inquiries with which all practitioners must be very familiar. To this point, the overarching areas typically covered in a mental health assessment are those related to: pregnancy, birth, and developmental milestones; family and upbringing; education; employment; social; religion; relationships; legal; medical; mental health; and substance use. Indeed, mental health and medical professionals receive many years of education and training on these issues as well as the many specific subtopics within each area. The paradox is that firearm-related violence and suicide have been noted to be such significant issues in our society that they have been classified as an *epidemic* by various professional organizations and groups (e.g., the American Public Health Association; see Greenberg, 2016). However, mental health and medical practitioners receive no formal education or training on firearm-related issues, and it is likely that many, if not most, do not know anything about firearms at all. Therefore, we are left with only an initial inquiry into a person's access to a firearm, with no follow-up or ability to assess the importance of the factor in context—a scenario that simply would be unacceptable in the assessment of any other potential risk factor.[1]

Community

Mental health issues are screened at most general medical settings in the community, including hospitals, clinics, and various types of doctor's offices. In these settings it is commonplace for patients to complete intake forms that include checklists of various medical and mental health conditions. As noted earlier (see *Mental Health Screening*), a majority of general medical visits are stress-related at some level, and the integration of primary care and mental health has become a routine and standard practice. Many mental health problems occur on a continuum and, as such, most of us experience some level of stress, anxiousness, moodiness, and sadness at times. These are normal experiences and often situational. However, medical professionals seek to screen for abnormal levels of these experiences, whereas concerns would arise when patients' daily functioning is affected or they experience discomfort above and beyond what is considered normal in the respective contexts. For instance, it is normal for someone to cry and feel sad when her dog dies—however, only to a point. In most cases, we would expect these feelings to be generally manageable and remit within months as the person grieves. On the other hand, it would be a problem if the person could not leave the house for 6 months and experienced suicidal thoughts as a result of the loss, for example. That said, there is no blanket set of behaviors or feelings we can ascribe to all situations to determine what is reasonable. Professionals should embrace a context-specific and culturally competent approach to their assessments because of the variability among patients and situations. Nevertheless, there is a range of so-called normal experiences we expect to see in certain circumstances, which are largely based on societal, cultural, and subcultural norms. Therefore, medical professionals working in hospitals, clinics, and private offices have a very important role in our society because they typically have the first (and most) contact with community members. This presents a critical responsibility and opportunity to provide care to those in need—either by providing treatment or by making referrals to appropriate professionals.

Mental health–related issues are also often addressed in the context of spiritual and religious centers, including churches, temples, and mosques. Indeed, many such places hold retreats and group meetings for their members and provide individual, couples, and family counseling. Pastoral counseling is a mainstay in most religions, whereby ministers, rabbis, priests, imams, and other psychologically trained religious leaders provide therapeutic services to their members. According to the American Association of Pastoral Counselors:

> Pastoral counseling is a unique form of counseling which uses spiritual resources as well as psychological understanding for healing and growth. Certified pastoral counselors are licensed mental health professionals who also had in-depth religious and/or theological

education or training. Clinical Services are non-sectarian and respect the spiritual commitments, theological perspectives and religious traditions of those who seek assistance without imposing counselor beliefs onto the client. (n.d.)

Pastoral counselors may be particularly helpful to those experiencing loss, illness, marital and family conflict, and conflicts with religious beliefs. Certainly, religious leaders often provide more or less formal "counseling" to their members, generally. At its core, open preaching in the form of a sermon, homily, *derasha*, or *khutbah* is a form of general counseling or teaching to the religious community; but more formal, case-specific counseling is also widely practiced among religious groups. Unlike medical and mental health professionals, religious leaders often have the opportunity to provide counseling to their members for positive, preparatory reasons (i.e., in the absence of problems). For example, in the Catholic faith, couples engage in marriage preparation programs, which are referred to as "Pre-Cana courses." Nevertheless, religious and faith-based settings often provide an outlet for community members to disclose concerns and seek support. Many people are even more comfortable addressing their problems with their leaders and peers in these communities, which may certainly include clinical concerns (e.g., depression, anxiety, suicidality, anger management). As a result, religious leaders have a great level of responsibility and set of opportunities to help community members receive mental health services. While religion, spirituality, or faith is not important to everyone, it is critical for mental health and medical professionals to provide services accordingly for those who do find it important. Formal coordination between religious leaders and treating professionals may also be beneficial and even necessary in some instances, especially among particular subcultures and community enclaves.

Of course, there are facilities and services in the community geared specifically toward mental health assessment, stabilization, and treatment. For instance, counties typically have mobile crisis services, whereby mental health screeners will respond to calls in the community to conduct on-site assessments. These situations usually also involve law enforcement personnel but may legally require mental health screeners to initiate involuntary commitment procedures that will be continued at county psychiatric emergency rooms or crisis centers. People may also go directly to hospitals when they are having a mental health emergency. Some hospitals have psychiatric emergency rooms or crisis units, whereas others may have mental health staff engaging in triage services out of their main emergency department. Regardless of the nuances that exist across counties and states in this regard, what is relevant here is that those tasked with conducting mental health screenings in crisis situations must be well versed in suicide and violence risk assessment among other areas. Therefore, the importance of education and training on firearm-related issues for these groups of professionals cannot be understated.

It is also worth noting the importance of community mental health centers and care management organizations (CMOs), which are available to many people and families in need. In 1963, President John F. Kennedy signed into law the Community Mental Health Act, which led to the development of community mental health centers throughout the United States and, therefore, was a significant part of the deinstitutionalization movement in this country. The act shifted the focus to community-based mental health care—a more effective approach for many Americans and a more cost-effective approach for the country, more generally. This concept, often referred to as *behavioral healthcare*, includes the integration of government and county-run agencies, in addition to nonprofit and private organizations, and funding is provided by a range of sources, including Medicaid; Medicare; county, state, and federal programs; private insurance; and self-paying clients. CMOs are county-based agencies that work with children and families to develop individualized service plans with the primary goal of keeping children in their homes, schools, and communities. As such, CMOs serve to gain access to and coordinate services for youth and families in need, which may include a wide range of services and service providers. Namely, CMO case managers may set up mental health evaluations and treatment for youth, including in-home, outpatient, and residential services; and they work closely with service providers as case managers. There are certainly many additional community resources and agencies available to those in need, including, but certainly not limited to, child and adult protective service agencies. Those working in the aforementioned community agencies encounter an extensive and unpredictable set of case circumstances and, therefore, must have the appropriate judgment, resources, and access to referral sources when particular issues arise. Mental health practitioners with expertise in firearm-related issues represent an important referral source.

Outpatient Settings

There are many types of community services, programs, and facilities that fall under the umbrella concept of *outpatient mental health*. What may come to mind first for most people is traditional psychotherapy in private practices, whereby mental health professionals provide individual, group, couples, and family therapy in their offices. Of course, there are also practitioners who provide on-site services, such as in patients' homes, institutions, or facilities in which they are residing (e.g., correctional, medical, and mental health facilities; schools; nursing homes). The field of teletherapy and telepsychiatry has also burgeoned in recent years, which involves the provision of mental health services remotely, online.

Recognition of the importance of outpatient mental health services has become widespread. For instance, employers often maintain employee assistance programs that set up referrals for employees, and many organizations even maintain their own in-house mental health services. For example, college counseling centers are available on campuses, and school psychologists and child study teams provide services to students, staff, and parents at the elementary, middle, and high school levels. In addition, there are numerous outpatient mental health clinics available to people, many of which are associated with hospitals, as well as services provided from various agencies, such as the US Department of Veterans Affairs (VA). There are also residential programs (e.g., group homes) and independent housing-based services for those with mental health needs, which represent an integral component of discharge planning for those being released from inpatient settings. Other options include intensive outpatient programs and partial hospitalization arrangements, which are intensive but encourage autonomy and independence in the community.

Some of the aforementioned programs may be associated with outpatient civil commitment provisions as well, which are essentially court-ordered treatment plans in the community. All states except Connecticut, Maryland, Massachusetts, and Tennessee, as well as the District of Columbia have assisted outpatient commitment laws, which is more commonly referred to as assisted outpatient treatment (see Treatment Advocacy Center, n.d.). These are *involuntary*, court-mandated plans aimed at reducing hospitalizations, arrests, and incarceration for those who qualify. There are also specialized mental health courts and jail diversion programs that have become available in recent years in many jurisdictions, which are for those who have legal troubles and are similarly aimed at reducing incarceration rates for non-violent offenders. Of course, probation and parole departments have been mandating mental health, substance abuse, anger management, and domestic violence programming for many years. Furthermore, consumer-run or peer programs, such as the very well-known 12-step program Alcoholics Anonymous has been internationally available for nearly 100 years. Others include those geared toward substance abuse and gambling (e.g., Narcotics Anonymous and Gamblers Anonymous) as well as those with dual diagnoses (i.e., clinical syndromes and substance use disorders), which are often referred to as "co-occurring" or "mentally ill chemical abuser" programs.

The range of outpatient mental health services available in this country is seemingly endless. It is a time of specialties and increased options for those seeking mental health support in the community, and therefore, outpatient providers must be prepared to work with a wide range of diverse clients. As such, they are very likely to encounter firearm-related issues or, at least, clients from one or more firearm subcultures—yet another reason driving the need for education and training on these issues and with these groups.

Inpatient Settings

Inpatient settings were the primary environments for medical and mental health services at one point in this country. However, the deinstitutionalization movement began in the mid-1950s in response to social pressures in the context of the civil rights movement and the advent of more effective medications. This was particularly true for the mental health arena. For instance, in 1955, there were 558,239 people diagnosed with severe mental illnesses in America's public psychiatric hospitals; by 1994, this number was reduced by 92% to 71,619 (Torrey, 1997). On the surface, deinstitutionalization seemed to be a major gain for patients; however, it ultimately led to what has been characterized as the criminalization of the mentally ill (Abramson, 1972). As a result, the nation's correctional facilities have been faced with a constant influx of offenders diagnosed with psychiatric conditions. This progression has not ceased, such that correctional institutions have been referred to as "the last mental hospital[s]" (Gilligan, 2001) and "the *de facto* state hospitals" (Daniel, 2007). In fact, the Los Angeles County Jail and Riker's Island in New York have become the largest psychiatric inpatient facilities in the United States, housing approximately 3,000 mentally ill inmates each (Torrey, 1999; Torey et al., 1992, 2010). Nevertheless, the ostensible push for outpatient (versus inpatient) treatment remains as medical and mental health facilities continue to close with some regularity. For example, according to the New Jersey Hospital Association (n.d.), 26 hospitals have closed in the state since 1992 and eight more have filed for bankruptcy since 2007. These include state psychiatric hospitals, such as the 2012 closure of Sen. Garret W. Hagedorn Psychiatric Hospital, the state's primary geriatric psychiatric facility. However, these numbers do not include the number of additional developmental centers and related mental health facilities that continue to close statewide. New Jersey is not unique in this regard. Many states are watching their psychiatric facilities close while their correctional facilities expand to house mentally ill offenders (e.g., see Sharp, 2016; Yates, 2016).

Despite the deinstitutionalization movement and associated closures, inpatient settings continue to serve as an important option in many cases. Certainly, correctional facilities provide the criminal justice system with a mechanism to enforce sanctions and secure those who pose a societal risk. The system includes juvenile detention centers, adult jails, prisons, and halfway houses. There is a range of security levels and specializations within each type of facility as well. For example, there are minimum, medium, maximum, and even "supermax" security prisons, as well as specialized prisons for particular offender groups (e.g., women, young adults, sex offenders). At this point, all facilities offer some level of medical and mental health care as well, and some even have medical and mental health units. As for hospitals, medical centers, and psychiatric and forensic psychiatric facilities, they are run at the private, county, and state levels. Inpatient substance abuse treatment rehabilitation centers are also widespread throughout the country, and 28-day programs have become quite popular in this regard.

Although private inpatient facilities theoretically have more control as to who they accept and treat, it is safe to say that most will encounter a fairly diverse clientele in terms of history and interests. Therefore, it is also a safe assumption that most mental health and medical professionals working in inpatient settings will interface with clients who have some connection with firearms, directly or indirectly. We must remember that all clients start off as community members but may find themselves in community-based, outpatient, or inpatient systems at any given time. In many cases, clients will be involved with more than one system over time, either via transfer during the same time period or at different points in their lives. Firearms may not be a primary concern in most matters, but it is important for practitioners to possess cultural awareness of firearm-related subcultures and issues, especially in high-stakes scenarios (e.g., assessment of violence, domestic violence, and suicide risk). We outline specific cultural competence considerations in the section that follows.

Cultural Competence

Developing and maintaining professional competence are ethical obligations for mental health and medical professionals, and cultural competence has become a well-recognized and critical component of professional competence. However, cultural competence has primarily centered on issues of race, religion, ethnicity, language, and nationality. To this point, there has been virtually no recognition in the professional literature or by professional groups of the need to develop firearm-related cultural competence. Such is a glaring omission, particularly in mental health and medical training and educational programs given the significant attention paid to gun-involved violence and other firearm-related issues. We are regularly reminded of the statistics surrounding firearm-involved suicide, violence and domestic violence, and crime, more generally. However, such is not met with equal (or virtually any) attention pertaining to the need for mental health and medical professionals who are adequately educated and trained on firearm-specific issues. We have recently set forth considerations in this regard (Pirelli & Witt, 2017), whereby we have noted the profound presence of firearms in our society:

> In addition to the military, firearms are present in various other contexts, such as law enforcement and corrections as well as among civilians. There are over one million active duty military personnel in the USA . . . ; approximately half a million full-time police officers . . . ; and almost as many correctional officers and jailers. . . . These numbers do not include retired officers or veterans, nor do they include other types of government agents or civilians who own firearms. Moreover, [it is] estimated that one in three households has a firearm and there are over 300 million firearms in the USA.

These numbers are compelling, particularly when we put them into the context of professional training, as there is considerable attention paid to very specific subgroups in this country. For instance, each year significantly less than 1% of the population dies by suicide (~35,000 of 319 million). Moreover, although the American public greatly overestimates, on average, that approximately

25% of people in this country identify as gay or lesbian, the actual number is 3.8% (Newport, 2015). Furthermore, according to Gallaudet University, approximately 0.38% of the US population over age 5 are "functionally deaf" (Mitchell, 2005). Of course, these are very important groups to understand, especially for mental health and medical professionals, who are relatively more likely than the average citizen to encounter a range of subgroups and are responsible for providing services to them. Undoubtedly, training and education with minority, disenfranchised, and vulnerable groups are important and necessary and should continue to develop. However, we cannot forget about the much (numerically) larger groups in the process, who also represent significant client bases. We also recognize that there will be people who either have been affected by or interact with firearms directly in all subgroups, including among minorities.

Kalesan, Villarreal, Keyes, & Galea (2016) examined the 2013 firearm ownership rates in the United States and the relationship between gun ownership and exposure to a social gun culture. Consistent with other estimates, they found that one-third of Americans reported owning a gun. Moreover, firearm ownership was 2.25 times greater among individuals who reported being a part of a social gun culture in comparison to those who did not. Kalesan and colleagues measured social gun culture using four questions that assessed whether an individual's "social circle thinks less of them if they did not own a gun," "family thinks less of them not owning a gun," "social life with family involves guns," and "social life with friends involves guns" (p. 216). They defined exposure to social gun culture if one of the four questions was answered yes. They concluded that gun violence prevention policies may need to take into consideration the social gun culture that is prevalent in America. However, people interested in firearms constitute one subculture. There are additional subgroups that have an association with firearms as well, and in some of our research work (Pirelli & Witt, 2017), we have outlined seven such groups: (i) Second Amendment (2A) groups; (ii) shooting sport groups; (iii) rod & gun clubs, hunting clubs, and shooting ranges; (iv) gun control and gun violence prevention groups; (v) military, law enforcement, and corrections; (vi) members of gangs, organized crime, and other criminal organizations; and (vii) victims of firearm-related suicide, violence, or domestic violence.

2A Groups

There are many 2A groups throughout the country. Members of these groups believe the US Constitution guarantees an individual right for US citizens to own firearms. Examples of these groups include: the National Rifle Association (NRA), Armed Citizens United, Firearms Policy Coalition, Jews for the Preservation of Firearm Ownership, the Second Amendment Foundation, Students for Concealed Carry on Campus, and Students for the Second Amendment. There are many more 2A groups throughout the United States, including those that primarily function at the state and local levels (see

Defend your rights, n.d.). What is important to note is that there is significant heterogeneity in the perspectives even among 2A groups. For instance, some maintain a "no compromise" stance, whereby they disagree with any negotiation related to gun control, whereas others are much more willing to compromise on various aspects of the issue—and, of course, there are many groups in between.

Shooting Sport Groups

These groups focus on education, training, and competitive forums for those interested in marksmanship-related activities and events, which may also include archery and the use of crossbows as well as rifles, shotguns, and pistols. Some of these activities, such as archery, date back at least 12,000 years; and many other shooting sports date back approximately 3,000 years. For example, according to the International Olympic Committee, the pentathlon was first held in the ancient Olympic Games in 708 BC and consisted of running, long jump, spear throwing, discus, and wrestling. The event was based on the types of skills needed to be a soldier. The more contemporary event is known as the "modern pentathlon" and consists of fencing, swimming, and horse riding, followed by a combined running and shooting event. It remains part of the Olympics, as are 15 other shooting sport events. The Paralympic Games also holds various shooting sport events with the use of air pistol, free pistol, and long rifle. In addition, shooting sports remain popular across colleges and universities throughout the country. According to the Association of College Unions International, there are at least 165 shooting collegiate teams and clubs, including those at Harvard, Yale, and Fordham universities, and the National Collegiate Athletic Association has held its rifle championship at the division I, II, and III levels for both men and women since 1980. Examples of other shooting sport groups include the National Shooting Sports Foundation, the Youth Shooting Sports Alliance, Shoot Like a Girl, and the International Defensive Pistol Association.

Rod & Gun Clubs, Hunting Clubs, and Shooting Ranges

There are seemingly countless clubs and ranges throughout the United States. It is axiomatic to say that hunting is an extremely popular activity throughout the country, and rod & gun clubs and shooting ranges are also present in essentially every region. Those who engage in these activities may or may not be involved in 2A groups or endeavors or other shooting sports. Therefore, it is incumbent upon mental health professionals to ascertain the nature and level of a person's acculturation and activities across firearm-related areas.

Gun Control and Gun Violence Prevention Groups

As with the 2A groups, there are many groups within this category, and there is also significant variability in their perspectives. At one end of the continuum, there are gun control and gun violence prevention groups that support the Second Amendment right to bear arms but advocate for stricter gun laws and policies; and, on the other end, there are groups essentially against all firearm ownership and use at the civilian level. As with the 2A groups, interested readers can easily locate local and regional groups in this regard, such as North Carolinians Against Gun Violence (n.d.) and New Yorkers Against Gun Violence (n.d.). There are many such groups throughout the country (for a representative list, see Gun Free Kids, n.d.). It is also important to note that many national groups represent mergers between and among various groups and, as such, many are campaigns and coalitions rather than stand-alone groups per se. Also, many groups are relatively new as they have been developed in response to particular mass shootings and tragic events, such as: Americans for Responsible Solutions, Everytown for Gun Safety, Moms Demand Action for Gun Sense in America, the Brady Campaign to Prevent Gun Violence, and the Newtown Action Alliance.

Military, Law Enforcement, and Corrections

Although active and retired military law enforcement and correctional personnel have received formal training on firearms, such exposure varies greatly among and within these groups. Perhaps the most homogeneity exists within law enforcement, whereas military personnel can range from soldiers in high-exposure infantry and combat training and scenarios to those who have not interacted with a firearm since basic training. Correctional officers are also very heterogeneous in their levels of firearm use and exposure given that it is a job that requires firearm training, ownership, and qualification but one that does not permit employees to actually carry firearms during the course of their work. A particularly important point to consider is that members of these groups may have service weapons, but this does not directly translate into the civilian world. In other words, one of us (G. P.) has conducted a number of evaluations on military and law enforcement officers who actively and legally possessed one or more service firearms but were still required to undergo a psychological firearm evaluation to be granted permission to own a personal firearm.

Gangs, Organized Crime, and Other Criminal Organizations

This subculture is perhaps best known to forensic and correctional mental health professionals. However, they may not readily associate individuals with firearms because the connection can be taken for granted. Nevertheless, while those engaged in illegal and otherwise nefarious activities are certainly not going to formally apply for a firearms identification card, members of these groups represent a primary source of much of the gun violence in our society.

Victims of Firearm-Related Suicide, Violence, and Domestic Violence

Victims of firearm-involved crimes and those affected by suicides involving firearms represent another very relevant subculture in this context. Therefore, professionals working with members of these groups should also be attuned to considerations relevant to firearms. It may also be the case that members of these groups will seek their own firearms at some point, particularly victims of violence and domestic violence who make efforts to protect themselves from potential threats. Indeed, some states have sought the loosening of firearm restrictions for such applicants (e.g., Governor Christie's initiatives in New Jersey).

Recommendations for Practitioners, Researchers, Academics, and Students

Given the significant proportion of our society that is associated with firearms in some way and the frequency with which issues in this area are discussed, it seems rather self-evident that mental health professionals need education and training in this area. We have recently set forth the following recommendations in this regard (Pirelli & Witt, 2017):

(1) All mental health professionals should develop their cultural competence by familiarizing themselves with the literature pertaining to firearms, which should extend well beyond the gun violence literature and into the full range of firearm-related matters, prosocial and otherwise.

(2) Additionally, practitioners should engage in formal continuing education efforts in this regard by taking courses in firearms and mental health. These types of   courses are rare; therefore, professionals may need to first take more general firearm courses at local gun ranges or conferences presented by various types of groups who are most familiar with firearms (e.g., law enforcement, public safety, or even Second Amendment groups). We also encourage taking courses or attending talks from the full range of groups associated with firearms, including gun violence prevention and even anti-gun groups; however, the goal is not to simply receive information on others' *perspectives*, but to receive education on firearm construction, use, safety, and the like. Put differently, appreciating the reasons why some are supportive of particular firearm laws is not going

to be useful for the practitioner who is conducting a domestic violence risk assessment and comes across firearm-specific information during the course of the evaluation. Awareness of the Second Amendment debate will have no utility in this context despite the fact that the professional literature is consumed with information pertaining to gun violence and perspectives on guns rather than information about firearms or those who are associated with them outside of violence and suicide (i.e., the vast majority of the population). In other words, appreciating the reasons why some are supportive of particular firearm laws is not going to be useful for the practitioner who is conducting a domestic violence risk assessment and comes across firearm-specific information during the course of the evaluation. For example: *The examinee has two boxes of 50 bullets—is that many or few? He owns a bolt-action rifle and a semi-automatic handgun—what is the difference, why does he own them, and what are the associated implications in this regard? How do the local norms (regional statistics) inform the assessment of risk?*

(3) Furthermore, practitioners interested in conducting firearm-specific evaluations should strongly consider visiting such places as gun ranges as well as other environments frequented by firearm owners and operators (e.g., gun shows, Second Amendment conferences), consistent with the principles underlying clinical training, more generally (i.e., the many years and thousands of hours of classroom education, independent reading and study, and participation in externships, internships, and other experiential practicum placements). Practitioners must stay within their areas of professional competence, which includes the types of services they provide *and* the types of clients for whom they provide them. Mental health professionals may develop new areas of professional competence, but such would necessitate gaining face-to-face, hands-on experience working with the new population and within the new type of service. Furthermore, practitioners should seek professional supervision or consultation until they have reached a point of independent proficiency in the area.

(4) Those who conduct research and teach in areas related to firearms to also develop and maintain their professional competence in this regard, as professional ethics codes also pertain to academicians, students and researchers Per the American Psychological Association's (EPPCC; APA, 2010):
  "Areas covered include but are not limited to the clinical, counseling, and school practice of psychology; research;

teaching; supervision of trainees; public service; policy development; social intervention; development of assessment instruments; conducting assessments; educational counseling; organizational consulting; forensic activities; program design and evaluation; and administration."

Consistent with such, the EPPCC is explicit about the responsibility of educators and researchers to engage in only such endeavors that are within their areas of professional competence:

"(a) Psychologists provide services, teach, and conduct research with populations and in areas only within the boundaries of their competence, based on their education, training, supervised experience, consultation, study, or professional experience." (Standard 2.01, Boundaries of Competence)

And, more specifically:

"(c) Psychologists planning to provide services, teach, or conduct research involving populations, areas, techniques, or technologies new to them undertake relevant education, training, supervised experience, consultation, or study." (Standard 2.01, Boundaries of Competence).

Consistent with the APA Ethics Code and with our aforementioned recommendations for practitioners, we recommend academics and researchers subscribe to a hierarchical approach to developing and maintaining their professional competence in the context of firearms and firearm subcultures. Thus, all educators and researchers who interface with firearm-related issues, directly or indirectly, should familiarize themselves with the broad literature pertaining to firearms and not solely on that which is related to gun violence. In addition, those conducting research and teaching in areas more closely connected with firearms should seek formal continuing education on firearm-specific topics, and those conducting research and teaching directly in the firearm arena should strongly consider getting exposure to various firearm-related subcultures, especially in natural environments, such as gun ranges. When 100 million Americans own a firearm and many more have some level of association with them, it is a matter of choice rather than availability to not receive professional exposure to firearms or firearm-related subcultures. (p. 68)

Psychological and Forensic Mental Health Assessment

Psychological Assessment

Mental health professionals receive education and training in the assessment of psychiatric symptoms and conditions. Psychologists are specifically trained to administer, score, and interpret psychological assessment measures, which may also be referred to as "instruments," "tests," "guides," and "checklists." Incorporating formal assessment measures in an evaluation can be very helpful in improving clinical judgment and facilitating decision-making; indeed, such is their purpose. While the clinical interview is a staple procedure in mental health evaluations, formal testing can add significant incremental validity to the process. Naturally, psychological test results may not be interpretable or may otherwise lack utility in a specific case, but they often provide an important and additional source of data for practitioners to consider. It is critical to gather and analyze data from different sources, consistent with the tenets of hypothesis testing and the scientific method, more generally. Nevertheless, there are cases where psychological testing is not indicated or may even be contraindicated, such as when there are no appropriate measures or comparison groups available—a somewhat common occurrence when evaluating clients across cultures. In fact, some may be surprised to know that most published psychological measures have not even been translated into Spanish and even those that have been are susceptible to a number of limitations (e.g., diverse dialects among Latino and Spanish subcultures). Test developers continue to work toward reducing bias when possible, however; and practitioners have many more options today than they once had (e.g., nonverbal and verbal intelligence measures, self-attribution and stimulus-attribution clinical and personality assessment measures—historically referred to as "objective" and "projective" tests).

Psychological tests are designed to *operationally define*, or measure, psychological constructs. Namely, the focus is on quantifying the concept in question (e.g., anger, intelligence, suicide risk) and, ideally, generating a score that has real-world value. Perhaps the best-known examples are intelligence quotient (IQ) scores and those related to academic achievement because of their widespread use throughout the educational system. Most of us have a general understanding of IQ, SAT, and ACT scores for that reason; and those familiar with higher education are likely familiar with the Graduate Record Examination, the Law School Admission Test, and the Medical College Admission Test. In the same way, mental health professionals have developed a multitude of tests to formally measure a wide array of constructs. For example, there are measures of intellectual functioning (e.g., the Wechsler Adult Intelligence Scale-fourth edition [Wechsler, 2008]), psychopathology and personality functioning (e.g., the Minnesota Multiphasic Personality Inventory-2-Restructured Form [Ben-Porath & Tellegen, 2008] and the Personality Assessment Inventory [Morey, 2007]), and those designed to assess many other, more specific issues, such as substance abuse problems (e.g., the Substance Abuse Subtle Screening Inventory-3 [Miller & Lazowski, 1999]) and those related to anger (e.g., the State-Trait Anger Expression Inventory-2 [Spielberger, 1999]). These types of measures are often referred to as "clinical assessment instruments," which are different from forensic assessment instruments or those that are forensically related.[2] Forensic assessment instruments are those that have been developed to address very specific psycholegal questions, such as adjudicative competency (e.g., the Fitness Interview Test-Revised [Roesch, Zapf, & Eaves, 2006]) and criminal responsibility (e.g., the Rogers Criminal Responsibility Assessment Scales [Rogers, 1984]). Forensically related measures are those designed to address constructs that are typically of importance in legal or administrative matters, such as those associated with violence and domestic violence risk. In the following section, we present an overview of this specialized type of psychological assessment, FMHA, which includes a set of evaluation types employed in various administrative, civil, criminal, and family legal matters. Forensic evaluations are not simply clinical assessments but part of the highly specialized subfield of forensic psychology and, therefore, warrant a formal overview.

Forensic Mental Health Assessment

Per the American Psychological Association's (APA) Specialty Guidelines for Forensic Psychology (SGFP; American Psychological Association, 2013b), forensic psychology:

> refers to professional practice by any psychologist working within any subdiscipline of psychology (e.g., clinical, developmental, social, cognitive) when applying the scientific, technical, or specialized knowledge of psychology to the law to assist in addressing legal, contractual, and administrative matters. (p. 7)

Of particular note is that adherence to the SGFP does not depend on practitioners' "typical areas of practice or expertise, but rather, on the service provided in the case at hand" (p. 7). In other words, it is not important how practitioners choose to label themselves—as forensic psychologists or not—but, rather, it is the nature of the services they provide that will or will not fall under the definition of *forensic psychology*. In other words, professionals who engage in forensic work cannot turn a blind eye to the SGFP and associated practice standards simply because they do not consider themselves to be forensic psychologists. Again, it is the nature of the services provided that carries professional obligations and responsibilities, not the provider per se. As we address in this section, there are significant differences between therapeutic and forensic roles. However, it is important to consider these issues in context; therefore, we first provide a brief overview of the field.

Forensic psychology has been said to have a long past but a short history. Although those such as James Cattell and Albert von Schrenck-Notzing began formally addressing psychological issues related to testimony and pretrial publicity in the early 1890s, the development of the field was forestalled many years. Professor Hugo Munsterberg of Harvard University wrote his now seminal text *On the Witness Stand* (1908) at the turn of the 20th century; however, it was harshly criticized by legal scholars, such as John J. Wigmore (1909), who claimed that Munsterberg exaggerated his claims pertaining to the benefits of applying psychological concepts to the law. As a result, the field as we now know it was delayed many years despite the fact that a number of social scientists continued to conduct research and publish on topics reflecting the intersection of psychology and law throughout the first half of the 20th century.

Psychologists also played a pivotal role in the development of formal psychological assessment measures to be used in various settings, such as those designed to assess aptitude and intellectual functioning for the military. Nevertheless, the field of forensic psychology did not catch its second wind until the 1960s and into the 1970s, at which point there was a proliferation of specialized journals, societies, and assessment measures. US Supreme Court and DC Circuit Court holdings also set the stage for psychologists to enter the legal arena in a way that had not previously been possible. Namely, the research conducted by psychologists Kenneth and Mamie Clark was cited by the Supreme Court in the pivotal school segregation case *Brown v. Board of Education* (1954), and psychologists were recognized as qualified expert witnesses on the issue of mental disease by the circuit court less than a decade later in *Jenkins v. United States* (1962). Still, forensic psychology has only been formally recognized as a specialty by the APA since 2001 thanks to decades of important work by numerous scholars and practitioners who contributed to its development. Over the last two decades or so, many formal academic and training programs in forensic psychology and psychology and law have been developed throughout North America (see, e.g., a listing of graduate programs set forth by the American Psychology–Law Society, Division 41 of the APA, in Graduate programs in psychology and law, n.d.).[3]

But what are the real distinctions between treating and evaluating professionals? That is, what distinguishes therapeutic from forensic roles among mental health professionals? After all, many of us would either be inclined or directed to consult a treating professional for a myriad of mental health–related issues, even in the case of legal or administrative matters. It is not uncommon for people to seek letters, notes, or reports from treating professionals to use in civil, criminal, and administrative cases, including, but not limited to, (i) when seeking disability or workers' compensation benefits; (ii) when claiming psychological injury in personal injury or employment harassment or discrimination matters; (iii) when one's fitness for duty or risk, more generally, must be evaluated to return to school or work; (iv) when child custody and other family court–related issues arise; (v) when mental capacity is at issue in legal guardianship matters or those associated with other types of legal decision-making; and, of course, (vi) when assessing risk or mental states is necessary in the context of various criminal and civil matters. While treating professionals may be able to provide some useful information in these types of situations, they would serve as fact witnesses who contribute data to the case but not as independent experts who directly address the psycholegal and administrative questions relevant to these matters.

In their seminal work, Greenberg & Shuman (1997, 2007) contrasted the role of the therapeutic clinician with that of the forensic evaluator. They outlined 10 differences between therapeutic and forensic relationships:

1. identifying the client
2. relational privilege
3. cognitive set and evaluative attitude
4. areas of competency
5. nature of the hypotheses tested
6. scrutiny applied to the information utilized
7. amount and control of the structure
8. nature and degree of "adversarialness"
9. goal of the professional
10. impact of critical judgment by the psychologist.

Perhaps the most notable differences are those that follow. One difference pertains to the determination of who the client is in the professional relationship—an issue first addressed by Monahan (1980). In a therapeutic context, identifying the client is typically straightforward; it is usually the person or people receiving therapy or therapeutic interventions (i.e., the individual patient, couple, or family). However, in a forensic context, there are often several clients, which may include the examinee (e.g., the defendant), the retaining attorney, the court, and the community. It is essential to identify the client(s) in each context to provide the foundation and associated considerations for the work moving forward.

A second difference is associated with the relational privilege. In the context of providing therapeutic services, privilege and confidentiality are generally protected and will be maintained barring any duty-to-warn– or duty-to-protect–related exceptions (à la *Tarasoff*). In forensic work, privilege may exist in limited circumstances, such as within the context of the attorney–client relationship (e.g., attorney work-product); however, no such privilege exists in other situations, such as in many administrative matters or court-ordered evaluations. As a result, an examinee's confidentiality will typically be very limited in a forensic evaluation. The aforementioned principles related to privilege are important for the practitioner to recognize for many reasons, particularly as they pertain to informed consent.

A third distinction—cognitive set and evaluative attitude—is one that clearly differentiates therapeutic and forensic practice. Treating professionals typically strive to be supportive, accepting, and empathic, whereas forensic practitioners are trained to be as neutral, objective, and (personally) detached as possible. In fact, some may contend that "empathy gets in the way" in forensic contexts, and a professional literature on the issue of *moral disengagement* has continued to grow.

A fourth difference pertains to the hypotheses tested in therapeutic and forensic work. Treating professionals test those hypotheses that may be associated with treatment goals, including considering differential diagnoses, family dynamics, and other relevant themes that may arise in therapy sessions. On the other hand, forensic practitioners test hypotheses related to the psycholegal question at hand (e.g., mental capacity to make decisions, the proximate cause of a psychological injury). As such, forensic practitioners must have an understanding of the law and be able to operationally define and clinically assess the relevant aspects of psycholegal constructs. For instance, when conducting a capacity evaluation in a legal guardianship case, a practitioner must know how to appropriately assess a defendant's competence-related abilities (i.e., understanding, reasoning, and appreciation).

The aforementioned difference (i.e., the nature of hypothesis testing) is closely associated with the ninth distinction outlined by Greenberg & Shuman (1997): the goal of the professional in each relationship. The primary goal of treating professionals is to help the patient via the therapeutic relationship, whereas the main goal of forensic practitioners is to address the psycholegal question at hand in order to assist the trier of fact (i.e., the judge or jury) in the legal decision-making process.

With an understanding of what forensic psychology is and what differentiates forensic and therapeutic practice, we can better appreciate concepts related to forensic evaluation, or what has been more formally referred to as FMHA. FMHA refers to the process of evaluating the emotional, behavioral, and cognitive functioning of a person whose mental state is at issue in a legal proceeding (Heilbrun, 2001). Although mental health professionals have conducted these types of evaluations for over 100 years, significant advances have occurred over the past few decades, including the publication of seminal texts (e.g., Grisso, 1986, 2003; Heilbrun, 2001; Heilbrun, DeMatteo, Brooks Holliday, & LaDuke, 2014; Heilbrun, Grisso, & Goldstein, 2009; Melton et al., 2007) as well as ethical standards as set forth in the "Ethical Principles of Psychologists and Code of Conduct" (American Psychological Association, 2002, 2010) and practice guidelines in the form of the SGFP (American Psychological Association, 2013b).

Per the APA, the SGFP:

> apply in all matters in which psychologists provide expertise to judicial, administrative, and educational systems including, but not limited to, examining or treating persons in anticipation of or subsequent to legal, contractual, or administrative proceedings; offering expert opinion about psychological issues in the form of amicus briefs or testimony to judicial, legislative, or administrative bodies; acting in an adjudicative capacity; serving as a trial consultant or otherwise offering expertise to attorneys, the courts, or others; conducting research in connection with, or in the anticipation of, litigation; or involvement in educational activities of a forensic nature. (p. 7)

Based on the definitions of forensic psychological practice and FMHA and consistent with professional practice standards, it is quite clear that psychological evaluations conducted in the context of firearm-related matters fall under the umbrella of forensic practice and FMHA, more specifically. This concept is unlikely to be particularly arguable among mental health or even legal professionals. However, we went a step further as we developed our earlier work on this topic and conceptualized psychological evaluations for firearm ownership as a unique area of forensic mental health assessment (Pirelli et al., 2015), which broadly consists of two types of assessments with civilians:

1. evaluations of new applicants referred subsequent to the discovery of identified concerns during standard application procedures, including routine background checks
2. evaluations of those seeking reinstatement of their firearm permits, licenses, and/or firearms subsequent to their revocation

Certainly, there are matters that do not necessarily fit neatly into the two aforementioned categories but still require a focus on the intersection between firearms and mental health among civilian groups. Moreover, there are associated areas very relevant to firearm matters but not necessarily specifically defined in that way. For instance, it is not uncommon for firearm applicants to engage in *expungement* efforts, whereby they seek to have prior records sealed, thereby blocking them from being flagged during background checks. Furthermore, in our earlier publications, we have noted the potential applications of these concepts to other types of firearm-related matters, such as fitness-for-duty evaluations for law enforcement and correctional officers or in other contexts where the need for a person to own or carry a firearm is necessary (e.g., federal agents, military personnel, security guards, armed guards). We will address these potential applications in greater detail in Chapter 9.

Those familiar with the assessment of psychopathology, violence, suicide risk, and competency will find that the foundational concepts within each of those areas underlie much of the necessary components of a psychological firearm evaluation. However, as we will see in the sections that follow, it is insufficient to simply employ general clinical assessment and FMHA concepts when conducting firearm evaluations because of the numerous *additional* considerations to take into account in this context. Namely, in addition to developing cultural competence related to various firearm subcultures, practitioners must attain a working knowledge of firearm basics and the various legal, administrative, and procedural issues that arise when someone is applying for a firearm permit or seeking for reinstatement of such. In Chapter 1 of this book, we provided a primer intended to serve as a useful reference for practitioners to begin to learn about firearm basics; and indeed, our aspiration is that this book as a whole will serve as a resource in this way by outlining the myriad issues relevant to firearms in our society today. However, reading this book represents only an initial step in developing one's professional competence in this area; certainly, those interested in conducting psychological firearm evaluations as well as research in this area of study should first review some of the primary sources we cite throughout this book, particularly the more recent, seminal publications (e.g., Gold & Simon, 2016; Pinals et al., 2015a, 2015b). A next step would be to begin to build one's cultural competence by reading about various firearm-related subcultures, prosocial and otherwise, such as the ones outlined in Chapter 1 of this book—for instance, familiarizing oneself with shooting sports, hunting, military, law enforcement, corrections, and 2A groups, as well as gun control, gun violence prevention, and antigun groups. In addition, it is important to gain an appreciation for the various other types of groups both directly and indirectly associated with firearms, such as the seven subcultures we have outlined.

Thus, it is quite clear that professionals who engage in clinical work or research related to the intersection of firearms and mental health must be well versed in numerous areas of study and must develop cultural competence associated with numerous types of populations. For treating professionals and those tasked with mental health screening in various settings, the group from which the next client comes (or may come) is simply unknown; and therefore, it would be unrealistic for most treating and evaluating professionals to avoid interfacing with firearms at some level, even if indirectly, given that one-third of the general population owns firearms and many more have had or will have some type of exposure to firearms or firearm-related issues.

Certainly, professionals interested in conducting firearm-related evaluations have an even greater responsibility to attain not only cultural competence in this area but also professional competence related to their areas of practice. This is obviously true for evaluators who conduct firearm-specific evaluations—where civilians are applying for a permit or seeking to have such reinstated—but it is also incumbent upon other types of evaluators to develop and maintain professional and cultural competence in this area. There are many cases that involve firearms, including, but not limited to, various types of violence, domestic violence, and suicide risk assessments, as well as a wide range of criminal matters where firearms were involved at some level. As we have noted, firearm-related considerations should be undertaken in much the same way as those associated with substance use, which are also relevant in many types of evaluation scenarios.

Moreover, practitioners interested in conducting firearm-specific evaluations should strongly consider visiting such places as gun ranges as well as other environments frequented by firearm owners and operators (e.g., gun shows, 2A conferences). The reason practitioners engage in many years and thousands of hours of externships, internships, and other experiential practicum placements prior to licensure is to ensure that they have gained ample *face-to-face* experience working with the populations they will ultimately serve in their practice. Once licensed, mental health professionals should maintain adherence to this principle because, although a license may permit practitioners to engage with the full range of potential clients, state licensing regulations and professional ethics codes certainly do not allow for such. Rather, professionals must practice within their areas of professional competence, which includes considerations for the types of services they provide *and* the types of clients for whom they provide them. Certainly, mental health professionals can develop new areas of professional competence at any point in their careers; but again, this type of venture would necessitate gaining face-to-face, hands-on experience working with the new population and within the new type of service. Furthermore, practitioners should seek professional supervision or consultation until they have reached a point of independent proficiency in the area.

Firearm Evaluations

We have contended that firearm evaluations are a specific type of FMHA (Pirelli et al., 2015); however, it is a concept that is very much in its early developmental stages. That said, the field of psychiatry has taken the lead in addressing the association between mental health and firearm-related issues. In 2015, the American Psychiatric Association set forth a position statement on firearm access, acts of violence, and the association to mental illness and mental health services (Pinals et al., 2015a), which outlined the principles and positions it supports in an effort to reduce morbidity and mortality due to firearm-related violence (Note: the interested reader should also review the association's resource document in this area; Pinals et al., 2015b). The position statement indicated that the association supports the following five principles and positions:

1. National and state legislation and regulation associated with requiring background checks, waiting periods, and safe storage; manipulating firearm characteristics to only allow owners or permitted others to use them; banning civilian carry in colleges, hospitals, and related institutions; and allowing doctors and other healthcare providers to inquire about the possession and access of firearms and to take steps to reduce suicide, homicide, and accidental injury.
2. Prioritizing research and training on the causes of firearm violence and related risk assessment and management considerations, including: removing barriers to federal funding; directing such resources toward developing risk assessment and identification methods; having the federal government develop and fund a national database on firearm injuries as well as homicides and suicides; training all physicians and other health professionals to assess and respond to those who are at elevated risk of engaging in violence or suicide, including education on speaking with patients about firearm access and safety; and increasing firearms safety education programs.
3. Reasonable restrictions on access to firearms, "but such restrictions should not be based solely on a diagnosis of mental disorder" (p. 196).
4. Prohibited categories of individuals should be clearly defined, and there "should be a fair and reasonable process for restoration of firearm rights for those disqualified on such grounds" (p. 197). Also, they suggested that non-adjudicated events, such as temporary hospital stays, "should not serve as sufficient grounds for a

disqualification from gun ownership and should not be reported to the NICS system" (p. 197).

5. Although improved recognition and access to care for those with psychiatric disorders may decrease the risk of firearm-related suicide and violence among those with such tendencies, such is likely to have "only a limited impact on overall rates of violence" because of "the small percentage of violence overall attributable to mental disorders (estimated at 3–5% in the U.S., excluding substance use disorders)" (p. 197).

The American Psychological Association has also set forth a position and policy document in the form of its panel of experts report (2013a) on gun violence prediction, prevention, and policy. Per the report, the association believes that gun violence prevention efforts should focus on a range of individual, family, school, peer, community, and sociocultural risk factors at the individual and community levels. Specifically, with respect to prevention efforts, the report noted the following:

> Although it is important to recognize that most people suffering from a mental illness are not dangerous, for those persons at risk for violence due to mental illness, suicidal thoughts, or feelings of desperation, mental health treatment can often prevent gun violence. . . . Prevention of violence occurs along a continuum that begins in early childhood with programs to help parents raise emotionally healthy children and ends with efforts to identify and intervene with troubled individuals who are threatening violence. . . . Firearm prohibitions for high-risk groups—domestic violence offenders, persons convicted of violent misdemeanor crimes, and individuals with mental illness who have been adjudicated as being a threat to themselves or to others—have been shown to reduce violence. (p. 2)

Dr. Liza Gold is a professor of psychiatry at Georgetown University and a preeminent leader in this field of study. In her 2013 editorial, she highlighted a number of additional critical points to consider, particularly in the context of mass shootings, media and legislative attention, and our resulting perspectives:

> The mass shootings that break our hearts are not representative of the behavior of most people with mental illness. Similarly, mass shootings are not representative of the much broader problem of gun violence in the United States. Despite the media attention that such incidents attract and the horror they cause, mass shootings by individuals with or without mental illness are a statistically rare event. (p. 337)
>
> Media coverage of mass shootings exacerbates negative attitudes toward people with serious mental illness. . .
>
> Pundits and politicians describe mass shooters as mentally ill, deranged, evil monsters, thus reinforcing the negative stigma. These polemics often conclude with the simplistic and equally mistaken

premise that the problem of gun violence can be resolved if we can keep guns out of the hands of mentally unstable individuals. Federal and state legislative measures proposed since the Newtown shootings follow this pattern, reflecting the mistaken belief that all those with mental illness are dangerous. . .

Legislation that mandates increased reporting of individuals with mental disorders and expanding categories of "mental defectives" in attempts to address the epidemic of gun violence is not likely to be more effective than extremist social proposals to create a so-called lunatic database. Such legislative attempts serve only to stigmatize those with mental illness further. . .

Media coverage and legislation based on the false premise that individuals with mental illness are a root cause of gun violence dehumanize patients, compromise patient privacy, threaten confidentiality, and interfere with the therapeutic relationship.

When discussing gun violence, the public and media seem unaware that the real link between mental illness and guns is suicide. (p. 338)

In conclusion, Dr. Gold indicated that gun violence is correlated with the prevalence of firearms and not mental illness; however, she readily acknowledged that "Most of this evidence demonstrates correlation and not causation" (p. 340). Nevertheless, she contended that public health interventions should focus on violence risk assessment and that legislation should also be linked to such and not solely based on the presence of a mental illness. As she articulated it:

By supporting a focus on dangerousness and violence risk assessment rather than on mental illness, we can help steer the national discussion toward nondiscriminatory approaches to reducing gun violence. (p. 342)

This sentiment has been echoed by many, including some gun violence prevention groups. For example, per the Coalition to Stop Gun Violence (n.d.):

It is undoubtedly true that people who are a danger to self and/or others because of mental illness should be prohibited from owning firearms. It is less clear, however, how to tailor new policies to better protect the American public while at the same time avoiding the stigmatization of Americans with mental illness. Any strategy to address the lethal intersection between guns and mental illness should focus on three key facts:

- A large majority of people with mental disorders will never engage in violence against others.
- Most violent behavior is due to factors other than mental illness.
- Psychiatric disorders such as depression are strongly implicated in suicide, which accounts for more than half of gun fatalities annually.

Unfortunately, very few states have engaged in a serious effort to look beyond the outdated (and somewhat arbitrary) federal standard regarding the purchase of firearms by the mentally ill. More needs to be done, by federal and state lawmakers alike.

As we discussed in Chapter 2, in *Tyler v. Hillsdale County Sheriff's Department* (2014), the Sixth Circuit Court of Appeals reversed and remanded a previous decision made by the District Court for the Western District of Michigan, which had dismissed Mr. Tyler's contention that the federal statute that prohibits individuals committed to mental institutions from possessing guns was unconstitutional as applied to him, especially as there was no relief program with an opportunity to challenge the prohibition in place. The appeals court held that he had cited a valid violation of the Second Amendment and that there was no lifelong prohibition based on mental illness per se. Although the court did not order that Tyler's rights be restored immediately, it provided him with the opportunity to prove that he had regained mental stability and that his mental illness did not pose a risk to himself or others. In his commentary on *Tyler*, Appelbaum (2017) noted the dilemmas that the case presented for mental health professionals. Namely, although most mental health organizations and professionals prefer stricter gun laws, restrictions in this context reinforce the stigmatization of mental illness, which the same groups have spent half a century fighting against. As he articulated it:

> As the Sixth Circuit's majority opinion noted, none of the data presented by the government to demonstrate increased risk of violence and self-harm associated with mental illness spoke to the degree of risk of someone who had a single episode of illness many years in the past and no problems since. Indeed, existing data suggest that the risk of violence to others drops quickly over the first several months after release from a psychiatric hospitalization. (p. 4)

Swanson & Felthous (2015) addressed this issue as well. They noted that, although evidence regarding physical conditions that should disqualify individuals from owning guns may be lacking, there is good evidence that individuals who are experiencing a mental health crisis are at an elevated risk for hurting themselves or others. Thus, they argued that emergency commitment would seem to be a valid criterion for at least temporary firearm prohibitions, such as California's short-term emergency commitment law (5150 law). Still, as they pointed out, "Mental illness *per se* explains very little of why people intentionally harm others with guns; it provides a somewhat better, if still incomplete, answer to the question of why people harm themselves" (p. 176).

Nevertheless, Appelbaum (2017) addressed the associated concerns with the prohibition of gun rights and the likely role of mental health professionals in these matters moving forward:

But the implications of Tyler transcend the clinical professions and extend beyond people with mental illness. Consistent with current interpretations of the Second Amendment, regulation of firearm access has focused on excluding classes of people, for example, persons dishonorably discharged from the armed forces, illegal aliens, or those with past convictions of misdemeanors involving domestic violence, whose status may bear little relationship to their current risk of violence. The decision in Tyler suggests that we may be moving toward more individualized determinations of risk for larger groups of people, for whom the predictors of violence are even less well specified. If that's true, the odds are that mental health professionals will once again be asked to undertake that role. (p. 5)

The concept of restoration of gun rights is likely to continue to be an area of particular relevance for legislatures as well as mental health professionals, and it is one that predates *Tyler*. For instance, Britton & Bloom (2015) reviewed Oregon's gun restoration legislation, which was set forth in 2010 and includes hearings in front of the state's Psychiatric Security Review Board. The process is as follows: prior to a hearing, petitioners are required to submit their mental health and court records associated with the prohibitor area (i.e., issue in question or "flagged" area of concern), a certified copy of their FBI juvenile and adult criminal histories, and an independent forensic mental health evaluation conducted within 90 days of the petition. The evaluation must be conducted by a licensed psychiatrist or psychologist and must include an opinion related to the petitioner's risk to others as well as self-harm. According to Britton & Bloom:

At a minimum, the assessment should include a review of the mental health adjudication records, police reports, if any, a clinical interview, psychological test results, diagnostic impressions, and a conclusion regarding the petitioner's risk to public safety if firearm privileges are restored. (p. 328)

Price & Norris (2010) addressed the roles and responsibilities of mental health professionals in firearm-related matters even prior to that:

Psychiatrists have always had, and will continue to have, a role in gun-management safety for patients, some of whom will, and some of whom will not, meet state or federal statutory definitions of prohibited persons.

Psychiatrists should be familiar with both state and federal firearm statutes.

Psychiatrists should remain alert to changes in state firearm statutes that may impose increased responsibilities on them for reporting patients. It is anticipated that as a result of the NICS Improvement Act, the numbers of persons reported to mental health registries will substantially increase. The NICS Improvement Act provides for an

> appeals process, and it is likely that patients will increasingly request that their psychiatrists participate in the "relief from disabilities" process. Psychiatrists should carefully consider the potential ramifications of accepting this professional responsibility. The new laws will likely impose new responsibilities on psychiatrists and create new challenges for them and their patients. (pp. 332–333)

Certainly, as we have noted throughout this book, firearm evaluations are independently conducted throughout the country even though formal or specific review boards are not in place in most jurisdictions. For example, Swanson & Felthous (2015) indicated that, in North Carolina, physicians are occasionally contacted by the sheriff's department to determine whether a patient, who is applying for a concealed carry permit, is suffering from "any physical or mental infirmity that prevents the safe handling of a handgun" (p. 171; N.C. Gen. Stat. §14-415.11). However, the authors appropriately questioned whether physicians are qualified to determine whether someone can safely operate a handgun as well as which health conditions should disqualify someone. They cited research conducted by Goldstein and colleagues (2015), which indicated that physicians from various specialties in North Carolina had fairly dissimilar views on competency and that their confidence to guide such decisions was lacking. The point is well taken, especially given the fact that there remains an almost unbelievable absence of research or commentary pertaining to evaluation and treatment with non-violent, non-suicidal civilians who interact with firearms despite the plethora of literature on gun violence and the important prevention and policy recommendations set forth by the American Psychological and Psychiatric Associations. This is particularly striking given that exponentially more Americans safely interact with firearms than not. However, the existing and proposed laws and policies usually do not account for this reality; therefore, while informative, much of the principles extracted from the firearm-related violence and suicide literature bases will not be applicable to the vast majority of examinees, clients, and patients seen by mental health professionals. This reality has prompted us to develop a comprehensive, empirically based model of assessment (i.e., the Pirelli Firearm-10 [PF-10]) that covers the full range of considerations relevant to those who interact with firearms, which we present in the section that follows.[4]

Civilian

Although media coverage and the professional literature in a number of relevant fields pertain almost exclusively to gun violence and firearm-involved suicide and injury, the reality is that the vast majority of those who own or otherwise interact with firearms do so safely. As we have cited numerous times throughout this book, there are 100 million civilian firearm owners in the country, in addition to those who use firearms in places such as gun ranges, and even more active and retired federal agents and law enforcement, correctional, and military personnel—all of whom have interacted with firearms in some capacity. These very high numbers are compelling in the context of available firearm statistics. Namely, firearm-related deaths represent about 1% of all deaths in the United States each year. There are approximately 33,000 firearm-related deaths annually in the United States, two-thirds of which are suicides; and most of the remaining third are homicides, with relatively few being the result of accidents. And although this information does not get published, it is rather safe to assume that many (if not most) firearm-involved homicides are committed by those who do not have gun permits and who are often using unregistered firearms during the commission of their crimes.

When the numbers are demarcated in this way, it becomes quite clear that it is firearm-involved suicide and not violence that is the primary issue in this context. As such, it is also important to recall that certain noncivilian groups, such as law enforcement, correctional, and military populations, have appreciably higher suicide rates compared to their civilian counterparts. For the sake of argument, though, let us assume for a moment that all 33,000 firearm-involved deaths each year were attributed to licensed civilian firearm owners with registered guns. This would represent 0.03% of all civilian firearm owners. This is actually a gross overestimate, however, because licensed civilian firearm owners are not responsible for most firearm-involved homicides; and while they certainly contribute much more to the suicide statistics, we must also take into account the aforementioned consideration related to the notably higher suicide rates among law enforcement, correctional, and military populations.

But what is the relevance of these statistics in the present context? It is that, although much less than 1% of all civilians who own or otherwise operate firearms are responsible for firearm-involved deaths each year in this country, firearm-related laws and policies affect 100% of them. Whether this should or should not be the case is a moral argument in which we will not engage as it should be left to "we the people" to decide through elected officials and those responsible for enacting and enforcing relevant policies (e.g., police chiefs). In other words, the fact that a base rate associated with a given issue is exceedingly low does not necessarily mean that there should not be laws and regulations associated with it. Indeed, many of our laws and regulations are based on low-frequency but potentially high-impact events (e.g., restrictions pertaining to the storage of explosives, parameters related to regional evacuation plans and routes). Again, the extent to which risk should be managed and mitigated in a society should be up to its citizens and their chosen leaders—ideally, with input and guidance from clinicians, educators, and researchers. However, what is relevant here is the disproportionate attention paid in the professional literature, media, legislation, and national debate, more generally, to non-violent, non-suicidal civilians who own, seek to own, or otherwise interact with firearms. Of course, gun violence and firearm-related suicide are very important issues, and they should continue to be studied and discussed.

However, we cannot hope to appropriately address 99 people by solely focusing on the issues related to 1.

In the social science arena, we refer to this misstep as *base rate neglect*. It is also referred to as *base rate bias* or *fallacy*. This occurs when insufficient weight is given to the base rates and too much weight is given to new, case-specific information. This bias is commonplace in civilian firearm-related matters, especially as it pertains to new applicants who have been flagged for a particular, often benign and dated, reason. The following example represents a fairly typical type of evaluation case for one of us (G. P.).

Jason is a 42-year-old man who applies for a firearms purchaser identification card because he would like to begin to go hunting with some new neighbors who have done so as a group for many years. Therefore, he goes to his local police department and hands in his application along with all necessary documentation and authorizations. Two weeks later, Jason receives a call from the town's detective in charge of processing these applications and is informed that he has been flagged due to a 3-day psychiatric hospitalization 22 years ago. Jason is taken aback because, while he recalls going to the hospital for a few days when he was 20 because he experienced depressive symptoms in response to his mother's unexpected death, he did not recall ever being involuntarily committed. He is informed that whether he was committed voluntarily or involuntarily is not relevant but that he will need a "doctor's certification," regardless. Jason first seeks to attain the hospital records, but they no longer exist because his admission was so long ago. He then goes to his primary care physician to ask for a letter for the department, indicating that he is psychologically healthy and stable; but the doctor does not want to be associated with firearms applications. He then calls a number of local therapists and doctors, but very few are willing to conduct such an assessment and even fewer have any experience or training with firearms or firearm-related issues. Jason ultimately finds a psychiatrist who is willing to see him and write a letter. The doctor subsequently sees Jason for 45 minutes and provides him with a one-page letter solely focused on Jason's current mental health status, without any mention of firearms; his past hospitalization; most of his history, more generally; or any inclusion of collateral documentation or interview data. Jason provides this letter to the detective and, after 3 more weeks of waiting, receives a letter from the chief of police indicating that he has been denied.

This scenario is fairly common in our experience.[5] Some applicants will stop there. Others may hire an attorney to either appeal the denial or first seek an expungement of their records. They may also retain a forensic psychological evaluator to conduct an assessment and provide a report to accompany the legal filing. Still others choose to proceed solely with the evaluator and without legal representation (i.e., pro se). Nevertheless, a paramount feature in Jason's case related to the issue of base rate neglect was the hyperfocus on his 3-day hospitalization over two decades ago by both law enforcement and the psychiatrist. Recall that no one inquired about firearms at all. The focus was solely on the flagged issue (i.e., the prohibitor area), and therefore, the context disappeared. It did not matter that the base rate of firearm-involved violence and suicide among gun owners is exceedingly low. It did not matter that he was seeking a long gun rather than a handgun and the associated implications of such. Local norms were not taken into account (see Wechsler et al., 2015), nor were any specific factors related to Jason that would be associated with even further reduced violence and suicide risk. Namely, it was not relevant if the hospitalization was two decades ago or 2 years ago. It did not matter if Jason was a military sniper for 20 years or if he had never seen a gun in his life. It did not matter if his reason for seeking the permit in the first place was grounded in paranoid beliefs about his neighbors or if he had become well versed in firearm safety over the past year. What mattered was that he was flagged because a notation arose on a database—one that was also without context. The detective had no (nor did he seek any) information as to why Jason was hospitalized or his diagnosis, treatment plan, or prior or subsequent mental health histories. The detective had no information about the multitude of additional factors relevant when assessing risk, including, but not limited to, prior or current considerations of: violence, domestic violence, conduct problems or antisocial behavior, relationships, employment, education, substance use, trauma, violent attitudes, suicidality, treatment, medical problems, attitudes, and insight. It is important to note that, even if such information is available in a given case, mental health professionals must still be used to analyze and interpret it. Therefore, any flag whatsoever in any mental health–related prohibitor domain (e.g., mental health, substance abuse, suicide, violence, domestic violence) would require the involvement of a mental health expert to decipher. Moreover, practitioners who become involved in these matters must appreciate base rates in this area and local norms and conduct a context-specific, comprehensive assessment that includes factors above and beyond the flag in question as well as addressing firearm-specific issues, such as the ones we address in the guide we have developed, presented below (i.e., *Pirelli Firearm-10*). First, we briefly explain the two most common types of civilian firearm evaluation scenarios—for initial applicants and owners seeking reinstatement.

Initial Applicants

One of the most commonly occurring situations in the civilian firearms arena is the discovery of identified concerns during standard initial application procedures. There are at least four opportunities for a flag to arise in this context: (i) per the applicant's self-report on an application, (ii) during a criminal background check, (iii) during a mental health background check, or (iv) in a reference letter. The last possibility is certainly the least likely by far as most people only seek letters of support from those they know well and who they know will support their application. Anecdotally, the others seem fairly split in terms of their frequency. Applications vary across jurisdictions with respect to their specific items and the language used but often consist of very broad questions. For example, item 26 on the New Jersey Application for Firearms Purchaser Identification Card and/or Handgun Purchase Permit reads:

> Have you ever been attended, treated or observed by any doctor or psychiatrist or at any hospital or mental institution on an inpatient or outpatient basis for any mental or psychiatric condition? If yes, give the name and location of the doctor, psychiatrist, hospital or institution and the date(s) of such occurrence. (see www.njsp.org/firearms/pdf/sts-033. pdf)

These types of very broad inquiries lead applicants to make more or less conservative interpretations of the item. For instance, confusion often arises when a person has seen a mental health professional privately, especially in the context of family or couples therapy or individually, for a relatively benign matter. Another issue that arises here is when the applicant was required to see a mental health professional for a work-related evaluation. For example, police officers are typically sent for a psychiatric assessment after critical incidents, such as shootings. Are they required to report such on this item? Again, think of all of the situations wherein administrative or legally driven mental health therapy and evaluations may arise (e.g., divorce, child custody, workers' compensation, fitness-for-duty determination, employment harassment, and discrimination). What is relevant to consider here is that those who answer affirmatively to this type of item will likely be required to produce documentation indicating their appropriateness for firearm ownership. Even if police departments suggest that the applicant can simply "get a letter" from the prior therapist or evaluator, this presents a dilemma because the mental health professionals involved in the prior matters were not retained to evaluate firearm-related issues. They did not conduct an assessment consistent with such and, therefore, should not opine on the applicant's appropriateness for firearm ownership. Moreover, while some may be willing to memorialize the nature of their work with the applicant if they are provided with consent to do so, it is not uncommon for professionals to refuse to become involved with firearm-related matters at all.

Thus, the applicant would have to seek an independent psychological firearm evaluation, which should be comprehensive and extend well beyond the flagged issue alone. As a result, these applicants find themselves in a difficult place, whereby the police department may only be asking for a brief written assurance from the mental health professionals who saw them—but those professionals either will not or cannot properly opine as to their appropriateness for firearm ownership. Therefore, an applicant would either have to pay a significant amount of money to be evaluated by a forensic practitioner to issue a comprehensive report or essentially go "doctor shopping" and find a mental health professional who is willing to issue a letter based on a brief assessment for a lesser fee, which is not particularly advisable for the applicant or the practitioner given the inherently high liability involved in these matters. Of course, it is not advisable for applicants to be dishonest on their applications either as this behavior may result in not only a denial but also charges for falsification in some cases. And, certainly, these issues can arise in the context of other application items as well (e.g., domestic violence, criminal activity, substance abuse histories).

In addition to being flagged at the self-report application level, issues can arise during the course of criminal and mental health background checks. As noted, there are particular problems with records and context in these situations. Namely, increases in the numbers of databases that are accessed do not necessarily equate to more information but often simply more flags and questions. In many cases, records will no longer be available because of the amount of time that has transpired since the event(s) in question. This poses a problem for all involved, including an evaluator who is tasked with addressing said issue. We have already seen an increase in access of various types of records, including those that are very old, including, but not limited to, juvenile records. Recall that in his 2016 executive order, President Obama also sought to tap into Social Security Administration records and remove barriers to reporting from the Department of Health and Human Services. This widening of the net has led to some peculiar scenarios for some applicants as well as existing firearm owners. Take the following example of Brenda, which represents a situation we have seen a number of times.

Brenda is 34 years old and has been a police officer for 12 years with a good work record. She has always received positive evaluations, and she has never had any complaints or disciplinary actions taken against her. Moreover, her fitness for duty has never been questioned. She is well respected in the department and in the community, more generally. In addition to her department-issued service weapon, she owns two personal handguns, one of which was willed to her by her late father. Brenda was issued her (civilian) firearm and handgun permits approximately 10 years ago, and she has had the handguns since that time. Six months ago, Brenda applied for an additional handgun permit as she would like to purchase a more manageable off-duty firearm. However, she was informed by her local detective that she was flagged for having a hospitalization as a juvenile. This sent Brenda into a panic as she was now worried about her job security and not simply about obtaining another gun. She could not understand how this could have come up now, after going through an extensive hiring process by her employer (police department) years ago and application procedures for two handguns. She was in a situation in which she has owned and operated three firearms (one service and two personal) for over a decade but is now being told that she is not appropriate to seek another.

This vignette illustrates a problem that can and does occur for military, law enforcement, and corrections personnel as well as civilians, more generally. It is an awkward scenario whereby the person may essentially be allowed to maintain his or her existing firearms, while being flagged as inappropriate to seek another. We have seen this with law enforcement, corrections, and military personnel as well as civilians who have dealer licenses and handle firearms daily but are not allowed to "personally" own them. In some cases like Brenda's, the person may seek an expungement, if such is possible. In other cases, he or she may either withdraw the application or seek to provide a professional clearance to the issuing department. The person may also seek an appeal if he or she was actually denied, although it is often the case that the process is paused when a flag arises and, therefore, no formal denial is set forth. Nevertheless, whether the person seeks an expungement, appeal, or to resubmit the application with a professional clearance, a formal psychological firearm evaluation conducted by a practitioner trained in this area is warranted.

Reinstatement (Forfeiture)

A second set of firearm evaluations pertain to those seeking reinstatement of their firearm permits, licenses, and/or firearms subsequent to their revocation. Perhaps the most commonly occurring situations in this context are those that pertain to domestic violence or psychiatric hospitalizations. However, there are countless scenarios associated with any one of the firearm prohibitor areas that could lead to a revocation, such as mental health–, substance abuse–, suicide–, violence–, and domestic violence–related issues. In many of these cases, the issue will arise when law enforcement is called to someone's home and firearms are present. As such, domestic violence calls are likely to prompt officers to ask if there is a firearm in the home, regardless of whether or not the situation involved firearms or threats associated with such. In many cases, though, officers cannot take a person's firearms without permission, unless they have a court order to do so or are acting in accordance with emergency procedures (see Chapter 5 in this book for a comprehensive review of issues in the domestic and intimate partner violence context). In other cases, the issue of firearm ownership may arise during the course of a mental health or medical screening at the community, outpatient, or inpatient level. In some of these situations, law enforcement personnel are present (e.g., on-site assessments in the community by mobile response teams or at crisis centers or psychiatric emergency rooms), but this is not typically the case (e.g., during mental health intakes or therapy sessions in a variety of outpatient and inpatient settings). These scenarios bring up mental health professionals' duty-to-warn-and-protect requirements associated with breaking client confidentiality, which are highly variable across jurisdictions. In most cases, however, a treating or examining professional is required to break confidentiality and report concerns about a client when there exists an imminent threat or risk to an identifiable third party or when he or she poses a foreseeable risk of self-injury. What is less clear and variable is how the duty is discharged by the professional. In states such as New Jersey, the professional can do so by arranging for the client's voluntary admission into a qualified psychiatric facility, initiating involuntary commitment procedures to a qualified psychiatric facility, or advising local law enforcement of the patient's threat and the identity of the intended victim (N.J.S.A. 2A: 62A-16). Proposed bills are also being set forth in some jurisdictions to expand the reporting role of practitioners in firearm-related contexts (e.g., see N.J. Assemb. A2938, 2016).[6]

In a civilian firearm reinstatement evaluation, the ultimate issue is related to a person's risk of engaging in future violence or self-injurious behavior in light of the event or concern that led to the revocation (e.g., a domestic violence incident, suicide attempt, destruction of property). In these evaluations, the suitability of reinstating a license and returning a firearm to the person is considered in the context of the identifiable concern or event, which would not usually be the case in evaluations for initial applicants. Although suicide and violence risk is certainly relevant in evaluations for initial applicants, other factors associated with firearm ownership may be just as salient in the absence of a history of violence or self-injury (e.g., the reason for seeking the license, experience with and plans for the use and storage of the firearm, plans for developing increased competence/continuing education regarding firearm use and safety). In reinstatement evaluations, these other factors are more likely to be overshadowed by the referral incidents. Consider the following example.

Warren is 27 years old, and he has had a firearms purchaser permit for 3 years. He owns a shotgun he uses for skeet shooting and a rifle for hunting, both of which he keeps in a large safe in the garage. He has been dating his girlfriend, Sandra, for 2 years; but their relationship has always been fairly rocky, such that they engage in verbal altercations multiple times per week. For the first time, however, their fighting escalated and became physical. Namely, 6 weeks ago, Sandra pushed Warren, prompting him to hold her down and scream at her, followed by him throwing her keys into the yard and smashing her cell phone on the deck. She stormed out of the house, drove down the street, and called the police. Sandra told the dispatcher that she was fearful of Warren because of his behavior, and she also noted that he owned guns. The responding police officers took statements, and although they found no basis for an arrest, they asked Warren if they could hold onto his firearms until the situation was settled; but he did not agree to this. Nevertheless, unbeknown to him, Sandra informed the officers that she wished to seek a temporary restraining order (TRO), which was ultimately granted and led to the revocation of Warren's permit and firearms anyhow. However, the couple reconciled within a month, Sandra dropped the TRO, and she began to help Warren find an attorney and a forensic evaluator in an effort to reclaim his firearms.

The case presented here is not an uncommon occurrence, particularly given the vacillation in relationship dynamics and sentiments that often occurs in domestic situations. It is not uncommon for TROs to be either dismissed or dropped relatively soon after they are granted, for example. At times, we have also found that the person who made the initial complaint and sought the TRO later advocates strongly for the reinstatement of the other party's permit and guns. As we discussed in Chapter 5, misdemeanor domestic and intimate partner violence scenarios (and those that do not result in charges at all) have a fairly weak correlation with firearm-related violence. Of course, context is key, and every situation requires an independent assessment in this regard; however, the vignette above is illustrative. The referral incident in this case did not involve a firearm at any level, nor did it consist of threats related to such. The couple has had a problematic relationship, although it has always been only verbally so up to this point. This was the first physical incident perpetrated by both parties, and, in fact, Angela initiated the physical altercation. Regardless of who is responsible, however, what is relevant to what we are addressing here is that in a reinstatement evaluation like this the focus will undoubtedly be on the relationship dynamics between the two parties and additional domestic violence–related risk factors associated with the person seeking reinstatement. Of course, we still recommend conducting a comprehensive psychological firearm evaluation, in which the full range of firearm-specific and prohibitor factors are addressed—just as in the case of an initial applicant. However, there must be increased focus paid to the issues surrounding the referral incident and associated risk factors in reinstatement evaluations. Moreover, it is important to point out that, in many of these cases, the use of formal risk assessment measures is now possible because the behaviors in question will likely be consistent with their definitions of violence or domestic violence.

Before turning to a review of the firearm evaluation guide we have developed, it is worth noting that options have become available for those who would benefit from safely storing their firearms outside of the home. For instance, Gun Sitters (n.d.), is a New Jersey–based company that offers firearms storage options for those involved in various situations, including precarious ones. Namely, the company maintains a very high-security storage facility for those in the midst of moving or involved in estate transitions (e.g., inherited firearms as family heirlooms), those going on vacations or military deployments, and those experiencing marital or legal problems. Although this option is not possible in some cases, such as once firearms are already revoked or court-ordered to be revoked, it can be a very useful option for those seeking to prevent such. This type of short- and long-term storage capability also provides evaluators with an additional option when making recommendations. Perhaps, instead of feeling they have to opine that the person should or should not have their firearms returned, they can consider recommending storage for a period of further observation or treatment. While this appears to be a promising idea, these facilities have yet to become available in most places. Moreover, it may not be an option at all in some cases, particularly in the context of legal matters. As such, it may serve as more of a preventive or proactive opportunity for some people rather than a viable option for evaluators to recommend at this time. Thus, mental health clinicians and medical practitioners should be aware of these type of storage facilities because they will be the ones who have the opportunity to intervene *before* a problem arises, whereas it will usually be too late by the time forensic evaluators become involved. Nevertheless, it is a very worthy option to explore in many cases.

Other noteworthy types of programs to point out include New York City's Cash for Guns program, whereby the New York City Police Department pays $100 to those, excluding active law enforcement personnel and gun dealers, who present guns in operative condition to any precinct, transit district, or police service area, 24-hours a day, 7 days per week. People can surrender as many guns as they want, but cash reimbursement is made for a maximum of three weapons. Of particular note is that no questions are asked and no identification is required as the identity of all individuals will remain anonymous (Gun buyback program, n.d.). These programs have been adopted across the country, but despite their popularity and feel-good nature, many contend that the empirical research simply does not support their effectiveness (Master, 2015; Wogan, 2013; Horn, 2013). Indeed, Kuhn and colleagues (2002) investigated buyback programs in Milwaukee County in the mid-1990s and found that the handguns recovered in the programs were not those most commonly associated with firearm-involved homicides and suicides. Therefore, they concluded that, while buyback programs may increase awareness of firearm-related violence, the relatively scarce resources designated for firearm injury prevention may be better allocated in other ways.

Models of Risk Assessment

Evaluators may employ unstructured, semistructured, or structured approaches to assess psycholegal constructs, such as appropriateness for firearm ownership. Although our conceptualization of firearm ownership suitability evaluations includes the assessment of firearm-specific factors as well as those associated with examinees' response styles, mental health, and substance use, these evaluations must be grounded in risk assessment principles. This is the case because the laws we are addressing in these contexts are primarily based on prohibitors associated with violence and suicide risk. As we have discussed, concerns related to accidental injury and death as a result of improper storage or handling are relevant (e.g., child access prevention laws), but the overarching focus is that of the more purposeful risk to self or others. We maintain that violence and suicide risk assessment in firearm evaluations is necessary but not sufficient given that most examinees will not have engaged in behaviors associated with these areas and that, therefore, additional factors should be addressed to conduct comprehensive firearm evaluations. Before we turn to the guide we have developed to assist those conducting these assessments, it is useful to provide a brief overview of violence risk assessment models to illustrate how the mental health field has developed in this regard and, ultimately, the way in which we developed our approach.

Various violence risk assessment models were developed throughout the 20th century, and methods to assess risk have been characterized as first, second, third, and fourth generation (Bonta & Andrews, 2007). The first-generation method of risk assessment refers to unstructured professional judgment, which was employed during most of the first half of the 1900s

(Grove et al., 2000; Rice, 1997). Within the context of this method, mental health professionals collect data from clinical interviews and other relevant sources and ultimately make judgments about a person's level of risk based on their professional training and experience (i.e., clinical intuition).

In the 1970s, actuarial, evidence-based assessment instruments were developed to replace the unstructured methods that were traditionally employed (Bonta & Andrews, 2007). This is considered the second generation of risk assessment. Much research was conducted on violence risk, particularly aimed at identifying which factors were most closely associated with violence and violent recidivism (e.g., those factors found to be most heavily weighted in statistical regression models). As such, actuarial assessment measures include static (i.e., historical, stable) factors that have been found to be correlated with violence and violent recidivism. The inclusion of static factors alone is not what constitutes an actuarial measure, however. A measure is considered actuarial if item scores are added to produce a total score that is associated with a probability, or quantitative estimate, of risk (Heilbrun, 2009). An example of an actuarial measure is the Violence Risk Appraisal Guide (Harris, Rice, & Quinsey, 1993; Quinsey, Harris, Rice, & Cornier, 1998).

Research demonstrated that actuarial risk assessment instruments were superior to unstructured clinical judgment in the prediction of violence (Bonta & Andrews, 2007; Heilbrun, 2009). As a result, a professional debate ensued over the utility of clinical versus actuarial methods of risk assessment. The seminal work of Paul Meehl (1954) regarding clinical versus statistical prediction was often cited to support the advantage of actuarial methods; however, arguments in this regard were largely misconstrued because what was referred to as clinical prediction or decision-making was typically unstructured clinical judgment as opposed to structured clinical judgment (Westen & Weinberger, 2004). Nevertheless, at least two shortcomings of second-generation, or actuarial, measures are identifiable: (i) they are atheoretical and (ii) they include static, or historical, factors, which do not account for recent or current changes in patients that may affect risk levels (e.g., treatment progress).

Test developers and researchers recognized these shortcomings and began to account for dynamic risk factors (i.e., current, changeable), thereby setting the stage for the third-generation risk assessment instruments (Andrews, Bonta, & Wormith, 2006; Bonta, 2002; Bonta & Andrews, 2007). These measures included static and dynamic factors as well as factors related to risk management and reduction. Included in this category is what is referred to as "structured professional judgment" (SPJ) measures. SPJ measures include empirically derived static and dynamic risk factors; however, scores are not aggregated (i.e., total scores are not used for clinical purposes). On an SPJ measure, a significant elevation on one risk factor may result in a patient being deemed high risk. An example of an SPJ measure is the Historical, Clinical, Risk Management-20, Version 3 (HCR-20^{v3}; Douglas, Hart, Webster, & Belfrage, 2013). Accounting for dynamic risk factors provides the evaluator with the ability to consider how the patient's present level of functioning affects his or her level of risk; it also allows the evaluator to estimate how a change in such factors may ultimately reduce risk level. This is critically important as we must consider risk, protective, static, and dynamic factors when assessing violence risk and focus on *prevention* rather than *prediction*. As Skeem & Monahan (2011) articulated it:

> The violence risk assessment field may be reaching a point of diminishing returns in instrument development. We might speculate that incremental advances could be made by exploring novel assessment methods, including implicit measures (Nock et al., 2010) or simple heuristics (Goldstein & Gigerenzer, 2009). But specific structured techniques seem to account for very little of the variance in predictive accuracy. If we are approaching a ceiling in this domain, there clearly are miles to go on the risk reduction front. We hope that forensic psychology shifts more of its attention from predicting violence to understanding its causes and preventing its (re)occurrence. (p. 41)

It is for these reasons and because our firearm evaluation approaches must be flexible enough to meet the demands of specific cases and legal standards that we have decided to model our guide consistent with an SPJ approach. Unstructured clinical assessment approaches are substandard and, therefore, out of the question. Actuarial approaches may have merit in certain contexts but are too limited in most firearm evaluation contexts for various reasons, including, but not necessarily limited to, the following: (i) they are premised on predictive rather than preventive models, and firearm-involved violence and suicide are extremely low base rate behaviors that do not lend themselves to prediction with any reasonable level of scientific accuracy; (ii) they tend to rely on static, or historical, risk factors rather than dynamic factors that are present- and future-oriented; (iii) they require the aggregation of item scores to be compared to a normative group—data that simply do not exist in this arena; and (iv) they require examinees to meet specific criteria based on definitions (e.g., violence) that do not apply to the vast majority of firearm applicants. It may be the case that actuarial measures can be incorporated in some firearm evaluations, particularly for those seeking reinstatement after a problematic incident, but they will still prove to be insufficient because they will not capture the full realm of factors relevant to assess in firearm-related matters. This area of assessment typically requires a more flexible, albeit evidence-based, approach but one that is also inclusive—in other words, one that provides evaluators with a semistructured format and a specific set of domains to address but also encourages them to use additional, supplemental measures as needed (e.g., measures of violence, domestic violence, and suicide risk; response style; psychopathology; substance use problems). It is also essential that firearm evaluations formally address firearm-specific factors. These are the types of considerations that led us to develop a specialized guide for those conducting firearm evaluations.

Pirelli Firearm-10 (PF-10)

The Pirelli Firearm-10 (PF-10) is a structured professional judgment guide designed to assist practitioners conducting firearm evaluations with civilians who are either first-time applicants or seeking to have their firearms reinstated. It may also have utility in other firearm-related matters, such as with law enforcement, correctional, governmental, and armed security personnel (see the following section, *Considerations for Law Enforcement and Related Professions*). The PF-10 consists of a 10-domain framework to be incorporated along with a semistructured interview for conducting firearm evaluations, which represents a specific type of FMHA. As noted above, the conceptual basis for the measure is grounded in the prohibitor areas typically included in firearm laws (i.e., domestic violence, violence, suicide risk; notable mental health or substance use concerns) as well as a number of firearm-specific factors. The PF-10 also identifies the assessment of response style as a specific, independent domain given its utmost importance in FMHAs. The conceptual model underlying the PF-10 is depicted in Figure 7.1.

Although there are seven overarching areas that comprise the conceptual framework of the PF-10, there are actually 10 domains assessed with the guide because the firearm-specific factors are addressed across four distinct item areas. These are presented in list form below, followed by a relatively detailed discussion of each item area.

1. Reason(s) for seeking licensure/reinstatement
2. Exposure to firearms
3. Knowledge of and perspectives on firearm safety precautions and relevant firearm regulations
4. Firearm use: experience, intent for use, storage, and continued education
5. Response style
6. Violence risk

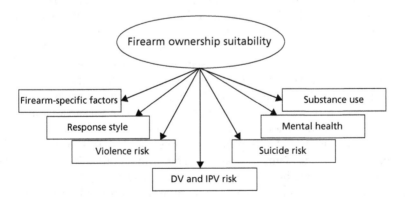

Figure 7.1. Pirelli Firearm-10 Conceptual Model of Firearm Suitability

  7. Domestic and intimate partner violence risk
  8. Suicide risk
  9. Mental health
  10. Substance use

1. Reason(s) for Seeking Licensure/Reinstatement

Evaluators must distinguish between initial applicants and those seeking re-instatement as those seeking reinstatement have likely lost their permit and/or firearm as a result of a particular circumstance, which would likely be the primary focus of the evaluation. It is critical to inquire about the examinee's reason(s) for seeking ownership of a firearm. Although evaluators should not impose moral judgments in this regard, the evaluator should assess the rationality of the examinee's intentions from a clinical standpoint. As such, we are focused more on the examinee's thought *process* than *content* within this particular domain. Certainly, some reasons for licensure or reinstatement will be problematic on their face (e.g., clearly paranoid or otherwise psychotic statements), but a fair amount of leeway should be given here. In other words, it generally should not matter to the evaluator if the examinee is seeking firearms for hunting, shooting sports, self-defense, or other legal purposes, unless there is a case-specific concern in this regard. The explanation behind the examinee's reason is what is of particular relevance, and someone can evidence a concerning thought process in the context of any one of these reasons.

Furthermore, the nature of the questions for those seeking a firearm for hunting or shooting sport purposes will usually differ compared to questions for those interested in self-defense. For instance, perceived risk of criminal victimization and a history of robbery victimization increase the probability of obtaining a firearm for self-protection (Kleck, Kovandzic, Saber, & Hauser, 2011). Thus, perceived risk is a powerful motivator and potentially a greater source of motivation to obtain a firearm than leisure or social reasons. Therefore, the examinee's motivation to obtain a firearm will affect the type of information the evaluator will seek.

In addition, evaluators should ask about the type of firearm being sought, which will inform the evaluator's subsequent inquiries as well as his or her ultimate opinions. For example, handguns are more likely than long guns to be involved in homicides. As we have noted a number of times, however, it is essential that evaluators who choose to practice in this area familiarize themselves with the relevant language and considerations associated with firearms. For instance, it is important to understand what is meant by such terms as "AR-15" and "semiautomatic" and how much ammunition is typically contained in a single box. Absent such context and perspective, evaluators' biases, misinformation, and general unawareness of firearm basics are likely to lead to ill-informed opinions.

2. Exposure to Firearms

As we have noted throughout this chapter, cultural considerations are particularly important in forensic work, and this is particularly true in firearm evaluations. Examinees' exposure to firearms is likely to have impacted their perceptions and views in this context. For instance, some people grew up in environments where hunting was an important part of their lives and family heritage. Others were raised in military or law enforcement families. And, of course, some may have been negatively exposed to firearms in the context of criminal activity, such as street gangs or organized crime. Others still may not have had previous exposure to firearms at all. Once again, there is not necessarily a right or wrong set of experiences here—the law certainly does not require any prior exposure in most cases; rather, this domain provides the evaluator with important context for the rest of the firearm-specific aspects of the evaluation.

Undoubtedly, negative exposure has been found to be correlated with problematic outcomes. For example, Garbarino, Bradshaw, & Vorrasi (2002) asserted that "exposure to gun violence also can desensitize youth to the effects of violence and increase the likelihood that they will use violence as a means of resolving problems or expressing emotions" (p. 74). Nevertheless, this is in contrast to prosocial or positive exposure, which has implications for learning and safety. Many examinees will have been exposed to firearms from an early age, as in the case of children of law enforcement officers and hunters; and they may very well have a positive association with them. Moreover, like most childhood learning in the home, they will have likely benefited from positive modeling in this regard (e.g., safety, handling, and general respect for firearms).

3. Knowledge of and Perspectives on Firearm Safety Precautions and Relevant Firearm Regulations

It is relevant to ascertain the examinee's base knowledge of and views on firearm safety as well as regulations, including local and federal laws. Again, there is no minimal requirement of knowledge here in most cases, especially not in the context of a clinical-forensic evaluation; however, the purpose of this domain is to provide the evaluator with yet another opportunity to assess the examinee's thought processes related to these areas.

Applicants should be assessed not solely by their experience with and exposure to firearms but also on their perspectives, which have likely been shaped by such experiences. We know that people's attitudes and perspectives affect their violence and suicide risk levels. For instance, researchers have found that antisocial and pro-violent attitudes, as well as social–cognitive distortions such as misperceiving hostile and/or aggressive intent or justification of criminal acts, can increase violence risk (Borum & Verhaagen, 2006; Dodge & Pettit, 2003). Factors in this domain should be considered in the context of the examinee's experience with and exposure to firearms, as well as his or her cultural and individual perspectives on violence and firearm usage. This domain should also include a review of any firearm safety, education, or instructional courses or session in which the examinee has engaged at any point.

Furthermore, prospective and current firearm owners should be adequately versed in federal and state law. That said, laws are ever-changing, complex, and voluminous; therefore, the examinee should not be expected to be a junior lawyer but rather should exhibit a general awareness and understanding of the most basic and critical laws. For instance, someone who has or would ever have children in his or her home should know child access prevention and storage laws. Moreover, all examinees should have a general appreciation for certain types of critical laws, such as those related to carry and transit. Again, it is not the evaluator's job to "test" the examinee's knowledge, but these inquiries are relevant to assessing one's judgment and decision-making abilities. It may be the case that the examinee is unaware of certain restrictions and requirements but is able to convey the ways in which he or she can go about acquiring the information. It is also important to note that this consideration may have already been addressed in situations in which an applicant has passed a written and/or hands-on examination as part of the application or reinstatement process. Regardless, it behooves evaluators practicing in this area to also become familiar with relevant firearm laws in order to adequately assess examinees' levels of knowledge.

In addition, this item calls for evaluators to inquire about examinees' perspectives on firearm laws and regulations and not solely their knowledge of such. Once again, a level of moral disengagement by the evaluator is critical here. Evaluators should develop opinions or judgments based not on examinees' positions on firearm regulations and laws per se but rather on their reasoning abilities when discussing them. In other words, someone can clearly and cogently explain his or her disagreement with particular laws or regulations, whereas another person may embrace a particular regulation but exhibit a problematic thought process when doing so. People are allowed to disagree with laws and regulations, even vehemently so; what they are not permitted to do is violate them. Therefore, addressing examinees' general knowledge and perspectives in this regard may provide clinical insights that inform the evaluation as a whole.

4. Firearm Use: Experience, Intent for Use, Storage, and Continued Education

This domain provides an opportunity for the evaluator to assess the examinee's personal (direct) experience with firearms as well as intent for use, storage, and education moving forward. For instance, it is relevant to know information such as the fact that someone has interacted with firearms for many years without any problems, especially if this was the case during the referral incident period. Once again, this is not a legal requirement, nor should it be clinically used against someone if he or she has never interacted with a firearm before; however, ascertaining this information will provide much context to the overall evaluation. It is also certainly relevant to gain perspective on how the examinee intends to use and store firearms moving forward, should he or she be approved to have them, and if he or she has any aspirations to learn more about firearms. As we have noted in the previous item, issues related to use and storage have legal and clinical implications; therefore, this item is aimed at determining how examinees plan on managing their own firearms. Also, just as an examinee does not need to have any direct prior experience with firearms, he or she will not be legally required to engage in continued education in most cases. Nevertheless, this is still a relevant area of inquiry in the context of a comprehensive psychological firearm evaluation.

While firearm operators and owners with more than minimal competence in the handling of firearms may be desirable, such considerations are largely dependent on intended use. For instance, an applicant who intends to use a rifle regularly during a particular hunting season would be expected to have a relatively high level of competence using that type of firearm compared to someone seeking to acquire a handgun for home protection only and, therefore, will likely never fire it outside of a practice range (if at all). This is not to say that competence is not important in all cases but rather that its significance is relative. Similar to the sentiment of previous PF-10 items, this is not a test of an examinee's competence to use a firearm, but a full assessment of a person's appropriateness for firearm ownership must account for a range of firearm- and context-specific factors.

It is important to assess the extent to which a person plans to uphold responsible firearm practices. Consistent with the NRA's Gun Safety Rules, it is particularly important to evaluate examinees' specific plans, including where the firearm and the ammunition will be kept, how it will be maintained, the anticipated frequency of use, and who will have access to it. Additional considerations may also be relevant in a given case, such as how children in the home will be introduced to and educated about the presence of a firearm or if anyone with any notable risk factors (e.g., history of violence, serious mental illness, and/or substance abuse) may have access. Per the American Academy of Pediatrics' Bright Future Pocket Guide (Hagan, Shaw, & Duncan, 2008), which includes recommendations for parents who keep firearms in the home, access to guns in the home increases the risk for suicide among adolescents. However, it has been contended that safe storage and preventing access to firearms reduce up to 70% of injuries (American Psychological Association, 2013a). Therefore, reviewing considerations within this domain with the examinee will provide useful information and context in these evaluations.

Evaluators should review collateral documentation if available and applicable, such as any firearm-related written or physical tests taken by examinees. Also, note that most (if not all) states require a hunter safety course and that some require firearms training prior to purchasing or acquiring a handgun.

For example, California's Basic Firearms Safety Certificate Program requires people to have a Handgun Safety Certificate, which is attained by passing a written test on firearm safety as well as successfully performing a safe handling demonstration (California Department of Justice, Office of the Attorney General, 2015). With regard to inquiring about the examinees' plans for seeking continued education, evaluators can ask about their plans for future firearm-related training and instruction, including frequenting shooting ranges, taking formal classes, and learning more from family or friends or via reading-related materials. The interested reader should note that the NRA provides access to an online database of education and training courses held throughout the country.

5. Response Style

As with any forensic evaluation, assessment of response style is paramount and consistent with the highest standards of practice in the field (Heilbrun, 2001; Heilbrun et al., 2009, 2014; Melton et al., 2007). There are many ways in which examinees may present in an evaluation session, and therefore, a number of different response style types have been delineated. A leading scholar in this area of study is Dr. Richard Rogers of the University of North Texas. For many years, he and his colleagues have contributed significantly to the professional literature pertaining to response styles, particularly in the form of his seminal text *Clinical Assessment of Malingering and Deception*, which is now in its fourth edition (Rogers & Bender, 2018). As articulated it in the opening line of the text, "Complete and accurate self-disclosure is a rarity even in the uniquely supportive context of a psychotherapeutic relationship"; and he also noted that "Most individuals engage in a variety of response styles that reflect their personal goals in a particular setting" (p. 3). Moreover, "In summary, all individuals fall short of full and accurate self-disclosure, irrespective of the social context" (p. 4). Rogers and his co-contributors go on to provide readers with a wide range of considerations related to the assessment of response styles across settings and populations, such as in the context of numerous mental health diagnoses, traumatic brain injury, substance abuse conditions, medical situations, and with children, sex offenders, and law enforcement personnel.

Given its importance, we have specifically demarcated this item because we recommend formally evaluating examinees' response styles in firearm evaluations, when possible. This can be accomplished in various ways, including by using an assessment instrument that contains validity scales, many of which will be additionally useful in assessing for the suicide, mental health, and substance use domains that follow. Most practitioners will be familiar with the concept of malingering, as previously described; but it would be very unlikely for examinees to engage in it in the firearms context because they usually want to present as healthy and stable. What would be more likely is the presence of *positive impression management* in these contexts, whereby the examinee may minimize his or her shortcomings and attempt to appear as better adjusted and psychologically healthier than he or she actually is. However, evaluators must be attuned to the reality that many people want to appear free of problems during the course of a forensic evaluation; therefore, it is incumbent on the evaluator to not make broad-based judgments about an examinee's truthfulness based on a single validity scale score, for example, particularly if the score is only somewhat elevated. It is critical to compare and contrast interview and collateral data. As with any clinical construct, evaluators must seek to gather data from multiple sources to determine if there is convergence or divergence. This consideration is relevant for all domains within this firearm evaluation framework, such that an evaluator should analyze information gathered from the interview (i.e., the examinee's self-report and behavioral observations) as well as information from available records and from interviews with collateral informants (e.g., family, friends, treating professionals).

6. Violence Risk

Most people diagnosed with mental illnesses per the *Diagnostic and Statistical Manual of Mental Disorders*, fifth edition (DSM-5; American Psychiatric Association, 2013) are not violent or "dangerous." Indeed, there are over 300 disorders listed across more than 900 pages, including learning disorders, eating disorders, sleep disorders, phobias, and various other conditions that have no ostensible connection to violence, especially firearm-involved violence. Even those conditions that are more associated with violence (e.g., disruptive, impulse control, and conduct disorders; antisocial personality disorder; and certain substance use disorders) are not necessarily dispositive of violence, including that which involves firearms. Moreover, according to the Department of Justice, 82% of those convicted of felonies in state courts in 2004 were characterized as "non-violent" felons, and it is also unclear how many non-violent ex-felons commit subsequent violent felonies because the literature in this area is lacking (see Bone, 2010).

Nevertheless, many years of research support the notion that evaluators are at least moderately able to identify individuals who are likely to commit serious acts of violence via conducting risk assessments. Although an assessment of violence (and suicide) risk represents only one aspect of a firearm ownership evaluation, it is an essential component. The reasons for this are self-evident and, therefore, will not be detailed here; but evaluators must decide how they will formally assess risk. However, for many of the reasons we have outlined throughout this chapter, most formal violence risk assessment measures will not be usable other than, perhaps, in reinstatement evaluations, where the examinee has committed an act of violence. Therefore, a measure such as the HCR-20[V3] (Douglas et al. 2013) may be more generally useful as an aide-memoire because it includes empirically based items related to violence risk. Regardless of the measure selected or approach employed, both individual and situational risk factors should be considered contemporaneously, in the adherence of a context-specific, idiographic assessment. This is imperative considering that empirical research has shown that acts of targeted violence are often carried out by individuals who are experiencing personal problems accompanied by feelings of desperation (American Psychological Association, 2013a).

With respect to violence risk factors, measures such as the HCR-20^{V3} delineate them into domains that account for issues related to the examinee's past, present, and future. Namely, the historical section (H) of the HCR-20^{V3} includes items related to past violence, antisocial behavior, relationships, employment, substance use, mental health diagnoses, traumatic experiences, violent attitudes, and treatment or supervision response. Its clinical section (C) accounts for current levels of insight, violent ideation or intent, mental health symptoms, instability, and treatment or supervision response. The final section pertains to factors associated with risk management (R), which are future-oriented factors to consider, namely, professional services and plans, living situation, personal support, treatment or supervision response, and stress or coping. Taken together, these are 20 empirically grounded factors associated with risk of engaging in future violence. However, it is important to point out the fact that violence risk does not necessarily equate to firearm-involved violence risk. Evaluators must take a step further to incorporate case-specific factors, the professional gun violence literature, and local norms to properly account for this domain on the PF-10.

Although published measures and structured guides may be very useful to incorporate when possible, evaluators must also assess case-specific data, such as risk factors unique to the examinee that may not specifically be captured by a particular risk assessment measure (e.g., threats involving firearms, recent problems in the workplace, an ongoing problem with a debtor). Evaluators should not only assess risk in context but also set forth opinions in context. In other words, it is insufficient (and often misleading) to opine that an examinee poses a violence risk. The thought must be completed: risk to *whom? when? where? why?* This clinical decision-making process is what Douglas and colleagues (2013) refer to as developing "likely scenarios"—that is, providing a context and accounting for *motivators, disinhibitors,* and *destabilizers.* A primary motivator in a case may be a person's intense desire to seek revenge, for example. Disinhibitors may relate to the person's negative self-concept, general alienation/isolated lifestyle, lack of insight and awareness, and lack of empathy. Destabilizers may be disturbed perceptions about the target of his or her anger, impaired reasoning and problem-solving in this matter, and unwavering, perseverative thoughts. This violence risk assessment model and type of case conceptualization may be applicable and quite useful in the context of assessing various types of violence risk, including, but not limited to, domestic and intimate partner violence (i.e., item 7).

7. Domestic and Intimate Partner Violence Risk

As we discussed in great detail in Chapter 5 of this book, problematic firearm use has been found to be associated with domestic violence (DV) and intimate partner violence (IPV) in some cases, particularly in the most serious matters. In addition to being a prohibitor in many legal statutes related to firearm ownership and use, the presence of DV or IPV in an examinee's history or in his or her current life certainly has clinical relevance. That said, the empirical literature tends to cite the more serious and violent situations as being a concern in this regard as opposed to those of the non-violent or minimally violent type (e.g., misdemeanors, dismissed or dropped restraining orders). Still, the presence of such constructs as power and control as well as serious physical violence (e.g., choking, beating) would certainly raise serious concerns about an examinee's suitability to possess a firearm.

In fact, the concept of gun violence restraining orders (GVROs) has been developed within the past few years (see Frattaroli, McGinty, Barnhorst, & Greenberg, 2015). This allows family members or intimate partners to request GVROs through the civil justice system if they observe behavior that they believe may be a precursor to violence. Once the court issues a GVRO, law enforcement is authorized to remove firearms from the respondent's possession, and he or she is prohibited from purchasing new guns. In September 2014, California's AB1014 was the first law to be enacted allowing GRVOs to be issued in an effort to prevent gun violence. As we have addressed throughout this book, especially in Chapter 2, there are a number of existing laws across the country that provide judges and law enforcement officers with discretion in DV and IPV cases. Of course, every jurisdiction also has a mechanism for traditional protective orders. However, the GVRO concept is one specifically geared toward concerns associated with firearm-involved violence.

As with all laws and regulations, however, much is left to interpretation; and appeals are permitted in most cases. Therefore, even cases involving mandatory, non-discretionary removal of firearms may be contested in a courtroom at some point. As such, forensic evaluators are likely to be called to conduct psychological firearm assessments. In these cases, formal violence risk assessment measures are likely to be applicable if the examinee was, in fact, accused of or charged with committing an act of violence. General risk assessment measures may be used in these cases; however, there are a number of published tools available specific to DV and IPV situations. For example, the Spousal Assault Risk Assessment, Version 3 (Kropp & Hart, 2015) is a structured professional judgment measure that was created by the same group that developed the HCR-20^{V3} and the Domestic Violence Risk Appraisal Guide (Hilton et al., 2008), and it is an actuarial measure that was developed specifically for use in this context. In addition, the Centers for Disease Control and Prevention provides a useful resource of measures that may be useful for evaluators' assessing DV- and IPV-related concerns (Basile, Hertz, & Back, 2007). Evaluation of issues within this domain should parallel the same type of form, approach, and case conceptualization involved with assessing violence and suicide risk within the PF-10 framework (items 6 and 8, respectively). As with those items, however, it is essential to highlight the fact that DV risk does not necessarily equate to firearm-involved DV risk. This requires an additional analysis and incorporation of case-specific factors, local norms, and the literature related to firearm-involved DV and IPV situations.

8. Suicide Risk

The contemporary empirical literature continues to suggest that the link between suicide and firearms is much stronger than that of violence (e.g., see Gold & Simon, 2016)—a concept we detailed extensively in Chapter 6 of this book. All clinicians should be aware that *access to weapons* is a primary consideration and area of inquiry to follow when assessing suicide risk, especially in terms of suicidal intent and presence of a plan. Therefore, evaluators are strongly encouraged to assess for suicide risk when conducting firearm evaluations and to develop their professional competence as it relates to firearm issues so that they can more adequately evaluate it in context and ask a series of informed questions in this regard.

Nevertheless, the title of the APA's November 2016 press release speaks for itself: "After Decades of Research, Science Is No Better Able to Predict Suicidal Behaviors" (American Psychological Association, 2016). The announcement was based on a recently published meta-analysis of 50 years of research in this area, whereby Franklin and colleagues (2017) analyzed 365 studies and concluded that suicide risk prediction was "only slightly better than chance for all outcomes" and "predictive ability has not improved across 50 years of research" (p. 187). For many forensic practitioners and researchers, this is not a particularly surprising or compelling finding as many of us have already moved from predictive to prevention-based approaches in the context of violence risk assessment (see Skeem & Monahan, 2011). As noted, this is a primary reason we endorse a structured professional judgment approach to conducting psychological firearm evaluations rather than one that relies on actuarial methods.

In addition to simply determining if an examinee has access to firearms, evaluators must ascertain if the person has planned or otherwise prepared to self-harm. A comprehensive suicide risk assessment will include identification and analysis of risk factors, warning signs, and protective factors, which are factors that reduce risk. Of particular note, however, is that the presence of suicide risk factors is not necessarily associated with firearm-involved suicide. A context-specific evaluation that is empirically based and incorporates case-specific factors and local norms is critical. Still, as with violence risk, it is imperative to assess general suicide risk when conducting firearm evaluations.

As Fowler (2012) outlined, risk factors include, but are not necessarily limited to, past suicide attempts, certain psychiatric diagnoses (e.g., major depression, bipolar disorder), severity of mental illness, genetic markers, and various psychological vulnerabilities. Demographic variables are also noteworthy given that it is also the case that males complete more suicides, whereas females attempt more. In addition, non-married people, those who are elderly, adolescents, and young adults as well as Caucasian groups are associated with increased suicide risk. With respect to warning signs, the presence of suicidal ideation or a plan, stressful life events, and post-hospitalization transitions may increase risk. Protective factors include religious affiliation and beliefs, identified reasons for living, marriage, children in the home, supportive social networks, therapeutic contacts, and certain psychotropic medications. Chapter 6 contains a more thorough review of risk and protective factors, inclusive of those that may be more pertinent to firearm-related contexts such as: certain professions (e.g., military), situations (e.g., family violence), geography (e.g., areas with less restrictive gun laws), traits (e.g., impulsivity), symptoms (e.g., anger/mania), and experiences (e.g., combat exposure).

There are many published suicide risk assessment tools available to practitioners, and in contrast to violence risk assessment measures, suicide measures are more readily usable across firearm assessment contexts because they do not necessarily require the occurrence of a self-injurious event, suicide attempt, or even suicidal ideation. It would likely be beneficial to incorporate a formal suicide assessment measure, such as the Columbia Suicide Severity Risk Scale (Posner et al., 2011) or the Suicidal Behaviors Questionnaire-Revised (Osman et al., 2001), to supplement this item area, especially when there is any notable concern regarding suicide risk in a particular case.

9. Mental Health

A significant portion of the population will meet DSM-5 criteria for a diagnosable mental health condition at some point in their lifetime, rendering the label of "mental illness" as one that is overly inclusive and lacks utility. As noted, there are over 300 disorders listed across more than 900 pages, including learning disorders, eating disorders, sleep disorders, phobias, and various other conditions that are not associated with the misuse of firearms. However, although there should not be a checklist of conditions that would bar someone from owning or interacting with firearms, there are certainly symptoms and conditions that may lead evaluators to recommend against such in certain contexts and during specific time periods. Indeed, the restoration of firearm ownership is becoming a more and more pressing issue. Nevertheless, certain conditions, symptoms, and mental states may be associated with suicide, violence, and DV risk or may otherwise lead the evaluator to feel that the examinee is not someone who is suitable for possessing firearms at that time.

For instance, depressive and bipolar disorders are more closely associated with suicide than other psychiatric disorders, and conditions such as borderline personality disorder are often associated with self-injurious behavior. Psychotic disorders and related conditions, such as schizophrenia and paranoid

personality disorder, may be associated with hallucinations, delusions, paranoia, and thought-disordered processes, more generally. Disruptive, impulse-
control, and conduct disorders, including antisocial personality disorder, are
typically associated with criminal behavior, which may include violence and
DV. Furthermore, criminal behaviors and incidents of violence and suicide
often involve drugs and/or alcohol, which are associated with those who meet
criteria for substance use disorders.

Again, the presence of these diagnoses alone is an insufficient criterion
to determine that someone is clinically inappropriate to use or own firearms.
Over the past half-century, great strides have been made to destigmatize
mental illness, including the advent and evolution of the Americans with
Disabilities Act of 1990 (ADA) and its 2008 revision (ADA Amendments Act
of 2008), which prohibits discrimination and ensures equal opportunity for
people with disabilities in the employment arena as well as in state and government services, transportation, and other public accommodations. Also, no
longer are the days when the presence of a mental illness alone precluded
someone from being afforded certain legal rights. For example, a diagnosis of
schizophrenia does not equal incompetence to make certain legal, medical,
vocational, financial, or educational decisions, although someone with that
diagnosis may certainly be found incompetent in one or more of those areas.
This concept applies to many areas of daily functioning in our society, including driving, home ownership, and having children. Interestingly, driving
is considered a privilege in our society, but a driver's license in one state is
sufficient to drive throughout the country, in contrast to permits for firearm
ownership.

Nevertheless, evaluators must conduct a *functional* assessment of the examinee at the symptom level and not simply take the diagnosis at face value
because of the significant heterogeneity even within diagnostic categories.
As we highlighted in Chapter 4, our mental health diagnostic system, the
DSM-5, is based on symptom combinations or clusters; therefore, there
is typically significant heterogeneity within diagnostic categories. For example, Galatzer-Levy & Bryant (2013) found that there are 636,120 possible
symptom combinations that can lead to a diagnosis of posttraumatic stress
disorder (PTSD) per the DSM-5. Most diagnostic categories lend themselves
to high numbers of symptom combinations as well. Therefore, knowing a diagnosis alone is rarely very informative and, in fact, can be quite misleading
when left up to the interpretive guesswork of the professional presented with
the information.

Therefore, evaluators should consider each examinee's symptom presentation in combination with other risk factors and across diagnostic categories.
Identification of comorbid illnesses and other historical information is important because research has shown that those diagnosed with comorbid substance use disorders (i.e., dual diagnosis) and histories of violence are more
likely to be violent than others who do not meet these criteria, even if they
were recently discharged from an institution (Wiebe, 2003). Nevertheless,

relatively few people commit acts of violence, DV, or suicide, even within diagnostic groups typically associated with these concerns. Moreover, firearm-related injuries and/or deaths occur in the absence of bona fide psychiatric disorders as well.

The task for evaluators is to assess the examinees' risk levels for engaging in firearm-involved violence and/or self-injurious behavior in the context of considering their mental health symptoms and overall psychological functioning. Therefore, traditional psychological assessment instruments, such as personality assessment inventories or cognitive tests, may be useful to incorporate in evaluations if evaluators believe constructs assessed by these types of measures may serve as moderating factors to consider in the appropriateness of examinees' firearm ownership (e.g., poor decision-making associated with cognitive deficits or psychosis).

10. Substance Use

Active substance use problems should raise concerns about an examinee's appropriateness to interact with firearms. However, having a history of such issues is likely to be a consideration that is less clear for evaluators. For some, their substance abuse was either episodic or otherwise isolated; for others, their use was more serious, and maintaining sobriety will be a lifelong process. Although it is not possible to draw a bright line as to who may be suitable to interact with firearms, evaluators should consider the history of the examinee's substance use in this context. For instance, one may consider: *Did examinees interact with firearms during the same time period they misused substances? If so, did they misuse firearms as well?* Again, the real utility of this guide, the PF-10, is to integrate firearm-specific considerations with those that are more generally associated with firearm-related problems (e.g., suicide, violence, and DV).

Research conducted by Wintemute (2015) has shown that acute and chronic alcohol misuse is associated with firearm ownership, risky behaviors involving firearms, and risk for firearm violence toward self and others. In addition, alcohol-related firearm deaths are equal to alcohol-related motor vehicle crashes among men. Based on his findings, Wintemute suggested that restricting access to firearms for those with an unambiguous documented history of alcohol misuse would be an effective prevention measure against violence. We would add that acute and chronic substance abuse problems, more generally, are likely to make most (if not all) examinees inappropriate for firearm use or ownership. Most substances are mind-altering and lead to impairments in various areas of daily functioning, which is the reason we expand the consideration to include the misuse of all substances and not just alcohol. As with other mental health problems, however, a functional assessment is warranted; and it is also important to point out the prescription medication problem that has developed in our society. There are a number of people who are taking medications as prescribed but whose medication may be overprescribed and, therefore, leads to impairments as well. There are also considerations related to the more recent legalization of marijuana and even medicinal marijuana, which has become an issue that varies state by state. Therefore, evaluators must remember not to focus solely on the legality of a substance but, again, the way in which it impacts the examinee's *functioning*— especially in the context of firearm use and ownership.

Considerations for Law Enforcement and Related Professions

For most law enforcement, correctional, and military personnel, their only interactions with mental health professionals have been during the pre-employment stage of their employment. Per the International Association of Chiefs of Police (IACP) Preemployment Psychological Evaluation Guidelines (2014):

> a preemployment psychological evaluation is a specialized examination to determine whether a public safety applicant meets the minimum requirements for psychological suitability mandated by jurisdictional statutes and regulations, as well as any other criteria established by the hiring agency. . . . In most jurisdictions, the minimum requirements for psychological suitability are that the applicant be free from any emotional or mental condition that might adversely affect the performance of safety-based duties and responsibilities and be capable of withstanding the psychological demands inherent in the prospective position. (p. 1)

Furthermore, the IACP indicates that the evaluation should include a job analysis, testing, an interview, and a review of relevant background information. In particular, it notes:

> Information about the required duties, responsibilities, working conditions, and other psychologically relevant job characteristics should be obtained from the hiring authority prior to beginning the psychological evaluation. This information should be directed toward identifying skills, behaviors, attributes and other personal characteristics associated with effective and counterproductive job performance. (p. 3)

Given that law enforcement officers are required to carry firearms in this country, we believe incorporating the PF-10 in these evaluations may very well be useful. As noted, however, the guide was developed for use with civilian populations, and it will be necessary to more formally investigate its potential utility in these types of pre-employment contexts. Nevertheless, this seems to be a worthy pursuit because evaluators do not necessarily formally assess firearm-specific factors during the course of these pre-employment evaluations. Although we know of no such research to directly speak to this issue, we hypothesize that firearm-related inquiries are not a major component of these assessments, if they are incorporated at all. We believe this is likely the case for correctional and military applicants, as well as others seeking employment in positions that require the use or carry of firearms (e.g., various federal and state agencies, as well as private agencies, as in the case of armed guards).

It is much more likely the case that firearm-specific factors are assessed in the context of fitness-for-duty evaluations, which are often required subsequent to critical incidents (e.g., officer-involved shootings). The IACP has also set forth psychological fitness-for-duty evaluation guidelines (2013), wherein they define a psychological fitness-for-duty evaluation (FFDE) as:

> a formal, specialized examination of an incumbent employee that results from (1) objective evidence that the employee may be unable to safely or effectively perform a defined job and (2) a reasonable basis for believing that the cause may be attributable to a psychological condition or impairment. The central purpose of an FFDE is to determine whether the employee is able to safely and effectively perform his or her essential job functions. (p. 2)

The IACP recommends inclusion of the following in FFDEs: a review of relevant background and collateral information; psychological testing; a comprehensive clinical interview and mental status examination; collateral interviews with relevant third parties, when applicable; and a referral to or consultation with a specialist, if necessary. Although the words *firearm* and *gun* are not included in the guidelines at all, we suspect that evaluators are much more inclined to inquire about firearm-related issues during the course of FFDEs compared to pre-employment evaluations. That said, such inquiries may still not be a primary or integral aspect of FFDEs for many examiners—at least not in a formal, structured manner. However, officers' suitability to carry and use firearms safely and effectively is an inherent and essential component of their fitness to return to work. Therefore, we also believe the PF-10 may have utility in FFDEs—again, a possibility that will require further consideration and investigation moving forward.

Law enforcement, correctional, and military positions are often very stressful and associated with high levels of stress as well as exposure to a myriad of potentially traumatic experiences, both directly and vicariously. As such, these positions are linked to risks related to the development of medical, mental health, and substance abuse problems as well as DV issues and suicide.

The commentary literature and empirical research base related to police stress is voluminous and long-standing (e.g., see Anderson, Swenson, & Clay, 1995; Brown & Campbell, 1994; Blum, 2000; Kates, 1999; Liberman et al., 2002; Reiser & Geiger, 1984; Robinson, Sigman, & Wilson, 1997; Terry, 1981; Van Hasselt, Sheehan, & Malcolm, 2008). The National Institute of Justice has noted that "for the law enforcement officer, the strains and tensions experienced at work are unique, often extreme, and sometimes unavoidable" (2000, p. 19), which led to the development of its Corrections and Law Enforcement

Family Support program. Officers are exposed to such stressors as criminality, accidents, complaints, verbal and physical altercations, death, periods of notable boredom followed by intense excitement, public and political pressures, and rotating shifts. There are also significant intradepartmental problems in many jurisdictions. For example, from 2009 to 2012, there were 148 legal settlements between New Jersey police officers against their departments—a $29 million cost to taxpayers, which was 45% more than the $20 million paid during that time period from the 117 lawsuits filed by civilians (Herships, 2014). This wide array of stressors can lead to a range of problems for police officers, which are very likely to affect their overall health and their work and home lives.

With regard to substance abuse, 11%–16% of urban officers drink alcohol at levels characterized as "at risk" according to the National Institute on Alcohol Abuse and Alcoholism (Ballenger et al., 2010), and more than one-third of officers have been found to engage in at least one problematic drinking behavior (Swatt, Gibson, & Piquero, 2007). Given that officers are less likely than others to report and seek help for these types of problems proactively, consistent with the so-called blue wall of silence, some have suggested that their rates of alcohol abuse may even double that of the general population (Kirschman, 2006; Violanti, 1999). Of course, work stress and substance abuse problems are often associated with increased medical problems, as well as problems associated with suicide and DV.

Professor John Violanti and colleagues conducted a large-scale study through the National Institute of Occupational Safety and Health, known as the Buffalo Cardio-Metabolic Police Stress study. This included more than 400 officers whom they tracked over time with questionnaires, blood tests, stress monitors, ultrasounds, and salivary cortisol samples. They found that officers over 40 years old had a higher 10-year risk of a heart attack compared to national standards; the majority of female officers and about half of male officers had higher cholesterol levels, pulse rates, and diastolic blood pressure levels than are recommended; and about one-quarter of officers reported more suicidal thoughts than the general population.[7] This finding is not particularly surprising as police suicides have received attention in recent years. Research has suggested that police officers may take their own lives at a rate double that of officer deaths by felons (see Nanavaty, 2015); however, national statistics are difficult to find in this regard because of reporting and related data collection challenges. As Stuart (2008) noted: "Owing to these unresolved methodological challenges, the epidemiology of suicide risk in police populations remains inconclusive" (p. 506). Nevertheless, state-level numbers are often more easily accessible, and they reflect serious concerns.

For example, according to the New Jersey Police Suicide Task Force Report (2009), suicide rates are greater among all active male officers in the state between 25 and 64 years old compared to same-aged male civilians. In fact, when correctional officers are included in the analysis, the rate is 30% greater than that for civilians. Moreover, the analysis showed that officer suicides are "far more likely to be committed with a firearm than suicide among similarly aged males" (p. 8). As a result of these significant statistics and the associated propensity for officers to avoid seeking help, New Jersey maintains a Cop 2 Cop service, which is a 24-hour anonymous helpline managed by Rutgers University Behavioral Health Care in conjunction with the New Jersey Department of Human Services (Cop 2 Cop, n.d.). The program is focused on suicide prevention and mental health support. It was mandated in 1998 by the Department of Personnel after a series of police suicides from 1996 to 1998. According to the program, it has helped to prevent more than 187 suicides over its initial 10 years, and it further notes:

> Though statistics have not been compiled nationally, most law
> enforcement experts believe the police suicide rate is higher than those
> of the general population, but because suicides among police officers
> are often reported as accidents or met with official silence, definitive
> numbers are hard to come by.

As noted, officer-involved DV is also a significant problem among police populations, such that officer families have been found to have higher rates of DV than non–police officer families (Cheema, 2016). In fact, the National Center for Women and Policing (n.d.) has cited research indicating that 24%–40% of police officer families experience DV compared to 10% in the general population. It further notes the unique vulnerabilities inherent to police officer victims in this context; namely, that the perpetrator has a gun, knows the location of battered women's shelters, and knows how to manipulate the system to avoid penalty and blame. Moreover, victims often fear calling the police because they are aware it will be handled by those who know the abuser. These concerns have led to the development of specialized programs to prevent and manage IPV among officer families, such as the Crystal Judson Domestic Violence Protocol Program (Federal legislation passed, n.d.), which was a Washington State–based initiative that became part of the reauthorization of the Violence Against Women Act and a model for many states that followed suit.

Consistent with the aforementioned suicide statistics, correctional officers have been found to have even higher levels of stress and DV-related problems than police officers (Summerlin, Oehme, Stern, & Valentine, 2010). In turn, substance abuse, divorce, and suicide rates are very high in correctional officer populations, relative to the general public but also compared to their police counterparts. The US Department of Justice (2000) has cited problems related to physical illness, substance abuse, burnout, excessive disability retirements, and damaged family relationships among correctional officer groups as well. Furthermore, consistent with the New Jersey statistics, Stack & Tsoudis (1997) found that they commit suicide at a rate twice that of both police officers and the general public and that the risk of suicide among correctional officers was 39% higher than that for all other professions combined. Nevertheless, there are significant barriers to treatment and prevention inherent to correctional officer subculture, just as there are in police populations. Perhaps two relatively recent headlines best illustrate this issue: "Prison Officers Need Help, But They Won't Ask for It" (Lopez, 2014) and " 'Prison Guards Can Never Be Weak': The Hidden PTSD Crisis in America's Jails" (Lisitsina, 2015).

Last, but certainly not least, are the multitude of serious concerns that face our active and retired military personnel. In the largest study of mental health risk ever conducted among the US military, Kessler and colleagues (2014) found that 25% of approximately 5,500 active-duty, non-deployed Army soldiers had some type of mental health disorder, 11% had more than one illness, and 13% reported severe role impairments. The rate of depression was five times greater than that for civilians, intermittent explosive disorder was six times greater, and PTSD was 15 times greater. Of particular note is that 50% of soldiers with at least one internalizing disorder diagnosis (e.g., depression, anxiety, PTSD) reported onset prior to enlistment, whereas more than 80% of externalizing disorders (e.g., intermittent explosive, substance use) developed after enlistment. According to the US Department of Veterans Affairs (n.d.b), substance use disorders (SUDs) co-occur with PTSD among veteran groups at problematic rates:

- More than 2 of 10 Veterans with PTSD also have SUD.
- War Veterans with PTSD and alcohol problems tend to be binge drinkers. Binges may be in response to bad memories of combat trauma.
- Almost 1 out of every 3 Veterans seeking treatment for SUD also has PTSD.
- The number of Veterans who smoke (nicotine) is almost double for those with PTSD (about 6 of 10) versus those without a PTSD diagnosis (3 of 10).
- In the wars in Iraq and Afghanistan, about 1 in 10 returning soldiers seen in VA have a problem with alcohol or other drugs.

The VA has further indicated that female veterans and active-duty military personnel are more likely than their civilian counterparts to experience IPV. Specifically, more than 35% of active-duty women have reported experiencing one or more types of such violence during their service, and 30%–70% have reported having these experiences at some point in their lives (US Department of Veterans Affairs, n.d.a). The Substance Abuse and Mental Health Services Administration has also set forth statistics that raise additional concerns for military personnel and their families (n.d.). For instance, the Army suicide rate reached an all-time high in 2012, which is consistent with 2014 statistics published by the VA indicating a rate of 20 veteran suicide deaths per day that year—a 21% greater rate than civilians—and accounting for 18% of all adult suicide deaths in the United States. Of particular note is that 66% of all veteran deaths were via firearm (VA Suicide Prevention Program, 2016).

As with many topics we address in this book, considerations related to law enforcement, correctional, and military personnel can and certainly do make up entire books specifically devoted to issues relevant to these groups. A comprehensive review of these issues is outside of the scope of this book; however, even our brief summary of the aforementioned concerns reflects the many risk factors inherent to these populations. Thus, the need to assess firearm-related factors when evaluating members of these groups seems clear. As such, there is a need for professional research and commentary investigating the utility of incorporating formal firearm assessment guides, such as the PF-10, into the various evaluations in which law enforcement, correctional, and military personnel are required to engage.

8

Treatment

Access to healthcare services, especially mental health care, is often cited as a necessary component of firearm-related violence and suicide prevention efforts. As we highlighted in the previous chapter, assessment is a necessary, albeit often overlooked, first step because it provides context and guidance for the types of interventions described in the present chapter. Nevertheless, many people, including government officials and politicians, frequently speak of the important role of mental health care in the firearm context without providing any specifics. It may be that they simply do not understand the nuances related to mental health treatment. However, citing the need for mental health care during broad discussions about guns lacks context, specificity, and utility. Which type of healthcare? Provided by whom? For whom? When? To what end? As we will illustrate, the answers to these questions are actually quite complex, when there are clear answers at all. In this chapter, we provide an overview of some of the more common contemporary treatment modalities, followed by a discussion of specific treatment considerations related to violence, domestic violence, and suicide and self-harm. We then address issues associated with therapeutic interventions for youth as well as general considerations for health and wellness and firearm safety precautions. In the subsequent section, we discuss some typical barriers to treatment, in addition to reviewing the burgeoning issues associated with restoration of gun rights. Lastly, we focus on the emerging roles for treating professionals in the context of firearm-related matters, including considerations related to vicarious trauma and self-care for practitioners. First, we present an overview of the history and science of psychology, followed by a primer on specific types of mental health treatment to provide context for those who are not particularly familiar with them.

Therapeutic Interventions

The recognition and treatment of psychological problems date back many thousands of years. Early societies ascribed emotional distress and erratic behaviors to divine or demonic entities, whereas the ancient Greeks were the first to recognize mental illnesses as medical conditions. For instance, Hippocrates (c. 460–c. 370 BC) studied brain pathology in this context, and although he was incorrect in his understanding of the exact etiology of certain conditions and their corresponding treatments (e.g., imbalance of the humors, bloodletting), he was significant in shifting the way in which mental health conditions were understood and treated. This waxed and waned over time, though, as the belief in the supernatural as the cause of mental illnesses resurfaced during some periods (e.g., the Middle Ages). Nevertheless, psychotherapies, initially conceptualized as "talking cures," were ultimately developed. Of particular relevance in our modern history is the significant contribution of two Austrian physicians, Josef Breuer (1842–1925) and Sigmund Freud (1856–1939), who developed theories and therapeutic approaches related to what we know as *psychoanalysis* (Breuer & Freud, 1955). As the following section will reflect, the modern-day mental health field has come quite a long way in conceptualizing and treating psychological disorders since the late 19th century. However, before we can fully appreciate the theoretical and empirical underpinnings of specific psychotherapy treatment modalities, we must become acclimated to the practical aspects of psychology as a science.

Psychology as a Science

As Baker, McFall, & Shoham (2009) articulated it: "The principal goals of clinical psychology are to generate knowledge based on scientifically valid evidence and to apply this knowledge to the optimal improvement of mental and behavioral health" (p. 69). They further contended that the nature of mental health care in the United States has significantly changed over the years, such that healthcare costs have increased significantly since the 1970s. These costs have been diverted from individuals to insurers and the government, and cost of mental health care has almost doubled over the past 30 years. However, it is more often delivered by primary care physicians in the form of psychotropic medication, and psychologists are being bypassed by primary care doctors and other licensed professionals (e.g., social workers). It is apparent that mental health care has continued to move toward managed care rather than fee-for-service providers (i.e., toward medical providers and away from psychologists).

Baker and colleagues (2009) further distinguished between the terms *efficacy* and *effectiveness* in the context of treatment outcomes. As they indicated, *effectiveness* refers to effects of the treatment intervention when applied to a situation that is very similar to one found in the real world, whereas *efficacy* refers to the treatment effects observed under controlled (e.g., laboratory) conditions. Thus, efficacy research typically occurs in the context of treatment studies or clinical trials at specific clinics or programs with volunteer research participants and predetermined facilitators, as in the case of randomized controlled trials (RCTs)—the gold standard in assessing treatment efficacy (Gartlehner et al., 2006). One can think of it in this way: efficacy trials, such as RCTs, are aimed at determining if a treatment works within a specific population and with respect to its particular mechanisms of change, whereas effectiveness trials seek to determine if the treatment benefits patients more broadly, in terms of both different populations and treatment outcomes. Simply put: efficacy is the treatment effect in ideal conditions (i.e., controlled) and effectiveness is the effect in the real world.

To maintain a balanced perspective, it is critical to recognize that the field of medicine did not function as a science for much of its history. In fact, it was not until well into the 1900s that the tenets of basic science were embraced, taught, and ultimately practiced by medical professionals (Baker et al., 2009). One can recall such practices as bloodletting and lobotomies and the use of substances such as heroin and cocaine to treat fairly common and benign ailments (e.g., cough, depression). However, the medical field has ultimately come to a point of standardized training and general consensus across many domains. Moreover, the medical model has embraced the integration of training, research, and practice, as evidenced by the many medical schools and teaching hospitals throughout the country and a general movement toward competency-based education. The mental health field remains much more disjointed, however; and there continues to be a focus on nonspecific and therapeutic alliance–related factors in terms of treatment effectiveness and efficacy. As Baker and colleagues (2009) indicated, the mental health field must also investigate causal effects on outcome variables and the sources of variance within such analytic models, the extent to which certain therapeutic skills can be trained and enhanced, and the overall impact of prolonged graduate training in mental health. These are the types of questions that will further move the mental health professions toward scientifically based practice. Failure to do so may very well lead to what seems to be happening in some respects and about which Baker and colleagues warned: low-cost providers without intensive training or skills.

Past American Psychological Association (APA) president Alan Kazdin (2008), spoke of the gap between research and practice inclinical psychology, particularly as related to evidenced-based treatments (EBTs) and practices. One primary concern is the generalizability of research findings to practice. This is an issue at the research design stage, however. Namely, patients in controlled research trials have been noted to have less severe conditions and fewer comorbid disorders than those who come to treatment in the real world. This issue is directly related to the exclusion and inclusion criteria set forth by researchers. It is also the case that controlled studies tend to incorporate certain types of therapeutic approaches that may not reflect treatment in actual treatment settings (e.g., manualized treatment with fixed content and a predetermined number of sessions). Kazdin also aptly points out that treatment studies tend to focus on symptoms and disorders in the context of the treatment *outcomes* rather than the *process*, which is very important for patients moving forward. As he articulated it:

> In clinical practice, much of psychotherapy is not about reaching a destination (eliminating symptoms) as it is about the ride (the process of coping with life). Psychotherapy research rarely addresses the broader focus of coping with multiple stressors and negotiating the difficult shoals of life, both of which are aided by speaking with a trained professional. In clinical practice, sometimes symptoms are the focus; even when they are the focus, over half of patients seen in therapy add new target complaints or change their complaints over the course of treatment . . . . Outcomes that seem loose and fuzzy (e.g., angst, quality of life, coping) or that are moving targets are rarely addressed in controlled therapy trials. Understandably, there is concern about applying many of the findings from research to practice. (pp. 147–148)

With regard to EBTs, specifically, Kazdin identified three particular concerns:

1. There are many different criteria for determining whether a treatment is evidenced-based or empirically supported.
2. The outcome measures in most psychotherapy studies raise concerns, conceptually, and apart from simply statistical issues.
3. There are often problems trying to aggregate findings within and between studies, such that some aspects of treatment may exhibit effects but only in certain contexts and only in particular studies.

The first issue is closely associated with a problem known as *vote-counting*, that is, the tendency for people to ascribe evidentiary support to specific findings based on the number of studies with significant or non-significant findings rather than the magnitude of effect sizes. For example, three studies finding a non-significant relationship between variables would likely be given more weight than one study with significant findings because effect size statistics are not calculated. In other words, the single study wherein significance was found may actually be better designed and less biased and demonstrate statistical effects that may be much greater, but this would not be relevant to the person who is simply interested in counting the number of studies with a particular set of findings. This concern supports the importance of *meta-analyses*, or studies that combine data from multiple studies to calculate total effect sizes and related statistics, rather than interpreting findings from individual studies in isolation—separate and apart from other research studies.

The second issue Kazdin noted relates to what is referred to as the use of *arbitrary metrics*. Blanton & Jaccard (2006) highlighted this issue in relation to psychological assessment instruments. They defined a metric as arbitrary when the location of an individual's observed score on the underlying psychological dimension is unknown or, if it is unknown, how the magnitude of a one-unit change in a score would be reflected on the underlying dimension. It is necessary for a metric to be linked to an external (i.e., real-world) event in order to be considered non-arbitrary; however, Blanton & Jaccard suggested that psychologists often attempt to infer non-arbitrary meaning by engaging in such actions as meter-reading strategies. *Meter-reading* refers to inferring a location on an underlying dimension from an individual's score on an arbitrary measure. For example, a psychologist would be engaging in meter-reading by inferring that an individual is severely depressed because he or she received a score of 45 out of 50 on a depression inventory. A scale's metrics end at some point—be it at a score of 3, 10, or 100 (i.e., the maximum score one can receive). Once the test developer "draws the line," he or she has effectively prevented individual scores from reaching the dimensional extremes. For example, an individual cannot score greater than 50 on the aforementioned depression inventory regardless of how high his or her levels of depression truly are; therefore, it is possible for various individuals to receive the same score but to differ in their true, underlying levels of depression. Lastly, category widths may differ across instruments. Imagine two depression inventories utilizing the same scoring (i.e., 0–50), and for illustration purposes, assume that the underlying psychological dimension of depression also ranged from 0 to 50. It is possible for a true score of 20 on the underlying dimension of depression to correspond to a score of 35 on the first depression inventory and a score of 45 on the second inventory. The inventories, particularly the second, would then lead to an inflated interpretation of the individual's level of depression.

The reality is that no metric is inherently arbitrary or non-arbitrary. Behavioral counts, such as the number of times an individual engages in a particular behavior, and physical metrics, such as height and weight, may be non-arbitrary metrics. For instance, if the variable of interest was "amount of coffee consumed daily" measured in cups, it would be easily understandable that scores of 3 and 4 indicate that the individual consumed three cups of coffee one day and four the next. Similarly, if told that a woman was 5 feet 5 inches tall and weighed 140 pounds, it would be possible to imagine her body type; and if she weighed 130 pounds on follow-up, it would be possible to appreciate her weight loss. However, even these physical metrics can be made arbitrary. For example, if told that a second woman was 1.65 meters tall and weighed 63.5 kilograms on a first weighing and 58.9 kilograms on a second, one could deduce that she lost weight, but the amount would not be meaningful or understandable to those unfamiliar with these metrics. In this example, the women are exactly the same height and weight and lost the exact same amount of weight; however, for those of us unfamiliar with the metric system, speaking in terms of meters and kilograms is virtually meaningless. Unless a metric has an external referent, it maintains its arbitrariness. For clinical practitioners and researchers using an instrument such as the aforementioned depression self-report tool, an individual's scores on the instrument are meaningless in terms of their real-world implications. In addition, it would be inappropriate to draw inferences from follow-up scores on the inventory. For instance, individual progress during the course of therapy cannot be deduced by changes of scores on the inventory if the metrics used are arbitrary.

The third issue Kazdin noted is associated with the fact that mental health treatment is multifaceted and it is commonplace for multiple outcome measures to be included in research studies as well. As a result, certain treatments cannot simply be dichotomously characterized as either effective or not. Rather, the results are often mixed, such that some aspects of the treatment may be effective for some people in certain respects but not necessarily in others or even in other studies. Replication research is a hallmark of science, but the medical and mental health research literatures are truly limited in this regard. Engber's (2016) recent article indicates: "we face a replication crisis in the field of biomedicine, not unlike the one we've seen in psychology but with far more dire implications. Sloppy data analysis, contaminated lab materials, and poor experimental design all contribute to the problem" (see also Freedman, Cockburn, & Simcoe, 2015).

As for mental health, the Association for Psychological Science (2013) noted: "Reproducing the results of research studies is a vital part of the scientific process. Yet for a number of reasons, replication research, as it is commonly known, is rarely published." The Association for Psychological Science highlighted the fact that the leading journal, *Perspectives on Psychological Science*, had launched an initiative to encourage researchers to conduct replication studies.

Undoubtedly, challenges remain and treatment efficacy studies remain in their early stages in the field as a whole. As McHugh & Barlow (2010) articulated it:

> Governments, public health authorities, and individuals suffering from psychological problems around the world are demanding increased access to psychological treatments, and the urgency of this demand has gotten ahead of the determination of best practices to achieve it. Scientists and clinicians must work together to meet this demand with the same sense of urgency expressed by health care policymakers and the individuals we serve. (p. 83)

With regard to future directions, they noted:

> Given the relative lack of data regarding the efficacy of specific dissemination and implementation procedures for increasing access to EBPTs [evidenced-based psychological treatments], evaluation is a particularly important topic for future research. For example, few programs have information on the number of clinicians (or clinical teams) who fail to reach competence standards after initiating training, which may have major implications for future initiatives. In order to determine the best practice for these efforts, examination of outcomes

in ongoing efforts is needed. Such examination should not be limited to clinical outcomes and should also include potential mediators of successful adoption, such as the duration of supervision necessary to achieve competence, the best procedures to facilitate sustainability (e.g., "train the trainer" models), and the most effective means of gaining stakeholder support and addressing negative perceptions about EBPTs among late adopters. (p. 81)

Some have gone so far as to contend that certain psychological treatments cause harm. Namely, Professor Scott Lilienfeld of Emory University referred to such as *potentially harmful treatments* (PHTs), or those that can lead to deterioration effects (Lilienfeld, 2007). He posited that the field of clinical psychology largely overlooked the topic of negative therapy effects, noting that there is no over-sight group equivalent to the Food and Drug Administration in psychology or in the mental health treatment arena, more broadly. Lilienfeld conceded that positive effects have been found for various types of psychotherapy approaches for a wide range of conditions when compared to no treatment or placebo treat-ment conditions. Still, he echoed the limitations associated with Empirically Supported Therapies (ESTs) and noted that, while it was traditionally thought that all psychotherapies work well and therapist- and client-specific variables explained the variance in outcomes, the developing psychotherapy outcome re-search has demonstrated that not all therapies are equally efficacious. Lilienfeld further noted that some research has shown that 3%–10% of clients become worse following psychotherapy (Mohr, 1995; Strupp, Hadley, & Gomez-Schwartz, 1977) and even 10%–15% in substance abuse treatment contexts (see Ilgen & Moos, 2005; Moos, 2005). Lilienfeld further indicated that there are multiple types of potential harm, including symptom worsening, the develop-ment of new symptoms, excessive dependency on therapists, reluctance to seek future treatment, and even physical harm. There may also be harm to others, such as relatives or friends (e.g., false allegations against family members), and there may be short-term or long-term deterioration effects. In his analysis, Lilienfeld characterized treatments as PHTs if they met three criteria:

1. They have demonstrated harmful psychological or physical effects in clients or others.
2. The harmful effects are enduring and do not merely reflect a short-term exacerbation of symptoms during treatment.
3. The harmful effects have been replicated by independent investigative teams.

Based on this, he developed a provisional list of PHTs, which are outlined below along with the associated potential harm. The primary sources from which the negative research findings were based were RCTs, meta-analyses, and low–base rate events in replicated case reports. The PHTs he set forth were:

- Critical incident stress debriefing
  - heightened risk of posttraumatic stress symptoms

- Scared Straight interventions
  - exacerbation of conduct problems
- Facilitated communication
  - false accusations of child abuse against family members
- Attachment therapies (e.g., rebirthing)
  - death and serious injury to children
- Recovered-memory techniques
  - production of false memories of trauma
- Dissociative identity disorder–oriented therapy (formerly, multiple personality disorder)
  - induction of "alter" personalities
- Grief counseling for individuals with normal bereavement reactions
  - increases in depressive symptoms
- Expressive-experiential therapies
  - exacerbation of painful emotions
- Boot-camp and peer-group interventions for conduct disorder
  - exacerbation of conduct problems
- Drug Abuse Resistance Education (D.A.R.E.) programs
  - increased intake of alcohol and other substances (e.g., cigarettes)
- Relaxation treatments for panic-prone patients
  - Induction of panic attacks

Lilienfeld reiterated that the last was intended to be provisional and open to revision contemporaneously with the evolving empirical research; moreover, he emphasized that these were being referred to as "potentially" harmful treatments because the presence of harmful effects is "not definitive" and "it is unlikely that any of the treatments on this list are harmful for all individuals exposed to them" (p. 59). The interested reader can refer to Lilienfeld's article directly for a detailed overview and analysis of each of the above PHTs.[1] Perhaps the main take-home message here is Lilienfeld's challenge to the assumption that "doing something is better than doing nothing," as he put it, and that therapy is, at worst, innocuous. He pointed out that there are over 500 "brands" of psychotherapy and most have not been investigated in controlled trials. He also contended that research on PHTs should come before that on ESTs. As he articulated it:

> Our field should therefore instead prioritize its efforts toward pinpointing treatments that are demonstrably harmful or ineffective and disseminating this information to current practitioners, students in training, potential clients, managed-care organizations, and the media. In addition, therapists who administer techniques that are associated with a significant risk of harm should be required to explicitly inform their clients of this risk. From the standpoint of the safety of mental health consumers, the lowermost end of the distribution of treatment efficacy is probably more critical than the uppermost end. . . .

> Both proponents and opponents of the EST movement should be able to find common ground on one central point: Treatments that have the potential to produce harm should either be avoided or, in the case of treatments that yield both positive and negative effects, implemented only with caution. A heightened emphasis on PHTs may therefore help to narrow the scientist–practitioner gap . . . by focusing the efforts of both EST proponents and opponents on a significant point of consensus—namely, the ethical injunction to first do no harm. (p. 63)

Despite all of these concerns and limitations, it is important to remember that there have been significant advances in psychotherapy research and mental health practice in a period of more than 60 years. The future looked quite bleak in the 1950s, but the development of RCTs, improved therapeutic intervention strategies, and increased consensus and standardization in mental health training have all contributed optimism to the field. Moreover, the gap between research and practice may still be present, but it is narrowing in many ways as scientist-practitioner models continue to prevail in response to accountability demands from stricter accrediting bodies and a savvier, better-informed public. In sum, conceptually grounded treatment approaches have been developed, they have been empirically supported in some respects, and they have absolutely helped some people in certain ways. We now turn to a review of some of the most common and contemporary models of psychotherapy—psychodynamic psychotherapy, cognitive-behavioral therapy, and dialectical behavioral therapy—as well as a notation on the many other types of interpersonal, systemic, and supportive and experiential treatment approaches that have been developed and remain active today.

An Overview of Contemporary Treatment Modalities

Pharmacotherapy, or the treatment of mental health conditions with medications, certainly has been beneficial for many people for a number of reasons; however, it is outside of the scope of this book, and therefore, we will solely focus on psychotherapy-based treatments. *Psychotherapy* has been defined as "an interpersonal process designed to bring about modifications of feelings, cognitions, attitudes and behavior which have proved troublesome to the person seeking help from a trained professional" (Strupp, 1978, p. 3). What you will come to realize in the subsections below is that different types of psychotherapy are distinguished essentially by: (i) the ways in which they conceptualize how mental health concerns arise and (ii) the most effective ways to treat these problems (i.e., in the context of mechanisms of change associated with specific theoretical orientations). A well-grounded case conceptualization is critical because it sets the foundation for the course of therapy. As Eells (2007) articulated it: "A psychotherapy case formulation is a hypothesis about the causes, precipitants, and maintaining influences of a person's psychological, interpersonal, and behavioral problems" (p. 4). Put differently,

a case formulation, or case conceptualization, provides the treating professional with a framework that guides treatment and that identifies markers for
change. Note that the operative term in the aforementioned definition is *hypothesis*, however, which reflects the fact that a case conceptualization is based
on available information at the onset of treatment and, therefore, can and
should be modified, with the patient's collaborative input (when possible), as
more information becomes available during the course of therapy. In this way,
mental health treatment, evaluation, and even research are comparable in that
they are all hypothesis-testing endeavors whereby professional opinions are
based on (and limited to) the data available. As Eells (2007) noted:

> As a hypothesis, a case formulation may include inferences about
> pre-disposing or antecedent vulnerabilities based on early childhood
> traumas, a pathogenic learning history, biological or genetic influences,
> sociocultural influences, currently operating contingencies of
> reinforcement, or maladaptive schemas and beliefs about the self or
> others. (p. 4)

Of additional note is that the nature of case formulations is dependent upon
the therapeutic orientation, or modality, employed by the clinician and that
treatment plans are developed based on such. We present three major types of
therapy approaches.

Psychodynamic Psychotherapy

Psychodynamic psychotherapy is an umbrella term that refers to a variety
of treatment approaches typically characterized as supportive, insight-
oriented, and interpretive in nature—all of which are historically rooted in
Freudian psychoanalysis, but many have evolved and, in turn, reflect notable
differences. Psychodynamic approaches primarily focus on unconscious and
subconscious psychological processes and conflicts. Clinical inferences about
a person's personality structure, mental health symptoms, dreams, fantasies,
and maladaptive patterns in interpersonal relationships are developed and
explored. Three overarching psychodynamic models more commonly seen in
North America are: traditional Freudian, object relations, and self psychology.
Traditional Freudian approaches are primarily based on Freud's drive model,
such that human behavior is determined by sexual and aggressive drives,
which are comprised of four components: a source, an aim, an impetus,
and an object. Behaviors are also a function of the *pleasure principle*, which
refers to the notion that people seek to maximize pleasure and minimize dis-
pleasure and pain. Moreover, it is believed that we have an id, ego, and su-
perego, which represent the hierarchical structure that ultimately determines
our decisions. A primary feature of Freudian conceptualization is the experience of unconscious fantasies and corresponding conflicts and how the interplay between them influences a person's behavior. In contrast, object relations
approaches emphasize the internal psychological representations of the self,

others, and the interaction between them (typically in terms of "good" and "bad" representations, such as the "good mother" or "bad self"). An important feature of this model is the idea that adults re-enact internalized object relations from their childhood, particularly those from conflicted or unresolved relationships (e.g., one prominent "object" is usually an internalized image of one's mother or maternal figure). Lastly, self psychology is based on the development and maintenance of a cohesive, healthy self, as opposed to a psychopathological, narcissistic self. This can arise when parents fail to empathically respond to children, precluding them from using the parents as "idealized selfobjects" or "mirroring selfobjects" (à la Kohut). To say that this is an overly simplistic and cursory description of psychodynamic and psychoanalytically based therapies is an understatement. However, while a more thorough and detailed review is outside of the scope of this book, the interested reader is directed to: Cabaniss, Cherry, Douglas, & Schwartz (2017); McWilliams (2004); Summers & Barber (2010); and the *Psychodynamic Diagnostic Manual*, second edition, edited by Lingiardi & McWilliams (2017).

But what does the empirical research literature indicate about the utility and benefits of these approaches? First, it is important to note that, although psychodynamic psychotherapy is one of the most commonly employed treatment approaches in clinical practice, it is often targeted and questioned with respect to its empirical research support. That said, many psychodynamic and psychoanalytically based treatments are not conducive to the level of control required in more rigorous empirical research designs that require a certain level of controlled conditions. As Leichsenring & Leibing (2007) bluntly noted: "the methodology of RCTs is not appropriate for long-term psychoanalytic therapy" (p. 220). Thus, psychoanalytic psychotherapy has been investigated in the context of *effectiveness* rather than efficacy research (e.g., Leichsenring, Biskup, Kreische, & Staats, 2005; Luborsky et al., 2001).

Generally, contemporary researchers have found it to be superior to treatment-as-usual and wait-list (i.e., control) conditions and as effective as cognitive-behavioral therapy approaches for the treatment of certain mental health disorders (e.g., see Leichsenring, Rabung, & Leibing, 2004). Leichsenring & Leibing (2007) reviewed the 24 published RCTs of psychodynamic psychotherapy that were available at the time. They found that it was superior in most cases to control conditions (e.g., treatment-as-usual or wait list), and they noted that 15 studies provided evidence for the efficacy of short-term (or "time-limited") psychodynamic psychotherapy (STPP) for a number of psychiatric conditions, including: depressive disorders, borderline personality disorder, eating disorders, somatoform disorders, posttraumatic stress disorder (PTSD), and alcohol and opiate dependence. In addition, longer-term psychodynamic psychotherapy (LTPP), defined as between 25 and 46 sessions or from 12 to 18 months, was found to have efficacy in eight RCTs for the following conditions: social phobia, eating disorders, borderline personality disorder, cluster C personality disorders, somatoform pain disorder, and opiate dependence.

More recently, Leichsenring et al. (2013) indicated that there is increasing evidence from RCTs supporting the efficacy of STPP and LTPP for certain psychiatric conditions. In this review, they noted that LTPP has been defined by at least 50 sessions or at least 1 year of psychodynamic psychotherapy. Based on their meta-analyses, Leichsenring and colleagues found that short-term psychotherapy is insufficient for many patients diagnosed with complex disorders, including chronic clinical syndromes and personality disorders. They meta-analyzed 12 RCTs of LTPP and found it to be effective, overall, and specifically to effectuate improvements in target problems, general symptoms, personality functioning, and social functioning compared to other forms of therapy or treatment-as-usual. The groups included those diagnosed with eating disorders, personality disorders, and depressive and anxiety disorders.

Perhaps Shedler (2010) summarized the state of psychodynamic psychotherapy best:

> There is a belief in some quarters that psychodynamic concepts and treatments lack empirical support, or that scientific evidence shows that other forms of treatment are more effective. The belief appears to have taken on a life of its own. Academicians repeat it to one another, as do healthcare administrators, as do healthcare policy makers. With each repetition, its apparent credibility grows. At some point, there seems little need to question or revisit it because "everyone" knows it to be so.
>
> The scientific evidence tells a different story: considerable research supports the efficacy and effectiveness of psychodynamic psychotherapy. The discrepancy between perceptions and evidence may be due, in part, to biases in the dissemination of research findings. One potential source of bias is a lingering distaste in the mental health professions for past psychoanalytic arrogance and authority. In decades past, American psychoanalysis was dominated by a hierarchical medical establishment that denied training to non-MDs and adopted a dismissive stance toward research. This did not win friends in academic circles. When empirical findings emerged that supported nonpsychodynamic treatments, many academicians greeted them enthusiastically and were eager to discuss and disseminate them. When empirical evidence supported psychodynamic concepts and treatments, it was often overlooked. (p. 9)

Cognitive-Behavioral Therapy

Cognitive-behavioral therapy (CBT) approaches have their origins in cognitive theories, such as those of Aaron Beck and Albert Ellis, as well as in learning theories (e.g., classical and operant conditioning, modeling). Behavioral therapy models focus squarely on behaviors and assume that unhealthy behaviors are learned and, therefore, can be changed. They are less concerned about internal mental processes (e.g., self-criticism) per se, but rather, focus on a person's learning history and how his or her behavior is generally reinforced. However, CBT approaches incorporate a cognitive component. Namely, they focus on maladaptive *thoughts* and beliefs about the self, others, the world, and the future. Generally speaking, CBT models assume that situations lead to (automatic) thoughts, which evoke feelings, followed by behaviors and/or physical reactions. Moreover, these thoughts, feelings, behaviors, and reactions can follow a cyclical pattern, thereby causing ongoing distress and problems for people. In a nutshell, CBT theories are based on mental health and behavioral problems being rooted in faulty thoughts, or cognitive distortions, which affect the way we view ourselves, others, the world, and the future. Cognitive distortions are many but include thinking styles like all-or-none/black-and-white thinking or catastrophizing (i.e., blowing something out of proportion). As such, we experience internal and external problems when our thoughts are faulty or distorted. CBT approaches have become very popular and widely used over the past half-century for a number of reasons, not the least of which is that their perspective of the brain is akin to that of a computer—the leading machine of the modern day[2]—and their use of manuals as well as individual and group homework assignments (e.g., thought journals, reading assignments, worksheets) makes them rather wide-ranging in terms of their utility and adaptability across settings. For much more comprehensive overviews of CBT as well as more purely behavioral and cognitive therapy approaches, readers are referred to: Beck (2011); Craske (2017); Josefowitz & Myran (2017); Riggenbach (2012); and Simmons & Griffiths (2013).

Given the use of assignments and the other ways in which CBT-based treatments track changes in symptoms and the like, they are highly quantifiable treatment approaches that have voluminous empirical research bases. Butler, Chapman, Forman, & Beck (2006) summarized the meta-analysis literature related to treatment outcomes of CBT for numerous mental health conditions. Specifically, they reviewed 16 methodologically rigorous meta-analyses comprised of nearly 10,000 patients across more than 330 studies, and they focused on CBT effectiveness by investigating treatment outcome effect sizes associated with CBT compared to control conditions across diagnostic groups. They found large effect sizes for CBT for unipolar depression, generalized anxiety disorder, panic disorder with or without agoraphobia, social phobia, PTSD, and childhood depressive and anxiety disorders. Moderate effect sizes were found for CBT of marital distress, anger, childhood somatic disorders, and chronic pain. Moreover, CBT was found to be somewhat superior to antidepressants in the treatment of adult depression but equally as effective as behavior therapy in the treatment of adult depression and obsessive–compulsive disorder. In addition, Butler and colleagues found uncontrolled effect sizes for bulimia nervosa and schizophrenia, which correspond to pre- and post-intervention effects *within* a group compared to groups receiving other types of treatments or those in control conditions. Taken together, the results are compelling and provide significant empirical support for the efficacy of CBT for the treatment of many psychiatric disorders.

More recently, Hofmann et al. (2012) conducted a much larger review of CBT meta-analyses; they investigated 106 meta-analyses that examined the efficacy of CBT for numerous psychiatric conditions: substance use disorder, schizophrenia and other psychotic disorders, depression and dysthymia, bipolar disorder, anxiety disorders, somatoform disorders, eating disorders, insomnia, personality disorders, anger and aggression, criminal behaviors, general stress, distress due to general medical conditions, chronic pain and fatigue, and distress related to pregnancy complications and female hormonal conditions. Based on their analyses, Hofmann and colleagues concluded that the strongest empirical support for CBT is associated with the treatment of anxiety disorders, somatoform disorders, bulimia, anger control problems, and general stress. It is also important to highlight the fact that, except for children and elderly populations, no CBT meta-analyses have been reported on specific subgroups (e.g., ethnic minorities or low-income/-socioeconomic status samples). Nevertheless, the evidence base of CBT is very strong overall, and it is associated with improvements in a number of other conditions as well.

That said, we are reminded of the nuances and limitations inherent to treatment outcome research, as we noted in the discussion of EBTs above in the "Psychology as a Science" section. For instance, Hofmann and colleagues found evidence for the efficacy of CBT for cannabis dependence and other substance dependence conditions, but its effect size was small compared to other interventions. Another example is that CBT was found to be effective in treating problematic gambling but only in conjunction with other non-pharmacological interventions, and it was still less efficacious than other briefer, less expensive treatments. This is the reality of treatment outcome research. It is exceedingly challenging to capture and quantify specific interventions and their effects at a granular level. Although some generalizations may be made, we are often left with very nuanced findings that do not readily translate into real-world practice. As Kazdin (2008) pointed out, there are often mixed results from these studies. There are many moderating and extraneous variables to consider, such as length of treatment, clinician adherence, treatment setting, and much more. Take, for example, Hofmann et al.'s (2012) findings related to CBT for the treatment of depression and dysthymia:

> CBT for depression was more effective than control conditions such as waiting list or no treatment, with a medium effect size. . . . However, studies that compared CBT to other active treatments, such as psychodynamic treatment, problem-solving therapy, and interpersonal psychotherapy, found mixed results. Specifically, meta-analyses found CBT to be equally effective in comparison to other psychological treatments. . . . Other studies, however, found favorable results for CBT. . . . For example, CBT [was found] to be superior to relaxation techniques at post-treatment. Additionally, CBT [was shown] to be

> superior to psychodynamic therapy at both post-treatment and at six months follow-up, although this occurred when depression and anxiety symptoms were examined together.
>
> Compared to pharmacological approaches, CBT and medication treatments had similar effects on chronic depressive symptoms, with effect sizes in the medium-large range. . . . Other studies indicated that pharmacotherapy could be a useful addition to CBT; specifically, combination therapy of CBT with pharmacotherapy was more effective in comparison to CBT alone.

In other words, the finding is not simply: "CBT is (or is not) effective for treating depression." In fact, we should be wary when treatment effects for any therapeutic modality are spoken of so casually and dichotomously. The fact that we cannot come to a bottom-line statement even after many years of research, whereby hundreds of empirical studies costing many millions of dollars have been conducted, is not an indictment of either researchers or clinicians. It is purely based on the reality that: (i) people are complex and enter treatment with an extensive set of variables that impact their mental health; (ii) neither treatment approaches nor clinicians are perfect, and they are not able to help every patient, at all times, in every way; and (iii) it is very challenging to operationally define (measure) each and every potentially relevant antecedent and outcome variable in a research study while preserving ecological validity (i.e., the ability to generalize findings to the real world). Still, CBT approaches lend themselves to measurement more easily than many other approaches because of the way in which techniques and outcome variables are conceptualized, which largely explains the extensive CBT empirical research literature. Despite this, the take-home message is similar to that which is associated with many other treatment interventions: CBT works for some people, some of the time, for particular issues.

Dialectical-Behavioral Therapy

Dialectical behavior therapy (DBT) is a manualized cognitive-behavioral treatment modality that was developed by Marsha Linehan in the early 1990s as an outpatient treatment for those diagnosed with borderline personality disorder who engaged in parasuicidal,[3] or self-injurious, behaviors (Linehan, 1993a, 1993b). However, it has become an extremely popular therapy approach that has been adapted and used across many contexts for a wide range of mental health problems—so much so that we have given it its own stand-alone section here, even though it is a cognitive-behavioral treatment type. Generally speaking, DBT can address four related domains of intervention in a behavior chain case formulation: emotional regulation, crisis management, interpersonal effectiveness, and mindfulness (Koerner, 2007). DBT integrates cognitive-behavioral and Eastern principles, particularly mindfulness. As Panos, Jackson, Hasan, & Panos (2014) articulated it:

DBT is partially based upon the theoretical belief that people with BPD [borderline personality disorder] significantly lack the ability to regulate emotions or to tolerate stress. Additionally, personal and environmental factors often block and inhibit the use of behavioral skills those people may have, thereby reinforcing dysfunctional behaviors. Theses [*sic*] deficits and difficulties combine and result in pervasive instability in moods and extensive pattern of self-harming acts. Therefore, a main overarching goal of DBT is to stabilize the clients and help them achieve behavioral control. Consequently, as noted previously, DBT has four main behavioral targets: (1) decrease life-threatening suicidal and parasuicidal acts, (2) decrease therapy-interfering behaviors, (3) decrease quality of life interfering behaviors, and (4) increase behavioral skills. (p. 222)

Furthermore, DBT seeks to enhance people's capabilities and their motivation to change and to ensure that new capabilities can be generalized to the natural environment. As the name implies, DBT is focused on identifying and targeting maladaptive behavioral patterns and dialectical dilemmas: (i) emotional vulnerability versus self-invalidation, (ii) active passivity versus apparent competence, and (iii) unrelenting crisis versus inhibited grieving. In its most traditional form, DBT is a very action-oriented treatment approach for the patient and therapist alike; in fact, some DBT providers remain "on call" 24 hours per day, 7 days per week to provide real-time coaching as needed. A combination of weekly individual and group therapy and skill-building sessions is typically required as well. Therapists are also trained to use a specific set of tools, language, and interventions.[4] DBT was designed as a four-stage treatment. In stage 1, behaviors that are life-threatening or therapy-interfering or that compromise the client's quality of life are targeted, in addition to deficits in behavioral capabilities necessary to make life changes. Stage 2 interventions target posttraumatic stress responses and traumatizing emotional experiences with the ultimate goal of getting the client out of ongoing emotional distress. In stage 3, treatment seeks to synthesize what has been learned while increasing self-respect and feelings of connectedness and continuing to resolve problems encountered in daily living. Lastly, stage 4 was designed to target the feelings of incompleteness that many people experience and to become fully mindful, thereby no longer needing reality to be different from what it is at present.

DBT has become a widely used treatment modality outside of self-injurious outpatients diagnosed with borderline personality disorder. For example, it has been adapted for use with such populations as adolescent and geriatric groups, couples, inmates, and those presenting with attention-deficit hyperactivity disorder, substance use, and eating disorder–related problems. As such, it has extended into community mental health, crisis, inpatient, partial hospital, and correctional settings (Robins & Chapman, 2004). DBT has further been established as a front-line effective treatment for suicide-related behavior (Comtois & Linehan, 2006). DBT remains particularly attractive because it is manualized, it includes individual and group formats, and it is easily adaptable because of such components as the use of social skills training and homework assignments. The interested reader is directed to the following sources for a more in-depth overview of DBT: Linehan (1993a, 1993b, 2014); McKay, Wood, & Brantley (2007); and Swenson (2016).

Despite its popularity and widespread use, the empirical research base for DBT is limited by relatively small sample sizes as well as the reality that many patients in traditional DBT treatment studies do not surpass the initial stages of treatment. At the time of Robins & Chapman's (2004) study, three published RCTs had investigated the efficacy of DBT for treating women with border-line personality disorder. In the first RCT, Linehan and colleagues randomized 44 women into treatment-as-usual and DBT treatment groups. Compared to those in the treatment-as-usual group, DBT participants showed greater reductions in the frequency and severity of parasuicidal behavior, frequency and length of inpatient hospitalizations, and better treatment retention (Linehan et al., 1991), as well as greater reductions in (trait) anger and social role functioning (Linehan, Tutek, Heard, & Armstrong, 1994) and the main-tenance of treatment gains at 6- and 12-month follow-ups (Linehan, Heard, & Armstrong, 1993). However, there were no significant differences between the treatment groups with respect to depression, hopelessness, suicidal idea-tion, or reasons for living. In the second RCT, Koons and colleagues (2001) investigated the efficacy of DBT with female veterans diagnosed with border-line personality disorder. They found that the 20 women assigned to 6 months of DBT evidenced greater improvements in suicidal ideation, parasuicidal be-havior, dissociation, hopelessness, depression, and anger expression compared to those in the treatment-as-usual group. There was no difference in the expe-rience of anxiety symptoms. The third RCT was conducted in the Netherlands by Verheul et al. (2003) with 58 women diagnosed with borderline personality disorder, half of whom also had a comorbid substance use disorder diagnosis. The women were treated for 12 months, and DBT patients exhibited greater reductions in parasuicidal behaviors and various impulse-control problem behaviors, such as substance abuse, binge-eating, gambling, and reckless driving. A significantly higher proportion of DBT patients remained with the same therapist for the entirety of the treatment, but there was no statistically significant difference between suicide attempts.

More recently, Panos and colleagues (2014) investigated the efficacy of DBT for the treatment of behaviors and symptoms related to borderline per-sonality disorder by meta-analyzing all RCTs that examined the efficacy of DBT in decreasing suicide attempts, parasuicidal behavior, attrition, or de-pressive symptoms in adults with this diagnosis. Of the 197 studies initially considered, only five RCTs met the full inclusion criteria (including the afore-mentioned studies reviewed by Robins & Chapman, 2004), corresponding to a total sample size of 345 patients—the vast majority of whom were women. Panos et al. found evidence for the efficacy of DBT in the treatment of sui-cidal and parasuicidal behavior; however, it was only marginally better than treatment-as-usual in reducing attrition and not significantly different in reducing depressive symptoms.

Additional Therapy Approaches

Admittedly, we have only scratched the surface when it comes to reviewing the myriad psychotherapy treatment modalities that have been developed over the past century or so. We have chosen to highlight psychodynamic, CBT, and DBT approaches because of the frequency of their use in many of the types of matters commonly seen in firearm-related contexts. As noted, however, there are literally hundreds more specific types of treatments available. Other overarching modalities include, but are certainly not limited to, existential-humanistic, interpersonal/relational, integrative and eclectic, family, marital (see Gurman & Messer, 2003, and Eells, 2007, for overviews of each), and many other types of interpersonal, systemic, and supportive and experiential treatment approaches, such as acceptance and commitment psychotherapy (see A-Tjak et al., 2015) and motivational interviewing (see Burke, Arkowitz, & Menchola, 2003). The interested reader is directed to the following sources for a review of the wide range of therapeutic approaches available: Capuzzi & Stauffer (2016); Seligman & Reichenberg (2014); VandenBos, Meidenbauer, and Frank-McNeil (2014); Yalom & Leszcz (2005); and Wampold (2012).

Treatment for Violence Risk and Violent Offenders

We have provided a broad overview of some of the most common types of therapeutic intervention modalities, but there are certainly more we did not address (e.g., existential, gestalt). Furthermore, there are literally hundreds of nuanced approaches even within those we did present. For our purposes, consistent with the scope of this book, our intention is not to zero in on treatment details and lose sight of the forest for the trees. Modifications are made even to the most structured, manualized therapeutic treatment approaches to increase their utility in certain settings, such as DBT in correctional facilities. Despite the myriad treatment approaches available, the question remains as to which to employ, when, at what levels of frequency and intensity, and for whom. This is especially relevant in the context of providing treatment for violence risk and violent offenders because of the significant heterogeneity in risk levels and needs among those who have engaged in violent acts or pose a particular risk of such. Fortunately, the importance of specifically matching interventions with these considerations in mind was recognized many years ago.

The risk–need–responsivity (RNR) model of risk assessment developed by Andrews, Bonta, & Hoge (1990) is one of the most influential and well-accepted models for the treatment and assessment of violent offenders. The RNR model is not a specific type of assessment or treatment but, rather, a model comprised of three core principles: risk, need, and responsivity. The *risk* principle relates to the notion that the level of service (i.e., intervention) provided should match the person's risk of reoffending. For instance, those most likely to engage in future violence should receive the most intensive interventions. The *need* principle pertains to evaluating the person's criminogenic and mental health needs, which will serve as treatment goals or targets. Criminogenic needs are dynamic risk factors directly related to violence. Recall that dynamic risk factors are those that can change (i.e., current and future-oriented), as opposed to those that are static or historical. The *responsivity* principle refers to a person's likelihood of responding to interventions developed to reduce his or her risk. In this regard, the aim is to maximize the person's ability to learn from interventions by tailoring such efforts to the person's learning style, motivation, abilities, and strengths. The responsivity principle consists of general and specific considerations. *General responsivity* refers to the assumption that social learning interventions are the most effective ways to teach new behaviors. Within general responsivity, two principles exist: the *relationship* principle (i.e., the need to establish a therapeutic/working alliance) and the *structuring* principle (i.e., influencing change via modeling, reinforcement, and problem-solving). *Specific responsivity* refers to the tenet that treatment interventions should consider individual strengths as well as sociobiological personality factors. A person's treatment is then tailored to best match his or her strengths and areas of need. The notion underlying this principle is that treatment can be enhanced if interventions are in line with personal factors that facilitate learning, with the ultimate goal of increasing motivation and decreasing treatment barriers.

The RNR model fits well within the context of violence risk assessment. As noted, treatment interventions and goals are developed based on a person's risk level, needs, and likely treatment response. It directs evaluators and treatment providers to focus on the interplay of these concepts, thereby requiring an ongoing assessment of risk, needs, and response to interventions, rather than setting forth a one-size-fits-all, cookbook approach to treatment that does not demand attention to treatment gains or the lack thereof. By not subscribing to an overarching model of violence risk assessment and treatment, medical and mental health professionals can focus too heavily on the granular aspects of evaluation and treatment, which can lead them to lose sight of the guiding principles and ultimate goal of these services: to manage and prevent violence.

As we addressed in Chapters 3 and 4 of this book, we have a general understanding of the types of clinical syndromes and personality disorders associated with those who engage in violence, more generally. Namely, the types of conditions commonly associated with interpersonal violence are certain substance use and personality disorders, particularly antisocial personality disorder (and psychopathy), as well as disruptive, impulse-control, and conduct disorders (e.g., oppositional defiant disorder, intermittent explosive disorder, conduct disorder) among others. As we outlined in the aforementioned chapters, many of these conditions are behaviorally based in terms of their clinical presentations and corresponding diagnostic criteria, and therefore, behavioral and cognitive-behavioral therapies predominate in this treatment context.

But which conditions are most commonly implicated in firearm-related violence, specifically? There is not necessarily a clear answer to this question because many people who engage in violent acts with firearms have never been formally diagnosed with a psychiatric condition or, if they have, it has not been made publicly available. The exception is the rare, yet more sensational mass shootings, including school shootings. Otherwise, we have some research on proxy variables, such as in the context of gun carrying. For example, in their analysis of the data from the National Comorbidity Study Replication, Swanson and colleagues (2015) found that people who engage in impulsive angry behavior and who carried firearms were more likely to meet the diagnostic criteria for a number of mental health conditions, including depressive, bipolar and anxiety disorders, PTSD, intermittent explosive disorder, pathological gambling, eating disorders, substance use disorders, and various personality disorders. However, of particular note is their finding that: "Very few persons in the risky category of having impulsive angry behavior combined with gun access had ever been hospitalized for a mental health problem" (p. 209). As a result, relatively few would be subject to current firearm restrictions because most will not be flagged during background checks.

Instead of recognizing this reality, however, the narrative we often hear is that there is a lack of mental health services available to people in need. This is often associated with large-scale firearm-related violence, such as mass shootings. Indeed, in his 2016 executive order on gun violence, President Obama allocated $500 million to increase mental health care for those in need (White House Office of the Press Secretary, 2016). Some have shared this sentiment. For example, in his editorial, Fawcett (2014) contended:

> Although there may be a political argument about freedom and the
> right to bear arms in this country, there is not much to argue about
> with regard to this country's failure to provide treatment to its seriously
> mentally ill citizens, not to mention its returning war veterans. (p. 206)

Fawcett added that, subsequent to Congresswoman Gabby Gifford's shooting, the sheriff of Pima County noted that their jail was the only mental health treatment facility in the county and Arizona had decreased its mental health budget nearly 40%. Fawcett further noted that the most distrustful, paranoid persons often refuse treatment, including medication, and represent one group at risk for engaging in mass murder. In fact, it has been found that the first episode of psychosis is associated with increased risk for homicide and serious violence (Nielssen, Yee, Millard, & Large, 2011), and some have suggested that diagnoses of bipolar disorder and schizophrenia may also be linked to a predisposition to homicide (Sher & Rice, 2015). However, the empirical research is clear that the presence of a major mental illness is a rather weak predictor of interpersonal violence and that there are a number of other conditions much more closely associated with such.

Treatment for Victims of Violence and Domestic Violence

Those who are the direct victims of violence may develop various types of mental health problems, including general depressive and anxiety-related conditions. However, some victims develop what are referred to in the *Diagnostic and Statistical Manual of Mental Disorders*, fifth edition (American Psychiatric Association, 2013), as trauma- and stressor-related disorders, which include adjustment disorders, acute stress disorder, and PTSD. An *adjustment disorder* is classified as the presence of emotional or behavioral symptoms in response to an identifiable stressor(s), developing within 3 months of the onset of such stressor(s). The condition may be acute or chronic (i.e., persists more than 6 months). Examples of stressors include harassment, workplace distress, and deaths of loved ones. The distress a person experiences must be above and beyond what would be expected, and the symptoms must cause marked distress and impairment in functioning. For instance, in the case of deaths, the distress one experiences must extend beyond the normal bereavement process.

In contrast, an *acute stress disorder* is caused by a trauma. Specifically, it includes exposure to actual or threatened death, serious injury, or a sexual violation; and it may include being the direct victim of, witnessing, or even learning about the incident. Additional symptom categories include intrusion symptoms (e.g., recurring, distressing memories), avoidance symptoms, negative alterations in cognitions and mood, and arousal symptoms (e.g., hypervigilance, irritability). A combination of these symptoms must be present for at least 3 days but no more than 1 month. If these symptoms persist for longer than 1 month, a PTSD diagnosis would be made. Given that the symptoms overlap and that time is essentially the only distinction between the two conditions, researchers have found that approximately 80% of people diagnosed with acute stress disorder will go on to develop PTSD (see Brewin, Andrews, Rose, & Kirk, 1999; Bryant & Harvey, 1998; Harvey & Bryant, 1998).

As noted, a person does not need to be the direct victim of violence to experience distress or mental health problems. Indeed, there is a voluminous and long-standing professional literature base pertaining to bereavement and loss, including Elisabeth Kübler-Ross' seminal book *On Death and Dying* (1969), wherein she delineated her five stages of grief model,[5] and Judith Viorst's *Necessary Losses* (1997). However, professional literature and research specifically pertaining to the emotional and psychological impact on those whose loved ones died violently are much scarcer. Nevertheless, there appears to be notable overlap in the themes relevant to loss across the spectrum. In a recent study, Bailey et al. (2013) investigated the cognitive processes of black mothers, who are disproportionately affected by homicide loss, in finding meaning and building resilience subsequent to the death of a child due to gun violence. They found that four themes emerged with respect to the way in which mothers changed the meaninglessness of their children's murder and built resilience: (i) belief that the death had a purpose, (ii) religious and spiritual beliefs, (iii) activism to honor their children, and (iv) renewed purpose for their lives. Of additional note is that the ability of these mothers to find meaning and achieve personal growth was influenced by social and cultural factors, including those related to race, social stigma, police interactions, and treatment within their social networks. Nevertheless, as Bailey and colleagues articulated it: "The process of finding meaning and building resilience reflects an overall shift in the mothers' sense of self and purpose for their lives, which had been fragmented by the violent deaths" (p. 344; see also Bailey, Sharma, & Jubin, 2013). As many readers will recognize, these are very similar concepts to those associated with the bereavement and loss literature, more generally.

But what about direct victims of violence? As we noted above, they may develop a range of problems, including depressive, anxiety, and trauma- and stressor-related conditions; and, of course, they may not develop any significant mental health problems at all. In many cases, trauma is not related to a single incident and can lead to a *complex trauma* condition. Recall that we devoted Chapter 5 of this book to issues related to domestic violence (DV), intimate partner violence (IPV), and battered woman syndrome, in particular. As Williams (2006) articulated it:

> When exposure to a catastrophic or violent event does not allow a person to resume living an undisrupted life, or if the type of trauma is both repetitive and cumulative, the result will be persistent complex manifestations that affect psychological, social, and biological systems. Referred to as complex posttraumatic stress disorders, as opposed to acute stress disorders, they exist independent of the causation situation. (pp. 321–322)

Complex trauma can result from various causes, including DV and IPV, as well as other types of emotional and physical abuse, neglect, disease, and exposure to war. It is important to highlight the fact that trauma can result even when no physical harm is present (e.g., neglect, psychological abuse, witnessing traumatic events). Williams also provided a concise and illustrative understanding of the trauma experience, more generally:

> People with posttraumatic and complex stress disorder have brains with altered responses that involve a sensitization of these systems to threats and alarm. In children, if violence and trauma are chronic and repeated, the actual development of the brain may be altered. This impacts both behavioral and emotional functioning . . . . Adolescents and adults tend to process internal and external stimuli in a maladaptive way; emotions become triggers of past trauma that are no longer clearly perceived. The result is a similar physiological reaction to a very different situation. The memory that caused the original reaction to threat is fixed in a part of the brain that has frozen its ability to access. . . . The body's response

to that original threat is replayed. The memory of the traumatic event is encoded, but the individual is missing the ability to make sense of the somatic sensations that are really implicitly felt memories of the event. (pp. 327–328)

Therefore, exposure-based treatments are often employed to treat trauma victims. Such treatment is focused on helping the person process the memories and become attuned to physical sensations and reactions. Triggers are revisited, assessed, and put back into context. The treatment seeks to develop empowerment and trust. Some people may seek to find meaning in their experiences and even "tell their stories," whereas others solely seek relief from their symptoms, a return to their baseline functioning, and to move forward (and away) from their experiences. As with all treatments, however, the modality to be used should be carefully chosen on a case-by-case basis. In this context, exposure-based treatments may be *contraindicated* for some people. Historically, it was believed that people exposed to traumatic events should "talk about them," but as Lilienfeld (2007) suggested, interventions such as critical incident stress debriefing can increase the risk of experiencing posttraumatic stress symptoms and recovered-memory techniques can potentially lead to the production of false memories of trauma. Treatment decisions should be made based on a careful assessment of the person, and situational factors must also factor into the decision. For example, a person may be a good candidate for exposure-based treatment; however, he or she may be in an environment not conducive to such (e.g., a correctional facility) or there may not be enough time to provide such treatment appropriately (e.g., the person is not expected to be in treatment for more than a month or two, or the therapist will likely be transferred in the near future).

Victims of DV and IPV often employ a wide range of strategies to cope with symptoms, such as seeking social support, relying on religious or spiritual coping, using electronic media and engaging in related hobbies (e.g., reading), and practicing deep breathing and relaxation exercises, but also potentially maladaptive coping mechanisms, such as substance use, sleeping, isolating, and avoiding trauma-related stimuli (Sullivan et al., 2017). Thus, a multidisciplinary approach that utilizes a mixture of contemporary treatment methods (e.g., technology-based) is frequently clinically indicated (Howell & Miller-Graff, 2016). Certainly, many traditional therapeutic principles apply as well. In her paper on ethical considerations for clinicians treating victims and perpetrators of IPV, McLaughlin (2017) highlighted the need to honor and incorporate general principles related to maximizing benefit and minimizing harm, respecting people's rights and dignity (e.g., if they choose to stay in an abusive relationship), and seeking and maintaining awareness of one's potential personal biases. More specific ethical considerations in this context include those related to limits of confidentiality, duty to warn and protect provisions (à la *Tarasoff*), professional competence, and assessing and managing suicide, violence, and child abuse risk. Namely, McLaughlin recommends that clinicians working in this area (i) assess violence and suicide risk regularly and thoroughly; (ii) familiarize themselves with the literature and relevant state laws, including those related to breaking confidentiality and mandatory reporting of concerns; (iii) seek consultation from those experienced in working with IPV clients; (iv) research local and national resources for both victims and perpetrators; and (v) maintain awareness of legal options available to victims.

It is also important to remember that DV is not solely comprised of spouses or significant others but also includes children, siblings, and other family members, such as grandparents. For this reason, family-based interventions may be warranted in some cases. Miller, Veltkamp, & Kraus (1997) presented a decision-tree model for clinicians who provide services in this regard, which is associated with a plan of action that includes the following components: (i) assessment, (ii) reporting and legal obligations, (iii) treatment/intervention, (iv) consults/assessments (with relevant specialists, such as medical doctors and forensic practitioners), and (v) victim/family education. The overarching premise is treating the family as one unit, consistent with a *family systems* approach to treatment (see, e.g., Gilbert, 2006; McGoldrick, Gerson, & Petry, 2008). As Miller and colleagues (1997) noted, risk factors in the context of family violence center around the notion that there are multigenerational patterns of abuse and victimization that are passed on to subsequent generations. They outlined the following risk factors:

- One parent may be extremely passive, dependent, and/or reluctant to assert self for fear of destroying the family unit.
- Poor marital relationship, a lack of constructive communication or poor interpersonal relationships.
- The perpetrator turns outside the family or toward the child to relieve and displace emotional tension and stress.
- The child may feel emotionally deprived and turn to the perpetrator for support and emotional nurturance, and in the process become abused.
- The issue of control is a significant factor in spouse- and child-abusing families. Perpetrators use control to force victims to comply with their wishes.
- Generational boundaries are often unclear between the perpetrator and child victim.
- There are a lack of social contacts outside the family.
- Parents have inadequate coping skills, particularly under stress.
- Family problems become family secrets, therefore not allowing change or intervention to occur within the cycle of violence.
- Alcohol and substance abuse is a common factor in cases involving domestic violence. (p. 429)

Furthermore, Miller and colleagues set forth a number of important areas for clinicians to consider in this context:

1. Should the therapist try to preserve the psychological attachment and maintain the psychological bond that victims of domestic violence experience? The victim's contact with the offender should be supervised and the child should not be forced to spend time with the perpetrator if he or she does not feel comfortable. Reducing the degree of environmental change is crucial for most victims. Maintaining the victim's relationship with peers, school, neighborhood, and church are [*sic*] also necessary to reduce risk of further problems.
2. Can the therapist help preserve continuity of the relationship between the victim and the perpetrator?
3. Does supervision by the therapist reduce risk for siblings?
4. When should the therapist evaluate to determine if siblings are showing symptoms as were observed in the victim?
5. The therapist should aid in assessing if the victim cannot be protected in the home or should be removed and placed in a safe environment. (p. 431)

In addition, they reiterated the types of community resources that should be available to clinicians engaging in these matters, which they had previously outlined (i.e., Veltkamp & Miller (1990, 1994): a safe shelter environment, a 24-hour crisis hotline, counseling and casework services, a legal advocacy program, a medical services advocacy program, a perpetrator's counseling program, and community education programs on DV-related issues for family members and clinicians but also to promote public awareness.

Treatment for Risk of Suicide and Self-Harm

As we discussed at length in Chapter 6 of this book, in order to set forth appropriate interventions to reduce and manage the risk of suicide and self-harm, we must first be able to identify risk factors and warning signs related to such, at which point we can seek to match risk levels with corresponding interventions. However, as we noted in Chapter 7, the healthcare fields have continued to shift toward *prevention-* rather than *prediction*-based approaches in the context of addressing violence and suicide risk, consistent with the sentiment of the American Psychological Association's recent press release (2016). As the corresponding synopsis reflects:

> Experts' ability to predict if someone will attempt to take his or her own life is no better than chance and has not significantly improved over the last 50 years, according to a comprehensive review of suicide research published by the American Psychological Association.

Per the lead author of the cited meta-analysis (Franklin et al., 2017):

> Our analyses showed that science could only predict future suicidal
> thoughts and behaviors about as well as random guessing. In other
> words, a suicide expert who conducted an in-depth assessment of risk
> factors would predict a patient's future suicidal thoughts and behaviors
> with the same degree of accuracy as someone with no knowledge of
> the patient who predicted based on a coin flip. This was extremely
> humbling—after decades of research, science had produced no
> meaningful advances in suicide prediction.

Risk factors and warning signs must be recognizable to set forth prevention
efforts. As Franklin and colleagues added:

> Warning signs are usually conceptualized as proximal indicators of
> suicide risk; risk factors are sometimes conceptualized as more distal
> indicators, but may also be proximal. (p. 189)

They also outlined suicide risk factors and warning signs set forth by several leading health- and suicide-focused organizations (see also Table 6.1,
Chapter 6, of this book for additional risk factors).

American Association of Suicidology
Risk Factors
- More than one warning sign; anticipated or actual losses or
  life stresses (e.g., romantic breakups, legal problems, academic
  failures); prior suicide attempts

Warning Signs
- Increased substance use; no reason or purpose for living; anxiety,
  agitation, or sleep problems; feeling trapped; hopelessness; social
  withdrawal; rage and anger; reckless or risky behaviors; dramatic
  mood changes

American Foundation for Suicide Prevention
Risk Factors
- Depression; bipolar disorder; schizophrenia; borderline or
  antisocial personality disorders; conduct disorder; psychotic
  disorders or symptoms; substance abuse disorders; serious or
  chronic physical health problems; exposure to others' suicide;
  access to lethal means; stressful life events; family history of
  suicide or mental health problems; childhood abuse; prior
  suicide attempt

Warning Signs
- Talking about suicide, having no reason to live, being a burden,
  feeling trapped, or unbearable pain; increased substance use;
  planning suicide; acting recklessly; social withdrawal; sleep
  problems; saying goodbye to people; giving away prized

possessions; aggression; depression; loss of interest; rage and irritability; anxiety; humiliation

Centers for Disease Control

Risk Factors

- Family history of suicide or childhood maltreatment; prior suicide attempt; mental disorders (especially depression); substance abuse; hopelessness; impulsive or aggressive tendencies; cultural or religious beliefs that suicide is noble; local suicide epidemics; social isolation; barriers to mental health treatment; loss; physical illness; access to lethal means; unwillingness to seek help due to stigma concerns

Warning Signs

- Talking about hurting oneself; increased substance use; changes in mood, diet, or sleeping patterns

National Institute of Mental Health

Risk Factors

- Mental disorders (especially depression and substance abuse); prior suicide attempt; family history of mental disorder, substance abuse, suicide, violence, or physical/sexual abuse; guns or firearms in the home; incarceration; being exposed to others' suicidal behaviors

Warning Signs

- Threatening or talking about killing oneself; planning suicide; hopelessness; rage or anger; reckless behaviors; feeling trapped; increased substance abuse; social withdrawal; anxiety, agitation, or sleep problems; dramatic mood changes; lack of purpose in life

World Health Organization

Risk Factors

- Mental disorders (especially depression and substance abuse); moments of crisis; chronic pain and illness; conflict, disaster, violence, abuse, and loss; being a refugee, migrant, indigenous person, prisoner, or non-heterosexual person; prior suicide

Warning Signs

- None noted

While it is important for healthcare providers to be attuned to the risk factors and warning signs, as Skerrett (2012), former executive editor of *Harvard Health Publications*, articulated it: "Every suicide, like every person, is different." Indeed, many suicides are impulsive acts, and we are not able to speak to those who have died by suicide—only those who have contemplated or survived it (Dadoly, 2011). Although these represent different groups, they are essentially the only compelling empirical data we have. In their study of those who engaged in near-lethal suicide attempts, Simon and colleagues (2001) found that 24% reported spending less than 5 minutes between the decision to attempt suicide and the actual attempt. Furthermore, suicidal crises are often self-limiting and acute, such that more than 90% of people who survive a suicide attempt, including lethal attempts, do not go on to die by suicide (Miller & Hemenway, 2008).

It is also very important to highlight the fact that some contemporary theories diverge from earlier ones in many respects. For example, in their interpersonal theory of suicide, Van Orden and colleagues (2010) conceptualized suicidal ideation as being caused by the simultaneous presence of two interpersonal constructs: *thwarted belongingness* (social isolation) and *perceived burdensomeness* (e.g., in the context of family conflict, unemployment, and physical illness).

As Van Orden and colleagues noted, older theories, such as that of Shneidman (1985, 1987, 1998), focused on individual factors, with *psychache* (i.e., psychological and emotional pain that reaches intolerable intensity) as the primary causal factor of suicide. However, according to Van Orden et al.:

> In contrast to Shneidman's model, we propose that the need to belong is the need central to the development of suicidal desire, consistent with the wealth of findings linking social connectedness to suicidal behavior.[6]
>
> Thus, the interpersonal theory is consistent with past theoretical accounts of suicidal behavior through its proposal for a key role for social connectedness. However, the interpersonal theory diverges from previous theories in its proposal that an unmet "need to belong" is the specific interpersonal need involved in desire for suicide. (p. 582)

Thus, individual factors in the context of "psychache" should not be necessarily assumed to be causal in the context of suicide attempts or completed suicides. In addition, we should not automatically assume the presence of fear leading up to the act. In fact, some models addressing the acquired capability for suicide suggest that "to die by suicide, individuals must lose some of the fear associated with suicidal behaviors" (Van Orden et al., 2010, p. 585). The interaction relevant here is that of *increased* pain tolerance and *reduced* fear of death. In fact, "fear of death or dying due to pain and suffering" is an empirically based primary *protective factor* associated with decreased risk of suicide attempt or death by suicide (e.g., see Columbia-Suicide Severity Rating Scale; Posner et al., 2011; Columbia Lighthouse Project, n.d., 2017).

We provided a more in-depth theoretical overview of various conceptualizations of suicide in Chapter 6 of this book, but let us consider the duties and responsibilities of clinicians in meeting standards of care for treating suicidal patients here. In their edited book *Risk Management with Suicidal Patients*, Dr. Bruce Bongar and colleagues set forth standards for those working in inpatient and outpatient settings who treat suicidal patients (1998). A particularly noteworthy theme that cuts across contexts is that of the need to conduct thorough assessments that lead to the formulation of formal treatment plans. This process must include an adequate history-taking and record review, when possible, and a mental status and diagnostic examination. Moreover, practitioners must provide appropriate environmental safeguards, monitoring, and support. They also emphasize that outpatient providers may need to increase their treatment options for suicidal patients, which may include 24-hour, holiday, and weekend ("on-call") coverage. In addition, pharmacological interventions are addressed throughout the book and it indicates that most patients experiencing suicidal ideation do not need hospitalization, they respond to outpatient treatment, and suicide risk is significantly reduced with proper medication for most patients. Additional treatment considerations include the importance of social support, individual and family therapy, and concurrent substance use treatment in many cases. Furthermore, medical consultations may be beneficial, as are psychoeducation and ready access to help. The emphasis is on realistic goals but with corresponding realistic interventions. For instance, clinicians should not simply rely on "no suicide contracts." As Silverman et al. (1998) noted in the fourth chapter of that volume:

> One of the common problems is when a therapist relies exclusively on a "suicide contract" with a patient. . . . The therapist may be feeling relieved that the patient has concurred with an agreement not to harm himself or herself while under the direct care of the therapist. However, the basis of a clinician–patient contract is a solid therapeutic relationship. . . . The therapist must know the patient and share a common language with the patient prior to engaging in the formulation of a contract. A contract entered into with a patient in a setting such as an inpatient unit, where behaviors may be extreme and risks for acting out have already been acknowledged to be high, must be understood as an enhancement of a therapeutic relationship, not a substitute for one. (p. 90)

In sum, the main duties and responsibilities of clinicians in meeting standards of care for treating suicidal patients set forth by Silverman et al. (p. 91) are:

- Appropriately diagnosing
- Appropriately foreseeing future behavioral problems
- Providing protection against harm (i.e., in the context of treatment planning)
- Supervising the patient appropriately
- Providing a safe, secure, and protective environment
- Treating conditions associated with suicidal behaviors, and using medication and other appropriate treatment modalities to do so
- Ensuring (clinician) adherence to the treatment plan
- Documenting clinical decisions
- Communication among providers
- Maintaining actively suicidal patients in the hospital or inpatient settings
- Providing post-discharge plans and care to those coming from inpatient settings

In a review of various expert sources concerning suicide prevention and assessment competencies for mental health professionals, Cramer and colleagues (2013) synthesized the broad literature of necessary skills for effective suicide risk assessment and management. Echoing many themes recommended by Silverman et al. (among others), this set of core competencies extends clinician responsibilities to managing one's own reaction and self-care as well. The specific set of competencies, applied in later pilot tests of competency-based training effectiveness for psychologists and other mental health professionals (Cramer et al., 2017; Cramer, Bryson, Stroud, & Ridge, 2016), is as follows:

1. Know and manage your own attitudes toward suicide
2. Maintain a collaborative, empathic stance toward the patient
3. Know and elicit evidence-based risk and protective factors in assessment
4. Focus on current plan and intent of suicidal ideation
5. Determine the level of risk
6. Develop and enact a collaborative evidence-based treatment plan
7. Notify and involve supportive others
8. Document risk, plan, and clinical reasoning
9. Know the law concerning suicide
10. Engage in debriefing and self-care

The interested reader is referred to Cramer and colleagues (2013) for a more thorough overview of the details for each competency.

The professional literature pertaining to interventions and programs specifically designed to address firearm-related suicide is much scarcer and, by and large, has been focused on firearm access prevention. For example, Johnson, Frank, Ciocca, & Barber (2011) evaluated a program called CALM (Counseling on Access to Lethal Means), which was developed and implemented by two of the authors through the Injury Prevention Center at the Children's Hospital at Dartmouth. CALM was a 2-hour workshop wherein community-based mental health professionals were instructed on the reduction of lethal means and suicide prevention efforts for at-risk clients and families. As Johnson and colleagues articulated it: "The goal of CALM was to increase the number of mental health care providers who talk with family members of youths at risk for suicide about access to guns and medications at home" (p. 260). The workshops were presented in seven community mental health centers in New Hampshire for a 5-month period in 2006, and follow-up surveys were administered approximately 2 months later. Of the 168 participants who completed the post-test questionnaire, most agreed that suicide could be prevented by restricting access to lethal means and that it was important to speak to parents about preventing access to firearms, and 65% reported that they had, in fact, counseled parents about these issues subsequent to the workshop. Ultimately, Johnson and colleagues opined that a brief workshop is an effective strategy for educating mental health professionals about reducing access to firearms among youth.

Simon (2007) noted:

> Guns in the home are associated with a five-fold increase in suicide. All patients at risk for suicide must be asked if guns are available at home or easily accessible elsewhere, or if they have intent to buy or purchase a gun. Gun safety management requires a collaborative team approach including the clinician, patient, and designated person responsible for removing guns from the home. A call-back to the clinician from the designated person is required confirming that guns have been removed and secured according to plan. The principle of gun safety management applies to outpatients, inpatients, and emergency patients, although its implementation varies according to the clinical setting. (p. 518)

In a very different context, Smith, Currier, & Drescher (2015) investigated firearm ownership and suicidality in a sample of military veterans (predominantly Vietnam veterans) entering residential treatment for PTSD. First, the frequency of firearm ownership was comparable to non-veteran estimates. They also found that those who experienced suicidal ideation and engaged in prior suicide attempts were less likely to own firearms compared to those who had only experienced suicidal ideation and those who had no suicide attempt histories. Moreover, more frequent combat exposure was associated with firearm ownership, but PTSD symptoms were not linked to such. Furthermore, most veterans endorsed safe storage practices. Taken together, Smith and colleagues opined that their findings may reflect increased awareness of firearm ownership risks with veteran groups as well as increases in *means-restricting counseling*. Specifically, they noted:

> Although means restriction counseling is important for all veterans seeking treatment for PTSD, this strategy appears particularly critical for those who have experienced combat in higher doses. It might also be important to consider more broad means counseling to veterans who have experienced combat given that veterans who die by suicide often do not exhibit typical psychiatric markers of suicide risk, such as lower rates of depression. (p. 223)

In addition, Smith et al. indicated that those at the greatest risk of suicide were those who endorsed the lowest rate of safe storage practices. Although this is an area of concern that warrants attention, they caution:

> Given the possible reluctance among many veterans with PTSD to entrust their firearms to friends or loved ones before an alleviation of their posttraumatic symptomatology via treatment, clinicians might first focus on safe storage practices and not take the risk of damaging their rapport by immediately challenging this possible avoidance strategy. (p. 223)

This sentiment is consistent with similar concerns related to law enforcement and correctional personnel, such that they may be less inclined to seek out professional help because of the risk of losing the ability to carry firearms in the context of being found unfit for duty, thereby jeopardizing their careers and livelihood (see also the sections *Considerations for Law Enforcement and Related Professions* in Chapter 7 and *Barriers to Treatment and Restoration of Firearm Rights* below).

A Note on Youth Interventions

As we discussed in Chapter 4, contemporary neuroscience research has dispelled the long-standing assumption that youth functioned in the same manner as their adult counterparts across a range of areas. Studies on brain anatomy and development led to the evolution of concepts such as *developmental immaturity*, which have helped us understand how young people make decisions and the many ways in which they differ from adults (see Steinberg & Scott, 2003, for an overview). We have also highlighted the need for evaluators to consider environmental (e.g., household, school, community) and individual (e.g., attitudes, behavior, psychiatric symptoms) factors when assessing youth, as well as tracking their response to interventions. The importance of assessing their home lives, family relationships and dynamics, and any problems their caregivers may be having that would affect them (e.g., legal, substance use, DV) cannot be overstated. Moreover, recall that mental health symptoms are often manifested quite differently in youth compared to adults. Taken together, it logically follows that therapeutic interventions with youth also require specialized approaches and considerations.

Weisz and colleagues (2017) recently conducted a meta-analysis on 50 years of youth psychological therapies. Specifically, their analysis included 447 studies published between 1963 and 2013, which included 30,431 youth participants. Ultimately, they concluded that treatment with youth has been moderately successful, overall, but that treatment impact significantly differed based on the target problems. Namely, treatment effects were largest for anxiety, whereas they were smallest for depression. In fact, treatments for depression were found to be *worse* than control conditions. Citing prior research also indicating weak treatment effects for youth depression, Weisz et al. suggest that this is an area that should be prioritized for future treatment development and evaluation. They also found even weaker treatment effects for treating multiple problems concurrently within the same treatment episode, prompting them to make a call for us to consider the ways in which we address youth comorbidity. With regard to the type of therapy used, the results were generally mixed and nuanced—consistent with the adult literature. As Weisz and colleagues articulated it:

> Taken together, the findings suggest that different treatments may differ in their effects, but in highly specific ways that require precise analysis and close attention to the source of outcome information. (p. 94)

Lastly, they found notable differences in treatment effects based on who reported the treatment progress or lack thereof (e.g., youth vs. parents vs. teachers). As such, Weisz et al. reminded us:

> The findings highlight the fact that youth therapy outcome is always, to some extent, in the eye of the beholder, and that different informants observe different samples of a youth's behavior, in different contexts, and bring different perspectives to what they observe. This being the case, much could be gained by linking therapy research and practice to the burgeoning effort to build multi-informant approaches to youth mental health assessment. (p. 95)

As noted, psychotherapies such as DBT have been modified for use with youth populations, particularly those at notable risk. However, their empirical research base is limited in many of the same ways as that of the corresponding adult treatments. For example, Freeman et al. (2016) reviewed studies on DBT for adolescents and found several inconsistencies, including, but not limited to, the use of different terms, definitions, and measures of self-harm; variations in diagnostic inclusion/exclusion criteria; inadequate use of self-harm outcome measures; variable lengths and intensities of treatment; and insufficient attention paid to clinicians' adherence to the DBT model. This is consistent with the concerns expressed by Singer, McManama O'Brien, and LeCloux (2017) in the context of their review study of three psychotherapies used to treat suicidal youth: attachment-based family therapy (ABFT), integrated cognitive-behavioral therapy (I-CBT), and DBT. They too found numerous limitations to the research and conceptual frameworks for these treatments (e.g., demographically and diagnostically narrow samples and overly specific treatment settings or conditions that limit generalizability). They also highlighted a number of considerations and limitations associated with the practical application of these approaches. Namely, they may not be particularly feasible (or available) given the amount of formal and specific training treating clinicians need to be able to appropriately provide these interventions. Nevertheless, Singer and colleagues noted that suicide is the second leading cause of death among youth, yet up to 40% never receive treatment. They also reminded us of the complexity of working with suicidal youth and the need to use theoretically grounded, efficacious treatments when available and possible:

> Although all three therapies have the goal of reducing suicide risk in youth, the differences in theoretical assumptions have important implications for how and when to intervene. Whereas ABFT and I-CBT provide guidance for when and how to work with families, DBT provides guidance for when and how to work in groups. ABFT is an affective-based therapy, whereas I-CBT and DBT are cognitive-based interventions. Although all three include skill-building, ABFT teaches skills to parents, and I-CBT and DBT teach skills to youth. While all treatments have been evaluated in outpatient settings, only

DBT-A has been evaluated in an inpatient setting. Each therapy was developed to address suicide risk within different psychiatric disorders, including depression (ABFT), substance abuse (I-CBT) and borderline personality disorders (DBT). These differences are not the eccentric whims of the developers, but are based on differing theoretical assumptions about what leads to change. (p. 104)

A number of treatment-related issues are important to point out here. For instance, as we addressed in Chapter 7, medical and mental health professionals play a very important gatekeeping role in our society in the firearm context, as illustrated in a study conducted by Bohnert et al. (2015). They noted that violence is a leading cause of injury among those between the ages of 15 and 24 and that it is often associated with substance use. Thus, they compared a sample of assault-injured youth who had used substances within 6 months prior to presenting at an urban emergency department ($n = 350$) to those presenting for non-assault-related care ($n = 250$). They found 57% of all youth to meet criteria for a substance use disorder and only 9% received prior treatment for such. Moreover, 25% of the assault-injured group intended to retaliate, and half of them had firearm access. In addition, the assault-injured (AI) youth had poorer mental health, had greater substance use, and were more likely to be on probation or parole and to report prior emergency department (ED) visits for assault or psychiatric evaluation. Based on their findings, Bohnert et al. concluded:

AI youth may have unmet needs for substance use and mental health treatment, including PTSD. These characteristics along with the risk of retaliation, increased ED service utilization, low utilization of other health care venues, and firearm access highlight the need for interventions that initiate at the time of ED visit. (p. 97)

In their article addressing the role of healthcare and mental health care providers in gun violence prevention efforts, particularly in the context of youth firearm-related homicide and suicide, Williamson, Guerra, & Tynan (2014) set forth the following risk factors:

Gun-Related Homicide

- Unsupervised access to firearms and ammunition
- Early onset of aggressive behavior
- High levels of early environmental and family stress
- Poor parent–child relationships, including harsh or inconsistent discipline and coercive interactions
- Positive individual or family-level normative beliefs about aggression, violence, and firearm usage as methods for problem-solving
- Affiliations with deviant and antisocial peers
- Academic disengagement and school failure or dropout

- Neighborhood disadvantage and exposure to community violence
- Exposure to violent media

Gun-Related Suicide

- Unsupervised access to firearms and ammunition
- Previous suicide attempts
- Male gender
- Non-Latino white ethnic background
- Psychological disorders and comorbidities, such as depression and substance use
- Other psychological vulnerabilities, such as impulsivity, hopelessness, feelings of burdensomeness, and a failed sense of belonging

While these factors are very important to identify, assess for, and manage, most are not particularly unique to firearm-involved homicides and suicides among youth compared to other means of violence and suicide. Moreover, many of the homicide-related youth risk factors cut across other types of acting-out behaviors (e.g., fire-setting, sexual offending), and, in fact, unsupervised access to firearms and ammunition may be the only unique risk factor in this regard (lending support to the attention paid to child access prevention and safe storage practices). In their review of the youth violence literature, Bushman and colleagues (2016) addressed the complexity of school shootings in relation to the much more common acts of street violence and contended that there is no single cause of the former. As they indicated:

> Following the Newtown shooting, Congress and the media focused on three risk factors for school shootings: (a) access to guns, (b) exposure to violent media, and (c) mental health. However, these are only three of a host of possible risk factors for youth violence. (p. 20)

Still, there are empirically based youth violence prevention factors that have been identified, such as those set forth by Bushman et al. (2016): (i) increasing self-control and social competence skills, (ii) strengthening effective parenting and family-based protective factors, (iii) minimizing violent media effects, (iv) reducing youth access to guns and alcohol and substance abuse in youth, and (v) improving school climates. These types of interventions are directly relevant to the above-mentioned risk factors and further substantiate the need to employ a multifaceted approach to manage such a multifaceted problem.

General Considerations for Health and Wellness

Many people pursue good health and wellness to ensure quality-of-life goals rather than to treat a mental health disorder per se, and this is typically accomplished via healthy eating and exercise or enjoyable activities (e.g., yoga, dance, sports). In contrast to clinical psychology, which tends to focus on psychopathology, the subfield of positive psychology assumes that large groups of people functioning in the "normal" range can achieve an even better well-being than they do. However, most people experience stress at some level and at some point in time, particularly in our society and in the context of work. As Johnson & Wood (2017) indicated:

> [there] is an overwhelming body of evidence suggesting that those individuals who might be considered within the normal range—that is, not in services, on medication or in therapy for mental health problems, and in employment—report symptoms of psychological disorder. For example, over 30% of consultant doctors demonstrate evidence of psychiatric morbidity . . . and 26% of both veterinarians . . . and teachers . . . report diagnosable rates of anxiety, depression or both. Even—as is the case for most people—when people score highly on measures of well-being such as life satisfaction . . . positive psychologists argue that these people can be helped more to live life to the full and "flourish." (p. 337)

de Bruin, Formsma, Frijstein, & Bögels (2017) also noted:

> Feeling tensed, restless, rushed, or overwhelmed as a result of daily stress is very common in western society. The lifestyle in the contemporary 24-h economy is characterized by speed, time pressure, competition, job insecurity, being constantly available due to modern telecommunication, an overload of stimuli, and multi-tasking in different roles that we fulfill. (p. 204)

They cited research indicating that work-related pressure is the primary source of stress in the United States and that 75%–90% of primary care visits are related to stress, 30% of work-related disorders are related to stress, and approximately half of the employment force in this country is estimated to be at a point of burnout. Thus, de Bruin and colleagues set out to investigate the potential benefits of a structured group training program called Mindful2Work (Formsma, de Bruin, & Bögels, 2015), which consists of six weekly, 2-hour sessions and a follow-up session, all of which are comprised of physical exercise (20 minutes), yoga (20 minutes), and mindfulness meditation and psychoeducation (80 minutes). The sessions are usually in the morning as energy levels are typically higher, and participants were also asked to practice mindfulness, yoga, and physical exercise at home. They found significant improvements related to physical and mental workability as well as for anxiety, depression, stress, sleep quality, and positive and negative affect. These effects remained significant and generally increased over time. In addition, risk of long-term dropout from work significantly decreased, and employees also worked a higher percentage of their contract hours each week. Taken together, de Bruin et al. contended that the Mindful2Work training was very feasible and promising.

The notion that these types of interventions would be effective is not surprising. Indeed, many contemporary psychotherapies incorporate such activities as those related to practicing mindfulness, relaxation techniques, and behavioral activation (e.g., CBT, DBT, and other behavioral and cognitive-behavioral treatments). Furthermore, specialized treatments have been developed over the years that inherently include these types of activities, such as art and music therapy. While the aforementioned activities and interventions are typically beneficial to the general public, they are often considered to be particularly important to those who have mental health disorders, especially severe mental illness. For instance, while the health benefits of healthy eating and exercise are clear, those diagnosed with serious mental illnesses have shorter life expectancies, largely due to poor diets and lack of exercise (Browne, Mihas, & Penn, 2016). In their study in this area, Browne and colleagues found that clients diagnosed with serious mental illnesses recognized the benefits of exercise but reported motivation, physical health complications, and safety as the three most cited barriers to such; and clinicians added that symptomatology and transportation-related issues were also barriers in this regard. Nevertheless, both clients and clinicians identified walking as the clients' primary form of exercise as it is the most accessible form of exercise to them and it also consists of a social interaction component—a critically important factor in healthcare. The take-home message in the context of all of the aforementioned considerations is that mental and physical health are interrelated concepts as we are whole people, mind and body.

Firearm Safety Precautions

In Chapter 1, we outlined specific firearm safety precautions set forth by the National Shooting Sports Foundation and the National Rifle Association (NRA). It is our contention that it is beneficial for mental health and medical providers to have an awareness of general firearm safety precautions and not solely focus on clients' access. In fact, it is not realistic for some clients, including youth, to have no access to firearms; and, as we will see in the *Emerging Roles for Treating Professionals* section below, clinicians lack formal firearm education and training, they typically do not address these issues with clients, and means-restricting counseling has notable limitations. Furthermore, many people live in households with law enforcement and correctional officers, other government agents, or hunters—situations that usually involve a regular exchange of firearms to and from gun safes. Moreover, those who own firearms for self-defense purposes are more likely to maintain them loaded at some level, especially those who own in states where carrying firearms is legal. Thus, with over 100 million firearm owners in this country, assuming that we can simply restrict access is unrealistic and too simplistic. It is also important to highlight the fact that this is an estimate of *legal* firearms. Given that a large portion of violent crimes are committed in nefarious environments, it is safe to assume that there are many illegal firearms available to those who are intent on securing them. Indeed, such is the primary purpose of gun buy-back programs, and we must also remember that even if a gun is not illegal per se, a person may not have the requisite legal permission to own or use it (e.g., straw sales).

As we have seen in other areas (e.g., sex education), abstinence-only education has significant limitations. Why then would we assume this concept would be more effective in the context of firearms access? While restricting access to vulnerable or at-risk persons is a necessary component to firearm safety, it is insufficient alone. Again, clinicians should familiarize themselves with firearm safety precautions; but also, it is necessary to take a risk management–, prevention-based approach rather than a risk prediction approach, as we have outlined throughout this book. However, as we address in the following section, there are significant barriers to treatment and the restoration of firearm rights for those who wish to own or interact with firearms.

Barriers to Treatment and Restoration of Firearm Rights

There continue to be notable efforts made by many politicians and involved others to make medical and mental health treatment more accessible to people in this country. Indeed, we have cited former president Obama's 2016 executive order numerous times throughout this book, wherein he allocated $500 million to increase access to mental health care and vowed to "help those suffering from mental illness get the help that they need" (White House Office of the Press Secretary, 2016). However, many of those pushing for such improvements in healthcare have contemporaneously promoted increases in restrictive firearm laws and the widening of the background check net. For example, President Obama sought to tap into Social Security Administration databases and remove barriers to reporting from the Department of Health and Human Services to identify those with mental health disorders in the context of conducting background checks for firearms. Despite the ostensible positive aspects of these efforts, they are likely to have a number of unintended consequences, including the likely paradoxical effect of *deterring* many people from seeking treatment (see also Luther, 2014, and his review of the Virginia Supreme Court Case *Paugh v. Henrico Area Mental Health and Developmental Servs.* (2013).[7]

Perhaps the title of the 2014 Gun Owners of America post is most illustrative: "See a Shrink, Lose Your Guns!" (Gun Owners of America, 2014). The article reads, in part:

As a Second Amendment organization representing over 500,000 members, Gun Owners of America is writing to express its opposition to Docket No. HHS-OCR-2014-0001-0001. This proposed rule would massively expand the ability to impose federal gun bans on Americans. The proposal from HHS would effectively say that federal health privacy laws (HIPAA) do not apply to the Second Amendment. The rule would waive federal privacy protections to "permit . . . disclosures of protected health information for purposes of reporting to the NICS. . . ." This isn't the first time that President Barack Obama has stuck his leering eyeballs into Americans' medical records and private affairs. From its Orwellian government database on Americans' health records to its voracious seizure of Americans' phone records, the Obama administration can't trample our personal privacy fast enough. But HHS Secretary Kathleen Sebelius' efforts to turn over personal mental health information to the government's gun ban blacklist (NICS) is particularly loathsome. . . . More than 150,000 law-abiding veterans have already lost their constitutional rights—with no due process whatsoever—because they consulted a VA therapist about a traumatic incident in Iraq, Afghanistan, or the Balkans. Under these new proposed regulations, tens of millions of police and firemen with Post Traumatic Stress Disorder—or people who, as kids, were diagnosed with Attention Deficit and Hyperactivity Disorder—could lose their constitutional rights without any court order, merely because they sought a benefit under a federal program. . . . But herein lies the problem: When Americans with Post Traumatic Stress Disorder and Attention Deficit Disorder realize that nothing they say to their therapist is really confidential, they're not going to be seeking treatment for very long.

On the one hand, we can chalk this sentiment up to that of a single group, albeit one with a half a million members. On the other hand, we must recognize that there are 100 million firearm owners and even more potential applicants who may be having similar types of concerns. Moreover, the notation related to police officers and firefighters is consistent with the reluctance that law enforcement, correctional, and military personnel have often exhibited in seeking mental health care that we have discussed in other parts of this book (e.g., see the *Considerations for Law Enforcement and Related Professions* section in Chapter 7). While efforts to increase and improve healthcare services to those in need are critically important, we must recognize that there are very real and significant barriers to treatment for civilians and public safety and military professionals alike—some are barriers related specifically to those in need, but many others are systemic and paradoxically originate from seemingly well-intended policies and procedures.

In this context, the contemporary issue of restoration of gun rights is particularly relevant and applies to those who have criminal as well as mental health histories. For instance, some states have an automatic restoration of various rights to felons once their sentences are completed, and many others have protocols through which ex-felons can seek to have their rights to firearm possession restored. Others, such as North Carolina, have an outright prohibition against the possession of firearms by ex-felons. In *Britt v. North Carolina* (2009), the North Carolina Supreme Court ruled that because Mr. Britt, an ex-felon, was not considered to possess a significant threat to public safety, the North Carolina law prohibiting the possession of firearms by ex-felons was unconstitutional as applied to him. This ruling was notably different from previous rulings, prompting Bone (2010) to suggest that other states may set forth similar rulings; and she further noted that it is unclear to what extent this specific ruling applies to other people in North Carolina who present with the same absence of lawlessness and dangerousness.

Issues concerning the restoration of firearm rights for those with mental health histories have begun to come to the fore. We have highlighted the recent case of *Tyler v. Hillsdale County Sheriff's Dept.* (2014) throughout this book in this regard as it is has set a legal foundation for the emerging roles of medical and mental health professionals in firearm-related matters. As the reader may recall, in *Tyler*, the Sixth Circuit Court of Appeals reversed and remanded a previous decision made by the District Court for the Western District of Michigan that dismissed a claim by Mr. Tyler, who had argued that the federal statute that prohibited individuals committed to mental institutions from possessing guns was unconstitutional as applied to him, particularly because there was no relief program with an opportunity to challenge the prohibition in place. The appeals court held that it was a valid argument regarding the violation of his Second Amendment rights, and the court noted that not everyone who was institutionalized is mentally ill at a later point, thereby making the law too broad. The court further noted that not everyone who was institutionalized or had a mental illness presents a sufficient risk to bar him or her from owning firearms—specifically, that Congress designed the law that enforces prohibitions on this group of people only during periods in which they are deemed dangerous, which does not necessarily equate to a lifelong prohibition. Even though the court did not order that Tyler's rights be restored immediately, it provided him with the opportunity to prove that he had regained mental stability and that his mental illness did not pose a risk to himself or others.

As we noted in Chapter 2, Britton & Bloom (2015) described two programs in Oregon designed to comply with federal gun laws pertaining to reporting requirements of individuals who have received mental health adjudications in criminal and civil courts. The second program requires the state to provide a qualifying gun restoration program for individuals who want to be requalified for gun ownership. Therefore, in 2009, Oregon's legislature developed an administrative approach to gun restoration, requiring the Oregon Psychiatric Security Review Board to conduct hearings for restoration of firearm rights. Only three completed petitions requesting restoration of gun rights have been set forth since the program's inception. Oregon also has a records reconciliation program, which began when the state legislature ordered the Oregon State Police to consolidate the three databases that had previously been held by separate organizations regarding who, under state and federal law, could not possess, transport, ship, or receive a firearm and electronically upload the appropriate names in the NICS. The petition for relief requirements includes a copy of mental health records relating to mental health disqualification, a copy of court records related to circumstances surrounding the firearms prohibitor(s), an FBI criminal history, and a forensic psychiatric assessment.

In the American Psychiatric Association's "Resource Document on Access to Firearms by People with Mental Disorders," Pinals and colleagues (2015) expressed "the need for fair procedures to restore firearms rights to individuals with histories of mental illness whose treatment history and behavior indicate that they are no longer at elevated risk for suicide or violence" (p. 187). They also addressed the concerns we noted above regarding barriers to treatment:

> Questions have also been raised about the possibly counterproductive effects of registries. Persons with treatable mental disorders may delay or avoid obtaining treatment because of concern about adverse consequences should their conditions become known to others or because they are unwilling to forfeit their right to use firearms for legitimate purposes (e.g., hunting), especially in regions of the country where recreational firearm use is deeply embedded in the culture. Although the statutes typically prohibit disclosures of registry information for purposes other than determining eligibility for firearms purchases, persons in need of psychiatric treatment may understandably question the security of the registries and the limitations on the use of the information they contain. (p. 190)

Nevertheless, Pinals and colleagues also noted the importance of restricting firearm access during a crisis, which is consistent with the empirical research in this regard. For example, Kolla, O'Connor, & Lineberry (2011) investigated whether certain patient subgroups were associated with firearm access among psychiatric inpatients. They conducted a retrospective record review of approximately 1,000 patients aged 16 and above who were admitted to the Mayo Clinic Psychiatric Hospital in Rochester, Minnesota, between 2007 and 2008. Kolla et al. found that approximately 15% of inpatients reported having firearm access; men were significantly more likely to report such access, whereas a previous history of suicide attempt(s) was associated with decreased access, as was older age. However, those who had a family history of suicide or suicide attempts reported increased access to firearms. That said, diagnostic categories did not significantly predict access. Nevertheless, Kolla et al. noted that many suicide attempts are impulsive and poorly planned, the primary method of suicide in the United States is firearm, and almost all people who attempt suicide with a firearm die. Therefore, they underscored the need for

limiting access to firearms for certain people at specific times given that suicide is often attempted in response to a psychosocial crisis or trigger. As such,
they contended that clinicians must screen for access to firearms with much
more frequency and structure as very few outpatient psychiatrists actually
do so (i.e., as few as 6%) and less than one-third have a routine system for
identifying patients who own firearms.

Still, Pinals and colleagues (2015) emphasized the importance of shifting
firearm policies from a focus on mental illness to that of "adjudicated conduct indicative of elevated violence risk, such as conviction for violent misdemeanor or repeated convictions for driving under the influence of alcohol or
drugs" (p. 190). They ultimately opined:

> An individual who is legally prohibited from purchasing a firearm
> due to a mental health adjudication should have a fair opportunity for
> restoration of the right to purchase a firearm after a suitable waiting
> period. These time periods should be reflective of the person's need
> for and participation in recommended psychiatric care. Psychiatric
> evaluations and testimony should be required when persons seek
> restoration of their firearm-related rights, because psychiatrists can
> describe and interpret the individual's mental health history and
> current mental health status, and the effects of treatment and other
> factors on improvement or exacerbation of the person's condition.
> However, ultimate decision-making about restoration of the right to
> purchase a firearm is best suited to administrative (e.g., review panels
> established by state agencies) or judicial bodies that can weigh the
> right to bear arms against the considerations of public safety in making
> restoration determinations.

In the context of his discussion of evolving firearm laws and regulations,
Simpson (2007) addressed the significant implications they have had and will
continue to have on mental health professionals. In addition to encouraging
clinicians to reflect upon the potential outcomes of their professional decisions
(e.g., loss of firearm rights as a result of involuntary commitment or treatment), Simpson further noted, "As the number of states with firearms prohibition laws has increased, it can be anticipated that the likelihood of a treating
clinician's being asked to give an opinion regarding restoration of the right
to own firearms will also increase" (p.336). However, he aptly suggested that
clinicians may wish to recommend that a forensic evaluation focused on risk
assessment be completed instead of a clinical assessment. Simpson concluded:

> Mental health practitioners should be aware of any laws in their
> jurisdiction affecting access to firearms by individuals with a history
> of mental illness or treatment. Such laws can have a significant impact
> on patients and may also present difficult challenges for treatment
> providers asked to give opinions about restoration. Despite some
> persisting questions about their appropriateness and fundamental

fairness, these types of laws are increasingly common and highly likely to remain on the books for the foreseeable future. (p. 6)

Emerging Roles for Treating Professionals

As we discussed in Chapter 2 of this book, Florida's 2011 Privacy of Firearm Owners Act prevents medical personnel from asking questions about gun ownership, documenting information concerning firearms in a patient's medical record, and denying care for patients who refuse to answer questions about firearm ownership. As noted, the Florida chapters of the American Academy of Pediatrics, the American Academy of Family Physicians, the American College of Physicians, and the American Medical Association filed a lawsuit challenging the law's constitutionality in *Wollschlaeger v. Farmer* (2011). Moreover, Falls (2011), a medical doctor, contended that it "interferes with physicians' personal liberties, ignores public health data and infringes on the fiduciary patient–physician relationship by contradicting standards of care and medical ethics" (p. 442). The contention was that doctors should be able to discuss these issues with their patients given that gun violence has been cited as a public health concern and professional organizations recommend such inquiries, psychoeducation, and risk assessment with patients.

In the context of suicide prevention, *means-restricting* efforts tend to be the predominant approach taken by professionals and policymakers alike. In this regard, child access prevention efforts have been a primary initiative in our society as research has shown that children will often interact with firearms should they find them. While education-based safety programs (e.g., the NRA's Eddie Eagle') have been applauded for teaching important information, they are also criticized for their reliance on such and lacking behavioral skills training, which would include providing instructions, modeling, rehearsing skills, and receiving feedback (see Himle & Miltenberger, 2004). However, even behavioral skills training programs with parents and children regarding firearm safety have evidenced mixed results, even in experimental studies investigating children's use of correct safety skills post-training (e.g., Gross et al., 2007). That said, there is some evidence to suggest improved acquisition of safety skills for young children when training has been conducted by a peer (Jostad, Miltenberger, Kelso, & Knudson, 2008). Still, the samples in these behavioral skills training studies are extremely small (i.e., a total of four and six children, respectively).

Of note, however, is that an evaluation of the Eddie Eagle GunSafe' Program found that, while the program was effective in teaching kids to reproduce the gun safety message, it was not effective for teaching them to perform gun safety skills during a supervised role play, nor were the skills used during assessments of real-life situations (Himle, Miltenberger, Gatheridge, & Flessner, 2004).

Although counseling families on the risk of having firearms in the home has been recommended by professional groups, such as the American Academy of Pediatrics, counseling alone has not necessarily been found to be effective—even among families who were specifically advised to remove their firearms (Brent et al., 2000). This has also been an issue with other groups as well, and it seems that a multifaceted approach is most effective. As Christoffel (2000) articulated it, "we must acknowledge that even if counseling is perfected, it cannot be effective all by itself" (p. 1228). As we have learned from the prevention of motor vehicle injuries over the years, a comprehensive approach is necessary; Christoffel noted the "4 Es" of injury prevention—*engineering, education, enforcement,* and *evaluation*: "Injury prevention efforts that skip any of these do not succeed. Gun injury prevention is no exception, and it cannot rely on education alone" (p. 1228).

There are often significant and inherent challenges to means-restricting efforts. One example is that of Walters and colleagues (2012), who investigated the feasibility and acceptability of interventions to delay gun access in the Department of Veterans Affairs (VA) mental health settings given that the majority of VA patient suicides are completed with firearms. However, they indicated that interventions that delay patients' gun access during high-risk periods may ultimately reduce suicide, but there are notable barriers to such (e.g., they may not be acceptable to VA stakeholders or be otherwise challenging to set forth). Therefore, Walters et al. conducted focus groups and interviews with 60 stakeholders, including VA mental health patients, mental health clinicians, family members, and VA facility leaders. They found that, although all stakeholders believed the VA providers had a role in increasing patient safety and highlighted the need for providers to address firearm access with at-risk patients, there was limited discussion regarding gun access during routine care contacts despite the fact that most patients and clinicians thought such screening was acceptable.

Another example is that of Sherman et al. (2001) and their investigation of the effectiveness of a firearms risk management program for 46 civilly committed psychiatric inpatients in Ohio. Their sample consisted primarily of men with substance abuse histories, who were diagnosed with personality disorders and who expressed intent to use a firearm to commit suicide. The intervention included an initial psychiatric risk assessment and multidisciplinary treatment team planning aimed at the patients' risk, including enrollment in a firearms treatment group. This group focused on self-control skills for interpersonal stressors, and it was designed specifically to address firearm-related issues. For example, patients learned to identify how they relied on external means, particularly firearms, to deal with their mental health problems. It was a cognitive-behaviorally based group, where patients learned about the interplay between thoughts, feelings, and behaviors and were trained to implement behavioral time-outs, relaxation techniques, and stress management exercises. Treatment goals focused on effective communication skills, problem-solving, and conflict resolution without the use of force or threats. In addition, a social worker completed a firearms flow sheet, which included the type and location of the firearm and identified potential victims. The social worker then corresponded with the patient's family, case manager, and law enforcement, as needed, to address issues related to the patient's access and threats. The intervention period also included regular monitoring through a quality assurance process ensuring that risk-related needs were being appropriately identified and addressed. The program also included consultation and discharge-related support for staff and patients, including continued monitoring in the community. Ultimately, 16 (35%) of the 46 patients were readmitted to the hospital within 24 months, and 5 threatened themselves or others with a firearm or regained access to a firearm. Thus, Sherman and colleagues found that the program was effective for approximately 90% of their sample.

The implications for mental health professionals are many, including that counseling efforts must be complemented with other steps, including, but not limited to, initiatives focused on assessment,[8] research, and public education. With regard to the latter, Price, Khubchandani, & Payton (2015) highlighted the disconnect between the number of firearm-involved injuries and deaths since the turn of the century and the relative lack of attention paid to firearm violence in health education–related journals. Specifically, they noted that firearms are associated with 30,000 deaths annually in the United States and approximately 1 million deaths and 2 million injuries over the prior three decades. However, in their study, Price and colleagues analyzed publications from 2000 to 2014 in health education–related journals and found that less than 0.5% of all research publications addressed firearm violence. The journals included and the corresponding number of empirical article publications related to firearm violence over this 14-year span are as follows:

- *American Journal of Health Education*, 5 out of 799
- *American Journal of Health Promotion*, 0 out of 851
- *American Journal of Health Studies*, 1 out of 372
- *Health Education & Behavior*, 5 out of 775
- *Health Promotion Practice*, 0 out of 820
- *Journal of American College Health*, 8 out of 850
- *Journal of School Health*, 3 out of 1,309

Thus, there were only 22 empirical articles published out of the 5,776 total published in these seven notable health education–related journals from 2000 to 2014. The dearth of firearm-related empirical research in health education journals (a key aspect of the broader public health scholarship) is clear, but such research is much needed. As Price and colleagues articulated it: "Research can guide evidence-based prevention practices, and health educators need adequate research available to them through their professional journals to plan, implement, and evaluate firearm violence prevention interventions and activities" (p. 319). Therefore, they recommended that journal editors take a more proactive approach in soliciting these types of submissions.

The exception to the general lack of firearms research in this arena is the leading public health journal, the *American Journal of Public Health*. Reflecting a shift since the turn of the century in thinking by federal agencies (e.g., the Centers for Disease Control and Prevention) that gun violence can be understood as a public health epidemic, the *American Journal of Public Health* offers considerable attention to the topic. At the time of the writing of this book, a search for the term *firearm* using the journal's general search engine (*American Journal of Public Health*, n.d.) produced 449 separate articles, with the vast majority appearing post-2000. This number can be expected to increase dramatically as the journal and the public health field are now actively treating firearm violence and death as public health concerns. Also echoing the trend in thinking of firearm violence in a public health framework is a recent conceptual piece in an online-mediated journal, *Frontiers in Public Health*. Health promotion and administration scholars Muni Rubens & Nancy Shehadeh (2014) outline considerations in a public health understanding of firearm violence prevention. Importantly, they highlight the need to attend to multiple levels of prevention efforts including: individual-level programs targeting parent–child relationships, interpersonal approaches facilitating contact between school staff and families, community-level strategies like multipronged media campaigns, and society-level approaches like legislation addressing penalties associated with violation of gun laws. While the efficacy of each of these specific approaches is beyond the scope of the present discussion, the critical point is this: mental and public health professionals hold the potential to engage in multilevel prevention programming.

What about the responsibility of clinicians as it corresponds to firearm-related matters? In his recent editorial, Huprich (2016) reflected on the 2016 Pulse nightclub shooting in Orlando, Florida:

> As personality assessment psychologists, we have to wonder what might have happened had these shooters been assessed carefully to determine the level and nature of their psychopathology and potential to act violently. Good multimethod assessment might have allowed clinicians to determine the extent to which the person acknowledged his or her troubles and what level of intervention was needed. At the time of writing this editorial, I am not aware of whether Mateen was ever formally evaluated, and if so, what recommendations were made. Yet, I wonder, and I suspect this kind of violence could have been prevented if access to assessment and treatment were more available, and if our society placed as much interest in psychological health as it does with physical health, or even more so, as it does with our national obsession with beauty and physical appearance. On a broader scale, I wonder if gun laws that were more carefully designed might have also prevented those with severe psychopathology from acting so readily. (p. 447)

Huprich added that mental health professionals, particularly personality assessment psychologists, must communicate publicly about what is known about personality and psychopathology, and professional task forces should be formed to assist in these efforts as well as to help inform policies and laws. He concluded, "No matter how great or small, a burden lies with us, the mental health community, to help alleviate this national epidemic" (p. 448).

As president of the Association for Behavioral and Cognitive Therapies, Professor Stefan Hofmann (2013) expressed his views on school violence as part of his "president's message" in *Behavior Therapist*. Citing statistics from a 2001 report and considering notable incidents that had transpired since, he concluded that "School shootings appear to be on the rise" (p. 53). Hofmann then indicated that "The purpose of this column is to share my personal view on school violence" (p. 55), followed by three recommended actions he contended can save lives:

1. Eliminating guns (citing the importance of gun buy-back programs)
2. Eliminating exposure to violent TV and video games (citing social learning theory and the types of games reportedly played by the Columbine and Sandy Hook perpetrators)
3. Identifying and providing adequate care to potential perpetrators (however, acknowledging that all three killers he cited—those of Columbine and Sandy Hook—had, in fact, been in contact with mental health experts prior to the shootings)

Professor Hofmann concluded:

As mental health experts, it is our job to separate fact from fiction, to dispel myths, to expose politically motivated opinions, to assist victims, to stop potential perpetrators, and to educate the policymakers and the general public—even if this means that we have to take a political stance. (p. 55)

Williamson and colleagues (2014) suggested that a comprehensive and active approach by healthcare providers, including mental health care professionals, across multiple settings is essential in gun violence prevention efforts, especially for youth populations. This would include screening for salient firearm violence–related risk factors, such as depression, anger management problems, impulsivity, homicidality and suicidality, carrying weapons, gang involvement, violence exposure, and access to firearms in various settings (e.g., home, school, other community settings). Williamson et al. also noted that healthcare providers can disseminate information about firearm safety, which has been found to reduce risk for involvement in gun-involved violence among youth. Of course, this presupposes that healthcare providers understand firearm safety concepts. Nevertheless, they recommended the following for practitioners:

- Integrate questions about firearm ownership and safe gun and ammunition storage into routine child wellness visits and mental health intakes and evaluations for all children, youth, and families.

- Integrate questions about youth aggressive behavior or violence, gun carrying, homicidality, and suicidality into routine pediatric and mental health visits for older children and adolescents.
- Use evidence-based screening tools for suicide and related risk behaviors.
- Provide basic counseling about gun safety to gun-owning families.
- Provide families and youth with educational handouts about firearms safety and the prevention of firearm-related youth homicide, accidental injury, and suicide.
- Provide families and youth with appropriate mental health treatment referrals when there is a risk for aggression, violence, homicidality, or suicidality.
- Seek training opportunities to learn more about gun safety counseling and other prevention practices.

The sentiment reflecting the need for much greater involvement in firearm-related matters has been set forth by those in the medical field as well (e.g., see the white paper issued by the National Physicians Alliance, 2013). The title of Selker, Selker, & Schwartz's (2013) editorial in the *Journal of General Internal Medicine* speaks for itself: "Gun Violence Is a Health Crisis: Physicians' Responsibilities." They drew parallels between firearms and cigarette smoking, noting that "Cigarettes' status has fallen from fashionable to toxic," noting that such was "a slow process—changes in advertising, education, films, and, eventually, laws, made it clear that smoking kills" (p. 601). Selker et al. indicated that clinicians, teachers, and researchers have opportunities to reduce preventable firearm-related deaths and injuries through: (i) counseling and increasing access to mental health services; (ii) opposing "government intrusion into the patient–doctor relationship" by not restricting discussions about firearm safety; (iii) educating and training physicians on issues associated with firearm-related injuries and deaths, including gun violence screening, counseling, and prevention; (iv) increasing research in this area of study; (v) registration of gun owners at the same level as that of motor vehicle drivers; and (vi) generally support gun safety efforts. They concluded:

> The modern Hippocratic Oath for physicians says, "I will remember that I remain a member of society, with special obligations to all my fellow human beings, those sound of mind and body as well as the infirm." The role of the physician brings a special obligation to society in the face of the preventable disability and death due to guns. We must take them on as we would for any other health crisis. (p. 602)

Based on their review of firearm statutes across all 50 states, the District of Columbia, and Puerto Rico and the Federal National Firearms Act, Norris, Price, Gutheil, & Reid (2006) opined:

> With firearm licensure statutes present in all 50 states, the District of Columbia, and Puerto Rico, it is likely that a psychiatrist will be asked at

some point in his or her career to provide a certificate or to perform an assessment for a firearm-related matter. A clinician must be cognizant of the professional responsibility inherent in this assessment. Many clinicians may not fully appreciate the ramifications of accepting such requests or evaluations, which may appear simplistic on their surface. (p. 1395)

While there is clearly a recognized need for medical and mental health professionals to become involved in firearm-related matters as well as broader initiatives, the primary questions are: Do they engage in routine, evidenced-based practices related to firearms? Are they even prepared and equipped to do so at this time by virtue of their training and education? Traylor et al. (2010) surveyed a national sample of 339 clinical psychologists and found that the vast majority (79%) believed that firearm safety issues were greater among those with mental health problems, but about the same number of psychologists (78%) also reported that they did not regularly chart or maintain a record of patients who owned or had access to firearms. Approximately half (52%) of the psychologists indicated that they would initiate firearm safety counseling for patients assessed to be at risk for self-harm or harm to others. That said, almost the same number of psychologists (46%) reported that they had not received any information on firearm safety issues themselves. It is also important to note that 20% of those who reported that they had received such information indicated that it was from the mass media, whereas only 13% received this information in graduate training and only 7% received it from reading professional journals. These compelling data led Traylor and colleagues to recommend that firearm safety counseling training be integrated into the graduate training of all clinical psychologists and for this to be a priority.

Price, Mrdjenovich, Thompson, & Dake (2009) examined college counselors' perceptions and practices regarding anticipatory guidance on firearms for student clients. Specifically, they surveyed a national sample of 213 counselors and found that very few (6%) were likely to provide anticipatory guidance in this regard and that only a somewhat greater number (17%) charted or kept records on client ownership and access to firearms. Of additional note is that the majority (54%) of counselors had never received any information on firearm safety and, of those who had, most reported receiving such information from mass media (15%), followed by graduate school training (14%). Less than 10% received firearm safety information from professional meetings, workshops, continuing education classes, or professional journals. Of concern, perhaps, is that despite the aforementioned rates, nearly all of the counselors felt at least moderately confident in their ability to:

- *ask* clients about the presence of firearms in their residence (97%)
- *advise* clients to remove the firearms from their residence (94%)
- *assess* the willingness of clients to remove firearms within the next 30 days (89%)

Furthermore, the majority of counselors felt at least moderately confident in their ability to *assist* clients in what to do with firearms removed from residences (59%) and *arrange* follow-up contact within 4 weeks to assess firearm removal (83%). Again, these data are concerning given counselors' self-reported lack of knowledge and training in the specific area of firearm safety.

Slovak, Brewer, & Carlson (2008) surveyed 697 licensed social workers from Ohio with regard to their attitudes, knowledge, and behaviors associated with client firearm assessment and safety-related counseling. They found that the vast majority of clinicians (85%) did not routinely counsel on firearm safety and that most (66%) did not routinely assess for firearm ownership and access. However, the likelihood of routine firearm assessment and counseling increased exponentially in cases where clients presented with depression or suicidality. Furthermore, media influences were notable; as Slovak and colleagues noted:

> The media's coverage of gun-related issues also affected responses to routinely assessing for firearms and counseling on firearm safety. If a social worker stated that media coverage motivated her or him to address gun-related issues with clients, the odds of routine firearm assessment and safety counseling increased by 320.6 percent and 465.9 percent, respectively. (p. 362)

In contrast, a number of factors were associated with a decreased likelihood of the social workers engaging in routine firearm assessment and counseling, such as if they believed: they were not adequately trained on the topic of firearm safety, it was not their responsibility, their clients were not at risk of firearm-related injury to self or others, there were more important topics to address, they were uncomfortable with the topic of firearms, and they were unaware of the risk associated with firearms in clients' homes. Of additional note is that very few social workers personally owned a firearm (9%) and only a somewhat larger number lived in a home with one (26%). Variables such as race, age, clinician gun ownership status, client gender, or practice setting (i.e., urban or suburban) were not associated with the likelihood to engage in firearm assessment and counseling. On the other hand, a primary significant factor was that of clinicians' firearm-specific education and training. Namely, if a social worker had prior firearm safety training, the reported likelihood of engaging in routine assessment increased by 257.7% and safety counseling by 479.3%. As Slovak and colleagues noted, "This illustrates the magnitude of firearm training for enhancing social work practice protocol" (p. 363).

Vicarious Trauma and Self-Care Considerations for Practitioners

Medical and mental health professionals are ostensibly the greatest proponents of healthcare and wellness; however, they are also groups that tend to neglect their own mental health (Dattilio, 2015). In their resource document titled "Promoting Prevention, Wellness, and Coping with Challenges," the American Psychological Association's Advisory Committee on Colleague Assistance echoed this concern about psychologists: "Self-care is obviously needed but often ignored" (n.d.). Wise, Hersh, & Gibson (2012) noted the importance of self-care for psychologists for many reasons, including ethical ones (i.e., in the context of professional competence). Undoubtedly, poor self-care can lead to impairments in work functioning, thereby affecting our clients directly or indirectly. Indeed, the concept of "burnout" is one that is frequently addressed in many employment contexts, especially among those in the helping professions. Wise et al. remind us that such professionals, including psychologists, are not immune to personal vulnerabilities and professional hazards. Moreover, they cite research that has indicated that notable proportions of psychologists, especially practicing psychologists, have experienced periods of emotional exhaustion and have admitted to working when they were too distressed to be effective, despite acknowledging that this is unethical.

Whereas work-related stress and burnout are not uncommon across employment settings, medical and mental health professionals can develop a much more serious condition, *vicarious trauma* (VT). VT consists of PTSD-like symptoms that these professionals can experience as a result of exposure to their clients' traumatic narratives, despite not being exposed directly to these events. Certain professions are generally more obviously susceptible to experiencing VT given the level of their involvement with traumatized clients, such as correctional healthcare nurses (Munger, Savage, & Panosky, 2015) and trauma therapists (Hernandez-Wolfe, Killian, Engstrom, & Gangsei, 2015); and those who maintain larger caseloads and spend more time with traumatized clients are at great risk of developing VT (Finklestein et al., 2015). However, Hernandez-Wolfe and colleagues (2015) remind us: "At the same time, therapists may experience personal and professional growth by being witness to and inspired by their clients' processes of resilience" (p. 156)—a concept referred to as *vicarious resilience*.

Nevertheless, burnout and VT are serious issues that mental health and medical professionals must maintain awareness of and prevention against. And it has been argued that clinician self-care is a necessary skill for mental health professionals working with high-risk clients (Cramer et al. 2013). So what can be done in this regard? Wise and colleagues (2012) highlighted four foundational principles for effective self-care for psychologists: (i) surviving versus flourishing, (ii) intentionality, (iii) awareness of reciprocity, and (iv) integrating self-care into daily practices and routines, which they articulated as:

> When we focus on *surviving*, we inadvertently maintain a barely good enough status quo and fixate on preventing the negative. In contrast, when we aspire to *flourish*, we invite a broader array of possibilities into our personal and professional lives, and we emphasize resilience-building attitudes and practices that reflect an overarching positive

orientation. Second is the act of *intentionally* choosing our self-care plan over time and being willing to change our attitudes and practices if (or as) they become unworkable. Third is the concept alluded to above that we have termed *reciprocity*, or the process of dynamic exchange of beneficial lifestyle attitudes and practices between psychologist and client. Fourth, we encourage the use of self-care strategies that are *integrated into* rather than added onto our already busy and stressful lives. (p. 488)

As such, they recommended mindfulness-based practices as well as interventions associated with acceptance and commitment therapy, and positive psychology. Furthermore, they highlighted the need for professionals to make *therapeutic lifestyle changes* when necessary, which additionally incorporates nutrition and exercise components aimed at improving physical health. Moreover, these changes would "also incorporate an awareness of our evolutionary need to be in nature and the negative impact of overexposure to contexts of hyperreality and media immersion" (p. 489). Similarly, Harrison & Westwood (2009) investigated VT in mental health therapists and identified nine predominant themes apparent across clinicians' narratives of protective practices: countering isolation (in professional, personal, and spiritual realms), developing mindful self-awareness, consciously expanding perspective to embrace complexity, active optimism, holistic self-care, maintaining clear boundaries, exquisite empathy, professional satisfaction, and creating meaning. In addition, the American Psychological Association's Advisory Committee on Colleague Assistance (n.d.) emphasizes the importance of being aware of stressors, engaging in self-assessment, coping skills, and other self-care actions, including those related to nutrition and exercise. Moreover, it highlights the importance of maintaining positive relationships, including those with our colleagues. In this regard, it suggests forming a peer consultation group and attending continuing education workshops to maintain and build our professional competencies.

Part IV

MAIN FINDINGS AND FUTURE DIRECTIONS
FOR PRACTICE, RESEARCH, AND POLICY

9

Main Findings and Future Directions in the Behavioral Science of Firearms

The average broadcast news soundbite is 9 seconds (The incredible shrinking soundbite, 2011), and the optimal length for most social media posts is 40 characters (Lee, 2014); but firearm-related issues are too great in number and too complex in nature to distill to a level anywhere near these parameters. In fact, the best we could do in our effort to be as concise as possible was 30—not seconds or characters but main findings related to the behavioral science of firearms. We present each of them in the following section, first in list form and then again along with their respective implications for practice, research, and policy. As always, and as our colleagues in psychology and law will appreciate, our conclusions are based on a reasonable degree of psychological certainty and are subject to change based on the advent of new information.

Main Findings

1. Firearms are inextricably linked to the history of the United States.
2. One-third of US citizens own firearms, and there are approximately 300 million firearms in this country.
3. Guns are different.
4. The "gun debate" is largely a political one.
5. Many media outlets provide disproportionate attention and inaccurate information about firearm-related issues, thereby contributing to the circulation of myths and misinformation in our society.
6. There is a lack of consensus among professional, government, and advocacy groups with respect to defining firearm-related terms and events; and there often is a restricted range of information and perspectives presented by them.

7. Firearm regulations have been present since United States' inception, many laws and landmark legal cases have followed, and the *individual rights* perspective is currently the prevailing view of the higher courts.
8. Research support for the effectiveness of firearm-related laws and policies is mixed.
9. The available firearm-related research is significantly limited because of an almost exclusive reliance on retrospective studies and proxy variables, a lack of interdisciplinary focus, and various systemic barriers.
10. Although some progress has been made in reducing illegal gun trafficking, regulating and holding firearm dealers legally liable has been much less successful.
11. Firearm-involved homicides account for approximately 11,000 deaths in the United States annually, or one-third of all gun deaths and two-thirds of all homicides, reflecting a mortality rate that has not changed in two decades.
12. State-level data indicate a correlation between firearm ownership and violent crime.
13. Mass shootings are very low–base rate but high-impact events that represent a very small proportion of firearm-involved deaths.
14. Concepts related to marginalization, damaged masculinity, and firearm access warrant increased attention in the context of threat assessment and the prevention of school shootings.
15. Only 3%–5% of all violence is attributable to even serious mental illness, and an even smaller percentage is associated with firearm-related violence. A primary concern is psychiatric crisis and not mental illness per se.
16. Firearms are rarely used in domestic violence (DV) and intimate partner violence (IPV) incidents, but they are implicated in DV and IPV homicides and homicide–suicides.
17. Restraining orders may be beneficial in some DV and IPV situations; however, implementation and enforcement problems pose significant challenges in this regard.
18. Two-thirds of firearm-involved deaths in the United States are suicides, nearly double that of acts of violence toward others.
19. Firearm-specific safety information is virtually absent in the professional medical and mental health literature.
20. There are many important emerging roles for medical and mental health professionals with respect to addressing firearm-related violence and suicide as they are our society's primary gatekeepers in this area.
21. Most medical and mental health professionals have not received formal education or training sufficient to develop professional competence on firearm-specific issues.

22. There are numerous firearm-related subcultures for whom practitioners, academics, and researchers should develop and maintain cultural competence.
23. Military, law enforcement, and correctional populations present with particular vulnerabilities and risk factors associated with firearm-involved violence, DV and IPV, and suicide.
24. Psychological firearm evaluations are a specific type of forensic mental health assessment that require specialized procedures and considerations.
25. Firearm-related violence and suicide risk assessments should follow prevention-, rather than prediction-, based models.
26. Restricting access to firearms is only one component of a comprehensive violence and suicide risk management and prevention plan for those at elevated risk.
27. There are various types of therapeutic interventions available that may reduce firearm-related violence and suicide risk, in addition to those associated with health and wellness, and firearm safety, more generally.
28. Many considerations for providing therapeutic interventions for at-risk youth are separate and distinct from those associated with adults.
29. There are significant systemic and case-specific barriers to treatment for some members of certain firearm-related subgroups.
30. The restoration of gun rights for those with mental health and related histories is a particularly novel and emerging area of consideration for medical, mental health, and legal professionals.

1. Firearms Are Inextricably Linked to the History of the United States

Firearms were brought to the United States in the 17th and 18th centuries by European settlers, and they played a critical role in securing independence and forming a new government. As such, guns have always had a direct and close relationship with the US military as well as with law enforcement and corrections. However, civilians have also maintained widespread involvement with firearms since this country's inception, and the Second Amendment of the US Constitution (1791) has remained in the spotlight in our modern era. In addition, many dignitaries, including most modern-day presidents and a number of Supreme Court justices, have either owned or at least used firearms in some capacity. Furthermore, the presence of firearms is pervasive in pop culture, including in American movies, television shows, music, books, theater, and video games; and a number of notable celebrities own or use firearms as well.

Practice

The historical and modern-day realities of firearm use and ownership in the United States are important for practitioners to consider, especially in the context of developing and maintaining their cultural competence (see finding 22 below).

Research

While there is a wealth of research available on such topics as the effects of exposure to violent video games and the like, the much subtler presence of firearms in our contemporary movies, television shows, and music has mostly been overlooked and not formally investigated. Much of what has been addressed in this regard has been in the form of celebrity liability debates, such as those related to the level of responsibility recording artists assume over the messages they may be sending in their music. However, these discussions tend to be primarily philosophical or moral in nature rather than empirically based. These debates would be better informed if researchers operationalized the firearm-related variables present in our contemporary movies, television, books, theater, and music. As noted, certain video games have received significant attention in this regard because of their inclusion of blatant violence, but other pop-culture mediums have been bypassed. As such, there is a disconnect in the professional literature. For example, most researchers employ correlational methods and use proxy variables to investigate such questions as the association between firearm ownership and violence in a city or state, but they have not looked at these other pop culture–specific variables that are, in fact, much more interwoven in people's daily lives—and, therefore, presumably impact their thoughts, feelings, and behaviors. Moreover, solely tracking the presence of firearms and firearm-related variables in films or songs is insufficient because context is likely quite important. For instance, it is not enough to identify how many Hollywood films simply include guns but also: How often and how many reflect principles of firearm safety? How do these exposures affect consumers, in terms of both their behaviors and attitudes?

Policy

Similar to practitioners, it would behoove policymakers, including, but not limited to, politicians and government officials, to recognize the cultural contours associated with firearms for most people in this country—firearm owners and operators but also those who are regularly exposed to guns in pop culture (see finding 22 below).

2. One-Third of US Citizens Own Firearms, and There Are Approximately 300 Million Firearms in This Country

The exact number of firearm owners and guns in the United States is unknown because there are no national registries, but most professional sources agree on these estimates. Although there may be some regional differences with respect to the number of firearm owners, the available data show that even the most politically liberal states have high numbers of background checks annually as well as many rod & gun/hunting clubs, shooting ranges, and the like. The Pew Research Center (Morin, 2014) found the following regional breakdown of households with a firearm: West (34%), Midwest (35%), South (38%), and Northeast (27%). That said, there are significant differences in ownership rates between some states (e.g., Delaware and Wyoming). Nevertheless, firearm use is widespread throughout the country and there is an even greater number of people who interact with firearms—above and beyond firearm owners. These additional people are part of a very diverse group with a wide-ranging set of firearm-related experiences: from the couple who go to an indoor shooting range one time on a whim to the young man who carries a gun illegally to facilitate criminal activity. Of course, the civilian estimates do not include military, law enforcement, or correctional personnel, either.

Practice

As noted in the context of the previous finding, practitioners must recognize that one out of every three civilians owns a firearm in this country and that an even greater number of people interact with or have been exposed to firearms at some level. Medical and mental health professionals receive formal education and training to work with numerous subcultures, many of which make up very small proportions of the US population. Developing and maintaining one's cultural competence are very important, however, because most practitioners provide services for clients who are diverse in some way (e.g., gender, race, ethnicity, socioeconomic status, religion, sexual orientation, disability). The absence of formal, firearm-specific education and training for medical and mental health practitioners reflects a gaping hole in this regard, especially because of the significant number of firearm owners and operators in this country (see finding 22 below). As such, firearm cultural competence represents a needed domain of continuing education moving forward.

Research

Academicians, researchers, and students are also ethically required to develop and maintain professional and cultural competence in areas of relevance to their work; but what is a very clear and compelling absence in the professional literature is the lack of empirical, prospective research that has been conducted with firearm owners and operators. Medical and mental health research has been conducted on the most obscure groups, and researchers will readily acknowledge the difficulty securing participants from even more accessible groups. However, firearm owners and operators are, perhaps, one of the most prevalent subgroups imaginable—behind only the most general ones (e.g., there are 162 million women in the country according to the US Census Bureau; FFF: Women's history month, 2016). Therefore, the fact that there is a dearth of prospective research with firearm owners and operators reflects a notable bias (in avoiding recruiting them as participants) rather than a research barrier based on limited availability and opportunity. This is tempered by established systemic barriers in conducting firearm-related research, ranging from individual university researchers avoiding firearm topics due to concerns over stakeholder backlash to society-level preclusion against conducting firearm-related research (e.g., prohibition with the Centers for Disease Control and Prevention [CDC] on conducting meaningful firearm-related research). These barriers must be deconstructed in order for the behavioral science of firearms to advance on knowledge and prevention programming moving forward.

Policy

Half of the people in this country support stricter laws covering firearm sales (Guns, n.d.), but more than one-third own and operate firearms—a substantial segment of the public. These significant numbers cut across party lines. Namely, approximately 50% of Republicans have a firearm in their home, but 36%–37% of Independents and 22%–32% of Democrats do as well (see Morin, 2014, and Carroll, 2006). While relatively more Republicans own firearms, Independents and Democrats still match the national average. As such, all politicians and policymakers should recognize that substantial numbers of people in this country own and operate firearms, regardless of their political party or region of residence. Therefore, wide-sweeping, broad-based firearm policy proposals are likely to continue to be met with significant resistance by large segments of the population, whereas those that are focused, are plausible, and seek to strike a balance between ownership rights and safety are more likely to receive public support.

3. Guns Are Different

In the case law and professional literature related to capital punishment, the concept that "death is different" reflects the qualitatively different considerations usually associated with death penalty cases. Firearms evoke a similar reaction. Guns are different. Despite the extremely low rates of firearm-related deaths and injuries (relative to other means), there continues to be much debate and concern about civilian firearm ownership rights, locally and nationally, because guns are different. In general, firearm-related incidents are very low-probability but very high-impact events; that is, although they rarely occur, the consequences are usually fatal when they do. This reality is true for acts of violence, including DV and suicide. This is likely what makes many people uneasy about firearms, including medical mental health professionals, who may be unwilling to conduct high-risk, high-liability evaluations. Even some law enforcement officials and judges may be uncomfortable around various firearm-related issues, and they are the ultimate decision-makers in these matters. Guns typically elicit strong emotions, both positive and negative; and issues related to firearms (e.g., gun control) are a well-established part of the gamut of social issues that continue to be hotly debated in this country. Public sentiment regarding guns spans the continuum and is quite nuanced, and there are certainly groups advocating for perspectives on all sides. In fact, advocacy groups and so-called apostrophe laws often arise in the wake of certain firearm-involved tragedies, such as particular school shootings; and there is very much an emotionally driven quality to the public and professional discussions and proposed policies that follow these events. Firearm-related issues are not usually met with apathy by the public or by legal, law enforcement, medical, or mental health professionals.

Practice

Medical and mental health practitioners work with a wide range of people with an equally wide-ranging set of perspectives on various social issues. Some professionals may see more homogenous groups of clients, but it is not advisable to make assumptions about their views on firearms (or any issue for that matter). As we noted above (finding 2), even one in four politically liberal people own firearms, and we contend that even greater numbers of people have had some exposure to firearms, directly or indirectly. Therefore, practitioners should not make assumptions about clients' views on guns or gun policies; rather, they should seek to elicit such directly from the client in situations where it is clinically indicated (e.g., during a firearm-related assessment or suicide risk assessment). In this context, it is also generally not advisable for professionals to impose their personal views regarding firearms on their clients; one exception, of course, is when practitioners believe their personal views may interfere with their ability to effectively and ethically provide services. Practitioners will certainly have perspectives on a range of social issues just as others do, but it is not usually the case that their personal opinions have particular relevance to the professional services at hand—and, in fact, their personal views can potentially impede service provision. Thus, we recommend that practitioners seek peer consultation for unfamiliar matters or those that elicit personal reactions so that they can determine their next steps.

Research

Statistics can be used and interpreted in many ways, but in many circumstances, emotions impact logic and can lead people to disregard the empirical basis of issues. It is incumbent upon social scientists to investigate firearm-related matters with adherence to the scientific method, objectively and dispassionately. While researchers may follow proper research methods—in terms of their procedures and analyses—they must also be aware of potential biases throughout the process. For example, a major tenet of science is hypothesis-testing, but it is the researchers themselves who develop the research questions and corresponding hypotheses. As such, there is the potential for bias before the study even starts due to the ways in which the questions are asked and the hypotheses worded. There are various types of biases that can arise during the procedural phases of a study as well, but even when they are sound, there is the potential for confirmation biases to interfere in the analysis and interpretation stage; after all, these are not "blind" studies, and the researchers are the ones who have constructed the research questions and hypotheses in the first place. These concerns are not an indictment on researchers but rather a recognition that these are known biases that *may* affect anyone in these circumstances. It is for this reason that we recommend that researchers seek outside consultation just as practitioners would, particularly from those with any notable interest in the study or the topic, more generally. There is often an inclination for researchers to consult with "content experts" when conducting research, but it is also a good idea to consult with experts in research and statistics to ensure objectivity in those contexts as well. Once a study is completed, the potential for additional biases arises, such as what is known as the "file-drawer problem" and related publication biases. In other words, researchers may simply not write a manuscript to submit to a professional journal if the findings turn out a certain way, and journals may not accept papers that do not contain statistically significant results. Therefore, researchers should always report their findings and submit them to journals or present them at conferences or other venues that may be more accepting of "non-significant" results, when applicable. Of additional note is that academics should recognize that their students are likely to subscribe to a range of perspectives on firearms and, therefore, should be cognizant and sensitive to this when teaching and advising students.

Policy

Similar to practitioners, policymakers would benefit from recognizing how polarizing firearm-related issues can be. While this may serve a political advantage in some respects at times, there is no simple or single answer to stop or even reduce firearm-involved violence and suicide. Rather, the professional literature consistently shows that a multifaceted approach that includes a diverse group of stakeholders is the most effective way to accomplish societal and individual goals in this area. Therefore, policymakers should employ non-partisan efforts grounded in psychological and social science to offer data-driven decisions in these matters.

4. The "Gun Debate" Is Largely a Political One

Politics are inescapable in our society, and this is reflected in much of what is played out in the public forum when it comes to firearms. Firearm-related issues are ever-present in the public eye but are brought to the forefront when a shooting tragedy occurs or during election periods. These topics are usually a part of national election debates, and many local politicians running for office engage in marketing efforts to make their positions on firearm-related issues clear. Moreover, although about one-quarter to one-third of Democrats and Independents own firearms, significantly more Republicans own them (50%). As such, although there is not a one-to-one correlation between political views and guns, generally, there is certainly a strong relationship in that regard. The primary justification for this specific finding—that the "gun debate" is largely a political one—is mainly based on the fact that the position statements set forth by leading professional groups seem to be generally ignored by many policymakers and government officials. For instance, despite their clear neutrality and objectivity on many firearm-related issues, information and recommendations in resource documents from such organizations as the American Psychiatric and American Psychological Associations do not seem to find their way into the speeches, proposed policies, or overall agendas of many policymakers.

Practice

Practitioners should be cautious as to their involvement into the political aspects of firearm-related issues. Although they certainly have a right to engage in advocacy-based efforts if they desire, professionals should make it very apparent as to where their personal and professional views begin and end. For example, the American Psychological Association's Ethical Principles of Psychologists and Code of Conduct makes it clear that it:

> applies to these activities across a variety of contexts, such as in person, postal, telephone, Internet, and other electronic transmissions. These activities shall be distinguished from the purely private conduct of psychologists, which is not within the purview of the Ethics Code. (p. 493)

In other words, there is certainly a distinction between professional and personal activities of psychologists as well as other mental health professionals and medical professionals. It is incumbent upon practitioners to be transparent in this regard, to self-monitor their actions, and to consult with peers when necessary. In addition, practitioners should be sensitive to the fact that firearm-related issues may evoke strong emotions in their clients, who would be best served by avoiding political discussions in most cases.

Research

There is certainly a place for the empirical study of sociopolitical issues, including those related to firearms. In particular, it would be beneficial to know more about the factors underlying people's perspectives on gun control and associated issues. Simply ascertaining the percentages of gun owners within each political party is not particularly informative. It would be useful to gather data on people's more specific views on firearm-related issues and investigate connections between not only their politic affiliation but their views on other social and political issues, more broadly. In this regard, a gap in gun-related knowledge has been noted in health-related scientific outlets. Moving forward, public health scholars and organizations may be able to play a pivotal role in illuminating what drives peoples' gun control and related policy attitudes.

Policy

Although some firearm-related policies and laws may be adopted initially via political channels, their implementation and ultimate success will often be dependent on apolitical means and by nonpartisan members of society. While a policy or law may make sense on the surface, many have unintended consequences and may prove to be ineffective after all (e.g., Drug Abuse Resistance Education [D.A.R.E.] and Scared Straight). Generally, there is a lack of policy- and intervention-based outcome research in the firearm arena. However, some exceptions exists; for instance, recent state-level research suggests potential positive impacts of waiting periods and universal background checks on reduction of suicide rates (Anestis & Anestis, 2015; Anestis, Anestis, & Butterworth, 2017). Thus, policymakers should set forth plans for analyzing effectiveness with timelines along with their proposals and bills to ensure transparency and accountability. It is laudable to fight for and pass certain laws, but it is even more praiseworthy to have the courage and wherewithal to modify or remove them if they are deemed ineffective.

5. Many Media Outlets Provide Disproportionate Attention and Inaccurate Information About Firearm-Related Issues, Thereby Contributing to the Circulation of Myths and Misinformation in Our Society

Some media outlets give significant and disproportionate attention to firearm-related interpersonal violence, especially mass shootings and sensational shootings, as opposed to firearm-involved suicide. It also seems to be the case that firearm-related violence in low-income areas is largely overlooked and absent from national and political discourse (see Parham-Payne, 2014), which is in line with Schildkraut & Muschert's (2014) contention that the media covers the "worthy victim" more than the shooter.[1] This issue has not gone unnoticed in pop culture, either. For example, in his 2000 song "The Way I Am," Eminem raps:

> When a dude's getting bullied and shoots up his school—
> And they blame it on Marilyn [Manson]—and the heroin—
> Where were the parents at? And look where it's at!
> Middle America, now it's a tragedy
> Now it's so sad to see, an upper-class city havin' this happening
>
> (Eminem, 2000)

As we noted in the beginning of this book, the *New York Times* presented a page-one editorial for the first time since 1920, entitled: "End the Gun Epidemic in America" (End the gun epidemic in America, 2015). Despite the fact that Americans' trust in the media is at its lowest point in 20 years (32%; Swift, 2016), many leading scholars and organizations note the influence the media has over public perception and misconceptions in this arena (e.g., see Fox & DeLateur, 2014;

McLeigh, 2015; Nekvasil, Cornell, & Huang, 2015; Perrin, 2016; Rocque, 2012; Swanson & Felthous, 2015). In particular, mental health has become connected with firearm legislation and policies for many reasons, including, but not limited to, sensational media portrayals of the stereotyped "mentally ill shooter," even though that is not at all representative of the behavior of most people with mental illness or a characteristic of most people who perpetrate interpersonal violence with guns (see Gold, 2013; Gold & Simon, 2016; Pinals et al., 2015a, 2015b; American Psychological Association 2013). It is the case that media portrayals usually lack an educational component, and it is also true that, although attention following noteworthy and tragic shooting events is warranted and understandable, the prosocial and appropriate use of firearms rarely, if ever, gains attention in our media, even though the vast majority of those who own or otherwise interact with firearms do so safely.

Practice

Although firearm-related violence and suicide continues to be considered a significant public health problem, (i) most mental health professionals do not routinely address firearm-specific issues in practice, (ii) approximately half have never received any education or training on firearm safety, and (iii) for those who have, their information has come from media sources more so than from professional ones (see Price, Mrdjenovich, Thompson, & Dake, 2009; Slovak, Brewer, & Carlson, 2008; Traylor et al., 2010). Of particular concern is that, despite these glaring gaps in education and training, most professionals express high levels of confidence in their abilities to assess and advise clients on firearm-specific issues.[2] We are not aware of any empirical research with medical professionals in this context but suspect similar rates. Nevertheless, what is most important to consider here is that media sources are serving as the basis of information for large numbers of practitioners as opposed to graduate training, professional meetings, workshops, continuing education classes, or professional journals. The level of public, media, and legislative attention that firearms receive must be met with equal—or even greater— careful attention by mental health and medical professionals. Therefore, clinical training programs must begin to incorporate firearm-specific education and training, and practicing medical and mental health professionals should actively seek continuing education in this regard. These efforts should include learning about guns, firearm subcultures, and prosocial firearm use in addition to issues related to firearm-related violence and suicide.

Research

The professional medical and mental health literatures are virtually devoid of research and commentary on firearm safety, firearm subcultures, and the prosocial ownership and use of guns. While many leading scholars have been instrumental in dispelling many of the myths and pieces of misinformation circulated by various media outlets, there remains an almost exclusive focus on the inappropriate and problematic use of guns, including firearm-involved violence and suicide. Of course, these are important areas that warrant ongoing attention and even prioritization; however, researchers are missing opportunities to increase professionals' understanding of various prosocial firearm subcultures and the appropriate use of guns—indeed, these groups are more representative of the types of people most practitioners will encounter. By solely focusing on "gun violence," researchers have created a very important but rather narrow literature base that addresses relatively rare events that most practitioners will never encounter. There is a real opportunity for researchers to develop a much more robust literature that would have utility for a far greater number of medical and mental health professionals, as well as professionals across other disciplines (e.g., law enforcement, education). We may in fact learn much from our public health colleagues who often deal with issues of "access" and "utilization." That is, to build a wider knowledge base concerning firearms, we suggest building a research literature concerning firearm "utilization" and "access" (with associated positive and negative drivers and implications). Furthermore, much of the research that has been conducted is based on correlational studies drawing from broad-based, publicly available databases. As a result, many important and more advanced questions remain unanswered (e.g., the *motivational, triggering,* and *disinhibiting* factors behind firearm-involved suicide by certain people as opposed to simply identification of their demographics). In addition, it is important to reiterate and highlight the reality that social science cannot compete with the media, including social media. As we have noted earlier in this book, a "breaking news" announcement, live feed, or online posting can "go viral" and reach millions of people within minutes, whereas properly conducted research studies can take well over a year before they are published, if they ever even get published (i.e., the file-drawer problem; see Rosenthal, 1979). While social scientists should not try to compete with media outlets, it is necessary for them to use various media and community platforms to educate the public on important findings once they are realized, just as they do with their peers at professional conferences, for example. Media outlets, including social media, can serve as the information *vehicles* they were intended to be and not the *sources* of information in and of themselves.

Policy

Politicians often possess great power—not only inherent to their positions but also because they can often direct media attention in certain directions (Lawrence & Birkland, 2004). However, with great power comes great responsibility, and policymakers should consider the opportunity they have to properly educate the public and the potential unintended consequences that often arise even from the best-intended efforts (think Newton's third law of motion: *For every action, there is an equal and opposite reaction*). We have seen this play out on large scales (e.g., alcohol prohibition) and smaller ones (e.g., local policies). In the firearm context, it has also been the case that some policies have resulted in unintended consequences. Perhaps one national headline put it best: "Obama Is the Best Gun Salesman in America" (Smith, 2016). Background checks reached record numbers under President Obama's tenure, and the gun industry grew 158% under his presidency. Specifically, the firearms and ammunition industry in the United States increased from $19.1 billion in 2008 to $49.3 billion in 2015, and full-time jobs related to gun-making nearly doubled during that time—from 166,000 to 288,000 (Miniter, 2016). Consideration of these numbers as well as those associated with the relatively high numbers of firearm owners and operators across political parties, and the low trust ratings for the mainstream media should give policymakers pause. Guns evoke emotions, in general, and tragic events significantly exacerbate them; however, policymakers may wish to respond in a more nuanced fashion rather than capitalizing on public emotion by pursuing wide-sweeping, hard-hitting legislation because once the high levels of emotionality dissipate, the potential for unintended consequences and ineffective or low-impact legislation remains.

6. There Is a Lack of Consensus Among Professional, Government, and Advocacy Groups with Respect to Defining Firearm-Related Terms and Events; and There Often Is a Restricted Range of Information and Perspectives Presented by Them

Most terms commonly used in firearm-related laws, policies, and initiatives, and the national debate, more generally, remain undefined or improperly defined. This leads to and perpetuates miscommunication and misunderstanding. There are many examples, ranging from general (e.g., *mental illness*) to specific (e.g., *AR-15*), and everything in between (e.g., *assault weapon*). It is very problematic when terms are defined differently but used as if they were one and the same. This issue is evident in professional, government, and advocacy groups. Even a classification we assume to be self-evident, such as "school shooting," is not even remotely so. For example, Everytown had emphasized the following statistic on its website for quite some time: "239 School Shootings in America Since 2013" (n.d.), followed by the statement:

> How many more before our leaders pass common-sense laws to prevent gun violence and save lives? Communities all over the country live in fear of gun violence. That's unacceptable. We should feel secure in sending our children to school—comforted by the knowledge that they're safe.

The statistic was also memorialized in a September 2017 press release by Moms Demand Action for Gun Sense in America (Washington Moms Demand Action, Everytown respond to fatal shooting at Freeman High School, 2017). In fact, the press release indicates:

> "Everytown research shows that this is at least the 31th school shooting nationwide this year, and the 239th school shooting nationwide since January 2013. It is also the second school shooting in less than 24 hours, following yesterday's shooting at St. Catherine University in St. Paul, Minnesota."

What is particularly noteworthy, though, is that the St. Catherine "school shooting" they were referencing was that of a university security officer who accidentally shot himself in the shoulder and fabricated a report of a gunman (see Horner, 2017 and Woltman, 2017). Now, it seems as though Everytown has begun to speak of "gunfire on school grounds" as opposed to "school shootings" per se, as evidenced by the new headline on their website previously linked to the aforementioned "239" headline.

While all shootings are serious and warrant attention, the type of stand-alone statistics such as "239 School Shootings in America Since 2013" can be quite misleading on its face as many people will associate it with the types of mass shootings we have seen in Columbine, Virginia Tech, and Newtown. However, a closer look at the statistic presented by Everytown reveals that it includes any incident whereby "a firearm was discharged inside a school building or on school or campus grounds, as documented by the press or confirmed through further inquiries with law enforcement," including fatal and nonfatal assaults, suicides, and unintentional shootings. As such, the school shootings statistic includes a very heterogenous set of incidents, ranging from those that stemmed from arguments to criminal and gang-related situations to those that occurred after school hours and coincidentally on school grounds in the absence of students. There are a number of examples in this regard, two of which are the shootings at Indian River State College in Fort Pierce, Florida, on February 7, 2013, and at Hillside Elementary School in San Leandro,

California, on February 13, 2013—both of which Everytown classifies under "Attack on Other Person(s) Resulting in Injury or Death." However, the Indian River State College shooting was actually a situation where a student was accidentally shot in the shoulder during a police shootout with a gunman who was not a student but someone who inadvertently ended up in the parking lot of the school's public safety complex. According to reports, Fort Pierce Police Chief Sean Baldwin believed the man ending up at the college was just "a coincidence" (Howk, 2013). With regard to the Hillside Elementary School shooting, it included two young adults who engaged in an altercation over an unpaid debt. Specifically, Taheer Randall shot and killed Trevion Foster at approximately 9:00 p.m. on the school grounds when he refused to pay him $5 after losing a dice game (Johnson, 2014). Of course, the statistic presented by Everytown includes some planned attacks targeting others with a firearm as well as suicides during school hours; but the school shootings it identified resulted in 59 deaths and 124 nonfatal gunshot injuries, and only a handful of the incidents it included would be classified as a mass shooting.

A related concern is that the range of information and views presented by many professional, government, and advocacy groups is often constricted. In fact, this was a major impetus for us to write this book. For instance, (i) gun-specific resources tend to focus on firearms in the context of their history, types, components, and functionality; (ii) Second Amendment resources usually focus on constitutional use and carry as well as issues related to prosocial shooting activities, such as target shooting and hunting, and issues pertaining to self-defense; and (iii) gun violence prevention resources typically focus on the inappropriate use of guns, such as firearm-involved violence, suicide, and shooting tragedies. This type of compartmentalization fosters the notable gaps of information and highlights the conceptual divides between groups rather than creating bridges and identifying common ground.

Practice

Medical and mental health practitioners can serve as objective experts in many contexts in our society, particularly when serving in forensic roles. By definition, forensic experts provide neutral professional opinions to assist the trier of fact, be it a judge or jury, in understanding advanced concepts in mental health. As such, practitioners have an opportunity to educate about firearm-related issues on a case-by-case basis. In addition, all practitioners (including non-forensic) who develop their professional and cultural competence related to firearms can give presentations in the community and to various professional groups on these issues. Nevertheless, it is essential for practitioners to avoid jargon and clearly define the clinical and firearm-related terms they use in all contexts. Moreover, practitioners must be able to sift through the statistics and focus on the scope of the question at hand. While all shootings are unfortunate and of great concern and we should aim to reduce them in our society, the types of prevention efforts relevant to cases that inadvertently occurred on school grounds are usually quite different from those related to the prevention of targeted mass shootings in schools (i.e., likely what many people think of when they hear the term *school shooting*).

Research

Consistent with the scientific method, researchers have a primary responsibility to operationalize variables and be transparent in their methods and analyses. However, these concepts can easily get lost when results are aggregated across studies. For example, *violence* may be defined differently in various studies, which may even be explicitly indicated; but the findings will usually be grouped together and discussed as if they were all the same. Therefore, research findings may be much less generalizable than we tend to believe. This is a particularly salient issue in large-scale databases that seem to be an inch deep and a mile wide, such as those made available by various government agencies. Variables that are crudely defined can only lead to similarly nonspecific interpretations and implications, and miscommunication and misunderstandings arise when terms are conflated or defined in otherwise non-conventional ways. Therefore, it would be beneficial for researchers to separate research findings based on the ways in which primary variables were operationalized. Those conducting qualitative and quantitative reviews must be particularly careful in this regard, consistent with the "garbage-in, garbage out" concept in meta-analytic methods. In addition, like practitioners, researchers also have an opportunity to educate in legal matters—especially in the form of amicus briefs. However, they must begin to provide a greater range of information and perspectives in all of their publications because the professional literature is very fragmented as it stands. As a result, there was no single source previously available wherein one could learn about guns, firearm safety, terms, and the myriad of issues related to firearms and mental health, violence, and suicide. Professional, government, and advocacy groups must acknowledge that we are all susceptible to confirmation bias and, therefore, many people will only actively seek out resources from those with whom they expect to agree. Thus, more objective publications that reflect a broader spectrum of information should help decrease misunderstanding and increase communication among those with different perspectives.

Policy

Policymakers should operationalize the terms they use as well, and none should be taken for granted. Even those that seem obvious, such as *mental illness*, are not obvious at all. For example, in his January 4, 2016, executive order on gun control, President Obama used the terms *mental health* and *mental illness* almost 30 times without ever defining them, despite the fact that the current *Diagnostic and Statistical Manual of Mental Disorders* (American Psychiatric Association, 2013) consists of over 300 mental health conditions, spanning approximately 900 pages. To say that speaking about "mental health" or "mental illness" is vague is an understatement. Such imprecision often contributes to inaccurate perceptions in the link between mental illness and firearm or overall violence. How can we ever come to a point of clarity and precise answers via nonspecific and ambiguous policies? It is also problematic when policymakers and government officials either change the way in which certain terms are defined (e.g., *mass killing*, *active shooter*) or aggregate data within overly inclusive terms (e.g., *gun violence*) because this affects previously constructed databases and corresponding analyses. We understand that while we can quantify a wide range of information, such as the number of lives that have been taken as a result of inappropriate firearm use, there is no way to quantify the importance of even one life. As a result, laws, policies, and initiatives will likely always be driven by emotion at some level and presented in that context—such as naming laws and initiatives after innocent victims (also known as "apostrophe laws"). However, this approach typically leads to morality-based rather than empirical, behavioral science–based debates. In fact, members of special interest groups, victims, families, and politicians are usually responsible for these laws, policies, and initiatives; and rarely are objective behavioral scientists and mental health professionals who can help foster scientifically grounded and more effective decision-making involved.

7. Firearm Regulations Have Been Present Since United States' Inception, Many Laws and Landmark Legal Cases Have Followed, and the *Individual Rights* Perspective Is Currently the Prevailing View in the Higher Courts

The Second Amendment was ratified in 1791, and, while some firearm laws were passed in the 1800s and early 1900s, the time period following the assassination of President John F. Kennedy represents a significant turning point in firearm legislation and policy in this country. Namely, the Gun Control Act of 1968 followed, as did the creation of the Bureau of Alcohol, Tobacco and Firearms in 1972, the Crime Control Act of 1990, the 1993 Brady Law and assault weapons ban, the National Instant Criminal Background Check (NICS) Improvement Act in 2008, and many other laws and policies. In addition, the landmark case *District of Columbia v. Heller* was decided in 2008, followed by *McDonald v. City of Chicago* in 2010. Collectively, these decisions affirmed that the Second Amendment protects an individual's right to possess a firearm for traditionally lawful purposes and that this applies federally but also to state and local governments. The two prevailing theories of the Second Amendment had traditionally been the *individual rights* and the *states'* (or *collective*) *rights* perspectives, and the individual rights perspective prevails in the higher courts at this time.

Practice

Medical and mental health practitioners should learn at least the most general federal and state firearm laws, such as those pertaining to storage, child access, and transportation. It may also be beneficial to become aware of local hunting regulations as well as those related to frequenting gun ranges and the like. Of course, they should already be familiar with their jurisdiction's duty-to-warn and -protect provisions in the context of breaking confidentiality and reporting risk-related concerns. However, it is also important for practitioners to recognize that it has been deemed to be a constitutional right for most people to own firearms. Regardless of their personal views on firearms and firearm laws, practitioners would be wise to familiarize themselves with relevant laws and regulations in this context as one-third of the population regularly interacts with guns at some level and, therefore, it is quite possible that a practitioner may become involved in a firearm-related matter at some point in his or her career. Indeed, all clinicians are taught to assess for the presence of firearms during their standard violence and suicide risk assessments; unfortunately, few are taught where to go from there. In addition, practitioners who directly engage in firearm-specific assessments should develop an even higher level of education and training on firearms and firearm laws so that they will be able to adequately assess clients' knowledge and perspectives in this regard. Overall, a good clinical practice guideline is to treat the client as the expert in his or her own beliefs. That is, when working with a client and firearm-related issues, it would be worth the clinician asking the client about the nature or quality of his or her "individual rights" or other beliefs. Doing so would not only likely improve clinical rapport but also lead to better mental health outcomes in instances where firearm concerns become pressing.

Research

It would be beneficial for researchers to retroactively assess the effectiveness of some of the more noteworthy firearm laws and policies, as well as the potential impact of landmark cases in this arena. Much of the professional firearm literature focuses on correlates of violence and related variables, but there is a dearth of empirical policy analysis research (see exceptions related to the suicide literature, as noted above). Still, retrospective, correlational research is inherently limited; therefore, it would be useful if researchers seek to conduct prospective studies at the state and local levels, commencing when policies are presented and moving forward. Comparative research that includes both baseline (i.e., before a policy is enacted) and post-policy data will likely prove to be much more informative and contributory.

Policy

Consistent with the aforementioned point in the context of research, policymakers should seek to collaborate with nonpartisan or at least bipartisan practitioners and researchers to conduct policy analyses. We have now entered 2018 with a citizenry that has access to a wealth of information—much of which is remotely available to them within seconds at the mere touch of a button. As such, it is likely that there will be an increasing push for policymakers to exhibit transparency, accountability, and responsibility in the context of their proposals and policy efforts.

8. Research Support for the Effectiveness of Firearm-Related Laws and Policies Is Mixed

Despite the sizable literature on gun-related violence and the significant attention these issues receive in the media and by legislators, there is a relatively scant empirical research base pertaining to the effectiveness of laws and policies in this area. The research that has been published primarily centers around background checks, the castle doctrine or "stand-your-ground" laws, right to carry (RTC) laws, and considerations related to child access prevention (CAP) and storage; and the findings are generally mixed. In general, more background checks have been found to be correlated with less firearm-involved violence and suicide at the state level; however, it is also the case that a number of mass shooters either already passed background checks or would have if they had gone through them. It is also important to highlight the likelihood that states that employ local agencies to conduct background checks place particular value and resources on gun control measures. There is even less research available on the castle doctrine or "stand-your-ground" laws, and that which is available shows no evidence of a deterring effect and even increases in crime and violence in some cases. Research findings on RTC laws are more mixed, but again, relatively few empirical studies have been conducted in that area. RTC on college campuses has become a more hotly debated issue, and that too reflects variable attitudes and practices (e.g., Cavanagh, Bouffard, Wells, & Nobles, 2012). Finally, research related to CAP and storage seems to indicate that keeping firearms locked and unloaded and storing ammunition locked and in a separate location are each associated with a protective effect against unintentional firearm-involved fatalities and may mitigate suicide risk for certain groups. However, findings associated with minimum age requirements and suicide overall, for example, are much less compelling.

Practice

Practitioners would be well served to focus on CAP and storage considerations in clinical practice. This is one of the few areas in the firearm arena that reflects significant agreement across the gun rights and control spectrum, and even leading Second Amendment groups (e.g., the National Rifle Association) have developed child safety programs in this regard. Access and storage considerations are also relevant to adults, especially those in crisis or who are psychologically unwell otherwise. Recently, a few local law enforcement agencies have offered free temporary firearm storage for those with mental health concerns, as have newly developed businesses that provide safe and secure firearm storage options for those in need.[3] Practitioners may do well to develop a priori relationships with local law enforcement in order to draw on such protective measures for clients in need. The other firearm laws and policies are potentially relevant to clinicians in some situations but likely more so in the context of assessing gun owners' attitudes and practices related to gun-carrying and home defense.

Research

Many research questions related to the aforementioned areas remain unanswered as many have yet to even be asked. There are very few empirical studies that have investigated the effectiveness of firearm-related laws and policies, and those that have primarily relied upon correlational, state-by-state analyses that are largely nonspecific and not particularly informative. Therefore, more intensive, prospective empirical investigations of the effectiveness of background checks, "stand-your-ground" laws, RTC laws, and CAP and storage efforts need to be undertaken. It would also be beneficial for researchers to include a range of outcome variables as well rather than such a heavy reliance on broad state-by-state violence and crime statistics. It would also be beneficial to conduct more case studies and local investigations, such as retroactively investigating the (potential) utility of background checks in various shootings, including, but not limited to, high-profile, mass shootings. Some, such as Dr. Peter Langman (2009), have already provided a solid foundation in this regard to expound upon. As for "stand-your-ground" and RTC laws, researchers should gather prospective data on the attitudes and practices of gun owners. This is also advisable for CAP and storage considerations, and experimental research is also needed in the context of CAP and storage as well as to investigate the effectiveness of firearm-related child safety programs, more specifically.

Policy

The empirical research literature pertaining to the effectiveness of firearm-related laws and policies is minuscule in relation to the disproportionate attention these efforts typically receive at the time of their inception, and that which is known is quite nuanced and relatively mixed. Therefore, policymakers should be transparent about the general lack of empirical support that exists for most firearm laws and policies that have already been implemented, and they should collaborate with medical and mental health practitioners and researchers who have expertise in firearm-related matters to conduct more policy evaluation studies, both retrospectively and prospectively.

9. The Available Firearm-Related Research Is Significantly Limited Because of an Almost Exclusive Reliance on Retrospective Studies and Proxy Variables, a Lack of Interdisciplinary Focus, and Various Systemic Barriers

Most of the professional literature regarding firearms reflects correlational analyses of variables from previously generated data sets, often compiled by government-based or related agencies. Moreover, researchers have relied heavily on proxy variables instead of conducting prospective studies to directly gather variables of interest. For example, instead of ascertaining how many people who legally own firearms engage in acts of interpersonal violence, many researchers will simply correlate the estimated number of firearm owners in a particular state with the number of violent crimes committed. In addition, there remains a disconnect across disciplines relevant to firearm-related issues; namely, there is a lack of interdisciplinary research efforts among those in the fields of medicine, mental health, public health, law, and law enforcement. Furthermore, there are inherent systemic barriers to conducting practice- and policy-oriented firearm research—some of which are common to these types of areas of study, but others seem to reflect more specific biases associated with guns.

Practice

Most practitioners never receive formal education or training on firearms or firearm-specific issues, and those who do are most likely to be exposed to broad-based, correlational research findings related to the inappropriate use of guns. However, medical and mental health practitioners must recognize that, while very important, research on "gun violence" and the like is not representative of the typical experience of most Americans who interact with guns. The disproportionate attention paid by many media outlets, policymakers, and researchers to improper firearm use and the extreme minority who pose risks in this context may lead practitioners to adopt a skewed perspective on firearms and firearm-related issues, however. Nevertheless, we share the sentiment of Perrin (2016) and Kaslow (2015), such that it is incumbent upon psychologists (and other mental health and medical practitioners) to translate the psychological science of mass shootings and the like for the media and public. It is also our contention, though, that the full range of firearm-related issues, including, but not limited to, firearm safety, prosocial firearm use, and firearm subcultural information be disseminated in this way.

Research

As we have noted, it is imperative for researchers to conduct prospective studies, seeking to gather data on direct rather than proxy variables. This will require, in part, inclusion of firearm owners and operators as research participants. In addition, researchers should seek to adopt a more collaborative interdisciplinary approach—as is recommended in gun violence prevention efforts—such that experts from the fields of medicine, mental health, public health, law, and law enforcement should develop research teams in an effort to increase the applicability and quality of studies. These are not particularly novel concepts. In fact, as La Valle (2013, p. 4) noted, the National Academy of Sciences issued a non-partisan critique of the extant gun policy research and raised concerns about:

(a) unacceptably high levels of aggregation such as states or counties,
(b) analytical dependence upon observably unreliable county-level
data . . . (c) artificial statistical confidence produced by excessively large
numbers of non-independent sample units, (d) the sensitivity of policy
effects to seemingly minor changes in overall model specification,
(e) questionably short or overly extended post-intervention periods,
(f) differences among the various statistical techniques of gun policy
outcome estimation, and finally, (g) the need for more data overall.

There are also significant barriers to conducting research in this area of study. One particularly salient issue pertains to funding as some cite cuts in federal funding to investigate such topics as "gun violence." Once again, this seems to be a very politically driven issue; and in our experience, there are clear barriers that cut across party lines and gun rights/control perspectives. For instance, some agencies seem to avoid funding firearm research due, in part, to partisan restrictions or fear of social and political blowback. Anecdotally, we have also experienced these barriers at the local level, whereby academicians, researchers, and publishers are hesitant to sign on to any projects involving firearms, again for reasons ranging from failure to subscribe to a particular predetermined set of research goals to fearing negative publicity and public ire. That said, it is true that hypothesis-testing is a major tenet of the scientific method; however, we must make more room for exploratory research questions in the firearm arena, or we will continue to run the risk of conducting biased or narrow studies. Moreover, research needs to be conducted by objective behavioral and social scientists rather than special interest or advocacy groups, and it must include a broader range of topics and not solely those associated with violence and suicide. For example, it would also be beneficial to gather more data on the attitudes and practices of members from various groups across the gun rights/control spectrum and from the range of firearm subgroups we have outlined throughout this book. Doing so holds great potential impact; for instance, we could begin to understand more of the nuanced factors that distinguish law-abiding firearm enthusiasts from those who do engage in improper firearm utilization. It is also important to conduct more policy evaluation research and to move away from a reliance on proxy variables and investigate such questions as: How many firearm deaths—homicides and suicides—involved illegal guns and unlicensed operators? What proportion of legal firearm owners interact with firearms appropriately and safely? Lastly, it would be useful for researchers to conduct quantitative research reviews (i.e., meta-analyses), once the literature improves and expands, to circumvent the many limitations inherent to qualitative research reviews and commentary-, rather than empirically, based investigations.

Policy

As we have noted in the context of other findings, policymakers should recognize the notable limitations associated with the extant research and seek to facilitate improvements moving forward in this regard. There is a dearth of empirical research on the effectiveness of various programs aimed at reducing firearm-related violence, including, but not limited to, such popularly advertised efforts as gun buy-back programs, whereas targeted policing intervention efforts are generally more promising terms of their empirical support (see Makarios & Pratt, 2012; Payne & Gainey, 2008; Phillips, Kim, & Sobol, 2013; Rosenfeld, Deckard, & Blackburn, 2014; Wyant, Taylor, Ratcliffe, & Wood, 2012). Nevertheless, politicians, other policymakers, and funding sources have an opportunity to foster interdisciplinary firearm research on a wider range of topics and to assist in removing barriers to conducting objective, non-partisan empirical studies.

10. Although Some Progress Has Been Made in Reducing Illegal Gun Trafficking, Regulating and Holding Firearm Dealers Legally Liable Have Been Much Less Successful

Illegal firearms are brought to and circulated throughout the United States in a variety of ways, but licensed firearm dealers have been noted to be a primary source for gun traffickers as they account for most of the guns diverted to the illegal market (Bureau of Alcohol, Tobacco and Firearms, 2000b). That said, it is only a small proportion of dealers that are associated with this problem; specifically, the Bureau of Alcohol, Tobacco and Firearms (2000a) found that only 1% of dealers initially sold more than 50% of all guns traced to crime. Still, while it remains the case that there is little or no regulation and enforcement of dealers in most states, those that do so have been associated with lower gun trafficking rates. Nevertheless, efforts to hold firearm dealers legally liable in more high-profile cases, such as mass shootings, have not gained much traction due, at least in part, to certain commerce protection laws—namely, the 2005 Protection of Lawful Commerce in Arms Act.

Practice

Although the aforementioned issues are not directly related to practitioners, they are understandably concerned about liability claims that can directly affect them; namely, ethics complaints and malpractice lawsuits. Two main topics emerge in this regard: (i) duty-to-warn and/or -protect requirements and (ii) inquiries about firearm-related matters, more generally. Medical and mental health practitioners receive copious amounts of education and training on such issues as maintaining client confidentiality, including, but not limited to, considerations related to the Health Insurance Portability and Accountability Act of 1996. It is the necessary breaking of confidentiality in elevated violence or suicide risk scenarios that is often a much more challenging endeavor. It is incumbent upon practitioners to familiarize themselves with their state's laws in this regard. Moreover, practitioners should also determine where their state stands with respect to firearm-specific inquiries and their associated responsibilities and restrictions (e.g., see the "Docs v. Glocks" lawsuit, or *Wollschlaeger v. Governor of Florida*, 2014). There is also much reason to believe that clinicians will increasingly be called upon to provide client information when firearm-related matters arise, which will accentuate issues related to confidentiality in purely clinical, therapeutic contexts. Of course, it is also likely that mental health professionals will be conducting firearm evaluations in a variety of contexts, including for new applicants and those seeking to have their firearms reinstated. As such, practitioner liability concerns will only continue to rise; therefore, treatment providers and evaluators would be wise to further develop and maintain their professional competence in these areas.

Research

It would be beneficial for researchers to more closely investigate the relationship between the regulation and enforcement of firearm dealers and outcome variables other than gun trafficking. Of course, a closer investigation into the sources of the other half of illegal drug trafficking and related crimes is needed. However, like other lines of research in this arena, analyses must go beyond identifying correlations between broad-based, state-level variables. This will require more in-depth and locally conducted prospective, policy analysis studies as well as those that include firearm dealers as participants. It would also be useful to assess public sentiment regarding dealer liability in shooting cases, especially high-profile shootings, to compare and contrast the perspectives of community members with those of the courts. In addition, it would be informative to investigate medical and mental health professionals' views—in therapeutic and forensic or evaluative contexts that involve firearms—with respect to their knowledge, training, and levels of comfort with their responsibilities and associated liability. Some research has been conducted with these groups regarding their attitudes and practices in these contexts (e.g., see Price et al., 2009; Slovak et al., 2008; Traylor et al.,

2010); but it has not been directly connected with liability-related concerns, and practitioners may express different perspectives if inquiries are made within a liability-based framework. Such work may also elucidate potential threats to clinician objectivity (e.g., negative attitudes toward firearms) that can be redressed in consultation and training.

Policy

As noted, the vast majority of firearm dealers are not associated with illegal gun trafficking or other crimes. In fact, it is a very small proportion that are responsible for at least half of these problems. Policymakers may decide to collaborate with researchers to identify the other half of the sources in this regard. Moreover, there is much work to do in terms of dealer oversight throughout the country given that most states do not require the retention of records, inspections, licenses, storage security requirements, and the reporting of stolen firearms. Efforts in this regard will require legislators to work directly with the dealers in their jurisdictions as well as the Second Amendment community, more generally. With respect to assigning added responsibilities and associated liability to medical and mental health professionals with regard to firearm-related matters, policymakers need to recognize that the overwhelming majority of these practitioners have never received formal education or training on firearms or most firearm-related issues. In addition, most clinicians are not forensically trained and, therefore, are likely to experience difficulties in certain areas, such as assessing firearm-related violence and suicide risk, discharging duty-to-warn and -protect requirements, and even interfacing with law enforcement or legal personnel. Therefore, policymakers should prioritize the firearm-specific education and training of medical and mental health professionals before seeking to pass widespread policies that would require even more involvement by practitioners in firearm-related matters as many are lacking advanced professional competence in this regard even with their current set of responsibilities.

11. Firearm-Involved Homicides Account for Approximately 11,000 Deaths in the United States Annually, or One-Third of All Gun Deaths and Two-Thirds of All Homicides, Reflecting a Mortality Rate That Has Not Changed in Two Decades

Every death is meaningful and should not be minimized. At the macro level, however, it is the case that the majority of firearm-involved deaths are suicides and not homicides. It is also the case that homicide rates have remained unchanged for more than two decades, and, in fact, some have noted a decline in death rates associated with certain types of firearm-involved violent acts. From an even broader perspective, some have also noted that interpersonal violence has decreased significantly over the course of human civilization (see

Pinker, 2011). Nevertheless, it is an important endeavor to work toward continued reductions in acts of violence, including those that involve guns.

Practice

First and foremost, practitioners must look well beyond national statistics and toward what are referred to as "local norms," or statistics associated with their particular states and regions. Although there are some similarities among firearm-related statistics across the country, there are often notable differences in some important respects—in terms of rates, laws, policies, procedures, and subcultural considerations. The concept of utilizing local norms, when possible, has become a widely accepted standard of practice in the psychological assessment arena; and we reiterate our call for its application to firearm-related matters (Wechsler, Pirelli, Struble, & Cramer, 2015). It is important to recognize that statistics often vary as a function of various subcultural classifications, including, but certainly not limited to, gender; ethnicity; marital, family, and socioeconomic status; and area of residence. In addition, practitioners should take a nuanced approach to assessment, whereby they consider case-specific details rather than basing their opinions wholly on broad diagnostic or criminal classifications. Consideration of local norms and general base rates is important, but analyzing the underlying factors that motivate, trigger, or otherwise destabilize people is critical—rather than primarily making inferences based on their diagnoses or criminal charges. Failure to do so results in aggregating cases that are clinically distinct, thereby approaching prevention efforts in an inappropriate one-size-fits-all manner (e.g., overly broad classifications of what are often very heterogenous school shootings).

Research

A primary consideration for researchers in this arena is to independently account for relevant variables during the data collection stages and make decisions to aggregate them during the analysis stages. In other words, researchers should seek to code for as many relevant variables as possible, such as separating data associated with violence, DV, and suicide. They may then decide to investigate their relevance as moderating variables in their analyses, but the premature aggregation of data often leads to overly broad classifications that, at best, lack utility and, at worst, are misleading. Perhaps the most salient example is the aggregation of all incidents that involved a discharged firearm on school grounds to comprise a data set of "school shootings" (see finding 6 above). In the context of firearm-involved homicides, it would be beneficial for researchers to seek to delineate the relevant statistics into their respective, distinct areas (e.g., mass school shootings, homicides committed during the course of a crime, or felony homicides) rather than presenting firearm-involved homicides as if it were a unitary construct and correlating it with other broad-based variables, such as the rates of background checks at the state level. How does the fact that a 42-year-old man sought approval for a hunting license and shotgun relate to a gang-related shooting on the opposite side of the state? Such a rhetorical question is axiomatic at the ground level but is lost during the process of data and construct aggregation. The advent of more focused, targeted research should lead to more focused, targeted interventions and relevant prevention efforts.

Policy

Politicians and other policymakers should clearly indicate to their constituents that, by and large, firearm-involved death rates have remained unchanged in many years. While important to address, politicizing rare yet tragic mass shootings fosters misunderstanding and miscommunication in our society, which contributes to a polarized, contentious climate among us. The vast majority of people in this country actually agree and want to prevent tragic shootings. However, the politicization of firearm-related issues highlights areas of disagreement—a surefire way to keep people divided. As such, policymakers should prioritize efforts to find the areas of common ground among most people in this country and refrain from sensationalizing tragic events that do not actually represent the majority of firearm-involved deaths. Therefore, they should avoid using overly inclusive terms and associated statistics when presenting their positions and proposals. For instance, just as practitioners and researchers, they should present information and statistics related to crime, suicide, and interpersonal violence separately. There are certainly overlapping considerations that cut across various firearm-related areas, but the ultimate focus must be on the underlying precipitants of these events to develop effective prevention efforts, laws, and policies.

12. State-Level Data Indicate a Correlation Between Firearm Ownership and Violent Crime

Rates of firearm ownership vary by state, ranging from Hawaii (26%) to Mississippi (77%), with an average of 58% across states countrywide (Siegel, Ross, & King, 2013). Although ownership rates have dropped nearly 10% since the 1990s, the United States still has relatively higher homicide rates than other developed countries; therefore, questions regarding the association between gun ownership and violence naturally arise. Although the research is correlational and few studies have been conducted in this area, that which has been published indicates a relationship between gun ownership and violent crime rates at the state level. That said, the implications of this finding are somewhat unclear because we are not able to ascertain which guns are involved in which crimes when we aggregate data in this way. In other words, it is difficult to say whether this correlation indicates that the presence of more guns in a state prompts violent crime or, rather, if this is simply not a good deterrent in regions with higher crime. Correlational research designs and analyses preclude us from speaking to causation. Nevertheless, it is a finding that warrants attention and further investigation.

Practice

As we have highlighted throughout this book, the vast majority of those who interact with firearms are law-abiding citizens who pose no notable risk of violence or suicide. However, if practitioners become aware that a patient or examinee interacts with or owns firearms, they should inquire further at relevant times, including, but not necessarily limited to, whenever someone's risk of violence or suicide is in question or when potentially vulnerable or at-risk others may have access to said firearms (e.g., children, adults in psychiatric crisis). Although access to firearms is a risk factor to consider in the context of assessing violence and suicide risk, it is not dispositive in and of itself. Put differently, medical and mental health professionals must ask about access to potentially lethal means in these situations; however, this inquiry alone is necessary but insufficient. Practitioners should further seek to gather such information as the amount and types of firearms and ammunition available, storage practices, and who has access. Moreover, the presence of firearms should be considered a moderating variable, such that practitioners seek to assess how such access might impact the risk of violence or suicide in a particular situation. That is, owning a gun does not cause someone to be suicidal or violent; moderation implies that it may worsen the chance of this occurring, however. It may be the case that treating professionals and some evaluators maintain a low threshold in this context, erring on the side of caution, as it were. However, some mental health professionals will ultimately be tasked with opining on certain people's suitability to own or interact with firearms, such as in matters of new applicants who have been flagged and those seeking reinstatement of their guns or to have their gun rights formally restored (see findings 24 and 30 below). Regardless, most medical and mental health professionals should develop and maintain their professional and cultural competencies associated with firearms and firearm-related subcultures given the roles and responsibilities they have in our society.

Research

It is imperative that researchers begin to directly connect firearm ownership with violence rather than correlating variables drawn from state-level databases. If the researchers seek to investigate the potentially deterring effects of the mere presence of legally owned guns in a region, then this line of research may have some value. However, if the hypotheses relate to the potential causal connection between legally owned firearms and violence, researchers must ascertain if it is these specific guns involved in violent crimes—and, therefore, what proportion of violent crimes are committed by lawful firearm owners with legal guns. In addition, more research is needed on the firearm storage and operation practices and attitudes of these lawful gun owners by including them as research participants. We may again learn from our colleagues in the health professions in this regard, this time from the notion of community-engaged participatory research. Community-engaged approaches, in short, place the community partner (e.g., health clinic) as an equitable partner in the research. What would happen if scholars partnered with firearm dealers or trainers in research in such a way? We suspect that access to willing research participants may become more feasible when the jointly presented survey and other studies are presented as a partnership between, for example, a university and a firearm dealer.

Policy

There will always be people who inappropriately attain and interact with firearms, regardless of the laws or policies in place. We suspect that the majority of such people do not follow the steps to acquiring or operating firearms appropriately—that they do not fill out applications or educate themselves on the proper storage and use of firearms. These are empirical questions, however; and policymakers can provide the assistance needed to acquire the data necessary to test these hypotheses. It has been contended that it is targeted law enforcement interventions in high-crime areas that may be effective in reducing firearm-involved violent crime (e.g., see Lindgren, 2015), which would render a primary focus on lawful firearm owners ineffective and, likely, rather distracting. It is critical that we begin to address these issues at the ground level rather than in manner that relies upon overly broad, nonspecific databases. Related to this, the stark lack of federal funding for firearm research is rather shocking. As noted, agencies like the CDC are often prohibited from engaging in such research themselves, and likely such barriers preclude the National Institute of Justice (NIJ), among others, from funding research. This is unfortunate because enhanced federal funding from the CDC and NIJ alike could actually serve as a catalyst for improved data-driven policymaking concerning many of the issues we have reviewed. Policymakers may revisit the funding and research concerns to re-evaluate the relative potential benefit of prioritizing a range of firearm-related topics.

13. Mass Shootings Are Very Low–Base Rate but High-Impact Events That Represent a Very Small Proportion of Firearm-Involved Deaths

Mass shootings represent less than 1% of all firearm-related homicides in the United States each year, an even lower proportion of firearm-involved deaths, and an exponentially lower percentage of deaths, in general. However, they receive disproportionate amounts of attention from some media outlets, politicians, and advocacy groups. In the context of our previously expressed sentiment, if guns are different, mass shootings are *very* different. Put differently, mass shootings are very high-impact events—in terms of both the death tolls and the corresponding emotions they evoke. This is akin to plane crashes. Most people possess an intellectual understanding that they are much more likely to be a victim of the many diseases we frequently encounter and the ostensibly benign daily tasks in which we engage, and neither mass shootings nor plane crashes come close to being one of the leading causes of death (Centers for Disease Control and Prevention, 2017). But people tend to have much different emotional reactions to mass shootings compared to chronic lower respiratory diseases—a reality that drives many mass shooters to engage in such sensational and terroristic acts. While we are fortunate that these types of shootings are relatively uncommon, their emotional impact often leads to divisiveness among various people and groups with regard to response and prevention efforts.

Practice

Like most community gatekeepers, one of the biggest fears of medical and mental health professionals is that one of their clients will engage in a serious act of violence or self-injury. Indeed, multimillion-dollar malpractice insurance policies are essentially premised on the fears of low–base rate, high-impact events. As we noted, firearm-involved homicides and suicides are rare enough, much less mass shootings. Therefore, prediction-based assessment and treatment efforts lack utility in this context and will only serve to exhaust valuable resources. We cannot predict mass shootings with any level of meaningful accuracy in terms of the perpetrators, event details, or victims. What we can do, however, is employ prevention-based approaches that focus on risk assessment and management rather than conjecturing if a specific event will happen in a particular way, at a given time, to a predetermined set of people. Medical and mental health professionals are neither psychics nor mind readers; they are essentially data analysts who can rely on their experience, training, and education—along with the contemporary professional literature—to assess risk levels and recommend corresponding prevention and intervention techniques. As such, practitioners should be clear to clients, relevant agencies and institutions, and the public, more generally, about their inability to predict specific events with any useful level of accuracy and about any other limitations associated with their opinions and recommendations.

Research

Some researchers have conducted qualitative reviews of high-profile mass shootings based on publicly available information and have found some commonalities and themes across shooters and situations; however, leading scholars and government agencies continue to recommend against profiling because these events are too rare. Therefore, quantitative, empirical studies on mass shootings investigating predictive models are likely to lack utility and may even be misleading. In this regard, it is critical to emphasize the importance of using more exclusive operational definitions for mass shooting and related variables, to avoid the aggregation of data from dissimilar events. Inclusion criteria solely based on the presence of a firearm or a specific number of deaths will continue to lead to overly inclusive databases of heterogenous offenders and situations. In most cases, it will be more beneficial to understand the motivations of perpetrators rather than the basic crime classification. For example, if we collect data based on a crude definition of mass shooting (e.g., a shooting resulting in three or more deaths), we run the risk of grouping conceptually different events, such as an impulsive gang-related shooting with a formally planned school shooting. Although another thwarted school shooting should be considered along with the one that was carried out, it would not be if the inclusion criteria are based on the number of people who died. The same would be true for foreign terrorist attacks that share the same motivation, regardless if the mechanism to do so is a plane, gun, or car. The type of research we are suggesting is complex. It is much simpler to analyze prepopulated and readily available data sets of "mass shootings." However, it is imperative that our research efforts evolve into more nuanced, in-depth studies that seek to analyze conceptually similar events—not primarily based on the means used or the number of victims but rather as a function of the perpetrators' intentions. We also embrace the recommendations made by Skeem & Monahan (2011), such that researchers should begin to investigate the effectiveness of risk management and reduction efforts, thereby shifting the focus from the predictive utility of risk factors.

Policy

It would be beneficial if politicians and other policymakers aligned their efforts with non-partisan, objective medical and mental health practitioners and social scientists. Mass shootings are extremely tragic and troubling events, but politicizing and sensationalizing them only serve to polarize the public and perpetuate myths and misconceptions. Policymakers can help foster firearm-involved violence prevention efforts by bringing together interdisciplinary teams comprised of experts in this arena.

14. Concepts Related to Marginalization, Damaged Masculinity, and Firearm Access Warrant Increased Attention in the Context of Threat Assessment and the Prevention of School Shootings

Although school shootings are too rare to allow for profiling or prediction with any real accuracy, commonalities and themes have certainly emerged from qualitative investigations of school shooters by leading scholars and organizations. As a practical matter, the fact that many of the school shooters in this country readily gained access to high-powered firearms should raise concerns and increased attention to issues related to gun storage and access, especially with young people who present with various risk factors. Still, it remains the case that many children and adolescents have access to firearms at some level, and the vast majority do not seek to use them inappropriately. In recent years, schools across the country have elevated bullying awareness to the forefront in the context of bullying-related laws and policies, such as New Jersey's harassment, intimidation, and bullying laws. However, a closer look at some of the most high-profile school shooters indicates that most were not victims of bullying, nor were they the stereotypical socially isolated loners. Langman (2009) highlighted these realities in his seminal work and addressed what appears to be the more salient issue of "damaged masculinity," comparable to Vandello & Bosson's (2013) concept of "precarious manhood." These constructs may help explain some of the extreme acts of violence committed by young males with physical, cognitive, and emotional deficits.

Practice

Within the context of their violence and suicide risk assessments, practitioners should pay particular attention to how issues related to self-image and psychosocial development affect potentially at-risk youth. Medical, mental health, and educational professionals widely recognize the importance of the numerous developmental milestones and challenges young people must overcome throughout their early lives. However, although considerations relevant to such areas as psychosexual development are readily acknowledged in "normally functioning" youth, these types of issues are often overlooked for those who present with concerns and needs in other areas that may be thought to be of greater priority (e.g., educational achievement). While schools must obviously focus on students' academic performance, it is necessary to recognize that many factors other than learning problems and disabilities can affect them, especially those pertaining to psychosocial development. Again, it is imperative to go beyond bullying and seek an understanding of youths' perceptions of their image, social status, and experience, including their view on masculinity and their development in that regard. These concepts are germane to healthy human development in our society and, therefore, should play a central role in assessments and interventions with at-risk youth. Prevention efforts in schools can benefit from the employment of a risk management and reduction approach to assessment. At the individual level, practitioners would likely find utility in using a structured professional judgment (SPJ) risk assessment approach in these matters. At the systemic level, schools would be well served by embracing an overarching threat assessment model to guide processes related to working with students of concern. Namely, we encourage practitioners and educational professionals to consider implementing the Virginia model for student threat assessment developed by Cornell & Sheras (2006) as it is well grounded in contemporary theory and behavioral science, and it has received empirical support (e.g., see Nekvasil & Cornell, 2015). In either case, it is imperative to engage in efforts that include much more than simply addressing youths' access to firearms.

Research

It would be beneficial for researchers to investigate the practices and attitudes of medical, mental health, and educational professionals with respect to their consideration of issues related to marginalization, damaged masculinity, and firearm access among youth. Furthermore, it would be informative to ascertain which risk assessment and intervention models schools use throughout the country and their associated effectiveness. In this regard, more empirical research is needed to investigate the effectiveness of Cornell & Sheras' Virginia model, which has evidenced significant promise to this point.

Policy

From a policy standpoint, risk and threat assessment efforts focused on practical prevention approaches should be prioritized over those that are much more dramatic and less realistic (e.g., active shooter drills). Policymakers should spearhead efforts to bring together medical, mental health, educational, legal, and law enforcement professionals with parents and various community stakeholders to facilitate communication and information-sharing among these groups. Analyses of high-profile (mass) school shootings suggest that many were rather well planned and that the perpetrators directly told others, gave off warning signs, or otherwise leaked relevant information related to their plans. Therefore, some of these tragic events may have been prevented if information was properly shared across sources and the proverbial pieces of the puzzle had been put together in advance rather than retrospectively. In some matters, professionals across disciplines can more effectively communicate with other involved professionals and family members. However, there are many times when such communication is hindered or outright precluded because of legal or procedural safeguards (e.g., confidentiality considerations, such as those related to the Health Insurance Portability and Accountability Act). Moreover, the various professionals and family members involved often have somewhat different objectives, responsibilities, and levels of liability. It is for these reasons that professional team–family approaches need to be looked at more closely by policymakers because, as it stands, there are many inherent barriers to communication in these scenarios and the relevant parties often function independently.

15. Only 3%–5% of All Violence Is Attributable to Even Serious Mental Illness, and an Even Smaller Percentage Is Associated with Firearm-Related Violence. A Primary Concern is Psychiatric Crisis and not Mental Illness Per Se.

The vast majority of people with mental health problems do not engage in acts of violence or suicide, with or without a gun. In fact, the overwhelming majority of those people diagnosed with even severe mental illnesses do not engage in firearm-related violence. This is an empirically based finding that has been consistently reflected in the contemporary professional literature, and the leading mental health organizations in this country have highlighted this as well. Namely, both the American Psychiatric Association (Pinals et al., 2015a, 2015b) and the American Psychological Association (2013) have come out with position statements from expert panels in this regard (see also Gold & Simon, 2016). Yet, mental illness continues to be closely linked to firearm-related violence by various media outlets, politicians, government officials, and advocacy groups. Indeed, in President Obama's gun control–based January 4, 2016, executive order, he used the terms *mental health* and *mental illness* almost 30 times without ever defining them, and he committed $500 million "to increase access to mental health care" (Fact sheet, 2016). In addition, the stereotyped image of the mentally ill shooter with an assault-style rifle is one that is often set forth to evoke emotional reactions and, therefore, galvanize support for certain legislation, especially in instances of domestic terrorism or school shootings. However, these efforts to tie mental illness to firearm-involved violence are far removed from reality and would only succeed in resetting the last 50-plus, hard-fought years of destigmatization efforts while contemporaneously *deterring* people from seeking mental health treatment.

Practice

Medical and mental health practitioners must consider relevant base rates in their assessments of clients, and, while they should address issues related to firearm access and risk more generally, it behooves them to integrate the very low base rates associated with firearm-involved violence into their analyses and ultimate opinions. In addition, clinicians should seek to identify certain types of active symptoms (e.g., paranoia, hopelessness) and emotional experiences (e.g., feeling burdensome or socially isolated), as such is likely to be much more useful than focusing on diagnostic labels. Furthermore, consistent with a public health education stance, practitioners should be leading efforts to educate others on mental health–related issues, including the public, legal professionals, and members of other professional groups. In particular, it is incumbent on medical and mental health professionals to promote awareness of the fact that mental illness is actually a weak predictor of firearm-involved violence. Practitioners' personal views on guns and gun control may negatively interfere with their assessments, and, therefore, they may decide that they will recuse themselves from matters that clearly involve guns. However, all practitioners need to attain competence in this arena because there is no way of knowing when a firearm-specific matter will arise in practice. Although many treating professionals may wish to avoid engaging in forensic matters, especially those related to guns, this is unrealistic because (i) they are most likely to be the first person contacted when someone is flagged while applying for a firearm permit or when there is a revocation subsequent to a problematic incident and (ii) firearm-related questions are a fundamental component of violence and suicide risk assessments, which are required when a client presents with concerns in this regard. Therefore, medical and mental health professionals must develop and maintain their professional competence via education and training on firearm-related matters, particularly for those issues most relevant to mental health. That said, reliance on broad and nonspecific classifications, such as psychiatric diagnoses, lacks utility and can be quite misleading. Rather, practitioners need to conduct functional analyses of *behaviors* while considering the potential moderating effects of certain variables (e.g., substance use, relationship status, access to a firearm) as it is the case that a relatively small number of people will be at elevated risk of engaging in violence with a firearm in certain contexts at particular times, and it is these people who warrant the majority of our attention and resources.

Research

The near entirety of the firearm-related professional literature in the medical and mental health arenas pertains to gun violence (and suicide). While very important, it is also essential to develop the literature to include a much fuller range of issues relevant to guns, including, but not limited to, the prosocial use of firearms by lawful and responsible owners. With respect to violence, it would be beneficial if researchers sought to identify precisely who engages in these acts with firearms as opposed to simply correlating various demographic and clinically relevant variables with state-level violence statistics. In addition, research in this area must become more granular; for example, firearm-involved violent acts perpetrated by those with mental health problems need to be investigated at the symptom rather than diagnostic level, as do firearm-specific factors well above and beyond ownership or access.

Policy

Laws, policies, and initiatives that primarily focus on associating mental illness with firearms, including but not limited to those in psychiatric crisis, perpetuate the stigmatization of those with mental health problems. In fact, the American Psychiatric Association's 2015 position statement on firearm-related issues specifically addresses this concern:

"Because privacy in mental health treatment is essential to encourage persons in need of treatment to seek care, laws designed to limit firearm possession that mandate reporting to law enforcement officials by psychiatrists and other mental health professionals of all patients who raise concerns about danger to themselves or others are likely to be counterproductive and should not be adopted. In contrast to long-standing rules allowing mental health professionals flexibility inacting to protect identifiable potential victims of patient violence, these statutes intrude into the clinical relationship and are unlikely to be effective in reducing rates of violence." (p. 198, Pinals et al., 2015a)

Moreover, although funding mental health treatment initiatives is imperative, doing so in the context of firearm legislation is very misguided. Furthermore, doing so significantly detracts from the focus on those who are actually at risk for engaging in inappropriate firearm use while deterring those with therapeutic needs who do not pose risks in this regard. Therefore, policymakers should seek to address those specifically at risk for firearm-involved violence (and suicide) rather than the exponentially larger group of people with mental illnesses who pose no notable risks in this regard. As such, proposing and pushing forward legislation with overly inclusive and nonspecific terms, such as *mental health* or *mental illness*, is likely to: (i) lack utility in reducing firearm-involved violence; (ii) stigmatize nearly all of the people with psychiatric diagnoses and histories who are not at particular risk in this context; (iii) deter those who develop mental health problems but also wish to own and operate firearms from seeking treatment, including civilians as well as law enforcement, correctional, and military personnel; and (iv) drain valuable resources needed to prevent firearm-related violence by seeking to identify, assess, and intervene with massive amounts of people who do not actually pose notable risks to others with guns. Increasing policy-oriented precision in terminology and targets may, for example, address symptom and diagnostic categories that are shown to be associated with firearm suicide or violence. Policy in this area could include provision of pro bono mental health services where problems are detected, potentially ameliorating stigma and avoidance of seeking mental health services.

16. Firearms Are Rarely Used in DV and IPV Incidents, but They Are Implicated in DV and IPV Homicides and Homicide–Suicides

The extant research indicates that the vast majority of DV and IPV incidents do not involve any weapon at all and that, when they do, firearms are present at rates comparable to or lower than other weapons. However, the presence of firearms has been associated with fatalities in these situations because they are often implicated in DV- and IPV-related homicides and homicide–suicides. This nuance is similar to what we see in the suicide arena, more generally.

Namely, there is a distinction between suicide attempts and suicide deaths, and firearms are much more associated with the latter because of the lethal effect of using them in that regard. Thus, just as those who attempt suicide are essentially a different group from those who die by it, there are distinctions between those who are involved in DV and IPV situations and those who ultimately commit homicides in these contexts.

Practice

Although practitioners should take all DV and IPV situations seriously, the presence of a firearm in the home (or access to one otherwise) should be considered a potentially exacerbating variable rather than a high-risk factor in and of itself. First, most DV and IPV situations do not involve firearms, and the fact that one person involved owns one may have no particular significance in a given situation because firearm-involved acts of violence and suicide are very rare events. Many DV and IPV situations are resolved or dismissed quickly, including those that result in temporary protective orders. However, there is a subset of situations that directly involve firearms and other notable risk factors. For example, in their large-scale review of over 1,300 DV restraining order applications in Los Angeles County from 2003 to 2004, Vittes & Sorenson (2006) found that a mention of a firearm was associated with eight abuse-related characteristics: threats to harm or kill, threats against others and to commit suicide, a history of choking and stalking, and a history of police involvement and injury. Moreover, those who have analyzed lethal and non-lethal attacks by a domestic abuser have pointed out that, in many cases, there was a child custody problem, the victim (usually female) either left the relationship or informed the abuser (usually male) that she was leaving, there was a physical assault within that year, and the abuser had problems with alcohol or other substances (e.g., see Farr, 2002). Again, practitioners should take all DV and IPV situations seriously and conduct thorough assessments of risk in these cases, but simply noting the presence of a firearm is insufficient. Practitioners must go well beyond determining if a person has access to a firearm and include a full assessment of the aforementioned risk factors that are associated with the more serious and lethal outcomes in DV and IPV matters.

Research

Researchers should also move beyond the basic correlational analysis of firearm ownership and access with DV and IPV risk. It is clear that the vast majority of those who legally own and operate firearms do so safely, and it is also the case that the majority of DV and IPV situations do not involve firearms or lethal outcomes related to guns. That said, there is a very concerning subset of these incidents that do; and, therefore, a much more precise, detailed focus on causal pathways from firearm ownership to DV/IPV is needed. Perhaps more focused research in this regard will lead to more focused assessments, interventions, policies, and laws.

Policy

There is some indication from the empirical research that laws in this context may be effective in preventing DV- and IPV-related homicides but not necessarily DV or IPV, in general—particularly misdemeanor-level situations. The research further indicates that the laws that seem to reduce homicides in these contexts do so for all types and not just for those that involve firearms (see Vigdor & Mercy, 2006). Thus, it seems that these laws may be generally effective in some situations but not necessarily because of their focus on firearms. Taken together, policymakers should certainly include firearm-related considerations in their proposals, but an overemphasis or sole focus on guns in these contexts will lead to missing the many other relevant risk factors that comprise the majority.

17. Restraining Orders May Be Beneficial in Some DV and IPV Situations; However, Implementation and Enforcement Problems Pose Significant Challenges in This Regard

As noted in the previous finding, there is some research support for protective orders in particular DV and IPV situations, including those where firearms have particular relevance. However, the available research also indicates that there are significant problems with the implementation and enforcement of these orders. Namely, there is significant variability across and within states in this regard. Generally speaking, there are problems identifying firearm owners in the first place because of inadequate record-keeping systems, but a more salient issue are the notable differences among the courts and law enforcement agencies throughout the country. One need not look from one state to another for evidence of this as this problem is evident at the local level among judges and police departments.

Practice

Practitioners should not consider the presence (or absence) of a protective order, past or present, as dispositive of risk because there are many frivolous restraining orders that are filed and ultimately dismissed, and there are also many situations where a protective order was never filed or granted. Certainly, the presence of a temporary or final restraining order warrants attention; but again, evaluators should focus on the risk factors related to the situation and not primarily on whether or not an order came to fruition. There may be relevant DV- or IPV-related risk factors in situations without protective orders, and there may also be very few, if any, notable risk factors identified in those with such orders. Again, there are many non-clinical reasons as to why a protective order is present or absent (e.g., false or exaggerated accusations, victims who do not want to file, variability in judges' thresholds and associated decision-making). Moreover, treating professionals need to appreciate the dynamics in these situations, such that abuse victims may have very valid reasons as to why they do not want to file for protective orders. Therefore, they can provide clients with information and support in this regard, provided that the situation does not escalate to a point where the practitioner has a duty to protect or warn and, therefore, breach confidentiality. Practitioners must be aware of their jurisdictions' laws in this respect, including, but not limited to, reporting requirements associated with child or elder abuse.

Research

It would be beneficial to have more studies conducted on the application, implementation, and effectiveness of protective orders throughout the country. It would be particularly informative to analyze which factors specifically account for the variability across cases—in relation to both systemic variables (e.g., differences among police departments, judges, prosecutors, laws) and those that are case-specific (e.g., demographics, historical and current risk factors). In addition, it would be useful to conduct research on the effectiveness of protective orders that include firearm-related considerations and restrictions. Given the very low base rates of firearm-involved acts of violence and suicide, researchers should incorporate other outcome variables of relevance, such as protective order violations and the commission of other offenses, and clinical factors related to therapeutic progress or those associated with social service agencies' involvement.

Policy

It is critical to begin to streamline DV- and IPV-related procedures across jurisdictions. The fact that someone owns a firearm does not necessarily indicate that he or she is at elevated risk of using a gun in the commission of a violent act. In fact, the contemporary empirical research suggests that firearms are involved in 16%–18% of these matters, often at comparable levels to knives and other weapons and well below the rates of violence via punching, hitting, kicking, and shoving. That said, protective orders that restrict firearm access are associated with a slightly decreased number of intimate partner homicides (e.g., see Vigdor & Mercy, 2006). As noted in finding 16, however, these very serious situations typically include a very specific set of risk factors that are not present in most DV and IPV situations. Therefore, policymakers should work with practitioners and researchers to contour more focused policies and laws geared toward identifying situations where the risk of firearm-involved violence is elevated.

18. Two-Thirds of Firearm-Involved Deaths in the United States Are Suicides, Nearly Double That of Acts of Violence Toward Others

As leading scholars and mental health organizations have continuously pointed out, the "real link" is between firearms and suicide rather than acts of interpersonal violence. The majority of firearm-involved deaths in the United States are suicides. Therefore, speaking of gun deaths resulting from such divergent acts as suicide, felony homicide, and school shootings collectively as "gun violence" can be confusing, particularly because many of the implications for risk assessment and management in these areas differ. In addition, using the broad term "gun violence" implies those who die by suicide are violent. In Chapter 6, we addressed the concept of *self-directed violence* in the context of suicide; however, many people do not think or speak of suicide in terms of violence. Nevertheless, various politicians, media outlets, special interest groups, and even professionals in a range of disciplines cite the country's total number of gun deaths when speaking about "gun violence." This presents a conceptual issue because there are approximately 45,000 suicides in the US each year and less than half are with guns, whereas two-thirds of gun deaths are suicides. It is generally no longer accepted to say someone "committed" suicide because it is thought to be offensive and insensitive, but suicides with a gun are being classified as "gun violence." Thus, if someone has hanged, many would say they have *died by suicide*; if they used a firearm, however, they are considered to have engaged in *gun violence*.

It is also the case that the presence of a firearm is a very significant risk factor for those who intend to attempt suicide because the lethality of guns makes suicide likely for those who make attempts. As Fowler, Dahlberg, Haileyesus, & Annest (2015) noted, 85% of people who use a firearm to attempt suicide die compared to those who use other methods, such as cut/pierce injuries (0.7%), poisoning (2.5%), and jumping/falling (19.9%). In addition, a much lower rate (20%) of victims die from firearm-related assaults. Furthermore, the highest proportions of the 20,000 firearm-involved suicides each year have been found for males (87%), non-Hispanic whites (87%), those who reside in the South (45%), and those over 65 years old (23%); however, when you combine the 15–24 and 25–34 year age groups, they account for 24% of suicides with guns. In fact, firearm-involved suicide rates for non-Hispanic whites are three to four times higher than those for their non-Hispanic black and Hispanic counterparts and over six times greater than those for non-Hispanic Asians/Pacific Islanders. In addition, whereas firearm-involved homicide rates are highest for adolescents and young adults and decrease with age, rates of suicide with guns are fairly comparable across age groups but actually *increase* with age. Of additional note is that law enforcement, correctional, and military groups tend to have disproportionally higher suicide rates compared to their same-aged peers, in general, but also specifically via firearm.

Practice

Practitioners should be generally well versed on suicide assessment and associated interventions and consider the presence of a firearm to be a potentially moderating risk factor. However, inquiries must extend beyond solely asking if clients have access to firearms (see Chapters 6–8). Therefore, it is essential that medical and mental health professionals receive education and training on firearms and firearm-related issues so that they can make professionally and culturally competent clinical decisions based on the contemporary professional literature in this arena. Most practitioners do not receive formal education or training on firearms or firearm-related issues, however, so it will be incumbent on them to develop their professional and cultural competence in this regard via continuing education efforts (see finding 21 below). We also echo recommendations in the literature (Cramer & Kapusta, 2017) that mental health professionals must think in multilevel terms to fully understand the potential associations, or lack thereof, of firearms and suicide. That is, while an individual may be at risk for suicide, factors at the individual (e.g., history of safe firearm usage and storage), interpersonal (e.g., support in removal of lethal means), and community or society (e.g., local laws) levels may mitigate or exacerbate the firearm-suicide death likelihood.

Research

We still have much to learn about firearm-involved suicide. To this point, researchers have generally focused on correlates of suicides with guns within broad-based databases that include firearm ownership and death statistics. As a result, we are left with data that support the notion that the presence of a firearm alone is a suicide risk factor. Of course, having access to a firearm is a necessary component of a firearm-involved suicide, but practitioners are in need of a much deeper understanding of the issue to be able to conduct evaluations that adequately distinguish between various levels of risk. For research to be useful to clinicians it must facilitate their decision-making, and they are tasked with offering context-specific opinions, such as foreseeability of risk, toward whom, and in which type of circumstances. As such, clinicians must also often assess clients' *motivations, triggers*, and *disinhibitors*. Identifying who has access to a firearm in the context of a suicide risk assessment is a critical step, but it is only the first step. Therefore, research that solely focuses on the correlation between firearm access and suicides will not be particularly useful for practitioners who must form opinions and make decisions about the person in front of them. Research in this area must become more closely tied to these types of clinical factors. In addition, databases are usually created around the death statistic (e.g., suicides with a gun), but doing so excludes very important comparison groups: (i) gun owners and those who have access to firearms, generally, and (ii) gun owners and those who have access to firearms who have experienced suicidality but did not die by suicide.

These represent the direct comparison groups most important to clinicians in this context because the population in question is *people with access to guns*, and research samples must be representative of the populations to which findings would be generalized. If more in-depth research is not conducted with these types of samples, we are unlikely to move beyond simply correlating gun access to suicide risk—a nonspecific finding that clinicians will continue to have difficulty integrating into their assessments and ultimate decisions. It is essential to parse out firearm-involved suicides from databases that include all gun deaths because failing to do so will conflate results and interpretations across various types of gun deaths.

Policy

Suicide prevention efforts should continue to be supported, advanced, and implemented throughout the country. These efforts should revolve around those who are at elevated risk for engaging in self-harm. Suicide prevention policies that focus solely on a possible method of suicide, such as guns, are likely to continue to exhaust resources and miss the higher-risk persons. There are 100 million gun owners in the country, and a very small percentage are at foreseeable risk for suicide. Comprehensive suicide prevention programming is multilevel in nature, addressing key influential agents at the individual through society levels (Cramer & Kapusta, 2017). Addressing firearm-related issues in prevention can certainly be a piece of prevention efforts (e.g., means reduction/safety counseling), especially for certain populations (e.g., military personnel); however, such efforts really need to be paired with broader prevention addressing high-risk persons and factors. Of course, those firearm owners, applicants, and related others who pose such a risk should continue to be identified and evaluated; but it is advisable for policymakers to work more closely with mental health professionals and researchers to develop more focused evidence-based approaches that are tied to plans for ongoing policy analyses. With regard to adopting a prevention-based approach to firearm suicide and suicide prevention more broadly, it has also been recommended that policymakers specifically address firearm misuse (as opposed to normative use) (Kapusta & Cramer, 2017). In doing so, prevention policies should deal with not only the availability of firearms but also universal causal factors of suicide in the general population (e.g., hopelessness, perceived insecurity), as well as the full range of violence outcomes (e.g., DV, IPV, suicide) together. Before effective policies can be developed and implemented, however, it is essential to stop speaking about all gun deaths collectively as "gun violence." Doing so leads to a mixing of data, results, and interpretations across what are often very different types of situations. For example, there are many separate and distinct considerations associated with a firearm-involved suicide, homicide, mass shooting, and accidental injury. However, we will not be able to get at the important nuances and associated implications if all gun deaths continue to be classified together as "gun violence."

19. Firearm-Specific Safety Information Is Virtually Absent in the Professional Medical and Mental Health Literature

The professional literature related to firearms in the medical and mental health arenas is almost exclusively centered around firearm-involved violence and suicide, or what is often referred to as "gun violence." However, despite the wealth of information available in this regard, there is an absence of corresponding information about firearm safety. In fact, research conducted with mental health clinicians has found that half of them have never received such education at all and that very few of those who have had some education gained it from graduate training or professional journals. In fact, Traylor and colleagues (2010) surveyed 339 clinical psychologists across the country and found that, of those who reported receiving education on firearm safety, 20% received it from the media, whereas 13% received it in graduate training and 7% from professional journals. These findings are nearly identical to those of Price and colleagues (2009), who surveyed 213 college counselors throughout the country and found that half had never received firearm safety education and that, for the remainder who had, 15% received it from the media, 14% from graduate training, and less than 10% from professional journals or other continuing education mediums. Clearly, there is a disconnect between the amount of attention that is paid to firearm-involved violence and suicide, in general, and firearm safety. As a result, the majority of mental health professionals do not know the components of safe and lawful firearm ownership and use. One is left to wonder whether lack of such critical knowledge among practitioners may negatively impact willingness to work with high-risk firearm-owning clients, especially in a culturally competent manner. We suspect that this reality extends beyond practitioners and applies to academicians and researchers as well, although we know of no published studies in which their knowledge in this regard was assessed.

Practice

Many medical and mental health practitioners are responsible for assessing violence and suicide risk, and one component of this pertains to firearm safety. However, as we have noted throughout this book and in finding 18, most clinicians solely inquire about access to guns in a forced-choice manner (i.e., yes or no). Via this line of thinking, more than 100 million people in this country automatically possess a violence and suicide risk factor. Whether or not this should be the case is somewhat of a red herring as the real issue is the lack of utility this basic information has for clinicians. Of course, some clinicians may be in a position at specific times to recommend completely restricting gun access, such as in emergency situations; but most practitioners are not functioning in these scenarios most of the time. Most clinicians are working with clients who are not in an acute psychiatric crisis or at elevated risk for engaging in violence or suicide. In other words, the majority of medical and mental health practitioners will find themselves in situations where they ask if clients have access to firearms but will have nothing to do with the information in and of itself. They would need to continue to provide services with a lingering potential violence and suicide risk factor that they do not know how to integrate into their case conceptualizations and associated clinical decisions. Therefore, it is essential for practitioners to at least learn basic firearm safety and familiarize themselves with local gun laws, such as those related to firearm use, storage, and transportation. This will require practitioners to read their relevant state laws and seek education from sources who interface with firearm owners and operators (e.g., firearm owners' and shooting sports associations, gun clubs and ranges). After all, if clinicians are unaware of the tenets of firearm safety or associated laws, how can they recognize clients' unsafe practices? Until they develop a basic level of competence in this regard, clinicians will be limited to solely asking if clients have access to a gun or not and will have little or nothing to do with the resulting information in terms of crisis response, safety, or other risk management planning. Although some have expressed the ostensibly logical sentiment that healthcare providers can play a role in educating clients and preventing some types of firearm-involved violence (e.g., see Williamson, Guerra, & Tynan, 2014), this presupposes that these providers understand firearm safety concepts. However, the research does not support this notion. Although practices such as means safety counseling (e.g., Stanley et al., 2016) have been recommended in suicide prevention and other relevant literatures, we contend that the competent ability to engage in such approaches first requires practitioner knowledge and competence in firearm-related matters.

Research

Those who conduct research and teach in firearm-related arenas should begin to include information about guns, gun safety, and relevant gun laws in their presentations and publications. A lot of important courses, presentations, and publications have been set forth in this area over the past three decades; and the literature has grown notably. But this also means that there have been many missed opportunities to educate medical, mental health, and related professionals and some members of the public on firearms and firearm safety. It is likely that many who conduct research and teach in areas related to firearms are unfamiliar with guns and gun safety principles, thereby precluding them from educating others in this regard. However, they are required to develop and maintain their professional and cultural competence in this area (see Pirelli & Witt, 2017). For example, per the American Psychological Association's ethics code, formally known as the Ethical Principles of Psychologists and Code of Conduct (American Psychological Association, 2010):

(a) Psychologists provide services, teach, and conduct research with populations and in areas only within the boundaries of their competence, based on their education, training, supervised experience, consultation, study, or professional experience. (p. 4, Standard 2.01, Boundaries of Competence)

(c) Psychologists planning to provide services, teach, or conduct research involving populations, areas, techniques, or technologies new to them undertake relevant education, training, supervised experience, consultation, or study. (p. 5, Standard 2.01, Boundaries of Competence)

Policy

Policymakers should work with medical and mental health professionals, including clinicians, academicians, and researchers, to ensure that firearm-related resources and publications include information about firearm safety, self-care, and emergency information. It is also important to bring together all relevant community groups (e.g., Second Amendment, shooting sports, rod & gun/hunting clubs, and gun violence prevention) to make this information more accessible to much broader groups of people. If information about guns, gun safety, and gun laws is presented in a purely factual and neutral manner, it should not differ based on the audience at hand. Experts in these areas should be brought together to develop resources in this regard. Of course, all of this information exists and is available, but it is often presented within partisan contexts rather than in mediums that are more accessible and palatable to diverse groups.

20. There Are Many Important Emerging Roles for Medical and Mental Health Professionals with Respect to Addressing Firearm-Related Violence and Suicide as They Are Our Society's Primary Gatekeepers in This Area

Medical and mental health professionals already have an important set of responsibilities in the context of assessing suicide and violence risk in emergency, outpatient, and inpatient settings; and a primary inquiry in these contexts pertains to access to guns. It also seems, though, that practitioners will increasingly be called upon in our society given the attention paid to firearm-related matters and the associated advent of laws and policies in this regard. For example, some legislators have proposed a greater role for clinicians in terms of identifying and reporting concerns when guns are at issue, particularly in matters involving elevated risk. Specialized evaluators will also be needed in much greater numbers moving forward as psychological firearm evaluations are a specific type of forensic mental health assessment

(FMHA) that requires specialized procedures and considerations (see finding 24 below).

Practice

Practitioners working in emergency rooms and crisis centers are primarily tasked with evaluating patients' acute risk of suicide and violence, and clinicians conducting intake evaluations across settings at least screen for such. Therefore, essentially all medical and mental health professionals should be regularly asking about firearms at some level. Moreover, treating professionals (e.g., primary care physicians, outpatient psychotherapists) are likely to be the first ones contacted by their patients and law enforcement agencies for a "clearance" letter when a flag is raised during the firearm ownership application process. While we do not advise practitioners to opine as to clients' suitability in this respect if they have not conducted an independent forensic evaluation, they would still need to provide a synopsis of their work with the client if the proper releases have been executed, such as in the form of a treatment summary or mental health screening report. These documents would generally include a notation of the presenting issue, the nature of services provided, diagnoses and symptoms, and the general treatment plan, if applicable. Again, because practitioners in these situations were not functioning as independent forensic evaluators, they would not be able to set forth an opinion about the psycholegal question at hand (i.e., suitability for firearm ownership or use). As such, these reports are unlikely to have any real value in the context of an application for firearm ownership or in gun forfeiture matters when people are seeking reinstatement of their guns and gun ownership rights. In fact, letters from treating or evaluating clinicians alone are more likely to lead to more questions than answers if they are set forth appropriately. In other words, if clinicians maintain the scope of their intended services and do not enter dual and forensic roles by addressing the ultimate issue—firearm ownership suitability—then, they will simply be providing law enforcement agencies and legal professionals with pure clinical information that would have to be appropriately interpreted and linked to the suitability issue anyhow. At best, this information alone will lack utility and, at worst, it will be misinterpreted and misapplied to the ultimate issue. Therefore, while practitioners should release relevant records and information when the proper consents are in place or when this is court-ordered, they should also avoid addressing the question of suitability for firearm ownership and make referrals to forensic practitioners with expertise in firearm evaluations in these instances.

Research

As noted, it would be beneficial to ascertain the practices of medical and mental health professionals with regard to the ways in which they integrate firearm-related inquiries and considerations into their suicide and violence risk assessments and intakes, more generally. Specifically, it would be useful to know if they go beyond solely asking if clients have access to firearms and, if so, the types of questions they ask. Across healthcare professionals, it would be further helpful to understand to what extent providers do actually inquire about firearms at all and the barriers and facilitators of doing so. Moreover, it is important to assess clinicians' attitudes about firearms, in general, but also their perspectives on being tasked with managing firearm-related matters. Furthermore, researchers should investigate practitioners' actual knowledge of guns and firearm-related issues rather than solely relying on their self-reported levels of competence and understanding in this regard.

Policy

Although medical and mental health practitioners are on the front line in out-patient and inpatient settings and, therefore, theoretically serve primary roles in relation to the intersection of firearms and mental health–related issues, the available research indicates that most do not ask, chart, or formally ad-dress these issues, nor are they adequately trained to do so. Much of the at-tention has been paid to what is referred to as *means-restriction counseling*, or the basic advisement against having access to guns; and most clinicians believe they are capable of intervening in this way despite the fact that they lack education and training on firearms. There is a pressing need for medical and mental health practitioners to receive formal training in their medical and graduate school and continuing education programs on firearms, firearm safety, and associated topics. In the context of the "docs vs. Glocks" issue, we believe that medical and mental health professionals need to be able to ask about firearm-related issues when they are relevant to the scope of their services, such as when assessing suicide and violence risk. However, very few general clinicians, including therapists, medical doctors, and nurses, have any specialized training in firearm-related issues; and much fewer have ex-pertise in conducting firearm-specific evaluations. In fact, firearm evaluations have only recently been recognized as a specialty area of FMHA (see Pirelli, Wechsler, & Cramer, 2015). As such, the education and training of med-ical and mental health professionals in this arena should be prioritized over enacting initiatives that seek their increased involvement in these contexts.

21. Most Medical and Mental Health Professionals Have not Received Formal Education or Training Sufficient to Develop Professional Competence on Firearm-Specific Issues

Although medical and mental health training programs pay significant amounts of attention to suicide risk assessment and management, they do not teach about firearms or firearm safety. This disconnect is puzzling given the association between firearms and suicide. It is also notable because some scholars and professional organizations have characterized firearm-involved violence and suicide as a public health epidemic. Still, it appears to be the case that most practitioners lack the professional competence to address many of the firearm-specific issues they may encounter in their work. As we have noted, the research in this regard indicates that half of clinical psychologists have never received any firearm safety education, only about 10% have received any via graduate training or professional journals, and approximately 8 out of 10 do not even include firearm-specific issues in their charting (Traylor et al. 2010). Of note is that almost identical numbers have been found with college counselors (Price et al., 2009). Despite these findings, Price and colleagues found that nearly all of the counselors in their sample were willing to *ask* clients about the presence of firearms in their residences (97%), *advise* clients to remove firearms from their residences (94%), and *assess* the willingness of clients to remove firearms within the next 30 days (89%). Furthermore, most counselors reported a willingness to *assist* clients in what to do with firearms removed from their residences (59%) and *arrange* follow-up contacts within 4 weeks to assess the firearm removals (83%). Once again, this is similar to the disconnect between experience and willingness to participate that we have seen in other areas of practice (see, e.g., Pirelli & Zapf, 2008).

Practice

Professional ethics codes and standards of practice are quite clear about the need to refrain from engaging in services outside of one's areas of competence. Professional competence is based on education, training, and skills developed within the context of formal programming and supervision. Based on these tenets, practitioners are in rather precarious situations when firearms or firearm-specific issues are of primary concern in their cases. As such, it is incumbent upon them to develop their professional competence in the context of firearms. Therefore, there is a pressing need for continuing education programs that provide medical and mental health professionals with information about and training on guns, gun safety, gun laws, and other relevant firearm-related issues. In addition, schools with medical and mental health programs have a responsibility to begin incorporating formal education and training in these areas.

Research

The professional medical and mental health literature needs fewer personally and politically driven viewpoints and more purely technical information about guns, gun safety, and gun laws. Researchers have an opportunity to educate practitioners in this way and conduct applied studies that will help inform clinical decision-making when guns are at issue. This will require researchers to develop their professional competence in firearm-specific areas and practitioners with this type of competence to contribute to the professional literature more frequently. It would also be beneficial for researchers to assist in developing content that may be incorporated into educational and training programs for medical and mental health students as well as more advanced professionals.

Policy

Policymakers, especially politicians, should not assume that medical and mental health professionals have the appropriate levels of professional and cultural competence to intervene in many firearm-related matters. In actuality, the research available in this regard indicates the opposite: the vast majority have never received formal education or training on guns or gun safety and, of those who have, very few gained it from professional journals or continuing education programs. Therefore, laws and policies that seek to elevate the roles of medical and mental health professionals in firearm-related matters at this time are premature. Instead, efforts should be primarily focused on educating and training clinicians as well as academicians and researchers on firearms, firearm safety, and other related topics. Medical and other professionals must develop their professional and cultural competence in the firearm arena before they can contribute ethically and meaningfully. State licensing boards also hold a potentially impactful role in ensuring competent firearm-related practice. Many states now mandate certain topics (e.g., ethics, suicide prevention, substance use) to be addressed during continuing education efforts in order to maintain licenses. Given the ubiquity of firearms in the United States and their inextricable clinical links to substance use, violence, and other topics, we wonder whether the time has come to mandate firearm-related continuing education content for maintaining licenses. Although likely to meet great resistance, we posit that such policy implementation would prove beneficial from a public health approach as it would enhance health professionals' skills (i.e., a medical determinant of health), offering improved mental health assessment and care for clients where firearms are in the clinical picture.

22. There Are Numerous Firearm-Related Subcultures for Whom Practitioners, Academics, and Researchers Should Develop and Maintain Cultural Competence

It is a well-recognized tenet that cultural competence is an essential aspect of professional competence as practitioners, educators, and researchers must familiarize themselves with the various other subcultures they may encounter in their work. Clinicians are instructed to incorporate such concepts as "local norms," levels of acculturation, and individual differences into their assessments, interventions, and decision-making, more generally. Researchers seek to gather samples that are representative of certain populations of interest, which requires attention to particularities at subcultural levels as well. Therefore, medical and mental health professionals receive formal diversity training throughout their student years and into their careers. However, the focus has primarily been to learn about considerations related to such factors as race, ethnicity, religion, language, gender, sexual orientation, and (dis)abilities. These areas include various subgroups that are necessary for practitioners, academicians, and researchers to learn about—including the approximate 3.8% of the population who identify as gay or lesbian (Newport, 2015) and the 0.38% over age 5 who are classified as "functionally deaf" (Mitchell, 2005); however, there are large subgroups that have been overlooked in this regard. Namely, more than 33% of the population owns firearms, and a much greater number has some connection to them. While training and education pertaining to minority, disenfranchised, and vulnerable groups is important, is necessary, and should continue to develop, it is essential for medical and mental health professionals to learn about firearm-related subcultures—especially in light of their emerging roles in relation to these groups. We have recently delineated seven such groups: (i) Second Amendment groups; (ii) shooting sport groups; (iii) rod & gun clubs, hunting clubs, and shooting ranges; (iv) gun control, gun violence prevention, and antigun groups; (v) military, law enforcement, and corrections; (vi) members of gangs, organized crime, and other criminal organizations; and (vii) victims of firearm-related suicide, violence, or DV (see Chapter 7 in this book as well as Pirelli & Witt, 2017).

Practice

As we outlined in Chapter 7, we believe practitioners should embrace a hierarchical approach to developing their cultural competence in this context. Namely, they should familiarize themselves with the firearm literature above and beyond that which is focused on "gun violence" and into a fuller range of firearm-related matters, including, but not limited to, prosocial uses and firearm safety. In addition, medical and mental health practitioners should receive formal (continuing) education by taking courses in the area of firearms and mental health. These types of courses are unlikely to be readily available for many at this time; therefore, practitioners may need to initially take more general firearm courses, such as those held at local gun ranges or conferences presented by various types of groups who are most familiar with firearms (e.g., law enforcement, public safety, or Second Amendment groups). Furthermore, practitioners who wish to conduct firearm-specific evaluations should strongly consider visiting such venues as gun ranges as well as other settings frequented by firearm owners and operators (e.g., gun shows, Second Amendment conferences), consistent with clinical training principles. They should also seek professional supervision or consultation until they develop their competence to a point of independent proficiency in this regard.

Research

Those who conduct research and teach in areas related to firearms must also develop and maintain their professional competence in this regard as professional ethics codes also pertain to academicians, students, and researchers. Therefore, all educators and researchers who work directly or indirectly with firearm-related issues should familiarize themselves with the broad literature pertaining to firearms and not only that which is related to "gun violence" or perspectives on the Second Amendment. Moreover, those who conduct research and teach in areas more closely connected with firearms should seek formal continuing education on firearm-specific topics. Furthermore, those who work directly in the firearm arena should strongly consider seeking exposure to various firearm-related subcultures, especially in natural environments, such as gun ranges.

Policy

Although some policymakers want medical and mental health professionals to increase their involvement in firearm-related matters, many (if not most) practitioners, academicians, and researchers need to first develop their cultural competence with firearm-related subgroups. Many of these professionals have never been exposed to firearms or firearm-specific issues in either their personal or professional lives. These professional groups already have a fair amount of involvement in this context and have generally not yet received the formal education and training they need to proceed with their current responsibilities and work. Therefore, policymakers should prioritize firearm-specific training for these groups before pushing for increased involvement or, at least, doing so contemporaneously. Again, state licensing boards may prove useful toward the goal of ensuring practitioner competence (see finding 21 above).

23. Military, Law Enforcement, and Correctional Populations Present with Particular Vulnerabilities and Risk Factors Associated with Firearm-Involved Violence, DV and IPV, and Suicide

Military, law enforcement, and corrections personnel are in high-risk professions that are often complicated by inherent intradepartmental stressors, such as lengthy and rotating shifts and the various challenges associated with hierarchical military and paramilitary organizational structures. The literature on mental health and related problems among members of these groups is robust and compelling. We delineated many of these issues in Chapter 7, including officers' elevated risks of acquiring medical and mental health conditions compared to their civilian counterparts and their proportionally higher substance use, DV, and suicide rates. Moreover, firearm-related concerns are often paramount in these contexts because of their static presence. As we noted in Chapter 6, more than two-thirds of military and 90% of law enforcement officer suicides involve guns (see Anglemyer, Miller, Buttrey, & Whitaker, 2016; McCarten, Hoffmire, & Bossarte, 2015; Violanti et al., 2012). Of course, there have also been a number of high-profile homicide–suicides among these groups.

Practice

Medical and mental health professionals who provide treatment and evaluation services to military, law enforcement, and correctional officers must familiarize themselves with the particular vulnerabilities and risks inherent to members of these groups. Consistent with this, these practitioners must develop their professional competence in the firearm arena, as it pertains to guns and gun safety but also the way in which firearms are particularly associated with acts of violence, DV, and self-harm with these groups. For example, skill using a firearm may enhance suicide risk among military veterans (York, Lamis, Pope, & Egede, 2013). In addition, practitioners conducting pre-employment and fitness-for-duty evaluations with military, law enforcement, and correctional officers should incorporate firearm-specific inquiries and considerations into their assessments. Although the need for officers to be "cleared" to interface with and even carry guns is well recognized, standard mental health assessment procedures in these contexts fall short of adequately covering firearm-specific domains. Therefore, practitioners may consider including areas of inquiry and considerations specific to guns, such as those that have been developed for use with civilians (see, e.g., the Pirelli Firearm-10 outlined in finding 24 below).

Research

There appears to be a general absence of research focused on the improper, unsafe, and otherwise dangerous use of firearms by military, law enforcement, and correctional officers. Although the professional literature has reflected the disproportionate rates of medical and mental health problems among these groups (including substance use, DV, and suicide), much of the research has focused on their work- and family-related stressors and not guns per se. On the other hand, much of the research in the corresponding civilian areas is centered on guns. This paradox of disproportionate attention being paid in the opposing direction is noteworthy. Although it is particularly challenging to conduct prospective research with military, law enforcement, and correctional personnel, efforts should continue to be made to understand the ways in which firearms may be associated with factors related to substance use, violence, and self-harm among them. As Wintemute (2015) noted, "Focusing on suicide will also require consideration of groups not ordinarily thought to be at high risk for firearm violence, such as current and former members of the military" (p. 8.10). As such, it would also be beneficial if researchers investigated the effectiveness (or lack thereof) of substance use, violence, and suicide prevention programs and interventions currently in place throughout our country's armed services, police, and correctional agencies.

Policy

Firearm-related laws and policies have been primarily focused on civilians despite the disproportionately higher rates of substance use, violence, and suicide among those in the military, law enforcement, and corrections. There are likely political and practical reasons for this; however, these groups are at particular risk for these types of problems and, therefore, represent firearm-related subgroups that should be prioritized in this regard.

24. Psychological Firearm Evaluations Are a Specific Type of Forensic Mental Health Assessment That Require Specialized Procedures and Considerations

Firearm-specific evaluations, such as those conducted with applicants who are flagged, people seeking reinstatement of their gun rights, and in the context of mental health expungement proceedings, are distinct from other types of psychological assessments because of the unique procedures and considerations required to perform them competently. These assessments are relevant to administrative and legal matters; therefore, they are a type of FMHA. However, psychological firearm evaluations do not fit well into one existing type of FMHA; rather, they require the compilation of aspects of other areas, such as competency and risk assessments, in addition to the inclusion of firearm-specific factors (Pirelli et al., 2015). We have developed a formal model to help guide evaluators address this unique set of considerations and domains, the Pirelli Firearm-10 (PF-10; see Chapter 7 for a full review). This SPJ-type guide includes 10 domains: four firearm-specific, one related to the assessment of response style, and five that map onto prohibitor areas common to most legal standards associated with firearm ownership and use. Specifically, the first four items address examinees' reasons for seeking a license or reinstatement; (historical) exposure to firearms; knowledge of and perspectives on firearm safety precautions and relevant firearm regulations; and firearm use as it relates to their experience interacting with guns and their intent for use, storage, and continued education. These factors are not legally required in most instances—for example, an examinee may have never seen a gun before, have no knowledge or experience with one, and have no interest in taking continuing education courses—however, these areas of inquiry help bring context to the assessment by providing the evaluator with a framework from which he or she can work to gain an understanding the examinee's association with firearms. In addition, assessing response style is a fundamental component of conducting; therefore, this is highlighted as a consideration as well. The second half of the assessment domains reflects areas specific to firearm-related prohibitor areas: violence risk, DV and IPV risk, suicide risk, mental health, and substance use. As we discussed in Chapter 7, measures that have been designed to assess these specific areas can and should be incorporated when clinically indicated. Furthermore, this framework likely has applications in other contexts as well, such as for pre-employment and fitness-for-duty evaluations for law enforcement and correctional officers or in other circumstances where the need for a person to own or carry a firearm is necessary (e.g., federal agents, military personnel, security guards, armed guards).

Practice

Practitioners who engage in firearm-specific evaluations, such as for civilians seeking gun licenses or reinstatement of their gun rights, should develop and maintain their professional competence in this specialized area. The professional literature is vast in the context of firearm-related issues, and there are important nuances practitioners must take into account when conducting assessments in this regard. By and large, medical and mental health educational and training programs do not teach about guns, gun safety, gun laws, firearm-related subcultures, prosocial firearm use, or the specific ways in which firearms are associated with violence and suicide. Continuing education programming is also lacking in this regard, and formal models of assessment in firearm matters have only just begun to develop. Therefore, practitioners who conduct firearm evaluations are most likely to approach them as they would a violence or suicide risk assessment. However, the vast majority of those advancing to the point of needing an evaluation will have had no history of engaging in violence or self-injurious behavior; thus, standard assessment procedures would lack utility. Nevertheless, these are important components to consider in all firearm evaluations, and they will likely have a more prominent place in reinstatement matters; but practitioners need to embrace a more inclusive and comprehensive approach. Namely, it is essential to inquire about firearms and firearm-specific factors in firearm evaluations. Although this may seem obvious, as we have pointed out numerous times throughout this book, most practitioners have no professional education or training in this area. Therefore, how can an evaluator assess the appropriateness of an examinee's firearm-specific practices, knowledge, or perspectives? Without developing their professional competence in the firearm arena, practitioners will either (appropriately) refrain from participating or move forward without the requisite set of knowledge and skills to ethically do so. These evaluators are likely to either avoid asking important firearm-specific questions or, if they do ask, not appropriately interpret the resulting data, which could result in misinformed and biased ultimate opinions. Of course, professionals who have not developed their professional competence in the firearm arena should not participate in these assessments, nor should those who are qualitatively against civilians' use or ownership of firearms. For the remaining forensic practitioners, it is essential to develop and maintain professional competence in this regard and to recognize that firearm evaluations are a specific type of FMHA that requires specialized procedures and considerations.

Research

Research efforts are currently underway to explore the utility of the PF-10, but it would be beneficial for researchers to investigate the current practices and attitudes of practitioners who are conducting firearm evaluations in administrative and legal matters. In particular, it would be informative to ascertain if they are including firearm-specific considerations in their evaluations and corresponding reports and if they are addressing all relevant prohibitor areas and not simply the issue that has been "flagged." More generally, it would be useful to know if these practitioners have specific expertise that relates to firearms and, if so, how they developed it. Furthermore, it would be beneficial to investigate practitioners' levels of cultural competence across firearm-related subgroups and how they developed this as well. A second important line of research pertains to the end users in these contexts: police detectives and chiefs, attorneys, and judges. It would be informative to ascertain their perspectives on the current practices of clinicians involved in firearm matters and the potential utility of SPJ-based firearm evaluations, such as those that incorporate the PF-10 or similar frameworks.

Policy

As we have noted repeatedly throughout this book, there is a pressing need to educate and train practitioners on firearm-specific issues. In the absence of such, many of the policies and laws that have been proposed and set forth lack viability. For example, while requiring mental health evaluations for every firearm applicant sounds good, it is simply impossible. In fact, much less is even possible. Take, for example, enhanced background checks. These tap into further databases conducted by more government agents and law enforcement personnel, which will equal more flags and questions rather than answers. The logic follows accordingly: more flags correspond to more legal responses by applicants, including appeals and expungement efforts. Recall President Obama's January 4, 2016, executive order, in which he indicated that the FBI was to overhaul its system so that it could conduct checks 24 hours a day, 7 days per week, while improving communication with local authorities when a prohibited person attempts to purchase a firearm; and the FBI was to hire more than 230 additional examiners and other staff to assist in the background check process. Further, he was to allocate $500 million to increase mental health treatment and reporting to the background check system, such that the Social Security Administration would begin to include information in the background. There is a glaring omission here—a complete oversight of the middle step; that is, who will conduct psychological firearm evaluations on all of these people? In his executive order, President Obama indicated that there were 63,000 NICS checks per day, on average, in 2015 alone. To put this number in context, competency to stand trial evaluations have been regarded as the most commonly pursued mental health evaluation in the system of criminal law, with national estimates of 60,000 per year (Bonnie & Grisso, 2000). The former president indicated that this was the daily number of checks conducted. Even if we underestimate and assume that only 10% of all NICS checks will result in a flag, we are left with 6,300 flags per day. And even if only half of those who are flagged seek an evaluation to accompany their appeal, this equals 1.15 million evaluations per year, or about 20 times as many as the most commonly conducted forensic evaluation in all of criminal law. These numbers are even more striking when we consider the fact that many forensic mental health professionals are very well trained, educated, and experienced in conducting competency evaluations and that the professional competency literature has remained robust for over 50 years. This is in stark contrast to firearm evaluations as most practitioners have no training, education, or experience in this area at all and the literature and guidance on conducting these evaluations with civilians is extremely thin and has only just begun to develop. Again, this is also why requiring all firearm applicants to submit to a mental health evaluation is completely unrealistic as it is not even realistic for a very low proportion of them to engage in such. Therefore, policymakers should prioritize efforts that will lead to the development of practitioners' professional competence in firearm-related matters.

25. Firearm-Related Violence and Suicide Risk Assessments Should Follow Prevention-, Rather Than Prediction-, Based Models

There has been a significant paradigm shift in the violence and suicide risk assessment arenas over the past 30 years—from *predicting dangerousness* to *assessing risk*—because research has elucidated the fact that practitioners are not able to predict a specific event with any compelling level of accuracy. Thus, leading scholars in the areas of violence and suicide risk assessment have implored practitioners to move toward risk management and reduction approaches. Indeed, the American Psychological Association recently issued a press release in this regard, "After Decades of Research, Science Is No Better Able to Predict Suicidal Behaviors" (American Psychological Association, 2016), which was based on Franklin et al.'s (2017) meta-analysis of 50 years of research in this area. Those in the violence (and sexual) risk arenas have embraced this notion for many years, which gave rise to the development of the SPJ approach to assessment in the early 1990s (see Hart, Douglas, & Guy, 2016, for an overview and historical account) as well as the risk–need–responsivity model developed by Andrews, Bonta, & Hoge (1990). These prevention-based models are premised on the notion that practitioners' decision-making is enhanced by: identifying the presence of evidenced-based risk factors, considering their relevance, developing a formulation of risk, identifying likely scenarios of future violence, developing interventions and plans in the context of risk management efforts, and communicating ultimate opinions about the risk. By employing a risk assessment rather than prediction approach, practitioners can connect their findings to interventions designed to manage and reduce risk as opposed to trying to determine the odds of someone engaging in a problematic act at some future point. One of the reasons practitioners' predictive accuracy is low in these contexts is the relatively low base rate associated with extreme acts of violence and suicide. The base rates are even lower for acts of violence and suicide with firearms, which is why efforts to predict, profile, or otherwise prognosticate with any real accuracy are futile at best and may have unintended consequences. For example, attempts to predict such low–base rate behaviors result in a high number of *false positives*, or incorrect indications that people will engage in particular acts, because this is the only way to correctly identify those of concern. To illustrate with an extreme example: if you predict that every single person who interacts with a firearm will engage in firearm-involved violence or suicide, you will have accurately identified all of those of concern, but you will also have been incorrect more than 99% of the time. It is for this reason that medical and mental health practitioners seek to balance the predictive accuracy of their assessments with considerations related to sensitivity (true positive), specificity (true negative), false positive, false negative, positive predictive value, and negative predictive value rates.

Practice

In low–base rate, potentially high-impact contexts like firearm evaluations, practitioners should forego prediction-based approaches and use those focused on risk assessment, management, and prevention. The SPJ approach to risk assessment is useful in firearm evaluations because it incorporates the consideration of evidenced-based risk factors along with a stepwise model that facilitates clinical decision-making. There are numerous violence assessment measures available to clinicians in this regard, such as the Historical-Clinical-Risk Management-20, Version 3 (Douglas, Hart, Webster, & Belfrage, 2013). Such empirically sound SPJs are currently lacking in the area of suicide assessment and prevention (Cramer & Kapusta, 2017), although certain self-report and interview-style instruments (e.g., the Columbia Suicide Severity Rating Scale; Posner et al., 2011) can be helpful. Practitioners conducting firearm-specific evaluations may wish to use a guide like the PF-10 to help structure their assessment, and those working in other environments, such as in the schools, would be wise to incorporate overarching threat assessment models into their safety planning (e.g., the Virginia model for student threat assessment; Cornell & Sheras, 2006).

Research

Much of the research conducted in the violence and suicide risk assessment arenas has focused on the psychometric properties of measures, especially their predictive validity. However, this continued focus is contrary to prevention-based models and has done little to advance the field any further.

As Skeem & Monahan (2011) put it:

> The violence risk assessment field may be reaching a point of diminishing returns in instrument development. We might speculate that incremental advances could be made by exploring novel assessment methods, including implicit measures . . . or simple heuristics. . . . But specific structured techniques seem to account for very little of the variance in predictive accuracy. If we are approaching a ceiling in this domain, there clearly are miles to go on the risk reduction front. We hope that forensic psychology shifts more of its attention from predicting violence to understanding its causes and preventing its (re)occurrence. (p. 41)

Hart and colleagues (2016) expressed a similar sentiment:

> The horizon is wide with respect to the scope of research needed to advance the SPJ approach further. As noted above, research on the "middle steps" in the administration process—formulation and scenario planning—is needed. What approaches to formulation are most fruitful, and under what circumstances for which types of professionals? Do formulations add value in terms of the quality and effectiveness of risk management, compared with the absence of formulation? Do they result in a reduction of risk? What types of scenarios—repeat, twist, escalation, or desistance—are most commonly relied upon? To what extent and in what ways are such scenarios valid, in that they are more likely to occur in the future relative to scenarios that were not identified? Do scenarios facilitate the development of risk management planning? Research on formulation and scenario planning should extend beyond reliability and validity, but also acceptability of these practices among practitioners engaging in them and consumers receiving them, such as judges and other triers of fact, administrators of agencies, and other end users of risk assessment reports. (p. 660)

The outstanding questions in the violence and suicide risk assessment arenas are very complex. It is much simpler to correlate scores on a test with a particular behavior than it is to investigate the multilayered factors underlying it. Moreover, treatment outcome research pertaining to violence and suicide prevention is generally lacking, and more advanced studies, such as randomized controlled trials are even scarcer (with noted exceptions such as suicide interventions for military personnel [e.g., Rudd et al., 2016] and suicide-specific problems [e.g., Jobes, 2012]). It would be beneficial if researchers conducted more prospective, longitudinal treatment outcome studies focused on the mechanisms of change and treatment progress (or lack thereof) for those at elevated violence or suicide risk.

Policy

Firearm-involved violence and suicides share some common risk and protective factors; however, the specific ways in which we need to address these issues in practice, research, and policy differ. Therefore, laws and policies targeting only means (e.g., firearms) rather than underlying motivations, triggers, and disinhibitors leading to such actions are likely to remain relatively ineffective. This may simply lead to a weapon substitution rather than an appreciable reduction in violence or suicide. Indeed, most acts of DV and IPV include means and weapons other than firearms. Policymakers should work with clinicians and researchers to determine the most effective interventions to prevent violence and suicide, particularly as related to those acts that involve firearms.

26. Restricting Access to Firearms Is Only One Component of a Comprehensive Violence and Suicide Risk Management and Prevention Plan for Those at Elevated Risk

Professional groups, such as the American Academy of Pediatrics, have recommended counseling families on the risk of having firearms in the home; and research has shown some promise for firearm safety counseling as a form of means restriction, generally (Johnson, Frank, Ciocca, & Barber, 2011; Stanley et al., 2016; Yip et al., 2012), and within specific groups, such as military veterans (Smith, Currier, & Drescher, 2015).

However, counseling alone has not necessarily been found to be effective—even for families specifically advised to remove their firearms (Brent et al., 2000). Instead, a comprehensive prevention-based approach is warranted. As Christoffel (2000) pointed out, we have learned this from the prevention of motor vehicle injuries over the years. In the context of the "4 Es" of injury prevention, *engineering, education, enforcement,* and *evaluation,* she noted: "Injury prevention efforts that skip any of these do not succeed. Gun injury prevention is no exception, and it cannot rely on education alone" (p. 1228). We concur, particularly given the notable barriers that exist in restricting firearm access (see, e.g., Walters et al., 2012) as well as the reality that some people will still pose risks with guns regardless of the overarching success of prevention efforts or given programs (see, e.g., Sherman et al., 2001). We must also remember that most practitioners lack education and training on firearms, firearm safety, firearm laws, and other firearm-specific issues, thereby limiting their assessment and counseling efforts in this regard. This presents two related practical concerns: (i) many clinicians will not know what to ask or what to do with the information they receive and (ii) this is likely to be obvious to their clients, which may deter them from disclosing information or even entering counseling in the first place. Nevertheless, it is incumbent on clinicians to address safety-related issues when risks are identified, and this must extend beyond means restriction in cases of elevated risk.

Practice

Practitioners should employ a comprehensive approach to their risk assessments and interventions with clients at potential risk of violence or self-injury. Williamson and colleagues (2014) set forth recommendations that would serve many practitioners well:

- Integrate questions about firearm ownership and safe gun and ammunition storage into routine child wellness visits and mental health intakes and evaluations for all children, youth, and families.
- Integrate questions about youth aggressive behavior or violence, gun carrying, homicidality, and suicidality into routine pediatric and mental health visits for older children and adolescents.
- Use evidence-based screening tools for suicide and related risk behaviors.
- Provide basic counseling about gun safety to gun-owning families.
- Provide families and youth with educational handouts about firearm safety and the prevention of firearm-related youth homicide, accidental injury, and suicide.
- Provide families and youth with appropriate mental health treatment referrals when there is a risk for aggression, violence, homicidality, or suicidality.

These recommendations are geared toward professionals who work with youth and families, but most can be applied to adult-only cases as well. Of particular note is their additional recommendation for practitioners to seek training opportunities to learn more about gun safety counseling and other prevention practices. This is key given that the aforementioned recommendations are predicated on the assumption that practitioners have a working knowledge of guns, gun safety, gun laws, and related issues—but they generally do not. We reiterate that practitioners should employ prevention-, rather than prediction-, based models at the individual and the system levels (see finding 25 above). The complete and foolproof restriction of gun access is unrealistic in the overwhelming majority of cases, and therefore, clinicians must be a part of comprehensive, multidisciplinary efforts to prevent firearm-involved suicide and violence in situations where risk is elevated. Where means restriction is necessary, we endorse the guidance provided by Simon (2007), who articulated several steps in engaging positive client social support in the removal of firearms for those who are being discharged from psychiatric hospitalization. Simon's recommendations include: (i) a collaborative approach between the clinician, patient, and the person responsible for removal of firearms; (ii) designate a willing, responsible person to remove and safely secure guns and ammunition outside the home, at a location unknown to the patient; (iii) call back and two-way contact between clinician and identified person is necessary (e-mail should not be used); and (iv) do not discharge from inpatient or emergency department care unless means removal is confirmed. Simon argues, and we concur, that these guidelines should apply to working with high-risk clients in any setting.

Research

As we highlighted in Chapter 8, health education–related journals have only recently begun to increase their attention to firearm-involved violence and related concerns. We have also detailed our concerns throughout this book with the lack of firearm-specific information readily available to medical and mental health professionals in professional forums, including, but certainly not limited to, peer-reviewed journals. Only a small portion of practitioners have received firearm safety information from professional journals, for example. More educative pieces on guns, gun safety, and gun laws published by those with professional competence in these areas are needed. Furthermore, much of the extant literature has focused on means restriction as a form of violence prevention rather than more comprehensive, multidisciplinary risk assessment and management approaches. Therefore, we reiterate and cannot overstate the need for treatment outcome research studies in this arena.

Policy

Most proposed policies and laws focus on means restriction in the form of classifying and reclassifying prohibited persons (think background checks, gun forfeiture and restraining orders, and specific gun and magazine capacity bans). In short, policymakers tend to be fixated on categorical prohibitions rather than empirically driven processes that seek to identify those at elevated risk of engaging in firearm-involved violence and suicide. Many of the legislators and government officials seeking to increase background checks and prohibitions have failed to recognize the inordinate number of appeals that are likely to follow, and, as we have noted numerous times throughout this book, there are not even enough practitioners available to appropriately address the existing firearm-specific matters. As we outlined in finding 24 above, the number of evaluations that would be needed for even the smallest proportion of the existing cases would far surpass those most commonly conducted in other legal areas, thereby serving to logjam the system. Therefore, the unintended consequences of increased, broader prohibitions are likely to be many.

Instead of embracing inch-deep, mile-wide approaches, it would be beneficial for policymakers to work with mental health and other violence and suicide risk experts to develop more precise policies and laws designed to identify those at elevated risk. Such engaged approaches to policymaking are ideally targeted at multiple levels of prevention at the society, community, interpersonal, and individual levels. Until then, we will continue to prioritize the raising of questions rather than the provision of answers. Instead, our primary focus should be on educating and training clinicians on guns, gun safety, gun laws, and related issues and to significantly increase the number of forensic mental health experts who develop their professional and cultural competence to conduct firearm-specific evaluations. Increased background checks, prohibitions, and access to mental health treatment may be worthwhile endeavors in some respects; but they do not address these other critical steps.

27. There Are Various Types of Therapeutic Interventions Available That May Reduce Firearm-Related Violence and Suicide Risk, in Addition to Those Associated with Health and Wellness, and Firearm Safety, More Generally

Not all psychotherapeutic interventions are beneficial to everyone at all times, and, in fact, some may even be potentially harmful in certain contexts. However, many developed over the past century have received empirical support for their treatment of specific conditions and people. Although psychotherapists often subscribe to a particular therapeutic modality, the leading contemporary approaches have all been found to be effective at some level. Namely, psychodynamic, cognitive-behavioral therapy (CBT), and dialectical-behavioral therapy (CBT) approaches have been found to be useful in treating people diagnosed with a range of mental health disorders and related problems. There are many additional types of approaches that have also been found to be beneficial for certain purposes, but CBT and DBT have become especially popular for the treatment of those who pose an elevated risk of violence and suicide. Moreover, these intervention models have been adapted for use with youth populations as well. An integration of established therapeutic interventions along with firearm safety–based counseling and assessment is warranted for those who pose the more specific risk of engaging in firearm-involved violence or suicide. Principles of firearm safety and health and wellness are critical to incorporate in these contexts, particularly because relatively few people will be completely prohibited from interacting with firearms in perpetuity— and even those who are (on paper) may very well gain access to firearms regardless. As noted, a comprehensive, multifaceted, and multidisciplinary risk management– and reduction-based approach is advisable when treating those at elevated risk.

Practice

In general, mental health practitioners are well versed on a range of effective interventions for adults and youth at risk for engaging in violence and suicide.

Of course, clinicians with particular expertise in these areas are critically important. However, all clinicians need to develop their professional and cultural competence pertaining to firearms and firearm-related subcultures so that they can provide adequate support and counseling in the context of firearm safety. Medical and mental health practitioners already represent the primary professional sources for reducing violence and suicide risk, and we fully expect that their involvement in such contexts will only increase given concerns about inappropriate firearm use and the like. One promising avenue for reduction in these areas is crisis response planning (Bryan et al., 2017), which may often include addressing firearms. Therefore, a comprehensive risk management and reduction approach in this regard should incorporate standard therapeutic principles and techniques as well as those associated with health and wellness and firearm safety.

Research

It would be beneficial for researchers to better delineate concepts related to violence and suicide compared to those that are firearm-specific. As it stands, much of the empirical literature and professional commentary simply adds the presence of a gun to existing concerns related to violence and self-harm, but this does little to inform about what distinguishes an act of violence or suicide from one that involves a gun. From a basic science standpoint, it may be sufficient to simply correlate variables of interest. However, this is inadequate from an applied science perspective, and practitioners are in need of firearm-related research that they can apply to their day-to-day work. As noted, many clinicians are already equipped to provide services for those at heightened risk of violence and suicide, but they are generally not informed as to the ways in which they can integrate firearm-specific considerations into such efforts. One necessary component is increasing practitioners' awareness of guns, gun safety, and gun laws through the literature and continued education programs; but another is the development of applied clinical research that elucidates what is effective in reducing firearm-involved risk, specifically. After all, if there are no discernable distinctions between these efforts and those that relate to situations that do not involve guns, then there seems to be no need for firearm-specific policies and laws. We do believe there are distinctions, as we have outlined throughout this book; but applied research in this area is sorely lacking and, therefore, clinicians engage in practice-as-usual approaches.

Policy

Lawmakers who set forth firearm-related proposals often resort to calls for increased access to mental health treatment, but these are not typically tied in with gun rights restoration mechanisms. In fact, mental health treatment issues are often brought up in the context of firearm-involved violence or suicide tragedies, but they are actually spoken about completely independently of gun rights. Put differently, it is not usually the case that a policymaker speaking in the context of firearm-related legislation calls for easier and increased access to mental health treatment for the purpose of restoring people's rights to own and operate guns. Therefore, it is unclear as to what the compelling connection is between mental health treatment and gun laws. One might argue that increasing access to treatment will make more people safer, in general; but this is a flawed conceptualization because relatively few people engage in firearm-involved violence—even those with diagnosable severe mental illnesses (i.e., less than 3%–5%). As we have noted numerous times, the more significant link is between guns and suicide, and there is relatively more promise in addressing firearm-specific concerns in these treatment contexts. However, broad-based legislation seeking to increase mental health services, generally, is unlikely to have any notable impact on firearm-involved violence or suicide rates. Instead, efforts should be focused on educating medical and mental health professionals about guns, gun safety, and gun laws and training them on how to integrate firearm-specific considerations into their clinical work. Less precise efforts that do not include such education and training, such as charging practitioners with the task of identifying risk and intervening in matters involving firearms, will only serve to heighten clinicians' apprehensions and associated liability in this regard. Increasing access to mental health services for people is important, generally, but is likely to have many unintended consequences when attached to firearm-related legislation—not the least of which is stigma and deterring people from seeking help.

28. Many Considerations for Providing Therapeutic Interventions for At-Risk Youth Are Separate and Distinct from Those Associated with Adults

Youth differ from adults in important ways; therefore, therapeutic interventions designed for those at elevated risk for violence and suicide must be adapted to meet their specific needs. Studies conducted in the neuroscience arena have illustrated the significant anatomical and corresponding functional differences between youth and adults, and concepts such as those related to developmental immaturity have continued to emerge in this context. In addition, it is particularly important to recognize that young people typically experience psychiatric symptoms and exhibit signs of such differently from adults. It is also essential to consider social, familial, and developmental factors when working with children and adolescents, including those associated with psychosocial and psychosexual development.

Practice

Medical and mental health practitioners must develop professional competence to work with youth, and those who work with at-risk children and adolescents must specialize even further. Still, all clinicians must be aware of violence and suicide risk factors among these groups, which include a range of environmental, familial, educational, mental health, medical, and social factors (see Williamson et al., 2014, for a review). One particular risk factor specific to guns relates to the unsupervised access to firearms and ammunition, which has prompted increased attention to CAP and storage laws throughout the country. Medical and mental health practitioners can certainly play a more active role in reducing access to at-risk youth once they develop their professional competence in this regard.

Research

The juvenile neuroscience and decision-making literature has flourished in recent years, and it has become a critical component in many major legal rulings, including those made by the higher courts in this country. There have also been significant advancements in the youth mental health evaluation and treatment arenas. However, many questions remain with regard to the use of firearms by young people who engage in violence and suicide. Much of what is discussed in this context is applicable to youth violence and self-harm, more generally, and not specific to guns per se. In fact, access to firearms is often the only distinguishing factor identified in this context. However, it is important to know if there are actual differences among youth who engage in violence or suicide with guns compared to those who do not use guns to harm others or themselves. Namely, are there identifiable individual differences that correspond to demographic, clinical, or psychosocial factors? Are there differences in their motivation, triggers, disinhibitors, or protective factors? Solely recognizing the fact that guns were used in particular acts of violence or suicide does not help us understand if there are distinctions between youth who choose to use such means versus those who do not. These more advanced questions require empirical investigation in order to provide practitioners who work with youth with information and guidance. Given that there are over 100 million firearm owners in this country and one-third of US households have at least one gun, many children have some level of exposure and potential access to guns. While unsupervised access (and not simply access) has been identified as a potential risk factor, this is still insufficient information for clinicians tasked with assessing risk, counseling, and intervening with youth and families. Again, it would be beneficial to determine which factors are more specifically associated with firearm-involved violence and suicide compared to the commission of these acts with other means. In addition, more program evaluation and policy analysis research is needed to assess the effectiveness of the various firearm safety programs for youth as well as for CAP and storage laws. The empirical literature in these areas is minimal and includes very small samples.

Policy

As noted, there is a dearth of empirical research on the effectiveness of firearm safety programs for youth and CAP and storage laws. Therefore, policymakers should work with clinicians and researchers to promote these lines of empirical study, and those proposing new policies and laws should set forth corresponding plans for contemporaneous policy analyses. They can also assist in efforts to identify youth who are at risk for engaging in firearm-involved violence and suicide as a subset of broader violence and suicide prevention initiatives.

29. There Are Significant Systemic and Case-Specific Barriers to Treatment for Some Members of Certain Firearm-Related Subgroups

There are structural and emotional barriers to mental health treatment for many people. For instance, there are practical considerations related to insurance coverage, costs, transportation and travel, time constraints, concern about stigma, and discomfort with disclosure. It is also not uncommon that the primary barrier is the very reason someone needs treatment in the first place (e.g., major depressive or anxiety-related symptoms). Nevertheless, 20% of those who enter psychotherapy drop out before completing treatment (Swift & Greenberg, 2012) and up to one-third do not return after the first session (Simon, Imel, Ludman, & Steinfeld, 2012).

These numbers notably increase for novice clinicians. The point remains that there are numerous existing barriers to treatment for people, generally, and even more for members of certain firearm-related subgroups. Namely, firearm owners may be deterred from seeking mental health treatment for fear that their gun rights will be held in question and their guns revoked. In addition, those wishing to apply in the future may be concerned with being flagged or having to disclose their involvement in treatment. It is generally well known that medical and mental health professionals tend to embrace more liberal ideologies, including increased gun control and even views counter to the Second Amendment individual rights perspective. Many people may also know that most practitioners have no firearm knowledge at all. Therefore, it would not be surprising if many gun owners or those who wish to own someday are deterred from seeking treatment. Indeed, this is a commonly expressed concern in the context of military, law enforcement, and correctional personnel. In those cases, the fear is "You lose your career if you lose your gun." Paradoxically, firearm policies and legislation related to increasing access to mental health services are likely to deter people further (see finding 15 above, particularly in light of the American Psychiatric Association's 2015 position statement; Pinals, 2015a). It is also the case that such effects can extend to family therapy and couples counseling, and even general medical contacts, as firearm owners may fear scrutiny in those contexts as well.

Practice

It is imperative for medical and mental health professionals to develop their professional and cultural competence associated with firearms and firearm-related subgroups. As noted, there are inherent and existing barriers to mental health treatment for the general population in even the most common scenarios. The barriers increase significantly when guns are involved. Just as in the case of ethnicity, sexual orientation, and the many other diversity-related considerations practitioners receive education and training on, they too need to familiarize themselves with concepts associated with guns and firearm-related subcultures. Those who work within specific subcultural enclaves will have a particular appreciation for the need to establish cultural competence in order to attract and retain group members. Moreover, concepts related to acculturation and the like are applicable to firearm-related subcultures as well. Ultimately, increasing access to mental health care for those associated with firearms will have little value if they are unwilling to enter treatment, regardless.

Research

It would be beneficial to conduct research on the attitudes of members of firearm-related subgroups toward mental health practitioners and treatment. In particular, it would be useful to assess if the treatment barriers among these groups are comparable to those associated with other groups. Furthermore, researchers should investigate the effects of firearm-related policies and legislation on mental health treatment with respect to both new and existing clients.

Policy

Policymakers should not assume that increasing access to mental health treatment by attaching such initiatives to firearm-related policies and legislation will actually increase the number of people who seek help. In fact, there is reason to believe that these efforts may actually have a paradoxical effect and deter people from entering or remaining in treatment. Policymakers should familiarize themselves with the existing treatment barriers and work with clinicians and researchers to identify the additional barriers specific to firearm-related subgroups. In most cases, client buy-in is a critical component of mental health treatment progress; therefore, it is essential to understand what may be deterring people from entering treatment in the first place. The assumption that the sole problem is a lack of treatment access for these groups is misguided. There are numerous other barriers that require attention, and policymakers should consider what may have been helpful in bringing reluctant members of other groups into treatment (e.g., maintaining anonymity as opposed to flagging them simply for entering treatment).

30. The Restoration of Gun Rights to Those with Mental Health and Related Histories Is a Particularly Novel and Emerging Area of Consideration for Medical, Mental Health, and Legal Professionals

As we have contended throughout this book, there are already numerous firearm-related contexts in which medical, mental health, and legal professionals are needed. However, various policies, laws, and legal cases have arisen that further necessitate the expertise and involvement of these types of professionals. One particularly noteworthy area is the restoration of gun rights. Recent legal rulings, such as that associated with *Tyler v. Hillsdale County Sheriff's Dept.* (2014), indicate the likelihood of increased involvement of these practitioners as well as the emergence of new roles (e.g., firearm-specific evaluations; see finding 24). Some states, such as Oregon, have already developed gun rights restoration programs to address these issues directly and in a specialized manner (see Britton & Bloom, 2015). These developments are not particularly surprising in light of the increased subscription to therapeutic jurisprudence principles and the corresponding proliferation of specialty courts in recent years (e.g., mental health and drug courts). Only a small proportion of people will be ordered to have an indefinite, lifetime revocation of their gun rights, and even those who ultimately fall under such a provision will have likely had the opportunity to contest it. Therefore, medical, mental health, and legal professionals would be needed regardless.

Practice

Medical and mental health practitioners are likely to be called on more frequently as gun rights restoration initiatives continue to develop. This presents an opportunity for forensic practitioners who wish to expand their practices to include conducting firearm evaluations. However, treating professionals are also likely to be involved in more firearm-related matters moving forward. As such, they need to develop their professional competence in this context by receiving education on guns, gun safety, gun laws, and firearm-involved violence, suicide, and related areas because they will continue to be first responders of sorts. Namely, they are responsible for assessing and managing risk, when applicable; and they are usually the first ones asked by their clients and attorneys to provide treatment-related information when issues associated with firearms arise.

Research

It would be beneficial for researchers to investigate the outcomes of situations where gun rights have been restored and revoked firearms reinstated (e.g., subsequent firearm-related problems). These data will be difficult to acquire, and therefore, researchers will need work more closely and develop rapport with gun groups and owners, more generally. In addition, policy analyses will be needed as gun restoration initiatives develop. Lastly, as we have suggested in various other contexts, it would be useful to assess medical and mental health practitioners' attitudes and practices regarding gun rights restoration, including their levels of professional and cultural competence associated with firearm-related matters and subgroups.

Policy

Gun rights restoration efforts are consistent with the perspectives of leading scholars and mental health organizations that indicate that firearm prohibitions should be based on risk levels and not mental health diagnoses, especially because such a small proportion of even those diagnosed with severe mental illnesses engage in acts of violence. McGinty and colleagues (2014) formed a consortium of national gun violence prevention and mental health experts to advance an evidence-based policy agenda on the issue of mental illness and firearms, and they agreed on a guiding principle for future policy recommendations:

> Restricting firearm access on the basis of certain dangerous behaviors is supported by the evidence; restricting access on the basis of mental illness diagnoses is not. (p. e22)

Therefore, policymakers should shift their focus to work with clinicians and researchers to develop evidenced-based gun rights restoration procedures. They should also prioritize the education and training of medical and mental health professionals on firearms and firearm-related issues.

Final Thoughts for a Fresh Start

There have been many significant efforts in the firearms arena over the years by people with various experiences and perspectives, including those associated with community and professional groups. Despite these efforts, many questions remain unanswered, there continues to be a general lack of agreement and compromise among us, and we are a long way from non-partisan collaboration. In addition, most of the research in this arena is limited, the effectiveness of firearm-related policies and laws is generally unknown, and our medical and mental health professionals are not educated or formally trained on firearms, firearm safety, firearm laws, or other firearm-specific issues. The challenge, then, is in channeling the existing energy and resources associated with firearms into process-, rather than content-, focused efforts. We have set forth many action points related to the main findings outlined in the present chapter, most of which necessitate conceptual and structural shifts in the ways in which we think about and handle firearm-related issues. They reflect non-partisan, scientifically based recommendations associated with the state of the field and our society, more generally. There has certainly been a lot of movement in the firearms arena since the 1960s, but does this have corresponding evidence of appreciable gains? Confirmation biases are strong, and statistics can be cherry-picked to fit a particular narrative. However, regardless of where one's personal views fall, there remain a number of areas requiring attention and intervention. These areas are often overshadowed by divisive, politically driven initiatives and media sensationalism.

Continuance of a broad-based, polarizing approach to addressing firearm-related issues will only strengthen our biases and interfere with our ability to develop evidence-based processes beneficial to our society, such as those designed to reduce firearm-involved violence and suicide. In fact, continuing to set forth far-reaching or otherwise unrealistic initiatives is very likely to lead to an exhaustion of resources, hopelessness about the topic of prevention, and unintended increases in firearm-related problems. For example, initiatives, policies, and laws that seek such requirements as mental health evaluations for all applicants are completely impractical and, essentially, impossible in any real sense. The logistics associated with these types of proposals are short-sighted, lack an empirical basis, and rely upon faulty assumptions (e.g., the current levels of competence among various professional groups).

Instead, it is necessary to take a stepwise, multifaceted approach rooted in non-partisan and multidisciplinary ideals. Education alone is insufficient, and practitioners, academicians, researchers, policymakers, and members of firearm-related subgroups (e.g., law enforcement, Second Amendment, and gun violence prevention groups) must find common ground and collaborate to address the concerns that are important to all. Our government officials, including our governors and president, can help to coordinate and facilitate these efforts. Many of the action points we have delineated associated with the 30 main findings above are complex because many firearm-related issues are complex. This may discourage those who believe there is an easy path, such as via sweeping prohibitions or the like. It may deter those seeking to engage in business as usual when it comes to handling firearm-related issues. However, our optimism has only increased since beginning our 2-year research effort because there are realistic, albeit challenging, action points that can lead to improvements in our society. The path will be long and difficult, but there is a path.

Appendix A

Glossary of Firearm-Related Terms

ACP: Automatic Colt pistol, a type of ammunition.

Action: The mechanism of a firearm involved with presenting the cartridge for firing, removing the spent casing, and introducing a fresh cartridge.

Airsoft Gun: A firearm pressurized by air to shoot non-metal projectiles.

Ammunition: A supply or quantity of bullets and shells which are fired from a firearm.

AR-15: ArmaLite Rifle, a semiautomatic firearm that is gas-operated.

Assault Weapon: An automatic firearm with a detachable magazine and a pistol grip, often a type of rifle typically for military use.

Automatic: A firearm which continues to fire as long as the trigger remains depressed.

Backstrap: The rear of two gripstraps on a handgun, which lies beneath the heel of the hand when gripping the gun.

Ball: A military term for standard, full metal–jacketed ammunition.

Ballistics: The science of cartridge discharge and the bullet's flight.

Barrel: The barrel serves the purpose of providing direction and velocity to the bullet; it is long and in the shape of a tube (cylinder).

BB Gun: A firearm that fires small pellets (BBs) using pressurized air.

Blowback: The backpressure in an internal combustion when firing a firearm.

Bluing: The chemical process of artificial oxidation (rusting) applied to gun parts so that the metal attains a dark blue or nearly black appearance.

Bore: The interior of a gun barrel.

Bore Diameter: The diameter of the inside of the barrel. The land-to-land diameter.

Breech: That portion of the gun that contains the rear chamber of the barrel; the action, trigger, or firing mechanism; and the magazine.

Breechblock: The part of the weapon that seals the rear of the chamber and supports the casehead when the cartridge is fired.

Bull Barrel: A heavier, thicker than normal barrel with little or no narrowing toward the end.

Bullet: The metal projectile, typically in the shape of a pointed cylinder, expelled from the mouth of a firing cartridge.

Butt: The part of a firearm which is held or shouldered, where the firing mechanism and barrel are connected.

Caliber: The diameter of the bore of a barrel measured from land to land, usually measured in tenths of an inch or in millimeters. It does not designate the actual diameter of a bullet.

Cannelure: A groove or indention around the circumference of a bullet.

Cartridge: In modern terms, a round of ammunition consisting of casing, primer, powder, and projectile. In the "percussion-cap" era, the cartridge consisted of the projectile and powder in a paper packet, with the primer cap separate.

Casing: A cylindrical tube closed at one end that holds the primer and powder of a cartridge. The cartridge bullet is crimped into the open end of the casing. They are typically made from brass but can be steel, aluminum, or even plastic.

Centerfire: A cartridge in which the primer or primer assembly is seated in a pocket or recess in the center of the base of the casing (the casing head). Also refers to a firearm which uses centerfire cartridges.

Chamber: The part of the firearm at the rear of the barrel that is reamed out so that it can contain a cartridge for firing.

Charger: A device typically made from stamped metal which holds a group of cartridges for easy and virtually simultaneous loading.

Choke: To keep the shotgun pellets in a tighter group there is a constriction of the shotgun bore at the muzzle.

Clip: This term is often used when referring to a detachable magazine. But, in fact, it is a device, usually of stamped metal similar to a charger, that holds a group of cartridges and is inserted along with the cartridges into certain magazines. It is expelled after the last round in the magazine is spent.

Cock: The term referring to the action of manually drawing the hammer back against its spring until it becomes latched against the sear, or sometimes the trigger itself, arming the hammer to be released by a subsequent pull of the trigger.

Concealed Carry: To carry a firearm on one's person that cannot be seen by the public.

Constitutional Carry: To carry a firearm in public that does not need to be concealed without a government permit.

Cylinder: A rotating cartridge holder in a revolver. The cylinder also contains the chamber portion of the revolver. Cartridges are held, and fired, within the cylinder. Cartridge chambers are evenly placed around the axis of the cylinder. The cylinder has a linkage to the firing mechanism, which rotates each chamber into alignment with the barrel prior to each firing.

Cylinder Stop: On a revolver, a spring-activated device housed in the bottom of the frame beneath the cylinder that engages alignment notches in the cylinder. It stops the cylinder's rotation and holds it in place each time a chamber in the cylinder is in alignment with the barrel.

Double-Action (DA): A revolver or pistol on which a long trigger pull can both cock and release the hammer to fire the weapon. In a revolver this action also rotates the cylinder to the next chambered round. DA also implies a single-action stage which can cock the gun separately, alternately called double action/single action, or DA/SA.

Double-Action Only: Typically on striker-fired pistols and spurless-hammer revolvers and referring to a trigger where the firing mechanism cannot be cocked in a single-action stage. Firing always occurs as a double-action sequence where pulling the trigger both cocks and then fires the gun.

Double Barrel: Two barrels that are side by side or one on top of the other, which bullets are shot through, typically on a shotgun.

Dovetail: A flaring machined or hand-cut slot that is also slightly tapered toward one end. Cut into the upper surface of barrels and sometimes actions, the dovetail accepts a corresponding part on which the sight is mounted.

Ears: Hearing protection

Ejector: The part on the firearm whose function is to throw a spent casing from the gun after firing.

Ejector Star: On a revolver, the collective ejector, manually operated through the center of an opened cylinder; when activated, clears all chambers at once.

Extractor: On a pistol, a part attached to the breechblock, which withdraws the spent casing from the chamber.

Eyes: Eye protection (safety glasses).

Firearms Identification Card: A permit issued by a state or local government allowing the sale, purchase, or ownership of a firearm.

Firing Pin: In a hammer fired gun, this is a hardened pin housed in the breechblock, centered directly behind the primer cap of a chambered cartridge. When struck by the hammer it impacts the primer cap of the cartridge, discharging the weapon.

Frame: The common part of a handgun to which the action, barrel, and grip are connected.

Front Strap: The part of a revolver or pistol grip frame that faces forward and often joins with the trigger guard.

Full Metal Jacket: A round of ammo where each bullet is encased in a stronger/harder metal.

GAP: Glock auto pistol, a type of ammunition.

Gauge: The amount of lead balls you can make from one pound of led of equal diameter to a shotgun's barrel.

Grip: The handle used to hold a handgun. Often refers to the side panels of the handle.

Gripstraps: The exposed portion of a handgun's frame, the front strap and backstrap, that provides the foundation for the handgun's grip.

Grooves: Spiral cuts into the bore of a barrel that give the bullet its spin or rotation as it moves down the barrel.

Gunpowder: A propellant explosive.

Half Cock: The position of the hammer in a hammer-activated firing mechanism that acts as a manual safety.

Hammer: That part of a revolver or pistol that impacts the firing pin or the cartridge directly, discharging the weapon. Its movement is rotational around its axis, which is fixed to the frame.

Hammerless: This general term can either refer to revolver or pistol designs that actually have hammers which are fully encased inside the frames, hammer designs where the spurs have been removed for concealment, or striker-fired pistols that are truly hammerless.

Hammer Spur: The thumb piece on the top rear of the hammer that enables it to be manually drawn back to full cock.

Handgun: A firearm, typically a pistol or revolver, which can be fired and held with one hand.

Handloading: The process of loading a firearm with cartridges assembled from the individual components (primer, shell casing, gunpowder, and bullet).

HMR: Hornady Magnum Rimfire, a type of ammunition.

Holster: A case (usually made of leather or fabric) which is on a person (typically on the hip) used to carry a firearm.

Ignition: The way gunpowder is lit.

Jacket: The casing surrounding a bullet.

Laser: A laser is used for accurately aiming a firearm in a quick manner.

LC: Long Colt, a type of ammunition.

Long Recoil: A semiautomatic pistol in which the barrel and breechblock are locked together for the full distance of rearward recoil travel, after which the barrel returns forward, while the breechblock is held back. After the barrel has fully returned, the breechblock is released to fly forward, chambering a fresh round in the process.

LR: Long rifle, a type of ammunition.

Machine Gun: A firearm where a single pull of the trigger fires multiple shots. An automatic weapon.

Magazine: A container, either fixed to a pistol's frame or detachable, which holds cartridges under spring pressure to be fed into the gun's chamber.

Magnum: A modern cartridge with a higher-velocity load or heavier projectile than standard.

Mainspring: Term often used for the hammer spring.

Master Marksman: A person who has mastered the use of a weapon.

Match Grade: When a modification is made to a firearm to increase accuracy.

Misfeed: Entering a round into a chamber incorrectly.

Misfire: A condition when firing a gun in which the cartridge fails to discharge.

Muzzle: The forward end of the barrel where the projectile exits.

Muzzle Velocity: The speed of the bullet, measured in feet per second or meters per second, as it leaves the barrel.

Neck: The constricted forward section of a bottle-necked cartridge casing—the portion that grips the bullet.

NICS (National Instant Criminal Background Check System): Used by Federal Firearms License holders for determining whether it is legal to sell a firearm to a prospective purchaser.

Ogive: A type of curve represented by the curved section of a bullet between its bearing surface and its tip.

Open Carry: To carry a firearm that is not concealed from the public.

Open Frame: Refers to a revolver frame that has no topstrap over the cylinder.

Pellet Gun: A firearm which fires a skirted pellet using pressurized air (CO_2).

Pistol: Refers generally to any handgun that is not a revolver. This includes self-loaders, manual repeaters, single-shots, double- or multiple-barrel pistols, and derringers.

Plinking: Shooting at inanimate objects, typically to practice shooting.

Polygonal: Rifling without hard-edged lands or grooves, typically consisting of flat surfaces that meet at angles around the bore.

Powder: A chemical that is ignited in order for a bullet to be fired.

Primer: A small detonating cap fitted in the head of a centerfire cartridge casing that, when struck by a firing pin, ignites the powder charge.

Primer Pocket: The counter bore in the center of the base of a centerfire cartridge casing in which the primer assembly is seated.

Primer Ring: Refers to a visible dark ring created by the primers in centerfire ammunition around the firing pin hole in the frame after much use.

Receiver: In handguns, this refers to the frame.

Recoil-Operated: Refers to a semiautomatic pistol whose barrel and breechblock both recoil rearward in reaction to the discharging bullet.

Revolver: A handgun that has revolving cylinder chambers which hold several cartridges, allowing several shots to be fired without reloading.

Rifle: A long gun with a grooved barrel, fired from shoulder level, which causes a bullet to spin for an increase in accuracy.

Rifling: Typically, a series of spiral grooves cut into the bore of the barrel. Rifling stabilizes the bullet in flight by causing it to spin. Rifling may rotate to the right or left. See *twist*.

Rimfire: A self-contained metallic cartridge where the primer is contained inside the hollow rim of the cartridge case. The primer is detonated by the firing pin striking the outside edge of the rim, crushing the rim against the rear face of the barrel.

Rimless: Refers to a cartridge in which the base diameter is the same as the body diameter. The casing will normally have an extraction groove machined around it near the base, creating a "rim" at the base that is the same diameter as the body diameter.

Round: A unit of ammunition consisting of the primer, casing, propellant, and bullet. A cartridge.

Safety: A mechanical device built into a weapon intended to prevent accidental discharge. It may be either manually operated or automatic.

Sawed-Off Shotgun: A shotgun that has a shorter barrel (usually under 18 inches) than a standard shotgun.

Sear: A pivoting part of the firing mechanism of a gun, either part of the trigger or an intermediate piece, that catches and holds the hammer or striker at full cock. Pressure on the trigger causes the sear to release the hammer or striker, allowing it to strike the firing pin and discharge the weapon.

Self-Loader: Another term for semiautomatic, more commonly refers to early designs of semiautomatic pistols.

Semiautomatic: A pistol that is loaded manually for the first round. Upon pulling the trigger, the gun fires. Energy from the discharging bullet is used to eject the fired round, cock the firing mechanism, and feed a fresh round from the magazine. The trigger must be released after each shot and pulled again to fire the next round.

Shell: An empty ammunition case.

Shotgun: A long gun with smoothbore barrels that usually fires shotshells. Shotshell cartridges contain numerous pellets that spread when fired.

Sights: A device on top of a barrel that allows a gun to be aimed accurately.

Silencer: A device placed over the muzzle of a firearm used to reduce/muffle the sound of gunfire.

Single-Action (SA): A pistol or revolver, in which the trigger is only used for firing the weapon and cannot be used to cock the firing mechanism. On SA revolvers, the hammer must be manually drawn back to full cock for each shot. On pistols, the recoil action will automatically recock the hammer for the second and subsequent shots.

Skeet: A shooting sport in which a clay target (pigeon) is thrown to simulate the flight of a bird.

Slide: The upper portion of a semiautomatic pistol that houses the barrel and contains the breechblock and portions of the firing mechanism. As its name states, it slides along tracks in the top of the frame during the recoil process, providing the linkage between the breechblock and barrel.

Slide Lever: Typically refers to a lever either on the left or right side of a pistol's frame that is used to release the slide for removal, maintenance, and cleaning.

Small Arms: Portable firearms.

Solid Frame: Refers to a revolver in which the cylinder window is cut into a single solid piece of frame stock. The construction is neither break-open nor open frame. This type of revolver is loaded by the cylinder flipping out of the solid frame or by feeding individual rounds into exposed chambers that are rotated out to the side of the frame.

Speed Loader: In revolvers in which the entire rear of the cylinder can be exposed for loading, the speed loader is a circular device or clip that holds a complete set of cartridges aligned to insert into all chambers of the cylinder simultaneously.

Stock: A frame which holds the action and barrel of a firearm that is held against one's shoulder when firing the gun.

Straw Purchase: A criminal act in which a person who is prohibited from buying firearms uses another person to buy a gun on his or her behalf, often related to a person wanting to remain unidentified.

Striker: In a handgun that does not have a hammer, the striker is a linearly driven, spring-loaded cylindrical part which strikes the primer of a chambered cartridge. The striker replaces both the hammer and firing pin found in hammer-driven pistols.

Topstrap: The part of a revolver frame that extends over the top of the cylinder and connects the top of the standing breech with the forward portion of the frame into which the barrel is mounted.

Trajectory: The arc described by a projectile traveling from the muzzle to the point of impact.

Trigger: Refers to the release device in the firing system that initiates the cartridge discharge. Usually a curved, grooved, or serrated piece that is pulled rearward by the shooter's finger, which then activates the hammer or striker.

Trigger Guard: Usually a circular or oval band of metal, horn, or plastic that goes around the trigger to provide both protection and safety in shooting circumstances.

Twist: The rate at which rifling grooves arc around the core of the barrel, measured in calibers, inches, or centimeters. Twists can arc from left to right or from right to left from the rear of the barrel. This is described as either a right-hand or a left-hand twist.

WCF: Winchester Centerfire, a type of ammunition.

WMR: Winchester Magnum Rimfire, a type of ammunition.

Appendix B

Glossary of Firearm-Related Law and Legal Cases

Armed Career Criminal Act of 1984: A federal law that increases penalties, through sentence enhancements, for individuals found in possession of firearms who are not qualified to own them (such as felons with three or more "violent felonies" and/or "serious drug offenses"). The law has since been revised numerous times as various terms were vague and difficult to interpret.

Brady Handgun Violence Prevention Act: Also referred to as the "Brady Act" or the "Brady Bill." This law mandated a 5-day wait period before the purchase of a handgun (until the NICS system was implemented in 1998). It also requires local law enforcement to conduct federal background checks on individuals attempting to purchase a handgun.

Caetano v. Massachusetts, **136 S.Ct. 1027 (2016):** The US Supreme Court sought to expound upon the meaning of the right "to keep and bear arms." Massachusetts had flatly banned stun guns from use by anyone other than law enforcement and military personnel. In this case, a woman threatened to use a stun gun against her ex-boyfriend, who had repeatedly assaulted her. The police found her in possession of the stun gun, however; and she was prosecuted. The Supreme Court came to a unanimous opinion to vacate Massachusetts' highest state court's upholding of the flat ban on possessing stun guns for personal self-defense.

Commonwealth v. McGowan, **464 Mass. 232 (2013):** A law which required firearms to be secured in a locked container or equipped with a safety device that would make the firearm inoperable by anyone other than the owner or an authorized user, when not carried by or under the control of the owner or other authorized user. The court stated the law exists to prevent accidents, violence, and suicide by those unlicensed to possess or carry a firearm.

Crime Control Act of 1990 (Public Law 101-647): Enacted to ban semiautomatic weapon production and importation into the United States. This law also encourages authorities to post "Gun-Free Zone" signs in school zones and increases the penalties for individuals found in possession of firearms in federal court facilities.

District of Columbia v. Heller, 554 US 570 (2008): A landmark case in which the Supreme Court of the United States held in a 5–4 decision that the Second Amendment to the US Constitution applies to federal enclaves and protects an individual's right to possess a firearm for traditionally lawful purposes, such as self-defense within the home. The decision did not address the question of whether the Second Amendment extends beyond federal enclaves to the states, which was addressed later by *McDonald v. Chicago* (2010). It was the first Supreme Court case to decide whether the Second Amendment protects an individual's right to keep and bear arms for self-defense.

Firearms Owners Protection Act (Public Law 99-308): A law that revised many of the provisions of the Gun Control Act of 1968. This law relaxed some of the restrictions on gun and ammunitions sales, while also establishing mandatory penalties for individuals who are in possession of a firearm during the commission of a crime. Some of the loosened restrictions included: a limited reopening of the interstate sale of long guns, legalizing the shipments of ammunitions through the US Postal Service, removal of the requirement to keep records on the sale of non-armor-piercing ammunition, and federal protection of individuals transporting firearms through states where firearm possession is illegal. The list of circumstances by which individuals would be prohibited from owning firearms was also modified.

Gun Control Act of 1968: An act that was passed after the assassinations of John F. Kennedy, Robert Kennedy, and Dr. Martin Luther King, Jr., which aimed to regulate interstate and foreign commerce of firearms. In an effort to impose stricter licensing and regulation of firearms, the Gun Control Act mandated the licensing of individuals and companies who sell firearms, established a new category of firearms offenses, and also prohibited the sale of firearms to certain persons, such as felons. The act required all newly manufactured firearms to bear a serial number. Finally, Congress reorganized the Alcohol Tax Unit and created the Alcohol and Tobacco Tax Division, which would enforce.

Law Enforcement Officers Protection Act (Public Law 99-408): A law that bans the possession, manufacture, and import of bullets that can penetrate bulletproof clothing, also known as "cop killer" bullets (with

minor exceptions). If someone is found in possession of armor-piercing
ammunition during the commission of a violent crime, there is an
additional mandatory sentence of no less than 5 years imposed.

***McDonald v. City of Chicago*, 561 US 742 (2010):** After *District of
Columbia v. Heller*, there was uncertainty regarding the scope of gun
rights as they applied to the states. While the *Heller* case reasoned that
the Second Amendment was applicable since the original Chicago
firearm ban was enacted under the authority of the federal government,
the *McDonald* case argued that the Second Amendment should also
apply to state and local governments. Essentially, the US Supreme Court
ruled that the Fourteenth Amendment included the Second Amendment
and applied it to the states, thereby finding Chicago's firearm ban to be
unconstitutional. Thus, the individual rights perspective (the individual
right to possess and use firearms for lawful purposes is a fundamental
American right) is the prevailing view at this time, at least in the higher
courts.

NICS Improvement Act of 2007: This act set to revise the National Instant
Criminal Background Check System (NICS) after the Virginia Tech
shootings. The law's intention was to address loopholes that allowed the
Virginia Tech shooter, Seung-Hui Cho, to buy firearms even though
he was previously deemed a danger to himself by a Virginia court.
However, because the Commonwealth of Virginia had not submitted
his disqualifying mental health adjudication to the NICS (which was all
too common across the country), Seung-Hui Cho was able to complete
the sale. The law enhanced the requirements that federal departments
and agencies provide relevant information to the NICS, through
implementation assistance to states and penalties for noncompliance,
among other things.

***Presser v. Illinois*, 116 US 252 (1886):** In 1886, Herman Presser was part of
an armed citizen militia group of over 400 German workers associated
with the Socialist Labor Party who was subsequently charged with
parading in the streets of Chicago on horseback and the like. They had
no license to do so, nor were they a recognized organization permitted
to engage in such by the government. Presser claimed that his Second
Amendment rights were violated, but the US Supreme Court held that
forbidding armed bodies of people to gather, drill or parade did not
violate an individual right to keep and bear arms.

***Printz v. United States*, 521 US 898 (1997):** The Brady Act required state
and local law enforcement officials to conduct background checks on
a temporary basis (until the national background check system was
computerized). According to this law, Congress cannot compel state
or local governments to implement or administer federal regulatory
programs under Tenth Amendment protections.

***Redford v. US Dept. of Treasury, Bur. of Alcohol, Tobacco and Firearms*,
691 F.2d 471 (1982):** A man challenged the seizure of his arsenal of

firearms due to a previous not guilty by reason of insanity (NGRI) determination, stating that the statutory prohibition against possession of firearms by individuals adjudicated as mentally incompetent was sufficiently vague (and perhaps would not include a finding of NGRI). But the court upheld the seizure, citing the belief that people of common intelligence would recognize that individuals found NGRI for a criminal charge would fall under the same category as those deemed mentally incompetent.

Tyler v. Hillsdale County Sheriff's Department, 775 F.3d 308 (2014): Twenty-eight years before this case, Tyler had been involuntarily hospitalized due to suicide risk following an especially difficult divorce. Many years later, he wanted to own a gun and argued that he was not mentally ill and, thus, should not be precluded from owning a firearm. Congress had previously created a program that would allow individuals who were otherwise restricted from owning firearms to seek relief so that they may regain their firearm rights. Tyler's state (Michigan) did not have a relief program in place; thus, he was unable to regain his Second Amendment right. The court held that Tyler should be able to exercise the right to bear arms in any state he chooses to live, regardless of whether the state has chosen to accept federal grant money to fund a relief program. The court further stated that Congress designed the law to enforce prohibitions only during periods in which the person is deemed dangerous, which does not necessarily equal a lifelong prohibition. Ultimately, the court did not order that Tyler's rights be restored immediately but provided him with the opportunity to prove that he had regained mental stability and that his mental illness did not pose a risk to himself or others.

United States v. Cruikshank, 92 US 542 (1875): This was the first case in which the U.D. Supreme Court interpreted the Second Amendment. In 1873, an armed White militia attacked and killed over 100 African American Republican freedman who gathered at a Colfax, Louisiana courthouse to prevent a Democratic takeover. Some of the White mob members were charged under the Eforcement Act of 1870 and part of the indictment suggested a conspiracy to prevent Blacks from exercising their civil rights, including bearing arms lawfully. The Court ultimately held that the Second Amendment only ensures that Congress will not infringe upon the right of gun ownership – it does not specifically set forth a right to own guns. Moreover, the Court cited that the Fourteenth Amendment protected individuals from the state and not from other individuals per se (i.e., the State Action Doctrine).

United States v. Miller, 307 US 174 (1939): This is a unique case wherein the US Supreme Court had the opportunity to apply the Second Amendment to a federal firearms statute. Namely, this involved a criminal prosecution under the National Firearms Act of 1934, which passed subsequent to the St. Valentine's Day Massacre. The Act, in part, banned fully automatic guns and short-barreled rifles and shotguns. In this case, Miller challenged certain aspects of Act as a violation of his Second Amendment rights, but the US Supreme Court ultimately held that banning a shotgun having a barrel less than 18 inches was not because it did not have any relation to a well-regulated militia or ordinary military equipment. Therefore, the Second Amendment would not guarantee a civilian's right to keep and bear such a firearm.

United States v. Portillo-Munoz, **643 F.3d 437 (5th Cir. 2011):** Portillo-Munoz, an undocumented immigrant, was arrested after he was found in possession of a handgun, which he stated was to protect chickens from coyotes on the ranch where he was employed. He was convicted of unlawfully possessing a weapon and sentenced to 10 months in prison. He appealed, and a Fifth Circuit panel held that the Second Amendment does not provide undocumented immigrants currently in the United States the individual right to bear arms. The panel noted that these undocumented immigrants are not among "the people" referred to in the Second Amendment.

United States v. Rehlander, **666 F.3d 45 (1st Cir. 2012):** A court case where Rehlander argued that a temporary hospitalization under an ex parte proceeding should not disqualify him from purchasing or possessing firearms under *Heller* as an ex parte proceeding does not qualify as a commitment for federal purposes. The court ultimately concluded that *Heller* did not apply to a temporary hospitalization, although this might be a different case if the Gun Control Act provided for a *temporary* prohibition from possessing firearms.

US v. Chamberlain, **159 F.3d 656 (1st Cir. 1998):** The court found that while a 5-day emergency detention is considered a "commitment" because it implies the potential for harm to self or others, it realized that there is a possibility of someone being mistakenly committed in such a fashion under other circumstances. The court noted that there are procedures in place that would allow an individual to seek relief from the firearms ban.

US v. Dorsch, **363 F.3d 784 (2004):** Dorsch was indicted after having been found in possession of firearms following an involuntary commitment to a psychiatric center. Dorsch argued that his commitment did not meet the statutory criteria according to the Gun Control Act, stating that his commitment was for observation only and not treatment. As such, he argued that the results of his case should be similar to the results of *US v. Hansel*. The court found that since Dorsch had the opportunity to appeal his commitment (and raise his inability to possess a firearm according to the Gun Control Act) but did not take advantage of the opportunity, his due process rights were not violated.

US v. Giardina, **861 F.2d 1334 (5th Cir. 1988):** Giardina was committed to a hospital in New Orleans for 2 weeks of treatment following the issuance of a physician's emergency certificate and a coroner's emergency certificate. After his release, he required no further treatment. Upon procuring two firearms, he signed federal paperwork stating he had never been committed to a mental institution (as he believed this particular hospital did not count as a mental institution). He was consequently indicted on two counts of receiving and possessing a firearm after having been committed to a mental institution. The Fifth Circuit Court of Appeals held that admission by emergency certificate did not constitute a commitment for the purposes of the Gun Control Act, stating that "[t]emporary, emergency detentions for treatment of mental disorders or difficulties, which do not lead to formal commitments under state law, do not constitute the commitment envisioned" (ref. 17, p. 1337).

US v. Hansel, **474 F.2d 1120 (8th Cir.1973):** Hansel was involuntarily committed for formal observation but not by judicial or administrative proceedings. In fact, after receiving a firearm following being committed to a mental institution and subsequently being convicted of two counts of violating the Gun Control Act of 1968, the examining physician testified at trial that Hansel did not have a serious mental illness, nor in need of hospitalization. Therefore, the appeals court found that Hansel was not committed for the purposes of the Gun Control Act. As such, the Gun Control Act's firearm restrictions would not apply to him.

US v. Waters, **23 F.3d 29, 30 (2d Cir. 1994):** Waters was indicted by a federal grand jury for illegally possessing a firearm following his commitment to a mental institution. Waters moved to dismiss the indictment on the grounds that there was no formal judicial order of commitment to the psychiatric hospital, especially as the federal gun control statute had not defined the term *commitment*. His motion was rejected by the court, which stated that Waters' commitment to the hospital (under New York State law) was sufficient under federal policy. This case set the precedent that while the question of whether an admission constitutes a commitment to a mental institution is a matter of federal law, the court reviewing such cases may seek guidance from state laws.

Violent Crime Control and Law Enforcement Act of 1994: A law that banned the manufacture of 19 military-style assault weapons, as well as certain high-capacity ammunition magazines. The law also established a firearm prohibition for individuals subject to family violence restraining orders and strengthened licensing standards for firearms dealers. Finally, the law created new crimes or penalties for drive-by shootings and the use of semiautomatic weapons.

Wollschlaeger v. Farmer, **814 F.Supp.2d 1367, 1384 (S.D.Fla.2011):** The petitioners argued that various provisions of the Firearm Owners Privacy Act, which barred physicians both from asking questions related to firearm possession and ownership and from entering related information into patients' medical records, violate the First and

Fourteenth Amendments of the US Constitution. In this matter, the plaintiffs stated that the act violated the First Amendment by preventing open communication with their patients about ways to reduce the safety risks posed by firearms. The court, in this case, issued a *preliminary* injunction against the provisions of the act, stating that they violated the First Amendment right of free speech.

***Wollschlaeger v. Farmer*, 880 F.Supp.2d 1251, 1267–69 (S.D.Fla. 2012):**
The court issued a *permanent* injunction against the provisions of the Firearm Owners Privacy Act (i.e., inquiry, record-keeping, discrimination, harassment) due to infringement upon doctors' free speech rights according to the First Amendment.

***Wollschlaeger v. Governor of Florida*, 760 F.3d 1195 (11th Cir. 2014):**
Dr. Wollschlaeger, other medical professionals, and various Florida chapters of medical organizations sued the governor of Florida and the state (officials) for setting forth the Firearm Owners Privacy Act. The Eleventh Circuit vacated the injunction and upheld the Firearm Owners Privacy Act, which banned medical doctors from asking their patients questions about firearm ownership. According to the court, because the law only restricts speech uttered in doctors' examination rooms, it is exempt from First Amendment scrutiny, which otherwise allows freedom of speech.

Notes

Frontmatter

1. "The Mice called a meeting and developed a plan to hang a bell around the Cat's neck, so they would be alerted when he approached. After much celebrating about this novel plan, an old Mouse praised the idea, but asked, 'Who will bell the Cat?'" (see Paxton, T., & Rayevsky, R. [1990]. *Belling the cat and other Aesop's fables*. New York: Morrow Junior).
2. Franke-Ruta, G. (2013, June 30). Justice Kagan and Justice Scalia are hunting buddies—Really. *The Atlantic*. Retrieved from www.theatlantic.com/politics/archive/2013/06/justice-kagan-and-justice-scalia-are-hunting-buddies-really/277401/.
3. See The incredible shrinking sound bite. (2011, January 5). NPR. Retrieved from www.npr.org/2011/01/05/132671410/Congressional-Sound-Bites; and Lee, K. (2014, October 21). Infographic: The optimal length for every social media update and more. Retrieved from https://blog.bufferapp.com/optimal-length-social-media, respectively.
4. Centers for Disease Control and Prevention. (2013). *WISQARS Leading Causes of Death Reports, 1999–2010*. Atlanta: National Center for Injury Prevention and Control.
5. Dahlberg, L., Ikeda, R., & Kresnow, M. (2004). Guns in the home and risk of a violent death in the home: Findings from a national study. *American Journal of Epidemiology, 160*(10), 929–936.
6. American Psychological Association. (2013). *Gun violence: Prediction, prevention, and policy*. Retrieved from www.apa.org/pubs/info/reports/gun-violence-prevention.aspx.

7. Barry, C. L., McGinty, E. E., Vernick, J. S., & Webster, D. W. (2013). After Newton—Public opinion on gun policy and mental illness. *New England Journal of Medicine, 368,* 1077–1081.

8. Jenson, J. M. (2007). Aggression and violence in the United States: Reflections on the Virginia Tech shootings. *Social Work Research, 31*(3), 131–134.

9. Pirelli, G., Wechsler, H., & Cramer, R. (2015). Conducting forensic mental health assessments for firearm ownership. *Professional Psychology: Research and Practice, 46*(4), 250–257; Pirelli, G., & Witt, P. (2015). Psychological evaluations for civilian firearm ownership in New Jersey. *New Jersey Psychologist, 65*(1), 7–9; Pirelli, G., & Witt, P. H. (2017). Firearms and cultural competence: Considerations for mental health practitioners. *Journal of Aggression, Conflict and Peace Research.* Retrieved from https://doi.org/ 10.1108/JACPR-01-2017-0268; Wechsler, H., Pirelli, G., Struble, C., & Cramer, R. (2015, August). Firearm ownership evaluations: A local norms perspective. Poster presented at the annual convention of the American Psychological Association, Toronto, Canada; Wechsler, H., Pirelli, G., & Cramer, R. (2014, May). Conducting forensic mental health assessments for firearm ownership. Poster presented at the 26th Annual Convention of the Association for Psychological Science, San Francisco, California.

Chapter 2

1. According to a post titled, The New D.A.R.E. Program—This One Works, from the www.dare.org website and published in *Scientific American*: "If you were one of millions of children who completed the Drug Abuse Resistance Education program, or D.A.R.E., between 1983 and 2009, you may be surprised to learn that scientists have repeatedly shown that the program did not work. Despite being the nation's most popular substance-abuse prevention program, D.A.R.E. did not make you less likely to become a drug addict or even to refuse that first beer from your friends. But over the past few years prevention scientists have helped D.A.R.E. America, the nonprofit organization that administers the program, replace the old curriculum with a course based on a few concepts that should make the training more effective for today's students. The new course, called keepin' it REAL, differs in both form and content from the former D.A.R.E." (Nordrum, 2014).

2. In January 2011, Assistant Attorney General of the Office of Justice Programs Laurie O. Robinson and Acting Administrator Jeff Slowikowski published an op-ed in the *Baltimore Sun* titled "Scary—and Ineffective: Traumatizing At-Risk Kids Is Not the Way to Lead Them Away from Crime and Drugs" (www. ncjrs.gov/html/ojjdp/news_at_glance/234084/op-ed.html). Per Robinson and Slowikowski, Scared Straight "is not only ineffective but is potentially harmful. And it may run counter to the law. . . . The fact that these programs are still being touted as effective, despite stark evidence to the contrary, is troubling. . . . In light of this evidence, the U.S. Department of Justice discourages the funding of scared straight–type programs. States that operate such programs could have their federal funding reduced if shown not to have complied with the Juvenile Justice and Delinquency Protection Act. . . . It is understandable why desperate parents hoping to divert their troubled children from further

misbehavior would place their hopes in a program they see touted as effective on TV, and why in years past policymakers opted to fund what appeared to be an easy fix for juvenile offending. However, we have a responsibility—as both policymakers and parents—to follow evidence, not anecdote, in finding answers, especially when it comes to our children" (see also, Office of Juvenile Justice and Delinquency Prevention: "Justice Department discourages the use of "Scared Straight" programs," www.ncjrs.gov/html/ojjdp/news_at_glance/234084/topstory.html).

3. The *Slaughter-House Cases* allowed for the first interpretation of the Fourteenth Amendment set forth by the Supreme Court. It held to a narrow interpretation of the Fourteenth Amendment, specifically that it protected the privileges or immunities of US citizens and did not affect rights based on state citizenship. Essentially, the decision made in these cases asserted that the Fourteenth Amendment only protected specifically federal rights.

4. Of further note is that a recent mass shooting at Fort Lauderdale Airport in early January 2017 perpetrated by Esteban Santiago led some Florida lawmakers to allow licensed gun owners with concealed carry permits to bring their firearms to the unsecured areas of their state's airports (Walsh, 2017).

5. Coincidentally, New Jersey has a law known as the Graves Act (N.J.S.A. 43-6[c]), but it was adopted in 1981 and named after the former mayor of Paterson and state senator Frank X. Graves, Jr. The act provides the mandatory minimum sentence (i.e., 3 years) and parole ineligibility for anyone found guilty of using a firearm in the commission of a crime. Certainly, the intention of the law was to target habitual criminals, gangs, and other common perpetrators of firearm-related crimes; but the law is very far-reaching and has been applied to people who have absolutely no criminal history or intent to harm with a firearm as it includes all illegal firearms, including air guns and BB guns, as well as the mere presence of a firearm in domestic disputes, for example.

6. As this book was being written, on October 13, 2016, New Jersey Senator Ronald L. Rice sponsored a bill that would require a firearms purchaser identification card, a permit to purchase a handgun, or a permit to carry a handgun for temporary transfer of a firearm at a firing range (see also New Jersey Bills A4179/S2666 and A4180/S2667). In the bill's closing statement, it reads in part, "this bill is in response to the recent fatal shootings that have occurred at New Jersey firing ranges." It is intended to prevent suicide and injury to others, including "emotional trauma," and is inherently reliant on background checks.

7. Storage- and access-related initiatives continue to be addressed throughout the country, for example, the California Wellness Foundation's Violence Prevention Initiative, a 10-year program geared toward reducing violence among the state's youth by limiting the availability of handguns to and increasing state resources for them (Wallack, Winett, & Lee, 2005).

8. Federal Firearms Prohibition Under 18 U.S.C. § 922(g)(4), revised May 2009, retrieved from www.atf.gov/file/58791/download.

9. We discuss cultural competence in greater depth in Chapters 7 and 8 of this book in the context of mental health evaluation and treatment.

10. Kopel and colleagues also set forth the idea that armed citizens would have fared better in protecting themselves in many regions throughout the

world in the past, such as Jewish people during the Nazi Holocaust—a view consistent with others, such as the Jews for the Preservation of Firearm Ownership, discussed in Chapter 1. For instance, Kopel and colleagues opined that citizens in Rwanda would have fared better during the genocide if they had been armed. They also believe that suicide rates would likely not decrease (given previous research on method substitution) if civilians were disarmed. The interested reader may also refer to Kopel, Mody, & Nemerov (2008), wherein they also contended that increased civilian firearm ownership has been associated with less corruption, more economic freedom, and more economic success. Nevertheless, they acknowledge the complex relationship that exists between guns and freedom (e.g., guns cause freedom, freedom causes guns, guns reduce freedom, freedom reduces guns) and suggest that there might be particular countries where reducing civilian firearm ownership might enhance freedom but maintain that "the data raise serious doubts about whether the gun-reducing agenda makes sense as a categorical imperative, at least if freedom ranks highly in one's hierarchy of values" (p. 31).

11. Salnikova (2013) addressed a topic one would be hard-pressed to find throughout the firearm literature: the potential right to bear arms of undocumented immigrants, also referred to as "illegal aliens." Salnikova noted that "the people" reference in the Second Amendment does not seem to include undocumented immigrants in *Heller*'s definition of "the people" (i.e., all members of the political community who are law-abiding, responsible citizens). Moreover, in *United States v. Portillo-Munoz* (2012), a Fifth Circuit panel held that the Second Amendment does not provide illegal aliens currently in the United States the individual right to bear arms. As such, Salnikova contended that this could mean that they are also excluded from all other Bill of Rights guarantees. Nevertheless, the interested reader should review this article as it includes a detailed account of *Portillo-Munoz* as well as a review of other cases that have been heard throughout the United States related to undocumented immigrants' possession of firearms. On page 673, she writes, "The aftermath of Portillo-Munoz has been nothing short of confounding, with some courts and thinkers accepting the decision without question as an accurate application of Heller, and others limiting its reach or entirely questioning its reasoning and/or ultimate conclusion."

Chapter 3

1. Unless otherwise indicated, the source for this section is the DSM-5.

Chapter 4

1. Please note that we focus on interpersonal violence in this chapter and not acts of terrorism or violent acts toward animals or property as each has its own set of considerations and literature base. We also cover domestic and intimate partner violence in Chapter 5 and suicide (i.e., self-directed violence) in Chapter 6.

2. We take the term *blood pressure* for granted today, but it is worth a brief look back to illustrate the point. The measurement of the pressure of the blood in the circulatory system, or *sphygmomanometry*, has its roots in the Egyptians' recognition of the palpitation of the pulse; however, the actual measurement of circulatory pressure began in the early to mid-18th century with the experiments of Stephen Hales (Booth, 1977). Incidentally, Hales' scientific research was first on tree and vegetable sap but progressed to the circulatory pressure in horses in 1733. His work was not extended until approximately one century later when the physician-physicist Jean Léonard Marie Poiseuille began studying the cardiovascular system with a mercury manometer in 1828, at which point he won the gold medal from the Royal Academy of Medicine for his doctoral dissertation on the instrument's use in measuring arterial blood pressure. Various innovations and advancements followed until the first sphygmomanometer was developed by Karl Vierordt in the 1850s. Of course, the instrument was cumbersome and invasive and not without significant criticism in the medical field; in fact, it was admonished by the *British Medical Journal* as an instrument that would actually *weaken* clinical accuracy. It was not until 1896 that an Italian medical doctor named Scipione Riva-Rocci developed the method upon which the present-day technique is based— namely, the compression of the arm around its full circumference to include a rubber bag, a cuff, a rubber bulb for inflation, and the traditional use of the mercury manometer. The most notable advancements came in the early 1900s from the Russian surgeon, N. C. Korotkoff, such as the use of a stethoscope over the brachial artery and other ways in which he ensured the accuracy and ease of measuring blood pressure that have essentially remained unchanged for the past century (Booth, 1977). Although seemingly tangential, it is important to acknowledge that the development of what is now considered a basic and routine medical measurement was met with fairly harsh criticism at the onset and ultimately took 175 years to perfect. This realization certainly puts social science constructs, such as violence, into perspective.

3. Some criminologists and other scholars and researchers have used an even lower number, such as two deaths, thereby changing the statistics even further (e.g., see Agnich, 2015).

4. Please note that hate-/bias-driven violence is a particularly important area of consideration as well, and it may be carried out via physical, sexual, and verbal means.

5. Incidentally, this is comparable to the shootings on Mother's Day weekend in Chicago in 2016, whereby 43 people were wounded and nine were killed as a result of gang violence (Huston, 2016).

6. Given the nature of this incident, Cho is briefly discussed again in Chapter 6 in the context of high-profile murder–suicides.

Chapter 5

1. Research studies pertaining to DV utilize similar definitions and often rely on empirical measures of violent behaviors to further investigate these types of violence. The Revised Conflict Tactics Scales–2 (CTS2; Straus, Hamby, Boney-McCoy, & Sugarman, 1996) is one of the leading self-report behavioral

checklists of dating violence and IPV (Cascardi & Muzyczyn, 2016). The CTS2 items measure verbal and passive aggressiveness, as well as physically aggressive behaviors, such as pushing, shoving, slapping, hitting, punching, licking, and throwing objects at an intimate partner.

2. This finding is also consistent with New Jersey's statistics. Namely, 99.8% of the approximately 62,000 DV incidents that occur in New Jersey annually do not involve a firearm. Per the 2015 state police report, 54% involved no weapon at all; 42% involved "hands, fists, etc."; 2.4% involved "other" weapons; 1.4% involved knives; and 0.2% involved firearms (New Jersey State Police, 2015).

3. National Domestic Violence Awareness Month evolved from the "Day of Unity" held in October 1981, set forth by the National Coalition Against Domestic Violence (see www.ncadv.org).

Chapter 7

1. We discuss means restriction counseling in Chapters 6 and 8, but this is limited for multiple reasons, including medical and mental health professionals' overall lack of firearm-specific education and training (see findings 21 and 26 in Chapter 9).

2. The interested reader is referred to the American Psychological Association's new and extensive database of psychological measures, scales, surveys, and related instruments, PsycTESTS', which now includes over 45,000 records (www.apa.org/pubs/databases/psyctests/index.aspx). According to the site, 76% of records include the actual test or test items.

3. The interested reader is directed to Ogloff (2000) for a comprehensive overview of the development of the field of forensic psychology.

4. Please note that relief-from-disability evaluations have been discussed in this context by leading scholars, and they are presented in a very comprehensive, empirically based manner (see Gold & Vanderpool, 2016). However, they do not include the firearm-specific arenas we believe are essential to incorporate into these evaluations.

5. It is also the case that people present with various mental health histories that have no particular connection with firearm-related issues per se (e.g., phobias, sexual dysfunctions, eating problems) or who are flagged for other unrelated prohibitors. This is true for certain criminal offense histories, such as those consisting of various types of misdemeanors (e.g., shoplifting) as well as even more serious charges (e.g., certain types of sexual offenses). These histories may be related to firearm concerns, but the point here is that they are unlikely to relate directly; therefore, a hyperfocus on the fact that someone has a mental health or criminal history alone is not dispositive of a firearm-related concern. Again, context is critical (e.g., see also Appelbaum, 2017).

6. New Jersey Assembly Bill 2938 (2016) sought to require firearms seizure when a mental health professional determines a patient poses threat of harm to self or others. Specifically:

If a licensed practitioner of psychology, psychiatry, medicine, nursing, clinical social work, or marriage counseling who currently is providing treatment services determines, in the exercise of reasonable professional judgment, that the patient is likely to engage in conduct that would result in serious harm to self or others, the licensee shall report, as soon as practicable to the Attorney General the patient's name and other non-clinical identifying information which the Attorney General shall only use to determine whether the patient has been issued a firearms purchaser identification card, permit to purchase a handgun, or any other permit or license authorizing possession of a firearm. If the patient has been issued a card or permit, the Attorney General shall arrange for any firearm possessed by the patient to be seized pending a hearing. The Attorney General shall issue guidelines governing the seizure of firearms pursuant to this subsection.

7. The interested reader is directed to the entire issue of the *International Journal of Emergency Mental Health*, volume 13, number 3, which can be accessed at: www.omicsonline.org/open-access/health-disparities-in-police-officers-comparisons-to-the-us-general-populations.pdf.

Chapter 8

1. Conversion or so-called reparative therapies are other examples of the dangers of applying "therapies" in the absence of data, and these have been denounced by leading organizations, such as the APA (see Cramer, Golom, LoPresto, & Kirkley, 2008, for a review).

2. A pattern has arisen historically (and metaphorically) in this regard. Namely, Descartes believed the brain was akin to a hydraulic pump, propelling the spirits of the nervous system through the body, whereas Freud compared the brain to a steam engine (Marcus, 2015).

3. *Parasuicidal behavior* is often defined as intentional, acute, self-injurious behavior with or without suicidal intent, including suicide attempts and acts of self-mutilation.

4. Dr. Marsha Linehan's company, Behavioral Tech, LLC, provides training and consultation to mental health care providers and treatment teams who work with complex patients and populations (www.behavioraltech.org).

5. Kübler-Ross' model was not empirically derived, and it was debunked rather quickly by Schulz & Aderman (1974) as they found no empirical support for the notion that patients near death pass through five psychological stages in a predictable order. To the contrary, they found that the process of dying seemed to be less rigid and even stageless. Supporters of Kübler-Ross' model subsequently contended that it was never intended to be taken literally, nor was it posited that every person experienced all stages, never mind in a stepwise fashion.

6. See Baumeister & Leary's (1995) article, "The Need to Belong: Desire for Interpersonal Attachments as a Fundamental Human Motivation."

7. Such paradoxical effects are not uncommon in response to prohibitive or tightened regulations. Perhaps the most salient example is that of the (alcohol) Prohibition era in the United States (1920–1933). In the context of firearms, however, we have noted the *doubling* of National Instant Criminal Background Check System (NICS) checks in New Jersey during President

Obama's tenure; namely, from 60,256 in 2011 to 120,071 in 2013 (Pirelli & Witt, 2015).

8. As we have emphasized in numerous places in this book, assessment and treatment are not necessarily distinct areas of practice. In some cases, evaluations are conducted separate and apart from therapeutic interventions (see Chapter 7); however, in all cases, *assessment*—more broadly defined— is an inherent, inextricably linked, and ongoing aspect of all therapeutic endeavors.

Chapter 9

1. The concept of the worthy victim can also be seen in death penalty sentencing, such that the racial disparity in who ultimately is sentenced to death is not primarily seen in the perpetrators per se but rather in the race of the victims (e.g., see Kleck, 1981; Klein & Rolph, 1991; Paternoster, 1984; Zeisel, 1981).

2. These findings are reminiscent of our earlier research on psychologists' participation in death penalty cases, such that even half of them who self-reported *not* having enough experience or training to participate in such matters indicated that they would engage in them anyhow and even notably higher rates of those who were *unsure* about their professional competence in that regard would still participate (Pirelli & Zapf, 2008).

3. One such company is GunSitters' (www.gunsitters.com). This company also maintains a nonprofit affiliate organization called Weapons Guard, which provides free firearm storage to members of the armed forces for a wide range of reasons (e.g., deployment, change of duty station, vacation, safety concerns, legal issues, divorce; see www.gunsitters.com/military-members.html).

References

Chapter 1

American Firearms Institute. (n.d.). Important dates in gun history. Retrieved from www.americanfirearms.org/gun-history/

Armed Citizens United. (n.d.). Retrieved from https://armedcitizensunited.com

Bateman v. Perdue, 881 F. Supp. 2d 709 (2012).

Barry, C. L., McGinty, E. E., Vernick, J. S., & Webster, D. W. (2015). Two years after Newtown: Public opinion on gun policy revisited. *Preventive Medicine, 79,* 55–58. doi:10.1016/j.ypmed.2015.05.007

Burke, A. (2015, March 12). Girls with guns: 8 celebrity women who exercise their Second Amendment rights. Newsmax. Retrieved from www.newsmax.com/FastFeatures/Girls-with-guns-Celebrity-Women-Second-Amendment/2015/03/12/id/629845

Burke, P. (2013, February 4). U.S. gun owners outnumbered hunters by 5 to 1 in 2011. CBS News. Retrieved from http://cnsnews.com/news/article/us-gun-owners-outnumbered-hunters-5-1-2011

Carroll, J. (2005, November 22). Gun ownership and use in America. Gallup. Retrieved from www.gallup.com/poll/20098/gun-ownership-use-america.aspx,%202005

Celebrities with gun licenses. (n.d.). Huffington Post. Retrieved from www.huffingtonpost.com/2012/05/31/celebrity-gun-owners-license_n_1557203.html?slideshow=true#gallery/229612/13

Ciyou, B. L. (2017). *2017 edition: Gun laws by state. Reciprocity and gun laws quick reference guide.* Indianapolis, IN: Peritus Holdings.

Confirmation bias. (n.d.). Science Daily. Retrieved from https://www.sciencedaily.com/terms/confirmation_bias.htm

Corporation for the Promotion of Rifle Practice and Firearms Safety, Title 36 U. S. C. §§ 40701-40733 (1996).

Denno, D. (2015, April 28). Kill lethal injection and bring back the firing squad. *Time*. Retrieved from http://time.com/3831515/execution-lethal-injection-supreme-court

Descriptions of execution methods. (n.d.). Death Penalty Information Center. Retrieved from www.deathpenaltyinfo.org/descriptions-execution-methods

District of Columbia v. Heller, 554 U.S. 570 (2008).

Eddie Eagle GunSafe Program. (n.d.). NRA. Retrieved from https://eddieeagle.nra.org

End the gun epidemic in America. (2015, December 4). *New York Times*. Retrieved from www.nytimes.com/2015/12/05/opinion/end-the-gun-epidemic-in-america.html?_r=0

Ezell v. City of Chicago, 651 F. 3d 684 (2011).

Firing squad. (n.d.). Crime Museum. Retrieved from www.crimemuseum.org/crime-library/firing-squad

For some British bobbies, a gun comes with job. (2009, October 23). NBC News. Retrieved from www.nbcnews.com/id/33448132/ns/world_news-europe/t/some-british-bobbies-gun-comes-job/#.Vu0-V9BhCQw

Furman v. Georgia, 408 U.S. 238 (1972).

Giffords Law Center to Prevent Gun Violence. (n.d.). Background check procedures. Retrieved from http://smartgunlaws.org/background-check-procedures-policy-summary

Gregg v. Georgia, 428 U.S. 153 (1976).

Guns 101. (n.d.). The firearms guide. Retrieved from www.thefirearms.guide/guns/guns-101

Hawkins, A. (2016, June 15). Ronald Reagan "carried his own gun" while president. Breitbart. Retrieved from www.breitbart.com/big-government/2015/06/15/ronald-reagan-carried-his-own-gun-while-president

Hollywood and guns: Weapons still prevalent in pop culture. (2013, June 24). Huffington Post. Retrieved from www.huffingtonpost.com/2013/06/24/hollywood-guns-weapons-revalent-pop-culture_n_3489996.html

Hunting. (n.d.). Retrieved from https://www.dec.ny.gov/outdoor/hunting.html

Jones, E. (2015, March 12). Firing squad bill fails. Wyoming Public Media. Retrieved from http://wyomingpublicmedia.org/post/fring-squad-bill-fails

Kappas, J. S. (2017). *2017 Traveler's guide to the firearm laws of the fifty states.* Covington, KY: Traveler's Guide.

Kelly, J. (2014, August 6). The British police on armed routine patrol. BBC News. Retrieved from www.bbc.com/news/magazine-28656324

Kleck, G. (2004). Measures of gun ownership levels for macro-level crime and violence research. *Journal of Research in Crime and Delinquency, 41*(1), 3–36. doi:10.1177/0022427803256229

Kleck, G. (2015). The impact of gun ownership rates on crime rates: A methodological review of the evidence. *Journal of Criminal Justice, 43*(1), 40–48. doi:10.1016/j.jcrimjus.2014.12.002

Kovandzic, T., Schaffer, M. E., & Kleck, G. (2013). Estimating the causal effect of gun prevalence on homicide rates: A local average treatment effect approach. *Journal of Quantitative Criminology, 29*(4), 477–541. doi:10.1007/s10940-012-9185-7

Largest caliber rifle ever: SSK .950 JDJ rounds are stronger than ten .30 rifles. (2013, August 2). *International Science Times*. Retrieved from www.isciencetimes.com/articles/5786/20130802/largest-caliber-rifle-ssk-950-jdj-rounds.htm

Longley, R. (2016, June 15). See a timeline of gun control in the United States. Retrieved from http://usgovinfo.about.com/od/rightsandfreedoms/fl/US-Gun-Control-Timeline.htm

Luciano, J. (2015). *Guns the right way: Introducing kids to firearm safety and shooting*. Iola, WI: Gun Digest Books.

McDonald v. Chicago, 561 U.S. 742 (2010).

McGinty, E. E., Webster, D. W., & Barry, C. L. (2013). Effects of news media messages about mass shootings on attitudes toward persons with serious mental illness and public support for gun control policies. *American Journal of Psychiatry, 170*(5), 494–501. doi:10.1176/appi.ajp.2013.13010014

McLeigh, J. D. (2015). The new normal? Addressing gun violence in America. *American Journal of Orthopsychiatry, 85*(3), 201–202. doi:10.1037/ort0000072

McNab, C. (2009). *Guns: A visual history*. New York: DK Publishing.

Mears, B. (2013, July 2). Kagan hunts with buddy Scalia, bags deer. CNN. Retrieved from www.cnn.com/2013/07/02/politics/kagan-deer-hunting

Moore v. Madigan, 702 F. 3d 933 (2012).

Morris, R. (2014, May 16). Will firing squads make a comeback in the US? BBC News. Retrieved from www.bbc.com/news/magazine-27303555

Mother's Dream Quilt Project. (n.d.). Retrieved from http://mothersdreamquilt.org

National Physicians Alliance. (n.d.). Retrieved from http://npalliance.org/

National Shooting Sports Foundation. (n.d.). Firearms safety—10 rules of safe gun handling. Retrieved from https://www.nssf.org/safety/rules-firearms-safety/

Noack, R. (2016, July 8). 5 Countries where most police officers do not carry firearms—and it works well. *Washington Post*. Retrieved from www.washingtonpost.com/news/worldviews/wp/2015/02/18/5-countries-where-police-officers-do-not-carry-firearms-and-it-works-well

NRA gun safety rules. (n.d.). Retrieved from http://training.nra.org/nra-gun-safety-rules.aspx

NRA trigger the vote. (n.d.). Retrieved from www.triggerthevote.org

Palm Pistol. (n.d.). Retrieved from http://constitutionarms.com/palm-pistol/

Perrin, P. B. (2016). Translating psychological science: Highlighting the media's contribution to contagion in mass shootings: Comment on Kaslow (2015). *American Psychologist, 71*(1), 71–72. doi:10.1037/a0039994

Pickhartz, E. (2016, June 27). These 10 U.S. presidents were packing heat. Wide Open Spaces. Retrieved from http://www.wideopenspaces.com/10-american-presidents-packing-heat-2/

Project ChildSafe. (n.d.). Retrieved from www.projectchildsafe.org

Richinick, M. (2015). Snoop Dogg asks fans to "unload" from guns. MSNBC. Retrieved from www.msnbc.com/msnbc/snoop-dogg-asks-fans-unload-guns

Rifle (n.d.). NCAA. Retrieved from www.ncaa.com/sports/rifle

Rowe-Finkbeiner, K. (2015, December 3). "Our hearts are breaking and we are more determined than ever to see common sense gun laws." MomsRising.org. Retrieved from https://www.momsrising.org/blog/%E2%80%9Cour-hearts-are-breaking-and-we-are-more-determined-than-ever-to-see-common-sense-gun-laws%E2%80%9D

Second Amendment. (n.d.). Cornell Law School. Retrieved from www.law.cornell.edu/wex/second_amendment

See a shrink, lose your guns! (2014, January 13). Gun Owners of America. Retrieved from www.gunowners.org/congress1132014.htm

Shea, M. (2017, July 25). Presidents' guns: Firearms and the commander-in-chief. *Outdoor Life*. Retrieved from www.outdoorlife.com/photos/gallery/guns/2013/02/presidents-guns-firearms-and-commander-chief/?image=12

Sonmez, F. (2013, January 28). Obama: "At Camp David, we do skeet shooting all the time." *Washington Post*. Retrieved from https://www.washingtonpost.com/news/post-politics/wp/2013/01/28/obama-at-camp-david-we-do-skeet-shooting-all-the-time

Supica, J. (n.d.). A brief history of firearms. NRA. Retrieved from www.nramuseum.com/gun-info- research/a-brief-history-of-firearms.aspx

Supica, J., Wicklund, D., & Schreier, P. (2011). *The illustrated history of firearms: In association with the national firearms museum.* New York: Chartwell Books.

The campaign to keep guns off campus. (n.d.). Retrieved from http://keepgunsoffcampus.org/

The genocide chart. (2002). Jews for the Preservation of Firearms Ownership. Retrieved from http://jpfo.org/filegen-a-m/deathgc.htm#chart

The history of firearms in law enforcement. (2016, February 26). Gun Vault. Retrieved from www.gunvault.com/blog/the-history-of-firearms-in-law-enforcement

Theodore Roosevelt biography in brief. (n.d.) Retrieved from www.theodorerooseveltcenter.org/Learn-About-TR/TR-Brief-Biography.aspx

Chapter 2

23 unusual laws around the world you probably didn't know about. (2016, June 9). *The Telegraph*. Retrieved from www.telegraph.co.uk/travel/galleries/Unusual-laws-around-the-world/law10/

Ajdacic-Gross, V., Killias, M., Hepp, U., Gadola, E., Bopp, M., Lauber, C., & . . . Rössler, W. (2006). Changing times: A longitudinal analysis of international firearm suicide data. *American Journal of Public Health, 96*(10), 1752–1755. doi:10.2105/AJPH.2005.075812

Allow doctors to talk about gun safety. (2017, March 10). *The Republic*. Retrieved from. www.therepublic.com/2017/03/11/allow-doctors-to-talk-about-gun-safety/

American Psychiatric Association. (2013). *Diagnostic and statistical manual of mental disorders* (5th ed.). Arlington, VA: American Psychiatric Publishing.

Amicus brief: *Wollschlaeger v. Governor, State of Florida*. (2015, August 28). Retrieved from https://everytownresearch.org/amicus-brief-wollschlaeger-v-governor-state-of-florida/

Appelbaum, P. S. (2017a). Does the Second Amendment protect the gun rights of persons with mental illness? *Psychiatric Services, 68*(1), 3–5.

Appelbaum, P. S. (2017b). "Docs vs. Glocks" and the regulation of physicians' speech. *Psychiatric Services, 68*(7), 647–649.

Arrigo, B. A., & Acheson, A. (2016). Concealed carry bans and the American college campus: a law, social sciences, and policy perspective. *Contemporary Justice Review, 19*(1), 120–141. doi:10.1080/10282580.2015.1101688

Artavia, D. (2013, July 22). Greece's health minister has reinstated a draconian measure that allows mandatory HIV testing, detention, and even eviction. Plus. Retrieved from www.hivplusmag.com/case-studies/world-news/2013/07/22/greece-reinstates-forced-hiv-testing

Baker, J., & McPhedran, S. (2015). Australian firearm related deaths: New findings and implications for crime prevention and health policies following revisions to official death count data. *International Journal of Criminal Justice Sciences, 10*(1), 1–9.

Barnhorst, A. (2015). California firearms law and mental illness. *Behavioral Sciences & The Law, 33*(2–3), 246–256. doi:10.1002/bsl.2177

Birkland, T. A., & Lawrence, R. G. (2009). Media framing and policy change after Columbine. *American Behavioral Scientist.* Online First: doi:10.1177/0002764209332555

Bobcat hunting seasons. (n.d.). New York State Department of Environmental Conservation. Retrieved from http://www.dec.ny.gov/outdoor/29475.html

Bouffard, J. A., Nobles, M. R., Wells, W., & Cavanaugh, M. R. (2012). How many more guns?: Estimating the effect of allowing licensed concealed handguns on a college campus. *Journal of Interpersonal Violence, 27*(2), 316–343. doi:10.1177/0886260511416478

Boyle, D. (2016, November 16). British tourist "gang-raped" in Dubai faces jail for having sex outside marriage. *The Telegraph.* Retrieved from www.telegraph.co.uk/news/2016/11/16/british-tourist-gang-raped-in-dubai-faces-jail-for-having-sex-ou/

Brady vs. Lucky Gunner. (n.d.). Lucky Gunner. Retrieved July 6, 2016, from www.luckygunner.com/brady-v-lucky-gunner

Braga, A. A., & Weisburd, D. L. (2015). Focused deterrence and the prevention of violent gun injuries: Practice, theoretical principles, and scientific evidence. *Annual Review of Public Health, 36*, 55–68. doi:10.1146/annurev-publhealth-031914-122444

Braga, A. A., & Hureau, D. M. (2015). Strong gun laws are not enough: The need for improved enforcement of secondhand gun transfer laws in Massachusetts. *Preventive Medicine: An International Journal Devoted To Practice And Theory, 79*, 37–42. doi:10.1016/j.ypmed.2015.05.018

Braga, A. A., Hureau, D. M., & Papachristos, A. V. (2014). Deterring gang-involved gun violence: Measuring the impact of Boston's Operation Ceasefire on street gang behavior. *Journal of Quantitative Criminology, 30*(1), 113–139. doi:10.1007/s10940-013-9198-x

Bratskeir, K. (2016, January 22). The craziest laws that still exist in the United States. Huffington Post. Retrieved from www.huffingtonpost.com/entry/weird-laws-in-america_us_56a264abe4b0d8cc1099e1cd

Bridge, M. (2012), Exit, pursued by a "bear"? New York City's Handgun Laws in the wake of *Heller* and *McDonald. Columbia Journal of Law & Social Problems, 46*(2), 145–206.

Britton, J., & Bloom, J. D. (2015). Oregon's gun relief program for adjudicated mentally ill persons: The Psychiatric Security Review Board. *Behavioral Sciences & The Law, 33*(2/3), 323–333. doi:10.1002/bsl.2167

Bureau of Alcohol, Tobacco and Firearms. (2000a). *Following the gun: Enforcing federal laws against firearms traffickers*. Washington, DC: US Department of the Treasury.

Bureau of Alcohol, Tobacco and Firearms. (2000b). *Commerce in firearms in the United States*. Washington, DC: US Department of the Treasury.

Butterfield, F. (1998, November 13). Chicago is suing over guns from suburbs. *New York Times*. Retrieved from www.nytimes.com/1998/11/13/us/chicago-is-suing-over-guns-from-suburbs.html

Caetano v. Massachusetts, 136 S.Ct. 1027 (2016).

Canadian firearms program. (2013, September 27). Royal Canadian Mounted Police. Retrieved from www.rcmp-grc.gc.ca/cfp-pcaf/faq/index-eng.htm#a2

Cavanaugh, M. R., Bouffard, J. A., Wells, W., & Nobles, M. R. (2012). Student attitudes toward concealed handguns on campus at 2 universities. *American Journal of Public Health, 102*, 2245–2247.

Chapin, J., & Coleman, G. (2003). Unrealistic optimism and school violence prevention programs. *North American Journal Of Psychology, 5*(2), 193–202.

Chappell, D. (2014). Firearms regulation, violence and the mentally ill: A contemporary Antipodean appraisal. *International Journal of Law And Psychiatry, 37*(4), 399–408. doi:10.1016/j.ijlp.2014.02.011

Ciyou, B. L. (2017). *2017 edition: Gun laws by state. Reciprocity and gun laws quick reference guide*. Indianapolis, IN: Peritus Holdings.

Clark, K. (2017, February 1). These are the gun law changes Florida lawmakers could take up in 2017. *Miami Herald*. Retrieved from www.miamiherald.com/news/state/florida/article126275869.html

Colorado school district to allow teachers to arm themselves. (2016, December 15). Associated Press. Retrieved from www.yahoo.com/news/colorado-school-district-allow-teachers-arm-themselves-092740426.html

Crifasi, C. K., Meyers, J. S., Vernick, J. S., & Webster, D. W. (2015). Effects of changes in permit-to-purchase handgun laws in Connecticut and Missouri on suicide rates. *Preventive Medicine: An International Journal Devoted To Practice And Theory, 79*, 43–49. doi:10.1016/j.ypmed.2015.07.013

Cukier, W. (2005). Commentary: Changing public policy on firearms: Success stories from around the world. *Journal Of Public Health Policy, 26*(2), 227–230. doi:10.1057/palgrave.jphp.3200023

DeAngelis, T. (2015). In search of cultural competence. *Monitor on Psychology 46*(3), 64.

Denniston, L. (2016, March 22). Constitution check: Where does the Second Amendment stand now? Retrieved July 5, 2016, from http://news.yahoo.com/constitution-check-where-does-second-amendment-stand-now-101610515--politics.html

DiGiacinto v. The Rector and Visitors of George Mason University, 704 S.E.2d 365, 369 (Va. 2011).

District of Columbia v. Heller, 554 U.S. 570, 595 (2008).

Dominguez, G. (2016). A look at Thailand's fervent gun culture. Retrieved March 2016 from www.dw.com/en/a-look-at-thailands-fervent-gun-culture/a-19060721

Donohue, J. (2015, June 24). How US gun control compares to the rest of the world. *The Conversation*. Retrieved from http://theconversation.com/how-us-gun-control-compares-to-the-rest-of-the-world-43590

Duggan, P. & Torry, S. (1998, October 31). New Orleans initiates suit against gunmakers. *Washington Post*. Retrieved from www.washingtonpost.com/archive/politics/1998/10/31/new-orleans-initiates-suit-against-gunmakers/2b612ee9-911b-438b-ba20-ec07ee664197/?utm_term=.d706cd002bd8

Duwe, G., Kovandzic, T., & Moody, C. E. (2002). The impact of right-to-carry concealed firearm laws on mass public shootings. *Homicide Studies, 6*(4), 271. doi:10.1177/108876702237341

Elson, M., & Ferguson, C. J. (2013). Gun violence and media effects: Challenges for science and public policy. *The British Journal of Psychiatry, 203*(5), 322–324. doi:10.1192/bjp.bp.113.128652

Ewing, C. P. (2005). *Tarasoff* reconsidered. American Psychological Association. Retrieved from www.apa.org/monitor/julaug05/jn.aspx

Fact sheet: New executive actions to reduce gun violence and make our communities safer. (2016, January 4). White House. Retrieved from https://obamawhitehouse.archives.gov/the-press-office/2016/01/04/fact-sheet-new-executive-actions-reduce-gun-violence-and-make-our

Falls, B. (2011). Legislation prohibiting physicians from asking patients about guns. *Journal of Psychiatry & Law, 39*(3), 441–464.

Federal appeals court ruling in Wollschlaeger v. Governor of Florida. (2017, February 16). ACLU. Retrieved from https://aclufl.org/resources/federal-appeals-court-ruling-in-wollschlaeger-v-governor-of-florida/

Firearms-control legislation and policy: South Africa. (n.d.). Library of Congress. Retrieved from www.loc.gov/law/help/firearms-control/southafrica.php

Fisher, C. E., Cohen, Z. E., Hoge, S. K., & Appelbaum, P. S. (2015). Restoration of firearm rights in New York. *Behavioral Sciences & The Law, 33*(2/3), 334–345. doi:10.1002/bsl.2171

Florida State law background. (n.d.). Giffords Law Center to prevent gun violence. Retrieved from http://smartgunlaws.org/gun-laws/state-law/florida/

Fox, J. A., & DeLateur, M. J. (2014). Mass shootings in America: Moving beyond Newtown. *Homicide Studies: An Interdisciplinary & International Journal, 18*(1), 125–145.

Frattaroli, S., & Vernick, J. S. (2006). Separating batterers and guns: A review and analysis of gun removal laws in 50 States. *Evaluation Review, 30*(3), 296–312. doi:10.1177/0193841X06287680

Friedman, D. (2017, January 6). New bill would force states to allow visiting gun owners to pack heat without a permit. *The Trace*. Retrieved from www.thetrace.org/2017/01/new-bill-congress-states-concealed-constitutional-carry-reciprocity/

Gagliardi, P. (2012). Transnational organized crime and gun violence. A case for firearm forensic intelligence sharing. *International Review of Law, Computers & Technology, 26*(1), 83–95. doi:10.1080/13600869.2012.646801

General hunting regulations. (n.d.). *New Jersey Hunting & Trapping Digest*. Retrieved from www.eregulations.com/newjersey/hunting/general-hunting-regulations

Gius, M. (2015). The impact of minimum age and child access prevention laws on firearm-related youth suicides and unintentional deaths. *The Social Science Journal, 52*(2), 168–175. doi:10.1016/j.soscij.2015.01.003

Gold, L. H., & Simon, R. I. (2016). *Gun violence and mental illness*. Arlington, VA: American Psychiatric Association.

Gorman, M. (2017, February 15). Trump overturns a mental health regulation on gun purchases. *Newsweek*. Retrieved from www.newsweek.com/trump-set-overturn-guns-mental-health-regulation-557237

Grossman, D. C., Mueller, B. A., Riedy, C., Dowd, M. D., Villaveces, A., Prodzinski, J., Nakagawara, J., Howard, J., & Harruff, R. (2005). Gun storage practices and risk of youth suicide and unintentional firearm injuries. *JAMA: Journal of the American Medical Association, 293*(6), 707–714.

Guns in America town hall with Obama transcript (full text). (2016, January 7). CNN. Retrieved from www.cnn.com/2016/01/07/politics/transcript-obama-town-hall-guns-in-america/

Hahn, R. A., Bilukha, O., Crosby, A., Fullilove, M. T., Liberman, A., Moscicki, E., . . . & Briss, P. A. (2005). Firearms laws and the reduction of violence. *American Journal of Preventive Medicine, 28*(2), 40–71.

Hallsworth, S., & Silverstone, D. (2009). 'That's life innit': A British perspective on guns, crime and social order. *Criminology & Criminal Justice: An International Journal, 9*(3), 359–377. doi:10.1177/1748895809336386

Hill, M. (2015, December 2). Second Amendment Society claims police departments delaying and denying handgun permits. NJTV News. Retrieved from www.njtvonline.org/news/video/second-amendment-society-claims-police-departments-delaying-and-denying-handgun-permits/

Jang, H., Dierenfeldt, R., & Lee, C. (2014). Who wants to allow concealed weapons on the college campuses? *Security Journal, 27*(3), 304–319. doi:10.1057/sj.2012.31

Jenson, J. M. (2007). Aggression and violence in the United States: Reflections on the Virginia Tech shootings. *Social Work Research, 31*(3), 131–134. doi:10.1093/swr/31.3.131

Junuzovic, M., & Eriksson, A. (2012). Unintentional firearm hunting deaths in Sweden. *Forensic Science International, 216*(1–3), 12–18. doi:10.1016/j.forsciint.2011.08.010

Kappas, J. S. (2017). *2017 Traveler's guide to the firearm laws of the fifty states.* Covington, KY: Traveler's Guide.

Karaffa, K. K., & Tochkov, K. (2013). Attitudes toward seeking mental health treatment among law enforcement officers. *Applied Psychology in Criminal Justice, 9,* 75–99.

Kazdin, A. E. (2006). Arbitrary metrics: Implications for identifying evidence-based treatments. *American Psychologist, 61,* 42–49.

Kazdin, A. E. (2008). Evidence-based treatment and practice: New opportunities to bridge clinical research and practice, enhance the knowledge base, and improve patient care. *American Psychologist, 63*(3), 146.

Keneally, M. (2016, December 14). 4 years after Sandy Hook, Obama leaves a legacy of little progress on gun laws. *Good Morning America*. Retrieved from https://gma.yahoo.com/4-years-sandy-hook-obama-leaves-legacy-little-111813067--abc-news-topstories.html

Kennedy, D. M., Piehl, A. M., & Braga, A. A. (1996). Youth violence in Boston: Gun markets, serious youth offenders, and a use-reduction strategy. *Law & Contemporary Problems, 59,* 147–196.

Killingley, J. (2014). Counterblast: Gun nuts or nuts about guns? *Howard Journal of Criminal Justice, 53*(5), 542–544. doi:10.1111/hojo.12101

Kmart held liable for selling gun to drunk man who shot woman. (1993, October 11). *New York Times*. Retrieved from www.nytimes.com/1993/10/11/us/kmart-held-liable-for-selling-gun-to-drunk-man-who-shot-woman.html

Kopel, D. B., Gallant, P., & Eisen, J. D. (2003). Global deaths from firearms: Searching for plausible estimates. *Texas Review of Law & Politics*, *8*(1), 113–140.

Kopel, D., Mody, C., & Nemerov, H. (2008). Is there a relationship between guns and freedom? Comparative results from fifty-nine nations. *Texas Review of Law & Politics*, *13*(1), 1–41.

Langmann, C. (2012). Canadian Firearms Legislation and effects on homicide 1974 to 2008. *Journal of Interpersonal Violence*, *27*(12), 2303–2321. doi:10.1177/0886260511433515

Lankford, A. (2016). Are America's public mass shooters unique? A comparative analysis of offenders in the United States and other countries. *International Journal of Comparative & Applied Criminal Justice*, *40*(2), 171–183. doi:10.1080/01924036.2015.1105144

Lawrence, R. G., & Birkland, T. A. (2004). Guns, Hollywood, and school safety: Defining the school-shooting problem across public arenas. *Social Science Quarterly*, *85*(5), 1193–1207. doi:10.1111/j.0038-4941.2004.00271.x

Longley, R. (2016, June 15). US gun control timeline. Retrieved from http://usgovinfo.about.com/blguntime.htm

Lucas, F. (2015, December 30). New gun laws for the new year: Three big changes coming for 2016 in these states. *The Blaze*. Retrieved from www.theblaze.com/news/2015/12/30/new-gun-laws-for-the-new-year-three-big-changes-coming-for-2016-in-these-three-states/

Luther III, R. (2014). Mental health and gun rights in Virginia: A view from the battlefield. *New England Journal on Criminal & Civil Confinement*, *40*(2), 345–358.

Makarios, M. D., & Pratt, T. C. (2012). The effectiveness of policies and programs that attempt to reduce firearm violence: A meta-analysis. *Crime & Delinquency*, *58*(2), 222–244. doi:10.1177/0011128708321321

Masters, J. (2016, January 12). U.S. gun policy: Global comparisons. Council on foreign relations. Retrieved from www.cfr.org/society-and-culture/us-gun-policy-global-comparisons/p29735

Mattaini, M. A. (2012). Guns: The data tell us. *Behavior and Social Issues*, *21*, 1–4.

McDonald v. City of Chicago, 130 S. Ct. 3020 (2010).

McDowall, D., Loftin, C., & Wiersema, B. (1995). Easing concealed firearms laws: Effects on homicide in three states. *The Journal of Criminal Law and Criminology (1973–)*, *86*(1), 193–206.

McGarrell, E. F., Corsaro, N., Melde, C., Hipple, N. K., Bynum, T., & Cobbina, J. (2013). Attempting to reduce firearms violence through a Comprehensive Anti-Gang Initiative (CAGI): An evaluation of process and impact. *Journal of Criminal Justice*, *41*(1), 33–43. doi:10.1016/j.jcrimjus.2012.11.001

McGinty, E. E., Frattaroli, S., Appelbaum, P. S., Bonnie, R. J., Grilley, A., Horwitz, J., & . . . Webster, D. W. (2014). Using research evidence to reframe the policy debate around mental illness and guns: Process and recommendations. *American Journal of Public Health*, *104*(11), e22–e26. doi:10.2105/AJPH.2014.302171

McGreevy, P. (2016, May 19). Here are the gun control proposals approved by the state senate. *Los Angeles Times.* Retrieved from www.latimes.com/la-pol-sac-essential-politics-here-are-the-gun-control-propo-1463685378-htmlstory.html

McPhedran, S. (2013). More guns . . . more or less crime? An Australian perspective on an international question. *Crime Prevention and Community Safety, 15*(2), 127–133. doi:10.1057/cpcs.2012.17

McPhedran, S. (2016). A systematic review of quantitative evidence about the impacts of Australian legislative reform on firearm homicide. *Aggression & Violent Behavior, 28*, 64–72. doi:10.1016/j.avb.2016.03.012

McPhedran, S., & Baker, J. (2008). The impact of Australia's 1996 firearms legislation: A research review with emphasis on data selection, methodological issues, and statistical outcomes. *Justice Policy Journal, 5*(1), 1–18.

McPhedran, S., Baker, J., & Singh, P. (2011). Firearm homicide in Australia, Canada, and New Zealand: What can we learn from long-term international comparisons?. *Journal of Interpersonal Violence, 26*(2), 348–359. doi:10.1177/0886260510362893

McPhedran, S., & Mauser, G. (2013). Lethal firearm-related violence against Canadian women: Did tightening gun laws have an impact on women's health and safety? *Violence & Victims, 28*(5), 875–883. doi:10.1891/0886-6708.VV-D-12-00145

Miller, L. (2004). Good cop–bad cop: Problem officers, law enforcement culture, and strategies for success. *Journal of Police and Criminal Psychology, 19*, 30–48.

Miller, M., Azrael, D., Hemenway, D., & Vriniotis, M. (2005). Firearm storage practices and rates of unintentional firearm deaths in the United States. *Accident Analysis and Prevention, 37*(4), 661–667.

Miller, T. W., & Kraus, R. F. (2008). School-related violence: Definition, scope, and prevention goals. In T. W. Miller (Ed.), *School violence and primary prevention* (pp. 15–24). New York, NY, US: Springer Science + Business Media. doi:10.1007/978-0-387-77119-9_2

Municipalities. (n.d.). State of New Jersey. Retrieved from www.nj.gov/cgi-bin/infobank/munisearch.pl

Nappen, E. F. (2015). *New Hampshire gun law.* Concord, NH: Fugio Press.

Nappen, E. F. (2017). *New Jersey gun law.* Concord, NH: Fugio Press.

Neil, B. A., & Neil, B. A. (2009). The *Heller* decision and its possible implications for right-to-carry laws nationally. *Journal of Contemporary Criminal Justice, 25*(1), 113–118.

Nieto, M. (2011). The changing landscape of firearm legislation in the wake of *McDonald v. City of Chicago,* 130 S. CT. 3020 (2010). *Harvard Journal of Law & Public Policy, 34*(3), 1117–1130.

Nordrum, A. (2014, September 10). The new D.A.R.E. program—This one works. *Scientific American.* Retrieved from www.scientificamerican.com/article/the-new-d-a-r-e-program-this-one-works/

Norris, D. M., Price, M., Gutheil, T. G., & Reid, W. H. (2006). Firearm laws, patients, and the roles of psychiatrists. *American Journal of Psychiatry, 163*, 1392–1396.

Number of municipal governments & population distribution. (n.d.). National league of cities. Retrieved from www.nlc.org/

build-skills-and-networks/resources/cities-101/city-structures/
number-of-municipal-governments-and-population-distribution

Olivero, A., & Pinals, D. A. (2015). The Right of Individuals with Mental Illness to Keep and Bear Arms. *Journal Of The American Academy of Psychiatry & The Law, 43*(3), 379–381.

Özalp, E., & Karakiliç, H. (2007). Gun ownership in Turkey: The legal dimension and mental health practices. *International Journal of Mental Health, 36*(3), 95–104. doi:10.2753/IMH0020-7411360311

Paglini, L. (2015). How far will the strictest state push the limits: The constitutionality of California's proposed gun law under the Second Amendment. *American University Journal of Gender, Social Policy & The Law, 23*(3), 459–485.

Parham-Payne, W. (2014). The role of the media in the disparate response to gun violence in America. *Journal of Black Studies, 45*(8), 752–768. doi:10.1177/0021934714555185

Parker, G. F. (2010). Application of a firearm seizure law aimed at dangerous persons: Outcomes from the first two years. *Psychiatric Services, 61*(5), 478–482. doi:10.1176/appi.ps.61.5.478

Parker, G. F. (2015). Circumstances and outcomes of a firearm seizure law: Marion County, Indiana, 2006–2013. *Behavioral Sciences & The Law, 33*(2–3), 308–322. doi:10.1002/bsl.2175

Patterson, W. R. (2010). Enforcing firearms laws at the local level: A case study of the Virginia Beach Police Department's Gun Trace Unit. *Police Journal, 83*(3), 268–282. doi:10.1350/pojo.2010.83.3.514

Paugh v. Henrico Area Mental Health & Developmental Servs., 286 Va. 85, 89, 743 S.E.2d 277, 279 (2013).

Payne, B. K., & Gainey, R. R. (2008). Guns, offense type, and Virginia exile: Should gun reduction policies focus on specific offenses? *Criminal Justice Policy Review, 19*(2), 181–195.

Petrosino, A., Campie, P., Pace, J., Fronius, T., Guckenburg, S., Wiatrowski, M., & Rivera, L. (2015). Cross-sector, multi-agency interventions to address urban youth firearms violence: A rapid evidence assessment. *Aggression & Violent Behavior, 22*, 87–96.

Phillips, S. W., Dae-Young, K., & Sobol, J. J. (2013). An evaluation of a multiyear gun buy-back programme: Re-examining the impact on violent crimes. *International Journal of Police Science & Management, 15*(3), 246–261. doi:10.1350/ijps.2013.15.3.315

Phillips, C. D., Nwaiwu, O., Lin, S., Edwards, R., Imanpour, S., & Ohsfeldt, R. (2015). Concealed handgun licensing and crime in four states. *Journal of Criminology, 20*, 151–158. doi:10.1155/2015/803742

Phillips, L., & Phillips, S. (2015, September 25). We lost our daughter to a mass shooter and now owe $203,000 to his ammo dealer. Huffington Post. Retrieved July 7, 2016, from www.huffingtonpost.com/lonnie-and-sandy-phillips/lucky-gunner-lawsuit_b_8197804.html

Piehl, A. M., Cooper, S. J., Braga, A. A., & Kennedy, D. M. (2003). Testing for structural breaks in the evaluation of programs. *Review of Economics and Statistics, 85*, 550–558.

Pinals, D. A., Appelbaum, P. S., Bonnie, R. J., Fisher, C. E., Gold, L. H., & Lee, L. (2015a). Resource document on access to firearms by people with mental disorders. *Behavioral Sciences & the Law, 33*(2/3), 186–194. doi:10.1002/bsl.2181

Pinals, D. A., Appelbaum, P. S., Bonnie, R., Fisher, C. E., Gold, L. H., & Lee, L. (2015b). American Psychiatric Association: Position statement on firearm access, acts of violence and the relationship to mental illness and mental health services. *Behavioral Sciences & The Law, 33*(2/3), 195–198. doi:10.1002/bsl.2180

Pirelli, G., Wechsler, H., & Cramer, R. (2015). Psychological evaluations for firearm ownership: Legal foundations, practice considerations, and a conceptual framework. *Professional Psychology: Research and Practice, 46*(4), 250–257.

Pirelli, G., & Witt, P. H. (2017). Firearms and cultural competence: Considerations for mental health practitioners. *Journal of Aggression, Conflict and Peace Research*, 10(1), 61–70. https://doi.org/10.1108/JACPR-01-2017-0268

Podnar, P. (2015, April 3). Gun laws around the world: Where does South America stand on firearms? Newsmax. Retrieved from www.newsmax.com/FastFeatures/gun-laws-mexico-south-america/2015/04/03/id/636379/

Polk, R. (2014). Want a gun in Egypt? Here's how. Retrieved March 2, 2016 from http://revolutionegypt.blogs.wm.edu/2014/10/19/want-a-gun-in-egypt-heres-how/

Price, M., & Norris, D. M. (2010). Firearm laws: A primer for psychiatrists. *Harvard Review of Psychiatry, 18*(6), 326–335.

Prickett, K. C., Martin-Storey, A., & Crosnoe, R. (2014). State firearm laws, firearm ownership, and safety practices among families of preschool-aged children. *American Journal of Public Health, 104*(6), 1080–1086. doi:10.2105/AJPH.2014.301928

Printz v. United States, 521 U.S. 898 (1997).

Redford v. U.S. Dept. of Treasury, Bureau of Alcohol, Tobacco and Firearms, 691 F.2d 471 (10th Cir. 1982).

Regents of the University of Colorado v. Students for Concealed Carry on Campus, 271 P.3d 496 (Colo. 2012).

Riker, M. S. (2016, May 24). Hawaii could be first to put gun owners in federal database. AP News. Retrieved from https://apnews.com/057945d6be7a4fb89d68bbf7d8b48bd8

Rosenfeld, R., Deckard, M. J., & Blackburn, E. (2014). The effects of directed patrol and self-initiated enforcement on firearm violence: A randomized controlled study of hot spot policing. *Criminology: An Interdisciplinary Journal, 52*(3), 428–449. doi:10.1111/1745-9125.12043

Rosenwald, M. (2016, May 18). Most mass shooters aren't mentally ill. So why push better treatment as the answer? *Washington Post*. Retrieved from www.washingtonpost.com/local/most-mass-shooters-arent-mentally-ill-so-why-push-better-treatment-as-the-answer/2016/05/17/70034918-1308-11e6-8967-7ac733c56f12_story.html?tid=sm_tw

Ruddell, R., & Mays, G. L. (2005). State background checks and firearms homicides. *Journal of Criminal Justice, 33*(2), 127–136. doi:1 0.1016/j.jcrimjus.2004.12.004

Saudi court tells girl aged eight she cannot divorce husband who is 50 years her senior. (2008, December 22). *Daily Mail*. Retrieved from www.dailymail.co.uk/news/article-1099447/Saudi-court-tells-girl-aged-EIGHT-divorce-husband-50-years-senior.html

Salnikova, O. A. (2013). "The People" of *Heller* and their politics: Whether illegal aliens should have the right to bear arms after *United States v. Portillo-Munoz*. *Journal of Criminal Law & Criminology, 103*(2), 625–662.

Schildkraut, J., & Hernandez, T. (2014). Laws that bit The bullet: A review of legislative responses to school shootings. *American Journal Of Criminal Justice, 39*(2), 358–374. doi:10.1007/s12103-013-9214-6

Schildkraut, J., & Muschert, G. W. (2014). Media salience and the framing of mass murder in schools: A comparison of the columbine and Sandy Hook massacres. *Homicide Studies, 18*(1), 23–43. doi:10.1177/1088767913511458

Sen, B., & Panjamapirom, A. (2012). State background checks for gun purchase and firearm deaths: An exploratory study. *Preventive Medicine: An International Journal Devoted to Practice And Theory, 55*(4), 346–350. doi:10.1016/j.ypmed.2012.07.019

Senate Bill 86, 217th Legislature. (2016). Retrieved from www.njleg.state.nj.us/2016/Bills/S0500/86_I2.HTM

Silver, J., Fisher, W. H., & Silver, E. (2015). Preventing persons affected by serious mental illnesses from obtaining firearms: The evolution of law, policy, and practice in Massachusetts. *Behavioral Sciences & The Law, 33*(2–3), 279–289. doi:10.1002/bsl.2170

Simpson, J. R. (2007). Bad risk? An overview of laws prohibiting possession of firearms by individuals with a history of treatment for mental illness. *Journal of the American Academy of Psychiatry and the Law, 35*, 330–338.

Slaughterhouse Cases, 83 U.S. 16 Wall. 36 (1872).

States with weak gun laws and higher gun ownership lead nation in gun deaths, new data for 2015 confirms. (2017, January 10). Violence Policy Center. Retrieved from www.vpc.org/press/states-with-weak-gun-laws-and-higher-gun-ownership-lead-nation-in-gun-deaths-new-data-for-2015-confirms/

Steinkopf, B. L., Hakala, K. A., & Van Hasselt, V. B. (2015). Motivational interviewing: Improving the delivery of psychological services to law enforcement. *Professional Psychology: Research and Practice, 46*(5), 348–354. doi:10.1037/pro0000042

Stidham, D. A. (2015). You have the right to bear arms, but not the ability? The evanescence of the second amendment. *New England Journal on Criminal & Civil Confinement, 41*(1), 137–158.

Sumner, S. A., Layde, P. M., & Guse, C. E. (2008). Firearm death rates and association with level of firearm purchase background check. *American Journal of Preventive Medicine, 35*(1), 1–6.

Supreme Court upholds wide reach of U.S. gun ban for domestic violence. (2016, June 27). NBC News. Retrieved from www.nbcnews.com/news/us-news/supreme-court-upholds-wide-reach-u-s-gun-ban-domestic-n599816

Swanson, J. W., & Felthous, A. R. (2015). Guns, mental illness, and the law: Introduction to this issue. *Behavioral Sciences & The Law, 33*(2–3), 167–177. doi:10.1002/bsl.2178

Swift, A. (2016, September 14). Americans' trust in mass media sinks to new low. Gallup. Retrieved from www.gallup.com/poll/195542/americans-trust-mass-media-sinks-new-low.aspx

Tan, A. (2016, April 19). Colorado school district to arm its security patrol with semi-automatic rifles. *ABC News*. Retrieved July 6, 2016, from http://abcnews.

go.com/US/colorado-school-district-arm-security-patrol-semi-automatic/
story?id=38513915

Tarasoff v. Regents of the University of California, 17 Cal.3d 425 (1976).

Texas state law background. (n.d.). Giffords Law Center to prevent gun violence.
Retrieved from http://smartgunlaws.org/gun-laws/state-law/texas/

Tomazic, M. (2015). Docs v. glocks: Restricting doctor's professional speech
in the name of firearm owner privacy – *Wollschlaeger v. Governor of
Florida. American Journal of Law & Medicine, 41*(4), 680–683. doi:10.1177/
0098858815622194

Tucker, G. (1803). *Blackstone's commentaries: With notes of reference*. Birch and
Small: Philadelphia.

Tyler v. Hillsdale County Sheriff's Department, 775 F.3d 308 (6th Cir. 2014).

United States v. Chamberlain, 159 F.3d 656, 665 (1st Cir. 1998).

United States v. Dorsch, 363 F.3d 784, 785 (8th Cir. 2004).

United States v. Giardina, 861 F.2d 1334, 1337 (5th Cir. 1988).

United States v. Hansel, 474 F.2d 1120, 1122–1123 (8th Cir. 1973).

United States v. Portillo-Munoz, 53 B.C. L. Rev. E-Supplement 75, 87 (2012).

United States v. Rehlander, 666 F.3d 45 (1st Cir. 2012).

United States v. Waters, 23 F.3d 29, 31–36 (2d Cir.), cert. denied, 513 U.S. 867, 115
S.Ct. 185, 130 L.Ed.2d 119 (1994).

University of Utah v. Shurtleff, 144 P.3d 1109 (Utah 2006).

US Department of Justice. (2006). *Survey of state procedures related to firearm sales
2005*. Washington, DC: Bureau of Justice Statistics.

Valle, J., & Glover, T. (2012). Revisiting licensed handgun carrying: Personal
protection or interpersonal liability? *American Journal of Criminal Justice,
37*(4), 580–601. doi:10.1007/s12103-011-9140-4

Vernick, J. S., McGinty, E. E., & Rutkow, L. (2015). Mental health emergency
detentions and access to firearms. *Journal of Law, Medicine & Ethics, 43*, 76–
78. doi:10.1111/jlme.12222

Vernick, J. S., Webster, D. W., Bulzacchelli, M. T., & Mair, J. S. (2006). Regulation of
firearm dealers in the United States: An analysis of state law and opportunities
for improvement. *Journal of Law, Medicine & Ethics, 34*(4), 765–775.
doi:10.1111/j.1748-720X.2006.00097.x

Voisine v. United States, 579 US ___ (2016).

Vigdor, E. R., & Mercy, J. A. (2006). Do laws restricting access to firearms by
domestic violence offenders prevent intimate partner homicide? *Evaluation
Review, 30*(3), 313–346.

Vizzard, W. J. (2015). The current and future state of gun policy in the United
States. *Journal of Criminal Law & Criminology, 104*(4), 879–904.

Wallace, L. N. (2014). Castle doctrine legislation: Unintended effects for gun
ownership? *Justice Policy Journal, 11*(2), 1–17.

Walsh, M. (2017, January 9). Florida lawmakers want more guns at airports. *Yahoo
News*. Retrieved from www.yahoo.com/news/florida-lawmakers-want-more-
guns-at-airports-214517227.html

Weaver, G. S. (2002). Firearm deaths, gun availability, and legal regulatory
changes: Suggestions from the data. *Journal of Criminal Law & Criminology,
92*(3/4), 823.

Webster, D. W., Vernick, J. S., & Bulzacchelli, M. T. (2009). Effects of state-level firearm seller accountability policies on firearm trafficking. *Journal of Urban Health, 86*(4), 525–537.

Webster, D. W., Vernick, J. S., Zeoli, A. M., & Manganello, J. A. (2004). Association between youth-focused firearm laws and youth suicides. *JAMA: Journal of the American Medical Association, 292*(5), 594–601.

Webster, D. W., & Wintemute, G. J. (2015). Effects of policies designed to keep firearms from high-risk individuals. *Annual Review of Public Health,* 3621–3637. doi:10.1146/annurev-publhealth-031914-122516

Wollschlaeger v. Farmer. 814 F.Supp.2d 1367 (2011).

Wollschlaeger v. Governor of Florida: Eleventh circuit upholds Florida law banning doctors from inquiring about patients' gun ownership when such inquiry is irrelevant to medical care. (2015). *Harvard Law Review, 128,* 1045.

Wyant, B. R., Taylor, R. B., Ratcliffe, J. H., & Wood, J. (2012). Deterrence, firearm arrests, and subsequent shootings: A micro-level spatio-temporal analysis. *JQ: Justice Quarterly, 29*(4), 524–545. doi:10.1080/07418825.2011.576689

Ziabari, K. (2012, December 19). How U.S. Mideast gun laws measure up. Retrieved from https://english.alarabiya.net/en/2012/12/19/How-US-Mideast-gun-laws-measure-up.html

Chapter 3

Ahmed, A. O., Green, B. A., McCloskey, M. S., & Berman, M. E. (2010). Latent structure of intermittent explosive disorder in an epidemiological sample. *Journal of Psychiatric Research, 44*(10), 663–672.

American Psychiatric Association. (2013). *Diagnostic and statistical manual of mental disorders,* 5th ed. Washington, DC: American Psychiatric Publishing.

Arnett, J. J. (2016). College students as emerging adults: The developmental implications of the college context. *Emerging Adulthood, 4,* 219–222.

Arnett, J. J. (2000). Emerging adulthood: A theory of development from the late teens through the twenties. *American Psychologist, 55,* 469–480.

Arulkadacham, L. J., Richardson, B., Staiger, P. K., Kambouropoulos, N., O'Donnell, R. L., & Ling, M. (2017). Dissociation between wanting and liking for alcohol and caffeine: A test of the incentive sensitisation theory. *Journal of Psychopharmacology, 31,* 927–933.

Beck, A. T., Freeman, A., & Davis, D. D. (2004). *Cognitive therapy of personality disorders.* New York: Guilford Press.

Behar, E., DiMarco, I. D., Hekler, E. B., Mohlman, J., & Staples, A. M. (2009). Current theoretical models of generalized anxiety disorder (GAD): Conceptual review and treatment implications. *Journal of Anxiety Disorders, 23,* 1011–1023.

Boland, E. M., Stange, J. P., LaBelle, D. R., Shapero, B. G., Weiss, R. B., Abramson, L. Y., & Alloy, L. B. (2016). Affective disruption from social rhythm and behavioral approach system (BAS) sensitivities: A test of the integration of the social zeitgeber and BAS theories of bipolar disorder. *Clinical Psychological Science, 4*(3), 418–432.

Brewin, C. R., & Holmes, E. A. (2003). Psychological theories of posttraumatic stress disorder. *Clinical Psychology Review, 23*(3), 339–376.

Carver, C. S. (1997). You want to measure coping but your protocol's too long: Consider the Brief COPE. *International Journal of Behavioral Medicine, 4*, 92–100.

Cherry, K. (2016). The Yerkes-Dodson law and performance. Retrieved from www.verywell.com/what-is-the-yerkes-dodson-law-2796027

Clark, D. A., & Beck, A. T. (2010). Cognitive theory and therapy of anxiety and depression: Convergence with neurobiological findings. *Trends in Cognitive Sciences, 14*(9), 418–424.

Coccaro, E. F., Fanning, J. R., Keedy, S. K., & Lee, R. J. (2016). Social cognition in intermittent explosive disorder and aggression. *Journal of Psychiatric Research, 83*, 140–150.

Coccaro, E. F., Solis, O., Fanning, J., & Lee, R. (2015). Emotional intelligence and impulsive aggression in intermittent explosive disorder. *Journal of Psychiatric Research, 61*, 135–140.

Fatemi, S. H., & Folsom, T. D. (2009). The neurodevelopmental hypothesis of schizophrenia, revisited. *Schizophrenia Bulletin, 35*(3), 528–548.

Haeffel, G. J., Hershenberg, R., Goodson, J. T., Hein, S., Square, A., Grigorenko, E. L., & Chapman, J. (2017). The hopelessness theory of depression: Clinical utility and generalizability. *Cognitive Therapy and Research, 41*(4), 543–555.

Howes, O. D., & Kapur, S. (2009). The dopamine hypothesis of schizophrenia: Version III—The final common pathway. *Schizophrenia Bulletin, 35*(3), 549–562.

Koerner, K., & Linehan, M. M. (2007). Case formulation in dialectical behavior therapy for borderline personality disorder. In *Handbook of psychotherapy case formulation*, edited by T. D. Eells (pp. 340–367). New York: Guilford Press.

Kraepelin, E. (1883; 1909–1915). *Compendium of psychiatry*. 8th ed. Leipzig: Earth. (First published as *Compendium der Psychiatrie*.)

Krol, N., Morton, J., & De Bruyn, E. (2004). Theories of conduct disorder: A causal modelling analysis. *Journal of Child Psychology and Psychiatry, 45*, 727–742.

Lieb, K., Zanarini, M. C., Schmahl, C., Linehan, M. M., & Bohus, M. (2004). Borderline personality disorder. *Lancet, 364*, 453–461.

McCrae, R. R., & Costa, P. T. (2003). *Personality in adulthood: A five-factor theory perspective*. New York: Guilford Press.

McGinn, L. K. (2000). Cognitive behavioral therapy of depression: Theory, treatment, and empirical status. *American Journal of Psychotherapy, 54*(2), 257–262.

Meloy, L. M., & Yakeley, J. (2014). Antisocial personality disorder. In *Gabbard's treatments of psychiatric disorders*, 5th ed., edited by G. O. Gabbard (pp. 1015–1034). Washington, DC: American Psychiatric Publishing.

Nusslock, R., Abramson, L., Harmon-Jones, E., Alloy, L., & Coan, J. (2009). Psychosocial interventions for bipolar disorder: Perspective from the behavioral approach system (BAS) dysregulation theory. *Clinical Psychology: Science and Practice, 16*(4), 449–469.

Otten, R., Mun, C. J., & Dishion, T. J. (2017). The social exigencies of the gateway progression to the use of illicit drugs from adolescence into adulthood. *Addictive Behaviors, 73*, 144–150.

Puhalla, A. A., Ammerman, B. A., Uyeji, L. L., Berman, M. E., & McCloskey, M. S. (2016). Negative urgency and reward/punishment sensitivity in intermittent explosive disorder. *Journal of Affective Disorders, 201*, 8–14.

Slavich, G. M., & Irwin, M. R. (2014). From stress to inflammation and major depressive disorder: A social signal transduction theory of depression. *Psychological Bulletin, 140*(3), 774–815.

Chapter 4

Adam Lanza. (2016, June 13). Biography. Retrieved from www.biography.com/people/adam-lanza-21068899

Agnich, L. (2015). A comparative analysis of attempted and completed school-based mass murder attacks. *American Journal of Criminal Justice, 40*(1), 1–22. doi:10.1007/s12103-014-9239-5

Aharoni, E., & Kiehl, K. A. (2013). Evading justice: Quantifying criminal success in incarcerated psychopathic offenders. *Criminal Justice and Behavior, 40*(6), 629–645. doi:10.1177/0093854812463565

Alfano, S. (2007, April 19). Va. Tech Killer Bought 2nd Gun Online. CBS News. Retrieved from www.cbsnews.com/news/va-tech-killer-bought-2nd-gun-online/

Altheimer, I. (2008). Do guns matter? A multi-level cross-national examination of gun availability on assault and robbery victimization. *Western Criminology Review, 9*(2), 9–32.

Altheimer, I., & Boswell, M. (2012). Reassessing the association between gun availability and homicide at the cross-national level. *American Journal of Criminal Justice, 37*(4), 682–704. doi:10.1007/s12103-011-9147-x

American Psychiatric Association. (2013). *Diagnostic and statistical manual of mental disorders* (5th ed.). Washington, DC: American Psychiatric Publishing.

An ex-Marine goes on a killing spree at the University of Texas. (n.d.). History.com. Retrieved from www.history.com/this-day-in-history/an-ex-marine-goes-on-a-killing-spree-at-the-university-of-texas

Andrew Kehoe. (2014, April 2). Retrieved from www.biography.com/people/andrew-kehoe-235986

Archer, R. P., Buffington-Vollum, J. K., Stredny, R. V., & Handel, R. W. (2006). A survey of psychological test use patterns among forensic psychologists. *Journal of Personality Assessment, 87*(1), 84–94.

Army major kills 13 people in Fort Hood shooting spree. (n.d.). History.com. Retrieved from www.history.com/this-day-in-history/army-major-kills-13-people-in-fort-hood-shooting-spree

Arseneault, L., Bowes, L., & Shakoor, S. (2010). Bullying victimization in youths and mental health problems: "Much ado about nothing"? *Psychological Medicine, 40*(5), 717–729. doi:10.1017/S0033291709991383

Ash, P. (2016). School shootings and mental illness. In *Gun violence and mental illness*, edited by L. H. Gold and R. I. Simon (pp. 105–126). Arlington, VA: American Psychiatric Association.

Augimeri, L., Webster, C., Koegl, C., & Levene, K. (2001). *Early assessment risk list for boys: EARL-20B*, version 2. Toronto, Canada: Earlscourt Child and Family Centre.

Aurora theater shooting. (n.d.). *Denver Post*. Retrieved from www.denverpost.com/tag/aurora-theater-shooting/

Babiak, P., & Hare, R. D. (2006). *Snakes in suits: When psychopaths go to work*. New York: Regan Books/Harper Collins Publishers.

Barber, C., & Hemenway, D. (2011). Too many or too few unintentional firearm deaths in official U.S. mortality data? *Accident Analysis and Prevention, 43*(3), 724–731. doi:10.1016/j.aap.2010.10.018

Barragan, M., Sherman, N., Reiter, K., & Tita, G. E. (2016). "Damned if you do, damned if you don't": Perceptions of guns, safety, and legitimacy among detained gun offenders. *Criminal Justice & Behavior, 43*(1), 140–155. doi:10.1177/0093854815611707

Basu, M. (2013, August 11). As Hasan trial starts, Fort Hood victims feel betrayed. CNN. Retrieved from www.cnn.com/2013/08/10/us/fort-hood-victims

Beck, J. (2016, June 7). Untangling gun violence from mental illness. *The Atlantic*. Retrieved from www.theatlantic.com/health/archive/2016/06/untangling-gun-violence-from-mental-illness/485906/

Bell, C. C. (2016). Gun violence, urban youth, and mental illness. In *Gun violence and mental illness*, edited by L. H. Gold and R. I. Simon (pp. 49–79). Arlington, VA: American Psychiatric Association.

Berkowitz, N. (2013, February 13). Members of Congress demand Obama administration classify Ft. Hood attack as an "act of terrorism." *ABC News*. Retrieved from http://abcnews.go.com/Blotter/members-congress-demand-obama-administration-classify-ft-hood/story?id=18493746

Blair, J. P., & Schweit, K. W. (2014). *A study of active shooter incidents, 2000–2013*. Washington, DC: Texas State University and Federal Bureau of Investigation, US Department of Justice.

Booth, J. (1977). A short history of blood pressure measurement. *Proceedings of the Royal Society of Medicine, 70*, 739–799.

Borum, R., Bartel, P. A., & Forth, A. (2006). *Structured assessment of violence risk in youth (SAVRY)*. Lutz, FL: Psychological Assessment Resource.

Boylen, M., & Little, R. (1990). Fatal assaults on United States law enforcement officers. *Police Journal, 63*(61), 61–77.

Braga, A. A., Papachristos, A. V., & Hureau, D. M. (2010). The concentration and stability of gun violence at micro places in Boston, 1980–2008. *Journal of Quantitative Criminology, 26*(1), 33–53. doi:10.1007/s10940-009-9082-x

Brandl, S. G., & Stroshine, M. S. (2011). The relationship between gun and gun buyer characteristics and firearm time-to-crime. *Criminal Justice Policy Review, 22*(3), 285–300. doi:10.1177/0887403410373510

Breiner, M. J., & Witt, P. H. (2017). Advances in assessments for risk of sex offender recidivism. *Sex Offender Law Report, 18*(6), 81–93.

Buchanan, L., Keller, J., Oppel, R., & Victor, D. (2016, June 12). How they got their guns. *New York Times*. Retrieved from www.nytimes.com/interactive/2015/10/03/us/how-mass-shooters-got-their-guns.html?_r=1

Burgason, K. A., Thomas, S. A., & Berthelot, E. R. (2014). The nature of violence: A multilevel analysis of gun use and victim injury in violent interpersonal encounters. *Journal of Interpersonal Violence, 29*(3), 371–393.

Bushman, B. J., Newman, K., Calvert, S. L., Downey, G., Dredze, M., Gottfredson, M., Jablonski, N. D., Masten, A. S., Morrill, C., Neill, D. B., Romer, D., & Webster, D. W. (2016). Youth violence: What we know and what we need to know. *American Psychologist, 71*(1), 17–39. doi:10.1037/a0039687

Buss, A. H., & Perry, M. (1992). The aggression questionnaire. *Journal of Personality and Social Psychology, 63*(3), 452–459. doi:10.1037/0022-3514.63.3.452

Camara, W. J., Nathan, J. S., & Puente, A. E. (2000). Psychological test usage: Implications in professional psychology. *Professional Psychology Research and Practice, 31*(2), 141–154.

Carbone, N. (2012, July 21). Colorado theater shooter carried 4 guns, all obtained legally. *Time.* Retrieved from http://newsfeed.time.com/2012/07/21/colorado-theater-shooter-carried-4-guns-all-obtained-legally/

Carlson, J. (2015). *Citizen-protectors: The everyday politics of guns in an age of decline.* New York: Oxford University Press.

Carter, P. M., Walton, M. A., Roehler, D. R., Goldstick, J., Zimmerman, M. A., Blow, F. C., & Cunningham, R. M. (2015). Firearm violence among high-risk emergency department youth after an assault injury. *Pediatrics, 135*(5), 805–815. doi:10.1542/peds.2014-3572

Centers for Disease Control and Prevention. (2017). Sexual violence. Retrieved from www.cdc.gov/violenceprevention/sexualviolence/

Centers for Disease Control and Prevention. (2012). Sexual violence: Facts at a glance. Retrieved from www.cdc.gov/ViolencePrevention/pdf/SV-DataSheet-a.pdf

Cerdá, M., DiGangi, J., Galea, S., & Koenen, K. (2012). Epidemiologic research on interpersonal violence and common psychiatric disorders: Where do we go from here? *Depression and Anxiety, 29*(5), 359–385. doi:10.1002/da.21947

Chavira, C., Bazargan-Hejazi, S., Lin, J., del Pino, H. E., & Bazargan, M. (2011). Type of alcohol drink and exposure to violence: An emergency department study. *Journal of Community Health: The Publication for Health Promotion and Disease Prevention, 36*(4), 597–604. doi:10.1007/s10900-010-9347-1

Ching, H., Daffern, M., & Thomas, S. (2013). A comparison of contemporary and traditional classification schemes used to categorise youth violence. *Journal of Forensic Psychiatry & Psychology, 24*(5), 658–674. doi:10.1080/14789949.2013.832351

Chuck, E. (2015, December 5). More than 80% of guns used in mass shootings obtained legally. MSNBC. Retrieved from www.msnbc.com/msnbc/most-guns-mass-shootings-obtained-legally

Chumley, C. K. (2014, August 29). Fort Hood shooter Nidal Hasan petitions to be "citizen" of Islamic State. *Washington Times.* Retrieved from www.washingtontimes.com/news/2014/aug/29/fort-hood-shooter-nidal-hasan-petitions-be-citizen/

Cillizza, C. (2016, January 5). President Obama cried in public today. That's a good thing. *Washington Post.* Retrieved from www.washingtonpost.com/news/the-fix/wp/2016/01/05/why-men-should-cry-more-in-public/

Cleckley, H. (1955). *The mask of sanity: An attempt to clarify some issues about the so-called psychopathic personality* (3rd ed.). St. Louis, MO: Mosby.

Coben, J. H., & Steiner, C. A. (2003). Hospitalization for firearm-related injuries in the United States, 1997. *American Journal of Preventive Medicine, 24*(1), 1–8. doi:10.1016/S0749-3797(02)00578-0

Coid, J. W., Ullrich, S., Keers, R., Bebbington, P., DeStavola, B. L., Kallis, C., Yang, M., Reiss, D., Jenkins, R., & Donnelly, P. (2013). Gang membership, violence, and psychiatric morbidity. *American Journal of Psychiatry, 170*(9), 985–993. doi:10.1176/appi.ajp.2013.12091188

Colin Ferguson—The Long Island Railroad gunman. (n.d.). Cornell Law School. Retrieved from www.law.cornell.edu/background/insane/lirr.html

Connecticut Office of the State Attorney. (2013). *Report of the state's attorney for the judicial district of Danbury on the shootings at Sandy Hook Elementary School and 36 Yoganada Street, Newton, Connecticut on December 14, 2012.* Retrieved from www.scribd.com/doc/187052598/Official-Sandy-Hook-Report

Cook, P. J., & Goss, K. A. (2014). *The gun debate: What everyone needs to know.* New York: Oxford University Press.

Cook, P. J., Parker, S. T., & Pollack, H. A. (2015). Sources of guns to dangerous people: What we learn by asking them. *Preventive Medicine: An International Journal Devoted to Practice and Theory, 79*, 28–36. doi:10.1016/j.ypmed.2015.04.021

Cornell, D. (2007). The Virginia model for student threat assessment. Public Entity Risk Institute (PERI) online conference. http://citeseerx.ist.psu.edu/viewdoc/download?doi=10.1.1.177.426&rep=rep1&type=pdf

Cornell, D., & Allen, K. (2011). Development, evaluation, and future directions of the Virginia student threat assessment guidelines. *Journal of School Violence, 10*, 88–106. doi:10.1080/15388220.2010.519432

Cornell, D., Sheras, P., Gregory, A., & Fan, X. (2009). A retrospective study of school safety conditions in high schools using the Virginia threat assessment guidelines versus alternative approaches. *School Psychology Quarterly, 24*, 119–129. doi:http://dx.doi.org/10.1037/a0016182

Cornish, D., & Clarke, R. (1987). Understanding crime displacement: An application of rational choice theory. *Criminology, 25*(4), 933–947.

Corrigan, P. W., & Watson, A. C. (2005). Findings from the National Comorbidity Survey on the frequency of violent behavior in individuals with psychiatric disorders. *Psychiatry Research, 136*(2-3), 153–162. doi:10.1016/j.psychres.2005.06.005

Covington, M. W., Huff-Corzine, L., & Corzine, J. (2014). Battered police: Risk factors for violence against law enforcement officers. *Violence and Victims, 29*(1), 34–52. doi:10.1891/0886-6708.VV-D-12-00022

Craun, S. W., Detar, P. J., & Bierie, D. M. (2013). Shots fired: Firearm discharges during fugitive apprehensions. *Victims & Offenders, 8*(1), 56–69. doi:10.1080/15564886.2012.745459

Cuffe, S. P., & Desai, C. V. (2016). Assessing adolescents. In *Dulcan's textbook of child and adolescent psychiatry,* edited by M. K. Dulcan and M. K. Dulcan (pp. 73–87). Arlington, VA: American Psychiatric Publishing.

Daftary-Kapur, T., & Zottoli, T. M. (2014). A first look at the plea deal experiences of juveniles tried in adult court. *International Journal of Forensic Mental Health, 13*(4), 323–336. doi:10.1080/14999013.2014.960983

Death Penalty Information Center. (n.d.). The U.S. military death penalty. Retrieved from https://deathpenaltyinfo.org/us-military-death-penalty

Declercq, F., & Audenaert, K. (2011). Predatory violence aiming at relief in a case of mass murder: Meloy's criteria for applied forensic practice. *Behavioral Sciences & The Law*, *29*(4), 578–591. doi:10.1002/bsl.994

Dem blames "political correctness" for Fort Hood "workplace violence" controversy. (2013, May 7). Retrieved from https://abcnews.go.com/News/dem-blames-political-correctness-for-fort-hood-massacre-controversy/blogEntry?id=19126011

DeMatteo, D., & Edens, J. F. (2006). The role and relevance of the Psychopathy Checklist-Revised in court: A case law survey of U.S. courts (1991–2004). *Psychology, Public Policy, and Law*, *12*(2), 214–241. doi:10.1037/1076-8971.12.2.214

DeMatteo, D., Edens, J. F., Galloway, M., Cox, J., Smith, S. T., & Formon, D. (2014). The role and reliability of the Psychopathy Checklist—Revised in U.S. sexually violent predator evaluations: A case law survey. *Law and Human Behavior*, *38*(3), 248–255. doi:10.1037/lhb0000059

DeMatteo, D., Murphy, M., Galloway, M., & Krauss, D. A. (2015). A national survey of United States sexually violent person legislation: Policy, procedures, and practice. *International Journal of Forensic Mental Health*, *14*(4), 245–266. doi:10.1080/14999013.2015.1110847

De Venanzi, A. (2012). School shootings in the USA: Popular culture as risk, teen marginality, and violence against peers. *Crime, Media, Culture*, *8*(3), 261–278. doi:10.1177/1741659012443233

Dolan, M., & Doyle, M. (2000). Violence risk prediction: Clinical and actuarial measures and the role of the Psychopathy Checklist. *British Journal of Psychiatry*, *177*, 303–311. doi:10.1192/bjp.177.4.303

Douglas, K. S., Hart, S. D., Webster, C. D., & Belfrage, H. (2013). *HCR-20^{V3}: Assessing risk of violence user guide*. Vancouver, Canada: Mental Health, Law, and Public Policy Institute, Simon Fraser University.

Duke, N. N., Pettingell, S. L., McMorris, B. J., & Borowsky, I. W. (2010). Adolescent violence perpetration: Associations with multiple types of adverse childhood experiences. *Pediatrics*, *125*(4), e778–e786. doi:10.1542/peds.2009-0597

Eckberg, D. (2015). Trends in conflict: Uniform Crime Reports, the National Crime Victimization Surveys, and the lethality of violent crime. *Homicide Studies*, *19*(1), 58–87. doi:10.1177/1088767914557810

Elkington, K. S., Teplin, L. A., Abram, K. M., Jakubowski, J. A., Dulcan, M. K., & Welty, L. J. (2015). Psychiatric disorders and violence: A study of delinquent youth after detention. *Journal of the American Academy of Child & Adolescent Psychiatry*, *54*(4), 302–312. doi:10.1016/j.jaac.2015.01.002

Ellis, R., & Chavez, N. (2017, October 20). *Las Vegas police again change timeline of mass shooting*. CNN. Retrieved from www.cnn.com/2017/10/13/us/las-vegas-shooting-investigation/index.html

Elsass, J. H., Schildkraut, J., & Stafford, M. (2015). Studying school shootings: Challenges and considerations for research. *American Journal of Criminal Justice*, *41*(3), 444–464. doi:10.1007/s12103-015-9311-9

Enger, J. (2015, March 18). The shooting at Red Lake: What happened. *MPR News*. Retrieved from www.mprnews.org/story/2015/03/18/red-lake-shooting-explained

Etter, G. W., & Swymeler, W. G. (2010). Research note: Courthouse shootings 1907–2007. *Homicide Studies*, *14*(1), 90–100.

Everytown. (2015). *Analysis of recent mass shootings.* Retrieved from https://everytownresearch.org/documents/2015/09/analysis-mass-shootings.pdf

Fact sheet: New executive actions to reduce gun violence and make our communities safer. (2016, January 4). White House Office of the Press Secretary. Retrieved from https://obamawhitehouse.archives.gov/the-press-office/2016/01/04/fact-sheet-new-executive-actions-reduce-gun-violence-and-make-our

Felson, R. B., Berg, M. T., & Rogers, M. L. (2014). Bring a gun to a gunfight: Armed adversaries and violence across nations. *Social Science Research, 47,* 79–90. doi:10.1016/j.ssresearch.2014.03.012

Ferguson, C. J., & Konijn, E. A. (2015). She said/he said: A peaceful debate on video game violence. *Psychology of Popular Media Culture, 4*(4), 397–411. doi:10.1037/ppm0000064

Fingerhut, L. A., & Christoffel, K. K. (2002). Firearm-related death and injury among children and adolescents. *The Future of Children, 12*(2), 25–37. doi:10.2307/1602736

First ever global report on violence and health released. (2002, October 3). World Health Organization. Retrieved from http://www.who.int/mediacentre/news/releases/pr73/en/

Fowler, K. A., Dahlberg, L. L., Haileyesus, T., & Annest, J. L. (2015). Firearm injuries in the United States. *Preventive Medicine: An International Journal Devoted to Practice and Theory, 79:* 5–14. doi:10.1016/j.ypmed.2015.06.002

Fox, J. A., & DeLateur, M. J. (2014). Mass shootings in America: Moving beyond Newtown. *Homicide Studies, 18*(1), 125–145. doi:10.1177/1088767913510297

Friedberg, A., & Davey, M. (2007, December 6). Gunman at Omaha malls kills 8 and himself. *New York Times.* Retrieved from www.nytimes.com/2007/12/06/us/06omaha.html?_r=0

Furlong, M., & Morrison, G. (2000). The school in school violence: Definitions and facts. In *Making schools safer and violence free: Critical issues, solutions, and recommended practices,* edited by H. M. Walker, M. H. Epstein, H. M. Walker, & M. H. Epstein (pp. 5–16). Austin, TX: PRO-ED.

Galatzer-Levy, I. R., & Bryant, R. A. (2013). 636,120 ways to have posttraumatic stress disorder. *Perspectives on Psychological Science, 8*(6), 651–662. doi:10.1177/1745691613504115

Gerard, F. J., Whitfield, K. C., Porter, L. E., & Browne, K. D. (2016). Offender and offence characteristics of school shooting incidents. *Journal of Investigative Psychology and Offender Profiling, 13*(1), 22–38. doi:10.1002/jip.1439

Gibbs, J. C., Ruiz, J., & Klapper-Lehman, S. A. (2014). Police officers killed on duty: Replicating and extending a unique look at officer deaths. *International Journal of Police Science & Management, 16*(4), 277–287.

Gilbert, F., & Daffern, M. (2011). Illuminating the relationship between personality disorder and violence: Contributions of the general aggression model. *Psychology of Violence, 1*(3), 230–244. doi:10.1037/a0024089

Gold, L. H., & Simon, R. I. (2016). *Gun violence and mental illness.* Arlington, VA: American Psychiatric Association.

Gookin, K. (2007). *Comparison of state laws authorizing involuntary commitment of sexually violent predators: 2006 update, revised.* Document No. 07-08-1101. Olympia: Washington State Institute for Public Policy.

Graham v. Florida, 130 S. Ct. 2011, 560 U.S. 48, 176 L. Ed. 2d 825 (2010).

Griffiths, E., & Chavez, J. M. (2004). Communities, street guns and homicide trajectories in Chicago, 1980–1995: Merging methods for examining homicide trends across space and time. *Criminology, 42*(4), 941–978.

Grimaldi, J. V., & Kunkle, F. (2011, January 9). Gun used in Tucson was purchased legally; Arizona laws among most lax in nation. *Washington Post.* Retrieved from www.washingtonpost.com/wp-dyn/content/article/2011/01/09/AR2011010901912.html

Grisso, T., Steinberg, L., Woolard, J., Cauffman, E., Scott, E., Graham, S., Lexcen, F. J., Repucci, N. D., & Schwartz, R. (2003). Juveniles' competence to stand trial: A comparison of adolescents' and adults' capacities as trial defendants. *Law and Human Behavior, 27*(4), 333.

Grommon, E., & Rydberg, J. (2015). Elaborating the correlates of firearm injury severity: Combining criminological and public health concerns. *Victims & Offenders, 10*(3), 318–340. doi:10.1080/15564886.2014.952472

Gunman shoots Philadelphia police officer "in the name of Islam." (2016, January 9). *CNBC.* Retrieved from www.cnbc.com/2016/01/09/gunman-shoots-philadelphia-police-officer-in-the-name-of-islam.html

Guy, L. S., Kusaj, C., Packer, I. K., & Douglas, K. S. (2015). Influence of the HCR-20, LS/CMI, and PCL-R on decisions about parole suitability among lifers. *Law and Human Behavior, 39*(3), 232–243. doi:10.1037/lhb0000111

Haas, H., & Cusson, M. (2015). Comparing theories' performance in predicting violence. *International Journal of Law and Psychiatry, 38,* 75–83. doi:10.1016/j.ijlp.2015.01.010

Hampson, R. (2013, June 12). "Apostrophe laws" named for kid victims on the wane. *USA Today.* Retrieved from www.usatoday.com/story/news/nation/2013/06/12/apostrophe-laws-on-the-wane-/2415963/

Hancock, L. (2011, June). Lee Hancock: The gun Nidal Hasan used to kill at Fort Hood. *Dallas News.* Retrieved from www.dallasnews.com/opinion/commentary/2011/06/17/lee-hancock-the-gun-nidal-hasan-used-to-kill-at-fort-hood

Hanson, R. K. (2003). Who is dangerous and when are they safe? Risk assessment with sexual offenders. In *Protecting society from sexually dangerous offenders: Law, justice, and therapy,* edited by B. J. Winick, J. Q. La Fond (pp. 63–74). Washington, DC: American Psychological Association. doi:10.1037/10492-003

Hare, R. D. (1980). A research scale for the assessment of psychopathy in criminal populations. *Personality and Individual Differences, 1*(2), 111–119. doi:10.1016/0191-8869(80)90028-8

Hare, R. D. (1991). *The Psychopathy Checklist Revised.* Toronto, Canada: Multi-Health Systems.

Hare, R. D. (2003). *The Psychopathy Checklist Revised,* 2nd ed. Toronto, Canada: Multi-Health Systems.

Hare, R. D. (1999). *Without conscience: The disturbing world of the psychopaths among us.* New York: Guilford Press.

Hare, R. D., & Neumann, C. S. (2008). Psychopathy as a clinical and empirical construct. *Annual Review of Clinical Psychology, 4,* 217–246. doi:10.1146/annurev.clinpsy.3.022806.091452

Harford, T. C., Yi, H., & Grant, B. F. (2013). Other- and self-directed forms of violence and their relationships to DSM-IV substance use and other psychiatric disorders in a national survey of adults. *Comprehensive Psychiatry*, *54*(7), 731–739. doi:10.1016/j.comppsych.2013.02.003

Harris, J. J., & Harris, R. B. (2012). Rampage violence requires a new type of research. *American Journal of Public Health*, *102*(6), 1054–1057. doi:10.2105/AJPH.2011.300545

Harter, S., Low, S. M., & Whitesell, N. R. (2003). What have we learned from Columbine: The impact of the self-system on suicidal and violent ideation among adolescents. *Journal of School Violence*, *2*(3), 3–26.

Hedges, C. (2003, July 6). What every person should know about war. *New York Times*. Retrieved from www.nytimes.com/2003/07/06/books/chapters/what-every-person-should-know-about-war.html

Hepburn, L., Miller, M., Azrael, D., & Hemenway, D. (2007). The US gun stock: Results from the 2004 national firearms survey. *Injury Prevention*, *13*(1), 15–19.

Hernandez, E., & Ingold, J. (2016, April 22). Judge imposes 12 life sentences plus 3,318 years on Aurora theater shooting gunman. *Denver Post*. Retrieved from www.denverpost.com/2015/08/26/judge-imposes-12-life-sentences-plus-3318-years-on-aurora-theater-shooting-gunman/

Hickman, M. J., Piquero, A. R., & Garner, J. H. (2008). Toward a national estimate of police use of nonlethal force. *Criminology & Public Policy*, *7*(4), 563–604.

Hoge, R. D., & Andrews, D. A. (2006). *Youth level of service/care management inventory: User's manual*. North Tonawanda, NY: Multi-Health Systems.

Hoskin, A. (2011). Household gun prevalence and rates of violent crime: A test of competing gun theories. *Criminal Justice Studies*, *24*(1), 125–136. doi:10.1080/1478601X.2011.544445

Howell, K. (2016, April 2). White House says "technical issue" caused omission of "Islamist terrorism" from video. *Washington Times*. Retrieved from http://m.washingtontimes.com/news/2016/apr/2/white-house-says-technical-issue-caused-omission-i/

Huang, Y., & Chou, C. (2010). An analysis of multiple factors of cyberbullying among junior high school students in Taiwan. *Computers in Human Behavior*, *26*(6), 1581–1590. doi:10.1016/j.chb.2010.06.005

Huston, W. T. (2016, May 9). Mother's Day weekend bloodbath: 43 wounded, 9 killed in Chicago gang violence. Breitbart. Retrieved from www.breitbart.com/big-government/2016/05/09/mothers-day-weekend-bloodbath-43-wounded-9-killed-in-chicago-gang-violence/

Ingraham, C. (2015, December 3). What makes a "mass shooting" in America [blog post]. Retrieved from www.washingtonpost.com/news/wonk/wp/2015/12/03/what-makes-a-mass-shooting-in-america/?utm_term=.50335b067883

In re Gault, 387 U.S. 1, 87 S. Ct. 1428, 18 L. Ed. 2d 527 (1967).

Investigative Assistance for Violent Crimes Act of 2012. Pub. L. 112–265, 126 Stat. 2436 (2013).

James Holmes (2015, July 17). Biography. Retrieved from www.biography.com/people/james-holmes-20891561

Jared Lee Loughner. (2015, January 2). Biography. Retrieved from https://www.biography.com/people/jared-lee-loughner

Johnson, K. L., Desmarais, S. L., Van Dorn, R. A., & Grimm, K. J. (2015). A typology of community violence perpetration and victimization among adults with mental illnesses. *Journal of Interpersonal Violence, 30*(3), 522–540. doi:10.1177/0886260514535102

Johnson, R. R. (2008). Officer firearms assaults at domestic violence calls: A descriptive analysis. *Police Journal, 81*(1), 25–45.

Kenbar, B. (2013, August 28). Nidal Hasan sentenced to death for Fort Hood shooting rampage. *Washington Post*. Retrieved from www.washingtonpost. com/world/national-security/nidal-hasan-sentenced-to-death-for-fort-hood-shooting-rampage/2013/08/28/aad28de2-0ffa-11e3-bdf6-e4fc677d94a1_story. html?utm_term=.913193c53dd8

Kent v. United States, 383 U.S. 541, 86 S. Ct. 1045, 16 L. Ed. 2d 84 (1966).

Kiehl, K. A., & Hoffman, M. B. (2011). The criminal psychopath: History, neuroscience, treatment, and economics. *Jurimetrics, 51*, 355.

Kieltyka, J., Kucybala, K., & Crandall, M. (2016). Ecologic factors relating to firearm injuries and gun violence in Chicago. *Journal of Forensic & Legal Medicine, 37*, 87–90. doi:10.1016/j.jflm.2015.11.003

Killias, M., van Kesteren, J., & Rindlisbacher, M. (2001). Guns, violent crime, and suicide in 21 countries. *Canadian Journal of Criminology, 43*(4), 429–448.

King, B. (2012). Psychological theories of violence. *Journal of Human Behavior in the Social Environment, 22*(5), 553–571. doi:10.1080/10911359.2011.598742

Kleck, G. (2004). Measures of gun ownership levels for macro-level crime and violence research. *Journal of Research in Crime and Delinquency, 41*(1), 3–36. doi:10.1177/0022427803256229

Kleck, G. (2015). The impact of gun ownership rates on crime rates: A methodological review of the evidence. *Journal of Criminal Justice, 43*(1), 40–48. doi:10.1016/j.jcrimjus.2014.12.002

Knoll, J. I., & Annas, G. D. (2016). Mass shootings and mental illness. In *Gun violence and mental illness*, edited by L. H. Gold and R. I. Simon (pp. 81–104). Arlington, VA: American Psychiatric Association.

Kohn, D. (2001, April 17). What really happened at Columbine? Did so many have to die? CBS News. Retrieved from www.cbsnews.com/news/ what-really-happened-at-columbine/

Krause, K. (2009). Beyond definition: Violence in a global perspective. *Global Crime, 10*(4), 337–355. doi:10.1080/17440570903248270

Krug, E. G., Mercy, J. A., Dahlberg, L. L., & Zwi, A. B. (2002). The world report on violence and health. *Lancet, 360*(9339), 1083–1088.

Langman, P. (2009). Rampage school shooters: A typology. *Aggression & Violent Behavior, 14*(1), 79–86. doi:10.1016/j.avb.2008.10.003

Larkin, R. W. (2009). The Columbine legacy: Rampage shootings as political acts. *American Behavioral Scientist, 52*(9), 1309–1326. doi:10.1177/ 0002764209332548

Leary, M. R., Kowalski, R. M., Smith, L., & Phillips, S. (2003). Teasing, rejection, and violence: Case studies of the school shootings. *Aggressive Behavior, 29*(3), 202–214. doi:10.1002/ab.10061

Lee, B. X. (2015). Causes and cures I: Toward a new definition. *Aggression and Violent Behavior, 25*, 199–203. doi:10.1016/j.avb.2015.10.004

Levene, K. S., Augimeri, L. K., Pepler, D. J., Walsh, M. M., Webster, C. D., & Koegl, C. J. (2001). *Early Assessment Risk List for Girls (EARL-21G)*. Toronto: Earlscourt Child and Family Centre.

"Loner" Jared Loughner spoke to Giffords in 2007. (2011, January 9). Face the Nation. Retrieved from www.cbsnews.com/news/loner-jared-loughner-spoke-to-giffords-in-2007/

Loughner moved to MN facility. (2016, March 4). *Tucson News.* Retrieved from http://www.tucsonnewsnow.com/story/30919983/loughner-moved-to-mn-facility

Margolin, J., & McKinley, C. (2016, Mar 3). Exclusive: Inside the prison assault on Aurora theater shooter James Holmes. ABC News. Retrieved from http://abcnews.go.com/US/exclusive-inside-prison-assault-aurora-theater-shooter-james/story?id=37339691

Marysville shooter texted before killings that he didn't want to "go alone." (2016, January 11). *Seattle Times.* Retrieved from www.seattletimes.com/seattle-news/crime/1400-page-report-on-marysville-school-shooting-cant-nail-down-motive/

Maskaly, J., & Donner, C. M. (2015). A theoretical integration of social learning theory with terror management theory: Towards an explanation of police shootings of unarmed suspects. *American Journal of Criminal Justice, 40*(2), 205–224. doi:10.1007/s12103-015-9293-7

Mattaini, M. A. (2012). Guns: The data tell us. *Behavior and Social Issues, 21*, 1–4.

Mayor Kenney on officer shooting: "It has nothing to do with being Muslim." (2016, January 8). CBS Philly. Retrieved from http://philadelphia.cbslocal.com/2016/01/08/mayor-kenney-on-officer-shooting-it-has-nothing-to-do-with-being-muslim/

McCarthy, T. (2015, March 18). The uncounted: Why the US can't keep track of people killed by police. *The Guardian.* Retrieved from https://www.theguardian.com/us-news/2015/mar/18/police-killings-government-data-count

McEllistrem, J. E. (2004). Affective and predatory violence: A bimodal classification system of human aggression and violence. *Aggression and Violent Behavior, 10*(1), 1–30. doi:10.1016/j.avb.2003.06.002

McGinty, E. E., Kennedy-Hendricks, A., Choksy, S., & Barry, C. L. (2016). Trends in news media coverage of mental illness in the United States: 1995–2014. *Health Affairs, 35*(6), 1121–1129.

McGinty, E. E., & Webster, D. W. (2016). Gun violence and serious mental illness. In *Gun violence and mental illness*, edited by L. H. Gold and R. I. Simon (pp. 3–30). Arlington, VA: American Psychiatric Association.

McMurran, M., Jinks, M., Howells, K., & Howard, R. C. (2010). Alcohol-related violence defined by ultimate goals: A qualitative analysis of the features of three different types of violence by intoxicated young male offenders. *Aggressive Behavior, 36*(1), 67–79. doi:10.1002/ab.20331

McMurran, M., Jinks, M., Howells, K., & Howard, R. (2011). Investigation of a typology of alcohol-related violence defined by ultimate goals. *Legal and Criminological Psychology, 16*(1), 75–89. doi:10.1348/135532510X486980

Medina, J. C. (2015). Neighborhood firearm victimization rates and social capital over time. *Violence & Victims, 30*(1), 81–96. doi:10.1891/0886-6708. VV-D-13-00092

Meloy, J. R. (2006). Empirical basis and forensic application of affective and predatory violence. *Australian and New Zealand Journal of Psychiatry, 40*(6–7), 539–547.

Mercado, C. C., Jeglic, E., Markus, K., Hanson, R. K., & Levenson, J. (2011). *Sex offender management, treatment, and civil commitment: An evidence based analysis aimed at reducing sexual violence.* Washington, DC: US Department of Justice.

Metzl, J. M., & MacLeish, K. T. (2015). Mental illness, mass shootings, and the politics of American firearms. *American Journal of Public Health, 105*(2), 240–249. doi:10.2105/AJPH.2014.302242

Meyer, G. J., Finn, S. E., Eyde, L. D., Kay, G. G., Moreland, K. L., Dies, R. R., Eisman, E. J., Kubiszyn, T. W., & Reed, G. M. (2001). Psychological testing and psychological assessment: A review of evidence and issues. *American Psychologist, 56*(2), 128–165. doi:10.1037/0003-066X.56.2.128

Miller v. Alabama, 132 S. Ct. 2455, 567 U.S., 183 L. Ed. 2d 407 (2012).

Miller, H. A., Amenta, A. E., & Conroy, M. A. (2005). Sexually violent predator evaluations: Empirical evidence, strategies for professionals, and research directions. *Law and Human Behavior, 29*(1), 29–54. doi:10.1007/s10979-005-1398-y

Miller, M., Hemenway, D., & Azrael, D. (2007). State-level homicide victimization rates in the US in relation to survey measures of household firearm ownership, 2001–2003. *Social Science & Medicine, 64*(3), 656–664. doi:10.1016/j.socscimed.2006.09.024

Mongan, P., Hatcher, S. S., & Maschi, T. (2009). Etiology of school shootings: Utilizing a purposive, non-impulsive model for social work practice. *Journal of Human Behavior in the Social Environment, 19*(5), 635–645. doi:10.1080/10911350902910583

Monuteaux, M. C., Lee, L. K., Hemenway, D., Mannix, R., & Fleegler, E. W. (2015). Firearm ownership and violent crime in the U.S.: An ecologic study. *American Journal of Preventive Medicine, 49*(2), 207–214. doi:10.1016/j.amepre.2015.02.008

Moreno, J. (2013, November 26). Sandy Hook killer took motive to his grave. *KTLA 5 News.* Retrieved from http://ktla.com/2013/11/26/sandy-hook-killer-took-motive-to-his-grave

Multi-Health Systems. (n.d.). MHS assessments. Retrieved from www.mhs.com

Muschert, G. W. (2007). Research in school shootings. *Sociology Compass, 1*(1), 60–80.

Muschert, G. W., & Spencer, J. W. (2009). The lesson of Columbine, part I. *American Behavioral Scientist, 52*(9), 1223–1226. doi:10.1177/0002764209332550

Najdowski, C. J., Cleary, H. D., & Stevenson, M. C. (2016). Adolescent sex offender registration policy: Perspectives on general deterrence potential from criminology and developmental psychology. *Psychology, Public Policy, and Law, 22*(1), 114–125. doi:10.1037/law0000059

National Council on Alcoholism and Drug Dependence. (2015, June 27). Alcohol, drugs, and crime. Retrieved from www.ncadd.org/about-addiction/alcohol-drugs-and-crime

Nekvasil, E. K., Cornell, D. G., & Huang, F. L. (2015). Prevalence and offense characteristics of multiple casualty homicides: Are schools at higher risk than other locations? *Psychology of Violence, 5*(3), 236–245. doi:10.1037/a0038967

Neumann, C. S., & Hare, R. D. (2008). Psychopathic traits in a large community sample: Links to violence, alcohol use, and intelligence. *Journal of Consulting and Clinical Psychology, 76*(5), 893–899. doi:10.1037/0022-006X.76.5.893

New photos taken inside "Dark Knight" theater show scene of James Holmes' deadly rampage. (2015, September 10). PIX11 News. Retrieved from http://pix11.com/2015/09/10/new-photos-show-scene-of-james-holmes-aurora-theater-shooting-his-booby-trapped-apartment/

Nicholls, T. L., Viljoen, J. L., Cruise, K. R., Desmarais, S. L., & Webster, C. D. (2010). *Short-Term Assessment of Risk and Treatability: Adolescent Version* (START: AV) (Abbreviated manual). Coquitlam, Canada: BC Mental Health and Addiction Services.

Nickeas, P., Wong, G., Chachkevitch, A., & Mahr, J. (2016, May 31). Memorial Day weekend closes with 69 shot in Chicago, many of them on West Side. *Chicago Tribune.* Retrieved from www.chicagotribune.com/news/local/breaking/ct-chicago-shootings-memorial-day-20160530-story.html

Orbis Partners. (2007). *Youth Assessment Screening Inventory (YASI).* Ottawa, ON, Canada: Orbis Partners.

Ousey, G. C., & Lee, M. R. (2010). The southern culture of violence and homicide-type differentiation: An analysis across cities and time points. *Homicide Studies: An Interdisciplinary & International Journal, 14*(3), 268–295.

Papachristos, A. V., Grossman, L. S., Braga, A. A., & Piza, E. (2015). The company you keep? The spillover effects of gang membership on individual gunshot victimization in a co-offending network. *Criminology, 53*(4), 624–649. doi:10.1111/1745-9125.12091

Pearson Education. (2017). Pearson assessments. Retrieved from www.pearsonassessments.com

Perez, E., Brown, P., & Almasy, S. (2016, June 17). Orlando shooting: Killer's behavior had long been an issue. CNN. Retrieved from www.cnn.com/2016/06/17/us/orlando-shooter-omar-mateen

Perrin, P. B. (2016). Translating psychological science: Highlighting the media's contribution to contagion in mass shootings: Comment on Kaslow (2015). *American Psychologist, 71*(1), 71–72. doi:10.1037/a0039994

Philipps, D., & Haag, M. (2017, October 2). Las Vegas gunman's criminal father vanished from sons' lives. *New York Times.* Retrieved from www.nytimes.com/2017/10/02/us/benjamin-paddock-stephen-paddock.html

Phillips, C. D., Nwaiwu, O., Moudouni, D. M., Edwards, R., & Lin, S. (2013). When concealed handgun licensees break bad: Criminal convictions of concealed handgun licensees in Texas, 2001–2009. *American Journal of Public Health, 103*(1), 86–91. doi:10.2105/AJPH.2012.300807

Phillips, D. A. (2007). Punking and bullying strategies in middle school, high school, and beyond. *Journal of Interpersonal Violence, 22*(2), 158–178.

Pinker, S. (2011). *The better angels of our nature: Why violence has declined.* New York: Viking.

Pirelli, G. (2016). Commonly contested issues in sexual risk assessment. *Sex Offender Law Report, 17*(3), 33–43.

Pirelli, G., & Witt, P. (2015). Psychological evaluations for civilian firearm ownership in New Jersey. *New Jersey Psychologist, 65*(1), 7–9.

Prentky, R. A., Barbaree, H. E., & Janus, E. S. (2015). *Sexual predators: Society, risk, and the law.* New York: Routledge/Taylor & Francis Group.

Pridemore, W. A., & Grubesic, T. H. (2013). Alcohol outlets and community levels of interpersonal violence: Spatial density, outlet type, and seriousness of assault. *Journal of Research in Crime and Delinquency, 50*(1), 132–159. doi:10.1177/0022427810397952

Psychological Assessment Resources. (2017). Retrieved from www4.parinc.com

Pulay, A. J., Dawson, D. A., Hasin, D. S., Goldstein, R. B., Ruan, W. J., Pickering, R. P., Huang, B., Chou, S. P., & Grant, B. F. (2008). Violent behavior and DSM-IV psychiatric disorders: Results from the National Epidemiologic Survey on Alcohol and Related Conditions. *Journal of Clinical Psychiatry, 69*(1), 12–22. doi:10.4088/JCP.v69n0103

Quinsey, V. L., Harris, G. T., Rice, M. E., & Cormier, C. A. (2006). *Violent offenders: Appraising and managing risk.* Washington, DC: American Psychological Association.

Reidy, D. E., Kearns, M. C., DeGue, S., Lilienfeld, S. O., Massetti, G., & Kiehl, K. A. (2015). Why psychopathy matters: Implications for public health and violence prevention. *Aggression and Violent Behavior, 24,* 214–225. doi:10.1016/j.avb.2015.05.018

Rice, M. E., & Harris, G. T. (1997). Cross-validation and extension of the Violence Risk Appraisal Guide for child molesters and rapists. *Law and Human Behavior, 21*(2), 231–241. doi:10.1023/A:1024882430242

Richardson, B. (2016, June 2). Media dedicate 54-times more coverage to gorilla than Chicago shooting spree. *Washington Times.* Retrieved from www.washingtontimes.com/news/2016/jun/2/media-dedicate-54-times-more-coverage-gorilla-chic/

Rocque, M. (2012). Exploring school rampage shootings: Research, theory, and policy. *Social Science Journal, 49*(3), 304–313. doi:10.1016/j.soscij.2011.11.001

Roesch, R., McLachlan, K., & Viljoen, J. L. (2008). The capacity of juveniles to understand and waive arrest rights. In *Learning forensic assessment*, edited by R. Jackson (pp. 265–289). New York: Routledge.

Roper v. Simmons, 543 U.S. 551, 125 S. Ct. 1183, 161 L. Ed. 2d 1 (2005).

Rosenthal, R. (1979). The file drawer problem and tolerance for null results. *Psychological Bulletin, 86*(3), 638–641.

Rosenwald, M. S. (2016, April 20). "Damaged masculinity" may help explain Columbine and other mass shootings. *Washington Post.* Retrieved from www.washingtonpost.com/news/local/wp/2016/04/20/damaged-masculinity-may-help-explain-columbine-and-other-mass-shootings/

Rutherford, A., Zwi, A. B., Grove, N. J., & Butchart, A. (2007). Violence: A glossary. *Journal of Epidemiology and Community Health, 61*(8), 676–680. doi:10.1136/jech.2005.043711

Sanburn, J. (2014, September 26). Why the FBI report that mass shootings are up can be misleading. *Time.* Retrieved from http://time.com/3432950/fbi-mass-shooting-report-misleading/

Schiffer, B., Müller, B. W., Scherbaum, N., Hodgins, S., Forsting, M., Wiltfang, J., Gizewski, E. R., & Leygraf, N. (2011). Disentangling structural brain alterations associated with violent behavior from those associated with substance use disorders. *Archives of General Psychiatry, 68*(10), 1039–1049. doi:10.1001/archgenpsychiatry.2011.61

Schomerus, G., Schwahn, C., Holzinger, A., Corrigan, P. W., Grabe, H. J., Carta, M. G., & Angermeyer, M. C. (2012). Evolution of public attitudes about mental illness: A systematic review and meta-analysis. *Acta Psychiatrica Scandinavica, 125*(6), 440–452. doi:10.1111/j.1600-0447.2012.01826.x

Scott, E. S., Reppucci, N. D., & Woolard, J. L. (1995). Evaluating adolescent decision making in legal contexts. *Law and Human Behavior, 19*(3), 221–244. doi:10.1007/BF01501658

Seung-Hui Cho. (2014, October 14). Biography. Retrieved from www.biography.com/people/seung-hui-cho-235991

Sevigny, E. L., & Allen, A. (2015). Gun carrying among drug market participants: Evidence from incarcerated drug offenders. *Journal of Quantitative Criminology, 31*(3), 435–458. doi:10.1007/s10940-014-9233-6

Shoener, N. (2016, October 10). Making a terrorist threat. LegalMatch. Retrieved from www.legalmatch.com/law-library/article/making-a-terrorist-threat.html

Siegel, M., Ross, C. S., & King, C. I. (2013). The relationship between gun ownership and firearm homicide rates in the United States, 1981–2010. *American Journal of Public Health, 103*(11), 2098–2105. doi:10.2105/AJPH.2013.301409

Simon, R. I., & Gold, L. H. (2016). Decreasing suicide mortality: Clinical risk assessment and firearm management. In *Gun violence and mental illness*, edited by L. H. Gold and R. I. Simon (pp. 249–289). Arlington, VA: American Psychiatric Association.

Skeem, J. L., & Monahan, J. (2011). Current directions in violence risk assessment. *Current Directions in Psychological Science, 20*(1), 38–42. doi:10.1177/0963721410397271

Spano, R. (2012). First time gun carrying and the primary prevention of youth gun violence for African American youth living in extreme poverty. *Aggression and Violent Behavior, 17*(1), 83–88. doi:10.1016/j.avb.2011.10.002

Spano, R., & Bolland, J. M. (2011). Is the nexus of gang membership, exposure to violence, and violent behavior a key determinant of first time gun carrying for urban minority youth? *JQ: Justice Quarterly, 28*(6), 838–862. doi:10.1080/07418825.2010.547868

Spano, R., Pridemore, W. A., & Bolland, J. (2012). Specifying the role of exposure to violence and violent behavior on initiation of gun carrying: A longitudinal test of three models of youth gun carrying. *Journal of Interpersonal Violence, 27*(1), 158–176. doi:10.1177/0886260511416471

Spiegel, A. (2011, May 26). Can a test really tell who's a psychopath? NPR. Retrieved from www.npr.org/2011/05/26/136619689/can-a-test-really-tell-whos-a-psychopath

Stanford v. Kentucky, 492 U.S. 361, 109 S. Ct. 2969, 106 L. Ed. 2d 306 (1989).

Steinberg, L. (2013). The influence of neuroscience on US Supreme Court decisions about adolescents' criminal culpability. *Nature Reviews Neuroscience, 14*(7), 513–518. doi:10.1038/nrn3509

Steinberg, L., & Cauffman, E. (1996). Maturity of judgment in adolescence: Psychosocial factors in adolescent decision making. *Law and Human Behavior, 20*(3), 249–272. doi:10.1007/BF01499023

Steinberg, L., Cauffman, E., Woolard, J., Graham, S., & Banich, M. (2009). Are adolescents less mature than adults? Minors' access to abortion, the juvenile death penalty, and the alleged APA "flip-flop." *American Psychologist, 64*(7), 583–594. doi:10.1037/a0014763

Steinberg, L., & Scott, E. S. (2003). Less guilty by reason of adolescence: Developmental immaturity, diminished responsibility, and the juvenile death penalty. *American Psychologist, 58*(12), 1009.

Stewart, D., & Bowers, L. (2013). Inpatient verbal aggression: Content, targets and patient characteristics. *Journal of Psychiatric and Mental Health Nursing, 20*(3), 236–243. doi:10.1111/j.1365-2850.2012.01905.x

Strait, M. D. (2010). Enoch Brown: A massacre unmatched. Retrieved from http://pabook2.libraries.psu.edu/palitmap/Enoch.html

Stroebe, W. (2013). Firearm possession and violent death: A critical review. *Aggression and Violent Behavior, 18*(6), 709–721. doi:10.1016/j.avb.2013.07.025

Teague, M., Ackerman, S., & Safi, M. (2016, June 12). Orlando nightclub shooter Omar Mateen was known to FBI, agent says. *The Guardian.* Retrieved from www.theguardian.com/us-news/2016/jun/12/omar-mateen-orlando-nightclub-attack-shooter-named

Teplin, L. A., Abram, K. M., & McClelland, G. M. (1994). Does psychiatric disorder predict violent crime among released jail detainees? A six-year longitudinal study. *American Psychologist, 49*(4), 335–342. doi:10.1037/0003-066X.49.4.335

The missing data on gun violence. (2016, January 21). *The Atlantic.* Retrieved from http://news.yahoo.com/missing-data-gun-violence-110000327.html.

Thompson v. Oklahoma, 487 U.S. 815, 108 S. Ct. 2687, 101 L. Ed. 2d 702 (1988).

Thorbecke, C. (2016, May 31). Cincinnati police launch criminal probe into gorilla incident at zoo. ABC News. Retrieved from http://abcnews.go.com/US/cincinnati-police-launch-criminal-probe-gorilla-incident-zoo/story?id=39500478

Trestman, R. L., Volkmar, F. R., & Gold, L. H. (2016). Accessing mental health care. In *Gun violence and mental illness*, edited by L. H. Gold and R. I. Simon (pp. 185–217). Arlington, VA: American Psychiatric Association.

University study documents gun violence injuries for African American youth. (2016, January 11). Danger Assessment. Retrieved from https://www.jbhe.com/2016/01/university-study-documents-gun-violence-injuries-for-african-american-youth/

van Kesteren, J. N. (2014). Revisiting the gun ownership and violence link: A multilevel analysis of victimization survey data. *British Journal of Criminology, 54*(1), 53–72. doi:10.1093/bjc/azt052

Violence Policy Center. (n.d.a). Where'd they get their guns? An analysis of the firearms used in high-profile shootings, 1963 to 2001. Retrieved from www.vpc.org/studies/wgun931207.htm

Violence Policy Center. (n.d.b). Where'd they get their guns? An analysis of the firearms used in high-profile shootings, 1963 to 2001. Retrieved from www.vpc.org/studies/wgun990420.htm

Violence Policy Center. (n.d.c). Where'd they get their guns? An analysis of the firearms used in high-profile shootings, 1963 to 2001. Selected high-profile shootings in the United States, 1963–2001. Retrieved from www.vpc.org/studies/wguncont.htm

Virginia Tech shooting leaves 32 dead. (n.d.). History.com. Retrieved from www.history.com/this-day-in-history/massacre-at-virginia-tech-leaves-32-dead

Virginia Tech shootings fast facts. (2017, April 3). CNN. Retrieved from www.cnn.com/2013/10/31/us/virginia-tech-shootings-fast-facts

Waddington, P. J., Badger, D., & Bull, R. (2005). Appraising the inclusive definition of workplace violence. *British Journal of Criminology, 45*(2), 141–164. doi:10.1093/bjc/azh052

Wallace, L. N. (2015). Responding to violence with guns: Mass shootings and gun acquisition. *Social Science Journal, 52*(2), 156–167. doi:10.1016/j.soscij.2015.03.002

Wallack, L., Winett, L., & Lee, A. (2005). Successful public policy change in California: Firearms and youth resources. *Journal of Public Health Policy, 26*(2), 206–226.

Warr, M. (2000). Fear of crime in the United States: Avenues for research and policy. In *Measurement and analysis of crime and justice*, Criminal justice 2000, vol. 4, edited by D. Duffee (pp. 451–489). Washington, DC: National Institute of Justice.

Waters, H. R., Hyder, A. A., & Rajkotia, Y. (2005). The costs of interpersonal violence: An international review. *Health Policy, 73*(3), 303–315.

Wellford, C. F., Pepper, J. V., & Petrie, C. V. (2004). *Firearms & violence: A critical review*. Washington, DC: National Academies Press.

Wevodau, A. L., Cramer, R. J., Gemberling, T. M., & Clark, J. I. (2016). A psychometric assessment of the Community Attitudes Toward Sex Offenders (CATSO) scale: Implications for public policy, trial, and research. *Psychology, Public Policy, and Law, 22*(2), 211–220. doi:10.1037/law0000066

White, M. D. (2016). Transactional encounters, crisis-driven reform, and the potential for a national police deadly force database. *Criminology & Public Policy, 15*(1), 223–235. doi:10.1111/1745-9133.12180

Willis, K. (2006). Armed robbery: Who commits it and why? *Trends & Issues in Crime & Criminal Justice*, (328), 1–6.

Wintemute, G. J. (2015a). Alcohol misuse, firearm violence perpetration, and public policy in the United States. *Preventive Medicine: An International Journal Devoted to Practice and Theory, 79*, 15–21. doi:10.1016/j.ypmed.2015.04.015

Wintemute, G. J. (2015b). The epidemiology of firearm violence in the twenty-first century United States. *Annual Review of Public Health, 36*, 8.1–8.15. doi:10.1146/annurev-publhealth-031914-122535

World Health Organization. (2014). *Global status report on violence prevention, 2014*. Geneva, Switzerland: World Health Organization.

World Health Organization. (1992). *The ICD-10 classification of mental and behavioural disorders: Clinical descriptions and diagnostic guidelines*. Geneva, Switzerland: World Health Organization.

Wu, X. J., Schepartz, L. A., Liu, W., & Trinkaus, E. (2011). Antemortem trauma and survival in the late Middle Pleistocene human cranium from Maba, South China. *Proceedings of the National Academy of Sciences, 108*(49), 19558–19562.

Zawitz, M. W. (1995). *Guns used in crime*. Bureau of Justice Statistics Selected Findings, publication NCJ-148201. Washington, DC: US Department of Justice.

Zhang, A., Musu-Gillette, L., & Oudekerk, B. A. (2016). *Indicators of school crime and safety: 2015*. NCES 2016-079, NCJ 249758. Washington, DC: National Center for Education Statistics.

Zwi, A., Garfield, R., & Loretti, A. (2002). Collective violence. In *World report on violence and health*, edited by E. Krug, L. Dahlberg, J. Mercy, A. Zwi, and R. Lozano (pp. 213–240) Geneva, Switzerland: World Health Organization.

Chapter 5

Alhabib, S., Nur, U., & Jones, R. (2010). Domestic violence against women: Systematic review of prevalence studies. *Journal of Family Violence*, *25*(4), 369–382.

Anderson, A. S., & Lo, C. C. (2011). Intimate partner violence within law enforcement families. *Journal of Interpersonal Violence*, *26*(6), 1176–1193. doi:10.1177/0886260510368156

Andrews, T. (2016, April 12). 40 percent of former NFL players suffer from brain injuries, new study shows. *Washington Post*. Retrieved from www.washingtonpost.com/news/morning-mix/wp/2016/04/12/40-percent-of-former-nfl-players-suffer-from-brain-damage-new-study-shows/

Bahk, D. (2016, April 5). NFL athletes with CTE who committed suicide. *Stony Brook Independent*. Retrieved from https://sbindependent.org/nfl-athletes-with-cte-who-committed-suicide/

Banks, L., Crandall, C., Sklar, D., & Bauer, M. (2008). A comparison of intimate partner homicide to intimate partner homicide–suicide: One hundred and twenty-four New Mexico cases. *Violence Against Women*, *14*(9), 1065–1078.

Barnard, G. W., Vera, H., Vera, M. I., & Newman, G. (1982). Till death do us part: A study of spouse murder. *Bulletin of the American Academy of Psychiatry & the Law*, *10*(4), 271–280.

Biggers, J. R. (2003). A dynamic assessment of the battered woman syndrome and its legal relevance. *Journal of Forensic Psychology Practice*, *3*(3), 1–22.

Billie Wayne Coble v. The State of Texas, AP-76, 019 (2010).

Blosser, J. (2015, February 10). Top 30 Hollywood republican celebrities: A Newsmax list. Newsmax. Retrieved from www.newsmax.com/t/newsmax/article/623957

Bond, C. W., & Jeffries, S. (2014). Similar punishment? Comparing sentencing outcomes in domestic and non-domestic violence cases. *British Journal of Criminology*, *54*(5), 849–872.

Brame family settles lawsuit against Tacoma. (2005, September 13). *Seattle Times*. Retrieved from www.seattletimes.com/seattle-news/brame-family-settles-lawsuit-against-tacoma

Bridges, F. S., Tatum, K. M., & Kunselman, J. C. (2008). Domestic violence statutes and rates of intimate partner and family homicide. *Criminal Justice Policy Review*, *19*(1), 117–130.

Bureau of Justice Statistics, US Department of Justice. (2007). Homicide trends in the U.S.: Intimate homicide. Retrieved from https://www.bjs.gov/index.cfm?ty=pbse&sid=31

Butt, J. (2015, February 9). Panthers' Greg Hardy has domestic violence case dismissed. *CBS Sports*. Retrieved from www.cbssports.com/nfl/news/panthers-greg-hardy-has-domestic-violence-case-dismissed

Byrne, M. (2016, July 1). Half of Maine homicides in 2014–15 stemmed from domestic violence, report says. *Portland Press Herald*. Retrieved from www.pressherald.com/2016/06/30/half-of-maine-homicides-stemmed-from-domestic-violence-report-shows/

Campbell, J. C., Glass, N., Sharps, P. W., Laughon, K., & Bloom, T. (2007). Intimate partner homicide. *Trauma, Violence & Abuse, 8*(3), 246–269.

Campbell, J. C., Webster, D., Koziol-McLain, J., Block, C., Campbell, D., Curry, M. A., Gary, F., Glass, N., McFarlane, J., Sachs, C., Sharps, P., Ulrich, Y., Wilt, S., Manganello, J., Xu, X., Schollenberger, J., Frye, V., & Laughon, K. (2003). Risk factors for femicide in abusive relationships: Results from a multisite case control study. *American Journal of Public Health, 93*(7), 1089–1097.

Cascardi, M., & Muzyczyn, B. (2016). Concordant responding on the physical assault/abuse subscales of the Revised Conflict Tactics Scales 2 and Conflict in Adolescent Dating Relationships Inventory. *Psychology of Violence, 6*(2), 303–312.

Centers for Disease Control and Prevention. (n.d.). Intimate partner violence. Retrieved from www.cdc.gov/violenceprevention/intimatepartnerviolence/index.html

Chesler, P. (2010). Worldwide trends in honor killings. *Middle East Quarterly, 17*(2), 3–11.

Coker, A. L., Davis, K. E., Arias, I., Desai, S., Sanderson, M., Brandt, H. M., & Smith, P. H. (2002). Physical and mental health effects of intimate partner violence for men and women. *American Journal of Preventive Medicine, 23*(4), 260–268.

Colpitts, J., & Niemczyk, K. (2012). Marital rape, strangulation, bail, firearms, and risk. *Domestic Violence Report, 18*(2), 17–30.

Corvo, K., & Dutton, D. (2015). Neurotransmitter and neurochemical factors in domestic violence perpetration: Implications for theory development. *Partner Abuse, 6*(3), 351–363.

Costanzo, M., & Krauss, D. (2010). *Forensic and legal psychology: Psychological science applied to law.* New York: Worth Publishing.

DA: Pa. dad took kids to theme park before killing family, self. (2016, August 15). *Crimesider*. Retrieved from www.cbsnews.com/news/pennsylvania-family-murder-suicide-mark-short-dad-took-kids-to-hershey-park-before-killing-family/

Davis, R. L. (2010). Domestic violence–related deaths. *Journal of Aggression, Conflict & Peace Research, 2*(2), 44–52.

Davoren, M., Kallis, C., González, R., Freestone, M., & Coid, J. (2016). Anxiety disorders and intimate partner violence: Can the association be explained by coexisting conditions or borderline personality traits? *Journal of Forensic Psychiatry and Psychology, 28*(5), 639–658. doi:10.1080/14789949.2016.1172659

DeJong, C., Pizarro, J., & McGarrell, E. (2011). Can situational and structural factors differentiate between intimate partner and "other" homicide? *Journal of Family Violence, 26*(5), 365–376.

Domestic abuse accusations: A look at celebrity cases. (2015, September 23). *Los Angeles Times*. Retrieved from www.latimes.com/entertainment/gossip/la-et-celebrity-domestic-abuse-pictures-photogallery.html

Ehrensaft, M., Knous-Westfall, H., & Cohen, P. (2016). Long-term influence of intimate partner violence and parenting practices on offspring trauma symptoms. *Psychology of Violence, 7*(2), 296–305.

Eichacker, C. (2016, August 17). Jefferson shooting that ended in death echoes other domestic violence cases in Maine. Centralmaine.com. Retrieved from www.centralmaine.com/2016/08/16/ex-boyfriend-shoots-wounds-woman-in-jefferson-then-kills-himself-after-fleeing-police/

Everytown for Gun Safety. (2015). *Analysis of recent mass shootings.* New York: Everytown for Gun Safety.

Everytown for Gun Safety. (2014). *Guns and violence against women.* New York: Everytown for Gun Safety.

Farr, K. A. (2002). Battered women who were "being killed and survived it": Straight talk from survivors. *Violence and Victims, 17*(3), 267–281.

Felton arrested on gun charges. (2014, February 25). ESPN. Retrieved from www.espn.com/new-york/nba/story/_/id/10514816/raymond-felton-new-york-knicks-arrested-weapons-charges

Folkes, S. F., Hilton, N. Z., & Harris, G. T. (2013). Weapon use increases the severity of domestic violence but neither weapon use nor firearm access increases the risk or severity of recidivism. *Journal of Interpersonal Violence, 28*(6), 1143–1156.

Frattaroli, S., & Teret, S. P. (2006). Understanding and informing policy implementation: A case study of the domestic violence provisions of the Maryland Gun Violence Act. *Evaluation Review, 30*(3), 347–360.

Frattaroli, S., & Vernick, J. S. (2006). Separating batterers and guns: A review and analysis of gun removal laws in 50 states. *Evaluation Review, 30*(3), 296–312.

Fry, C. (2011, June 4). Official: Arizona gunman targeted ex-wife, friends. *USA Today.* Retrieved from http://usatoday30.usatoday.com/news/nation/2011-06-04-arizona-shootings_n.htm

Frye, V., Manganello, J., Campbell, J. C., Walton-Moss, B., & Wilt, S. (2006). The distribution of and factors associated with intimate terrorism and situational couple violence among a population-based sample of urban women in the United States. *Journal of Interpersonal Violence, 21*(10), 1286–1313.

Garcia, L., Soria, C., & Hurwitz, E. L. (2007). Homicides and intimate partner violence: A literature review. *Trauma, Violence & Abuse, 8*(4), 370–383.

Gershon, R. (2000). *Police stress and domestic violence in police families in Baltimore, Maryland, 1997–1999.* ICPSR Study No. 2976. Baltimore, MD: Johns Hopkins University.

Getlen, L. (2014, September 6). Inside the murder of Phil Hartman. *New York Post.* Retrieved from http://nypost.com/2014/09/06/inside-the-murder-of-phil-hartman/

Glass, N., Laughon, K., Rutto, C., Bevacqua, J., & Campbell, J. C. (2008a). Young adult intimate partner femicide: An exploratory study. *Homicide Studies, 12*(2), 177–187.

Glass, N., Perrin, N., Hanson, G., Bloom, T., Gardner, E., & Campbell, J. C. (2008b). Risk for reassault in abusive female same-sex relationships. *American Journal of Public Health, 98*(6), 1021–1027.

Gordon, M. (1996). *Validity of "woman syndrome" in criminal cases involving battered women.* Bethesda, MD: National Institute of Mental Health.

Gwinn, C. (2006). Domestic violence and firearms: Reflections of a prosecutor. *Evaluation Review, 30*(3), 237–244.

Hanlon, R. E., Brook, M., Demery, J. A., & Cunningham, M. D. (2016). Domestic homicide: Neuropsychological profiles of murderers who kill family members and intimate partners. *Journal of Forensic Sciences, 61*(Suppl. 1), S163–S170.

Heide, K. M. (2013). Matricide and stepmatricide victims and offenders: An empirical analysis of U.S. arrest data. *Behavioral Sciences & the Law, 31*(2), 203–214.

Hemenway, D., & Hicks, J. G. (2015). "May issue" gun carrying laws and police discretion: Some evidence from Massachusetts. *Journal of Public Health Policy, 36*(3), 324–334.

Hopkins, K., Gecan, A., & Park, K. (2016, September 30). Philip Seidle sentenced to 30 years in prison. app.com. Retrieved from www.app.com/story/news/local/courts/2016/09/29/seidles-childrens-plea-put-dad-jail/91164272/

Ibn-Tamas v. United States, 407 A 2d 626 (1979).

Islam, T. (2010). The fourth circuit's rejection of legislative history: Placing guns in the hands of domestic violence perpetrators. *American University Journal of Gender, Social Policy & The Law, 18*(2), 341–366.

Jenkins, K. (2016, August 5). Attorney pleads guilty to domestic violence shooting. *The Spectrum*. Retrieved from www.thespectrum.com/story/news/2016/08/05/attorney-pleads-guilty-domestic-violence-shooting/88316186/

Jerry "The King" Lawler busted for domestic violence, pistol involved. (2016, June 17). Retrieved from www.yahoo.com/celebrity/jerry-the-king-lawler-busted-for-domestic-154647058.html

Johnson, J. A., Lutz, V. L., & Websdale, N. (1999). Death by intimacy: Risk factors for domestic violence. *Pace Law Review, 20*, 263.

Johnson, M. P. (1995). Patriarchal terrorism and common couple violence: Two forms of violence against women in U.S. families. *Journal of Marriage and the Family, 57*, 283–294.

Jouriles, E. N., McDonald, R., Norwood, W. D., Ware, H. S., Spiller, L. C., & Swank, P. R. (1998). Knives, guns, and interparent violence: Relations with child behavior problems. *Journal of Family Psychology, 12*(2), 178–194.

Kern, R., Libkuman, T. M., & Temple, S. L. (2007). Perceptions of domestic violence and mock jurors' sentencing decisions. *Journal of Interpersonal Violence, 22*(12), 1515–1535.

Kernsmith, P., & Craun, S. (2008). Predictors of weapon use in domestic violence incidents reported to law enforcement. *Journal of Family Violence, 23*(7), 589–596.

Kids saw police chief shoot wife, kill self. (2003, April 28). *ABC News*. Retrieved from http://abcnews.go.com/GMA/story?id=125208&page=1

Kimmel, S., & Friedman, S. H. (2011). Limitations of expert testimony on battered woman syndrome. *Journal of the American Academy of Psychiatry and the Law, 39*(4), 585–587.

Klein, A. K., Salomon, A., Huntington, N., Dubois, J., & Lang, D. (2009). *A statewide study of stalking and its criminal justice response*. Final report to the National Institute of Justice. Washington, DC: US Department of Justice, National Institute of Justice.

Klinoff, V. A., Van Hasselt, V. B., & Black, R. A. (2015). Homicide–suicide in police families: An analysis of cases from 2007–2014. *Journal of Forensic Practice, 17*(2), 101–116.

Knicks' Raymond Felton will plead guilty in gun case. (2014, June 23). *USA Today*. Retrieved from www.usatoday.com/story/sports/nba/2014/06/23/no-jail-offer-for-knicks-felton-in-ny-gun-case/11258321/

Kunz, J., & Bahr, S. J. (1996). A profile of parental homicide against children. *Journal of Family Violence, 11*(4), 347–362.

Leal, W., Gertz, M., & Piquero, A. (2015). The National Felon League?: A comparison of NFL arrests to general population arrests. *Journal of Criminal Justice, 43*(5), 397–403.

Lewis, R. J., Mason, T. B., Winstead, B. A., & Kelley, M. L. (2016, January 21). Empirical investigation of a model of sexual minority specific and general risk factors for intimate partner violence among lesbian women. *Psychology of Violence, 7*(1), 110–119. Retrieved from http://dx.doi.org/10.1037/vio0000036

Logan, T., & Walker, R. (2010). Civil protective order effectiveness: Justice or just a piece of paper? *Violence and Victims 25*(3), 332–348.

Logan, T., & Walker, R. (2009). Civil protective order outcomes: Violations and perceptions of effectiveness. *Journal of Interpersonal Violence 24*(4), 675–692.

Messing, J. T., & Heeren, J. W. (2009). Gendered justice: Domestic homicide and the death penalty. *Feminist Criminology, 4*(2), 170–188.

Morgan, S., Nackerud, L., & Yegidis, B. (1998). Domestic violence gun ban: An analysis of interest-group conflict. *Affilia, 13*(4), 474–486.

Morgan, W., & Wells, M. (2016). "It's deemed unmanly": Men's experiences of intimate partner violence (IPV). *Journal of Forensic Psychiatry & Psychology, 27*(3), 404–418.

Muddaraj, R., & Chapin, J. (2016, July 7). New details emerge of mom who shot, killed 2 daughters. KHOU 11. Retrieved from www.khou.com/news/crime/fbcso-mom-called-family-meeting-then-shot-her-2-daughters/257414793

National Coalition Against Domestic Violence. (2015). Domestic violence national statistics. Retrieved from https://www.speakcdn.com/assets/2497/domestic_violence.pdf

National Stalking Awareness Month. (2013). *Domestic Violence Report, 18*(2), 26.

National Violent Death Reporting System. (n.d.). Retrieved from https://wisqars.cdc.gov:8443/nvdrs/nvdrsDisplay.jsp

Neidig, P. H., Russell, H. E., & Seng, A.F. (1992). Interspousal aggression in law enforcement families: A preliminary investigation. *Police Studies: The International Review of Police Development, 15*, 30–31.

New York State Office for the Prevention of Domestic Violence. (n.d.). Domestic violence and traumatic brain injury information guide. Retrieved from http://www.opdv.ny.gov/professionals/tbi/dvandtbi_infoguide.html

New Jersey State Police. (2015). *Domestic violence in New Jersey*. Retrieved from http://www.njsp.org/ucr/pdf/domesticviolence/2015_domestic_violence.pdf

Oehme, K., Siebert, D. C., Siebert, C. F., Stern, N., Valentine, C., & Donnelly, E. (2011). Protecting lives, careers, and public confidence: Florida's efforts to prevent officer-involved domestic violence. *Family Court Review, 49*(1), 84–106.

Okano, M., Langille, J., & Walsh, Z. (2016). Psychopathy, alcohol use, and intimate partner violence: Evidence from two samples. *Law and Human Behavior*, *40*(5), 517–523.

Pace, G. (2005, December 21). Letterman fights restraining order. *CBS News*. Retrieved from www.cbsnews.com/news/letterman-fights-restraining-order

Parrish, J. (1996). Trend analysis: Expert testimony on battering and its effects in criminal cases. *Wisconsin Women's Law Journal 11*, 75–173.

P.L. 104-208. Omnibus Consolidated Appropriations Act, 1997. Volume 110, Title VI, Section 658 U.S. Statutes at Large, 104th Congress (1996).

Police: Officer who killed family and raped wife. (2014, 17 July). Retrieved from www.yahoo.com/news/police-officer-killed-family-had-raped-wife-235805261.html?ref=gs

Presidential proclamation—National domestic violence awareness month, 2012. (2012, October 1). The White House. Retrieved from https://obamawhitehouse.archives.gov/the-press-office/2012/10/01/presidential-proclamation-national-domestic-violence-awareness-month-201

Price, M. S. (2014). All's fair in love and war—or is it? Domestic violence and weapons bans. *American Journal of Family Law*, *28*(2), 79–86.

Ramos, B. M., Carlson, B. E., & McNutt, L. (2004). Lifetime abuse, mental health, and African American women. *Journal of Family Violence*, *19*(3), 153–164.

Robinson, S. (2013, April 21). 10 years later: Looking back at former Tacoma police chief David Brame. Retrieved from www.thenewstribune.com/news/special-reports/article25860805.html

Rose, B. (2014, May 14). Details emerge in arrest of Carolina Panthers defensive end Greg Hardy. *Sports Illustrated*. Retrieved from www.si.com/nfl/audibles/2014/05/14/details-emerge-greg-hardy-arrest-carolina-panthers

Saltzman, L., Mercy, J., O'Carroll, P., Rosenberg, M., & Rhodes, P. (1992). Weapon involvement and injury outcomes in family and intimate assaults. *Journal of the American Medical Association*, *267*, 3043–3047.

Saunders, D. G., Prost, S. G., & Oehme, K. (2016). Responses of police officers to cases of officer domestic violence: Effects of demographic and professional factors. *Journal of Family Violence*, *31*(6), 771–784.

Seave, P. L. (2006). Disarming batterers through restraining orders: The promise and the reality in California. *Evaluation Review*, *30*(3), 245–265. doi:10.1177/0193841X06287675

Schuller, R. A., & Vidmar, N. (1992). Battered woman syndrome evidence in the courtroom: A review of the literature. *Law and Human Behavior*, *16*(3), 273–291.

Shuman, R. D., Jr., McCauley, J., Waltermaurer, E., Roche, W. P. III, Hollis, H., Gibbons, A. K., Dever, A., Jones, S., & McNutt, L. (2008). Understanding intimate partner violence against women in the rural south. *Violence & Victims*, *23*(3), 390–405.

Slovak, K., Carlson, K., & Helm, L. (2007). The influence of family violence on youth attitudes. *Child & Adolescent Social Work Journal*, *24*(1), 77–99.

Smith, P. H., Moracco, K. E., & Butts, J. D. (1998). Partner homicide in context. *Homicide Studies*, *2*(4), 400–421.

Snider, B. (2013, August 5). 50 Cent must turn in guns in domestic violence case. *FindLaw*. Retrieved from http://blogs.findlaw.com/celebrity_justice/2013/08/50-cent-must-turn-in-guns-in-domestic-violence-case.html

Sorenson, S. B. (2006). Firearm use in intimate partner violence: A brief overview. *Evaluation Review, 30*(3), 229–236.

Sorenson, S. B., & Shen, H. (2005). Restraining orders in California: A look at statewide data. *Violence Against Women, 11*(7), 912–933.

Sprinkle, J. E. (2007). Domestic violence, gun ownership, and parental educational attainment: How do they affect the aggressive beliefs and behaviors of children? *Child & Adolescent Social Work Journal, 24*(2), 133–151.

Straus, M. A., Hamby, S. L., Boney-McCoy, S., & Sugarman, D. (1996). The Revised Conflict Tactics Scales (CTS2). *Journal of Family Issues, 17,* 283–316.

Tacoma police chief shoots wife before killing himself, authorities say. (2003, April 28). *New York Times.* Retrieved from www.nytimes.com/2003/04/28/us/tacoma-police-chief-shoots-wife-before-killing-himself-authorities-say.html

Terrance, C. A., Plumm, K. M., & Kehn, A. (2014). Battered women who kill: Impact of expert testimony type and timing. *Psychiatry, Psychology and Law, 21*(1), 1–15.

Tree, O. (2011, July 25). "I hope I'm making the right decision": Wife of Texas gunman withdrew protection order against him months before he shot her and family dead at son's roller rink birthday party. *Daily Mail.* Retrieved from www.dailymail.co.uk/news/article-2018167/Texas-gunman-Tan-Do-shot-wife-Trini-family-dead-sons-birthday-party.html

Trostle, L. C., Barnes, A. R., & Atwell, C. L. (2000). Including domestic violence restraining orders in Brady Bill background checks: The Alaska experience. *Criminal Justice Policy Review, 11*(4), 329.

Truman, J. L., & Morgan, R. E. (2014). *Nonfatal domestic violence, 2003–2012.* Washington, DC: US Department of Justice, Bureau of Justice Statistics.

United States v. Hayes, 482 F.3d 749, 752 (4th Cir., 2007).

United States v. Hayes, 129 S. Ct. 1079, 1083–84 (2009).

US Department of Justice. (n.d.). Domestic violence. Retrieved from https://www.justice.gov/ovw/domestic-violence

Utah Department of Health. (2006). *Domestic violence fatalities (2005).* Salt Lake City: Utah Department of Health. Retrieved from http://utah.ptfs.com/awweb/guest.jsp?smd=1&cl=all_lib&lb_document_id=11805

van Wormer, K. (2008). The dynamics of murder–suicide in domestic situations. *Brief Treatment and Crisis Intervention, 8*(3), 274–282.

Vest, J. R., Catlin, T. K., Chen, J. J., & Brownson, R. C. (2002). Multistate analysis of factors associated with intimate partner violence. *American Journal of Preventive Medicine, 22*(3), 156–164.

Vigdor, E. R., & Mercy, J. A. (2006). Do laws restricting access to firearms by domestic violence offenders prevent intimate partner homicide? *Evaluation Review, 30,* 313–346.

Violanti, J. M. (2007). Homicide–suicide in police families: Aggression full circle. *International Journal of Emergency Mental Health, 9*(2), 97–104.

Violence against women. (2017). World Health Organization. Retrieved from www.who.int/mediacentre/factsheets/fs239/en/

Violence Against Women Act of 1994, Title IV of the Violent Crime Control and Law Enforcement Act, Public Law Number 103–322 (1994).

Vittes, K. A., & Sorenson, S. B. (2006). Are temporary restraining orders more likely to be issued when application mention firearms? *Evaluation Review, 30,* 266–275.

Vittes, K. A., Webster, D. W., Frattaroli, S., Claire, B. E., & Wintemute, G. J. (2013). Removing guns from batterers: Findings from a pilot survey of domestic violence restraining order recipients in California. *Violence Against Women, 19*(5), 602–616.

Von Glinow, K. (2012). Celebrity gun owners: Stars who are packing heat. Retrieved from https://www.huffingtonpost.com/2012/05/31/celebrity-gun-owners-license_n_1557203.html

Walker, L. (1979). *The battered woman.* New York: Harper & Row.

Walker, L. E. (1991). Post-traumatic stress disorder in women: Diagnosis and treatment of battered woman syndrome. *Psychotherapy: Theory, Research, Practice, Training, 28*(1), 21–29. doi:10.1037/0033-3204.28.1.21

Walker, L. E. A. (1984). *The battered woman syndrome.* New York: Springer.

Walsh, J. A., & Krienert, J. L. (2014). My brother's reaper: Examining officially reported siblicide incidents in the United States, 2000–2007. *Violence and Victims, 29*(3), 523–540.

Webster, D. W., Frattaroli, S., Vernick, J. S., O'Sullivan, C., Roehl, J., & Campbell, J. C. (2010). Women with protective orders report failure to remove firearms from their abusive partners: Results from an exploratory study. *Journal of Women's Health, 19*(1), 93–98.

Webster, D. W., & Wintemute, G. J. (2015). Effects of policies designed to keep firearms from high-risk individuals. *Annual Review of Public Health, 36,* 21–37.

Weinbaum, Z., Stratton, T. L., Chavez, G., Motylewski-Link, C., Barrera, N., & Courtney, J. G. (2001). Female victims of intimate partner physical domestic violence (IPP-DV), California 1998. *American Journal of Preventive Medicine, 21*(4), 313–319.

Williams, B. (2015, March 6). 50 Cent shares his thoughts on past domestic violence cases. Huffington Post. Retrieved from www.huffingtonpost.com/2015/03/06/50-cent-domestic-violence-accusations_n_6818370.html

Wilson, A. (2012, December 1). Kansas City Chiefs player Jovan Belcher kills girlfriend, himself. *Baltimore Sun.* Retrieved from http://articles.baltimoresun.com/2012-12-01/sports/bal-chiefs-linebacker-jovan-belcher-murder-suicide-1201_1_david-lindaman-practice-facility-ravens

Wincentak, K., Connolly, J., & Card, N. (2016). Teen dating violence: A meta-analytic review of prevalence rates. *Psychology of Violence, 7*(2), 224–241. http://dx.doi.org/10.1037/a0040194

Wintemute, G. J., Frattaroli, S., Claire, B. E., Vittes, K. A., & Webster, D. W. (2014). Identifying armed respondents to domestic violence restraining orders and recovering their firearms: Process evaluation of an initiative in California. *American Journal of Public Health, 104*(2), e113–e118.

Withers, B. (2015). Without consequence: When professional athletes are violent off the field. *Journal of Sports and Entertainment Law, 6*(2), 373–412.

Wolfgang, M. E. (1958). *Patterns in criminal homicide.* Philadelphia: University of Pennsylvania Press.

World Health Organization. (2002). *World report on violence and health.* Geneva, Switzerland: World Health Organization.

Yardley, W. (2009, April 5). Wife was leaving man who killed 5 children. *New York Times.* Retrieved from www.nytimes.com/2009/04/06/us/06killings.html

Zeoli, A. M., & Webster, D. W. (2010). Effects of domestic violence policies, alcohol taxes and police staffing levels on intimate partner homicide in large US cities. *Injury Prevention, 16*(2), 90–95.

Chapter 6

Abramson, L. Y., Alloy, L. B., Hogan, M. E., Whitehouse, W. G., Cornette, M., Akhavan, S., & Chiara, A. (1998). Suicidality and cognitive vulnerability to depression among college students: A prospective study. *Journal of Adolescence, 21*, 473–487.

Abramson, L. Y., Metalsky, G. I., & Alloy, L. B. (1989). Hopelessness depression: A theory-based subtype of depression. *Psychological Review, 96*, 358–372.

American Association of Suicidology. (n.d.). Warning signs & risk factors. Retrieved from www.suicidology.org/ncpys/warning-signs-risk-factors

American Foundation for Suicide Prevention. (n.d.). Suicide statistics. Retrieved from https://afsp.org/about-suicide/suicide-statistics/

American Psychiatric Association. (2013). *Diagnostic and statistical manual of mental disorders*, 5th ed. Washington, DC: American Psychiatric Publishing.

Ammerman, B. A., Kleiman, E. M., Uveji, L. L., Knorr, A. C., & McCloskey, M. S. (2015). Suicidal and violent behavior: The role of anger, emotion dysregulation, and impulsivity. *Personality and Individual Differences, 79*, 57–62.

Anestis, M. D., & Anestis, J. C. (2015). Suicide rates and state laws regulating access and exposure to handguns. *American Journal of Public Health, 105*, 2049–2058.

Anestis, M. D., Dixon-Gordon, K. L., & Gratz, K. L. (2015). Suicidal behavior and personality disorders. In *Advancing the science of suicidal behavior: Understanding and intervention*, edited by D. A. Lamis & N. J. Kaslow (pp. 405–420). Hauppauge, NY: Nova Science Publishers.

Anglemyer, A., Horvath, T., & Rutherford, G. (2014). The accessibility of firearms and risk for suicide and homicide victimization among household members: A systematic review and meta analysis. *Annals of Internal Medicine, 160*, 101–110.

Anglemyer, A., Miller, M. L., Buttrey, S., & Whitaker, L. (2016). Suicide rates and methods in active duty military personnel, 2005 to 2011: A cohort study. *Annals of Internal Medicine, 165*, 167–174.

Arias, E. A., Schlesinger, L. B., Pinizzotto, A. J., Davis, E. F., Fava, J. L., & Dewey, L. M. (2008). Police officers who commit suicide-by-cop: A clinical study with analysis. *Journal of Forensic Sciences, 53*, 1455–1457.

Barnes, S. M., Bahraini, N. H., Forster, J. E., Steams-Yoder, K. A., Hostetter, T. A., Smith, G., Nagamoto, H. T., & Nock, M. K. (2017). Moving beyond self-report: Implicit associations about death/life prospectively predict suicidal behavior among veterans. *Suicide and Life-Threatening Behavior, 47*(1), 67–77.

Baxter v. Montana, 224 P.3d 1211 (2009).

Beck, A. T., Rush, A. J., Shaw, B. F., & Emery, G. (1979). *Cognitive therapy of depression*. New York: Guilford Press.

Beck, A. T., & Steer, R. A. (1991). *Manual for the Beck Scale for Suicidal Ideation.* San Antonio, TX: Psychological Corporation.

Beck, A. T., Steer, R. A., & Brown, G. K. (1996). *Beck Depression Inventory (BDI-II) Manual,* 2nd ed. San Antonio, TX: Psychological Corporation.

Bernard, V., Geoffroy, P. A., & Bellivier, F. (2015). Seasons, circadian rhythms, sleep and suicidal behaviors vulnerability. *Encephale, 41*(Suppl. 1), S29–S37 (in French).

Betz, M. E., Miller, M., Barber, C., Beaty, B., Miller, I., Camargo, C., & Bourdeaux, E. (2016). Lethal means access and assessment among suicidal emergency department patients. *Depression and Anxiety, 33,* 502–511.

Brent, D. A., & Bridge, J. (2003). Firearms availability and suicide: Evidence, interventions, and future directions. *American Behavioral Scientist, 46,* 1192–1210.

Bryan, C. J., & Rudd, M. D. (2006). Advances in the assessment of suicide risk. *Journal of Clinical Psychology: In Session, 62,* 185–200.

Byard, R. W., Veldhoen, D., Kobus, H., & Heath, K. (2010). "Murder–suicide" or "murder accident"? Difficulties with the analysis of cases. *Journal of Forensic Sciences, 55,* 1375–1377.

Cacioppo, J. T., & Petty, R. E. (1982). The need for cognition. *Journal of Personality and Social Psychology, 42,* 116–131.

Cain, C. L. (2016). Implementing aid in dying in California: Experiences from other states indicates the need for strong implementation guidance. *Policy Brief: UCLA Center for Health Policy Research,* (PB2016-4), 1–7.

Calear, A. L., Christensen, H., Freeman, A., Fenton, K., Busby Grant, J., van Spijker, B., & Donker, T. (2016). A systematic review of psychosocial suicide prevention interventions for youth. *European Child and Adolescent Psychiatry, 25,* 467–482.

California Assembly Bill No. 15. AB-15 End of life (2015).

Centers for Disease Control and Prevention. (n.d.a). Definitions: self-directed violence. Retrieved from www.cdc.gov/violenceprevention/suicide/definitions.html

Centers for Disease Control and Prevention. (n.d.b). The social-ecological model: A framework for violence prevention. Retrieved from www.cdc.gov/ViolencePrevention/pdf/SEM_Framewrk-a.pdf/

Centers for Disease Control and Prevention. (n.d.c). Suicide: Risk and protective factors. Retrieved from www.cdc.gov/violenceprevention/suicide/riskprotectivefactors.html

Centers for Disease Control and Prevention. (2015). Suicide: facts at a glance. Retrieved from www.cdc.gov/violenceprevention/pdf/suicide-datasheet-a.pdf

Centers for Disease Control and Prevention. (2016). Deaths: Final data for 2013. Retrieved from www.cdc.gov/nchs/data/nvsr/nvsr64/nvsr64_02.pdf

Costa, P. T., Jr., & McCrae, R. R. (1992). *Revised NEO Personality Inventory (NEO-PI-R) and NEO Five-Factor Inventory (NEO-FFI) professional manual.* Odessa, FL: Psychological Assessment Resources.

Cramer, R. J., Bryson, C. N., Gardner, B. O., & Webber, W. (2016). Can preferences in information processing aid in understanding suicide risk among emerging adults? *Death Studies, 40,* 383–391.

Cramer, R. J., Desmarais, S. L., Johnson, K. L., Gemberling, T. M., Nobles, M. R., Holley, S. R., Wright, S., & Van Dorn, R. (2017). The intersection of interpersonal and self-directed violence among general adult, college student, and sexually diverse samples. *International Journal of Social Psychiatry, 63*(1), 78–85.

Cramer, R. J., Moore, C. E., & Bryson, C. N. (2016). A test of the trait-interpersonal model of suicide proneness in emerging adults. *Personality and Individual Differences, 102*, 252–259.

Crifiasi, C. K., Meyers, J. S., Vernick, J. S., & Webster, J. W. (2015). Effects of changes in permit to-purchase handgun laws in Connecticut and Missouri on suicide rates. *Preventive Medicine, 79*, 43–49.

Crosby, A. E., Ortega, L., & Melanson, C. (2011). *Self-directed violence surveillance: Uniform definitions and recommended data elements*, Version 1.0. Atlanta, GA: Centers for Disease Control and Prevention, National Center for Injury Prevention and Control.

DeGue, S., Fowler, K. A., & Calkins, C. (2016). Deaths due to use of lethal force by law enforcement. *American Journal of Preventive Medicine, 51*(Suppl.), S173–S187.

De Leo, D., Burgis, S., Bertolote, J. M., Kerkhof, A. J., & Bille-Brahe, U. (2006). Definitions of suicidal behavior: Lessons learned from the WHO/EURO multicentre study. *Crisis, 27*, 4–15.

Drapeau, C. W., & McIntosh, J. L. (for the American Association of Suicidology). (2015). *U.S.A. suicide: 2014 Official final data*. Washington, DC: American Association of Suicidology.

Durkheim, E. (1897). *Le suicide*. Paris: Alcan.

Ellis, T. E., Rufino, K. A., & Green, K. L. (2016). Implicit measure of life/death orientation predicts response of suicidal ideation to treatment in psychiatric inpatients. *Archives of Suicide Research, 20*, 59–68.

Fainaru-Wada, M., Avila, J., & Fainaru, S. (2013, January). Doctors: Junior Seau's brain had CTE. ESPN. Retrieved from www.espn.com/espn/otl/story/_/id/8830344/study-juniorseau-brain-shows-chronic-brain-damage-found-other-nfl-football-players

Fowler, K. A., Dahlberg, L. L., Haileyesus, T., & Annest, J. L. (2015). Firearm injuries in the United States. *Preventive Medicine, 79*, 5–14.

Franklin, J. C., Ribeiro, J. D., Fox, K. R., Bentley, K. H., Kleiman, E. M., Huang, X., Musacchio, K. M., Jaroszewski, A. C., Chang, B. P., & Nock, M. K. (2017). Risk factors for suicidal thoughts and behaviors: A meta-analysis of 50 years of research. *Psychological Bulletin, 143*(2), 187–232.

Gius, M. (2015). The impact of minimum age and child access prevention laws on firearm-related youth suicides and unintentional deaths. *Social Science Journal, 52*, 168–175.

Glanz, K., Rimer, B. K., & Lewis, F. M. (eds.). (2015). *Health behavior: Theory, research, and practice*, 5th ed. San Francisco: Jossey-Bass.

Gratz, K. L. (2001). Measurement of deliberate self-harm: Preliminary data on the Deliberate Self-Harm Inventory. *Journal of Psychopathology and Behavioral Assessment, 23*, 253–263.

Gratz, K. L. (2003). Risk factors for and functions of deliberate self-harm: An empirical and conceptual review. *Clinical Psychology: Science and Practice, 10*, 192–205.

Grinshteyn, E., & Hemenway, D. (2016). Violent death rates: The US compared with other high-income OECD countries, 2010. *American Journal of Medicine, 129,* 266–273.

Hagan, C. R., Podlogar, M. C., & Joiner, T. E. (2015). Murder–suicide: Bridging the gap between mass murder, amok, and suicide. *Journal of Aggression, Conflict and Peace Research, 7,* 179–186.

Hasley, J. P., Ghosh, B., Huggins, J., Bell, M. R., Adler, L. E., & Shroyer, A. L. (2008). A review of "suicidal intent" within the existing suicide literature. *Suicide and Life-Threatening Behavior, 38,* 576–591.

Hayes, A. F. (2013). *Introduction to mediation, moderation, and conditional process analysis: A regression-based approach.* New York: Guilford Press.

Hempstead, K., Nguyen, T., David-Rus, R., & Jacquemen, B. (2012). Health problems and male firearm suicide. *Suicide & Life-Threatening Behavior, 43,* 1–13.

Hoyt, T., & Duffy, V. (2015). Implementing firearms restrictions for preventing U.S. Army suicide. *Military Psychology, 27,* 384–390.

Hunter S. Thompson. (n.d.). Biography. Retrieved from www.biography.com/people/hunter s-thompson-9506260#video-gallery

Ivanoff, A. (1989). Identifying psychological correlates of suicidal behavior in jail and detention facilities. *Psychiatric Quarterly, 60,* 73–84.

Molski, H. (2015, June). Chief: Suspect who killed cop texted plans for suicide. Retrieved from https://www.usatoday.com/story/news/nation/2015/06/19/police-officer-dead/28980727/

Jobes, D. A. (2009). The CAMS approach to suicide risk: Philosophy and clinical procedures. *Suicidology, 14,* 3–7.

Joe, S., Marcus, S. C., & Kaplan, M. S. (2007). Racial differences in the characteristics of firearm suicide decedents in the United States. *American Journal of Orthopsychiatry, 77,* 124–130.

Johnson, S. M., Cramer, R. J., Conroy, M. A., & Gardner, B. O. (2014). The role of and challenges for psychologists in physician-assisted suicide. *Death Studies, 38,* 582–588.

Johnson, S. M., Cramer, R. J., Gardner, B. O., & Nobles, M. R. (2015). What patient and psychologist characteristics are important in competency for physician assisted suicide evaluations? *Psychology, Public Policy and Law, 21,* 420–431.

Joiner, T. E. (2005). *Why people die by suicide.* Cambridge, MA: Harvard University Press.

Kahneman, D., & Frederick, S. (2002). Representativeness revisited: Attribute substitution in intuitive judgment. In *Heuristics and biases: The psychology of intuitive judgment,* edited by T. Gilovich, D. Griffin, & D. Kahneman (pp. 49–81). New York: Cambridge University Press.

Kaplan, M. S., McFarland, B. H., & Huguet, N. (2009). Characteristics of adult male and female firearm suicide decedents: Findings from the National Violent Death Reporting System. *Injury Prevention, 15,* 322–327.

Kapusta, N. D., Etzersdorfer, E., Krall, C., & Sonneck, G. (2007). Firearm legislation reform in the European Union: Impact on firearm availability, firearm suicide and homicide rates in Austria. *British Journal of Psychiatry, 191,* 253–257.

Katz, C., Bolton, J., & Sareen, J. (2016). The prevalence rates of suicide are likely underestimated worldwide: Why it matters. *Social Psychiatry and Psychiatric Epidemiology, 51,* 125–127.

Khazem, L. R., Houtsma, C., Gratz, K. L., Tull, M. T., Green, B. A., & Anestis, M. D. (2016). Firearms matter: The moderating role of firearm storage in the association between current suicidal ideation and likelihood of future suicide attempts among United States military personnel. *Military Psychology*, *28*, 25–33.

Kurt Cobain. (n.d.). Biography. Retrieved from www.biography.com/people/kurt-cobain/9542179#related-video-gallery

Lankford, A. (2012). A comparative analysis of suicide terrorists and rampage, workplace, and school shooters in the United States from 1990 to 2010. *Homicide Studies*, *17*, 255–274.

Lester, D. L. (1994). A comparison of 15 theories of suicide. *Suicide & Life-Threatening Behavior*, *24*, 80–88.

Lester, D. L. (1999). The social causes of suicide: A look at Durkheim's *Le Suicide* one hundred years later. *Omega*, *40*, 307–321.

Linehan, M. M., Goodstein, J. L., Nielsen, S. L., & Chiles, J. A. (1983). Reasons for staying alive when you are thinking of killing yourself: The Reasons for Living Inventory. *Journal of Consulting and Clinical Psychology*, *51*, 276–286.

Lundh, L. G., Karim, J., & Quilisch, E. (2007). Deliberate self-harm in 15-year-old adolescents: A pilot study with a modified version of the Deliberate Self-Harm Inventory. *Scandinavian Journal of Psychology*, *48*, 33–41.

Ma, J., Batterham, P. J., Calear, A. L., & Han, J. (2016). A systematic review of the predictions of the interpersonal-psychological theory of suicidal behavior. *Clinical Psychology Review*, *46*, 34–45.

Maio, G. R., & Esses, V. M. (2001). The need for affect: Individual differences in the motivation to approach or avoid emotions. *Journal of Personality*, *69*, 583–615.

Mathews, E. M., Woodward, C. J., Musso, M. W., & Jones, G. N. (2016). Suicide attempts presenting to trauma centers: Trends across age groups using the National Trauma Data Bank. *American Journal of Emergency Medicine*, *34*, 1620–1624.

McCarten, J. M., Hoffmire, C. A., & Bossarte, R. M. (2015). Changes in overall and firearm veteran suicide rates by gender, 2001–2010. *American Journal of Preventive Medicine*, *48*, 360–364.

McCrae, R. R., & Costa, P. T. (2003). *Personality in adulthood: A five-factor theory perspective*. New York: Guilford Press.

McNally, M. R., Patton, C. L., & Fremouw, W. J. (2016). Mining for murder-suicide: An approach to identifying cases of murder–suicide in the National Violent Death Reporting System Restricted Access Database. *Journal of Forensic Sciences*, *61*, 245–248.

Merrill, E. (2010, July 4). The woman forever tied to Steve McNair. ESPN. Retrieved from www.espn.com/espn/otl/news/story?id=5347315

Miller, M., Barber, C., Azrael, D., Hemenway, D., & Molnar, B. E. (2009). Recent psychopathology, suicidal thoughts and suicide attempts in households with and without firearms: Findings from the National Comorbidity Study Replication. *Injury Prevention*, *15*, 183–189.

Miller, M., Warren, M., Hemenway, D., & Azrael, D. (2013). Firearms and suicide in US cities. *Injury Prevention*, *31*, e116–e119.

Murray, A. L., & Booth, T. (2015). Personality and physical health. *Current Opinion in Psychology*, *5*, 50–55.

National Institute of Mental Health. (2015). Suicide in America: Frequently asked questions. Retrieved from www.nimh.nih.gov/health/publications/suicide-faq/index.shtml

Nock, M. K., & Prinstein, M. J. (2004). A functional approach to the assessment of self-mutilative behavior. *Journal of Consulting and Clinical Psychology, 72,* 885–890.

O'Carroll, P. W., Berman, A. L., Maris, R. W., Moscicki, E. K., Tanney, B. L., & Silverman, M. M. (1996). Beyond the tower of Babel: A nomenclature for suicidology. *Suicide & Life- Threatening Behavior, 26,* 237–252.

O'Connor, R. C. (2011). The integrated motivational–volitional model of suicidal behavior. *Crisis, 32,* 295–298.

O'Hara, A. F., & Violanti, J. M. (2009). Police suicide: A web surveillance of national data. *International Journal of Emergency Mental Health, 11,* 17–24.

Oregon Death with Dignity Act. Or. Rev. Stat. §§127.800-127.995 (1995).

Panczak, R., Geissbuhler, M., Zwahlen, M., Killias, M., Tal, K., & Egger, M. (2013). Homicide suicides compared to homicides and suicides: Systematic review and meta-analysis. *Forensic Science International, 233,* 28–36.

Pirelli, G., Wechsler, H., & Cramer, R. J. (2015). Psychological evaluations for firearm ownership: Legal foundations, practice considerations, and a conceptual framework. *Professional Psychology: Research and Practice, 46,* 250–257.

Pirelli, G., & Witt, P. (2015). Psychological evaluations for civilian firearm ownership in New Jersey. *New Jersey Psychologist, 65,* 7–9.

Project Implicit. (n.d.). Retrieved from https://implicit.harvard.edu/implicit/

Randall, J. R., Rowe, B. H., Dong, K. A., Nock, M. K., & Colman, I. (2013). Assessment of self-harm risk using implicit thoughts. *Psychological Assessment, 25,* 714–721.

Regoeczi, W. C., Granath, S., Issa, R., Gilson, T., & Sturup, J. (2016). Comparing homicide–suicides in the United States and Sweden. *Journal of Forensic Sciences, 61,* 1524–1530.

Reinhard, M. (2010). Need for cognition and the process of lie detection. *Journal of Experimental Social Psychology, 46,* 961–971.

Schneidman, E. S. (1981). A psychological theory of suicide. *Suicide & Life-Threatening Behavior, 11,* 221–231.

Selby, E. A., Anestis, M. D., Bender, T. W., & Joiner, T. E. (2009). An exploration of the emotional cascade model in borderline personality disorder. *Journal of Abnormal Psychology, 118,* 375–387.

Selby, E. A., Anestis, M. D., & Joiner, T. E. (2008). Understanding the relationship between emotional and behavioral dysregulation: Emotional cascades. *Behaviour Research and Therapy, 46,* 593–611.

Sen, B., & Panjamapirom, A. (2012). State background checks for gun purchase and firearm deaths: An exploratory study. *Preventive Medicine, 55,* 346–350.

Seung-Hui Cho. (n.d.). Biography. Retrieved from https://www.biography.com/people/seung-hui-cho-235991

Shenassa, E. D., Rogers, M. L., Spalding, K. L., & Roberts, M. B. (2004). Safer storage of firearms at home and risk of suicide: A study of protective factors in a nationally representative sample. *Journal of Epidemiology and Community Health, 58,* 841–848.

Silverman, M. M., Berman, A. L., Sanddal, N. D., O'Carroll, P. W., & Joiner, T. E. (2007). Rebuilding the tower of Babel: A revised nomenclature for the study of suicide and suicidal behaviors. Part 2: Suicide-related ideations, communications, and behaviors. *Suicide & Life-Threatening Behavior, 37*, 264–277.

Silverman, M. M., & De Leo, D. (2016). Why there is a need for an international nomenclature and classification system for suicide. *Crisis, 37*, 83–87.

Simon, R. I. (2007). Gun safety management with patients at risk for suicide. *Suicide and Life- Threatening Behavior, 37*, 518–526.

Slovak, K., & Brewer, T. W. (2010). Suicide and firearm means restriction: Can training make a difference? *Suicide & Life-Threatening Behavior, 40*, 63–73.

Sorenson, S. B., & Vittes, K. A. (2008). Mental health and firearms in community-based surveys: Implications for suicide prevention. *Evaluation Review, 32*, 239–256.

Stanley, I. H., Horn, M. A., Rogers, M. L., Anestis, M. D., & Joiner, T. E. (2016). Discussing firearm ownership and access as part of suicide risk assessment and prevention: "Means safety" versus "means restriction." *Archives of Suicide Research, 13*, 1–17.

Steve McNair biography. (n.d.). JockBio.com. Retrieved from www.jockbio.com/ Bios/McNair/McNair_bio.html

Stroebe, W. (2013). Firearm possession and violent death: A critical review. *Aggression and Violent Behavior, 18*, 709–721.

Substance Abuse and Mental Health Services Administration. (2014). Counseling on access to lethal means. Retrieved from www.samhsa.gov/ samhsaNewsLetter/Volume_22_Number_2/preventing_suicide/lethal_means. html

Suicide Prevention Resource Center. (n.d.). Understanding risk and protective factors for suicide: A primer for preventing suicide. Retrieved from www.sprc. org/sites/default/files/migrate/library/RiskProtectiveFactorsPrimer.pdf

Swogger, M. T., Van Orden, K. A., & Conner, K. R. (2014). The relationship of outwardly directed aggression to suicidal ideation and suicide attempts across two high-risk samples. *Psychology of Violence, 4*, 184–195.

Tex. Health & Safety Code §574.101 (2012a).

Tex. Health & Safety Code §574.034 (2012b).

Treatment Advocacy Center. (2014). State standards for assisted treatment. Retrieved from www.treatmentadvocacycenter.org/storage/documents/ Standards_-_The_Text-_June_2011.pdf

Van Orden, K. A., Witte, T. K., Cukrowicz, K. C., Braithwaite, S. R., Selby, E. A., & Joiner, T. E. (2010). The interpersonal theory of suicide. *Psychological Review, 117*, 575–600.

Van Orden, K. A., Witte, T. K., Gordon, K. H., Bender, T. W., & Joiner, T. E. (2008). Suicidal desire and the capability for suicide: Tests of the interpersonal-psychological theory of suicidal behavior among adults. *Journal of Consulting and Clinical Psychology, 76*, 72–83.

Vars, F. E. (2015). Self-defense against gun suicide. *Boston College Legal Review, 56*, 1465–1499.

Vars, F. E., McCullumsmith, C. B., Shelton, R. C., & Cropsey, K. L. (2017). Willingness of mentally ill individuals to sign up a novel proposal to prevent firearm suicide. *Suicide & Life-Threatening Behavior, 47*(4), 483–492.

Vermont Patient Choice and Control at the End of Life Act (2013). Retrieved from http://www.leg.state.vt.us/docs/2014/acts/act039.pdf

Violanti, J. M., Mnatsakanova, A., Hartley, T. A., Andrew, M. E., & Burchfiel, C. M. (2012). Police suicide in small departments: A comparative analysis. *International Journal of Emergency Mental Health, 14*, 157–162.

Violence Policy Center. (2015). American roulette: Murder–suicide in the United States. Retrieved from www.vpc.org/studies/amroul2015.pdf

Washington Death with Dignity Act, Wa. Rev. Code, chap. 70. §§245.010–70.245.904 (2008).

Whetton, D. A. (1989). What constitutes a theoretical contribution? *Academy Management Review, 14*, 490–495.

World Health Organization. (2015). *Global status report on violence prevention, 2014*. Retrieved from www.who.int/violence_injury_prevention/violence/status_report/2014/en/

Yip, P. S., Caine, E., Yousuf, S., Chang, S. S., Wu, K. C., & Chen, Y. Y. (2012). Means restriction in suicide prevention. *Lancet, 379*, 2393–2399.

Chapter 7

Abramson, M. (1972). The criminalization of mentally disordered behavior. *Journal of Hospital & Community Psychiatry, 23*, 101–105.

ADA Amendments Act of 2008, Publ. L. 110-325 (2008).

American Association of Pastoral Counselors. (n.d.). Retrieved from www.aapc.org

American Psychiatric Association. (2013). *Diagnostic and statistical manual of mental disorders*, 5th ed. Washington, DC: American Psychiatric Publishing.

American Psychological Association. (2002). Ethical principles of psychologists and code of conduct. *American Psychologist, 57*(12), 1060–1073. doi:10.1037/0003-066X.57.12.1060

American Psychological Association. (2010). 2010 Amendments to the 2002 "Ethical principles of psychologists and code of conduct." *American Psychologist, 65*(5), 493. doi:10.1037/a0020168

American Psychological Association. (2013a). Gun violence: Prediction, prevention, and policy. Retrieved from www.apa.org/pubs/info/reports/gun-violence-prevention.aspx

American Psychological Association. (2013b). Specialty guidelines for forensic psychology. *American Psychologist, 68*(1), 7–19. doi:10.1037/a0029889

American Psychological Association. (2016). After decades of research, science is no better able to predict suicidal behaviors. Retrieved from www.apa.org/news/press/releases/2016/11/suicidal-behaviors.aspx

Americans with Disabilities Act of 1990, 42 U.S.C. § 12101 *et seq.* (1990).

Anderson, W., Swenson, D., & Clay, D. (1995). *Stress management for law enforcement officers*. Englewood Cliffs, NJ: Prentice Hall.

Andrews, D. A., Bonta, J., & Wormith, J. S. (2006). The recent past and near future of risk and/or need assessment. *Crime & Delinquency, 52*(1), 7–27. doi:10.1177/0011128705281756

Appelbaum, P. S. (2017). Does the Second Amendment protect the gun rights of persons with mental illness? *Psychiatric Services, 68*(1), 3–5.

Ballenger, J. F., Best, S. R., Metzler, T. J., Wasserman, D. A., Mohr, D. C., Liberman, A., Delucchi, K., Weiss, D. S., Fagan, J. A., Waldrop, A. E., & Marmar, C. R. (2010). Patterns and predictors of alcohol use in male and female urban police officers. *American Journal on Addictions, 20,* 21–29.

Basile, K. C., Hertz, M., & Back, S. (2007). *Intimate partner violence and sexual violence victimization assessment instruments for use in healthcare settings,* version 1. Atlanta, GA: Centers for Disease Control and Prevention, National Center for Injury Prevention and Control.

Ben-Porath, Y. S., & Tellegen, A. (2008). *The Minnesota-Multiphasic Inventory-2 Restructured Form: Manual for administration, scoring, and interpretation.* Minneapolis: University of Minnesota Press.

Blum, L. N. (2000). *Force under pressure: How cops live and why they die.* New York: Lantern Books.

Bone, D. (2010). The *Heller* promise versus the *Heller* reality: Will statutes prohibiting the possession of firearms by ex-felons be upheld after *Britt v. State*? *Journal of Criminal Law & Criminology, 100*(4), 1633–1658.

Bonta, J. (2002). Offender risk assessment: Guidelines for selection and use. *Criminal Justice and Behavior, 29*(4), 355–379. doi:10.1177/0093854802029004002

Bonta, J., & Andrews, D. A. (2007). Risk–need–responsivity model for offender assessment and rehabilitation. *Rehabilitation, 6*(1), 1–22.

Borum, R., & Verhaagen, D. (2006). *Assessing and managing violence risk in juveniles.* New York: Guilford Press.

Britton, J., & Bloom, J. D. (2015). Oregon's gun relief program for adjudicated mentally ill persons: The psychiatric security review board. *Behavioral Sciences & the Law, 33*(2–3), 323–333. doi:10.1002/bsl.2167

Brown v. Board of Education, 347 U.S. 483, 74 S. Ct. 686, 98 L. Ed. 873 (1954).

Brown, J. M., & Campbell, E. A. (1994). *Stress and policing: Sources and strategies.* New York: Wiley.

California Department of Justice, Office of the Attorney General. (2015). *Firearms safety certificate study guide.* Retrieved from www.oag.ca.gov/sites/all/files/agweb/pdfs/firearms/forms/hscsg.pdf

Cheema, R. (2016). Black and blue bloods: Protecting police officer families from domestic violence. *Family Court Review, 54*(3), 487–500. doi:10.1111/fcre.12226

Coalition to Stop Gun Violence. (n.d.). Retrieved from http://csgv.org/issues/guns-and-mental-health

Community Mental Health Act of 1963, 42 U.S.C. § 2685 (1963).

Cop 2 Cop. (n.d.). Retrieved from http://ubhc.rutgers.edu/cop2cop/

Daniel, A. E. (2007). Care of the mentally ill in prisons: Challenges and solutions. *Journal of the American Academy of Psychiatry and the Law, 35,* 406–410.

Defend your rights. (n.d.). Retrieved from www.allgungroups.org

Dodge, K. A., & Pettit, G. S. (2003). A biopsychosocial model of the development of chronic conduct problems in adolescence. *Developmental Psychology, 39*(2), 349–371. doi:10.1037/0012-1649.39.2.349

Douglas, K. S., Hart, S. D., Webster, C. D., & Belfrage, H. (2013). *HCR-20V3: Assessing risk of violence—User guide.* Burnaby, Canada: Mental Health, Law, and Policy Institute, Simon Fraser University.

Edwards, T. M., Stern, A., Clarke, D. D., Ivbijaro, G., & Kasney, L. M. (2010). The treatment of patients with medically unexplained symptoms in primary care: A review of the literature. *Mental Health and Family Medicine, 7*(4), 209–221.

Federal legislation passed: The Crystal Judson domestic violence protocol program. (n.d.). Retrieved from www.lanejudson.com/4_Brame_tragedy_spurs_federal_dv_program.htm

Fowler, J. C. (2012). Suicide risk assessment in clinical practice: Pragmatic guidelines for imperfect assessments. *Psychotherapy, 49*(1), 81–90.

Franklin, J. C., Ribeiro, J. D., Fox, K. R., Bentley, K. H., Kleiman, E. M., Huang, X., Musacchio, K. M., Jaroszewski, A. C., Chang, B. P., & Nock, M. K. (2017). Risk factors for suicidal thoughts and behaviors: A meta-analysis of 50 years of research. *Psychological Bulletin, 143*(2), 187–232. doi:10.1037/bul0000084

Frattaroli, S., McGinty, E. E., Barnhorst, A., & Greenberg, S. (2015). Gun violence restraining orders: Alternative or adjunct to mental health-based restrictions on firearms? *Behavioral Sciences & the Law, 33*(2/3), 290–307. doi:10.1002/bsl.2173

Galatzer-Levy, I. R., & Bryant, R. A. (2013). 636,120 ways to have posttraumatic stress disorder. *Perspectives on Psychological Science, 8*(6), 651–662. doi:10.1177/1745691613504115

Garbarino, J., Bradshaw, C. P., & Vorrasi, J. A. (2002). Mitigating the effects of gun violence on children and youth. *The Future of Children, 12*(2), 73–85. doi:10.2307/1602739

Gilligan, J. (2001). The last mental hospital. *Psychiatric Quarterly, 72,* 45–61.

Gold, L. H. (2013). Gun violence: Psychiatry, risk assessment, and social policy. *Journal of the American Academy of Psychiatry and the Law, 41*(3), 337–343.

Gold, L. H., & Simon, R. I. (2016). *Gun violence and mental illness.* Arlington, VA: American Psychiatric Association.

Gold, L. H., & Vanderpool, D. (2016). Relief from disabilities: Firearm rights restoration for persons under mental health prohibitions. In *Gun violence and mental illness,* edited by L. H. Gold & R. I. Simon (pp. 339–380). Arlington, VA: American Psychiatric Association.

Goldstein, A. O., Viera, A. J., Pierson, J., Barnhouse, K. K., Tulsky, J. A., & Richman, B. D. (2015). Physician beliefs about physical and mental competency of patients applying for concealed weapon permits. *Behavioral Sciences & the Law, 33*(2–3), 238–245. doi:10.1002/bsl.2169

Goldstein, D. G., & Gigerenzer, G. (2009). Fast and frugal forecasting. *International Journal of Forecasting, 25*(4), 760–772.

Graduate programs in psychology and law. (n.d.). American Psychology–Law Society. Retrieved from www.apadivisions.org/division-41/education/programs/index.aspx

Greenberg, D. (2016, June 13). APHA mourns Orlando shootings. Retrieved from www.apha.org/news-and-media/news-releases/apha-news-releases/2016/apha-mourns-orlando-shootings

Greenberg, S. A., & Shuman, D. W. (1997). Irreconcilable conflict between therapeutic and forensic roles. *Professional Psychology: Research and Practice, 28*(1), 50–57. doi:10.1037/0735-7028.28.1.50

Greenberg, S. A., & Shuman, D. W. (2007). When worlds collide: Therapeutic and forensic roles. *Professional Psychology: Research and Practice, 38*(2), 129–132. doi:10.1037/0735-7028.38.2.129

Grisso, T. (1986). *Evaluating competencies: Forensic assessments and instruments.* New York: Plenum.

Grisso, T. (2003). *Evaluating competencies: Forensic assessments and instruments,* 2nd ed. New York: Kluwer Academic/Plenum Publishers.

Grove, W. M., Zald, D. H., Lebow, B. S., Snitz, B. E., & Nelson, C. (2000). Clinical versus mechanical prediction: A meta-analysis. *Psychological Assessment, 12*(1), 19–30.

Gun buyback program. (n.d.). Retrieved from www.nyc.gov/html/nypd/html/community_affairs/gun_buyback_program.shtml

Gun Free Kids. (n.d.). Resources. Retrieved from http://www.gunfreekids.org/resources

Gun Sitters. (n.d.). Retrieved from www.gunsitters.com

Hagan, J. F., Shaw, J. S., & Duncan, P. M. (2008). *Bright futures: Guidelines for health supervision of infants, children, and adolescents,* 3rd ed. Elk Grove Village, IL: American Academy of Pediatrics.

Harris, G. T., Rice, M. E., & Quinsey, V. L. (1993). Violent recidivism of mentally disordered offenders: The development of a statistical prediction instrument. *Criminal Justice and Behavior, 20*(4), 315–335. doi:10.1177/0093854893020004001

Heilbrun, K. (2009). *Evaluation for risk of violence in adults.* New York: Oxford University Press.

Heilbrun, K. (2001). *Principles of forensic mental health assessment.* New York: Kluwer Academic/Plenum Press.

Heilbrun, K., DeMatteo, D., Brooks Holliday, S., & LaDuke, C. (eds.). (2014). *Forensic mental health assessment: A casebook,* 2nd ed. New York: Oxford University Press.

Heilbrun, K., Grisso, T., & Goldstein, A. M. (2009). *Foundations of forensic mental health assessment.* New York: Oxford University Press.

Herships, S. (2014, June 17). Good cop, bad cop: How infighting is costing New Jersey taxpayers. Retrieved from www.wnyc.org/story/good-cop-bad-cop-how-infighting-coasting-nj-taxpayers/

Hilton, N. Z., Harris, G. T., Rice, M. E., Houghton, R. E., & Eke, A. W. (2008). An indepth actuarial assessment for wife assault recidivism: The domestic violence risk appraisal guide. *Law and Human Behavior, 32*(2), 150–163. doi:10.1007/s10979-007-9088-6

Horn, D. (2013, January 13). Gun buybacks popular but ineffective, experts say. *USA Today.* Retrieved from www.usatoday.com/story/news/nation/2013/01/12/gun-buybacks-popular-but-ineffective/1829165

International Association of Chiefs of Police. (2014). Preemployment psychological evaluation guidelines. Retrieved from www.theiacp.org/portals/0/documents/pdfs/psych-preemploymentpsycheval.pdf

International Association of Chiefs of Police. (2013). Psychological fitness-for-duty evaluation guidelines. Retrieved from www.theiacp.org/portals/0/documents/pdfs/psych-fitnessfordutyevaluation.pdf

Jenkins v. United States, 307 F.2d 637 (D.C. Cir. 1962).

Johnson, S. K. (2008). *Medically unexplained illness: Gender and biopsychosocial implications.* Washington, DC: American Psychological Association.

Kalesan, B., Villarreal, M. D., Keyes, K. M., & Galea, S. (2016). Gun ownership and social gun culture. *Injury Prevention, 22*(3), 216–220.

Kates, A. R. (1999). *Copshock: Surviving posttraumatic stress disorder.* Tucson, AZ: Holbrook Street Press.

Kessler, R. C., Heeringa, S. G., Stein, M. B., Colpe, L. J., Fullerton, C. S., Hwang, I., Naifeh, J. A., Nock, M. K., Petukhova, M., Sampson, N. A., Schoenbaum, M., Zaslavsky, A. M., & Ursano, R. J.; Army STARRS Collaborators. (2014). Thirty-Day prevalence of DSM-IV mental disorders among nondeployed soldiers in the US Army. Results from the Army study to assess risk and resilience in service members (Army STARRS). *JAMA Psychiatry,71*(5), 504–513. doi:10.1001/jamapsychiatry.2014.28

Kirschman, E. (2006). *I love a cop: What police families need to know,* rev. ed. New York: Guilford Press.

Kleck, G., Kovandzic, T., Saber, M., & Hauser, W. (2011). The effect of perceived risk and victimization on plans to purchase a gun for self-protection. *Journal of Criminal Justice, 39*(4), 312–319. doi:10.1016/j.jcrimjus.2011.03.002

Kropp, P. R., & Hart, S. D. (2015). *SARA-V3: User manual for version 3 of the Spousal Assault Risk Assessment guide.* Vancouver, BC, Canada: ProActive ReSolutions.

Kuhn, E. M., Nie, C. L., O'Brien, M. E., Withers, R. L., Wintemute, G. J., & Hargarten, S. W. (2002). Missing the target: A comparison of buyback and fatality related guns. *Injury Prevention, 8*(2), 143–146.

Liberman, A. M., Best, S. R., Metzler, T. J., Fagan, J. A., Weiss, D. S., & Marmar, C. R. (2002). Routine occupational stress and psychological distress in police. *Policing: An International Journal of Police Strategies and Management, 25,* 421–439.

Lisitsina, D. (2015, May 20). "Prison guards can never be weak": The hidden PTSD crisis in America's jails. *The Guardian.* Retrieved from www.theguardian.com/us-news/2015/may/20/corrections-officers-ptsd-american-prisons

Lopez, O. (2014, May 27). Prison officers need help, but they won't ask for it. *Newsweek.* Retrieved from www.newsweek.com/2014/06/06/prison-officers-need-help-they-wont-ask-it-252439.html

Master, K. (2015, July 17). Police trade cash for thousands of guns each year. But experts say it does little to stem violence. *The Trace.* Retrieved from www.thetrace.org/2015/07/gun-buyback-study-effectivness/

Meehl, P. E. (1954). *Clinical versus statistical prediction: A theoretical analysis and a review of the evidence.* Minneapolis: University of Minnesota Press. doi:10.1037/11281-000

Melton, G. B., Petrila, J., Poythress, N. G., Slobogin, C., Lyons, P. J., & Otto, R. K. (2007). *Psychological evaluations for the courts: A handbook for mental health professionals and lawyers,* 3rd ed. New York: Guilford Press.

Miller, F. G., & Lazowski, L. E. (1999). *The adult SASSI-3 manual.* Springfield, IN: SASSI Institute.

Mitchell, R. E. (2005, February 15). Can you tell me how many deaf people there are in the United States? Retrieved from https://research.gallaudet.edu/Demographics/deaf-US.php

Monahan, J. E. (1980). *Who is the client? The ethics of psychological intervention in the criminal justice system.* Washington, DC: American Psychological Association.

Morey, L. C. (2007). *Personality Assessment Inventory professional manual,* 2nd ed. Odessa, FL: Psychological Assessment Resources.

Munsey, C. (2008). At least one in 10 Americans are prescribed psychotropics. *Monitor on Psychology, 39*(2), 52.

Munsterberg, H. (1908). *On the witness stand: Essays on psychology and crime.* New York: Doubleday, Page.

Nanavaty, B. R. (2015, September 8). Addressing officer crisis and suicide: Improving officer wellness. Retrieved from https://leb.fbi.gov/2015/september/addressing-officer-crisis-and-suicide-improving-officer-wellness

National Center for Women and Policing. (n.d.). Police family violence fact sheet. Retrieved from http://womenandpolicing.com/violenceFS.asp#notes

National Institute of Justice. (2000). *On-the-job stress in policing—Reducing it, preventing it.* NCJ Publication No. 180079. Retrieved from www.ncjrs.gov/pdffiles1/jr000242d.pdf

National Institute on Drug Abuse. (2015, September). Chart of evidence-based screening tools for adults and adolescents. Retrieved from www.drugabuse.gov/nidamed-medical-health-professionals/tool-resources-your-practice/screening-assessment-drug-testing-resources/chart-evidence-based-screening-tools-adults

N.C. Gen. Stat. § 14-415.11. Retrieved from https://www.ncleg.net/gascripts/statutes/statutelookup.pl?statute=14-415.11

New Jersey Hospital Association. (n.d.). Retrieved from www.njha.com

New Jersey Police Suicide Task Force report. (2009, January 30). Retrieved from www.nj.gov/oag/library/NJPoliceSuicideTaskForceReport-January-30-2009-Final(r2.3.09).pdf

Newport, F. (2015, May 21). Americans greatly overestimate percent gay, lesbian in U.S. Retrieved from www.gallup.com/poll/183383/americans-greatly-overestimate-percent-gay-lesbian.aspx

N.J. Assemb. A2938. Reg. Sess. 2016-2017 (2016).

N.J.S.A. 2A: 62A-16. Retrieved from https://law.justia.com/codes/new-jersey/2013/title-2a/section-2a-62a-16/

Nock, M. K., Park, J. M., Finn, C. T., Deliberto, T. L., Dour, H. J., & Banaji, M. R. (2010). Measuring the suicidal mind: Implicit cognition predicts suicidal behavior. *Psychological Science, 21*(4), 511–517.

Ogloff, J. R. P. (2000). Two steps forward and one step backward: The law and psychology movement(s) in the 20th century. *Law and Human Behavior, 24*(4), 457–483.

Osman, A., Bagge, C. L., Gutierrez, P. M., Konick, L. C., Kopper, B. A., & Barrios, F. X. (2001). The Suicidal Behaviors Questionnaire—Revised (SBQ-R): Validation with clinical and nonclinical samples. *Assessment, 8*(4), 443–454. doi:10.1177/107319110100800409

Pinals, D. A., Appelbaum, P. S., Bonnie, R., Fisher, C. E., Gold, L. H., & Lee, L. (2015a). American Psychiatric Association: Position statement on firearm access, acts of violence and the relationship to mental illness and mental health services. *Behavioral Sciences & the Law, 33*(2/3), 195–198. doi:10.1002/bsl.2180

Pinals, D. A., Appelbaum, P. S., Bonnie, R. J., Fisher, C. E., Gold, L. H., & Lee, L. (2015b). Resource document on access to firearms by people with mental disorders. *Behavioral Sciences & the Law, 33*(2/3), 186–194. doi:10.1002/bsl.2181

Pirelli, G., Wechsler, H., & Cramer, R. (2015). Psychological evaluations for firearm ownership: Legal foundations, practice considerations, and a conceptual framework. *Professional Psychology: Research and Practice, 46*(4), 250–257.

Pirelli, G., & Witt, P. (2015). Psychological evaluations for civilian firearm ownership in New Jersey. *New Jersey Psychologist, 65*(1), 7–9.

Pirelli, G., & Witt, P. H. (2017). Firearms and cultural competence: Considerations for mental health practitioners. *Journal of Aggression, Conflict and Peace Research, 10*(1), 61–70. Retrieved from: https://doi.org/10.1108/JACPR-01-2017-0268

Posner, K., Brown, G. K., Stanley, B., Brent, D. A., Yershova, K. V., Oquendo, M. A., Currier, G. W., Melvin, G. A., Greenhill, L., Shen, S., & Mann, J. J. (2011). The Columbia-Suicide Severity Rating Scale: Initial validity and internal consistency findings from three multisite studies with adolescents and adults. *American Journal of Psychiatry, 168*(12), 1266–1277. doi:10.1176/appi.ajp.2011.10111704

Price, M., & Norris, D. M. (2010). Firearm laws: A primer for psychiatrists. *Harvard Review of Psychiatry, 18*(6), 326–335. doi:10.3109/10673229.2010.527520

Quinsey, V. L., Harris, G. T., Rice, M. E., & Cormier, C. A. (1998). *Violent offenders: Appraising and managing risk.* Washington, DC: American Psychological Association.

Reiser, M., & Geiger, S. (1984). The police officer as a victim. *Professional Psychology: Research and Practice, 15*, 315–323.

Rice, M. E. (1997). Violent offender research and implications for the criminal justice system. *American Psychologist, 52*, 414–423.

Robinson, H. M., Sigman, A. R., & Wilson, J. P. (1997). Duty-related stressors and PTSD symptoms in suburban police officers. *Psychological Reports, 81*, 835–845.

Robinson, J. (2013, May 22). Three-quarters of your doctor bills are because of this. Huffington Post. Retrieved from http://m.huffpost.com/us/entry/3313606

Roesch, R., Zapf, P. A., & Eaves, D. (2006). *Fitness Interview Test-Revised: A structured interview for assessing competency to stand trial.* Sarasota, FL: Professional Resource Press.

Rogers, R. (1984). *Rogers Criminal Responsibility Assessment Scales (R-CRAS) and test manual.* Odessa, FL: Psychological Assessment Resources.

Rogers, R., & Bender, S. D. (2018). *Clinical assessment of malingering and deception*, 4th ed. New York: Guilford Press.

Sharp, J. (2016, August 15). As Alabama shuts down psychiatric hospitals, one jail is expanding to house mentally ill. Retrieved from www.al.com/news/mobile/index.ssf/2016/08/one_alabama_county_looks_to_ex.html

Skeem, J. L., & Monahan, J. (2011). Current directions in violence risk assessment. *Current Directions in Psychological Science, 20*(1), 38–42.

Spielberger, C. D. (1999). *State-Trait Anger Expression Inventory-2.* Lutz, FL: Psychological Assessment Resources.

Stack, S. J., & Tsoudis, O. (1997). Suicide risk among correctional officers. A logistic regression analysis. *Archives of Suicide Research, 3*, 183. doi:10.1023/A:1009677102357

Stuart, H. (2008). Suicidality among police. *Current Opinions in Psychiatry, 21*, 505–509.

Substance Abuse and Mental Health Services Administration. (n.d.). Veterans and military families. Retrieved from www.samhsa.gov/veterans-military-families

Summerlin, Z., Oehme, K., Stern, N., & Valentine, C. (2010). Disparate levels of stress in police and correctional officers: Preliminary evidence from a pilot study on domestic violence. *Journal of Human Behavior in the Social Environment, 20*(6), 762–777. doi:10.1080/10911351003749169

Swanson, J. W., & Felthous, A. R. (2015). Guns, mental illness, and the law: Introduction to this issue. *Behavioral Sciences & the Law, 33*(2–3), 167–177. doi:10.1002/bsl.2178

Swatt, M. L., Gibson, C. L., & Piquero, N. L. (2007). Exploring the utility of general strain theory in explaining problematic alcohol consumption by police officers. *Journal of Criminal Justice, 35*(6), 596–611.

Tarasoff v. Regents of the University of California, 17 Cal. 3d 425, 551 P.2d 334, 131 Cal. Rptr. 14 (Cal. 1976)

Terry, W. (1981). Police stress: The empirical evidence. *Journal of Police Science and Administration, 9*, 61–75.

Torrey, E. F. (1997). *Out of the shadows: Confronting America's mental illness crisis.* New York: John Wiley & Sons.

Torrey, E. F. (1999). Reinventing mental health care. *City Journal* (Autumn).

Torrey, E. F., Kennard, A. D., Eslinger, D., Lamb, R., & Pavle, J. (2010). *More mentally ill persons are in jails and prisons than hospitals: A survey of the states.* Arlington, VA: National Sheriffs Association and Treatment Advocacy Center.

Torrey, E. F., Stieber, J., Ezekiel, J., Wolfe, S. M., Sharfstein, J., Noble, J. H., & Flynn, L. M. (1992). *Criminalizing the seriously mentally ill: The abuse of jails as mental hospitals.* Collingdale, PA: DIANE Publishing.

Treatment Advocacy Center. (n.d.). Retrieved from www.treatmentadvocacycenter.org

Tyler v. Hillsdale County Sheriff's Department, 775 F.3d 308 (6th Cir., 2014).

Van Hasselt, V. B., Sheehan, D. C., & Malcolm, A. S. (2008). The Law Enforcement Officer Stress Survey (LEOSS): Evaluation of psychometric properties. *Behavior Modification, 32*(1), 133–151.

US Department of Justice. (2000). *Addressing correctional officer stress: Programs and strategies.* NCJ Publication No. 183474. Retrieved from www.ncjrs.gov/pdffiles1/nij/183474.pdf

US Department of Veterans Affairs. (n.d.a). Intimate partner violence. Retrieved from www.ptsd.va.gov/public/types/violence/domestic-violence.asp

US Department of Veterans Affairs. (n.d.b). PTSD and substance abuse in veterans. Retrieved from www.ptsd.va.gov/public/problems/ptsd_substance_abuse_veterans.asp

VA Suicide Prevention Program. (2016, July). Facts about veteran suicide. Retrieved from www.va.gov/opa/publications/factsheets/suicide_prevention_factsheet_new_va_stats_070616_1400.pdf

Violanti, J. M. (1999). Alcohol abuse in policing: Prevention strategies. *FBI Law Enforcement Bulletin, 68*(1), 16–20.

568 References

Webster, C. D., Douglas, K. D., Eaves, D., & Hart, S. D. (1997). *HCR-20: Assessing risk for future violence*, version 2. Vancouver, BC, Canada: Simon Fraser University.

Wechsler, D. (2008). *Wechsler Adult Intelligence Scale*, 4th ed. San Antonio, TX: Pearson Assessment.

Wechsler, H., Pirelli, G., & Cramer, R. (2014, May). Conducting forensic mental health assessments for firearm ownership. Presented at the 26th Annual Convention of the Association for Psychological Science (APS), San Francisco, CA.

Wechsler, H., Struble, C., Pirelli, G., & Cramer, R. (2015, August). Firearm ownership evaluations: A local norms perspective. Presented at the 2015 Annual American Psychological Association (APA) Convention, Toronto, Canada.

Westen, D., & Weinberger, J. (2004). When clinical description becomes statistical prediction. *American Psychologist, 59*(7), 595–613. doi:10.1037/0003-066X.59.7.595

Wiebe, D. J. (2003). Homicide and suicide risks associated with firearms in the home: A national case-control study. *Annals of Emergency Medicine, 41*(6), 771–782.

Wigmore, J. H. (1909). Professor Munsterberg and the psychology of testimony: Being a report of the case of *Cokestone v. Munsterberg. Illinois Law Review, 3*, 399–445.

Wintemute, G. J. (2015). Alcohol misuse, firearm violence perpetration, and public policy in the United States. *Preventive Medicine: An International Journal Devoted to Practice and Theory, 79* 15–21. doi:10.1016/j.ypmed.2015.04.015

Wogan, J. B. (2013, March). Cities rethink gun buyback programs. Retrieved from www.governing.com/topics/public-justice-safety/gov-cities-rethink-gun-buyback-programs.html

Yates, R. (2016, October 8). With Pennsylvania mental hospitals full, jails become way stations. Retrieved from www.mcall.com/news/local/mc-pa-long-waits-at-state-mental-hospitals-incompetency-20161008-story.html

Chapter 8

American Journal of Public Health. (n.d.). Retrieved from http://ajph.aphapublications.org/

American Psychiatric Association. (2013). *Diagnostic and statistical manual of mental disorders*, 5th ed. Washington, DC: American Psychiatric Publishing.

American Psychological Association. (2016, November 15). After decades of research, science is no better able to predict suicidal behaviors. Retrieved from www.apa.org/news/press/releases/2016/11/suicidal-behaviors.aspx

American Psychological Association's Advisory Committee on Colleague Assistance. (n.d.). Tips for self-care. Retrieved from www.apapracticecentral.org/ce/self-care/acca-promoting.aspx

Andrews, D. A., Bonta, J., & Hoge, R. D. (1990). Classification for effective rehabilitation: Rediscovering psychology. *Criminal Justice and Behavior, 17*, 19–52.

Association for Psychological Science. (2013, March 5). Leading psychological science journal launches initiative on research replication. Retrieved from www.psychologicalscience.org/news/releases/initiative-on-research-replication.html

A-Tjak, J. L., Davis, M. L., Morina, N., Powers, M. B., Smits, J. J., & Emmelkamp, P. G. (2015). A meta-analysis of the efficacy of acceptance and commitment therapy for clinically relevant mental and physical health problems. *Psychotherapy and Psychosomatics, 84*(1), 30–36. doi:10.1159/000365764

Bailey, A., Hannays-King, C., Clarke, J., Lester, E., & Velasco, D. (2013). Black mothers' cognitive process of finding meaning and building resilience after loss of a child to gun violence. *British Journal of Social Work, 43*(2), 336–354.

Bailey, A., Sharma, M., & Jubin, M. (2013). The mediating role of social support, cognitive appraisal, and quality health care in black mothers' stress-resilience process following loss to gun violence. *Violence and Victims, 28*(2), 233–247.

Baker, T. B., McFall, R. M., & Shoham, V. (2009). Current status and future prospects of clinical psychology toward a scientifically principled approach to mental and behavioral health care. *Psychological Science in the Public Interest, 9*(2), 67–103.

Baumeister, R. F., & Leary, M. R. (1995). The need to belong: Desire for interpersonal attachments as a fundamental human motivation. *Psychological Bulletin, 117*(3), 497–529.

Beck, J. S. (2011). *Cognitive behavior therapy: Basics and beyond.* New York: Guilford Press.

Blanton, H., & Jaccard, J. (2006). Arbitrary metrics in psychology. *American Psychologist, 61*, 27–41.

Bohnert, K. M., Walton, M. A., Ranney, M., Bonar, E. E., Blow, F. C., Zimmerman, M. A., Booth, B. M., & Cunningham, R. M. (2015). Understanding the service needs of assault-injured, drug-using youth presenting for care in an urban emergency department. *Addictive Behaviors, 41*, 97–105. doi:10.1016/j.addbeh.2014.09.019

Bone, D. (2010). The *Heller* promise versus the *Heller* reality: Will statutes prohibiting the possession of firearms by ex-felons be upheld after *Britt v. State? Journal of Criminal Law & Criminology, 100*(4), 1633–1658.

Bongar, B., Berman, A. L., Maris, R. W., Silverman, M. M., Harris, E. A., & Packman, W. L. (1998). *Risk management with suicidal patients.* New York: Guilford Press.

Brent, D. A., Baugher, M., Birmaher, B., Kolko, D. J., & Bridge, J. (2000). Compliance with recommendations to remove firearms in families participating in a clinical trial for adolescent depression. *Journal of the American Academy of Child & Adolescent Psychiatry, 39*(10), 1220–1226. doi:10.1097/00004583-200010000-00007

Breuer, J., & Freud, S. (1955). Studies on hysteria. In *The standard edition of the complete psychological works of Sigmund Freud,* edited and translated by J. Strachey (Vol. 2, pp. 1–311). London: Hogarth Press. (Original work published 1893–1895)

Brewin, C. R., Andrews, B., Rose, S., & Kirk, M. (1999). Acute stress disorder and posttraumatic stress disorder in victims of violent crime. *American Journal of Psychiatry, 156*, 360–366.

Britt v. North Carolina, 681 S.E.2d 320 (N.C., 2009).

Britton, J., & Bloom, J. D. (2015). Oregon's gun relief program for adjudicated mentally ill persons: The psychiatric security review board. *Behavioral Sciences & the Law, 33*(2–3), 323–333. doi:10.1002/bsl.2167

Browne, J., Mihas, P., & Penn, D. L. (2016). Focus on exercise: Client and clinician perspectives on exercise in individuals with serious mental illness. *Community Mental Health Journal, 52*, 387–394.

Bryant, R. A., & Harvey, A. G. (1998). The relationship between acute stress disorder and posttraumatic stress disorder following mild traumatic brain injury. *American Journal of Psychiatry, 155*, 625–629.

Burke, B. L., Arkowitz, H., & Menchola, M. (2003). The efficacy of motivational interviewing: A meta-analysis of controlled clinical trials. *Journal of Consulting and Clinical Psychology, 71*(5), 843.

Bushman, B. J., Newman, K., Calvert, S. L., Downey, G., Dredze, M., Gottfredson, M., Jablonski, N. G., Masten, A. S., Morrill, C., Neill, D. B., Romer, D., & Webster, D. W. (2016). Youth violence: What we know and what we need to know. *American Psychologist, 71*(1), 17–39.

Butler, A. C., Chapman, J. E., Forman, E. M., & Beck, A. T. (2006). The empirical status of cognitive-behavioral therapy: A review of meta-analyses. *Clinical Psychology Review, 26*(1), 17–31.

Cabaniss, D. L., Cherry, S., Douglas, C. J., & Schwartz, A. R. (2017). *Psychodynamic psychotherapy: A clinical manual*, 2nd ed. Malden, MA: Wiley.

Capuzzi, D., & Stauffer, M. D. (2016). *Counseling and psychotherapy: Theories and interventions.* Alexandria, VA: American Counseling Association.

Christoffel, K. K. (2000). Commentary: When counseling parents on guns doesn't work: Why don't they get it? *Journal of the American Academy of Child & Adolescent Psychiatry, 39*(10), 1226–1228. doi:10.1097/00004583-200010000-00008

Columbia Lighthouse Project. (n.d.). About the scale. Retrieved from http://cssrs.columbia.edu/the-columbia-scale-c-ssrs/about-the-scale/

Columbia Lighthouse Project. (2017, March 25). The Columbia Suicide Severity Rating Scale (C-SSRS): Supporting evidence. Retrieved from http://cssrs.columbia.edu/wp-content/uploads/CSSRS_Supporting-Evidence_Book_2017-04.pdf

Comtois, K. A., & Linehan, M. M. (2006). Psychosocial treatments for suicidal behavior: A practice-friendly review. *Journal of Clinical Psychology, 62*(2), 161–170.

Cramer, R. J., Bryson, C. N., Eichorst, M. K., Keyes, L. N., & Ridge, B. E. (2017). Conceptualization and pilot testing of a core competency-based training workshop in suicide risk assessment and management. *Journal of Clinical Psychology, 73*, 233–238.

Cramer, R. J., Bryson, C. N., Stroud, C. H., & Ridge, B. E. (2016). A pilot test of a graduate course in suicide theory, risk assessment and management. *Teaching of Psychology, 43*, 238–242.

Cramer, R. J., Golom, F. D., LoPresto, C. T., & Kirkley, S. M. (2008). Weighing the evidence: Empirical assessment and ethical implications of conversion therapy. *Ethics & Behavior, 18*(1), 93–114.

Cramer, R. J., Johnson, S. M., McLaughlin, J., Rausch, E. M., & Conroy, M. A. (2013). Suicide risk assessment for psychology doctoral programs: Core competencies and a framework for training. *Training and Education in Professional Psychology, 7*, 1–11.

Craske, M. G. (2017). *Cognitive-behavioral therapy*, rev. ed. Washington, DC: American Psychological Association.

Dadoly, A. (2011, March 21). Suicide is forever but the stress leading up to it is often temporary. Retrieved from www.health.harvard.edu/blog/suicide-is-forever-but-the-stress-leading-up-to-it-is-often-temporary-201103211957

Dattilio, F. M. (2015). The self-care of psychologists and mental health professionals: A review and practitioner guide. *Australian Psychologist, 50*, 393–399.

de Bruin, E. I., Formsma, A. R., Frijstein, G., & Bögels, S. M. (2017). Mindful2Work: Effects of combined physical exercise, yoga, and mindfulness meditations for stress relieve [*sic*] in employees. A proof of concept study. *Mindfulness, 8*, 204–217.

Eells, T. D. (2007). History and current status of psychotherapy case formulation. In *Handbook of psychotherapy case formulation*, 2nd ed., edited by T. D. Eells (pp. 3–32). New York: Guilford Press.

Engber, D. (2016, April 19). Cancer research is broken. Slate. Retrieved from www.slate.com/articles/health_and_science/future_tense/2016/04/biomedicine_facing_a_worse_replication_crisis_than_the_one_plaguing_psychology.html

Falls, B. (2011). Legislation prohibiting physicians from asking patients about guns. *Journal of Psychiatry & Law, 39*(3), 441–464.

Fawcett, J. (2014). Mass murder, non-treatment of severe mental illness, and available firearms: The perfect storm. *Psychiatric Annals, 44*(5), 206. doi:10.3928/00485713-20140502-01

Finklestein, M., Stein, E., Greene, T., Bronstein, I., & Solomon, Z. (2015). Posttraumatic stress disorder and vicarious trauma in mental health professionals. *Health & Social Work, 40*(2), e25–e31.

Formsma, A. R., de Bruin, E. I., & Bögels, S. M. (2015). Mindful2Work training protocol: a combination of mindfulness meditation, yoga, and physical exercise. Internal publication. Amsterdam: UvA Minds You & University of Amsterdam.

Franklin, J. C., Ribeiro, J. D., Fox, K. R., Bentley, K. H., Kleiman, E. M., Huang, X., Musacchio, K. M., Jaroszewski, A. C., Chang, B. P., & Nock, M. K. (2017). Risk factors for suicidal thoughts and behaviors: A meta-analysis of 50 years of research. *Psychological Bulletin, 143*(2), 187–232. doi:10.1037/bul0000084

Freedman, L. P., Cockburn, I. M., & Simcoe, T. S. (2015). The economics of reproducibility in preclinical research. *PLoS Biology, 13*(6). doi:10.1371/journal.pbio.1002165

Freeman, K. R., James, S., Klein, K. P., Mayo, D., & Montgomery, S. (2016). Outpatient dialectical behavior therapy for adolescents engaged in deliberate self-harm: Conceptual and methodological considerations. *Child Adolescent Social Work Journal, 33*, 123–135.

Gartlehner, G., Hansen, R. A., Nissman, D., Lohr, K. N., & Carey, T. S. (2006). *Criteria for distinguishing effectiveness from efficacy trials in systematic reviews.* AHRQ Publication No. 06-0046. Retrieved from www.ncbi.nlm.nih.gov/books/NBK44029/?report=reader

Gilbert, R. M. (2006). *The eight concepts of Bowen theory.* Lake Frederick, VA: Leading Systems Press.

Gross, A., Miltenberger, R., Knudson, P., Bosch, A., & Breitwieser, C. B. (2007). Preliminary evaluation of a parent training program to prevent gun play. *Journal of Applied Behavior Analysis, 40*(4), 691–695. doi:10.1901/jaba.2007.691-695

Gun Owners of America. (2014, January 13). See a shrink, lose your guns! Retrieved from www.gunowners.org/congress1132014.htm

Gurman, A. S., & Messer, S. B. (2003). *Essential psychotherapies: Theory and practice*, 2nd ed. New York: Guilford Press.

Harrison, R. L., & Westwood, M. J. (2009). Preventing vicarious traumatization of mental health therapists: Identifying protective practices. *Psychotherapy: Theory, Research, Practice, Training, 46*(2), 203–219. doi:10.1037/a0016081

Harvey, A. G., & Bryant, R. A. (1998). The relationship between acute stress disorder and posttraumatic stress disorder: A prospective evaluation of motor vehicle accident survivors. *Journal of Consulting and Clinical Psychology, 66*, 507–512.

Hernandez-Wolfe, P., Killian, K., Engstrom, D., & Gangsei, D. (2015). Vicarious resilience, vicarious trauma, and awareness of equity in trauma work. *Journal of Humanistic Psychology, 55*(2), 153–172.

Himle, M. B., & Miltenberger, R. G. (2004). Preventing unintentional firearm injury in children: The need for behavioral skills training. *Education & Treatment of Children, 27*(2), 161–177.

Himle, M., Miltenberger, R., Gatheridge, B., & Flessner, C. (2004). An evaluation of two procedures for training skills to prevent gun play in children. *Pediatrics, 113*, 70–77.

Hofmann, S. G. (2013). School shooting: A call for action. *Behavior Therapist, 36*(3), 53–55.

Hofmann, S. G., Asnaani, A., Vonk, I. J., Sawyer, A. T., & Fang, A. (2012). The efficacy of cognitive behavioral therapy: A review of meta-analyses. *Cognitive Therapy and Research, 36*(5), 427–440.

Howell, K. H., & Miller-Graff, L. E. (2016). Clinical considerations when intervening with individuals exposed to violence. *Psychology of Violence, 6*(3), 478–483.

Huprich, S. K. (2016). Psychologists should help curb the wave of U. S. gun violence. *Journal of Personality Assessment, 98*(5), 447–448. doi:10.1080/00223891.2016.1204832

Ilgen, M., & Moos, R. (2005). Deterioration following alcohol-use disorder treatment in Project MATCH. *Journal of Studies on Alcohol, 66*, 517–525.

Johnson, J., & Wood, A. M. (2017). Integrating positive and clinical psychology: Viewing human functioning as continua from positive to negative can benefit clinical assessment, interventions and understandings of resilience. *Cognitive Therapy Research, 41*, 335–349.

Johnson, R. M., Frank, E. M., Ciocca, M., & Barber, C. W. (2011). Training mental healthcare providers to reduce at-risk patients' access to lethal means of suicide: Evaluation of the CALM Project. *Archives of Suicide Research, 15*(3), 259–264. doi:10.1080/13811118.2011.589727

Josefowitz, N., & Myran, D. (2017). *CBT made simple: A clinician's guide to practicing cognitive behavioral therapy*. Oakland, CA: New Harbinger Publications.

Jostad, C. M., Miltenberger, R. G., Kelso, P., & Knudson, P. (2008). Peer tutoring to prevent firearm play: Acquisition, generalization, and long-term maintenance of safety skills. *Journal of Applied Behavior Analysis, 41*(1), 117–123. doi:10.1901/jaba.2008.41-117

Kazdin, A. E. (2008). Evidence-based treatment and practice: New opportunities to bridge clinical research and practice, enhance the knowledge base, and improve patient care. *American Psychologist, 63*(3), 146–159.

Koerner, K. (2007). Case formulation in dialectical behavior therapy for borderline personality disorder. In *Handbook of psychotherapy case formulation*, edited by T. D. Eells (pp. 340–367). New York: Guilford Press.

Kolla, B. P., O'Connor, S. S., & Lineberry, T. W. (2011). The base rates and factors associated with reported access to firearms in psychiatric inpatients. *General Hospital Psychiatry, 33*(2), 191–196. doi:10.1016/j.genhosppsych.2011.01.011

Koons, C., Robins, C. J., Tweed, J. L., Lynch, T. R., Gonzelez, A. M., Morse, J. Q., Bishop, G. K., Butterfield, M. I., & Bastian, L. A. (2001). Efficacy of dialectical behavior therapy in women veterans with borderline personality disorder. *Behavior Therapy, 32*, 371–390.

Kübler-Ross, E. (1969). *On death and dying.* New York: Macmillan.

Leichsenring, F., Abbass, A., Luyten, P., Hilsenroth, M., & Rabung, S. (2013). The emerging evidence for long-term psychodynamic therapy. *Psychodynamic Psychiatry, 41*(3), 361.

Leichsenring, F., Biskup, J., Kreische, R., & Staats, H. (2005). The effectiveness of psychoanalytic therapy. First results of the Göttingen study of psychoanalytic and psychodynamic therapy. *International Journal of Psychoanalysis, 86*, 433–455.

Leichsenring, F., & Leibing, E. (2007). Psychodynamic psychotherapy: A systematic review of techniques, indications and empirical evidence. *Psychology and Psychotherapy: Theory, Research and Practice, 80*(2), 217–228. doi:10.1348/147608306X117394

Leichsenring, F., Rabung, S., & Leibing, E. (2004). The efficacy of short-term psychodynamic therapy in specific psychiatric disorders, a meta-analysis. *Archives of General Psychiatry, 61*, 1208–1216.

Lilienfeld, S. O. (2007). Psychological treatments that cause harm. *Perspectives on Psychological Science, 2*(1), 53–70.

Linehan, M. M. (1993a). *Cognitive-behavioral treatment of borderline personality disorder.* New York: Guilford Press.

Linehan, M. M. (2014). *DBT skills training manual*, 2nd ed. New York: Guilford Press.

Linehan, M. M. (1993b). *Skills training manual for treating borderline personality disorder.* New York: Guilford Press.

Linehan, M. M., Armstrong, H. E., Suarez, A., Allmon, D., & Heard, H. L. (1991). Cognitive-behavioral treatment of chronically suicidal borderline patients. *Archives of General Psychiatry, 48*, 1060–1064.

Linehan, M. M., Heard, H. L., & Armstrong, H. E. (1993). Naturalistic follow-up of a behavioral treatment for chronically parasuicidal borderline patients. *Archives of General Psychiatry, 50*, 157–158.

Linehan, M. M., Tutek, D., Heard, H. L., & Armstrong, H. E. (1994). Interpersonal outcome of cognitive-behavioral treatment for chronically suicidal borderline patients. *American Journal of Psychiatry, 51*, 1771–1776.

Lingiardi, V., & McWilliams, N. (2017). *Psychodynamic diagnostic manual*, 2nd ed. New York: Guilford Press.

Luborsky, L., Stuart, J., Friedman, S., Diguer, L., Seligman, D. A., Bucci, W., Pulver, S., Kraus, E. D., Ermold, J., Davison, W. T., Woody, G., & Mergenthaler, E. (2001). The Penn psychoanalytic treatment collection: A set of complete and recorded psychoanalyses as a research resource. *Journal of the American Psychoanalytical Association, 49*, 217–234.

Luther, R., III. (2014). Mental health and gun rights in Virginia: A view from the battlefield. *New England Journal on Criminal & Civil Confinement, 40*(2), 345–358.

Marcus, G. (2015, June 27). Face it, your brain is a computer. *New York Times*. Retrieved from www.nytimes.com/2015/06/28/opinion/sunday/face-it-your-brain-is-a-computer.html

McGoldrick, M., Gerson, R., & Petry, S. (2008). *Genograms: Assessment and intervention*, 3rd ed. New York: W. W. Norton & Company.

McHugh, R. K., & Barlow, D. H. (2010). The dissemination and implementation of evidence-based psychological treatments: A review of current efforts. *American Psychologist, 65*(2), 73–84.

McKay, M., Wood, J. C., & Brantley, J. (2007). *The dialectical behavior therapy skills workbook: Practical DBT exercises for learning mindfulness, interpersonal effectiveness, emotion regulation & distress tolerance.* Oakland, CA: New Harbinger Publications.

McLaughlin, K. D. (2017). Ethical considerations for clinicians treating victims and perpetrators of intimate partner violence. *Ethics & Behavior, 27*(1), 43–52.

McWilliams, N. (2004). *Psychoanalytic psychotherapy: A practitioner's guide.* New York: Guilford Press.

Miller, M., & Hemenway, D. (2008). Guns and suicide in the United States. *New England Journal of Medicine, 359*(10), 989–991. doi:10.1056/NEJMp0805923

Miller, T. W., Veltkamp, L. J., & Kraus, R. F. (1997). Clinical pathways for diagnosing and treating victims of domestic violence. *Psychotherapy, 34*(4), 425–432.

Mohr, D. C. (1995). Negative outcome in psychotherapy: A critical review. *Clinical Psychology: Science and Practice, 2*, 1–27.

Moos, R. (2005). Iatrogenic effects of psychosocial interventions for substance use disorders: Prevalence, predictors, prevention. *Addiction, 100*, 595–604.

Munger, T., Savage, T., & Panosky, D. M. (2015). When caring for perpetrators becomes a sentence: Recognizing vicarious trauma. *Journal of Correctional Health Care, 21*(4), 365–374.

National Physicians Alliance. (2013). *Gun safety & public health: Policy recommendations for a more secure America.* Retrieved from http://smartgunlaws.org/wp-content/uploads/2013/09/gunsafety-and-publichealth.pdf

Nielssen, O. B., Yee, N. L., Millard, M. M., & Large, M. M. (2011). Comparison of first-episode and previously treated persons with psychosis found NGMI for a violent offense. *Psychiatric Services, 62*(7), 759–764. doi:10.1176/appi.ps.62.7.759

Norris, D. M., Price, M., Gutheil, T., & Reid, W. H. (2006). Firearm laws, patients, and the roles of psychiatrists. *American Journal of Psychiatry, 163*(8), 1392–1396. doi:10.1176/appi.ajp.163.8.1392

Panos, P. T., Jackson, J. W., Hasan, O., & Panos, A. (2014). Meta-analysis and systematic review assessing the efficacy of dialectical behavior therapy (DBT). *Research on Social Work Practice, 24*(2), 213–223. doi:10.1177/1049731513503047

Paugh v. Henrico Area Mental Health & Developmental Servs., 286 Va. 85, 89, 743 S.E.2d 277, 279 (2013).

Pinals, D. A., Appelbaum, P. S., Bonnie, R. J., Fisher, C. E., Gold, L. H., & Lee, L.-W. (2015). Resource document on access to firearms by people with mental disorders. *Behavioral Sciences and the Law, 33*, 186–194. doi:10.1002/bsl.2181

Pirelli, G., & Witt, P. (2015). Psychological evaluations for civilian firearm ownership in New Jersey. *New Jersey Psychologist, 65*(1), 7–9.

Posner, K., Brown, G. K., Stanley, B., Brent, D. A., Yershova, K. V., Oquendo, M. A., Currier, G. W., Melvin, G. A., Greenhill, L., Shen, S., & Mann, J. J. (2011). The Columbia-suicide severity rating scale: Initial validity and internal consistency findings from three multisite studies with adolescents and adults. *American Journal of Psychiatry, 168*(12), 1266–1277. doi:10.1176/appi.ajp.2011.10111704

Price, J. H., Khubchandani, J., & Payton, E. (2015). Vision impaired or professionally blind: Health education research and firearm violence. *Health Promotion Practice, 16*(3), 316–319. doi:10.1177/1524839914566456

Price, J., Mrdjenovich, A. J., Thompson, A., & Dake, J. A. (2009). College counselors' perceptions and practices regarding anticipatory guidance on firearms. *Journal of American College Health, 58*(2), 133–139. doi:10.1080/07448480903221350

Riggenbach, J. (2012). *The CBT toolbox: A workbook for clients and clinicians*. Eau Claire, WI: PESI, Inc.

Robins, C. J., & Chapman, A. L. (2004). Dialectical behavior therapy: Current status, recent developments, and future directions. *Journal of Personality Disorders, 18*(1), 73–89.

Rubens, M., & Shehadeh, N. (2014). Gun violence in United States: In search for a solution. *Frontiers in Public Health, 3*, 2–17.

Schulz, R., & Aderman, D. (1974). Clinical research and the stages of dying. *OMEGA–Journal of Death and Dying, 5*(2), 137–143.

Seligman, L. W., & Reichenberg, L. W. (2014). *Theories of counseling and psychotherapy: Systems, strategies, and skills*. Boston, MA: Pearson.

Selker, H. P., Selker, K. M., & Schwartz, M. D. (2013). Gun violence is a health crisis: Physicians' responsibilities. *Journal of General Internal Medicine, 28*(5), 601–602. doi:10.1007/s11606-013-2408-2

Shedler, J. (2010). The efficacy of psychodynamic psychotherapy. *American Psychologist, 65*(2), 98–109.

Sher, L., & Rice, T. (2015). Prevention of homicidal behaviour in men with psychiatric disorders. *World Journal of Biological Psychiatry, 16*(4), 212–229. doi:10.3109/15622975.2015.1028998

Sherman, M. E., Burns, K., Ignelzi, J., Raia, J., Lofton, V., Toland, D., Stinson, B., Tilley, J. L., & Coon, T. (2001). Firearms risk management in psychiatric care. *Psychiatric Services, 52*(8), 1057–1061. doi:10.1176/appi.ps.52.8.1057

Shneidman, E. S. (1987). A psychological approach to suicide. In *Cataclysms, crises, and catastrophes: Psychology in action*, Master Lectures, edited by G. R. VandenBos (pp. 147–183). Washington, DC: American Psychological Association.

Shneidman, E. S. (1985). *Definition of suicide.* New York: Wiley.

Shneidman, E. S. (1998). Perspectives on suicidology: Further reflections on suicide and psychache. *Suicide and Life-Threatening Behavior, 28*, 245–250.

Silverman, M. M., Berman, A. L., Bongar, B., Litman, R. E., & Maris, R. W. (1998). Inpatient standards of care and the suicidal patient: Part II. An integration with clinical risk management. In *Risk management with suicidal patients,* edited by B. Bongar, A. L. Berman, R. W. Maris, M. M. Silverman, E. A. Harris, & W. L. Packman (pp. 83–109). New York: Guilford Press.

Simmons, J., & Griffiths, R. (2013). *CBT for beginners,* 2nd ed. Los Angeles: Sage.

Simon, R. I. (2007). Gun safety management with patients at risk for suicide. *Suicide and Life-Threatening Behavior, 37*(5), 518–526.

Simon, T. R., Swann, A. C., Powell, K. E., Potter, L. B., Kresnow, M., & O'Carroll, P. W. (2001). Characteristics of impulsive suicide attempts and attempters. *Suicide and Life-Threatening Behavior, 32*(Suppl.), 49–59. doi:10.1521/suli.32.1.5.49.24212

Simpson, J. R. (2007). Issues related to possession of firearms by individuals with mental illness: An overview using California as an example. *Journal of Psychiatric Practice, 13*(2), 109–114. doi:10.1097/01.pra.0000265768.10248.d7

Singer, J. B., McManama O'Brien, K. H., & LeCloux, M. (2017). Three psychotherapies for suicidal adolescents: Overview of conceptual frameworks and intervention techniques. *Child Adolescent Social Work Journal, 34*, 95–106.

Skerrett, P. J. (2012, September 24). Suicide often not preceded by warnings. Retrieved from www.health.harvard.edu/blog/suicide-often-not-preceded-by-warnings-201209245331

Slovak, K., Brewer, T. W., & Carlson, K. (2008). Client firearm assessment and safety counseling: The role of social workers. *Social Work, 53*(4), 358–366.

Smith, P. N., Currier, J., & Drescher, K. (2015). Firearm ownership in veterans entering residential PTSD treatment: Associations with suicide ideation, attempts, and combat exposure. *Psychiatry Research, 229*(1–2), 220–224. doi:10.1016/j.psychres.2015.07.031

Sorenson, R. L., Gorsuch, R. L., & Mintz, J. (1985). Moving targets: Patients' changing complaints during psychotherapy. *Journal of Consulting and Clinical Psychology, 53*, 49–54.

Steinberg, L., & Scott, E. S. (2003). Less guilty by reason of adolescence: Developmental immaturity, diminished responsibility, and the juvenile death penalty. *American Psychologist, 58*(12), 1009.

Strupp, H. H. (1978). Psychotherapy research and practice—an overview. In *Handbook of psychotherapy and behavior change,* 2nd ed., edited by A. E. Bergin & S. L. Garfield (pp. 3–22). New York: Wiley.

Strupp, H. H., Hadley, S.W., & Gomez-Schwartz, B. (1977). *Psychotherapy for better or worse: The problem of negative effects.* New York: Wiley.

Sullivan, T. P., Weiss, N. H., Price, C., Pugh, N., & Hansen, N. B. (2018). Strategies for coping with individual PTSD symptoms: Experiences of African American victims of intimate partner violence. *Psychological Trauma: Theory, Research, Practice, and Policy, 10*(3), 336–344. doi:10.1037/tra0000283

Summers, R. F., & Barber, J. P. (2010). *Psychodynamic therapy: A guide to evidence-based practice.* New York: Guilford Press.

Swanson, J. W., Sampson, N. A., Petukhova, M. V., Zaslavsky, A. M., Appelbaum, P. S., Swartz, M. S., & Kessler, R. C. (2015). Guns, impulsive angry behavior, and mental disorders: Results from the National Comorbidity Survey Replication (NCS-R). *Behavioral Sciences & the Law*, *33*(2–3), 199–212. doi:10.1002/bsl.2172

Swenson, C. R. (2016). *DBT principles in action: Acceptance, change, and dialectics.* New York: Guilford Press.

Traylor, A., Price, J. H., Telljohann, S. K., King, K., & Thompson, A. (2010). Clinical psychologists' firearm risk management perceptions and practices. *Journal of Community Health: The Publication for Health Promotion and Disease Prevention*, *35*(1), 60–67. doi:10.1007/s10900-009-9200-6

Tyler v. Hillsdale County Sheriff's Dept., 775 F.3d 308 (6th Cir., 2014).

VandenBos, G. R., Meidenbauer, E., & Frank-McNeil, J. (2014). *Psychotherapy theories and techniques: A reader.* Washington, DC: American Psychological Association.

Van Orden, K. A., Witte, T. K., Cukrowicz, K. C., Braithwaite, S. R., Selby, E. A., & Joiner, T. J. (2010). The interpersonal theory of suicide. *Psychological Review*, *117*, 575–600.

Veltkamp, L. J., & Miller, T. W. (1994). *Clinical handbook of child abuse and neglect.* Madison, CT: International Universities Press.

Veltkamp, L. J., & Miller, T. W. (1990). Clinical strategies in recognizing spouse abuse. *Psychiatric Quarterly*, *61*(3), 181–189.

Verheul, R., van den Bosch, L. M. C., Koeter, M. W. J., de Ridder, M. A. J., Stijnen, T., & van den Brink, W. (2003). Dialectical behavior therapy for women with borderline personality disorder. *British Journal of Psychiatry*, *182*, 135–140.

Viorst, J. (1997). *Necessary losses: The loves, illusions, dependencies, and impossible expectations that all of us have to give up in order to grow.* New York: Free Press.

Walters, H., Kulkarni, M., Forman, J., Roeder, K., Travis, J., & Valenstein, M. (2012). Feasibility and acceptability of interventions to delay gun access in VA mental health settings. *General Hospital Psychiatry*, *34*(6), 692–698. doi:10.1016/j.genhosppsych.2012.07.012

Wampold, B. E. (2012). *The basics of psychotherapy: An introduction to theory and practice.* Washington, DC: American Psychological Association.

Weisz, J. R., Kuppens, S., Ng, M. Y., Eckshtain, D., Ugueto, A. M., Vaughn-Coaxum, R., Jensen-Doss, A., Hawley, K. M., Krumholz Marchette, L. S., Chu, B. C., Weersing, V. R., & Fordwood, S. R. (2017). What five decades of research tells us about the effects of youth psychological therapy: A multilevel meta-analysis and implications for science and practice. *American Psychologist*, *72*(2), 79–117.

White House Office of the Press Secretary. (2016, January 4). Fact sheet: New executive actions to reduce violence and make our communities safer. Retrieved from https://obamawhitehouse.archives.gov/the-press-office/2016/01/04/fact-sheet-new-executive-actions-reduce-gun-violence-and-make-our

Williams, W. I. (2006). Complex trauma: Approaches to theory and treatment. *Journal of Loss and Trauma*, *11*, 321–335.

Williamson, A. A., Guerra, N. G., & Tynan, W. D. (2014). The role of health and mental health care providers in gun violence prevention. *Clinical Practice in Pediatric Psychology*, *2*(1), 88–98. doi:10.1037/cpp0000055

Wise, E. H., Hersh, M. A., & Gibson, C. M. (2012). Ethics, self-care and well-being for psychologists: Reenvisioning the stress–distress continuum. *Professional Psychology: Research and Practice, 43*(5), 487–494.

Wollschlaeger v. Farmer, 814 F. Supp. 2d 1367 (S.D. Fla., 2011).

Yalom, I., & Leszcz, M. (2005). *Theory and practice of group psychotherapy.* New York: Basic Books.

Chapter 9

239 school shootings in America since 2013. (n.d.). Retrieved August 6, 2017 from https://everytownresearch.org/school-shootings/; https://momsdemandaction. org/washington-moms-demand-action-everytown-respond-to-fatal-shooting-at-freeman-high-school/

American Psychiatric Association. (2013). *Diagnostic and statistical manual of mental disorders,* 5th ed. Washington, DC: American Psychiatric Publishing.

APA [American Psychological Association] (2002). Ethical principles of psychologists and code of conduct. *American Psychologist, 57,* 1060–1073. doi:10.1037/0003-066X.57.12.1060

American Psychological Association. (2016, November 15). After decades of research, science is no better able to predict suicidal behaviors. Retrieved from www.apa.org/news/press/releases/2016/11/suicidal-behaviors.aspx

American Psychological Association. (2010). 2010 Amendments to the 2002 "Ethical principles of psychologists and code of conduct." *American Psychologist, 65*(5), 493. doi:10.1037/a0020168

American Psychological Association. (2013). Gun violence: Prediction, prevention, and policy. Retrieved from www.apa.org/pubs/info/reports/gun-violence-prevention.aspx

Andrews, D. A., Bonta, J., & Hoge, R. D. (1990). Classification for effective rehabilitation: Rediscovering psychology. *Criminal Justice and Behavior, 17,* 19–52.

Anestis, M. D., & Anestis, J. C. (2015). Suicide rates and state laws regulating access and exposure to handguns. *American Journal of Public Health, 105*(10), 2049–2058. doi:10.2105/AJPH.2015.302753

Anestis, M. D., Anestis, J. C., & Butterworth, S. E. (2017). Handgun legislation and changes in statewide overall suicide rates. *American Journal of Public Health, 107*(4), 579–581. doi:10.2105/AJPH.2016.303650

Anglemyer, A., Miller, M. L., Buttrey, S., & Whitaker, L. (2016). Suicide rates and methods in active duty military personnel, 2005 to 2011: A cohort study. *Annals of Internal Medicine, 165,* 167–174.

Bonnie, R. J., & Grisso, T. (2000). Adjudicative competence and youthful offenders. In *Youth on trial: A developmental perspective on juvenile justice,* edited by T. Grisso & R. G. Schwartz (pp. 73–103). Chicago: University of Chicago Press.

Brady Handgun Violence Prevention Act, Pub. L. 103–159, 107 Stat. 1536 (1993).

Brent, D. A., Baugher, M., Birmaher, B., Kolko, D. J., & Bridge, J. (2000). Compliance with recommendations to remove firearms in families participating in a clinical trial for adolescent depression. *Journal of the*

American Academy of Child & Adolescent Psychiatry, 39(10), 1220–1226. doi:10.1097/00004583-200010000-00007

Britton, J., & Bloom, J. D. (2015). Oregon's gun relief program for adjudicated mentally ill persons: The psychiatric security review board. *Behavioral Sciences & the Law, 33*(2–3), 323–333. doi:10.1002/bsl.2167

Bryan, C. J., Mintz, J., Clemans, T. A., Leeson, B., Burch, T. S., Williams, S. R., Maney, E., & Rudd, M. D. (2017). Effect of crisis response planning vs. contracts for safety on suicide risk in U.S. Army soldiers: A randomized clinical trial. *Journal of Affective Disorders, 212*, 64–72. doi:10.1016/j.jad.2017.01.028

Bureau of Alcohol, Tobacco and Firearms. (2000a). *Commerce in firearms in the United States.* Washington, DC: US Department of the Treasury.

Bureau of Alcohol, Tobacco and Firearms. (2000b). *Following the gun: Enforcing federal laws against firearms traffickers.* Washington, DC: US Department of the Treasury.

Carroll, J. (2006, February 16). Gun ownership higher among Republicans than Democrats. Gallup. Retrieved from www.gallup.com/poll/21496/gun-ownership-higher-among-republicans-than-democrats.aspx

Cavanaugh, M. R., Bouffard, J. A., Wells, W., & Nobles, M. R. (2012). Student attitudes toward concealed handguns on campus at 2 universities. *American Journal of Public Health, 102*(12), 2245–2247. doi:10.2105/AJPH.2011.300473

Centers for Disease Control and Prevention. (2017, May 3). Deaths and mortality. Retrieved from www.cdc.gov/nchs/fastats/deaths.htm

Christoffel, K. K. (2000). Commentary: When counseling parents on guns doesn't work: Why don't they get it? *Journal of the American Academy of Child & Adolescent Psychiatry, 39*(10), 1226–1228. doi:10.1097/00004583-200010000-00008

Cornell, D. G., & Sheras, P. L. (2006). *Guidelines for responding to student threats of violence.* Dallas, TX: Sopris West Educational Services.

Cramer, R. J., & Kapusta, N. D. (2017). A social-ecological understanding of theory, assessment, and prevention of suicide. *Frontiers in Psychology, 8*, 1756.

Crime Control Act of 1990, Pub. L. No. 101–647, 104 Stat. 4789 (1990).

District of Columbia v. Heller, 552 U.S. 1254, 128 S. Ct. 1695 (2008).

Douglas, K. S., Hart, S. D., Webster, C. D., & Belfrage, H. (2013). *HCR-20V3: Assessing risk of violence—User guide.* Burnaby, Canada: Mental Health, Law, and Policy Institute, Simon Fraser University.

Eminem. (2000). The way I am. On *The Marshall Mathers LP* [CD]. Santa Monica, CA: Aftermath Entertainment.

End the gun epidemic in America. (2015, December 4). *New York Times.* Retrieved from www.nytimes.com/2015/12/05/opinion/end-the-gun-epidemic-in-america.html?_r=0

Fact sheet: New executive actions to reduce gun violence and make our communities safer. (2016, January 4). Retrieved from https://obamawhitehouse.archives.gov/the-press-office/2016/01/04/fact-sheet-new-executive-actions-reduce-gun-violence-and-make-our

Farr, K. A. (2002). Battered women who were "being killed and survived it": Straight talk from survivors. *Violence and Victims, 17*(3), 267–281.

FFF: Women's history month: March, 2016. (2016, February 10). Retrieved from www.census.gov/newsroom/facts-for-features/2016/cb16-ff03.html

Fowler, K. A., Dahlberg, L. L., Haileyesus, T., & Annest, J. L. (2015). Firearm injuries in the United States. *Preventive Medicine: An International Journal Devoted to Practice and Theory, 79*, 5–14. doi:10.1016/j.ypmed.2015.06.002

Fox, J. A., & DeLateur, M. J. (2014). Mass shootings in America: Moving beyond Newtown. *Homicide Studies, 18*(1), 125–145. doi:10.1177/1088767913510297

Franklin, J. C., Ribeiro, J. D., Fox, K. R., Bentley, K. H., Kleiman, E. M., Huang, X., Musacchio, K. M., Jaroszewski, A. C., Chang, B. P., & Nock, M. K. (2017). Risk factors for suicidal thoughts and behaviors: A meta-analysis of 50 years of research. *Psychological Bulletin, 143*(2), 187–232. doi:10.1037/bul0000084

Gold, L. H. (2013). Gun violence: Psychiatry, risk assessment, and social policy. *Journal of the American Academy of Psychiatry and the Law, 41*(3), 337–343.

Gold, L. H., & Simon, R. I. (2016). *Gun violence and mental illness.* Arlington, VA: American Psychiatric Association.

Gun Control Act of 1968, § 101, Pub. L. No. 90–618, 82 Stat. 1213 (1968).

Guns. (n.d.). Gallup. Retrieved from http://news.gallup.com/poll/1645/guns.aspx

Hart, S. D., Douglas, K. S., & Guy, L. S. (2016). The structured professional judgment approach to violence risk assessment: Origins, nature, and advances. In *The Wiley handbook on the theories, assessment and treatment of sexual offending: Assessment*, vol. 2, edited by L. Craig & M. Rettenberger (pp. 643–666). Chichester, UK: Wiley Blackwell.

Health Insurance Portability and Accountability Act of 1996. Pub. L. No. 104–191, 110 Stat. 1936 (1996).

Horner, S. (2017, December). St. Catherine University security guard who falsely said black man shot him will avoid jail time, at least for now. Retrieved from https://www.twincities.com/2017/12/18/st-catherine-university-security-guard-who-falsely-said-black-man-shot-him-will-avoid-jail-time-at-least-for-now/

Howk, A. (2013, February 7). One student injured in shooting at Indian River State College. PalmBeachPost. Retrieved from www.palmbeachpost.com/news/crime--law/one-student-injured-shooting-indian-river-state-college/K0ubcIzadvyXKgDED1H3QO/

Jobes, D. A. (2012). The Collaborative Assessment and Management of Suicidality (CAMS): An evolving evidence-based clinical approach to suicidal risk. *Suicide and Life-Threatening Behavior, 42*(6), 640–653. doi:10.1111/j.1943-278X.2012.00119.x

Johnson, A. (2014, June 14). Man sentenced to prison for fatal 2013 shooting at Hillsdale Elementary. San Leandro Patch. Retrieved from https://patch.com/california/sanleandro/man-sentenced-to-prison-for-fatal-2013-shooting-at-hillside-elementary

Johnson, R. M., Frank, E. M., Ciocca, M., & Barber, C. W. (2011). Training mental healthcare providers to reduce at-risk patients' access to lethal means of suicide: Evaluation of the CALM Project. *Archives of Suicide Research, 15*(3), 259–264. doi:10.1080/13811118.2011.589727

Kapusta, N. D., & Cramer, R. J. (2017). Firearm suicide in the United States from a broader preventive perspective. *American Journal of Psychiatry, 174*, 77–78.

Kaslow, N. J. (2015). Translating psychological science to the public. *American Psychologist, 70*(5), 361–371. doi:10.1037/a0039448

Kleck, G. (1981). Racial discrimination in criminal sentencing: A critical evaluation of the evidence with additional evidence on the death penalty. *American Sociological Review, 46*(6), 783–805.

Klein, S. P., & Rolph, J. E. (1991). Relationship of offender and victim race to death penalty sentences in California. *Jurimetrics, 32*(1), 33–48.

Langman, P. (2009). Rampage school shooters: A typology. *Aggression & Violent Behavior, 14*(1), 79–86. doi:10.1016/j.avb.2008.10.003

La Valle, J. M. (2013). "Gun control" vs. "self-protection": A case against the ideological divide. *Justice Policy Journal, 10*(1), 1–26.

Lawrence, R. G., & Birkland, T. A. (2004). Guns, Hollywood, and school safety: Defining the school-shooting problem across public arenas. *Social Science Quarterly, 85*(5), 1193–1207. doi:10.1111/j.0038-4941.2004.00271.x

Lee, K. (2014, October 21). Infographic: The optimal length for every social media update and more. Retrieved from https://blog.bufferapp.com/optimal-length-social-media

Lindgren, J. (2015). Forward: The past and future of guns. *Journal of Criminal Law & Criminology, 104*(4), 705–716.

Makarios, M. D., & Pratt, T. C. (2012). The effectiveness of policies and programs that attempt to reduce firearm violence: A meta-analysis. *Crime & Delinquency, 58*(2), 222–244. doi:10.1177/0011128708321321

McCarten, J. M., Hoffmire, C. A., & Bossarte, R. M. (2015). Changes in overall and firearm veteran suicide rates by gender, 2001–2010. *American Journal of Preventive Medicine, 48*, 360–364.

McDonald v. City of Chicago, Ill., 130 S. Ct. 3020, 561 U.S. 742, 177 L. Ed. 2d 894 (2010).

McGinty, E. E., Frattaroli, S., Appelbaum, P. S., Bonnie, R. J., Grilley, A., Horwitz, J., Swanson, J. W., & Webster, D. W. (2014). Using research evidence to reframe the policy debate around mental illness and guns: Process and recommendations. *American Journal of Public Health, 104*(11), e22–e26.

McLeigh, J. D. (2015). The new normal? Addressing gun violence in America. *American Journal of Orthopsychiatry, 85*(3), 201–202. doi:10.1037/ort0000072

Miniter, F. (2016, April 12). The gun industry says it has grown 158% since Obama took office. *Forbes*. Retrieved from www.forbes.com/sites/frankminiter/2016/04/12/the-gun-industry-says-it-has-grown-158-since-obama-took-office/#7778cbcf7f4e

Mitchell, R. E. (2005, February 15). Can you tell me how many deaf people there are in the United States? Gallaudet University. Retrieved from https://research.gallaudet.edu/Demographics/deaf-US.php

Morin, R. (2014, July 15). The demographics and politics of gun-owning households. Pew Research Center. Retrieved from www.pewresearch.org/fact-tank/2014/07/15/the-demographics-and-politics-of-gun-owning-households/

NCIS Improvements Amendments Act, H.R. 2640, Pub. L. 110–180 (2008).

Nekvasil, E. K., & Cornell, D. G. (2015). Student threat assessment associated with safety in middle schools. *Journal of Threat Assessment and Management, 2*(2), 98–113.

Nekvasil, E. K., Cornell, D. G., & Huang, F. L. (2015). Prevalence and offense characteristics of multiple casualty homicides: Are schools at higher risk than other locations? *Psychology of Violence, 5*(3), 236–245. doi:10.1037/a0038967

Newport, F. (2015, May 21). Americans greatly overestimate percent gay, lesbian in U.S. Gallup. Retrieved from www.gallup.com/poll/183383/americans-greatly-overestimate-percent-gay-lesbian.aspx

Parham-Payne, W. (2014). The role of the media in the disparate response to gun violence in America. *Journal of Black Studies, 45*(8), 752–768. doi:10.1177/0021934714555185

Paternoster, R. (1984). Prosecutorial discretion in requesting the death penalty: A case of victim-based racial discrimination. *Law & Society Review, 18*(3), 437–478.

Payne, B. K., & Gainey, R. R. (2008). Guns, offense type, and Virginia exile: Should gun reduction policies focus on specific offenses? *Criminal Justice Policy Review, 19*(2), 181–195.

Perrin, P. B. (2016). Translating psychological science: Highlighting the media's contribution to contagion in mass shootings: Comment on Kaslow (2015). *American Psychologist, 71*(1), 71–72. doi:10.1037/a0039994

Phillips, S. W., Kim, D. Y., & Sobol, J. J. (2013). An evaluation of a multiyear gun buy-back programme: Re-examining the impact on violent crimes. *International Journal of Police Science & Management, 15*(3), 246–261.

Pinals, D. A., Appelbaum, P. S., Bonnie, R., Fisher, C. E., Gold, L. H., & Lee, L. (2015a). American Psychiatric Association: Position statement on firearm access, acts of violence and the relationship to mental illness and mental health services. *Behavioral Sciences & The Law, 33*(2–3), 195–198. doi:10.1002/bsl.2180

Pinals, D. A., Appelbaum, P. S., Bonnie, R. J., Fisher, C. E., Gold, L. H., & Lee, L. (2015b). Resource document on access to firearms by people with mental disorders. *Behavioral Sciences & the Law, 33*(2–3), 186–194. doi:10.1002/bsl.2181

Pinker, S. (2011). *The better angels of our nature: The decline of violence in history and its causes.* New York: Viking.

Pirelli, G., Wechsler, H., & Cramer, R. (2015). Psychological evaluations for firearm ownership: Legal foundations, practice considerations, and a conceptual framework. *Professional Psychology: Research and Practice, 46*(4), 250–257.

Pirelli, G., & Witt, P. H. (2017). Firearms and cultural competence: Considerations for mental health practitioners. *Journal of Aggression, Conflict and Peace Research, 10*(1), 61–70. https://doi.org/10.1108/JACPR-01-2017-0268

Pirelli, G., & Zapf, P. A. (2008). An investigation of psychologists' practices and attitudes toward participation in capital evaluations. *Journal of Forensic Psychology Practice, 8*(1), 39–66.

Posner, K., Brown, G. K., Stanley, B., Brent, D. A., Yershova, K. V., Oquendo, M. A., Currier, G. W., Melvin, G. A., Greenhill, L., Shen, S., & Mann, J. J. (2011). The Columbia-Suicide Severity Rating Scale: Initial validity and internal consistency findings from three multisite studies with adolescents and adults. *American Journal of Psychiatry, 168*(12), 1266–1277. doi:10.1176/appi.ajp.2011.10111704

Price, J., Mrdjenovich, A. J., Thompson, A., & Dake, J. A. (2009). College counselors' perceptions and practices regarding anticipatory guidance on firearms. *Journal of American College Health, 58*(2), 133–139. doi:10.1080/07448480903221350

Protection of Lawful Commerce in Arms Act, Pub. L. 109–92, 119 Stat. 2095 (2005).

Rocque, M. (2012). Exploring school rampage shootings: Research, theory, and policy. *Social Science Journal, 49*(3), 304–313. doi:10.1016/j.soscij.2011.11.001

Rosenfeld, R., Deckard, M. J., & Blackburn, E. (2014). The effects of directed patrol and self-initiated enforcement on firearm violence: A randomized controlled study of hot spot policing. *Criminology, 52*(3), 428–449.

Rosenthal, R. (1979). The file drawer problem and tolerance for null results. *Psychological bulletin, 86*(3), 638.

Rudd, M. D., Bryan, C. J., Wertenberger, E. G., Peterson, A. L., Young-McCaughan, S., Mintz, J., Williams, S. R., Arne, K. A., Breitbach, J., Delano, K., Wilkinson, E., & Bruce, T. O. (2015). Brief cognitive-behavioral therapy effects on post-treatment suicide attempts in a military sample: Results of a randomized clinical trial with 2-year follow-up. *American Journal of Psychiatry, 172*(5), 441–449. doi:10.1176/appi.ajp.2014.14070843

Schildkraut, J., & Muschert, G. W. (2014). Media salience and the framing of mass murder in schools: A comparison of the Columbine and Sandy Hook massacres. *Homicide Studies: An Interdisciplinary & International Journal, 18*(1), 23–43. doi:10.1177/1088767913511458

Sherman, M. E., Burns, K., Ignelzi, J., Raia, J., Lofton, V., Toland, D., Stinson, B., Tilley, J. L., & Coon, T. (2001). Firearms risk management in psychiatric care. *Psychiatric Services, 52*(8), 1057–1061. doi:10.1176/appi.ps.52.8.1057

Siegel, M., Ross, C. S., & King, C. I. (2013). The relationship between gun ownership and firearm homicide rates in the United States, 1981–2010. *American Journal of Public Health, 103*(11), 2098–2105. doi:10.2105/AJPH.2013.301409

Simon, G. E., Imel, Z. E., Ludman, E. J., & Steinfeld, B. J. (2012). Is dropout after a first psychotherapy visit always a bad outcome? *Psychiatric Services, 63*(7), 705–707. doi:10.1176/appi.ps.201100309

Simon, R. I. (2007). Gun safety management with patients at risk for suicide. *Suicide and Life-Threatening Behavior, 37*, 518–526.

Skeem, J. L., & Monahan, J. (2011). Current directions in violence risk assessment. *Current Directions in Psychological Science, 20*(1), 38–42. doi:10.1177/0963721410397271

Slovak, K., Brewer, T. W., & Carlson, K. (2008). Client firearm assessment and safety counseling: The role of social workers. *Social Work, 53*(4), 358–366.

Smith, A. (2016, January 6). Obama is the best gun salesman in America. CNN. Retrieved from http://money.cnn.com/2016/01/06/news/obama-gun-control-sales/index.html

Smith, P. N., Currier, J., & Drescher, K. (2015). Firearm ownership in veterans entering residential PTSD treatment: Associations with suicide ideation, attempts, and combat exposure. *Psychiatry Research, 229*(1–2), 220–224. doi:10.1016/j.psychres.2015.07.031

Stanley, I. H., Horn, M. A., Rogers, M. L., Anestis, M. D., & Joiner, T. E. (2016). Discussing firearm ownership and access as part of suicide risk assessment and prevention: "Means safety" versus "means restriction." *Archives of Suicide Research, 13*, 1–17.

Swanson, J. W., & Felthous, A. R. (2015). Guns, mental illness, and the law: Introduction to this issue. *Behavioral Sciences & the Law, 33*(2–3), 167–177. doi:10.1002/bsl.2178

Swift, A. (2016, September 14). Americans' trust in mass media sinks to new low. *Gallup*. Retrieved from www.gallup.com/poll/195542/americans-trust-mass-media-sinks-new-low.aspx

Swift, J. K., & Greenberg, R. P. (2012). Premature discontinuation in adult psychotherapy: A meta-analysis. *Journal of Consulting and Clinical Psychology, 80*, 547–559.

The incredible shrinking soundbite. (2011, January 5). NPR. Retrieved from www.npr.org/2011/01/05/132671410/Congressional-Sound-Bites

Traylor, A., Price, J. H., Telljohann, S. K., King, K., & Thompson, A. (2010). Clinical psychologists' firearm risk management perceptions and practices. *Journal of Community Health: The Publication for Health Promotion and Disease Prevention, 35*(1), 60–67. doi:10.1007/s10900-009-9200-6

Tyler v. Hillsdale County Sheriff's Dept., 775 F.3d 308 (6th Cir., 2014).

Vandello, J. A., & Bosson, J. K. (2013). Hard won and easily lost: A review and synthesis of theory and research on precarious manhood. *Psychology of Men & Masculinity, 14*(2), 101.

Vigdor, E. R., & Mercy, J. A. (2006). Do laws restricting access to firearms by domestic violence offenders prevent intimate partner homicide? *Evaluation Review, 30*, 313–332.

Violanti, J. M., Mnatsakanova, A., Hartley, T. A., Andrew, M. E., & Burchfiel, C. M. (2012). Police suicide in small departments: A comparative analysis. *International Journal of Emergency Mental Health, 14*, 157–162.

Vittes, K. A., & Sorenson, S. B. (2006). Are temporary restraining orders more likely to be issued when application mention firearms? *Evaluation Review, 30*, 266–275.

Walters, H., Kulkarni, M., Forman, J., Roeder, K., Travis, J., & Valenstein, M. (2012). Feasibility and acceptability of interventions to delay gun access in VA mental health settings. *General Hospital Psychiatry, 34*(6), 692–698. doi:10.1016/j.genhosppsych.2012.07.012

Washington Moms Demand Action, Everytown respond to fatal shooting at Freeman High School. (2017, September). Retrieved from https://momsdemandaction.org/washington-moms-demand-action-everytown-respond-to-fatal-shooting-at-freeman-high-school/

Wechsler, H., Pirelli, G., Struble, C., & Cramer, R. (2015, August). Firearm ownership evaluations: A local norms perspective. Presented at the 2015 Annual American Psychological Association Convention, Toronto, Canada.

Williamson, A. A., Guerra, N. G., & Tynan, W. D. (2014). The role of health and mental health care providers in gun violence prevention. *Clinical Practice in Pediatric Psychology, 2*(1), 88–98. doi:10.1037/cpp0000055

Wintemute, G. J. (2015). The epidemiology of firearm violence in the twenty-first century United States. *Annual Review of Public Health. 36*, 5–19. doi:10.1146/annurev-publhealth-031914-122535

Wollschlaeger v. Governor of Florida, 760 F.3d 1195 (11th Cir., 2014).

Woltman, N. (2017, September). St. Catherine guard shot himself, made up the gunman-on-campus story, police.

Retrieved from https://www.twincities.com/2017/09/13/
st-catherine-resumes-classes-after-campus-shooting-offers-counseling/

Wyant, B. R., Taylor, R. B., Ratcliffe, J. H., & Wood, J. (2012). Deterrence, firearm arrests, and subsequent shootings: A micro-level spatio-temporal analysis. *Justice Quarterly, 29*(4), 524–545.

Yip, P. S., Caine, E., Yousuf, S., Chang, S. S., Wu, K. C., & Chen, Y. Y. (2012). Means restriction in suicide prevention. *Lancet, 379,* 2393–2399.

York, J. A., Lamis, D. A., Pope, C. A., & Egede, L. E. (2013). Veteran-specific suicide prevention. *Psychiatric Quarterly, 84,* 219–238.

Zeisel, H. (1981). Race bias in the administration of the death penalty: The Florida experience. *Harvard Law Review, 95*(2), 456–468.

Index

revolvers, double-action, 31
Rice, Tamir, 192
Richardson, H. L., 49
rifles, 32
rifling, 4–5
right to carry (RTC), 92–95, 437
rimfire, 32–33
risk assessment, 342–57, 474–77
risk factors, 276, 279–84
Risk Management with Suicidal Patients (Bongar), 391–92
risk–need–responsibility model, 381–82
Roberti-Roos Assault Weapons Control Act (1989), 77
Robins, C. J., 380
Rocque, M., 220
Rodger, Elliot, 218–19
rod & gun clubs, 59, 316
Rogers, Richard, 350
Roosevelt, Franklin Delano, 9
Roosevelt, Theodore, 6–7, 9, 38–39
Roper v. Simmons, 169–70
Rosenfeld, R., 113–14
RTC (right to carry), 92–95, 437
Rudd, M. D., 276
Ruddell, R., 91
Ruger, William B., 6–7, 36
Ruiz, J., 194
Rutkow, L., 100
Rydberg, J., 184–85

SAF (Second Amendment Foundation), 51–52
safety, 39–41, 84, 400–1, 461–63
SAF Reporter, 51
sale
  straw, 118, 202–3
same-gender relationships, 239
Sanchez, Daniel, 262–63
Sanders, Dave, 202–3
Sandy Hook Elementary shooting, 42, 123, 207–8
Sandy Hook Promise (SHP), 69–70
Saunders, D. G., 244
Scalia, Antonin, 9, 169–70
Scared Straight programs, 72–73

SCCC (Students for Concealed Carry on Campus), 52
Schaffer, M. E., 11
Schildkraut, J., 110–11, 123, 223–24
schizophrenia, 144, 159
Schneidman, E. S., 285
school shootings, 109–11, 200–1, 215–22, 449–51. *See also* mass shootings
school violence, defined, 217
Schreier, P., 4
Schwartz, M. D., 411
Scott, E. S., 169–70
SCOV (southern culture of violence), 186
SDV (self-directed violence), 166–67, 275
Seau, Tiana Baul "Junior," 297
Seave, Paul, 270–71
Second Amendment, 8–9, 44, 79–80
  and right to carry, 92–94
Second Amendment Foundation (SAF), 51–52
Second Amendment (2A) groups, 44–54
  Armed Citizens United, 46–47
  Bullets & Bagels, 47
  Citizens Committee for the Rights to Keep and Bear Arms, 47–48
  confirmation bias in, 3
  Firearms Policy Coalition, 48
  Gun Owners of America, 49
  Jews for the Preservation of Firearm Ownership, 49–50
  Keep and Bear Arms, 50
  National Association for Gun Rights, 50–51
  National Rifle Association, 44–45
  Second Amendment Foundation, 51–52
  social gun culture in, 315–16
  stance of, 44
  Students for Concealed Carry on Campus, 52
  Students for the Second Amendment, 53–54
  US Concealed Carry Association, 54